SO-AJC-788

New Paradigms for Treating Relationships

New Paradigms for Treating Relationships

Edited by
Jill Savege Scharff and
David E. Scharff

JASON ARONSON
Lanham • Boulder • New York • Toronto • Oxford

Published in the United States of America
by Jason Aronson

An imprint of Rowman & Littlefield Publishers, Inc.
A wholly owned subsidiary of
The Rowman & Littlefield Publishing Group, Inc.
4501 Forbes Boulevard, Suite 200, Lanham, Maryland 20706
www.rowmanlittlefield.com

PO Box 317
Oxford
OX2 9RU, UK

British Library Cataloguing in Publication Information Available

Library of Congress Cataloging-in-Publication Data

New paradigms for treating relationships / edited by Jill Savege Scharff
and David E. Scharff.
    p.   cm.
Includes bibliographical references and index.
ISBN-10: 0-7657-0437-4 (cloth : alk. paper)
ISBN-13: 978-0-7657-0437-5 (cloth : alk. paper)
1. Family psychotherapy.   I. Scharff, Jill Savege.   II. Scharff, David
E., 1941– .
[DNLM: 1. Family Therapy.   2. Couples Therapy.   3. Marital Therapy.
WM 430.5.F2 N5326   2006]
RC488.5.S3655   2006
616.89'156—dc22   2005029980

Printed in the United States of America

Contents

v

Figures

Tables

Preface and Acknowledgments

David E. Scharff, M.D., and Jill Savege Scharff, M.D.

Freud began the process of applying psychoanalysis to group process, art, civilization, and war, but he did not extend his analytic reach to the family. He saw the couples that were parents to early patients such as Dora and Hans as supporting cast, not as principals in his patients' dramas—hindrances or helpers of the main character. Nevertheless, others have been able to construct plausible family histories from Freud's keen observations of his analysands' families, and to imagine alternate therapeutic strategies that might have involved the families. When analytic family therapists do this, it is not to second-guess Freud, but to document alternate paths for psychoanalytic understanding.

We credit John Bowlby, at the Tavistock Clinic's Children's Department, with the introduction of family treatment. Sometime around 1950, he is said to have made an almost offhand remark to John Elderkin Bell about his belief in seeing the families of the children he studied. Bowlby meant that it was important to meet with the parents, but Bell took the cue and began to see whole families, and he was followed in this by Nathan Ackerman. Bowlby enthusiastically approved of this development and also began to see families, as did a few other analysts. But the field of family therapy, with Americans in the lead, became nonanalytic because classical theory did not transfer well to a group setting. Later family therapy became pointedly anti-analytic out of criticism of analysts' ignoring of the family and, we believe, partly as a political strategy to establish the autonomy of the field of family therapy by giving it an identity in opposition to that of an identifiable enemy.

Some analysts continued to believe in conjoint therapy. The Tavistock was a hotbed of applied psychoanalysis, including work on organizational consultation, education, and understanding marital and family dynamics. In the 1930s Enid Balint founded The Family Discussion Bureau, later called the Tavistock Institute for Marital Studies, now called the Tavistock Centre for Couple Relationships. In the 1950s Henry Dicks studied spouses being treated in parallel psychotherapies in the Adult Department at the Tavistock Clinic. In the 1970s at the Tavistock Clinic the Family Therapy Workshop was developing analytic concepts for applying to family life. Meanwhile in the United States, Ackerman's pioneering family work, which was solidly built on analytic principles, was taken over by nonanalytic followers who stressed systems and strategic approaches to family therapy. Nonanalytic approaches became dominant in the United States, even at the Ackerman Institute itself. The field of family therapy evolving in contradistinction to psychoanalysis depended on cognitive-behavioral, systemic, and structural techniques to effect symptom change.

Lyman Wynne and Roger Shapiro and their groups at the National Institutes of Health continued the analytic approach to families in their clinical research. Roger Shapiro and John Zinner moved to George Washington University, and eventually into private practice where they continued practicing family therapy with adolescents and training many family therapists. In the 1980s we began our writing on couple, sex, and family therapy from an object relations perspective and edited The Library of Object Relations. The object relations approach emphasizes insight into the defensive, communicative, and structure-building functions of unconscious processes, resistance, and working in the transference. To psychoanalysts, object relations theory offers a way of thinking about the development of the person and interaction of personalities in a language that is near to family experience. To couple and family therapists who think that affect is a manipulation and insight is unnecessary for change, object relations theory communicates complex psychoanalytic ideas about the unconscious in a practical, acceptable format.

Washington continues to be the center for the development of object relations family and couple therapy in the United States. But we are not alone. Analysts in Europe and South America have continued to value analytic family and couple therapy, where systemic therapy has not been dominant. Unfortunately for analytic family therapists in the United States, unfamiliarity with these analysts' languages and psychoanalytic traditions left us unenlightened by their contributions. That state of ignorance began to change when the International Psychoanalytic Association accepted our proposal for a workshop in family therapy, and we invited some of the analysts we met there to present at the International Psychotherapy Institute Conference on Object Relations Couple and Family Therapy held in New Orleans in 2003 (at which some of the chapters in this book were first conceived of and presented as papers). Analytic family therapy got another boost in 2004, when analysts from France, Italy, Germany, Canada, Argentina, Great Britain, the United States, and other parts of Europe and South America met in Paris at the first International Psychoanalytic Family Therapy Congress and made proposals for an International Association of Analytic Family Therapy and for a second conference in Montreal in 2006. With simultaneous translation into three languages, the Paris conference provided a unique window through which to sample the rich ideas in the non-English literature. In 2005, the Society of Couple Psychoanalytic Psychotherapists in the United Kingdom in association with the Scottish Institute of Human Relations presented a conference in Edinburgh on the theme of power and attachment in couple relationships. *New Paradigms for Treating Relationships* brings these previously unheard voices from many countries together with our model of object relations couple and family therapy to create a global perspective that brings depth and breadth to psychoanalytic couple and family therapy.

In this volume, we reach into the international analytic family therapy community to present contributions from home and abroad that complement one another. To contributions from English-speaking Great Britain, Australia, Panama, and the East and West Coasts of the United States, we bring those from Argentina, France, Germany, Italy, and Slovenia, written by the authors in English or translated for them, with further editorial assistance by Jill Scharff. We bring together research on neurophysiology, affect regulation, infant attachment, adult attachment, couple relating, divorce, and remarriage; clinical insights on sibling rivalry and play; and concepts of defense against annihilatory and Oedipal anxieties from theories of individual object relations and marital interaction. This rich input from related fields augments the psychoanalytic approach to families (in part 1) and couples (in part 2).

The contributors discuss the levels of communication in a family, sibling and parental relationships, and the stress of severe illness, psychosis, divorce, and remarriage on individual and family functioning. They write from Freudian, object relations, intersubjective, relational, and systemic perspectives, but the dominant orientation (although not exclusively so) is object relations theory, the one the editors find most flexible. Some of the contributors describe straightforward clinical applications in the consulting room. Others propose new models of applied therapy requiring technical innovation in concert with psychoanalytic insight.

Some of the chapters could have been placed in either part 1 or part 2. For instance, one might argue that the Losso chapter on divorce should be in part 2 on couple therapy because it applies to couples, but the author's emphasis on the family, social, and legal ramifications of divorce led to the decision to keep it in part 1 on family therapy. Similarly, Nicolò's chapter on folie à deux is about a couple, but it sits in part 1 on families, because it is paired with her chapter on the family, psychosis, and transpersonal pathologies, and together they provide models for understanding transpersonal disorders. We have arranged the chapters so that each part stands alone, but each must be read in the context of the overlap of couple and family.

Many, many thanks to our wonderful administrator Anna Innes and her assistant Ana Granados without whom we would be totally lost under a mountain of paper, and to our colleagues at the International Psychotherapy Institute, especially the hard-working co-chairs of the conference on Object Relations Couple and Family Therapy in New Orleans—Carl Bagnini and Michael Kaufman, who gracefully prepared presenters and coordinated panels, and Walt Ehrhardt, who made superb local arrangements. As always we are grateful for the inspiration of our publisher Jason Aronson and his colleagues at Rowman and Littlefield. Last but not least, we are most grateful to the couples and families who have worked with all of us in couple or family therapy, especially those who generously agreed to videotape for teaching purposes. Most of the couples and parents in *New Paradigms for Treating Relationships* happen to be heterosexual, but as Suzanne Iasenza illustrates, the theories and techniques apply to gay and lesbian couples too. All identifying details have been changed throughout the book to protect the couples' and families' confidentiality, but the clinical process is presented exactly as the contributors remembered it.

I
FAMILY THERAPY

Introduction to Part 1: Family Therapy

The image of the family is changing rapidly in the twenty-first century. More than half of all marriages end in divorce. More than half of women work outside the home. There are two-mom families, two-dad families, and families in which an independent woman is supporting a child alone. The global economy means that families migrate away from the previous generation, and thus many children grow up without ready access to their grandparents. The family sits uneasily in a rapidly changing context. So we need new ideas for family therapy—analytic concepts and techniques that can reach in to the depth of disquietude.

Part 1 opens with the Scharffs' established ways of thinking and their new ideas about couple and family therapy. David Scharff illustrates his overview of a psychoanalytic model of the mind in couple and family therapy in a clinical example of a family therapy session with three young children at play expressing the family's negative transference to a separation from their therapist. This is followed by Jill and David Scharff's chapter on new paradigms in couple and family therapy, in which they enrich their object relations point of view with findings from current thinking in psychoanalysis, attachment research, trauma theory, neuroscience, and chaos theory.

We also need input from family therapists who live in cultures other than the American and who read languages other than English. Roberto Losso, from Argentina, delves deep into the French and Spanish psychoanalytic literature to cull the concepts fundamental to his views on levels of communication of affect and experience in couples and families. He holds that symptoms arise from the transpsychic level of communication, and that therapy needs to re-create the transitional space in which family members can acknowledge the otherness of one another, and then establish the healthier interpsychic mode of transmission.

From Italy where she works in a systems family training institution, Lilia

3

Gagnarli looks to object relations theory to help a family gain access to what remains unexpressed. She uses two clinical examples of listening to what is said and sensing how she and the family use the consultation space so as to help the family members connect with their feelings.

Another example of integrating analytic ideas into a systems framework comes from Slovenia. Robert Cvetek, Katarina Kompan Erzar, Tomaz Erzar, and Christian Gostecnik demonstrate an innovative model of therapy called Relational Family Therapy that integrates aspects of general systems theories with object relational theories, self psychology, and interpersonal analysis to conceptualize the structure of the mind on all levels and in all aspects of human life: intrapsychic, interpersonal, and systemic, in real life and in fantasy, on the conscious and unconscious domains of personal experience.

Family and couple therapy can be invaluable approaches for severe disturbances. In paired chapters, Anna Nicolò from Italy brings her analytic perspective to pathological symptomatic constellations and their connection to the psychotic potential of the family of origin. In her first chapter she gives the example of an adolescent with fragile differentiation between ego and object, and describes the reciprocal interactions between his symptoms and the hidden psychosis in his family. In her second chapter, she illustrates her ideas in relation to folie à deux. She shows the connection between the symptoms of each partner in the couple and their connection to their families' psychotic potential.

A troubled child's parents are a couple with their own issues apart from their parenting problems. Molly Ludlam from Scotland ponders the boundary between a child's feelings of rivalry and persecution and the child's parents' own conflict, and illustrates an approach through which a therapist can tactfully help a parental couple resolve the present crisis in their family and in their relationship.

Siblings are too often overlooked by psychoanalysts, even by family therapists. Sylvie Angel of France makes the point that the sibling bond, marked by complex conscious feelings and unconscious revolt, jealousy, passion, hatred, nostalgia, complicity, and disappointment, is actually more durable than the marriage contract and should be of much more concern in psychoanalysis.

Jill Scharff values the siblings as well as the identified patient. She advocates seeing the whole family at play to get whole family understanding, nowhere more important than when one member of the family is a baby who might otherwise get left at home. She gives clinical vignettes of families dealing with the impact of very young children from a few months to two years of age, and revisits sibling issues in latency and adolescence, showing how children's issues complement those of their parents.

Not all families stay together with the parents as a couple at the center of the family. The couple separates and the family takes on a new shape. Studying the divorce process, Roberto and Ana Losso show how impasses keep divorcing individuals from moving on to the next phase of their life, and entrap their dependent children. The partners may fail to live up to the ideal expected of them, become controlling and possessive, or simply grow apart as life goes on. Their unconscious collusive links are disrupted. Family therapy needs to work with the social and legal system to address the issue of divorce and help the families re-establish sustaining links.

Some divorcing families enter a state of extreme agitation, with vicious recriminations and allegations of neglect and abuse that involve the legal system. Kate Scharff describes therapeutic supervision, an object-relations-based methodology that she has developed for working with families of high-conflict divorce. While supporting the visitation rights of a parent in a custody dispute, the supervisor, who is a therapist, studies conflict among the family members, detects patterns of behavior that stem from their losses, and intervenes interpretively to secure the family's functioning in its emerging form with two single parents.

Divorce may be followed by remarriage, and new hopes are heaped upon old losses. Working with a stepfamily, Carl Bagnini describes a complex treatment arrangement for relationship difficulties and problems with self-regulation in a family years after divorce, and illustrates the reworking of the conflicts, traumatic memories, and losses of the divorced parents so as to repair the trauma that their children otherwise continue to enact.

HIV infection has cast its shadow over families in many parts of the world, but less commonly studied is the fear of AIDS when there is no HIV infection. Hans-Jürgen Wirth of Germany gives a detailed study of the family of a man suffering from phobia of AIDS, showing how an analytic understanding of the individual family members, their dyads, and their family roles contributes to a comprehensive understanding of the family and to effective family and couple intervention.

When family members not only live together but work together, their family therapist needs an understanding of business principles as well as therapeutic skill. For consulting to the uniquely intense phenomena generated in a family business, Mike Stadter applies object relations theory in his brief intervention model that combines the dynamics of the family and the workplace.

Part 1 closes with Jenny Berg and Penny Jools's Australian outline of progression along a developmental sequence from narcissistic, autistic contiguous, and paranoid-schizoid levels to depressive position functioning. They illustrate their theory in ongoing couple therapy with two parents. They help the parents as a couple bear depression, give up manic solutions, grieve losses together, and move toward a satisfying reality that appropriately makes room for both of them and for their child.

1

Models of the Mind for Couple and Family Therapy

David E. Scharff

The object relations theory of mind highlights the interactive origin of psychic function and the beginnings of mental structure in the infant's relationships within the family group. Based on this model, psychoanalytic family and couple therapy employs the interactions between family and therapist to detect and work with developmental failures in holding and containment, skewed family projective identification, and attacks on linking, which characterize pathological and traumatized families. The coming together of transference generated by the family as a group and the therapist's countertransference and the family are the fulcrum on which such therapy turns. An extended vignette of a session illustrates the application of object relations theory to the therapeutic process of family therapy.

The object relations model of the mind is a bridge between our understanding of the individual and of the couple and family, both in development and in treatment. For many years we have been developing this model for work with families and couples because it connects the development of the individual psyche to the dyad of early development and to the larger family group in which most children grow, and because it provides in-depth understanding of the dyad on which many families are built and in which procreation takes place (D. Scharff 1982, 1994; Scharff and Scharff 1987, 1991, 1998).

The components of the theory of the mind that make this possible include:

1. An interactive theory of mental development;
2. A theory of the family as a small group;

7

3. A model of growth and change that includes the larger family—the father, siblings, and others, such as babysitters or grandparents—and its relations with wider society.

AN INTERACTIVE THEORY OF MIND

Fairbairn wrote that mind developed as an introjection of unsatisfying experience with the mother. The infant inevitably experiences her as unsatisfying at times, even though she is a good-enough mother, and as a defense, builds an image of her in its own ego through identification. Having introjected the image of the mother as unsatisfying, the infant now experiences the maternal *internal* object as unsatisfying, and so performs the next mental defensive operation. The infant self splits off and represses the unsatisfying maternal part-object from the satisfying "ideal object" that is connected to the central ego (or self). This unsatisfying object is further split into two types, which gives rise to two areas of split-off and repressed function that express the two classes of "bad object relations" (bad because they feel affectively painful): (1) the exciting object that represents the parent that is excessively exciting of unsatisfiable need and the part of the self (the libidinal ego) that anxiously craves satisfaction; and (2) the rejecting or persecuting object representing the unsatisfying parental object and the part of the self (the anti-libidinal ego or internal saboteur) that angrily or sorrowfully adheres to the rejecting object. In the case of all three ego-and-object constellations, the affect characterizing the relationship is the mental organizer of the experience and, in the treatment situation, informs the therapist about the quality of the relationship being expressed consciously and unconsciously (Fairbairn 1952, 1954; Scharff and Scharff 1998). The point here in so briefly summarizing this complex theory is that the inner world is made up of split and repressed constellations of self and object which monitor relations with the external object world, and which are themselves subject to internal dynamic shifts.

Klein's (1946) theory of projective and introjective identification and Bion's (1970) theory of container/contained offer a psychoanalytic model for the formation of the infant's mind through continual interaction with the parent's unconscious. In this model, the infant puts its unstructured and intolerable anxieties into the mother through unconscious, nonverbal methods of communication known as projective identification. She takes them in through introjective identification, that is, she identifies with them and unconsciously responds to the infant. The infant's unverbalized anxieties and experiences are taken in by the parents, tolerated, and understood unconsciously and intuitively. They resonate with the mother's own psychic organization through a process Bion called maternal "reverie," in which she sorts them out, identifies with them, and projects them back into the infant in less toxic, more structured ways that gradually imbue experience with both affective and cognitive meaning. The infant now introjectively identifies with the mother's tolerance and with her mental structure derived from the sojourn through the mother's mind (Scharff and Scharff 1998).

In one of his seminal papers, "Attacks on Linking," Bion (1967) describes patients who destroy the connections between their own thoughts, and between affect and cognition. This disconnect is based on the failure of container/contained to provide a cycle of links that begins in the interaction of the psyches of child and parent. Schore (2001) makes the point that the mechanism of projective identification resides in humans' capacity to read each other affectively through instantaneous decoding of facial gesture, gaze pattern, vocal tone, small-motor movements, and postural shifts. This capacity for mutual reading adds up to a right-brain-to-right-brain communication that is dominant in infancy, as the child grows in interaction with the mother and father. The affective right brain of the infant predominates for the first eighteen months. These cyclical interactions nurture the infant's brain and mind and result in the periodic "entrainment" of the brains of child and parent. These earliest developmental processes are the basis of projective and introjective identification and affective cueing, which in turn are the basis of transference and countertransference, the center of technique in object relations therapy.

Winnicott's (1963) study of the mother-infant relationship differentiated two groups of maternal (or parental) functions. The first is the "arms-around" holding function of the mother and/or primary caretakers who secure the environment to facilitate the infant's development. Within that envelope, the mother focuses on the infant "eye-to-eye" and "I-to-I," which establishes a relationship of mutual subjectivity, interest, and desire. Linking these contextual and focused ways of relating is a potential mental space within which the transitional phenomena occur that foster thinking about the other and about the self in relationship (Winnicott 1963; Scharff and Scharff 1987, 1998). This eventually forms a space for thinking, for mentalizing emotional relationships, for reflective function (Fonagy et al. 1991; Fonagy 2001), and for symbolic manipulation of experience. It is also a space for empathy and creativity. We extend Winnicott's division of parental function into the environmental and object mother to conceptualizing two types of transference/countertransference—contextual and focused. The contextual transference derives from the arms-around parental function expressed toward the therapist as the one who provides a therapeutic potential space for growth and who protects the patient or family's safety. The focused transference occurs when the patient then explores and makes use of the therapist as an object on whom to project libidinal and aggressive object relations. I believe that in family and couple therapy, unlike the clinical situation of psychoanalysis, the therapist is subject primarily to forces of contextual transference because the family transfers problems from deficits in their own capacity to provide developmental holding to the relationship to the therapist.

THE FAMILY AS A SPECIAL SMALL GROUP

W. R. Bion and S. H. Foulkes have derived models for thinking about groups from analytic experience. Bion (1959) taught that in any group, two organizations of group life exist simultaneously: the task group and the basic assumption group. An unconscious group organized by what Bion called "basic assumptions" underlies the conscious task organization of all groups. In any family or group, an observer can assess the degree to which unconscious organization supports or undermines the conscious and rational task-organization of the family or group. The unconscious organization of a family can be described as constituted by "shared family assumptions" (Zinner and Shapiro 1974). These organize the pattern of family thought and activity and the pattern and distribution of group projective identifications. In dysfunctional families, the dynamic in which one family member is seen as responsible for all the badness or another for all the goodness is created by shared family assumptions regarding unconsciously assigned roles as family scapegoats or heroes.

Foulkes (1948, 1974) described individuals in a group forming an interlocking, mutually influential matrix in which extremes of anxiety usurp the free flow of information and affect, clog the matrix, or isolate the overly anxious individual. Foulkes's understanding of blockages to group function applies equally to family and couple interaction where one member monopolizes the matrix and the network—a telltale sign of neurosis. When we see one member of a family or couple who chronically monopolizes the flow of conscious and unconscious communication, we recommend individual therapy either instead of or in addition to family therapy.

Principles of group dynamics apply in families, but whenever a family is together, unlike a group of strangers, the primary objects internalized by each family member are also literally present as people. It is not only the children who have introjected objects based on experience with their parents. For those parents, their children represent two aspects of the object world. First, the children have been the recipients of parental projections of internal objects whose identity derived from the parents' own parents. In this way, the children also house aspects of the parents' parents and come to stand in for them. Second, the children become, from the time of conception, new internal objects for the parents, ones who have a standing that is just as important as the internal maternal and paternal objects. This aspect of internal object life, the ordinary birth of new internal objects in marriage and childbearing, is important in both family therapy and psychoanalysis, but its lessons are only gradually being imported from family therapy into psychoanalysis (Scharff and Scharff 1998).

A group is a larger context for growth than the dyads and triads that are the usual focus of psychoanalysis. A series of concentric circles operates in family development:

The mother holds the child, who holds her in return.
The father holds the two of them (and they hold him).
The larger nuclear family (siblings, a babysitter, a resident grandparent) participates in family group holding. All members are held by each other.
The extended family holds the nuclear family.
The family is held by the social groups among which it lives.
Social groups are held by the wider society.

There is mental and social exchange among all levels of group organization in which the family and individual live. These wider levels of support and organization are represented mentally in each individual's psychic organization as a complex and comprehensive group construct. In analytic therapy with individuals or in family therapy, transference to the therapist stems not only from the individual, dyad, or Oedipal triad, but also from the nuclear family group, extended family, social group, and society. All of these levels of organization are represented in each individual and each family's mind, so in the transference, all are presented (Scharff and Scharff 1998; Hopper 2002).

CLINICAL EXAMPLE

Tom and Irene Smith, parents in their late thirties, and their children Eric, age ten, Mike, age seven and a half, and Jennifer, age five and a half, have been in weekly family therapy for eighteen months. Tom, a pilot, is withdrawn. Irene, depressed and angry, is also in intensive individual therapy. The couple has been in sex therapy weekly for fifteen months for their sexual dysfunction—her sexual aversion and his premature ejaculation. Irene was physically abused by her father and had sexual interaction just short of penetration with an older brother. As a ten-year-old boy, Tom was sodomized by his father as the father's way of explaining sex. The sex therapy has gone well but slowly. This session draws on the developmental themes of the parents as individuals and as a couple, and illustrates these themes in the family context.

I had been away the two previous weeks. As this session begins, Irene, the mother, looks depressed and has a severe headache. The three children are playing on the floor. Jennifer makes a paper airplane and builds a fence around it with blocks. "Here's his hiding place, Momma," she calls out. I think silently that her play refers both to my absence and to father's hiding from the family. The boys build with blocks. Ten-year-old Eric plays with two toy fighter planes chasing each other in a battle.

The parents watch the play as they talk about having a disappointing setback to their progress during the past two weeks. I understand they are referring indirectly to their sex therapy. I find my thoughts fixing on Jennifer's comment about the airplane's hiding place and Eric's play of two airplanes chasing each other as if in an aggressive primal scene.

I ask the parents, "Do you think your backsliding had to do with feeling abandoned in my absence?"

Irene answers, "I can say 'yes' for myself, and I don't know about Tom."

Tom shakes his head and says, "I really wouldn't know."

I say, "Well, it's likely that without my support over the last two weeks, you have felt shakier emotionally and physically. But I don't think you, Tom, can connect that to my being away, because you have trouble making links." I had in mind Bion's concept of attacks on linking as a reflection of traumatic disconnection. I attribute Tom's difficulty to the integrity of his mental functioning having been invaded by sexual abuse.

Jennifer and Mike are playing with a toy helicopter and a small doll in a bathtub. Jennifer speaks for the small doll who calls to Mike's helicopter as it flies away, saying, "Goodbye! See you tomorrow." As the older boy, Eric, continues playing with planes, one of them is shot down by the other and he throws it forcefully to the floor.

I notice how the children's play is a combative reaction to my absence, which confirms my idea that the rejection it carries for the family has organized the events of their week, and now is organizing the session. I say to Tom, "I think you would have missed me if you could have thought about it. That's what the children are showing in their play. Eric is playing an angry chase, and Jennifer and Mike are playing a missing helicopter."

"I wouldn't know," Tom repeats, smiling wanly and shaking his head in a mixture of disbelief and chagrin.

Suddenly a puppet pig interrupts us by snorting loudly from behind the play table, demanding everyone's attention. "I'm hungry!" says Eric, speaking for the pig. Jennifer and Mike join Eric, taking puppets, too. "We're having a picnic," says Jennifer. "We're eating carrots," she says, as her pink rabbit puppet and Mike's cow chew on my pencils because they are so hungry. Then they bring me a purple furry monster puppet to put on my hand. The children's animal puppets bite and twist the nose of my purple monster while saying, "Honk! Honk!" They do this in a voracious, teasing, and even loving way. I turn to Irene and Tom and say, "Here's the evidence that some people are mad at me for leaving them hungry."

"Yes," says Irene, now smiling from underneath her headache. "I think they aren't the only people who might want to bite your nose." She makes a gesture with her hand as though she were honking my puppet's nose too—or perhaps my actual nose.

I say, "Maybe if you could talk about that, you wouldn't have such a headache."

"Maybe so," she agrees, slowly widening her smile.

Tom joins in with his own impish grin, saying to Irene, "Why don't you go over there and honk his nose, too?"

His teasing obviously gets through to me, because before I know it, I find myself saying, "No! Why don't you just talk about it?" I feel sheepish as soon as I realize how Tom's teasing has caught me.

Jennifer now stops honking my puppet's nose and strides away from me. Her heels click loudly on the floor. Then she turns around and strides back.

"Hello!" she says. "I've been away for a trip." Her pink rabbit starts to chew on my purple monster's nose again.

"What's happening?" I ask.

"I'm honking someone's nose," she says. "He's been mean to us, so we're being mean to him!"

I feel I now have vivid evidence and language for reaching Tom, knowing that Irene had already understood me. So I say, "The whole family has been missing me and is mad at me about being away. It's true for you, too, Tom. But you can't link the two things up—my being away and your trouble functioning with Irene. The trouble you have linking things like that goes back to the situation when you asked your father to help you, and he hurt you instead. So now you can't trust me to support you." (I left the more specific language about his father's sexually abusing him for the following couple session out of deference to the children.)

Tom says, "My first impression is: 'You don't even think about it!'"

Seizing on the grammatical construction of his speech, in which I knew he meant "a person doesn't think about it," I say, "What you have just said, Tom, is that I don't think about it, that I don't think about what I mean to you."

"I meant that I don't think about it," he protests.

I say, "That's not what you said, though. You *said* that '*I* don't think about it.'"

Before I could say more, Irene joins in, teasing him and making the emotional link more powerfully than I could. "Nyah, nyah, nyah. You got caught in a Freudian slip!" she teases. Tom playfully slaps her knee, acknowledging her point.

I now continue to elaborate on the way Tom had been unable to know that he missed me, and had retreated from Irene and the family in his hurt instead. While I talk directly with Tom and Irene, a final piece of play confirms the theme of the family's transference anger. Eric uses a toy ambulance to knock down the building that Jennifer and Mike have been building over the last few minutes. Tom notices and says, "Eric, stop trying to distract us." I agree with Tom that Eric is trying to divert our attention, and say, "Eric, I know you've been upset today, too. Those airplanes have been having a real battle, and the plane you've been enjoying throwing on the floor is my toy. Now the ambulance is knocking down the building. And you know, ambulances are connected to doctors."

"I can see it," says Irene. "The ambulance-slash-doctor knocked down the building." As she says this, she makes a gesture with her hand of the grammatical "slash" that indicates that two words are joined together by the slash (ambulance/doctor).

Taken with the word *slash,* thinking of its meaning as the wound a knife makes, and joining their teasing mode, I say, "I liked the part about the ambulance-slash-doctor."

"Oh, yes," she says, laughing now. "I see. 'Slash the doctor!' Yes. I see."

Tom lets out a laugh. As the session ends, Jennifer laments, "I don't want to go!"

FAMILY GROUP HOLDING
AND CONTAINMENT

Let me relate this vignette to some points, first to the model of mind, and then to the action of family therapy. The Smith family's group holding capacity was challenged in the transference by my absence and the abandonment the family group experienced. The couple's sexual function "fell apart" in their words, standing for a failure of parental attachment, interfering with the mental capacity to make links emotionally, physically, and cognitively, and evoking the traumas of their early development. Each individual's experience of separation in the transference contributes to the family's overall experience of loss. Each of them speaks, in play or in words, for the experience of rejection, thereby showing individual areas of difficulty that combine as a group experience that expresses the family's vulnerability to retraumatization in the transference—where it can be recognized and modified by interpretation and working-through.

In the family's past, which I had seen represented in the early days of the family therapy when similar absences had resulted in a more through parental collapse, the children as a subgroup would become distressed and disorganized. Their play deteriorated into quarreling and whining, Eric's attacking Mike, Mike's soiling during the session or frantically knocking down block structures, and Jennifer's running to cling to her mother. We could see the disruptions at both group and individual levels. The collapse was developmentally rooted in the malfunction of the circles of parental and social holding in which each parent grew up, and it was conveyed to the children through projective identification. In the chain of events, failures of holding and containment in the family and social group resulted in adulthood in easily disrupted parental psychic states, and these were conveyed by action, angry and despairing facial expressions, and words accompanied by threatening and threatened cadences to the children, where the effects showed up in disrupted mood and behavior through projective identification.

The session shows that the children have grown much more resilient, able to sustain play without regression, to use play to give meaning to the shared family group distress. We usually think of this as a parental function, but in an impaired family, it is common for the parental capacity for holding and containment to collapse. In this session, Irene's headache and depression and Tom's inability to make links are signs of collapse, but at this stage in treatment, they are transitory. The children have been directly expressing family-wide feelings about my absence, and they also respond first to my interpretation by playing with the hungry animals eating and then attacking the puppet monster they give me so it can receive their anger. They do what children often do in healthy families—they help their parents function. And it works. Their efforts to offer containment to the parents help to restore the parents' capacity for linking and reflection with humor. After the children's intervention, the parents get going again: Tom once again becomes an active father, telling Eric not to disrupt his siblings' play, and Irene interprets her own slip and shows the family their anger at me.

A MODEL OF ANALYTIC
FAMILY GROUP THERAPY

While family therapy affects each individual, family group experience in therapy is more than the sum of individual experience. In this session, the group's overall expression of object-hunger speaks for each of them and for the group as a whole. All the elements of individual analytic treatment are relevant to work with families and couples. We value understanding offered through opening a potential space for exploration, supported by the holding relationship, and offered by accepting individual and family projective identifications, allowing them to form in us as introjective identifications and resonate with our own internal object relations, feeding them back to the patient, often in words, as we translate nonverbal experience into more cognitively structured and verbalized experience. But we also know that we convey a great deal to patients and families through our nonverbal behavior. When I reflexively responded to Irene and Tom that they should not literally honk my nose but should talk about it, I knew that I conveyed my anxiety about their aggression. But I also conveyed that together we could both stand and understand them. Even though we could all see the potential for micro-breakdown, we could repair together. Not every moment in therapy works out as well, but not every moment needs to. It is only necessary that enough of them work out that family and therapist can maintain a sense of continuing development. Families even take solace that we therapists are fallible in ways similar to the ones in which they feel vulnerable—that we too struggle with our vulnerability and recover. If we present ourselves as invulnerable, we increase their sense that they can never achieve the level of maturity they believe they see in us.

Transference-countertransference exchange is as powerful in family therapy as in psychoanalysis. In this session, we see a developmental regression in the family generated in the transference, and we see the family work with it to repair their sense of loss. My retort to Tom's teasing threat that Irene should honk my nose was a visible indicator of my countertransference, but there was, of course, much more going on inside me. I was caught up in confronting how on guard Tom was with me, and how he thereby guarded the whole family group from directly knowing and expressing their anger and disappointment. Silently, I was feeling quite guilty for letting them down, and hoping they would not voice this. Because of my guilt, I had my own internal block to linking. When they finally did manage to get through to me, I felt relieved. The humor the family mustered in using the children's play helped us all find a dignified way through. By the time we joined forces to find the "slash the doctor" metaphor for my transference betrayal of them and their group transference response to it, I felt we were working securely and creatively together.

The subgroups (the couple, the children) and individuals that make up each family generate a group transference that influences individual psychic organization. When parents in family therapy are able to grow a capacity for holding and containment in full view of the children, internalized versions of the parents embedded in each child are deeply affected. The family members receive analytically informed understanding as individuals. Evidence of growth in the parents and children is itself growth promoting and combines with a family group experience of holding and containment that provides space for the reorganization of the internal object relations set of the family. Through these continuous interactions, family members refashion their individual psychic structures.

Object relations family and couple therapy is first and foremost an application of psychoanalysis. Its technique derives directly from core analytic theory to understand mental development and to promote growth for the whole family.

REFERENCES

Bion, W. R. 1959. *Experiences in Groups.* New York: Basic Books (1961).
———. 1967. Attacks on Linking. In *Second Thoughts*, pp. 93–109. London: Heinemann.
———. 1970. *Attention and Interpretation.* London: Tavistock.
Fairbairn, W. R. D. 1952. *Psychoanalytic Studies of the Personality.* London: Routledge.
———. 1954. The nature of hysterical states. In *From Instinct to Self: Selected Papers of W. R. D. Fairbairn*, vol. 1, ed. D. E. Scharff and E. F. Birtles, pp. 13–40. Northvale, NJ: Jason Aronson (1994).
Fonagy, P. 2001. *Attachment Theory and Psychoanalysis.* New York: Other Press.
Fonagy, P., G. S. Moran, H. Steele, and A. C. Higgitt. 1991. The capacity for understanding mental states: The reflective self in parent and child and its significance for security of attachment. *Infant Mental Health Journal* 13:200–216.
Foulkes, S. H. 1948. *Introduction to Group-Analytic Therapy: Studies in the Social Integration of Individuals and Groups.* London: Heinemann.
———. 1974. *Group Analytic Psychotherapy: Method and Principles.* London: Gordon and Breach.
Hopper, E. 2002. *The Social Unconscious: Selected Papers.* London: Jessica Kingsley.
Klein, M. 1946. Notes on some schizoid mechanisms. In *Envy and Gratitude and Other Works: 1946–1963*, pp. 1–24. London: Hogarth.
Scharff, D. E. 1982. *The Sexual Relationship: An Object Relations View of Sex and the Family.* Northvale, NJ: Jason Aronson.
———. 1994. *Refinding the Object and Reclaiming the Self.* Northvale, NJ: Jason Aronson.
Scharff, D. E., and J. S. Scharff. 1987. *Object Relations Family Therapy.* Northvale, NJ: Jason Aronson.
———. 1991. *Object Relations Couple Therapy.* Northvale, NJ: Jason Aronson.
———. 1998. *Object Relations Individual Therapy.* Northvale, NJ: Jason Aronson.
Schore, A. N. 2001. The right brain as the neurobiological substratum of Freud's dynamic unconscious. In *The Analytic Century: Freud's Legacy for the Future*, ed. D. E. Scharff, pp. 61–88. New York: Other Press (2001).
Winnicott, D. W. 1963. Communicating and not communicating leading to a study of certain opposites. In *The Maturational Processes and the Facilitating Environment*, pp. 179–92. London: Hogarth.
Zinner, J., and R. Shapiro. 1974. The family group as a single psychic entity: Implications for acting out in adolescence. *International Review of Psycho-Analysis* 1(1): 179–86.

2

New Paradigms for Treating Relationships

David E. Scharff and Jill Savege Scharff

Our original formulation of object relations couple and family therapy (D. Scharff and J. Scharff 1987, 1991) drew primarily from Fairbairn (1952) and Winnicott (1965, 1974); Klein (1975a, 1975b) and Bion (1959, 1970); and Dicks's (1967) synthesis of Fairbairn's endopsychic situation and Klein's projective identification. Adding to this an emphasis on intimacy and sexuality informed by the work of Masters and Johnson (1970), Helen Singer Kaplan (1974), and other sexologists, and an understanding of child development and play therapy from child analytic training, we came up with a model of analytic conjoint therapy that addresses the couple's intimate life and the family's role in development. Since then we have been more specific about our use of dreams in family therapy, couple therapy, and sex therapy. Over the past decade, we have been culling findings from trauma research and theory, attachment theory, neuropsychoanalysis, and chaos theory, but until now we have written about them mainly in connection with individual therapy. We now summarize these new developments and apply them to couple and family therapy. We propose an updated view of how object relations family therapy and couple therapy work, along with clinical lessons derived from these ideas. Often such developing areas of research as those from which we draw are regarded as though one of them is *the* new area, the hot area to be given precedence, as if all that came before is old-fashioned, and so should be relegated to the archaic sciences of yesteryear. That was so, for instance, with Masters and Johnson's understanding of sexuality of a generation ago, which was then supplanted by later advances in understanding the

19

biology and pharmacology of sex. The concepts we discuss here all offer promise of our increased understanding of couples and families, although none is a panacea, and all are works in progress.

NEUROPSYCHOANALYSIS AND INFANT RESEARCH: AFFECT REGULATION AND THE ORIGIN OF THE SELF

Brain researchers and analysts have been adding to our knowledge of affect regulation and the interpersonal stimuli required for growth of the infant's brain in the first months. Alan Schore (2003a, 2003b) drew this work together in his remarkable two-volume work, while Fonagy (2001) and his colleagues synthesized research findings on early infant-parent attachment and child development.

It is now clear that the earliest attachment is of evolutionary value not only for the physical survival of the young organism, as Bowlby (1988) proposed a generation ago, but for the development of a mind that processes interpersonal relations, and that moves from co-regulation of affect in infancy to a fair degree of self-regulation by middle childhood. In this process, a self is born, housed first in the physical experience of the infant's body in interaction with the parents. In psychological interaction, infants increasingly recognize themselves as instrumental in determining the course of their relationships. The culture medium for the growth of the brain is a positively toned relationship with primary attachment figures, that is, with the parents. In the first eighteen months the right orbitofrontal lobes—the executive center of affective experience—are dominant. During these early months, mother and infant experience each other from inside carefully coordinated, mutually cued interactions of high affective value and significance. Within this context, the infant's brain is entrained by its association with the mother's more developed brain.

According to experiments, the infant's cue-and-response interactions make a crucial shift at three months of age from preferring contingent to noncontingent marking (Fonagy, Gergely, Jurist, and Target 2002). If something hurts, or if it feels good, newborn infants prefer their caretakers to mark the facial expression or sound with a similar, but exaggerated expression or vocalization that is very close to their own. This is called "contingent marking." To put it differently, young babies prefer that their parents mirror hurt or pleasure with responses at the same level of intensity and volume at which the babies communicated their feelings to their parents. But at three months, they prefer "noncontingent marking"—that is, a response that is nearly the same but clearly not the same. The parent gives meaning to the child's experience by mirroring with a slight, but definite, difference. In this way, painful experience can be "down-regulated" before it becomes overwhelming, and pleasurable experience can be validated, played with, and extended. This research detail provides the specifics of Bion's concept of containment.

From such new ways of studying the processes of mirroring and containment, we can develop a more specific language for couple and family therapy. Problems arise, for instance, when a parent requires a child to accept nearly identical marking when the need and preference for that is long past, or when the parent intrudes by using the mirroring process to insert the parent's own affective and object relations agenda into the child instead of responding to the child's need for affect down-regulation. The mother of a school phobic child may respond to an expression of anxiety by marking it too exactly, thereby "up-regulating" it and so reinforcing it (as Bion might say, "reflecting unconscious dread"). Or she may down-regulate it, saying in essence, "I see your worry, but it's not so bad, and I'm here to help you through it." Mothers or fathers with an overload of their own anxieties may not only mark their children's anxious responses but move them up a notch, implying that their children should fear more than they know.

This research confirms the value of object relations concepts such as the holding environment and projective identification. Firm holding means secure attachment. Poor holding leads to insecure or disorganized attachment styles. Parents with insecure, fearful attachment styles have inner object relations that transmit to their children by projective identification. Parents with secure attachment styles have good mentalizing capacities and give their children a way of dealing with anxiety by reflecting on their experience—in Bion's language, the mother a is good container, transforming beta bits into alpha function. The reflective function of the infant's self evolves from being aware of affecting the other person, eventually discovering that those effects can be intentional, to being fully aware of being a person in a life drama, an autobiographical self, beginning between four and five years of age. The self continues to evolve throughout the rest of life, and especially in relation to significant others in couples and families.

The child developmental researchers have given us ideas that are not totally new, but their close focus does give us new tools for seeing how couples and families work at the co-regulation of affect. We can use their paradigms to examine how partners and families provide safety, holding, and containment for one another, how they mark anxiety, how they exaggerate distress, and how they calm one another by the objectivity of their own point of view to provide a soothing parental transformation of experience.

ATTACHMENT RESEARCH: COMPLEX ATTACHMENTS

The real-life attachments of couples have been described by Christopher Clulow's colleagues, Fisher and Crandell (2001), as "complex attachments" in distinction to the relatively simplified classifications of infant attachment made for research purposes, and based on findings from structured tests—the Strange Situation for infants, and the Adult Attachment Interview (Ainsworth et al. 1978; George, Kaplan, and Main 1985; Main, Kaplan, and Cassidy 1985). How much more complex, then, are the multiple attachments forged in families over time, attachments not only to the parents but also to siblings, grandparents, and other extended family members, all reinforced by subgroups interacting within the family? When we see couples and families for therapy, we see these attachments in vivo, and in the transference when we become crucial attachment figures. Then the coming-and-going of the family at the beginning and end of sessions, or before and after breaks and vacations, constitutes a repeated strange situation where the family's attachment behavior can be experienced and clinically decoded (Clulow 2001).

CLINICAL STUDIES OF TRAUMA

Trauma causes a constriction of mentalization (the capacity to freely assess one's own and another's mental state) and a defect in affect regulation, leading to post-traumatic startle responses, hypervigilance, and distress over stimuli apparently unrelated to the trauma. The traumatized person seeks the familiarity of fearful attachments that militate against symbolization and has a diminished repertoire of adaptive responses and types of interaction patterns. People who are overwhelmed by recent trauma will experience it in terms of any previous trauma. Partners may try to dissociate from current trauma and events that trigger recall of earlier trauma by splitting off their awareness of traumatic experience and sequestering it in deeply buried traumatic nuclei inside the individual psyche, the marriage, or the family. An apparently satisfactory marital relationship and a family organized in a highly controlled or overexciting way may cover these traumatic nuclei or gaps. In that case, couple and family therapists may get access to the dissociated material by analyzing their own feelings of discomfort or by examining gaps in the treatment process. When the material inside the nuclei is too toxic to be managed, affect explosions or absences of affect and motivation may bring the couple or family into treatment. That is how the couple we now describe came to see Dr. D. Scharff (described more fully in J. Scharff and D. Scharff 1994).

Tony and Theresa

Tony and Theresa had an apparently strong, happy marriage with an active sex life. They enjoyed their three children, shared the responsibility of supporting them, and both of them kept house. Following a routine medical procedure, Tony got a fulminating infection in his right arm, which then had to be amputated. Easygoing Tony bounced back from surgery, but then he realized what the loss of his arm would mean, and he got too depressed to work or think about a prosthesis. Theresa had to work double time, and then he complained that he missed her. They began to argue daily, and then their children got depressed, stayed away from home, and did badly at school.

Telling the story of the trauma to the therapist as a witness relieved their stress initially, and usefully led to their revealing the earlier trauma that they shared. Each of them had been physically abused by their parents, and had stepped in to take the abuse so that younger children were spared. Their marriage contract was based on a promise that they would never hit each other. If they got angry, they would hit something else, such as a wall. Dealing with Tony's passive, dejected reaction to his trauma, Theresa hit the wall more and more. The bricks and mortar absorbed her rage until a wall had formed between them and their feelings. Without his punching arm, Tony had no way to express his rage and grief.

With therapy Tony and Theresa became more able to acknowledge anger in words, but then they fell silent in some sessions, and skipped others altogether. The therapist, who had felt in tune with them, now felt out of touch. He guessed that the gap between them and him might reflect a gap in their shared marital personality so as to cover yet a deeper traumatic nucleus. The therapist asked if they were avoiding some other feeling, perhaps of a sexual nature. Theresa replied sadly that they used to have lots of sex, but since her hysterectomy she had had continuous vaginal infections that made sex extremely painful. Theresa had not told Tony this—another instance of leaving a gap to cover a trauma.

Even before the couple lost Tony's arm (standing for the management of aggression), they had lost Theresa's well-functioning, sexually responsive vagina (standing for their loving connectedness); both crucial aspects of their bond. They would need plenty of time in couple therapy to mourn all their losses, rebuild a safe holding environment, and find new ways to express love and anger.

Couples like Tony and Theresa compulsively avoid any repetition of abuse as a way of trying to forget it, but the control exerted tends also to squash spontaneity of expression. This impoverishes their relationship and is transmitted as a trauma to the next generation despite their best efforts. Some couples tend to invoke abusive behavior in one spouse by repeating the abuse instead of remembering it. Some up-regulate affective experience and cause an escalating cycle of out-of-control interactions. Some do not mark experience at all. The couple and family therapist puts words to experience, and so demonstrates a new way of marking it. We engage with the family in a dynamic experience of down-regulation that is responsive and flexible and reduces the occurrence of explosive traumatic replays. Object relations couple and family therapy helps couples and families develop a shared family narrative of the abuse history, and competent, sensitive affect regulation, as an alternative to the reenactment of trauma and the defenses against it.

CHAOS THEORY: INTERACTING PERSONALITIES AS SELF-ORGANIZING SYSTEMS

Chaos theory is the understanding of self-organizing systems (Gleick 1987). Chaos theory applies to the study of the evolving self in its matrix of relationships and to the dynamics of interacting couples and families. Mathematical study of complex systems shows that it is impossible to predict the effects on a system of small changes, especially at the point of origin. Similarly, therapists cannot predict how people will relate to one another after they have been exposed to the more organized, caring system of a therapeutic relationship, but we do see that they tend to be influenced toward a more mature relationship. Traumatized couples and families are more predictable and more likely to resist change than families where there has been no trauma because their patterns are numbingly repetitive and do not adapt to changing circumstances. A healthy family has repeating, characteristic patterns but they differ slightly in each iteration, and in that area of difference lie possibilities of change and adaptation. The healthy family is capable of a wider range of adaptive variation and its members have a wider range of responses to different stimuli and varying circumstances.

To put this in mathematical language of chaos theory, we describe the unhealthy pattern as "self-same," governed by a *limit-cycle attractor,* a system that always follows the same narrow range of expression, like an electric pendulum. In the most stuck families, the attractor is a *fixed-cycle attractor* that draws all patterns to the same point, like the pendulum of a clock that has wound down. In healthy families, the pattern is "self-similar," governed by a relatively stable *strange attractor,* a system that moves the pattern into chaos and back again to a slightly different point in what is a new, yet recognizable pattern. Movement between chaos and reorganization allows for adaptation and creativity.

All psychology, including object relations theory, is a concretization and simplification of the patterns of flux in mental development. These patterns are a synthesis of responses to multiple influences on already established, but modifiable patterns. In the terms of chaos theory, stimuli from new *perturbations* in association with strange attractors disrupt the self-same patterns of limit-cycle attractors, and even affect the rigid patterns of fixed-cycle attractors. An individual's mental organization is made up of an internal object relations set that functions as a *basin of attraction* that, like a whirlpool, pulls new experience toward old patterns, and of strange attractors that open the personality system to learning from experience. When that individual comes into intimate relationship, the loved one's basin of attraction may pull in the direction of old, maladaptive patterns that keep the couple or family locked in limited ways of behaving and feeling. On the other hand, association with the strange attractors of a loved one's internal object relationships may exert a healing effect across the interpersonal space.

CLINICAL EXAMPLE FROM FAMILY THERAPY

Eleven-year-old Seth Darnell can never get up on time, and so he misses the school bus and has to be driven to school most days. Mrs. Darnell is terribly afraid for his well-being, and regards him as fragile and unhappy. She dotes on him and spends every evening with him helping with homework. Bedtime drags on so that even she is sleep deprived. Mr. Darnell can set limits, but Mrs. Darnell has to undermine them. For Mr. and Mrs. Darnell, sex is vanishingly rare. When he protests that he is pushed aside by his wife when she is overindulgent of Seth, she ignores his protestations and denies his accusations. Their thirteen-year-old daughter, Mary, is an excellent and reliable student, but she has severe daily headaches and tension in her jaw, and bites her nails to the quick. She is furious at Seth for getting so much attention, and complains bitterly that their mother has no time for her. In compensation for missing her mother, Mary and her father have an intense relationship.

Seth is frequently between his parents in their bed, he showers in his mother's bathroom, and she still helps him with homework. Why does she feel compelled toward him? Seth triggers her guilt over not being more helpful to her own brother, a boy with extreme social and academic problems that got her parents' constant attention, and who is now a schizophrenic man. She monitors Seth constantly to guard against his decline to such a state, but his difficulty going to school only makes her more fearful. Her constant babying of Seth diminishes her relationship to her husband. The trauma of her brother's illness and its impact on her family has led to Mrs. Darnell's continuing anxiety and insecure attachments to her husband and children, thus creating similar patterns in the current family to the ones she grew up with. Her incomplete development of mentalizing capacity means that, like her mother, she cannot imagine and empathize with her son's reality so as to detoxify his fears. Instead she up-regulates them. In the basin of attraction created by her overtly powerful interactional pattern of anxious clinging with Seth, we see the swirl of other anxious attachments. A family culture of anxiety is reflected in Mr. Darnell's resigned passivity, Mary's tension headaches, Seth's anxious phobic behavior, and Mrs. Darnell's excited way of relating to him.

At the next family session, Mrs. Darnell began. She said that things had been good over the holidays. She told of a humorous incident in which she had teasingly asked Seth if he would like a carrot. But it was an old one, and when he went to take it from her, he had found it limp. He had asked her what it was and then asked if she had cut off his dad's penis. Seth blushed, and said, "What did you have to tell him that for?" Mary said, "Eww! Let's talk about something else." Mr. Darnell silently raised his hands in a gesture of "What can you do?"

Apparently changing the topic, Seth said to his mother, "I don't want you to come in to comfort me in the morning. It makes it too hard to get up. And I want to go to school."

"You don't want me to come in and wake you up?" she asked incredulously. "But you need me because it's so hard for you."

"Let's think about why you have to baby him," I said. "What was the morning like for you as a child?"

Mrs. Darnell answered, "When I was five, I cried every day about going to school. My mother would talk to me for hours about what I should wear, which of eleven dresses, and, since I hated getting cold feet, she would carry me across the cold tiles. I worry for Seth like that."

"You were five," I said. "Seth is eleven! You are treating him like a scared little girl. He needs to be free to grow up."

"I don't want you to treat me like a baby or a little girl," he said, surprisingly assertively. "I want to grow up, and you make it too hard."

We discussed how this limited-cycle, repetitive, obligatory pattern between Seth and his mother pushes the relationship between the parents into the shadows, and serves to create the compensatory relationship between Mary and her father. I said that Mrs. Darnell offers Seth many carrots, and doing so is part of making any carrots that Mr. Darnell could offer him become limp, and so the children see him as weak.

Mary said that I was right. She said that she likes her father a lot, but she wants some of her mother too, and there isn't enough to go around because she is preoccupied with Seth. Mr. Darnell reminded me that he objected to her indulgence of the boy, but she wouldn't listen, and so what could he do?

I said, "This pattern leaves no time for Mom and Dad to have a relationship of their own, which they miss. The carrot story is a sexual joke between Mom and Seth about how there is less of a relationship between Mom and Dad than there is between Mom and Seth."

Seth was nodding, so I continued. "What Seth needs is not a limp carrot joke between Mom and Seth. He and Mary both need two parents who stand up strongly for themselves as a couple."

"That's a good joke," said Seth. "I like it."

Mrs. Darnell's carrot story captures the essence of her excited, sexualized relationship with Seth, and his joking comment refers to the implied castration of his father. The group-wide dynamic reflects a pattern of dependence on others, and alternating fragmentation and merged confusion. This changes as the therapist introduces new, more adaptive patterns into the family group. Seth sets a limit on his mother's babying. Mary states her needs, but she will need to modify her entrenched contempt for Seth if they are to develop a better sibling relationship. Mr. Darnell speaks of his despair, and asks for help in being effective in opposition to his wife's overindulgence of their son. In association to the male therapist, the family system is reaching for the fresh carrot of a strengthened male presence, which will act as a strange attractor around which the family can reorganize.

THE INDIVIDUAL'S REPETITIVE DREAM ADDRESSED IN COUPLE THERAPY

Repetitive dreams generally represent a trauma that a person has been unable to metabolize. When receiving such a dream from one of the partners in couple therapy, the couple therapist works with the couple to detoxify the trauma and its contribution to underlying conflict in the couple relationship. The repetition feature of the dream reflects the dream as a limit-cycle attractor, not open to re-organization by the unconscious process of dreaming. The participation of the partner creates turbulence in the telling of the dream and in associating to it. The effect of the partner's object relations set on the dream material connected to the dreamer's object relations acts as a strange attractor that can change the closed system of the dream process and open it to the added strange attractor effect of the therapist's interpretive work.

Madge and Laurence

Madge and Laurence, each forty years old, had been living together in Madge's apartment, but Laurence, who suffered from incapacitating depression and anxiety, could not commit to marrying Madge, who went into rages because of feeling that no one could love her. It was a vicious cycle. Often in a fury, she berated him for his lack of commitment, at which he sat in mute silence with his head hung in shame, which inflamed her rage at his passivity. Nevertheless they were at times close, appreciative, and understanding of one another's difficulties. They spent time together, they had an excellent sex life, and the relationship seemed to be moving along. Then Laurence was offered a transfer to his company's Middle East sales office.

If Laurence accepted the position abroad, Madge could not work there without a work permit, and so could only go as a wife, but Laurence still did not agree to marry her. Madge went into a tailspin, hysterically demanding that he prove his love for her, and saying that if he could not, it would prove that she was indeed as unlovable as she had thought and might as well be dead. There was no one else Laurence wanted to be with, he loved Madge, but he felt that he was too depressed and low in energy to be a good husband.

In the following session, Laurence told a dream that he has two or three times a week. Laurence began, "My dream always takes place in a place I'm not sure I'm supposed to be. It's not a place that I'm forbidden, but I don't know where I fit in. I feel very uncomfortable being there. I sense someone may come in and find me there. I'm not in a lot of trouble, but I would have to explain myself and I'm not sure why I'm there."

He said he thought this dream was emblematic of the difficulty of knowing who he is and what he is doing. It describes how unsure and uncertain he feels about his job and where his relationship is going.

Madge responded, "Laurence is more frightened in the dream than he is saying. Sometimes it's a nightmare, and it wakens me up. His explanation of uncertainty doesn't ring true to me. It's more profound than, 'Should I marry this woman? Am I choosing the right career?'"

Laurence replied, "There is uncertainty about whether my life is worth living."

Madge said, "You didn't need to stay uncertain. You could ask someone in the dream if you were in the wrong place."

Thinking of Laurence's schizoid aloneness, I said, "I thought there was no one in this dream for Laurence to ask."

Madge said, "Yes there is. He's left them out. Oh, sorry, I'm like that Thurber story about the man who has to die because his wife tells all his stories."

Petulantly, Laurence said, "Can I tell my own dream? Often there's no one there. There *is* another part of the dream where I am with people, but I don't really know them, and I'm not sure what they think about me. [I wondered if these other people might be standing for me, the therapist, in various sessions, my feelings about him not addressed directly.] It's not obvious that they like me or dislike me, and it's not obvious that I don't fit in, because I seem to be accepted. It's more that I have a feeling of alienation and of being alone. There's no one I can ask to figure out where I stand. It's up to me to try to figure out where I stand, and in the dream, I never do."

Laurence's dream operated like a limit-cycle attractor, always returning in slightly different ways to the same question of who he was and whether he should be there. The dream conveyed to me an image of a lost and lonely little boy with an insecure attachment and a floating sense of identity. This image acted like a basin of attraction, pulling relationships toward him in that dimension. I saw him with no one and then with some people he is not sure he fits in with, including me. I immediately thought of an actual adoption, or an Oedipal romance fantasy. In doing so, I was moving defensively to nail down the gaps that are characteristic of any kind of trauma, and moving away from the transference of myself as not able to connect with him. I asked rather concretely, "Do you think that there's a secret about where you come from?"

He said, "I don't understand the question."

I said, "I'm wondering if you have a fantasy or had a fantasy as a child about where you came from and where you really belonged."

Madge jumped in to say, "You don't look like your parents."

Laurence corrected her, "I don't look like my brother. It's not an impossible stretch to see my mother in me, but I have been struck by the differences in my brother and me in a lot of ways. I never had serious doubts about whether we were really brothers, but I have to admit we are so different, and I wonder why. He's a couple of inches shorter that I am. He's extremely muscular. He has blue eyes, and no intellectual interest. He hasn't read a single book. He's a mechanic—an aircraft maintenance supervisor. Culture and intellect are important to me and totally unimportant to him. He lives in a small town in Ohio with three kids and a wife. He doesn't care about his life the way I do. He was damaged too, but he made his peace."

Madge said, "You told me you think he wrestles with the same things you do, but in a different way. This notion of him being satisfied and at peace is not what you've offered up to me before."

Laurence said, "He's come to terms with his life."

"Who's come to terms with what happened?" Madge challenged him. "Tell about his accident with the pipes."

Laurence said, "Well, okay, when I was four and he was two, we lived next to a construction project where big sewer pipes were exposed. My brother and I were playing on these and my mom was there. The pipes opened up and closed above his head. Two five-hundred-pound weights smashed on his skull, and my mother couldn't pull him out. She told me, 'Go get your dad.' But he was on the phone, and he said it was important, and he couldn't talk to me. I said, 'We need you. Mom wants you right away.' But he dismissed me. I ran back to Mom. Somehow or other, Mom pulled the pipes apart, and got my brother out, and took him to the hospital. They said he had only had a concussion, but he stopped talking and he couldn't focus his eyes. I remember it, completely. He could do everything else, like eat and walk, but he was not communicative for a couple of months. He seems to have recovered fully in the physical sense, and in the emotional sense, but he just doesn't have the intellectual capacity that I do. And I feel really bad about what happened to him. Why did it happen to him and not me? All my parents said was that we were really fortunate he wasn't killed, and then it was never talked about again."

I said, "Being the kid that didn't get hurt seems to have left you feeling guilty. Unlike your brother, from whom you feel so different, you find it hard to deserve pleasure in your work, to claim the woman you say you love, and to choose to be married. It's as if you feel you must let him be the only one to have those things to make up for his not having the intellect you do."

Laurence became more assertive after this interpretation. I was congratulating myself that my intervention had interrupted the limit cycle and that therapy had functioned as a strange attractor pulling toward the chaos of remembering traumatic experience and then toward reorganization. But then he accepted the new job, and left without Madge, and so the couple therapy came to a bitter end. Laurence continued to insist that he loved Madge but just didn't want to be married. He met a woman in the Middle East, and Madge moved on, but she was devastated when he married, less than a year from the end of the couple therapy. The couple's analysis of the repetitive dream relieved Laurence of a guilty inhibition that had kept him unmarried. Unfortunately for Madge, it also freed him from his insecure attachment to her. She had become too tied to his distancing, rejecting internal object to survive the reorganization of his internal object relations.

In Laurence's dream, the sense of not belonging shows up in many iterations. The dream presents him with the bleakness, hopelessness, and personal uncertainty that follow from his dismissive, distancing style of relating. He tells his dream but he leaves out some details, and Madge provides them for him, like a mother who thrusts her own needs and personality into her less-developed child, and pries open his closed personality, thus providing hope of relating intimately but also generating his need to resist. She intrudes to get her points in. This sets up a perturbation that usefully stimulates new associations. Then Laurence tells the memories of his brother's accident that had left him feeling estranged and guilty. He self-organizes in a new way and develops a set of capacities with more autonomy, but he does so by jettisoning his object—his old dismissive pattern.

In terms of adult attachment theory, Madge's pattern is preoccupied, insecure, and clinging while Laurence has a dismissive attachment pattern with a fearful element based in trauma. Their attachment patterns are limit-cycle attractors producing patterns of interaction and views of the self that are repetitive—self-same, not self-similar—and, from one behavioral cycle to another, leave no area of difference in which to experience turbulence, healthy confusion, adaptation, and change. Self-similar patterns carry the identity of the couple relationship over time and yet leave room for growth and development as circumstances change. Therapy provides a strange attractor that breaks up the limit-cycle profile of their interaction, moves it into chaos, and back to a new state of organization. This provides a stimulus for growth and new choices. Laurence chooses to separate from the couple relationship. This destroys Madge's pattern of clinging to a frightened, distancing man, and catapults her into her deepest fear of being unlovable. However, this also leaves her free to reorganize as a single woman who wants to be in love with a loving man rather than a woman who wants marriage to an elusive lover.

CONCLUSION

Attachment theory, trauma theory, and chaos theory illuminate the dynamics of family interaction. Chaos theory also offers a way of relating new systems of thought to each other and to Freud's early theories within the context of complex understanding now available. Freud's theories are not absolute, any more than Newton's physics are. They both offer useful observations of rules of behavior, but they do not account for all natural phenomena, and certainly not those at the edge of chaos. Freud joins other systems in offering useful approximations of development, each of them most applicable to contemporary pathologies. We now see the complexity of self and family development, the essential unpredictability of life, and the way in which theories, although useful guides to understanding, are still in formation, still woefully inadequate, still only partial explanations of life's infinite variety. Older concepts from drive theory, psychosocial stages of development, the repetition compulsion, or the centrality of the Oedipal situation help us with specific clinical problems. Object relations theory, self psychology, sexual research, and family therapy theories focused on the person and the relational context for growth and adult development; attachment theory, theories of affect regulation and neurological development; and trauma theory also give partial explanations toward our understanding of complex self-organizing systems, but none of them offers total explanation. We think it is important to integrate knowledge from each of these clinical fields, research, and theory, so as to help us recognize patterns of complexity, tolerate continued uncertainty, and embrace understanding as an evolving state of knowledge.

In the new paradigm, experience with the therapist becomes the new organizer. The attentive therapist is the new attachment figure that attracts the past attachment anxieties so that they can be recognized, and also attracts them toward more secure types of attachment with greater flexibility and resilience. The therapist, open to experience and able to tolerate ambiguity and uncertainty, is a basin of attraction that pulls in the current affective response patterns, and then as a new strange attractor throws them into confusion, but, having a sturdy belief in self organization, is not sucked permanently into the old basins of attraction, and does not perseverate on one theme or one theory. Couples and families move from co-regulation in close relation to the therapist, to self-regulation in identification with the therapist whose presence is no longer required. The therapist is not a limit-cycle attractor, but is a strange attractor in proximity to which couples and families are drawn to new levels of organization. The therapist's action as a strange attractor takes place through the therapeutic relationship and the transference, which is similar to that of the couple's or family's object relations set, at a different level of scale. In mathematical terms, the transference is a fractal of the object relations set. Change in the transference reverberates along all levels of the couple and family system.

Chaos theory, attachment theory, trauma theory, and dream analysis enrich current models of object relations couple and family therapy to help couples and families reach their potential as self-organizing systems, attachment groupings, affect regulators, and environments for the personality development of individual family members.

REFERENCES

Ainsworth, M. D. S., M. C. Blehar, E. Waters, and S. Wall. 1978. *Patterns of Attachment: A Psychological Study of the Strange Situation.* Hillsdale, NJ: Lawrence Erlbaum.

Bion, W. 1959. *Experiences in Groups.* New York: Basic Books.

———. 1970. *Attention and Interpretation.* London: Heinemann.

Bowlby, J. 1988. *A Secure Base: Clinical Applications of Attachment Theory.* London: Routledge.

Clulow, C. 2001. Attachment theory and the therapeutic frame. In C. Clulow, ed., *Adult Attachment and Couple Psychotherapy.* London and Philadelphia: Brunner-Routledge.

Dicks, H. V. 1967. *Marital Tensions.* London: Routledge and Kegan Paul.

Fairbairn, W. R. D. 1952. *Psychoanalytic Studies of the Personality.* London: Routledge.

Fisher, J., and L. Crandell. 2001. Patterns of relating in the couple. In C. Clulow, ed., *Adult Attachment and Couple Psychotherapy.* London and Philadelphia: Brunner-Routledge.

Fonagy, P. 2001. *Attachment Theory and Psychoanalysis.* New York: Other Press.

Fonagy, P., G. Gergely, E. Jurist, and M. Target. 2002. *Affect Regulation, Mentalization, and the Development of the Self.* New York: Other Press.

George, C., N. Kaplan, and M. Main. 1985. The Adult Attachment Interview. Unpublished manuscript, University of California, Berkeley.

Gleick, J. 1987. *Chaos.* New York: Viking Penguin.

Kaplan, H. S. 1974. *The New Sex Therapy. Active Treatment of Sexual Dysfunctions.* New York: Brunner/Mazel.

Klein, M. 1975a. *Envy and Gratitude and Other Works: 1946–1963.* London: Hogarth.

———. 1975b. *Love, Guilt and Reparation and Other Works: 1921–1945.* London: Hogarth.

Main, M., N. Kaplan, and J. Cassidy. 1985. Security in infancy, childhood and adulthood: A move to the level of representation. In I. Bretherton and E. Waters eds., *Growing Points of Attachment Theory and Research.* Monograph of the Society for Research and Child Development. Serial No. 209, Vol. 50, nos. 1–2.

Masters, W. H., and V. E. Johnson. 1970. *Human Sexual Inadequacy.* Boston: Little Brown.

Scharff, D., and J. Scharff. 1987. *Object Relations Family Therapy.* Northvale, NJ: Jason Aronson.

———. 1991. *Object Relations Couple Therapy.* Northvale, NJ: Jason Aronson.

Scharff, J., and D. Scharff. 1994. *Object Relations Therapy of Physical and Sexual Trauma.* Northvale, NJ: Jason Aronson.

Schore, A. N. 2003a. *Affect Regulation and the Repair of the Self.* New York: Norton.

———. 2003b. *Affect Dysregulation and Disorders of the Self.* New York: Norton.

Winnicott; D. W. 1965. *Maturational Processes and the Facilitating Environment.* London: Hogarth Press and the Institute of Psycho-Analysis.

———. 1974. *Playing and Reality.* Harmondsworth: Penguin.

3

Intrapsychic, Interpsychic, and Transpsychic Communication

Roberto Losso

In families and couples, various psychic phenomena occur in association with three modalities of the transmission of affect and experience: intrapsychic, interpsychic, and transpsychic transmissions. One of the aims of family and couple psychoanalysis is to help family members defuse the impact of transpsychic transmission, re-create the transitional space in which they can acknowledge the otherness of one another, and then establish the interpsychic mode of transmission. The development of effective preconscious function fosters this process.

Let's begin with "Group Psychology and Analysis of the Ego" (1921) where Freud affirms: "In the individual's mental life someone else is invariably involved, as a model, as an object, as a helper, as an opponent; and so from the very first individual psychology, in this extended but entirely justifiable sense of the words, is at the same time social psychology as well" (p. 69). The fact that individual psychology is social is nowhere more evident than in the couple relationship where the real, concrete other is present as a model, as an object, as a helper, and as an opponent.

Now let's turn to Pichon Rivière's (1979, pp. 21–33) theory of the link. Infants have needs that must be met if they are to survive the situation of helplessness. They need the other if they are to stay alive. This is the archaic level of the need for a link. The couple relationship is a particular kind of link. In every link, structure, subject, and object interact in a dialectic relationship. During this interaction, the link structure is internalized, acquiring thus an intrasubjective dimension. What was interpsychic becomes intrapsychic. The process goes from intersubjectivity to intrasubjectivity.

These internalized link structures—the intrasubjective relations articulated in an internal world—comprise what Pichon Rivière has called the internal group (his modification of the Kleinian concept of internal world). That internal group (which is basically the internalization of family links modified by the individual's needs) functions as a stage on which to build the internal reconstruction of external reality. The internal group is similar to the internal representation of family links that Laing has called the "family" (between quotation marks, to distinguish it from the external family). Eiguer (2003) has described three levels in the link: an archaic, narcissistic, preverbal, and pre-objectal level; an oneiric level related to the desire, the expectations, and the projects of the subjects of the link; and a mythical level, related to the family myth and transgenerational transmission of affect and experience.

At a narcissistic level where there is no acknowledgment of the other as different, a man falling in love chooses, as Freud (1914, p. 90) said, "what he himself is, what he himself was, what he himself would like to be, someone who was once part of himself." At the oneiric level, where there is already an acknowledgment of the other as different, the person falling in love chooses a partner based on desire displaced from the Oedipal situation: "I want to be loved by, and receive the penis from a man, as a paternal representative; I want to be loved by, and penetrate a woman, as a maternal representative." The oneiric includes an anaclitic aspect: "I search for the woman who feeds me or the man who protects me." The couple forms not only between the adult parts of the partners, but also from the more archaic aspects in the individual's psychological functioning.

The partners in every couple relationship make a narcissistic investment in one another, and they organize and maintain their relationship around positive elements such as reciprocal admiration and being in love, common identifications, a community of ideals and beliefs, satisfactory fulfillment of desires, confirmation and reaffirmation of their narcissism, and a safe space for the expression of a useful level of aggression.

The couple is also organized and maintained by negative elements, when the partners, setting aside psychic contents, disavow aspects of their affect and experience and renounce ambitions through unconscious agreement in which certain aspects of the link remain repressed, denied, or encysted in the mental space of both subjects. Kaës (1989, pp. 130–69) called this the *pacte dénégatif*. This means a pact of denial. The contents of the pact, and the pact itself, remain unconscious. On the one hand, the *dénégatif* pact fulfills an organizing function of the link and of the ensemble of contents, and, on the other hand, it has a defensive function. Depending on the intensity and the quality of this defensive aspect, as well as other elements, the couples and families will be more or less functional. Good enough, functional couples with a satisfactory life are capable of constituting families with a strong couple at the center of the children's experience (Meltzer and Harris 1983), while more dysfunctional couples with difficulties in their couple life have less potential to fulfill parental functions and build adequate families.

In summary, partners bring to the couple relationship their desires, expectations, and fantasies; ideals of their own, their parents, and previous generations; conscious and unconscious ideas and affects; and their individual intrapsychic constellations. They bring together both individual "family" or internal groups, which become entangled to constitute a new internal constellation, that we have called the *couple's internal group*, in which the couple's unconscious action drama evolves (Losso and Packciarz Losso 1987, 1988).

THE COUPLE, THE FAMILY, AND THE TRANSMISSION PHENOMENA

Following Kaës (1993a, pp. 31–36), we consider three different types of transmission: intrapsychic, interpsychic (or intersubjective), and transpsychic.

Intrapsychic Transmission

In intrapsychic transmission, described by Freud in his theory on dreams, the transmission of the psychic contents takes place from the unconscious to the preconscious or conscious systems. In this type of transmission, Kaës points out the importance of the preconscious, a system in which some of the unconscious contents are subject to transformation so that they can return to consciousness, "a system tied to the associative and interpretative capacity of the psyche, as a place of connection of the pulsion, of the meaning and of the link" (page 33).

In clinical work with families and couples, we find that in certain situations, or in relation to certain subjects, this transmission is blocked. Certain contents are not in consciousness because some of them have been consciously negated, others have been repressed or encysted in a *pacte dénégatif*.

Interpsychic (or Intersubjective) Transmission

Interpsychic (or intersubjective) transmission originates in the family group. In infancy when the infantile psyche is constituted from narcissistic investments and separation experiences within the context of the narcissistic contract (Aulagnier 1975), intersubjective links that generate a psychic space among the subjects and identifications that lead to the formation of the ego and of the superego are all transmitted. Each family transmits to the newborn its model of capturing the external world and of organizing the internal one. This type of transmission implies a historical dimension of *the family psychic apparatus* (Kaës 1976, Ruffiot 1984). This family psychic apparatus for the articulation, circulation, and transformation of the psychic contents mediates between the family group level and the internal group level of each of the members of the family, and it generates a transitional psychic space between the subjects.

Interpsychic transmission is only possible in couples and families where there is a psychic family apparatus with adequate functioning of the preconscious and the recognition of others as different, with their own particular affiliative needs, sexual desires, expectations, projects, and anxieties and where there is a transitional space of play and creativity. In the case of "dysfunctional" families and couples, this space is missing, or it is not properly constituted, and good interpsychic transmission is not possible and what happens is transpsychic transmission instead.

Intergenerational transmission represents a particular aspect of intersubjective transmission. A family history is organized and elaborated by the individual members each taking the necessary elements to create their own myth. These transmitted contents are incorporated into the psyche of the new generation.

Transpsychic Transmission

Transpsychic transmission comes direct from parents, grandparents, greatgrandparents, and significant characters of their family mythology straight through to the subject's psyche without transformation in the preconscious because the transitional space, which lets the previously transmitted contents turn into one's own elements, is missing, and the intersubjective space is severely limited. What was transmitted is not transformed, and the transmission is not performed between the subjects: it is performed through them. The transpsychic transmission abolishes the boundaries among the subjects. Intersubjective and transpsychic transmission may coexist in the same subjects through different channels.

Transpsychic transmission deals with contents in the rough, with no possibility of being elaborated. What was transmitted may be felt as something strange, alienating, and disturbing or as something enervating that withdraws vitality. It is a brutish process. Transpsychic transmission of narcissistic imperatives and traumatic experiences unelaborated by the preceding generations is a sort of transgenerational violence. For defensive reasons of protecting their own narcissism, parents have received the command to transmit what they have not been able to elaborate, so as to maintain their own psychic life. This mechanism corresponds to what Laing has named "transpersonal defenses," in which each subject intends to control the other's internal worlds, by acting on the other's experiences, in order to be able to maintain their own psychic balance (Laing 1969, p. 13).

These contents that are still in the rough are present in all subjects, but when they take up a lot of space within the psyche of one or both of the members of the couple and/or the siblings, symptoms and incomprehensible acts ensue. Narcissistic transpersonal defenses are put in place, which significantly contribute to the development of collusive ties in the couple and the family.

The transgenerational imperatives may be strong enough to impede the subject from recognizing the other as such, and therefore he/she presses the other to meet with impossible demands that are, in fact, demands from mythical characters, rough contents that have been transmitted with no modification. These contents are embodied and encysted (Abraham and Torok 1978) but cannot be introjected. Framo (1965) has named them "fossil remains" in reference to their nearly undisturbed preservation throughout time. Abraham and Torok (1978) have defined them as ghosts (*fantômes*) that dwell in crypts.

Transpsychic transmission may also occur between the members of the couple. By using the transpersonal defenses, each member of the couple modifies the experience of the other one in order to maintain his or her own psychic balance. Racamier (1990) has described this process as a gearing:

> a sort of psychic organization provided with an interactive perspective, that takes place between at least two subjects, for which everything felt, thought about, dreamed of, desired by one of the members of the couple has an immediate resonance for the other one. . . . An own fantasy experienced by one of them is directly expressed by the acting of the other one. What one imagines in silence, perhaps without even having the own inside space to really imagine it, will be put in action by the other one. (pp. 84–85)

Intergenerational transmission occurs in the interpsychic (intersubjective) realm. It transmits the positive: the narcissistic continuity, the ideals, the values, the identifications, and the defensive modalities. This is a structuring transmission that implies multigenerational support from the family group. I have named this *trophic transmission* (Losso 2001a, p. 157). In this transmission, each subject's ego reaches out to the family myths and does the individual psychic work of re-encountering and re-creating the elements of his history that have been transmitted outside conscious knowledge. Trophic transmission allows for the elaboration of secondary fantasies, and so makes possible successive and necessary transformations of mandates and legacies from one generation to another. To become conscious of one's own lineage is very important for one's own sense of identity. Trophic transmission with the support from the multigenerational family group is fundamental in the constitution of individual and family identity. This makes it possible to bring together the past and the present as a fruitful encounter of two complementary cultures.

Unlike intergenerational transmission, transgenerational transmission is a type of transpsychic transmission that is highly traumatic and pathogenic. It is transmitted from one generation to another with no modification. Like Freud's individual concept of the compulsion to repeat, transgenerational transmission is compelled toward repetition. All the negative, all that cannot be contained or elaborated, all that is shameful, transgressive, and denied, and all the mourning that has not been properly elaborated, all are transmitted by the transpsychic route.

POSITIVE AND NEGATIVE TRANSMISSION IN THE COUPLE

The members of the couple, each of whom has created new intrapsychic products of the elements derived from different origins, gathering aspects of the cultures of their own and earlier generations, now add new ones from the partner to create a collage. When the transmission of the negative is predominant, unconscious abusive legacies remain in place and tie the subjects to invisible loyalties (Boszormenyi-Nagy and Spark 1973). The partners are forced to take care of their ancestors' demands much more than of their own desires. There is a libidinal disinvestment of the family and life as a couple while outstanding debts must be paid to the preceding generations. Therefore, the family, and especially the designated patient, is unable to do anything but suffer, supporting the abusive legacy or the self-punitive mandate (Stierlin 1977) even though it de-structures, alienates, and paralyzes the self. Subjects are to fulfill the mission of the family myth—no matter their own desires.

DEFENSIVE COLLUSION

Transpsychic transmission creates *dénégatif* pacts for which the unconscious agreements require more severely defensive characteristics. This is the way that collusions are established (Laing 1961, pp. 103–18, Spanish edition). Collusion derives from *ludere* (to play), and also from *illudere* (to deceive). A collusion is a shared illusion, a shared deceit.

In couples, each one is to play the role that the other one assigns, and at the same time each plays his or her own role. When a synthesis of both themes is reached, the couple creates the collusive couple's action drama

(Losso and Packciarz Losso 1987, p. 180). Collusion is the result of two intrapsychic scenes that are mutually strengthened and constitute a new central scene with frequent updates. The central scene and its updates are key scenes for expressing the collusion. They are pathogenic scenes, given that they repeat themselves and increase the couple's disturbance, lack of satisfaction, misunderstanding, and resentment, through constant reinforcement. They stamp in the collusive mechanisms by repetition and create a *dénégatif* pact in which primitive projective identification, splitting, denial, and massive idealization dominate the transpersonal defenses.

There also are identifications with transgenerational objects, in which a partner may intend to do to the other what was done to him or her. These identifications are a caricature of idealized or denigrated characters of the family mythology. I call them trivial, meaning well-known and well-traveled, in that they are conscious, repeated, hand-me-downs that seem false (Losso 2001a, p. 80).

Endless, vengeful reproaches may be thrown at the spouse when they should be aimed at the primary object. This implies proof of fidelity to that primary object, as if to proclaim that there is nothing better than the original family. In this destructive sadomasochist dynamic, the object must be preserved in order to receive the reproaches and maintain the transpersonal defenses. The old object should not be lost, and the spouse who contains that object must not be lost. These are the couples that "together they kill each other and separated they die" (Caillot and Decherf 1989, p. 54).

In families or couples that consult because of symptoms related to severe pathologies in one of their members, we find a persisting narcissistic functioning with a predominance of the transpsychic transmission mechanisms, and an interpsychic transmission deficit, which impedes the psychic spaces and the sexual and generational roles being properly differentiated. In other words, the preconscious functioning fails.

To make intersubjectivity possible, the presence of the preconscious is needed; and vice versa, the preconscious requires intersubjectivity. In a functional couple or family, a transforming activity of the preconscious exists, which is in touch with the psychic activity of each partner. Couples and family members can help one another do the work of linking and transforming that they may be unable to do themselves. This is the meta-preconscious function of the other (Kaës 1993b, p. 274).

In couples and families, the possibility of developing this as a mutual function makes the growth and development of the couple's relationship and that of the entire family possible. This curative aspect of the couple and family links is missing in dysfunctional couples and families. One of the tasks of couple and family psychoanalytic therapy is to reveal the alienating unmetabolized contents that are transmitted by the transpsychic route—what is split, what myths are enacted, which ghosts are let loose, and which symbolic debts with the ancestors are being paid. De-alienation becomes possible by learning the myths and then transforming rigid myths into flexible ones adapted to the present situation and to the subjects' needs, and to recognizing differences between the members of the couple and among the generations. We help the subjects create a transitional space between them in which they recognize the other as different, and this allows for the interpsychic transmission mode.

We believe that to discriminate among these three modalities of transmission allows for a much better comprehension of the couple's or family's problems, especially of severe pathology related to narcissistic problems. The sufferings of the members of the couple or of the family are not only connected to the history of the individual, the couple, and the family of origin, but also to that of preceding generations.

The therapeutic team brings to the table a well-developed meta-preconscious function. They lend their own preconscious to the members of the family, in order for the family to turn the disturbing psychic contents from defensive ways of relating into thinkable material that can be analyzed. One of the purposes of psychoanalytic couple and family therapy is to develop the preconscious of each of the subjects, by allowing them to share in and internalize the therapist's reflective function or mentalization (Fonagy 2000).

Cotherapy is invaluable for keeping alive and active this meta-preconscious function. With a more developed preconscious and an improving capacity for interpsychic transmission, the partners of the couple will have the capacity to take charge of their own individuality and to be alone (Winnicott 1958) within a more sustaining relationship.

REFERENCES

Abraham, N., and M. Torok. 1978. *L'écorce et le noyeau*. Paris: Flammarion.

Aulagnier, P. 1975. *La violence de l'interprétation. Du pictogramme à l'énoncé*. Paris: PUF.

Baranger, M. and W. Baranger. 1961–1962. La situación analítica como campo dinámico. *Revista Uruguaya Psicoanál* 4(1): 3–54.

Boszormenyi-Nagy, I., and C. Spark. 1973. *Invisible Loyalties*. New York: Harper & Row.

Caillot, J. P., and G. Decherf. 1989. *Psychanalyse du couple et de la famille*. Paris: A. PSY. G. Editions.

Ciccone, A. 1997. Empiètement imagoïque et fantasme de transmission. In *Le psychisme à l'épreuve des generations*, eds. Tisseron et al., Clinique du fantôme. Paris: Dunod.

Décobert, S., and N. Soulé. 1972. La notion de couple thérapeutique. *Revue Française Psychanalyse* 326:83.

Dicks, H. 1967. *Marital Tensions. Clinical Studies towards a Psycho-Analytic Theory of Interaction.* London: Routledge and Kegan Paul.

Eiguer, A. 1983. *Un divan pour la famille. Du modèle groupal à la thérapie familiale psychanalytique.* Paris: Le Centurion.

———. 2003. Personal communication.

Fonagy, P. 2000. Attachment and borderline personality disorder. *Journal of the American Psychoanalytic Association* 48(4): 1129–46.

Framo, J. 1965. Systemic research on family dynamics. In I. Boszormenyi-Nagy and J. L. Framo, eds., *Intensive Family Therapy.* New York: Harper & Row.

Freud, S. 1898. Sexuality in the etiology of the neurosis. *Standard Edition* 3:259–86.

———. 1912. Recommendations to physicians practising psycho-analysis. *Standard Edition* 12: 109–120.

———. 1914. On narcissism: An introduction. *Standard Edition* 14:67–104.

———. 1916–17. Introductory lectures on psycho-analysis. *Standard Edition* 15:13–240.

———. 1921. Group psychology and analysis of the ego. *Standard Edition* 18: 65–144.

Kaës, R. 1989. Le pacte dénégatif dans les ensembles trans-subjectifs. In A. Missenard et al., *Le négatif, figures et modalités,* pp. 130–69. Paris: Dunod.

———. 1993a. Introduction au concept de transmission psychique dans la pensée de Freud. In *Transmission de la vie psychique entre générations,* pp. 17–58. Paris: Dunod.

———. 1993b. *Le groupe et le sujet du groupe.* Paris: Dunod.

Laing, R. 1961. *Self and Others.* London: Tavistock.

———. 1969. *The Politics of the Family and Other Essays.* London: Tavistock.

Lemaire, J. 1971. *Les thérapies du couple.* Paris: Payot.

———. 1979. *Le couple: sa vie, sa mort.* Paris: Payot.

Losso, R. 1990. La Teoría psicoanalítica y el psicoanálisis familiar. *Revista de Psicoanálisis* 47(5–6): 923–35.

———. 1996. Il transfert nella terapia di coppia (intervista/dibattito). *Interazioni* 2:126 – 29.

———. 1999. Teoría del campo y psicoanálisis de familia y de pareja. In *Volviendo a pensar con Willy y Madeleine Baranger. Nuevos desarrollos,* ed. and comp. L. Kancyper, pp. 237–55. Buenos Aires: Lumen.

———. 2000. Le mythe familial, source de transferts familiaux. Transfert et contre-transfert dans la thérapie familiale psychanalytique. *Le Divan familial* 4:25–37.

———. 2001a. *Psicoanálisis de la familia. Recorridos teòrico-clínicos.* Buenos Aires: Lumen. Italian version: *Psicoanalisi della famiglia. Percorsi teorico-clinici.* Milano: Franco Angeli.

———. 2001b. Il mito familiare: fonte dei transfert familiari. *Interazioni* 15:59–67.

———. 2002. Vigencia de Enrique Pichon-Rivière. *Revista de Psicoanálisis* 49(4): 883–89.

Losso, R., and A. Packciarz Losso. 1982. Crónica del tratamiento psicodramático psicoanalítico de una pareja. In: *Desarrollos en psicoterapia de grupo y psicodrama,* ed. J. L. Marti i Tusquets e L. Satne, pp. 287–98. Barcelona: Gedisa.

———. 1987. Psicoanálisis de la pareja. In *Temas Grupales por Autores Argentinos,* pp. 179–90. Buenos Aires: Ediciones Cinco.

———. 1988. La coppia vista dalla psicoanalisi. In *Terapia Familiare Notizie*, n. 7–8.

Meltzer, D., and M. Harris. 1983. *Child, Family and Community: A Psycho-analytic Model of the Learning Process*. Paris: OECD.

Moreno, J. L. 1966. Psicodrama de un matrimonio. In *Psicoterapia de Grupo y Psicodrama*. México: Fondo de Cultura Económica.

Nachin, C. 1993. *Les Fantômes de l'âme*. Paris: L'Harmattan.

Pichon Rivière, E. 1971. *Del Psicoanálisis a la Psicología Social*. Buenos Aires: Galerna.

———. 1979. *Teoría del Vínculo*. Buenos Aires: Nueva Visión.

Racamier, P. C. 1990. A propos de l'engrénement. *Gruppo* 6:83–95. Paris: Apsygée.

Ruffiot, A. 1984. La terapia familiar psicoanalítica: Un tratamiento eficaz del terreno psicótico. *Revista Argentina Psicología y Psicoterapia de Grupo* 7(1): 134–46.

Stierlin, H. 1977. *Psychoanalysis and Family Therapy*. Northvale, NJ: Jason Aronson.

Willi, J. 1975. *Die Zweier-beziehung*. Hamburg: Rowohlt Verlag. Spanish version: *La pareja humana: relación y conflicto*. Madrid: Morata, 1978.

Winnicott, D. W. 1951. Transitional objects and transitional phenomena. In *Through Paediatrics to Psycho-Analysis*, pp. 229–94. London: Hogarth Press, 1987.

———. 1958. The capacity to be alone. In *The Maturational Process and the Facilitating Environment*, pp. 29–36. London: Tavistock Publications, 1965.

4

Family Process and Individual Evolution

Lilia Gagnarli

Listening is fundamental to the analyst's role. Listening means accepting the patient's communication and giving meaning to the words that are said. The listening attitude fosters engagement in the encounter between patient and therapist and facilitates the emergence of transference. It creates conditions that make it possible to stage and unravel the unconscious web of fantasies underlying the emotional pain and the symptoms that prompt the patient to seek help.

Listening is also fundamental to the family therapist's role, but since the patient is now a group of people, there are some additional aspects to the listening. In work with couples and families, much of the listening attitude is focused on the visuals. Body language and gestures deserve particular attention. The nonverbal aspects intertwine with the verbal exchanges to lend more, or less, congruity to what is being said and to establish alliances or conflicts which trigger intense feelings.

When we open the door to receive a patient or family, we immediately pick up an image based on the way they use space, how they greet us, and how they look at each other. All the nonverbal aspects taken together evoke emotions and thoughts that prepare us to listen to their stories and construct a pattern of meanings. We note whether and to what extent the nonverbal aspects are consistent with the content and modes of telling. We find out whether the image transmitted to the therapist is shared by some or all of the family members. We think about how the external image correlates with the characters (the internal objects) that populate each one's inner world.

43

Understanding family function follows from the observation of two fundamental aspects, the somatic and the psychic. The use of space, the posture of the individuals, and all the nonverbal aspects comprise the somatic aspect, while the psychic factors are the sum of individual intrapsychic aspects and current interpersonal relationships, as well as the transgenerational aspects deriving from transpsychic transmission. We find that some families are emotionally illiterate on the somatic and intrapsychic levels. This creates stasis, an immobility that is the result of failure to resolve a double source of conflict: The individuals are unable to express emotions; and at the family level, emotions are not communicated from one individual to the other.

More and more frequently, we meet families whose members are successful, but they cannot recognize their own emotions and do not know what to do with them or how to manage them. These emotional handicaps at the individual and family levels are the focus of our therapeutic work regardless of the problem or symptom that brought the family to therapy. This emotional illiteracy unites their way of being: Emotions are managed by trying to hide them, repress them, or prevent them from occurring at all by avoiding all occasions that could lead to feeling. Clearly expressing one's needs, problems, or discomforts, or making one's own feelings an occasion for comparison and sharing, is often impossible because it would activate the emotional channel that is feared and avoided. The therapeutic effort actually activates the presenting problem.

In the histories of the families we meet, the parents almost always experienced this mode in their original families. Unable to integrate the affective world as part of themselves, they take refuge in formalized, stereotypical relationships. Thus, they, in turn, become parents who, in their relationships with their own children, place emphasis on roles and/or functions, or often make the children carry out parental tasks. There is a lack of warmth, and little experience in having another person with whom to resonate emotionally. Roccato (1998) maintains that it is rare to encounter total illiteracy of all emotions. It is more common to find various degrees of difficulty in experiencing some or grasping others, and he calls this "emotional daltonism." Emotional experiences are taken in, but not fully differentiated, as if they were only different shades of the same color. This mode is also supported by today's culture of seeing things in black and white, which makes it difficult to experience subtle conflicting feelings or to tolerate either one's own ambivalence or that of other family members.

Having constructed a relationship based on listening to each of the people in the room, and to the couple or family as a whole, we can proceed to describe the experience and fantasy of the whole. We attend to movements, glances, tone of voice, misunderstandings, or clashes, in order to grasp the unconscious transfer of emotion and overlapping of emotion and its imposition on the others. Complex reciprocal family relationships are constituted by the assignment of roles or positions that each family member must accept in order to guarantee the continuity and cohesion of the whole family group, which is, at the same time, also a support for each individual's identity and personal subjective experience.

The basis of psychic well-being is the perception of self as valued, as being worthy of love, without that value being perceived as conflicting with that of other family members. One of the objectives of the therapeutic process is to make it possible for each member of the family to recognize shared unconscious fantasies by tracing them from the emotions that emerge during family interactions, and during the interaction of the family with the therapist. In therapy, a gradual approach to long-ignored emotional levels permits the eventual expression of feelings and the recognition and acceptance of well-endowed, pleasing aspects of the self as well as fragilities and weaknesses. Then the family does not need to pressure one family member to be the sole carrier of problems in a family life of denied emotions and unacknowledged roles.

The integration of emotion is essential for the health of a family group, just like the integration of part objects is essential for healthy development early in childhood. Lack of emotional integration causes suffering and pathology in the individual just as it does in the family group.

One of the motivations most significant in pushing families to seek therapy is depression in response to loss. In adulthood depression takes the familiar form of low energy, crying spells, self-destructiveness, and sad and angry mood. In children, depression often takes on various forms, such as low self-esteem, which are less easily recognized as depression. Family-wide fantasies of abandonment have so much poignancy that the children often acquire a central emotional position between the parents, which offers some reassurance to the parents, and at the same time separates them. Taking their place between their parents allows children to carry out protective roles, but as they take on their parents' emotional difficulties, they subtract vital energy from their own self-development and their own personality, with negative repercussions on the quality of their school lives and relationships outside the family.

The working through of the Oedipus complex—a constellation of romantic and murderous fantasies organized by the child to protect himself from feelings of exclusion by the parental couple—is more complicated when children experience real-life overinclusion by their parents. When such children occupy a space in which they feel captured by their parents' problems, they are filled with claustrophobic fantasies, which are transformed into the opposing fantasies of rejection and loss of both parents. If the couple is not well integrated and separate from the children, it cannot be considered a third object with which to establish both imaginary and real relationships and which can be installed in the child's personality as an internal couple.

CLINICAL VIGNETTE: FEDERICO, FABIOLA, AND FAMILY

At the first session with a family, the mother, the father, and their two daughters sat down in the following order: Franca, age seventeen, Federico, the father, Fabrizia, age eleven years, and Fabiola, the mother. The father explained that they had requested the meeting because the younger daughter is no longer able to apply herself. She is very slow in doing her homework, distracted, sloppy in the house, but efficient and focused when she is doing something she likes, such as singing at church.

I get a strong feeling of being closed into a tight space from several elements: the way in which they are seated, the fact that all their names start with the same letter, the uncertainty with which the mother speaks, which gets me thinking about difficulties in differentiation, and mainly the visual appearance of the family: this pretty, petite little girl seated between her parents. All this triggers a discomfort in me. The story they tell makes me think that there are two couples: Franca, the seventeen-year-old, with her father, both efficient and confident, and the eleven-year-old, Fabrizia, with her mother, who both come across as inadequate and insecure.

I ask Fabrizia: "Whom do you feel closer to?"
Fabrizia: "I try to stay near Mom as much as possible."

The diagnostic picture lights up and the therapeutic course begins with attention to the special configuration of these two couples in the room and with the underlying claustrophobic and exclusion fantasies.

During the couple's crisis little Fabrizia had become her mother's emotional support, filling lonely empty spaces by spending a great deal of time together. In the relationship that developed, Fabrizia's identification processes were compromised: It was difficult to identity with such an inadequate mother, and while clinging to her, it was impossible to get close to her father whom the family considered more competent and solid and who might have been a better model for identification. During the course of the therapy, however, the father's frailties in all areas of relating emerged, in his case expressed by an obsessive need to control everything around him according to a model derived from his family of origin. For Fabrizia, getting close to him would create a fear of betraying the bond with her mother and a fear of indulging her desire to replace her sister in her father's affections. Oedipus complex and sibling complex feelings were all around. Fabrizia's parents were the object of both her aggression and her desire, making separation and detachment impossible. Fabrizia had aggressive fantasies that she kept actively under control, and so they took the form of an attack on herself expressed through feelings of inadequacy. This individual emotional configuration is not only applicable to Fabrizia, but to all the members of the family: The father and Franca are efficient at doing things, but feel inadequate in relationships; Mother and Fabrizia feel totally ineffective.

My interpretation was that Fabrizia's profound discomfort in the relationship with both parents was an expression of fantasies of abandonment in the family. This interpretation triggered an evolutionary process that released Fabrizia and Franca from rigid and inappropriate roles and allowed the entire family to encounter previously unknown and unrecognized emotional levels. The parents as a couple begin to regain their own functions and to create room for a sexual life that had been missing.

These children had been so entrenched in the space between the two parents that they had been paralyzed there out of fear of losing the closeness, the physical contact, and the affection of one or both parents. In their immobility, they experienced inhibition of thought, reduction of creative abilities, a tendency to stay at home, refusal of contact with peers, and an overall decrease of vitality. When the parents could not achieve an integration as a couple out of fear of encountering feelings of exclusion and rejection themselves, they lost their ability to transform their unconscious affects into emotions that could be shared between themselves and with their children as separate individuals of different generations and with different roles.

CLINICAL VIGNETTE: CARLA AND FAMILY

This family consists of a father, mother, twenty-four-year-old son, and the index patient, Carla, who is sixteen. The father says that for five months Carla has had an irritating cough that only stops when she is in bed, or seated almost lying down so that she can no longer attend school. She has been examined by specialists in many parts of Italy who have not discovered the cause of the cough.

In the first family meeting, I am struck by Carla's frequent coughing accompanied by a smiling attitude that minimizes the situation. At the same time, her mother, her head tilted sadly, is completely withdrawn into herself.

Illness has left a deep mark on the family over the past few years: the mother has had heart surgery the previous year; the father has a herniated disc; the brother who had plans to marry has postponed the wedding until his sister's serious cough is cured. Both children say that, although little is spoken in the family, they are extremely close. The parents' mutual disappointment is expressed in a war of compromised positions: The father has had to accept his wife's refusal to have virtually any contact with the outside world; the mother has had to adjust to the husband's violent and authoritarian personality, which she handles by trying to dampen any possible conflict. The presence of the children is indispensable in this war, because getting too close to the themes of conflict would be dangerous. The parents might either explode or the children could be left in painful solitude. The cough that diminishes only when Carla is lying down and the overall family atmosphere evoke thoughts of death in me. In this family, growth and the threat of separation of the children creates anxiety, because without them the family (and especially the couple) would have an experience of solitude, sadness, and death. Carla's coughing symptom combines two irreconcilable things in a protest—against the fact that her father's ideas dampen the family's vitality (like her cough does to her), and against her mother's desperate desire to avoid conflict in order to guarantee family unity. All this is according to the parents' wishes. It prevents Carla from functioning as a normal young woman with a future, and keeps her brother at home, also unable to grow. It protects them from facing the challenge of developing couples of their own.

CONCLUSION

At the beginning of this short chapter, I spoke of somatic or bodily aspects: I listed them at the start because in the observation process at the beginning of therapy, what we see (the visual channel) precedes what we hear (the auditory channel). In the two clinical vignettes, the first image I perceived concerned something that was unnaturally static, a spatial position of the two daughters in pain, sitting too tightly together between their parents. That led me to think of a difficulty in getting loose, and a fear of "losing" significant relationships.

Coping with the loss of the object is at the center of the depressive problem and plays an essential role in the normal development of the individual. This brings us to the early concept of loss that occurs in the transition from relating to partial objects to relating to total objects. In normal development there is a gradual integration of those objects when infants learn that memories of the loving breast and memories of the hated breast are memories of the same breast at various times, and that the happy mouth and the irate mouth are the same mouth.

Just as this integration of whole objects is important for the harmonious development of the individual, it is essential that during growth the child introject a sufficiently integrated parent couple, capable of mutual listening and exchange. The child needs parents each of whom can recognize in self and partner, both efficiency and inadequacy, tenderness and roughness, power and fragility, closeness and distance. Children who realize that their mother and father are capable of functioning at both poles find it easier to deal with the parents as the whole objects of the depressive position and can tolerate ambivalent feelings about them. That mature parental couple is able to support the child in accepting limits and in containing the love and hate that emerges from the loss of the idealized aspects of these parents.

Parents bring with them the family style acquired in their family of origin, for instance the habit of staying in contact with the vast range of emotions or the limited potential to favor only one type of feeling. In the families I describe here, we find efficient and apparently secure fathers, and uncertain, sad mothers—each parent embodying only one kind of feeling. With this polarization, it is difficult for them to build understanding for themselves and for their children, and instead they live with opposed positions, competition, and feelings of suffering that create a distance that ultimately becomes profound solitude. They cannot deal with their sadness because they cannot tolerate the ambivalence that would be required for grieving.

The onset of symptoms and discomfort in one of the children is a first move. It is the prelude to the encounter with underlying emotions that allows the entire family to deal with the situation of emotional stasis. Work on the fear of losing significant relationships mobilizes the family; it reveals rigid identifications and reactivates in the parents reflections on their individual histories. It allows them to work through conflicts experienced with significant persons in the past, those toward whom in childhood and adolescence they had vindictive feelings that became encysted. Boszormenyi-Nagy and Framo wrote that "the reasons that determine the actions of a person can be found in another's need for identification" (1977, p. 62). Sentiments that are unexpressed, denied, and closed in are transmitted and reproduced in internal relational models. With insecure, affectionless, distant parents, children experience situations of insecurity, leading often to a loss of desire for objects in general. The experience of loss can also lead to ambivalent feelings that generate aggression and guilt with denial of the aggression for fear of destroying the objects. Then symbolic and creative aspects of personality become inhibited, self-esteem is lost, and in turn the children become insecure and unaffectionate themselves. Only by working through the ambivalence and aggression, the guilt, and the inhibitions, is the attack on the self overcome, and the move begun that lets the family understand that these matters concern not only the designated patient, but the entire family.

Work with families gives voice to emotions that have been removed and denied, and mobilizes a process that involves all members of the family, making it possible to work through processes of identification in which depressive affects with their intolerable experiences of loss, difference, and distance become the motor instead of the brake on the individuals' ego functioning and capacity for symbolic thinking. When the stasis yields, life begins again, and the denial of the many colors of emotion begins to relinquish its power. Only then is it possible to gain control over ambivalence and aggression, and to free the family as a group and as individuals to express their problems, needs, reactions, and wishes for the future.

REFERENCES

Algini, M. L., ed. 1997. *La Depressione dei Bambini.* Rome: Borla.

Boszormenyi-Nagy, I., and J. L. Framo. 1977. *Psicoterapia Intensiva della Famiglia.* Turin: Bollah Boringhieri.

Losso, R. 2000. *Psicoanalisi della Famiglia.* Milan: Franco Angeli.

Mitchell, S. A. 1995. *Speranza e Timore in Psicoanalisi.* Turin: Bollati Boringhieri.

Nicolò Corigliano, A. M. 1997. L'importanza diagnostica delle interazioni nella valutazione della famiglia e delle sue difese transpersonali. In *Interazioni* 10(2): 53–66.

Palacio Espasa, F. 1995. *Psicoterapia con i Bambini.* Milan: Cortina.

Reiss, D. 1991. La famiglia rappresentata e la famiglia reale: Concezioni contrastanti della continuità familiare. In *I Disturbi delle Relazioni nella Prima Infanzia*, ed. A. L. Sameroff and R. N. Emde. Turin: Bollati Boringhieri.

Resnik, S. 1990. *Spazio Mentale.* Turin: Bollati Boringhieri.

Roccato, P. 1998. Dal paziente freudiano al paziente catodico. *MicroMega* 3:218.

Savege Scharff, J., ed. 1999. *I Fondamenti della Terapia Familiare Basata sulle Relazioni Oggettuali.* Milan: Franco Angeli.

Scott, W. Clifford M. 1966. Concetto psicoanalitico dell'origine della depressione. In *Nuove vie della Psicoanalisi*, ed. M. Klein, P. Heinemann, and R. E. Money-Kyrle. Milan: Il Saggiatore.

Stern, D. N. 1987. *Il Mondo Interpersonale del Bambino.* Turin: Bollati Boringhieri.

———. 1992. Il dialogo fra l'intrapsichico e l'interpersonale: una prospettiva evolutiva. *Interazioni* 0:79–88.

5

Relational Family Therapy

Robert Cvetek, Katarina Kompan Erzar, Tomaz Erzar, and Christian Gostecnik

In this chapter we demonstrate an innovative model of therapy called Relational Family Therapy. This model of therapy integrates aspects of general systems theories with relational models combining the object relational theories, self psychology, and interpersonal analysis. The Relational Family model radically changes the understanding and perception of human experience and consequently also the therapeutic approach. This model traces the structure of the mind on all levels and in all aspects of human life: intrapsychic, interpersonal, and systemic, in real life and in fantasy, on the conscious and unconscious domains of personal experience. The Relational Family model, therefore, also dramatically changes the ways therapists understand their practice.

THE RELATIONAL PERSPECTIVE

The relational model, which was developed by Mitchell (1988, 2000, 2002), studies human experience from the perspective of the self (Winnicott 1965, 1971, 1975; Kohut 1984), object relations (Fairbairn 1952), and affect (Sullivan 1972), which is created on intrapsychic and also on interpersonal levels between the self and the object (Mitchell 1988, 1993, 1997, 2000, 2002). We propose that human experience can be studied in a similar way among the members of the family and also on a systemic level even though this perspective is not explicitly mentioned in relational theories. We contend that ultimately only thorough elaboration of all four aspects can sufficiently and definitively explain the family system as a whole.

From our standpoint, humans are regulated from all four aspects of their experiences: from the self, from relations with others, from the affect which develops and in the psychic arena between the self and the object, and also from the systems atmosphere. All together, they consist of a whole family system that contains and maintains the basic affect. In these four psychic domains, constant affect regulation (Schore 1994, 2003) creates the affective psychic construct where the functional development is blocked. In other words, when affect regulation is restricted, emotion such as anger or anxiety is not sufficiently addressed and is denied instead. A split-off, affective psychic construct is developed which functions as a defense mechanism that blocks further development or functional responsiveness. A person's affective psychic construct may consist of irrational thoughts such as obsessive derogatory feelings of worthlessness or, on the other hand, omnipotence with which the person guards against painful issues of rejection and abandonment. The affective psychic construct serves as a defense against painful, unacceptable mental contents.

In our model of therapy, we are interested in developing and maintaining a relatively stable and coherent sense of self, improving the reliability of perception and affect, fostering the appropriate expression of affect, and facilitating the creation and maintenance of permanent relations with others in terms of the individual intrapsychic world, the interpersonal, and the social system. All these dynamics mutually influence each other to reach systemic equilibrium. The capacity for affect regulation which develops as the self grows in relation to others creates a specific family atmosphere that is maintained and repeated from one generation to the other, based on powerful mechanisms of projective and introjective identification (Scharff 1992).

The complex dialectic between self-definition, interpersonal relations, and systemic levels creates a specific affective psychic construct that may be quite dramatic at times and incapacitating to individual, couple, and family. Then conflict among these dynamics on the intrapsychic, interpersonal, and systemic levels obscures basic anguish and pain. Self and object relations and systemic dynamic processes may be in good balance working well together or may be in a state of contradiction, which leads to painful conflicts. Intrapsychic, interpersonal, and systemic components interpenetrate and influence one another through the powerful mechanism of projective and introjective identification. Via the repetition compulsion, they consolidate in various ways with a characteristic set of affects, mechanisms, conflicts, and split-off aspects of self, object, and systemic relational configurations (Scharff 1989, 1992).

When the three models—self psychology, object relation theories, and interpersonal psychoanalysis—are interwoven and integrated with systems theory, the resulting systemic Relational Family model gives the most sophisticated and profound synthesis of the dimensions of human experiences, intricate dynamics, and relational configurations in the conscious and unconscious matrix.

THE SYSTEMS PERSPECTIVE

Our model is not only a combination of integrated relational models and theories, but is a new, more elaborate family system relational model of therapy that transcends the combined relational models (Gostecnik 2002). Integrating all three relational perspectives is made possible by the concepts of mutuality of affect and valency (Kompan Erzar 2001b, Scharff and Scharff 1998). The family entity embraces all relational configurations, intrapsychic, interpersonal, and systemic aspects, to become a dynamic family system. In this synthesis of interactions, a family system gives the entire tapestry of family relations a more profound form, new meaning, a new conceptual framework, and mostly, a sophisticated explanation of the dynamics of their interrelatedness. A system by itself has its own principles, its own needs and desires, and, therefore, produces profound affects that penetrate all relations that influence the system as a whole, regulates affect, and gives rise to affective psychic constructs (Gostecnik 2004).

In this regard, the family system affirms all relational configurations and creates a new frame in which to understand them in combination with their affects, traumas, and conflicts. A system gives a new conceptual and dynamic framework, which allows the therapist to understand individuals and their relations with others in a more holistic way. Consequently, the therapist using the family systemic relational approach can arrive at a more comprehensive understanding. The various relational and systemic bonds in the family produce idiosyncratic dynamics and characteristic forms of relatedness. The therapist has to deal with a sense of burden and pain. Levels of activity and spontaneity, bodily processes, sexuality, and aggression affect the experience of conflict, compromise formation, affect regulation, and the production of affective psychic constructs. The drama is shaped in interactions among the members of the family or between the partners of a couple and also between them and their therapists. From our perspective, different family system relational interventions can therefore focus on various facets of the Relational Family matrix.

THE RELATIONAL FAMILY MODEL

In the Relational Family model of therapy all three analytic models—interpersonal analysis, object relations, and self psychology—have their place, each of them concentrating on a specifically defined subsystem.

Interpersonal analysis focuses on basic affects that govern interpersonal relations in a family system. In this subsystem, the therapist observes the affect regulation and affective psychic construct produced in this dynamic. Object relations theories address the fundamental early object relations that formed the affective psychic construct and the mechanism of affect regulation (Scharff 1989, 1992). Self psychology is interested in the development of intrapsychic images of self and others on the basis of which the self develops and is maintained (Kohut 1984). Self psychology and object relations theories both address the impact of experiences with the most significant members of the family of origin on the development of affect regulation and the constitution of the affective psychic construct (Winnicott 1971, Kohut 1984). In combination, the interrelated intrapsychic subsystems produce a unique system of intrapsychic, relational, and systemic dynamics which governs individual experience to which each individual also contributes meaning (Mitchell 1993, 2000). Various aspects of the self, the object, and the affects that connect them are intrapsychically split off, projected, and introjected in a complex relational matrix (Scharff 1989, 1992). In reciprocal unconscious interaction with others, these split aspects of self and object can be later projected into the interpersonal and systemic world, where they gain new meaning and regulatory dynamics governed by new affect regulation and affective psychic constructs.

On the intrapsychic level, mechanisms of mutual projective and introjective identification ensure that the dynamics of the intrapsychic domain are produced or reproduced and repeated in intrapersonal and interpersonal relational systemic configurations (Gostecnik 2002). On the interpersonal level, two individual selves are in mutual interaction, projecting and consequently introjecting the various aspects of split-off ego, object, and affect, and so maintaining affect regulation and affective psychic construct. In cases of trauma, these relational sequences are subject to the repetition compulsion (Scharff and Scharff 1994) through which the individual self consolidates intrapsychic mental contents and creates the interpersonal dimension of experience. In other words, affects and experiences, specifically those associated with trauma, are repeated in adult life, generally among intimate partners who promise the relatedness without which humans cannot strive and survive.

DISCUSSION

We propose that only the Relational Family model and its intrapsychic and interpersonal subsystems produce a holistic model of human perception, activity, and meaning, a comprehensive view of human experience, and therefore an adequate approach to therapy. The same individual and group dynamics and processes create the intrapsychic and interpersonal dimensions of human experience, constitute affect regulation and affective psychic construct, and regulate and govern the whole system. Only on a family system level can all the relational configurations be definitively understood.

Example: Tatiana and Mario

Tatiana and Mario came to therapy because of long-standing marital conflict that almost completely incapacitated them in their functioning as partners. They initially presented their problem as one relating to their child, Robert, who does not want to stay in school. Interventions on a systemic level alone did not work. No matter how much the therapist tried to reorganize their parenting roles, Mario and Tatiana were constantly defeating each other, blaming each other, and hating each other for reasons not yet disclosed. It was soon obvious that Robert's problem is needed to divert them from their marital discord. So the therapist looked more deeply and discovered that Mario and Tatiana are actually scared and afraid of one another, each feeling alone and cut off from one another because of a shared fear of intimacy.

As the therapy progressed, it became apparent that they both came from families of origin where they were mistreated and emotionally abused. They both served as parentified children. As a child, Tatiana was responsible for the family household, in the absence of her parents who were rarely home, her father being a long-distance truck driver, and her mother, a busy social organizer. Tatiana had to stay home taking care of her two younger brothers and maintaining the household, even though it was beyond her capacities and made her anxious. She was scared to reveal her anxiety because she feared being scolded and abandoned.

Mario came from a family where he was also a parentified child, especially after his father died early from alcoholism. In her grief, Mario's mother was emotionally unavailable to parent Mario, and expected him to be her emotional husband instead of her child. He also had to take care of his younger siblings and was not allowed to complain about that. He was afraid to tell his mother that all this was too much for him in case she detached herself from him in all ways. Before long she died of grief, and Mario felt totally abandoned.

Mario and Tatiana each had a deep fear of being abandoned that carried over into adulthood. Now that they are together, they again fear abandonment, this time by one another. This is the shared affective psychic construct that prevents intimacy. They focus on Robert's dysfunction so as to avoid their marital conflict and the underlying fears of not being worthy of each other's attention, not being deserving of happiness together, and being abandoned if they become too close. By blaming one another for ineffective parenting, they project the deepest, most vulnerable affects of abandonment and rejection. To avoid recognizing that they are afraid of being found inept and therefore rejected, they shame each other, reject, misunderstand, and misperceive one another, experiencing one another like their parents when they were growing up.

The Relational Family therapist helped them to penetrate those areas of relatedness, from systemic and interpersonal viewpoints and then from the intrapsychic realm where the key issues are hidden. When Mario and Tatiana discovered their affective intrapsychic construct which prevented them from being functional parents and partners, they experienced great relief. They discovered that they argued over their child in order to hide painful abandonment issues in their own lives. They also discovered how the parenting styles of their parents influenced their own parenting and created their distorted self-images. Mario and Tatiana, after discovering and confronting all those painful issues, started life afresh, not without conflicts, but with the resources to tackle the challenges of being intimate partners as well as parents.

Understanding the whole system enables the Relational Family therapist to penetrate, understand, interpret, and intervene on all levels of relatedness. The therapist uncovers the residues of mental contents that block affective regulation and affective psychic construct formation on systemic, interpersonal, and intrapsychic levels. Locating the part of the system from which the problem derives is almost impossible and therefore the therapist has to *figure it out* in a progression from systemic to interpersonal and finally to intrapsychic levels. The basic rule of this process of intervention is to proceed from the broadest horizon of human experience which stems from the system as a whole and discover what makes the system dysfunctional. If that sort of intervention on a systemic level does not produce any meaningful result, the therapist delicately advances to more intricate areas of interpersonal and intrapsychic arenas of human relatedness. Then the therapist can discover the wounded self with the injured object relations, which influences all other relationships, and uncovers the affect that has led to the particular type of affect regulation and affective psychic construct. The therapist works on elaborating the profound historic residues of early childhood experiences, which, unconscious, unresolved, and unexplained, still govern the perceptions of that individual in the present through the mechanism of projective and introjective identification. Poignantly, the individual creates the same atmosphere, affects, meaning, and way of relating with a significant other in the present as in the past.

The affect-based self and object subsystems and the hierarchical equilibrium are important in all intimate relationships. In this intrapsychic, unconscious realm the most profound relations between the self and the objects are formed and they modulate through the mechanism of projective and introjective identifications all adult relationships. At the same time the intrapsychic world of the individual with its characteristic type of affect regulation and affective psychic construct is established on the basis of experiences created in the interpersonal world of family systems.

These systems—intrapsychic, interpersonal, and systemic—are in constant reciprocal interactions of mutual influence at all levels. If either the self or the object overpowers the other or both are flooded by affect, intrapsychic systemic disequilibrium will follow. If there is fusion of self and other, the result will be inappropriate perceptions of self and others, poor affect regulation, and a disturbed affective psychic construct. The intrapsychic relational structure always influences interpersonal and systemic configurations of relatedness by being constantly repeated and re-created via the mechanism of projective and introjective identification. That structure influences and is influenced by the other systems or subsystems as well as by the system as a whole.

Example: Irene and Tim

Irene and Tim had been fighting for a number of years. Finally, Irene threatened to leave Tim, and that brought them to therapy. The therapist initially worked in a strategic format to consolidate their busy working schedules so they could see each other more. Irene had many outside activities that were not absolutely necessary and did not produce any money. Tim was constantly traveling from one place to another, having two jobs, and looking for a third one for weekends. They had a fancy house with lots of rooms where their two children constantly created a mess. They had to employ a maid. This additional expense gave Tim more reason for a third job. The children were placed in child care during the week, and therefore the family was rarely together. There were continual visits from the grandparents, which further complicated their family life, robbed them of privacy, and created even greater enmeshment.

The therapist saw that the problem was deeper than mismanagement of scheduling. They fought over not having enough time together so that they could avoid their deeper conflicts of intimacy. The therapist changed gears and inquired what would happen if Tim and Irene allowed for more time together. They became defensive and accused the therapist of misunderstanding them. The therapist sensed that their present conflicts serve as an avoidance of long-standing feelings. He guessed that their constant quarreling, bickering, and shaming of one another was a repetition of how they themselves were shamed and belittled as children. So he inquired what it was like with their families of origin. Tim and Irene were reluctant to go into those vulnerable areas. Their promise to themselves was that their hidden affective constructs that were filled with shame and disgust would never be open to anyone.

The therapist sensitively approached those issues of abandonment and shame. He found that Irene and Tim had suffered greatly as children. Irene had felt replaced by her younger sister who had become their father's doll. Her father left the family for another woman and took her younger sister with him. Tim had felt replaced by a baby brother, at the same time that his father left the family. Both Irene and Tim had worried about being further abandoned by their mothers if they did not behave.

When Tim and Irene got married those hidden abandonment issues started pressing on them outside their awareness. They acted out their frustrations on each other. They created an atmosphere in which they repeatedly experienced fear of neglect and abandonment. It was not until those painful issues were uncovered and understood, and placed in the proper perspective—that is, in their families of origin—that they became more flexible and could create a functional couple.

CONCLUSION

The Relational Family model is a synthesis and integration of relational theories. It integrates object relations theories with interpersonal psychoanalysis and specific trends of self psychology into a systemic relational model. Our basic premise is that the pursuit and maintenance of human relatedness is not just a maturational process: It is the fundamental motivation, the basic thrust of life. Disturbances in early relationships with caretakers lead to serious distortions of subsequent relatedness, not by freezing infantile needs in place, as some theories of self psychology might suggest, but by setting in motion a complex projective and introjective identificatory process through which the child (and later the adult) builds an interpersonal and systemic world that further consolidates affect regulation and the affective psychic construct.

This dynamic process can be repeated from one generation to the other and can seriously distort and damage not only the individual in a system but also the most significant intimate relationships between partners and the entire multigenerational family system. Family members can be affected by these damaging influences in all aspects of their psychic lives without really knowing why they suffer so much or why they experience the same conflicts and traumatic relationships with others over and over again. They seek compatible persons with whom to re-create the only model of relatedness they know. Everything else is for them unfamiliar and therefore dangerous.

The Relational Family model works not only to expand conscious awareness of deprivation and missed early experiences, but also to correct affect regulation, dismantle a dysfunctional affective psychic construct, and alter the basic structure of the individual interpersonal and relational systemic world. The Relational Family therapist looks for sufficient resolution of the problem of affect regulation and affective psychic construct on a systems level, then goes deeper into the interpersonal level, and finally unravels the most basic intrapsychic contributants. The Relational Family model approaches intrapsychic components and processes from various angles within the relational matrix: self organization, object ties, transactional patterns, interpersonal patterns, and the dynamics of the system. The Relational Family therapist tries to make sense of these mental contents from the past in terms of their powerful influence on the present life of the individual, the couple, or the family system.

From the point of view of the subsystem of self psychology, the therapist helps the individual, couple, or family to recover, reconnect, and fully experience aspects previously disavowed but projected into the interpersonal and/or systemic world. After exploring distortions of the individual self and its subsequent affect regulation and affective psychic construct, the therapist encourages new interactions that lead to new ways of experiencing relatedness.

In object relations theory, the therapeutic process is described in terms of intervention to modify internal object relational sets that are formed complementary to the character structure of significant others. Deprived individuals form the same object relations with others in later life as in early childhood with the purpose of maintaining a sense of attachment and connectedness. These powerful links to the past are expressed in ways of relating in the present in the transference to the therapist and are received in the countertransference. The therapist feels the pull toward past forms of relatedness but behaves in ways that are different from early figures. The therapist can put experiences into words. The therapist's use of the countertransference to generate an interpretation of the transference links between past and present leads the individual, couple, or family toward new ways of relatedness to the self, to others, and to the whole family system. The powerful mechanism of countertransference, drawn from the object relations tradition, is the essential component of the Relational Family model of therapy.

Lastly, interpersonal analysis facilitates changes in the transactional patterns of an individual, couple, and family. Repetitive rituals and patterns of relatedness define the experience of both self subsystem and object subsystem and prevent new ways of relating. By discovering patterns of affect regulation and articulating the affective psychic construct, the therapist encourages the individual, couple, or family system to try a new interpersonal experience where more functional patterns of behavior are possible.

SUMMARY

We present in this chapter our innovative model of therapy called Relational Family Therapy and illustrate our way of working. The basic premise of this model of therapy is that the three levels of interactions, systemic, interpersonal, and intrapsychic, mutually and reciprocally influence and are influenced by one another, establish the mode of affect regulation, and produce the affective psychic construct. We describe how the intrapsychic subsystems as conceptualized by self psychology, object relation theories, and interpersonal psychoanalysis, all defined as relational models, directly affect an individual, a marital relationship, and a system as a whole. We also demonstrate that affective psychic constructs and related forms of affect regulation appear on the systemic level as symptoms of distorted interpersonal and systemic relational configurations.

REFERENCES

Cvetek, R. 2004. Predelava disfunkcionalno shranjenih stresnih izkusenj ter metoda desenzitizacije in ponovne predelave z ocesnim gibanjem. Unpublished doctoral thesis. Ljubljana: Univerza v Ljubljani, Oddelek za psihologijo.

Fairbairn, W. R. D. 1952. *An Object Relations Theory of the Personality.* New York: Basic Books.

Framo, J. L. 1992. *Family of Origin Therapy: An Intergenerational Approach.* New York: Brunner/Mazel.

Gostecnik, C. 2002. *Sodobna Psihoanaliza (Modern Psychoanalysis).* Ljubljana: Brat Francisek.

———. 2004. *Relational Family Therapy.* Ljubljana: Brat Francisek.

Kohut, H. 1984. *How Does Analysis Cure?* Chicago: University of Chicago Press.

Kompan Erzar, K. 2001a. *Odkritje odnosa (The Discovery of the Relationship).* Ljubljana: Brat Francisek in Franciskanski druzinski institut.

———. 2001b. Neuropsihologija in relacijska psihoterapija. *Psiholoska Obzorja* 10(4): 119–34.

Lachkar, J. 2004. *The Narcissistic/Borderline Couple: New Approaches to Marital Therapy* (2nd edition). New York: Brunner-Routledge.

Mitchell, S. A. 1988. *Relational Concepts in Psychoanalysis.* Cambridge: Harvard University Press.

———. 1993. *Hope and Dread in Psychoanalysis.* New York: Perseus Books Group.

———. 1997. *Influence and Autonomy in Psychoanalysis.* Hillsdale, NJ: The Analytic Press.

———. 2000. *Relationality: From Attachment to Intersubjectivity.* New York: The Analytic Press.

———. 2002. *Can Love Last? The Fate of Romance over Time.* New York: W. W. Norton.

Pines, A. M. 1999. *Falling in Love: Why We Choose the Lovers We Choose.* New York: Routledge.

Scharff, J. S. 1989. *Foundations of Object Relations Family Therapy.* Northvale, NJ: Jason Aronson.

———. 1992. *Projective and Introjective Identification and the Use of Therapist's Self.* Northvale, NJ: Jason Aronson.

Scharff, J. S., and D. E. Scharff. 1991. *Object Relations Couple Therapy.* Northvale, NJ: Jason Aronson.

———. 1998. *Object Relations Individual Therapy.* Northvale, NJ: Jason Aronson.

———. 2000. *Tuning the Therapeutic Instrument: Affective Learning of Psychotherapy.* Northvale, NJ: Jason Aronson.

Schore, A. N. 1994. *Affect Regulation and the Origin of the Self.* Hillsdale, NJ: Lawrence Erlbaum.

———. 2003. *Affect Regulation and the Repair of the Self.* New York: W. W. Norton.

Slipp, S. 1996. *Healing the Gender Wars: Therapy with Men and Couples.* Northvale, NJ: Jason Aronson.

Solomon, M. F., R. J. Neborsky, L. McCullough, M. Alpert, F. Shapiro, and D. Malan. 2001. *Short-Term Therapy for Long-Term Change.* New York: W. W. Norton.

Sullivan, H. S. 1972. *Personal Psychopathology.* New York: W. W. Norton.

Winnicott, D. W. 1965. *The Maturational Processes and the Facilitating Environment.* New York: International Universities Press.

———. 1971. *Playing and Reality.* New York: Basic Books.

———. 1975. *Through Paediatrics to Psycho-Analysis.* New York: Basic Books.

6

The Family and Psychosis
Transpersonal Pathologies

Anna Maria Nicolò

REVIEW OF STUDIES OF
PSYCHOTIC FUNCTIONING

For several years, many people have discussed the characteristics of psychotic functioning, whether or not unique family configurations exist, what weight external reality places on the origin and perpetuation of serious pathologies, and how easily these patients can become chronic in the minds of their attendants. The treatment of such patients raises numerous questions, not least of which is the relationship between healing, progress, and adaptation to the context, given that in certain situations improvement that is too fast can aggravate their awareness of suffering and impede adaptation to the environment.

These patients have facilitated advances in psychological understanding and treatment techniques as no others have. No patients so thoroughly try their therapists and force them to confront their limits and examine their techniques. In psychosis, as in other serious pathologies, the environment is involved in its origin and maintenance, and so psychosis falls under the rubric of transpersonal pathologies. Psychotic pathology is found in the encounter between the patient and the world outside the self, and, according to Aulagnier, it occurs between the ego and the "psychotic potentiality" and consists of "a specific organization of the space outside the psyche and the surrounding discourse" (Aulagnier 1975, p. 246).

The psychotic personality is held in common by members of a family. Yet

63

each member will hold it in a unique way, reacting variously, according to their experience and abilities. The one who becomes the spokesperson for all the stakeholders in this psychosis-generating potentiality is the one who will become the psychotic patient, but each family member has his or her own part in the puzzle, both in its origin and in its maintenance, or in suffering or defending themselves from its pull. Particular types of bonds are generated, which in turn become pathological and pathogenic.

We have come a long way in our understanding of psychosis since the days when Sullivan (1953) or Fromm-Reichmann (1950) in the United States pointed their fingers at the schizophrenogenic mother, indicating the child as her passive victim. Nevertheless these early studies usefully shifted attention away from the index patient and onto environmental treatment, and connect with present-day understanding of the importance of empathic attunement between the child and the parent. In Europe during the same period, Winnicott (1960) underlined the importance of the environment in the treatment of the child. He said that the environmental object constituted an element of the self. Winnicott held that environmental privation was the central cause of psychosis. Reviewing the literature, I find a progressive enlarging of the environmental context as a factor involved in the origin of these disturbances.

Searles (1959) laid the groundwork for a relational explanation of psychotic disturbance in his article, "The effort to drive the other person crazy—An element in the aetiology and psychotherapy of schizophrenia," in which he described interactions with psychotic patients and attributed the motivation for driving the other person crazy to the "desire to exteriorize, in this way freeing one's self from the threatening craziness that one feels in the self" (Searles, p. 254). The patient therefore becomes "a deposit for the foolishness present in the other members" (Searles, p. 254), because of the failure of the differentiation process. In the atmosphere of a symbiotic-pathologic relationship, the mother who is loving her child to death transmits to the child the idea that the mother's mental health depends on the child's care of her. The child experiences the desire to be of help to the sick parent, which is natural. However, Searles remarks, "It is often noticeable in the history of schizophrenic patients how one or both parents had the chronic tendency to solicit liking, sympathy, and we could say, therapeutic treatment from the child, but at the same time refused his or her efforts to help; in this way, the kindness and genuine desire to be of use that the child had felt, became mixed with feelings of guilt, anger, and perhaps overall, a sense of powerlessness and personal worthlessness" (1959, p. 246). Then the child "will experience his or her own desire to madden the mother" (p. 260). The psychotic person wants to alleviate feelings of loneliness by selecting a soul mate, which can press the soul mate into craziness.

Searles explained the unconscious reasons for mutual projections between patient and parent and illustrated particular types of pathological interactions that incite emotional conflict in the other into whom various opposing sectors of the personality have been projected. He detected various interactive partners including: (1) sexually arousing the other in a context in which obtaining gratification is not permitted, (2) simultaneously stimulating and frustrating various types of needs, and (3) suddenly changing the emotional depth of the relationship. All these are techniques that threaten reliance and trust in one's self, one's own perception of reality, and they weaken the ego.

The attention that Searles gave to the communicative interactions was uncommon in the field of psychoanalysis in his day, when the focus was intensely intrapsychic and provided the basis for an analytic approach to psychosis, which is still relevant and invaluable. At the same time, other authors were conducting research at the systemic level. Wynne et al. (1958) identified a "pseudo-reciprocal" relationship in the parental couples of schizophrenic individuals. The impression of the parents' reciprocal adaptation was hollow, an impression achieved by using elastic, rubbery, slippery defenses avoiding confrontation and trivializing conflict. Many years later (1984) Wynne illustrated another type of psychotic transaction using rigid defenses that created a hardening of the roles and an inflexible family superego, which hinders individual growth. An emotional environment, characterized by "pseudo-hostility," defends against the need for intimacy. These confusing and contradictory interactions preclude the child from having the necessary good introjective identification with steady parental figures.

Attention has progressively shifted from the individual to the environment, the dual interaction between the child and the mother, including the father, and so to the broader realm of familial transactions.

Bowen (1960) placed psychosis within a trigenerational dynamic. In this view, the parents are no longer implicated as the guilty parties, but rather, a vicious cycle comes to light that expresses itself in the parents' conflicts and shortcomings as much as in the index patient's problems. The level of differentiation of the parents and the emotional climate prevalent in the family of origin determines the level of individual autonomy early in childhood.

Bowen's concept of the patient as a symptom of a family problem was further developed by Bateson and Jackson of the Palo Alto school, whose somewhat mechanistic conception of the family in terms of unitary system and double bind (Bateson and Jackson 1956) was nevertheless remarkably advanced. More recent authors have continued the work. Like Searles, Racamier dealt with craziness and its impact on the other person. Racamier (1989) wrote that craziness appears to be an active mental and relational strategy that is subject to rules that are not well known but are precise nevertheless. He affirms that every case of schizophrenia is a battlefield in which the shots aim to render the other crazy. The victims of these strategies become schizophrenic. We would be mistaken if we thought of psychosis as a voluntary strategy, or a mental filicide of which the parents are guilty. The parents are themselves victims of a learned way of functioning that has enshrouded them since birth.

THE INTERACTIVE ORGANIZATION OF THE PSYCHOTIC FAMILY

Treating families or parents with psychotic adolescents, we face complex familial organizations with specific mechanisms, at the levels of conscious interaction and unconscious fantasy. To understand this type of functioning, and to facilitate therapeutic treatment, we need to focus both on unconscious familial fantasy and the interactions that circulate in these families.

The family as a whole uses transpersonal defenses to deal with anxiety or mental pain that cannot be expressed by evacuating it into the other or passing it through the other into a space that is separate from one's own mind. In psychotic families intrapsychic and interpersonal conflicts are related to experiential deficits. Each member of the psychotic-potential family, since the beginning of life, has been immersed in a specific interactive climate and has learned to privilege certain forms of communication and mental mechanisms. For instance, nonverbal interactions are normally subordinate to verbal communication, but in psychotic families, nonverbal messages contradict the verbal messages and the real emotional, relational messages take place at the nonverbal level. This leads to continuous control over emotion and pressure to understand the other person's thoughts, even if they are not communicated directly.

CLINICAL EXAMPLE

Two married women who were raised as sisters twenty years apart in age, sisters in a family with a schizophrenic patient, take turns caring for their mother, who is now elderly, physically frail, and prone to injury. Every time the mother is a guest in the home of one of the sisters, she telephones the other with veiled allusions to not feeling well and to having been robbed of her belongings by the daughter who is caring for her. In the course of these phone calls, the custodial sister takes the phone from her mother's hand and, accusing her sister of having neglected their mother and causing her injury, affirms that *she* is caring for the mother as she should. The noncustodial sister is dumbfounded, guilty, and confused.

The mother always implicates whichever sister is absent. The goals of this behavior are multiple: (a) to wield control over all her children, inciting jealousy and rivalry, (b) to prevent separation and individuation (an objective in which hate is much more effective than love), and (c) to deny any need of affection and dependence. She inverts the relationship, as if to say that it is the children who need their mother, and not vice versa. The final goal is to find out the *real* intentions of the other. The mother, like each of her daughters, does not feel deserving of love from anyone, and is therefore predisposed to doubt the other's words, always seeking to discover some hidden meaning.

The mother's manipulation unleashes a persecutory reaction in one sister who projects the fault onto the other sister, who then feels guilty instead. Suffering and guilt are evacuated into the other. The actual content of the messages is not addressed and dealt with because the point of the messages is to induce a feeling state in the other.

This example leads us on to recalling other characteristics of these families. A tyrannical organization of control substitutes for any genuine family solidarity. The relational schemas are of the "controller-controlled" and "persecutor-victim" types. Family members alternate in taking one or the other role, controlling or being controlled. The control is exercised not so much on one's own behavior as on everyone else's emotions and thoughts. The other is not recognized as a person different from one's self, but as one who must be possessed and colonized. In these families, *every bond is open to attack because it is experienced as dangerous.* Within the psychotic potential family, each individual is always trying to prevent solid bonding because the third party might feel excluded from the coalition of the other two. Any external bond is experienced as dangerous because it involves dependency, which has been characterized since the beginning as being inferior. Emotionally surrendering one's self to another is seen as depicting oneself as a needy, debased, and worthless being who will be degraded by the other. When this happens between the parents, the marriage loses any potential to be a transformative container. Then the remainder of the bonds of submission of each of the parents to their family of origin are directed against one another. Removing one's self from the original submissive relationship is perceived as dangerous, because among other things it means re-creating another submission, this time to the partner, which, being by choice, is much more debasing and dangerous. Similarly, these families find it dangerous to accept help from a therapist.

Keeping secrets is an attempt at setting boundaries in a situation where personal space is disregarded, but it creates coalitions that exclude the third party, be it a family member or a therapist. What is usually kept private in normal families, such as the parents' sexuality (the bedroom doors are often not closed) and the adolescents' bodily development, is publicized in psychotic-potential families, while events worthy of the participation of everyone are apparently kept secret. These secrets are sometimes passed on down the generations, from grandparent to grandchild. A subverted aspect of family functioning interrupts or perverts the family associative chains like a fetish object in family life (Racamier 1992). This is transmitted from one generation to another with the pathogenic effect of renewing a need for secrets. We must explore the function of the secret in the intrapsychic and interpersonal economy of the subject and the family. The very act of creating or perpetuating a secret can mean an active sequestering of parts of the individual or aspects of the family emotional life, which is handed down the generations. The content and the function of the secret are sequestered in a potential space where an elaborative reciprocity is set up between it and the ego of the self and the other. The unelaborated, traumatic event contained in the secret perpetuates itself, and time stops. Identity formation proceeds in parallel paths, one in consciousness, and one in the sequestered reality. The continued, parallel existence of these two registers within the family and inside the subject perpetuates a state of splitting because it is difficult to integrate an alienating and sequestered aspect of the self that has not been experienced and known personally. The most serious thought disorder and psychosomatic manifestations are expressions of identity diffusion between these two registers and a paradoxical solution for the coming into contact with these two parallel paths (Nicolò 1993, pp. 145–46).

Perplexity *and confusion* abound in these families. Searles (1965a) described a reactive confusion against the emergence of intolerable affects caused by projective, reciprocal, and mutually contradictory identifications in the familial world at different levels, and between different partners in the relationship. In my opinion, this contradiction that the subject is forced to submit to is another cause of perplexity and confusion. Meltzer (1979, p. 38) has described this phenomenon on the individual plane as a geographic and zonal confusion.

The confusion that characterizes the internal world of these patients can also be seen when one member in a family misattributes intentions, desires, and needs to another. When a therapist asks a question of a child, a parent replies, attributing to a child a taste or ambition that the child does not have. For instance, the mother says, "My child loves cheese," when the child has never tasted it; or, "My son will definitely study engineering, like all the men in my family for many generations," even when the child has never been good at math. The highest level of confusion is reached when the fragile subject, who has been invaded by the parent's projections, injunctions, and solicitations and who is rendered unable to understand his own needs and desires, respects the injunctions as if they were his own, and as if he were not facing an alienation of the self by colonization of his mind. This illustrates Searles's description of a psychotic family as a symbiotic, collective ego that replaces each individual ego (Searles 1965b).

This pathological confusion is an element of pathogenic importance: the parent is unable to recognize the otherness of the child and so pushes him toward identities that alienate him from the real aspects of his self. In this way, experiences are produced in which not only is there a lack of empathic sharing, but in which there is a violent intrusion into the identity. Many authors have described such processes, among them Winnicott, Cahn, and Garcia Badaracco, to whose contributions I turn in the following paragraphs.

A direct consequence of the existing confusion is the *inversion* of the roles and functions between the generations and the sexes. A child can precociously play a parental role, while the parent is discounted as an incompetent child. A father who is weak, passive, and submissive is incapable of opposing the possessive and authoritative influence of an intrusive mother. Resolving the Oedipus complex is impossible because there is no recognition of the third party as different from the self, there is no link to the sense of reality, no paternal prohibition, and no independent thought.

These patterns become chronic over time. In a constantly reverberating vicious cycle they trap the family members in their roles, because these roles are the only ones recognized by the other members and so guarantee them a glimmer of a coherent identity. For example, a brother may always be seen as the only one capable of making decisions, even if in reality he appears fearful, confused, or incompetent to an outside observer; sister may be the one who is seen as weak, silly, incapable, and needing of guidance, even if over the years she has proven dependable. Consequence and cause of all these family dynamics is the family's inability to function as a container of suffering, a space for thinking, and a nurturing organization with a consonant unconscious life.

These families amplify and speed up emotions or defend them by denial, splitting, or shifting into the other because of the fragility of each member's personal boundaries and the absence of a sufficient distance between one member and another within the family. There is a collapsed transitional space because it is saturated with persecuting ghosts and filled with crises and catastrophes.

There is no space for thinking and no metaphor. This is the biggest problem in these families. Their sessions are filled by concrete problems and arguments over facts or events. Dreams are absent or scanty, and their eventual appearance can signal a turning point in treatment. Ruffiot et al. (1981) observed that in these families, communication and thinking are dominated by concrete operations. They use a rigorous, dry logic to stick to their version of reality, explain away everything, and close off discussion. For instance, the parent of an adolescent suffering a breakdown explains, "My son started feeling bad after his friends pressured him to smoke marijuana," or "my daughter started failing in school when her boyfriend left her." In this case, the triggering event gives the parent a ready explanation that puts an end to any curiosity or anxiety. The concrete dimension eclipses anxiety, cuts off thinking from feeling and fantasy, and blocks elaboration and sublimation.

Sensitive therapy picks up on the fact that beyond their defensive script lies another reality. In every psychosis, there is a person in retreat, hidden and inaccessible because of avoiding pain. Confusedly, the family knows that something different is true. Being trapped in a labyrinth, every clue is useful. An exit is possible, but at the same time, the paths for finding it are blocked. A few psychotic adolescents, in order to affirm their own existence, can only attempt suicide. Encountering the truth is equivalent to encountering the monstrosity of the primal scene and the enormous task of integrating instinctual and representational elements, and undoing sexual and generational confusion. The omnipotent therapist who takes this on blindly crashes and burns. While areas of unconscious fantasy life are empty or concretized, a few areas may be so saturated with content and ghosts that they become difficult to reach in words, and remain expressed in delusions and hallucinations.

THE UNCONSCIOUS ORGANIZATION IN THE PSYCHOTIC FAMILY

Racamier illustrated a constellation that is characteristic of psychotic functioning, which he has called "the anti-Oedipal." The rich potential of this idea has not been fully realized but it is central to the understanding of these cases. I will therefore try to summarize it. The anti-Oedipal is a constellation that can be found at the junction between object-relating and narcissistic functioning, between the individual and the familial. It tends to oppose the drives and to counterbalance the anxieties of the Oedipal complex, but overall, it precedes it. In this way, it may be said to be ante-Oedipal as well as anti-Oedipal. In the symbiotic phase this constellation is characterized by a relationship of narcissistic seduction in which a reciprocal fascination between mother and child is established. This primary narcissistic fascination aims to preserve a constant world protected from internal and external excitement. This constant, narcissistic order is disturbed only by the impact of external events, spurts in the child's growth, and by various drives and desires (Racamier 1989).

The goal of such a constellation, founded since the beginning of the family, is that of preempting the mourning and anxiety of separation, maintaining the omnipotent fusion with the mother, protecting against the excitement of external stimuli, growth spurts, Oedipal conflicts, castration anxiety of the primitive scene, and averting anxieties activated by differences between the sexes and the generations. While the Oedipal fantasy based on generational and gender differences is one of taking the parents' place and killing them, the anti-Oedipal fantasy is one of rendering both parents useless and so becoming self-generating. This anti-Oedipal functioning opposes arriving at the depressive position with concern for the object. Eroticization and actual incest bind the patient within the familial tissue.

Garcia Badaracco (1986), an Argentine psychoanalyst, developed two important related concepts: *alienating identification* and *the maddening object*. In his view, the problem central to psychosis is that of the constitution of identity, which is based on identifications constructed in relation to the other family members, which in these families are pathological and alienating to the self. Alienating identifications with the object's unconscious burdens the process of becoming one's own person. The nonelaborated unconscious contents of the parental couple intrude on the child's mind. This intrusion repeats in turn the intrusion that the parents themselves had suffered in childhood. These dominating, pathological identifications are maddening objects, split off, hidden, and demanding. They subordinate other areas of mental functioning and compel restructuring of the psyche. Behind these pathological alienating identifications, we always find a history of traumatic situations, or of intense psychic suffering. The ego, not being able to defend itself, develops a false pathological self or, even more likely, is forced to transform itself by assuming aspects of the other's fantasies. The ego has been invaded by a foreign object that expropriates it and threatens its identity and its becoming a subject.

Children enjoying ordinary good environmental care are allowed to discover their objects for themselves, to find the object and size it up (Davies and Wallbridge 1981). Children have omnipotent control over the objects they have created and found for themselves. In psychotic-potential families the mother imposes too many objects on the child or presents too few objects to be discovered. She imbues them with too much meaning and too little meaning. This impedes the child from the extraordinary moment of spontaneity in the hiatus between finding the presented object and creating a new object that is separate from the mother, and that is normally the beginning of subjectivity. The mother who cannot let go of control attributes her own meanings or lack of meaning to everything and cannot allow meaning to emerge, and she squashes her child's healthy omnipotence and creativity.

The psychotic child must confront an excess. The mother is the carrier of an excess of meanings from the previous generation and is not capable of tolerating an unpredictable and creative child who looks for new meanings. On the other hand the child may confront a lack. In that case, the mother has never invested the child with any meaning and fails to offer objects and meanings to her child. Then the child must self-organize defensively against an absence that has become a persecutory presence.

Pathological identifications remain disassociated and organize themselves as unconscious internal objects that are evil and maddening and must be kept under control by rigidly defensive mechanisms, with a permanent expense of energy. Unable to integrate stimuli coming from the external world, from the internal world, and from the body (as in the course of adolescence, for example), the psychotic child reaches an impasse and develops a false self, following the parents' unconscious regulations inside the self. This organization is unstable. Threatened by developmental challenges, these rigid defenses are revealed as brittle and break down. The self that breaks down is at the same moment trying to break out and find affirmation by getting help outside the family system.

Adapted to another person's mandate and deprived of the chance to exist in one's own identity, the psychotic individual can experience delusions of passive influence and reference or may appear to be an inanimate caricature—both outcomes of transpersonal pathology. The parents hold a caricature of a child in mind as they do not really know their actual child. The child obeying parental injunctions develops a mask to hide the real self, and this effort may cause a robotic demeanor. In an effort to do their best, they want their child to adapt completely in conformance to their plan governed by a transgenerational mandate.

This roboticizing of the child captures the mechanical qualities of affective functioning in the family. Tenderness, indulgence, fragility, and compassion must be resisted, hidden, split, and denied. In therapy we notice a mechanization of the normal atmosphere of the sessions, except during moments of crisis.

THE PARENTAL COUPLE OF THE PSYCHOTIC INDIVIDUAL

The parents, however, are certainly not to blame for this situation, as they in turn are victims. Each of them has been led by the unconscious choice of a partner to create the shared psychotic potentiality. If one of the parents ceased to be involved in the maintenance of this organization, that would change the situation radically. This is not possible, however, given that they are prisoners of their history and of the bond that unites them.

A healthy degree of autonomy is impossible for them. Caught up in a sadomasochistic dialectic, each is the persecutor-victim of the other. Their hate and pain strengthen their incestuous bond with their child, in an attempt to vindicate themselves and marginalize the power of their partner. The real problem lies at the beginning of the marriage when each spouse, glued to the family of origin by unelaborated trauma and failed mourning, fails to develop as an autonomous individual capable of becoming a subject in a marriage.

The nurturing mother whom each would have liked to find in the other, given their primitive frustrations, is there only to demand and disappoint. The original rancor for the past becomes confused with rancor for the present. The membrane of the couple does not carry out an effective function of delineation; rather, the incestuous bond existing between one of the parents and the child often renders the other peripheral and impotent and obliterates the boundary that the couple should have established. The couple's intermediate space does not serve a containing function. The bond is not between spouses but between a parent and a child. The deepest commitment is shown in an extrafamilial relationship, or in a strong commitment to work—all to the exclusion of the spouse.

CLINICAL EXAMPLE

Cassio is a fifteen-year-old boy, whose father has made a request for hospitalization because the boy has become progressively isolated (for a full report on this case see Nicolò 1992). He stays in his room, afraid of being contaminated in his relationships with other boys or random objects on the street, which he fears could make him homosexual. Cassio seems to be on the verge of a breakdown. He does not shake hands with the doctor out of fear, remains silent, and looks around with a suspicious air. In the first session, Cassio's father, who presents himself as an artist and philosopher, tells us about his doubts and worries. The mother seems hardly to be paying attention to what her husband says. She is an austere woman, with lovely blond hair pulled back from her face. She interrupts only to communicate her notion of reality, entrusting her husband with all other comments. The father commandeers the space of his son, who is becoming more and more quiet and intimidated.

Cassio is similar to him, doubtful, and perplexed. He used to play the guitar and participate on a soccer team, but after a fight with a teammate, he was expelled from the team. In the previous months he had already found it difficult to be in the locker room with his other teammates. His father, who is Cassio's only confidant, now feels that he cannot care for his son by himself.

In the course of the next session, the father, Eolo, tells his own story and that of the family. Cassio is the youngest of four children, to each of whom Eolo has given a specially significant name. Eolo tells us that Cassio is like the name of one of Caesar's assassins, Cassius, who, unlike Brutus, was "more insecure, thoughtful, and doubting." Eolo is the son of an artisan, who was anarchic, authoritarian, but full of "Eros." Eolo, who had always hated his own father and only felt liberated when he died, maintains that it was natural for him to have had homicidal feelings toward his father. Perhaps if he, Eolo, died, Cassio would be free. Eolo speaks disparagingly about his paid work as an employee and tells instead of books of poetry that he has written, and of his younger days, in which, despite being married, he was a Don Juan by prenuptial agreement.

Cassio's mother, Maria, confirms this fact, adding that the agreement also stipulated that her husband would leave her most of his salary and the children to manage. She, on the other hand, had come from a unified family: her father, a modest artisan, worked at home in the company of her mother. According to Eolo, Maria does not have Eros. He says that she refused his request that she cut her hair, and then he reads us a poem dedicated to her, titled "You Are No Longer a Woman." Maria seems upset by this, then adds that she will never cut her hair, because the request is merely a whim of her husband's. While on this subject, the father adds that he is worried that his son is constantly trimming the first fine whiskers from his face, while the mother maintains in a reassuring tone that Cassio is only doing it to reinforce the growth of his beard.

The parents then tell us how, unlike their other children, Cassio has been particularly doted on by his father since the age of nine, following a time during which Eolo was afraid of dying of severe depression. After a hospital stay Eolo felt reborn, began to be interested in his child again, and spent a lot of time raising and teaching him.

While these family sessions are taking place, Cassio is undergoing consultation with a colleague. The first consultation proves difficult and tiring. In the next two, Cassio allows himself a more trusting and cooperative attitude, to the point of talking about his worries and his passions, for music and especially for the song, "Romeo and Juliet." He speaks of his worry about having to leave his family if he is preselected for the juvenile soccer team. He offers his hand spontaneously to his interviewer and talks of how he feels that he is much less capable than his father, in his understanding of reality and profundity of thought.

In the last session with the parents, each one tells of their dreams. Maria says that the night before the session, she had dreamed that Cassio was a small child who was still nursing at her breast, and she was complaining about the fact that he still had not grown. Eolo complains that Maria has "incestualized" her relationship with their son, and in the next breath invites her to go with him to Jamaica, a free and exciting land. Eolo confesses a dream that he had had prior to the initial family consultation in which Cassio was trying to penetrate a woman with an unknown face, but he, Eolo, intervened and moved the boy's penis, so that he ejaculated outside of her, at which Cassio then started to cry. Eolo comments that he may have done it out of fear of Cassio contracting AIDS.

REFLECTIONS ON IDENTITY, ANXIETY, AND THE USE OF COUPLE DREAMS

We could direct our attention to many points in the family situation described. First of all, we might note that the specific moment in which the request for intervention took place was adolescence, where the theme of remodeling the identity is in the foreground. We could also examine the dangerous, continuous intrusion into the son's mental space on the part of an overinvested father who gave his son the name Cassio, the doubting murderer. We could observe not only Cassio's anxiety, but his father's patricidal fantasies, which he feared that his son could act out against him. A paradoxical situation has been created: a father, in order to allow his son to exist, must permit his killing and in reaction takes up the care for his son. We could explore the nature of the two dreams that the couple presented in the last session, which reflect both the relationship between the couple and the son, and the relationship between the spouses. In both dreams, there are similar contents: the mother tells of a small child who is still nursing at her breast; the father tells of preventing his son from concluding an adult sexual act and spoiling his creative possibilities.

In both dreams, the son appears as a dependent, impotent, crying child. We may ask ourselves if the Cassio of the dream does not also represent the father-husband as childlike and still attached to the breast, and as an impotent teenager, subjected to an internal parental object that attacks him narcissistically and humiliates him. In the dreams of the parents, we see the correspondence between their internal worlds and real interactions. The son in the dreams represents both his own self and his parents' inability to give him space to be himself. He stands for the father who cannot define his own identity with respect to his own father.

This case shows how a symptomatic constellation, a family mode of functioning, and a confusion of identities can be ascribed on the one hand to the vicissitudes of personal history, and on the other to interactive characteristics of the family, especially of the particular nature of the reciprocal functioning of the parental couple. We can see this particularly clearly in an adolescent case like this because the continuous oscillations in self-concept at this age, the revisiting of identity, and the instability of personal boundaries are more marked than in other stages of life. Finally, we may note a coincidence between the weakness of the adolescent boundaries and the psychotic potential family characteristic of fragile differentiation between the ego and the other.

REFERENCES

Aulagnier, P. 1975. *La violenza dell'interpretazione*. Rome: Borla.

Bateson, G., and D. Jackson. 1956. Verso una teoria della schizofrenia. In C. E. Sluzki and D. C. Ransom, eds., *Il doppio legame*. Rome: Astrolabio, 1979.

Bowen, M. 1960. Interpretazione della schizofrenia dal punto di vista della stuttura familiare. In D. D. Jackson, ed., *Eziologia della schizophrenia*, pp. 421–52. Milan: Feltrinelli, 1964.

Cahn, R. 1991. *Adolescence et folie*. Paris: Press Universitaires de France (PUF).

Davies, M., and D. C. Wallbridge. 1981. *Introduzione all'opera di D. W. Winnicott*. Florence: Martinelli, 1994.

Fromm-Reichmann, F. 1950. *Principi di psicoterapia*. Milan: Feltrinelli, 1962.

Garcia Badaracco, J. 1986. Identification and its vicissitudes in the psychoses. The importance of the concept of the "maddening object." *International Journal of Psychoanalysis* 67:133–46.

Meltzer, D. 1979. Un approccio psicoanalitico alle psicosi. *Quaderni di Psicoterapia Infantile* 2:31–49. Rome: Borla.

Nicolò, A. M. 1992. Versione del Sé e interazioni patologiche. *Interazioni* 0:37–48.

———. 1996. Il transgenerazionale tra mito e segreto. *Interazioni* 1(7): 138–52.

Racamier, P-.C. 1989. *Antedipo e i suoi destini*. Milan: CeRP, 1990.

———. 1992. Il "figurante predestinato." In *Il genio delle origini*. Milan: Cortina, 1993.

Ruffiot, A., A. Eiguer, D. Litovsky, E. Liendo, M. C. Gear, and J. Perrot. 1981. *Terapia Familiare Psicoanalitica*. Rome: Borla, 1983.

Searles, H. F. 1959. The effort to drive the other person crazy—An element in the aetiology and psychotherapy of schizophrenia. *British Journal of Medical Psychology* 32: 1–18. (Italian edition: Il tentativo di far impazzire l'altro partecipante al rapporto: Una componente dell'etiologia e della psicoterapia della schizofrenia. In *Scritti sulla schizophrenia*, pp. 243–71. Turin: Boringhieri, 1974.)

———. 1965a. Funzione psicoadinamica della perplessità, della confusione, della diffidenza e degli stati mentali affini. In *Scritti sulla schizophrenia*, pp. 67–107. Turin: Boringhieri, 1974.

———. 1965b. Integrazione e differenziazione nella schizofrenia: Una visione globale del problema. In *Scritti sulla schizophrenia*, pp. 304–35. Turin: Boringhieri, 1974.

Sullivan, H. S. 1953. *Teoria interpersonale della psichiatria*. Milan: Feltrinelli, 1962.

Winnicott, D. W. 1960. The theory of the parent-infant relationship. In *Maturational Processes and the Facilitating Environment*, pp. 37–55. London: Hogarth Press, 1975.

Wynne, L. C., I. Ryckoff, J. Day, and S. I. Hirsch. 1958. Pseudomutuality in the family relations of schizophrenia. *Psychiatry* 21:205–220.

———. 1984. The epigenesis of relational systems: A model for understanding family development. *Family Process* 23(3): 297–318.

7

Folie à Deux as a Model for Transpersonal Disorders

Anna Maria Nicolò

Understanding the folie à deux requires a shift from an intrapsychic vision of the mind's functioning to a relational and interpersonal perspective. The folie à deux derives from the tight correlation between two internal worlds and the mutual influence of one subject's internal world and external reality. One of the questions posed by the early investigators that still is waiting for an answer is this: Does the folie à deux appear simultaneously (Régis 1880) in two individuals with no distinction as to who started it, or is it imposed on, or communicated by, the one who is clearly the originator (Lasègue and Falret 1873) to the other who is the follower, even if each is in a different generation?

Moving beyond the twosome, we see the imposition or emergence of the folly in groups, referred to in the early literature as "psychic contagion" (Lucas 1833; Esquirol 1838; Baillarger 1860; Despine 1870; Moreau de Tours 1875). We see it in family groups with serious psychopathology especially. We can see a core of nonrealistic, misperceiving, or even delusional modes shared by the members of a family or between parent and child.

In *Metapsychology*, Freud (1915) wrote that a person's unconscious can react to another person's unconscious outside conscious control. In the *Uncanny* (1919), he discussed direct transmission among persons' unconsciousnesses, subject to yet unknown rules. In *Psychoanalysis and Telepathy* (1921a), *Dream and Telepathy* (1922), *Some General Additions to* The Interpretation of Dreams (1925), Freud discussed the relation between dreams and telepathic phenomena by relating thought transmission to the activation of unconscious wishes. It is not any irrelevant communication that is transmitted: it is an extraordinarily intense wish that manages to obtain conscious expression, even if slightly disguised, using a second person who is in a special relationship to the transmitter. This is analogous to the use of a light-sensitive plate to detect the invisible part of the spectrum, seen as a colored appendage. The intensity of the affect that is communicated (and the nature of the relationship) amplifies—as if on a light-sensitive plate—aspects, emotions, conflicts, parts of the self that would otherwise have remained invisible.

In an essay of this same period, *Group Psychology and Analysis of the Ego* (1921b), Freud further discussed the issue of psychic contagion, quoting the example of a girl in a boarding school who responds to receiving a letter from a young man she secretly loves by having a hysterical seizure. Becoming aware of the letter, some of her friends also develop seizures by psychic contagion. The egos of the infected friends mirror and resonate with the ego of the hysterical young woman and a transpersonal symptom takes form. Freud also mentioned the young women's sharing the same environment as an important contributing factor.

In short, four elements are necessary for folie à deux to occur: (1) the intensity of the communicated feeling, (2) the special nature of the relationship, (3) the significant correspondence with an aspect of the other's unconscious, and (4) the sharing of a common context.

In 1938, Deutsch discussed this issue in a clinical and theoretical essay, addressing in particular the mechanisms of dependence and identification that are, in her opinion, the basic elements of delusional contagion. By suggestion and induction the subject receives a communication that is not foreign to the ego. According to her model, folly is the outcome of the combination of two unconscious worlds. The person who can become infected through hysterical suggestion or schizophrenic induction is led toward the unconscious wish to take in the present object or recover the lost object.

In his classic 1965 paper, Searles described the effort to drive the other person crazy and wrote about induction as a component of the aetiology and psychotherapy of schizophrenia. Induction is a suggestive term with a debatable meaning. According to Searles, interpersonal interaction is aimed at inducing (or perhaps provoking) emotional conflict in the other by activating opposing sectors of the other's personality. The other person's wish for psychosis connects with the schizophrenic's aggressive wish to drive the other crazy and achieve psychic death—analogous to the wish to kill and eliminate the other physically. Further aims of induction are to externalize the folly that threatens the self in order to get rid of the threat, the conflict, and the lack of resolution, and to establish a symbiotic relationship, to find a twin soul that alleviates the intolerable sense of loneliness. On a positive note, induction is useful to help the other think from more than one point of view and so reach intrapersonal integration and interpersonal relatedness. To realize oneself through induction is in a sense the essence of a loving relationship.

From its earliest days psychoanalysts tried to study the changes induced in internal or external reality by omnipotent affects and fantasies in the subject's mind, and to describe interpersonal processes as part of an intrapsychic mechanism, and vice versa. In subsequent years, this effort continued with discussions on projective identification as an intrapsychic defense, as a one-body or two-body phenomenon, as a constructivist-interpersonal vision of projective identification, culminating in an indiscriminate use of the concept (J. Scharff 1992). Similar or related concepts are Grinberg's (1981) projective counteridentification, A. Freud's (1936) identification with the aggressor, or Brodey's (1965) externalization. More recently and from a different purview, Sandler (1976) talked of "role responsiveness" where the analyst reacting to the material of the session enacts the role assigned by the patient.

Folie à deux includes all these elements of induction and more complicating aspects besides. According to Meltzer (1983), the mechanisms of folie à deux go beyond projective identification to include narcissistic identification, such as adhesive identification, and depend on basic assumptions linking the group of two, as they link subgroups in a work group described by Bion (1959). In the case of folie à deux, when one of the two can get rid of delusional ideas, the other becomes crazier. Meltzer thinks of folie à deux as if the two structures of personality are uniting in order to form a new structure still to be defined. What this particular kind of structure is, and how it is formed, are the basic questions posed by this pathology.

FOLIE À DEUX AS A BASIC MODEL FOR A RELATIONSHIP

Using Freud's metaphor of the light-sensitive plate that makes the final part of the spectrum visible, we can say that, in some interactional contexts, complementary, mutually reverberating aspects of two personalities trigger the mutual influencing and amplification of contained affects or parts of the self, which would otherwise remain dormant. The relevant aspect is not so much the complementarity, but rather this highlighting of new aspects that had always belonged to that person, but might not ever come to light or be analyzed without the experience of that relationship context.

In a previous essay (Nicolò 1992) referred to in chapter 6, I suggest that in the relation to the other any person can activate a complementary version of the self that in extreme cases can overwhelm what had up to that moment been the identity known by that individual and by others. I also suggest many multifaceted possible uses of the other in the relationship—for providing normal stabilization of personality, maintaining consistency, and defining the self, or pathological colonization and parasitizing of the other (never a passive receptor) so that the suffering enacted by, or evacuated into, the other finds a mental or somatic container that can repeat it or elaborate it.

The folie à deux is located at the pathological end of the spectrum, but it can be viewed as a universal model of a bipersonal psychological functioning in that it not only describes the representations in an individual's mind but rather the bond as central element. In this case the bond itself can activate and induce aspects in each of the personalities as they interact and relate to their context. The idea of the sudden appearance of these dormant aspects of the self seems far more acceptable if, instead of conceiving the subject's self as a single unchangeable structure, we try to see it as a complex organization of various parts, each representing an aspect of identity.

The context is fundamental for determining the rules of the relationship, and also for giving meaning to the events and words, and indeed for all mental processes (Bateson 1979). The context, as Modell (1984) reminds, allows for the selection of certain aspects that are seen as existing just because they are understandable within a binding context.

CASE HISTORY: MARIA AND ROBERTO

I now present a clinical vignette that illustrates this situation.

A middle-aged woman calls me for couple therapy. On the telephone and again in the first consultation session, she tells me the reason she requests treatment is to convince her husband that she is not cuckolding him.

As they walk into the consulting room, I get the impression of an elegant couple. Maria and Roberto have been married for twenty years and have no children. Maria is a pleasant, well-educated woman who spends all her time managing the home. Roberto is a manager spending most of his time at work. Roberto looks somewhat sad and tired but is quite handsome nevertheless.

Maria immediately affirms her trust for her husband and the esteem in which she holds him for his professional capability. She feels loved and understood. Their marriage has always worked well, even if no children were born. She had tried to discover why she was sterile, but no specific cause was identified. He could have tried to find out, too, but refused to do it. Remembering her father and how he prided himself on his masculinity, she says that she can understand how humiliating this kind of investigation can be for a man.

Roberto says, however, that they had agreed that it was not important to have children and they have had a good marriage. He says that he only came to therapy to please his wife. But the story changes when they both start talking about finding a strategy for a small problem.

Maria says that she would like to reassure Roberto about her fidelity. She says she is flattered by Roberto's love expressions, but at times she is also embarrassed by the extent of his distrust. Before my more and more astonished eyes, she tells that Roberto powders the floor to check if she goes out and ties threads to the door handles so the threads will break when the doors are opened. Her litany reaches its climax. "Every Friday a boy comes to bring six eggs. Usually Roberto is at home to collect them, but last Friday there was a problem. . . ." At this point a terrible fight starts. Roberto states that on Wednesday there were still six eggs left, while he had eaten two eggs the day before. How come there were six? He assumes that Maria had put two new ones in there, meaning that the boy had come when he was not at home. So Maria must be having an affair with the boy. At this point he takes a gun out of his pocket. Maria does not seem scared and explains, "He is worse than a Sicilian man." Any effort on my part to show that Roberto's reactions are exaggerated and that the problem goes far beyond jealousy has no effect. The couple cannot believe there might be other explanations.

In the following sessions I learn that Maria's life is filled with the task of following the rituals imposed by her husband. Before that, her life was burdened with suicidal depression due to feeling persecuted and devalued by her sister whom she found more beautiful and capable than herself. Curiously, that depression had disappeared now that she had such a problem with Roberto. Gradually, covert maneuvers employed by Maria to trigger her husband's jealousy come to light.

Maria's ability to see her husband's disorder, with his jealous delusions, covered her activation of her husband's pathology. Maria and Roberto shared a delusional core, formerly expressed by Maria with her sister and now by Roberto in relation to Maria and her supposed lovers. Roberto's pathological jealousy of Maria is a later edition of Maria's envy of her sister.

The bond uniting Maria and Roberto, organized by mutual control and the exclusion of a persecutory third, ends up being claustrophobic, but it is seen as the only way to survive, keeping psychic death under control. The idea of killing oneself or the envied other is alarmingly present in each one's mind and so is kept under control by various defensive measures, at first by turning murderous rage into a suicide attempt, and then by projecting it into the couple where it is kept under brittle control by defensive rituals. The pathology is egosyntonic for both of them. In the couple's space each one's intrapsychic pathology is split off and externalized, and each one is an accomplice to that fact. Couple therapy is indicated, but the resolution of the delusional bond is a dangerous undertaking. Functioning structures like the ones enacted by this couple are useful to keep at bay other pathologies that would otherwise threaten the subject's mental and physical health.

Analyzing the use of the rituals can produce imbalance in one of the two, which therapy tries to contain but may not always succeed in doing. Individual therapy is doomed to failure. It is equally difficult to treat each of them separately as the important element is their bond into which all their pathology is projected. The partners are not aware of the delusional nature of their problem, precisely because both contribute to create it.

Maria and Roberto share the need to control and dominate the other as a way of feeling accepted, acknowledged, loved, and belonging in a family. Each triggers the pathology in the other where the symbols of the unconscious are given flesh. It is difficult to move back from the concrete level to arrive at an understanding of the impact of unconscious fantasy. The underlying fantasy of death that is so clear to the therapist is totally foreign to the mind of the couple acting in this way.

FOCUSING ON THE BOND

In some couples, in some contexts, we see unconscious sharing that can end up creating transpersonal psychopathologic organizations, which cannot be separated from the interacting partners. The members of such a couple in another context or with other partners might not have become ill. The pathologic aspect of their bond might not have emerged, whereas in the marriage of Roberto and Maria the folie à deux served the economic and dynamic needs of both partners.

The intensity of the affects, the nature of the bond, the similarity to aspects of the other's fantasy world, and the sharing of a particularly evocative context create the necessary conditions for the foundation of a folie à deux. Rather than the two individuals coming together from separate healthy positions they live inside their bond, which is co-constructed from archaic fantasies and a few structural elements.

The expression of pathological aspects of a couple's bond may be triggered by changes, breakups, separations, and family deaths. The threat of breakup activates jealousy. Delusional jealousy has the effect of producing an undifferentiated needy state in the partner. But when the bond is one in which each partner feels narcissistically satisfied only insofar as the other is subdued, controlled, intruded upon, and unable to exist autonomously, then separations question the very essence of the self. Archaic fantasies and anxieties about annihilation and death of the self are let loose, since the death of the bond is seen as the breakup of that symbiotic bond that has supported the self up to that moment. The partner has never been established as a separate object, but has been considered as part of the self.

I propose to apply understanding of the shared pathology of the folie à deux pattern seen at the extreme end of the continuum of types of interpersonal functioning to more normal interactions, although in different degrees and with different modes. Viewing interpersonal relations in the light of folie à deux sheds light on the normal person's ability to change constantly, to learn from experience, to allow various aspects of the self to come forth according to needs and situations. Although it is a clearly pathological dyad, I think that it may be found deep in ordinary couples, not expressed explicitly, but mutually biasing the partnership. In normal couples, the bond exists as a relational potential or as a background, a stage for their life as a couple, and does not become a character in their drama unless the partners encounter unusual demands in their roles.

To varying extents the other in an intimate relationship can never be fully known. Nevertheless, significant others have their unconscious effect on their partners and use them, as their partners affect and are used by them in a real and a fantasy relationship. An internal object relationship re-created in a partnership produces an exchange with the external object and leads to a mutual projective identification that becomes the couple's projective identificatory system (Teruel 1966, J. Scharff 1992). Bion (1974) confirmed the usefulness of the concept of projective identification in clinical work, but he was also seeking a broader explanation for how the patient affected the analyst (p. 181). I propose that each intimate partner and each family member is both an object of projection and a contributing subject with an external reality that is separate, offers the partner a new experience of reality, and pushes toward change. Beyond the effect that subject and object have on one another in reality and fantasy, they also create and are held together in their characteristic form of relationship by a unique bond.

In situations of serious pathology, where acting prevails on thinking, talking, and representing, where there is a sort of short circuit of consciousness, the subject receiving the projection feels changed by unseen factors and thereby induced to have behaviors, experiences, and emotions and act them unknowingly. But we should not describe these events in causal terms or look at who started it and induced the other to do something, because it is always mutual. There is not one person parasitizing the other. The victim becomes the persecutor and vice versa, both of them entrapped by the nature of their bond.

Following on studies of bonds in couples and families (Berenstein 2000, Berenstein and Puget 1997, Eiguer 1998, and Kaës 1996), I define bonds as those mutual and interdependent relations that are co-constructed by members of a couple or family as a third object operating between them and influencing them powerfully. I think that the use of the term *bond* addresses effectively the bilateral or multilateral nature of these relations in which the other is a subject in reality as well as an object of projection. A bond is the third object co-constructed by two or more mutually interdependent

Table 7.1. Specific characteristics of the bond in folie à deux

- It is a shared unconscious co-construction by the partners.
- It influences the partners who co-constructed it.
- It is unseen, but
    expressed in behaviors, dreams, or symptoms
    becomes evident if it biases the subject's freedom of expression
    may become conscious after working through.
- It pulls from each partner various versions of it.
- It is the backdrop for the object relationships.
- It is obvious only in pathological situations.
- It is powerful enough to prevent the development of personality.
- It controls against the emergence of psychotic and depressive dynamics.
- It can be detected in countertransference feelings, dreams, interactions, and gestures.

members of a family. The bond is expressed in family behavior, individual symptoms, and dreams (Nicolò, Norsa, and Carratelli 2003).

Although the bond is created by the parties in their interaction, it becomes a third element that functions almost autonomously to affect both parties. The bond enacts a specific version of the self, leaving the other versions of the self dormant. In pathological situations, it is the folie à deux that expresses extremely disturbed aspects of both partners, and the healthy parts of the self lie dormant, blocked from differentiation. In healthy relationships, the folie à deux lies dormant.

I conclude that it would be better to describe the events in terms of the bonds that unite or trap rather than the actions of the individual partners, one upon the other.

REFERENCES

Baillarger J. 1860. Quelques exemples de folie communiquée, *Gazette des Hôpitaux*, Paris.

Bateson, G. 1979. *Mente e Natura*. Milan: Adelphi, 1984.

Berenstein, I. 2000. El vinculo y el otro. *Revista de Psicoanalisis* 58(3, 4): 677–88.

Berenstein, I., and J. Puget. 1997. *Lo Vincular*. Buenos Aires: Paidos.

Bion, W. R. 1959. *Experiences in Groups*. London: Tavistock.

———. 1974. Seminari brasiliani. In *Il Cambiamento Catastrofico* (1974): 102–83. Turin: Loescher, 1981.

Brodey, W. M. 1965. On the dynamics of narcissism: I. Externalization and early ego development. *Psychoanalytic Study of the Child* 20:165–93.

Despine P. 1870. *De la contagion morale*, Camoin, Marseille.

Deutsch, H. 1938. Folie à deux. *Psychoanalytic Quarterly* 7:307–18.

Eiguer, A. 1998. *Clinique Psychanalytique du Couple*. Paris: Dunod.

Esquirol. 1838. *Traité des maladies mentales*. In Babini V.P. (ed), *Folie à deux*, Métis, Lanciano, 1992.

Freud, A. 1936. *L'Io e i Meccanismi di Difesa*. Florence: Martinelli, 1977.

Freud, S. 1915. *Metapsicologia*. *Opere* 8:3–118. Turin: Boringhieri, 1976.

———. 1919. *Il perturbante*. *Opere* 9:79–118. Turin: Boringhieri, 1977.

———. 1921a. *Psicoanalisi e telepatia*. *Opere* 9:345–61. Turin: Boringhieri, 1977.

———. 1921b. *Psicologia delle masse e analisi dell'Io*. *Opere* 9:259–330. Turin: Boringhieri, 1977.

———. 1922. *Sogno e telepatia*. *Opere* 9:383–407. Turin: Boringhieri, 1977.

———. 1925. *Alcune aggiunte d'insieme alla* Interpretazione dei sogni. *Opere* 10:151–64. Turin: Boringhieri, 1978.

Grinberg, L. 1981. *Psicoanalisi, Spetti Teorici e Clinici*. Turin: Loescher, 1983.

Kaës, R. 1996. A proposito del gruppo interno, del gruppo, del soggetto, del legame e del portavoce nell'opera di Pichon-Rivière. *Interazioni* 1(7): 18–38.

Kohon, G. 1989. Qtd. in R. D. Hinshelwood (1989). *Dizionario di Psicoanalisi Kleiniana*, p. 627. Milan: Cortina, 1990.

Laplanche, J., and J. B. Pontalis. 1967. *Enciclopedia della Psicoanalisi*. Laterza: Bari, 1968.

Lasègue, C., and J. P. Falret. 1873. *La folie à deux ou folie communiquée*. In V. P. Babini (a cura di), *Folie à Deux*, pp. 93–127. Lanciano: Métis, 1992.

Lucas, P. 1833. *De l'Imitation Contagieuse ou de la Propagation des Névroses et des Monomanies*. Paris: Thèse.

Meltzer, D. 1983. Commento a M. Harris, Folie à deux: un caso clinico. *Quaderni di Psicoterapia Infantile* 12:39–79. Rome: Borla, 1985.

Modell, A. H. 1984. *Psicoanalisi in un Nuovo Contesto*. Milan: Cortina, 1992.

Moreau de Tours. 1875. *De la contagion du suicide*, Patient, Paris.

Nicolò, A. M. 1992. Versioni del sé e interazioni patologiche. *Interazioni* 0:37–48.

Nicolò, A. M., and F. Borgia. 1995. Tra l'intrapsichico e l'interpersonale. La folie à deux come ipotesi-modello di un funzionamento interpersonale. *Interazioni* 1(5): 40–51.

Nicolò, A. M., D. Norsa, and T. Carratelli. 2003. Playing with dreams: The introduction of a third party into the transference dynamic of the couple. *Journal of Applied Psychoanalytic Studies* 5(3): 283–96.

Pichon Rivière, E. 1979. *Teoria del Vinculo*. Buenos Aires: Nueva Vision.

Régis, E. 1880. La folie à deux ou folie simultanée. In V. P. Babini (a cura di), *Folie à deux*, pp. 131–205. Lanciano: Métis, 1992.

Sandler J. 1976. Countertransference and role-responsiveness, *Int.Rev.Psychio-Anal.*, 3.

Scharff, J. S. 1991. La teoria delle relazioni oggettuali e la sua applicazione alla terapia familiare. In *I Fondamenti della Terapia Familiare*, pp. 29–36. Milan: Angeli, 1999.

———. 1991. La terapia familiare basata sulle relazioni oggettuali: Introduzione storica. In *I Fondamenti della Terapia Familiare*, pp. 23–28. Milan: Angeli, 1999.

Searles, H. F. 1965. Il tentativo di far impazzire l'altro partecipante al rapporto: Una componente dell'etiologia e della psicoterapia della schizofrenia. In *Scritti Sulla Schizofrenia*, pp. 243–71. Turin: Boringhieri, 1977.

Teruel, G. 1966 (trad. it.). Considerazioni per una diagnosi nella psicoterapia coniugale. *Interazioni* 2(12): 12–18, 1999, and *British Journal of Psychology* 39:231–36.

8

Psychotherapy for the Parents as a Couple

Molly Ludlam

When a family in crisis seeks help, what we can offer them is greatly affected by our therapeutic stance and our perspective. In my view, the symptoms are part of a tangle of relatedness—between children, parents, couples, and families in their internal and external worlds, between family and therapist, and between the modalities of couple and parent psychotherapy. Crises enveloping a parents' relationship with their children often threaten to spill over into their relationship as a couple. Family therapists have developed our understanding of the circular causality of troubled family relationships, showing that a child's distressing behavior both reflects and exacerbates unresolved conflict between the parental couple. Object relations theories also help us to understand how couples use projective identification to try and resolve childhood losses and disappointments in their adult partnerships.

Where is the boundary between the child's feelings of rivalry and persecution and the parental couple's own conflict? What approaches are most suited to help a parental couple to resolve their present crisis? What is the relationship between supportive psychotherapy with them as parents and analytic psychotherapy with them as a couple? And how manageable and compatible are these approaches, particularly for couples who feel as if they have to choose between family or couple breakdown? I want to discuss the nature of the task a psychotherapist undertakes with parents seeking help to address a crisis presented by their child's distressing behavior. I explore the issue theoretically and illustrate it with reference to work with a family where the placement of an adopted child was at risk of breaking down. I present two clinical illustrations drawn from short-term family therapy and other concurrent child and parent therapies.

THE GREEN FAMILY

This family's crisis seems to typify the kind of challenge presented where family roles and boundaries become entangled and where a careful assessment is the prerequisite to a successful choice of intervention.

Jenny Green was aged nine when she was referred with behavioral problems to a Child and Family Service. She was loud and quarreled fiercely with her younger sister. Her schoolteachers complained that she was bullying smaller children in the playground. In the family interview Jenny took the lead in criticizing her parents, Craig and Anna, frankly drawing my attention to factual errors in their account of her wrongdoings. Craig and Anna explained that she was touchy and sensitive to their attempts to discipline her. They complained that they could spend very little time as a couple on their own. After rows at suppertime, Jenny was inconsolable and hard to put to bed and Craig and Anna would quarrel about how to discipline her. Jenny's nightmares prompted frequent visits to her parents' bed at night.

Further enquiry revealed that Jenny had been born with a heart condition, necessitating treatment in intensive care and heart surgery. Her parents had not expected her to survive and from her infancy had restrained themselves when correcting her. Happily, she now was strong and sturdy, but she was allowed a license she now found frightening. Her behavior tested all the boundaries, as if to say, "Will you still love me if . . . ?" Sadly she had become unlovable and this terrified her.

We agreed upon a course of treatment that aimed to find a balance in the economy of needs. Having learned about Jenny's birth, her parents' distress, and their need to protect their vulnerable baby, I could see that they had kept her alive by fostering in her an aggressive life force, which was now counterproductive. Together we explored how Jenny herself needed to test their resilience as parents and as a couple. For all their sakes, Craig and Anna now had to establish a firm parental boundary, to protect and exclude Jenny and to be alone together as a couple.

In this instance, family therapy in four meetings with the whole family sufficed to help Craig and Anna strengthen their couple relationship and their parental understanding, so allowing Jenny the security to speak about, rather than to discharge, her worries in behavior. Had the family's difficulties been more entrenched, a range of separate therapies might also have been offered; with individual psychotherapy for Jenny, and perhaps including either concurrent supportive psychotherapy with Craig and Anna as parents or couple psychotherapy for them.

In making such choices about what we can offer as therapists, we must consider the strength of our own resources as well as the family's capacities for understanding. When we are weighing up what might be the most helpful approach to offer the adults in a family, whether parent or couple psychotherapy, how are we to evaluate these different and complementary therapeutic modes of working? To consider this more fully, it might be helpful to reflect on their shared perspectives as well as their differing characteristics.

SHARED PERSPECTIVES OF PSYCHOTHERAPY WITH PARENTS AND COUPLES

Both approaches have an interest in and concern with what the child represents for parents, or for the couple. This is often thought about as the place the child has "in the mind of the parents" or "in the mind of the couple." Both approaches share an interest too in the nature of the adults' experiences of childhood and of being parented. Couple psychotherapists often wonder with the partners how their own parents managed differences and difficulties as a couple. And both parent and couple therapists are interested in how the partners as children were caught up in the instigation or resolution of their own parents' tensions as a couple.

CHARACTERISTICS OF THERAPY WITH COUPLES

To meet with a couple for psychotherapy is to meet and work with at least three families! In *Object Relations Couple Therapy* (1991) David and Jill Scharff explain the way in which partners in an intimate couple relationship take on transferences from parent, sibling, and peer relationships. So they have the potential to re-enact previous harmful relationships with one another, as well as to contain and change them; the balance is between being negatively repetitive and positively mutative. A couple therapist who is able to tolerate the partners' transference to each other and to the therapist enhances the capacity of the couple relationship itself to assist the partners in performing this function for each other. This is another way of saying that in couple therapy the patient is the partnership, and the aim is to help the couple relationship function in attachment terms as a "secure base." From such a secure base, the couple can risk thinking about other troubling relationships, such as those between parents and children.

The efficacy of couple psychotherapy depends upon the therapist's capacity to provide a good *holding environment* (Winnicott 1960), *contain* the couple's anxieties (Bion 1970), and hold a *couple state of mind* (Morgan 2001). This involves holding the couple relationship centrally in mind against all pressures to make one partner, or even a child, the focus. Additionally the therapist must be able to adopt *a third position* (Britton 1989), so as to relate to the two individuals, while observing them as a couple from outside the relationship. The therapist's *third* position stands for the outside objective figure, necessary for confirmation that they are a couple. In the transference, the *therapist-third* may also stand for the relationship itself and represents a containing entity that can think about and care for the relationship. With this concept Morgan has built on the ideas of marriage as a *psychological container* (Colman 1993) and of *the creative couple* (Morgan and Ruszczynski 1998) to stress that the couple in the mind of the therapist is truly containing when it is felt to be *a creative couple state of mind*, one that can envisage mutual nurturing and growth.

CHARACTERISTICS OF THERAPY WITH PARENTS

One of the distinguishing characteristics of child psychotherapy is that working with children in mind invariably involves working with a network embracing other services and professionals and, of course, importantly, the child's parents. (By contrast, couple psychotherapy does not necessarily involve cooperation with a network.) In Britain, psychotherapy with parents is undergoing an exciting period of growth, incorporating parent-infant psychotherapy, as described by Fraiberg (1980) and Daws (1985), and brief work with under-fives. This development has been led for the most part by child psychotherapists.

Thanks to the development of parent-infant psychotherapy, we can draw a more complete picture of parent-child relationships. Using both attachment theory and object relations, Selma Fraiberg in *Ghosts in the Nursery* (1980) explored the ways in which the parents' past experiences affected their relationship with their baby in the present. So, as Hopkins (1992) notes, for the therapist, "the primary focus of the work is on understanding the parents' transference to their baby, rather than on understanding their transference to the therapist" (p. 5). Fraiberg developed a style of working that combined interpretation with *developmental guidance.* In this she aimed to give parents emotional support, to show them their unique importance to their child, help them observe and understand their child's stage of development, and consider the reasons for their child's behavior. Working in this way, therapists provide parents with the holding environment and containment, which Winnicott and Bion discerned as crucial to therapeutic engagement.

THE AIMS OF THERAPY WITH PARENTS

In *Dialogues with Parents* (1998) Rustin reviewed work with parents and usefully described four main categories of work in terms of the therapeutic aims listed below (see table 8.1).

Rustin notes that cases often call for the therapist to veer from one to another of these aims. When therapists are explicit with patients about any proposed change in the mode of working, patients can give their real consent, and therapists can gain clarity about therapeutic objectives and better understanding of the relationship between parent therapy and couple therapy for their patients' best interest.

UNCONSCIOUS DYNAMICS DIRECTING THE FOCUS OF THE WORK

In choosing the focus for the therapy and the style of working, we may be pulled in by unconscious dynamics, including the need for a sense of competence. How then do we decide on the most appropriate focus for the work? Rustin (1998) argues strongly that child psychotherapists are particularly suited to work with parents, because their capacity for attunement to the infantile in their child patients has prepared them to recognize and address the disturbances in adult and parental functioning. This endorses the therapist's need to stay with the troubled conflicts at the heart of the work. A baby's cry often tips parents into a maelstrom of feelings of compassion, jealousy, tenderness, and terror of helplessness. The ensuing Oedipal struggles do not belong to the baby alone, nor even to the parents. There is a widespread assumption that fathers need not be involved in parent-infant work, as Barrows's (1997) critique of Stern (1995) and Cramer (1993) points out. Powerful forces operate in defense of pairing. The psychotherapist is continually being invited into alliances with one parent/partner versus another, or against another service. The parent or couple therapist can always find reasons for preferring to see one parent on their own, as if to

Table 8.1. Therapeutic aims in work with parents

- To gain the support of parents to protect and sustain the child's therapy.
- To support parents in their parental functioning during developmental crises.
- To change family functioning as part of a whole treatment approach, which may also involve marital therapy, individual therapy focusing on intrafamily relationships, or family therapy.
- To provide individual psychotherapy for one or both parents, as patients in their own right, even though the presenting concern was for their child.

say, "Let's not complicate matters by drawing Father in. Mother and I will sort it out!" Then Oedipus "rides again"!

One way of conceptualizing the crisis of early parenthood is to see the couple relationship that is under stress as a defense of the pair against a hostile environment. A couple may have children to confirm their coupling, but when two becomes three, the pair can only be re-created if one is excluded. Oedipal conflict creates and compounds the hostile environment. The excluded other is shrouded with feelings of guilt, resentment, jealousy, and persecution, particularly if the parents' own early Oedipal conflicts remain unresolved. How can the new threesome relationship contain the double task of managing both past and present struggles?

However carefully psychotherapists try to create a holding environment, they risk re-creating a hostile one instead, where the pair is under attack from the intrusion of the therapist whose observations are seen as critical and a threat to the couple alliance. The therapist has much in common with the child in this respect. If therapists take the child's view of the parents, without at the same time confirming the couple as a couple, they must expect to be fended off in the same way as the child is excluded.

Working with parents, then, can we be more than *child* centered? Called in at a time of crisis involving a child, especially one who has been abused, inevitably we are mobilized to care for the most vulnerable member of the family and to focus on the needs of the minor. Rightly, such an obligation is enshrined in our organizational protocols. But, recalling the Green family, what can we do to ensure there is also appropriate support for the couple relationship under assault from the envious attacks of the child?

It seems to me that we should continually examine our own unconscious motives in designing our services. Services often enact a difficulty, such as that of thinking about the parental couple consulting us as parents only and not as a couple. This may be expressed by addressing parents directly as Mom and Dad, rather than using Mr. and Mrs. or their first names. In this way their parental identity in the therapy is fixed and the therapist's child-centered approach limits the relationship with the parents. It reflects the therapist's difficulty of functioning in a triangle, having to think about oneself as both part of, and excluded by, the relationship of the other two. When faced with helplessness, we desperately need to feel competent. All of this underlines the importance of creating agencies where therapists can enact having both the child in mind and the creative couple in mind, and this means nurturing and tolerating relatedness between child, parent, and couple therapy.

I should like now to illustrate these issues by describing work with a family in crisis in which I was the couple therapist working with the parents, and a child psychotherapist met with their child.

THE BROWNE FAMILY

Richard and Susan Browne, a couple in their late thirties, sought help from our Children and Young People's Team because their adoption of Tom, aged six, was at risk of breaking down. Taken into their family permanently at four years of age, Tom initially seemed to settle well, but the transition of going to school threw up all kinds of difficulties that threatened to be unmanageable. His solution to feeling vulnerable was to tough it out, getting into fights with other children, tearing and dirtying his clothes, and wrecking his toys. He could not explain his distress, only behave it. Susan and Richard were at a loss to understand him, and, feeling that they could not identify with him, they feared that he was too damaged to become their son.

The team agreed on the formulation that Tom was afraid he did not belong and that, as he had already moved from his birth mother to foster parents, surely he would now be sent away again. It was decided that a child psychotherapist colleague would offer Tom intensive psychotherapy, while I would meet fortnightly with Susan and Richard. Without parallel sessions for them, parents feel excluded and may even enviously attack the child's therapy, because they have never themselves received such a nurturing experience. Since our team was part of a wide network of services, Susan found many other mothers on whom to be dependent and to witness her transition to motherhood, which filled a need in her since her own mother had died two years before the adoption.

Enormous anxiety, which often seemed overwhelming, attended this work from the outset. Regular collaboration between me and the child's psychotherapist was crucial for processing our countertransference experiences and for facing the fundamental question: If psychotherapy failed, might Tom be returned to care, his parents' hopes of creating a family lost forever? While ostensibly I was recruited to help his parents make a tolerant space for Tom, my experience was one of being asked continually to hold in mind a space in which they might grieve the loss of a family and yet become a creative couple.

At our first meeting, I learned that the Brownes had applied to adopt two children and still held open the hope that Tom's little birth sister might in time also join them. I realized that they were wary of any scrutiny on my part that might suggest their rejection as suitable parents.

Richard said at the start, as if preempting any focus on them, "Look, we are just here to sort out Tom. We don't need to revisit all that third degree pre-adoption stuff."

Susan laughed anxiously. "What Richard means is that we have gone through all that, all those hurdles and we know why we want children; and that we—he and I—are OK. We don't want to live our lives like we are on public show. We just want Tommy to settle, don't we, so we can love him like our own."

I could see that they must be reexperiencing painful echoes of uncertainty and critical enquiry undergone in the pre-adoption assessment and that I would need to try, delicately, to separate my work with them from it. Work with adoptive parents has taught me that the preselection process of assessment can leave them feeling raw, exposed, and needing to retreat into their shell. Careful scrutiny pre-adoption is vital and maybe even serves to test a couple's resilience. But perhaps the fear of being seen as struggling soon after the adoption deters couples from seeking help early on, rather than when it is too late to support them not just as parents, but as a couple.

So I acknowledged Susan and Richard's deep concern about Tom needing child therapy with my colleague and I appreciated that they too needed something at this time of crisis. As Tom would find his sessions sometimes disturbing, our meetings would offer a place where they could think about what was going on for him and how that affected them both. They looked relieved. Then, in what became a familiar retreat into a child-centered structure, they took out a list of concerns and plunged into an agenda, filling the space with a shopping list of worries. They wanted to be businesslike. The list provided them with a secure base, as if free-floating thinking might expose them to the risk of feeling overwhelmed. So I could not ask them to put it aside but I had to struggle not to feel inadequate. Our meetings consequently often seemed to be driven by worries, like a school parents' meeting, instead of a place to address hurt and disappointments.

Ever-present anxiety that dogged the work steered me away from asking what I felt were intrusive, or critically loaded, questions that might upset their place with me. I felt curious about their childlessness, about how much they had felt supported by one another in that, but it felt like exploring very thin ice to broach such questions. They clearly needed time to spill out all their frustrations and concerns, and the time allotted was easily filled.

Susan and Richard continued to keep a tight hold on the agenda. While Tom was their prime preoccupation, occasionally they spoke wistfully about his little sister, who seemed to represent a lost child. These preoccupations held them in their role as parents, rather than as a couple.

My task in the first few months was primarily to hear their complaint, recognize their disappointment, and try to give them another emotional language with which to read Tom's desperate, confused, and confusing messages. This was a slow process because their appointments with me, it seemed, could only be made at best every fortnight, and for a phase once a month. Although they faithfully brought Tom for his thrice-weekly sessions, they would only allow themselves what felt like a minimum with me, a toe-hold in the door. Their determination to give Tom priority, to put him in the van of their defensive relationship with us, had the effect of marginalizing them. It was as if most of their needs—their own hunger—had to be met through him. Through this process of projective identification, Tom threatened to become a cuckoo in their nest, with themselves as anxious parent birds so preoccupied with meeting his insatiable appetite that they could not afford to be aware of their own. Susan and Richard appeared naively unprepared for Tom's testing of their love. Richard had been strictly brought up never to be physically aggressive and when Tom got into trouble at school for fighting, his anger with Tom frightened him and made him want to reject his son. Sent to his room, Tom wrecked his bed and his toys. His parents felt he would have to go; it wasn't working.

Initially I was swept up with the anxiety everyone involved seemed to share, that Tom would be sent away. But my role was to help steady the boat, to enable Susan and Richard to understand and tolerate Tom's turbulence. There was a delicate line to tread in translating the possible messages of Tom's behavior, while supporting adult responses in the parents. It seemed helpful to interpret the projective identification by explaining that Tom communicated with them by getting them to feel as he did, frightened, rejected, and angry; now that he felt relatively safe with them, he was asking them to help him express all the feelings that really belonged to his relationship with his birth family. Having established this way of thinking, it felt safer to explore all the infantile feelings Tom evoked in his parents, which they then needed one another to understand and contain. It was also then possible to reflect with them on the ways in which Tom came between them, partly out of an envious wish to split them up, but also to test the strength of their relationship, to see if they would stay together for him.

After several months of Tom's psychotherapy, the threat of the breakdown of his adoption receded. It was then apparent that Susan and Richard's possessiveness of their parental roles in our meetings stemmed from fear that losing Tom meant that parenthood itself would also be lost to them. Such a loss would have been devastating. This fear had enhanced their transference to me as a superior, critical parent. I wondered how much their concept of themselves as a couple was dependent on being procreative like their parents. At last I felt secure enough with them to risk asking about their inability to have children of their own. I acknowledged that it had not been always easy to meet with me.

Richard shook his head ruefully. "I think we just longed to be a 'normal' couple, no questions asked—two reasonably happy adults with two reasonably happy kids."

It was evident that their ideal internal couple was complete with two children, certainly not with only two adults.

Susan said, "I wonder if we need a problem, you know, like other people need a drink—or a dog! Somehow we can't let it go, as if we need a problem to worry about."

I said, "And Tom has become the problem you can't let go?"

"Yes, perhaps. After we talked here about what our parents expected of us, I've been thinking how it's wrong to expect Tom to be the child we dreamed of having. There's no such thing as a perfect little boy, or a perfect person. I was watching him playing the other day and he was having a lovely time covered in paint, and I thought I wouldn't change him for anything. It's enough to see him being himself. I don't think it's right for Tommy that we should try to adopt his sister. I don't think he's ready yet to have a sister."

Richard agreed. He acknowledged how much he wanted to give Susan the family she had so wanted and that had been withheld from her.

It seemed to me that they were both able to grieve a little more and to let unrealistic hopes go.

Working with this couple meant witnessing a gradual process of relinquishment. Holding on to a problem was like holding on to disappointment. Because the disappointment was unbearable, it was projected into Tom, who could so easily identify with it. This meant that their grief for the perfect child, who could never be theirs, was not expressed. They had unconsciously hoped to contain their loss of a birth child by assuaging the losses of a foster child through adoption. They had, however, been unprepared for what felt like the undeserved assault that such a damaged and deprived little boy could make on their love and idealization. Moreover, they were undergoing the crises that any recently reconstituted family might expect, experiencing all the trauma of the arrival of the new baby without the preparation time afforded by pregnancy. There was not even a period of physical infancy. This child arrived believing he must immediately prove his acceptability and so tried not to display any vulnerability. He came straight into the lap of parents who were themselves anxious that they might not prove adequate. In their turn, the parents had to refind themselves as a couple, without being the ideal family they had imagined.

My hypothesis was that they had been relating to critical, withholding internal parents who denied them the right to put their needs first. Such inner parents found external forms in the hospital and social services, our service, and their own bodies. But such perceptions might be safely explored only after Tom's psychotherapy had safely ended.

My initial parent therapy role to help safeguard Tom's therapy meant tolerating the parental transference and projection of almost overwhelming anxiety about not being adequate. As the work progressed, however, it proved increasingly vital to hold in mind a grieving couple, for whom there was still hope of becoming the creative couple they longed to be.

REFERENCES

Barrows, P. 1997. Parent-infant psychotherapy: A review article. *Journal of Child Psychotherapy* 23(2): 255–64.

Bion, W. 1970. *Attention and Interpretation*. London: Tavistock Publications.

Britton, R. 1989. The missing link: Parental sexuality in the Oedipus complex. In *The Oedipus Complex Today: Clinical Implications*, ed. J. Steiner, pp. 83–101. London: Karnac.

Colman, W. 1993. Marriage as a psychological container. In *Psychotherapy with Couples*, ed. S. Ruszczynski, pp. 70–96. London: Karnac.

Cramer, B., and F. Palacio-Espasa. 1993. *La Pratique des Psychotherapies Mere-Bebes*. Paris: Presses Universitaires de France.

Daws, D. 1985. Two papers on work in a baby clinic. *Journal of Child Psychotherapy* 11(2): 77–96.

Fraiberg, S., ed. 1980. Ghosts in the nursery. In *Clinical Studies in Infant Mental Health*. London: Tavistock.

Hopkins, J. 1992. Infant-parent psychotherapy. *Journal of Child Psychotherapy* 18(1): 5–14.

Morgan, M. 2001. First contacts: The therapist's "couple state of mind" as a factor in the containment of couples seen for consultations. In *Brief Encounters with Couples, Some Analytical Perspectives*, ed. F. Grier, pp. 17–32. London: Karnac.

Morgan, M., and S. Ruszczynski. 1998. The creative couple. Unpublished paper presented at Tavistock Marital Studies Institute 50th Anniversary Conference.

Rustin, M. 1998. Dialogues with parents. *Journal of Child Psychotherapy* 24(2): 233–42.

Scharff, D., and J. Savege Scharff. 1991. *Object Relations Couple Therapy*. Northvale, NJ: Jason Aronson.

Stern, D. 1995. *The Motherhood Constellation*. New York: Basic Books.

Winnicott, D. W. 1960. The theory of parent-infant relationship. In *The Maturational Processes and the Facilitating Environment*, pp. 37–55. London: Karnac, 1990.

9

Sibling Relationships

Sylvie Angel

Be sure to make many friends, because your mother's womb will provide you with your enemies.

African proverb

For many years psychoanalytic thinking has ignored the sibling story in describing family sagas. Nevertheless, the sibling bond is marked by complex conscious feelings and unconscious affects. It is commonly filled with revolt, jealousy, passion, hatred, nostalgia, complicity, and disappointment. It rarely leaves its protagonists indifferent. In fact it has a profound effect on the psychic development of the child. Rivalries are always present, even though minimized by the family. In adolescence the accompanying emotions of the sibling bond are amplified, ranging from hatred to passion, and even to incest in some dysfunctional family organizations.

THE SIBLING COMPLEX AND
THE OEDIPUS COMPLEX

We owe to the works of Sigmund Freud our basic understanding of the main mental mechanisms of psychic organization. By taking up the myth of Oedipus, from the tragedy of Sophocles, Sigmund Freud constructs a theory of psychological development, but without taking account of sibling rivalries. Daniel Marcelli objected: "What Sigmund kills at first is not the father, it is the siblings, because it is the emergence of the sibling that awakens anger, frustration, and disappointment in the mother; then it is to the siblings that

99

the hatred and the jealousy spread, protecting the figure of the parents" (Marcelli 1993, p. 239). Siblings rarely appear in the works of Freud, or indeed in other psychoanalytical writings. For a long time, fraternal jealousy was interpreted as a displacement of the Oedipus complex. Rene Kaës (1993) shows that there is also a sibling complex, which differs from the Oedipus complex in that there is not the inhibiting factor of the difference between generations. In my view, the sibling relationship represents a fundamental object constellation in the psychic organization of the individual.

Jacques Lacan (1938) took up and developed ideas presented by Wallon. In an article on the family, Lacan outlines the sibling complex, of which the main features are aggressive identifications among the rivals, the spectacular ambiguity of the structure of sibling narcissism, and the drama of jealousy. He shows the contribution of sibling jealousy to paranoid ideation. Dadoun (1978) shows that sibling violence is not the simple reflection of the violence of the father, but it is "a specific energy registered in a definite network of feelings, events, action" (Dadoun, p. 42). Kaës (1993) holds that the sibling relationship contributes to the construction of the identity.

The sibling bond stems from belonging in the family. The siblings are part of a set connected by genetically endowed physical resemblance and their shared experience of domestic life and family customs—managing the household, taking care of appearances, and regulating the tone of voice and rhythm of speech, and so on. The daily sharing of the same story and repetitive feelings strengthen the attachments, and so the sibling link is established, even when there are no biological ties, as in the case of children adopted or placed temporarily in foster families.

SIBLING RIVALRY AND JEALOUSY

At the birth of a younger sibling, older children are frustrated by being held at a distance from their mother whose attentions are now centered on the baby. Primarily they resent the rival brother or sister as a competitor for maternal love. They also identify with their brothers and sisters and a relationship of reciprocity is built. The problem is that they have to share their mother with the baby as well as with their father, and that baby symbolizes the link between the couple, which they envy. They experience ambivalence about their mother as both nurturer and betrayer.

As Jean-François Rabain puts it: "To define the rivalry is inevitably to question this dual and symmetrical relationship which connects someone to another and which leads to an aggressive tension linked to the competition of two protagonists for the same role or for the same object. Rivalry conceived in this way is connected to the implicit identification with the model of the other who is at the same moment the representative of the obstacle to the desire" (1995, pp. 231–51).

The arrival of a sibling in the family awakens jealousy in the existing child. The classic psychoanalytical model describes this feeling as the result of a displacement of the Oedipus conflict. In fact, the situation is more complicated: a mixture of various projections and identifications in the family group with various emotional exchanges. Jealousy is there, but it does not always express itself in easily observable or predictable ways. It can be sublimated, or repressed. In early childhood, the reactions of hostility and jealousy are most pronounced when the age gap is between two and four years. When the children are less than two years apart, they are brought up like twins, as a sort of couple, and this diminishes feelings of exclusion. Jealousy diminishes as the age gap increases, depending on the personality of the child and the domestic context. But each story is different, and feelings of jealousy and hatred can be present even with children far apart in age, as the following example shows:

> *Michael arrived "too early" for his working-class parents, who were aspiring to improve their standard of living and quality of life, and so Michael was given over to be raised by his grandmother. Eight years later, his parents were ready to have a second child and provide for their children. By that time the grandmother was too attached to him to permit him to return home. Three years later, his grandmother died and so, at the age of eleven, Michael began to live with his parents. His feelings of jealousy toward his younger brother Jack were always extremely strong and remain so in adulthood. Michael has never forgiven his parents for having "abandoned" him and for having kept his younger brother with them from birth. Jack reacted to Michael's rivalry and jealousy with a feeling of opposition toward Michael with whom he maintains only a superficial relationship.*

Hostility, jealousy, and hatred are more marked in same-gendered sibling relationships, such as those found in mythological tales, for example, Romulus and Remus, Seth and Osiris, Polynice and Etéocle. Rivalries and murderous feelings in the sibling are reinforced by parental attitudes, which shape the structure of the sibling relationship. We see this clearly in Biblical stories.

The Bible gives us several examples to illustrate the impact of favoritism on the lives of the children: Cain and Abel, Jacob and Esau, Joseph and his half-brothers.

> *Cain, the farmer, was the elder brother of Abel, the shepherd. They followed the custom of making offerings to God. To them, God seemed dissatisfied with the products of the earth but delighted with Abel's most beautiful lambs. Cain, jealous of Abel receiving approval from God, threw himself on his brother and killed him.*

Isaac, the father of Esau and Jacob, had become blind and wanted to make the ritual promises to Esau, his elder son. The boys' mother Rebecca dressed her favorite, Jacob, in an animal skin so that he would feel more like Esau who was "a hairy man" and that was how she made sure that her favorite received the father's blessing.

Joseph was the favorite of his father, Jacob. His half-brothers could not bear this situation, and decided to kill him.

THE ATTITUDE OF THE PARENTS TOWARD THE SIBLINGS

Parents unconsciously project onto their children what they experienced previously with their own brothers and sisters. They do not understand their children's hostility to one another if they recall a loving relationship with their own siblings, even if this memory is not entirely accurate. On the other hand, they may be surprised to see that their children are so close if their childhood consisted of sibling rivalry and aggression. Parents who have not had enough contact with their brothers and sisters will have difficulty in strengthening the bond between their children. Parents who are jealous of a sibling may play favorites with their children, which reinforces sibling jealousy, rivalry, and a sense of injustice. When alliances are established among a parent and a child of the same sex, or between a parent and child of the opposite sex, the children of the other sex are left out. The father or the mother may appropriate a child according to personal needs or indeed may do so at birth when, for example, the first name of the child is chosen by the father or by the mother, without taking into account the wishes of the spouse or their family of origin.

Mohammed insisted that his children have a Moslem first name while his wife, Mari, from a Welsh family, wished to give them a Celtic first name. They decided that the elder son would be called Ali, and the second child, the daughter, would be called Gwenaëlle.

The importance of the parents in defining sibling relationships has been largely neglected in literature. An exception, however, is Walter Toman's (1987) book, which deals with the importance of the rank of the sibling in the choice of a spouse. This point of view clarifies the attitude of the parents toward their offspring; however, its typology of sibling links as the determinants of future action is too simplistic.

NEITHER TOO CLOSE NOR TOO FAR

When childhood sibling rivalry has not been sublimated in appropriate social conduct, sibling relationships can lead to extreme situations: to hatred, violence, and incestuous relationships.

The prohibition of incest is a necessity to protect our couples, our families, and our psychic life. Incest entails a major trauma for anyone who has experienced it as victim or bystander. Sibling incest occurs in association with the games of childhood more frequently than one might believe. The parents do not notice the physically intrusive and seductive nearness of their children and proudly encourage their close-knit relationship. The boundaries of physical contact are left vague, and the emotional connection confused with eroticism. These games usually remain occasional, occurring only under the family conditions that favor them, but sometimes those conditions are such that the games lead to sexual relations.

Often the premature death of a parent strengthens the sibling ties and fills it with passion, but then in adolescence, the passionate sibling relationship (like Byron and his sister) can become incestuous (as for Virginia Woolf, whose elder brother raped her). Loving passionate relations occur more frequently between an elder sister and a younger brother. Serious sexual abuse experienced during childhood in dysfunctional families leads to major consequences in the psychological development of all its members.

FINDINGS FROM FAMILY THERAPY

Since the creation in 1980 of our institution, Centre Monceau (the Family Therapy Center), more than eight thousand families have attended for help, many of them for problems of drug addiction. In these family configurations, the consultation is often motivated by concern over a child, but working with these families soon reveals the suffering of other family members. The participation of the children in the sessions is essential for the following reasons (see table 9.1):

In numerous families, the transgressions are found repeated in future generations: the parents, having lived a particular type of relationship, reproduce it with their children.

We have developed the following hypothesis, concerning heroin-addicted patients: Heroin use protects against the incestuous act, in both parent-child

Table 9.1. Reasons to include all the children in family therapy

- All the members of the family are affected by and concerned about the suffering of the designated patient with the presented problem.
- Each member has his or her perception of the family story.
- The other children of the family will become symptomatic.
- The psychological work done with the brothers and sisters reduces the risk of symptoms and decompensation in other family members when the designated patient gets better.
- The presence of siblings clarifies the family roles and puts the generations in perspective.

and sibling relationships. Heroin is at the same time euphoric and anesthetizing. It cancels the sexual urges while producing extremely strong sensations of pleasure. The sharing of the ritual and the gathering of the paraphernalia—preparing the powder, mixing in the lemon, warming it in a spoon, applying the tourniquet, filling the syringe, and making the injection—is a displaced sexual coming together, but without genital action.

Difficulties other than addiction appear in the course of family and sibling sessions, but the suffering of the user is the central concern for all the protagonists. In a review of our files, 50 percent of the parents present major troubles such as depression, alcoholism, or serious illness that compromise the course of their existence; and among brothers and sisters, 75 percent show academic failure, truancy, suicide attempts, or eating disorders. Brothers and sisters feel the full brunt of domestic trials and tribulations. The suffering of the healthy brothers and sisters of the addict expresses itself in the emergence of symptoms sooner or later once therapy is undertaken—or in the choice of a career in the caring professions or humanitarian activities.

In every dysfunctional family system therapists notice confusion in the roles and between the generations, emotional deprivation of the children, the absence of rules, and perhaps a history of bereavements during childhood or adolescence that strengthens the sibling ties. The premature death of a brother or sister—whether from addiction, illness, or accident—has a painful echo. The work of mourning is at the center of the family task. Often, the parents idealize the deceased child. The suffering of the parents amplifies the tensions of their intimate relationship, which weakens and sometimes breaks the couple bond. Some bereaved parents never resign themselves to their loss, and this blocked mourning reflects on the other children who, incapable of being as good as the deceased sibling, feel abandoned. The mourning appears to be even more traumatizing when the dead child had a meaningful connection with the other brothers and sisters.

Mary, Frank, and Julie still mourn their younger brother Mark who died in an accident that occurred when they were walking with their favorite babysitter. Mark ran after their ball, which rolled onto the road. A car came, tried to brake, but too late. Taken to hospital, Mark died some days later. Very shocked, the family decided to relocate so as "to forget." Mary, Frank, and Julie lost their network and missed their school friends. They lost their mother who had sunk into a state of deep melancholy. Crippled by heartache, she remained inconsolable. The children grew up in this atmosphere of blocked mourning. The parents went out very little and did not receive anyone at home. The children felt very guilty, but attempted to be perfect, which meant that they were well behaved and successful at school. It was only at the time of leaving home at the end of adolescence that they expressed their suffering, in the form of adult depression.

THE EVENTS OF ADULT LIFE MAY
WEAKEN THE SIBLING BOND

When Susan chose sailing for a profession, she moved away from her brothers and sisters to the Caribbean, returning only once a year to her country of origin. For her family she represents the adventuress of the twentieth century. Her parents and her siblings created a myth of Susan as a free woman living under the Caribbean sun, which they envy. The reality is not so enviable, because Susan, passionate about sailing, suffers terribly for not having found a companion and not having managed to start a family.

But the events of adult life also strengthen the sibling links. Maternity brings sisters closer even if their spouses have personalities that do not mesh well.

Catherine and Françoise Labordes (two well-known journalists) found that their extremely close relationship as sisters was strengthened by motherhood and by their fate as adults. Over forty, they found themselves alone, each with two children to raise, and they used each other to form a couple of solidarity and mutual support.

CONCLUSION

Relationships in adulthood are modified according to individual choices about fitting into the social world, choosing a partner, and developing one's own family. One's choice of spouse considerably alters one's sibling relationships. What can we say of the strength of the sibling link today? At the dawn of the twenty-first century, the sibling link is more durable than the marital bond. Our brothers and our sisters accompany us throughout life—for better, rather than for worse.

REFERENCES

Angel, P., and P. Mazet. 2004. *Guérir les Souffrances Familiales.* Paris: PUF.

Angel, S. 1996. *Des Frères et des Sœurs.* Paris: Ed. R. Laffont.

———. *Ah, Quelle Famille.* Paris: Ed. R. Laffont.

Angel, S., and P. Angel. 2003. *Les Toxicomanes et leurs Familles.* Paris: Ed. Armand Colin.

Dadoun, R. 1978. Frères ennemies, la violence fondatrice en psychanalyse entre chien et loup. Paris: Imago, 1984.

Kaës, R. 1993. Le complexe fraternel. In *Topique les Jumeaux et le Double*, pp. 5–42. Paris: Ed. Dunod.

Labordes, C., and F. Labordes. 1997. *Des Soeurs, des Mères et des Enfants.* Paris: J.-C. Lattes.

Lacan, J. 1938. Le complexe concret de la psychanalyse familiale. In *La Famille,* pp. 840, 842. Paris: Encyclopédie Française VIII.

———.1966. *Motifs du crime paranoïaque: Le crime des soeurs Papin.* Ecrits. Paris: Le Seuil.

Marcelli, D. 1993. Oedipe, fils unique. In *Visage de la Fratri—Revue Adolescence* 11(2): 239. Paris: Ed. Greupp.

Rabain, J.-F. 1995. La rivalité fraternelle. In *Nouveau Traité de Psychiatrie de l'Enfant et de l'Adolescent* (ed. M. Soulé, S. Lebovici, and R. Diatkine), pp. 231–51. Paris: Ed. PUF.

Toman, W. 1987. *Constellations Fraternelles.* Paris: Ed. ESF.

10

Play and Family Therapy

Jill Savege Scharff

I am making a plea for psychotherapists to include young children in family therapy sessions. I want to encourage adult family therapists to learn how to include children in family therapy, and individual child therapists how to work with families. I present a brief theory of play as well as an overview of object relations theory and its application to the family as a group. I illustrate my idea of the effective use of play as a mode of communication in family therapy in clinical examples of family sessions with babies, latency-age children, and adolescents. Play and fun support learning and growth of children and their families and help the therapist to reach into all the developmental levels represented in the session, and so gain whole family understanding.

FAMILY THERAPY, PLAY, AND HOLDING

In family therapy, my task is to provide a helpful environment for the whole family, babies included. A recent study showed that marriage and family therapists are unwilling to include young children in their family therapy sessions, because they have not been trained to understand children (Sori and Sprenkle 2000). Learning about development and the nature of communication in play along with experience in individual play therapy or child analysis are essential preparations for the family therapist. Using play as much as verbal interaction, I aim at providing a context in which every member of the family can express themselves and show the family's usual patterns of relating. These derive from the complex interaction of present relationships in the family, previous experiences with significant others in the family of origin, and experiences with the present family during earlier periods of development.

OBJECT RELATIONS THEORY AND FAMILY THERAPY

Object relations theory derives from study of the therapeutic relationship. It focuses on the nature of relationships between the self and others and between parts of the self and its objects in the internal world. Because of this focus, I find it to be the analytic theory most easily applicable to therapeutic work with groups and families (D. Scharff and J. Scharff 1987). The family is a small group with the job of supporting its members through the life cycle. As family therapists we step in when one of its members needs more than the family group can offer. At this point, the family is blocked in doing its work and our job is to help the family understand why. What are the defensive purposes served by their repeating patterns of interaction and inaction? What are the unnameable anxieties that are being avoided? As we help the family to explore its defensive structures, basic assumptions, and underlying anxieties, we build skills for dealing with the current problem and for future developmental challenges.

OBJECT RELATIONS FAMILY THERAPY

Object relations family therapy uses nondirective analytic techniques invented by Freud (1912). Listening for the unconscious theme in word, silence, and gesture is augmented by the value of watching and responding to the play. Following the affect is easy when play gives us a direct route to the child's feelings expressed in relation to the toys. Working with dreams and fantasies takes on a graphic dimension when we see them put into the form of the family doing something fun together, for instance, painting. Repeating defensive patterns are detected in the repetition of play sequences and the family's typical reactions to the play. Throughout the session, we tune into the unconscious communication in the play and notice how it makes us feel. This helps us to detect how the parents feel about their children and how the whole family as a group feels about us, the therapist, the outsider to their family process. Playing with the children, or sitting quietly but engaging with the play in a playful attitude, we resonate with the unconscious themes. Play helps us reach deep inside our own experience, to make a connection with the family's pain, and to find a way to speak to them about it, either directly in words, or through our response to the play.

PLAY IN FAMILY THERAPY WITH VERY YOUNG CHILDREN

Freud recommended the analyst's stance: maintaining a neutral position of equal distance from superego, ego, and id. Similarly, the family therapist maintains a stance that gives equal weight to the contributions of various generations of the family. That means we must be able to talk and play at the same time and work with groups and not just individuals. We must also be willing to tolerate noise, mess, and confusion.

Example

A family asked for help with their seven-year-old boy's tantrums. This boy and his five-year-old brother played well with rockets while their parents talked. The next session, they brought the baby. The five-year-old played as before, but the seven-year-old brought the skunk puppet and pretended that it was farting, pooping, and spraying me. I linked this to angry feelings about Mommy having the baby on her lap and there being no room there for him. He responded by tying me to my chair with wool thread, taping my mouth shut with adhesive tape, blocking my ears with tissue taped to my face, and he wound pipe-cleaners round my fingers. I pretended that Stinky the Skunk said to me that the boy had taped me up because he didn't want me to be able to see or hear what was happening in the family and certainly not to speak about it because it made him feel bad. He then spun me in my swivel chair. I again used Stinky to say how much he wanted to separate me from the family so I couldn't see or say anything about how people felt about the baby on Mom's lap. The baby got off Mom's lap. The father observed my situation with amusement and made the perfect comment to describe the role of the family therapist. He said, "I've just learned that to be a family therapist you have to be able to hit a moving target while tied down and spinning."

WHOLE FAMILY UNDERSTANDING

Why have the young children there? Unless you do, you cannot get whole family understanding (Zilbach 1986). Having the children present gives a vivid picture of problems that have less impact when only spoken about. The youngest children make deeper problems more visible and therefore intervention can happen earlier.

Example: Eduardo and Guido

A mother complained that her nine-year-old, Eduardo, was violent at home, tormenting his brother, Guido, and even punching his mother. In an individual session, Eduardo was a delight to talk to about how he didn't mind his sister, Valentina, but he couldn't stand Guido always interrupting him when he was trying to do his homework. He refused to play with me because he no longer liked Legos, and he didn't want to draw, because he only played games with balls, now that he was nine. At school and at home he only played football, baseball, and street hockey. I offered to play indoor catch with the soft Nerf ball but he said that wouldn't be fun.

Later in a family meeting with the parents, Eduardo, Guido, and two-year-old Valentina, I noted how the family sat in total silence, their attention riveted adoringly on Valentina as she trotted around the room with no inhibition and engaged me with paper and crayons. Eventually, the boys began to color. Guido simply tested all the colors and made a color chart, while Eduardo drew a rattlesnake in the desert. No longer the focus of attention, Valentina got fussy and Mother offered her some crackers. Now the boys talked about fighting, the main problem. Guido said that Eduardo starts the punching to get Guido to leave him alone, but Eduardo said that Guido really starts the fights by bugging Eduardo to play with him. Eduardo's inability to enjoy play at his brother's level was the cause of the fights. Eduardo said that he only liked sports and he couldn't play with Guido because Guido couldn't throw straight or far enough. Guido tried to appeal to Eduardo by telling him he had played football with older kids.

Guido said, "I was playing with the fifth graders and the quarterback fumbled the ball, but I was right there and I caught it. So then I was playing quarterback and they all said it was a great play."

Eduardo squashed him by explaining, "Yes, you could recover the fumble but no, you couldn't suddenly become the quarterback. You're still playing defense. And no, you didn't get a touchdown, no, you didn't score, so it wasn't a great play at all."

I said, "Eduardo knows so much more about football than I do, that if I try to argue the point, I'll end up getting defeated like Guido. What I do know is that Guido is trying hard to join Eduardo and appeal to his interests, but Eduardo doesn't want to be drawn into being friends with him because he alone wants to be the oldest and the best."

"Yes," Eduardo agreed. "I'm in fourth grade now and I just don't care about toys anymore."

By having the whole family present I could see how the mother focused attention on the baby and got the whole family to join her in doing that. This clued me in to how excluded her firstborn, Eduardo, could have felt at the time of Guido's birth. Eduardo's need to distance himself from longing to be his mom's baby meant that he had rejected his brother, put him down, and gave up the toys of childhood that might have let them bond together.

This play example is quite easy to understand. That is not always the case.

Example: Good Play

A student was reporting a family session to me. I noticed that she was telling me information that the parents had told her and was not giving me a sense of the session. I asked her to describe the children's play. She said that she hadn't seen any "good play" to report. I told her that there is no such thing as "good play." There is only play that we can understand and play whose message we don't yet receive. The important thing is to report what happened whether you understand it or not. Simply describing the play to yourself as it is happening and monitoring how it makes you feel can make the meaning clear. I then found out that she had not provided any toys. Without toys, of course there is no good play because the children feel that the therapist expects them to behave and be quiet, instead of feeling free and being expressive.

We want to create an environment in which children will play so that they can feel comfortable and communicate their hopes, conflicts, and fears. This does not require masses of toys, but some toys and art media are necessary to stimulate the play activity and to give the message that play is welcomed.

HOW IS PLAY EFFECTIVE?

Children express their ideas and feelings both directly and symbolically in play. The inhibited child who is fearful of the family's disapproval sits quietly on the chair and may be too afraid to play at all. The aggressive child may attack the paper with such gusto that he breaks the pencil. The anxious child may flit around the room unable to settle at one play area. The attitude toward the toys and the art media offered to the family is as important as the message conveyed thematically. For instance, a child may fill the page with colorful hearts and rainbows. The hearts and rainbows may represent parents and siblings and the way that they are arranged in size and in order may tell a lot about the family dynamics. Equally important may be the child's wish to give an impression of happiness and normality, and the physical pleasure of painting with color rather than drawing with pencil. In another family, one brother may make a block building that expresses how concerned he is with big blocks and little blocks and which of the children has the most attention from the parents, while another brother may simply want to knock down the building. This could be simply about the sibling relationship or it might also reflect the mother's wish to discuss her feelings and the father's wish to get rid of tension. Sometimes the play follows the words and the family therapist realizes that the children and the adults share an understanding of the family problem. Sometimes it seems to be on a totally different track, leading the therapist to ask about matters that had been kept out of the discussion but which the child's play reveals as important.

Children need to play in the office as they do at home and at school. This gives them an environment that is child-centered, a familiar place where they can behave as usual, even while doing the difficult task of dealing with conflict and the mystery of family life. Very young children play with much movement and bodily contact. They use their bodies to relate to the toys, and in so doing they find physical release for pent-up energy and anxiety. Children of school age play in a less physical way than younger children. They conceptualize and execute a plan. Perhaps they write diaries, make paintings individually or in series, establish families of animals, or dolls, create armies, or re-create lesson plans in schoolroom scenes. Adolescents often pretend that they don't play, but they will fiddle with their hair, pull on their clothing, and try out different positions on the floor, the couch, and so on. Babies play, too. They play at holding on and dropping their toys, waiting for a parent to fetch the lost object. They play hide and seek. They play with their mother's body.

The therapist must tune in to the type of play that the particular family brings to the session, sometimes commenting on it, and sometimes being content to let it unfold. Using tact and a good sense of timing, the therapist may enter into the play in order to make a point conveyed by one of the characters in the play or may use the play to illustrate what the family has been talking about. The play may then become an arena in which the family can find solutions to their problems.

PLAY IN THERAPY WITH A
LATENCY CHILD AND A BABY

Ana and her husband Pedro complained about their six-year-old Maria's temper, her stubborn behavior, and her failure to build a good relationship with Pedro, her stepfather, even though she was close to his seven-year-old daughter, Arion, who didn't live with them. Ana and Pedro have a six-month-old, Pedro Junior, a large, blond, beautiful baby who is able to sit upright but who is not yet crawling. Propping Pedro up by the arms, Maria walked him into the session as if he were a one-year-old, teasing him about deciding where to sit, and telling him to sit forward in the couch. I said that she wanted him to grow up quickly, walk, and play games with her.

Mother explained that Maria had a horrible tantrum on Saturday night. But, as soon as Pedro said it was awful, Mother pointed out that Maria had gotten in control of it. During this disagreement between Mother and Pedro as to how awful the tantrum was, Maria pretended to be asleep.

I said, "If I were Maria, I'd be glad that Mom noticed I did better, but I wouldn't be able to see why Pedro and Mom saw it so differently. Maybe that's why Maria is closing her eyes."

Mother said that she and Pedro often disagree and see behavior differently, depending on whether it is her daughter or his daughter whose behavior is at issue. Maria suddenly woke up and asked for lunch. It felt like a startling change of subject. Suddenly I got the idea that her request might be motivated by sensing that the baby was about to be fed. I asked if this was so, and the mother said yes, she was just getting ready to breastfeed Pedro Junior. Maria had a little bit of a tantrum, grabbed her mother's leg, and began to mouth it.

I said, "Maria is showing us one of the things that leads her to feel like having a tantrum, that is when the baby is going to be breastfed and lie close to Mom. Then Maria feels hungry and feels like grabbing and biting on Mom, too. What was happening on Saturday night before Maria had her tantrum?"

Mother remembered that the baby was being fed then, too. She explained, "Pedro Junior wakes up at 4 o'clock in the afternoon. He feeds a lot off and on, and especially from 8:30 to 9:30 P.M. Maria goes to bed at 7:30 P.M., so she gets jealous that he gets to stay up with us after she has gone to bed, when he is younger than she is."

As Mom explained this and the baby nursed, Maria lay on Mom's foot. Then Mom took him off the breast momentarily and Maria put him back on. She then pulled off Mom's dangling earring. Mom checked her for interrupting when she was trying to talk to me.

I said, "No, Maria's playing is her way of talking to us. She's putting the baby on the breast and she's taking Mom's earring off. The earring comes off, and Maria can play with that, but the breast stays where it is. It doesn't come off and she can't take control of it, because it is only there for the baby."

Maria then switched her attention to the other earring. This happened just before Mom was ready to put the baby on the other side. Suddenly Mom was soaked by Pedro Junior. The feeding had to be interrupted while the baby was changed. During this changing, Maria played with both her mother's earrings. I asked her to come over and talk to me about them. She showed them to me, dangled them to make them move, and said, "There are two earrings, and each of them is a circle with another circle." I now saw the earrings clearly. Each one was a big hoop with a small circle inside it. The two of them looked like a pair of mobile breasts each with a nipple in the middle. She turned to place the earrings back on Mom's ears at the same moment that the baby went back on the breast. I was struck by how Mom was surrounded by children while Pedro, the father, was sitting by himself. I asked how he felt.

He said, "Fine, not jealous. I'm just waiting until we can interact again."

I said, "Pedro, you're a grown-up and it's okay for you to wait. But for Maria waiting is more difficult and that's what leads to tantrums."

In this example, the presence of the whole family provided a vivid illustration of the family dynamic around the new baby and its connection to the presenting symptom of the index patient.

WORKING WITH A LATENCY CHILD AND A PUBERTAL CHILD

Mrs. Silver is a widow, an ambitious professional and devoted single mother with Ruth, her twelve-year-old girl, and Liz, her nine-year-old (described at greater length in J. Scharff 1992). Liz and Mother are often nasty to each other, because Liz is irritating, refuses to help, clings to her mother, and has trouble making friends. They asked for an early morning appointment but they are often late and one week they missed altogether. This week they came in sleepily as usual, but the girls got to work at the desk. They were angry that their mother was staying too late at work, but she explained that she had to get her work done so that she could get away to take them to a bar mitzvah in the South where she was from. Liz was upset because she felt excluded by the other cousins at the bar mitzvah anyway. Mrs. Silver talked about being excluded for being so aggressive and successful, not what had been expected of her as a Southern woman.

As she talked, the girls drew at the desk. Liz produced a painting of a witch with long, red, raggedy fingernails. Ruth noticed that Liz had mistakenly spelled it w-h-i-c-h.

Thinking of her outspoken mother, and looking down at my own chipped red nail polish, I said, "W-h-i-c-h is the real title. Which witch is it?"

In her Southern phrasing, pausing after *what*, Mrs. Silver asked, "What—do you mean Dr. Scharff?"

I said, "Yes, I do mean Dr. Scharff. My nails are like the witch's. I wonder if there are witchy things about me that are bothering you, Liz."

Ruth said, "I made the red for the nails, so that can't be true."

I connected the red nails to drops of blood and I said, "I remember Ruth had been angry at me for mentioning the fact of her getting her first period last week when she wanted it to be kept a secret from her sister who might blab. You thought that was mean of me, and perhaps you aren't the only one."

Mrs. Silver took the opening to confront me quite aggressively. She said at length how mean I was for charging them for that missed session some weeks earlier. When I said I knew that was hard for her, especially as the only breadwinner, she smiled and said, "I'm glad I told you. I wasn't going to say anything, but Liz's drawing helped me to get to it."

Liz beamed at her helpfulness being appreciated.

By recognizing and naming the witch transference I detoxified it so that Mrs. Silver could express her own witchiness toward me while confronting my witchiness, and this reduced the witchiness between mother and Liz. It was the girls' play that made this possible.

TESTING THE RESPONSE TO INTERPRETATION IN A FAMILY WITH ADOLESCENTS

In both family meetings sixteen-year-old Ashley sat in a chair in the corner, while the parents sat with thirteen-year-old Deirdre between them on the couch (also described in D. Scharff and J. Scharff 1987). Mother and Father took turns cuddling with Deirdre, even though she seemed too old for that. I said that from their angry exchanges I had learned that the parents and children were disappointed in each other and had spoken as if there were nothing of the loving or positive sort going on.

From Mother's and Father's cuddling with Deirdre, I could see that each parent was demonstrating a need for affection and closeness between them, while Deirdre was representing for herself and Ashley a wish to fill the emptiness. The parents agreed, and said that they had used Ashley that way, too. They were already disappointed in each other before she was conceived, and when she was born they turned to her with wonder and delight. I said that Ashley became a perfect, doted-on child who fulfilled their need for an ideal object until adolescence. Incidentally, in subsequent sessions, Deirdre took her own chair.

To find her own identity and to separate from her parents, Ashley had to rebel against this projection into her. When she did so, it was with the vehemence of the return of the more repressed projection she had also received, that of the disappointing, rejecting object that has been destroyed or made "shitty" by greed and rage.

Following my interpretation, Ashley reached quietly for the paper and markers which she had been talked out of using earlier in the session when her parents made fun of drawing pictures. She drew a picture of an attractive young girl's face, which I took to be the need-exciting object on which my comments had focused. No sooner had I thought this, than she "spoiled" the beauty of the drawing by writing "Aargh" coming from the mouth. In this way, I thought, she had demonstrated and confirmed what I had just said to the family, that for her parents she had been a "beautiful" tantalizing object who had been spoiled by growth and the family situation.

The interpretation in the session focused on the way the rejecting and angry elements operated to secondarily repress unrequited mutual longing in this couple. They were angry at Ashley and cozy with Deidre to avoid the intolerable pain coming from a sense of failed love in their relationship. The couple's capacity to accept this statement with little defensiveness, and to make use of it to spur further understanding, provided positive evidence of their ability to work therapeutically. As they did this, Ashley provided evidence not only of her unconscious agreement with my interpretation, but of the family's capacity to work productively and even creatively in the family therapy situation, when she drew a picture illustrating and "fleshing out" what I had been saying.

In a couple's session that followed, I referred back to the family meeting and asked the couple about the emptiness in their relationship. They said they had no sexual life recently, and very little since Ashley's birth. Mrs. Brown felt too angry to want it and often caused a fight before bedtime. She was angry that this was important to Mr. Brown when other things like being more ambitious about earning money to provide for them were not. Mr. Brown was unhappy and felt frustrated, but he did not pursue his sexual aim assertively.

The family came for treatment when Ashley, at sixteen, was no longer willing or able to substitute as their idealized exciting object but instead was becoming tentatively interested in her own adolescent sexuality. This is often a point of stress for an empty couple's relationship, since it brings back longing and hope from earlier years and sometimes an unbearably envious response.

The Browns accepted a recommendation for family therapy in which the couple would meet once a week and the family once a week. Ashley, who had been the index patient, refused individual assessment or therapy, because she felt her parents' relationship needed so much work. Although she was resisting the emergence of her unconscious, she was nevertheless handing back to the parents their projection of the good-object-gone-bad.

FINAL COMMENTS

Children who may not do well in individual therapy can do well and learn about themselves in the family setting. If their attachments are insecure, proximity to family members may be helpful. Some children who deny that they have any difficulty can be confronted in the family and at the same time have the therapist's support. Children who cannot conceptualize their individual difficulties, and have no insight into themselves, can see the problem as a group problem and work on it in the group. Even so, therapy is an anxiety-provoking undertaking, and play helps them to release their tension in bodily displays of energy and to cope with anxiety by doing what is familiar. Play makes it fun, and that encourages the family to stay with the therapy task. Fun moves the learning forward.

REFERENCES

Freud, S. 1912. Recommendations to physicians practicing psycho-analysis. *Standard Edition* 12:111–20.

Scharff, D. E., and J. S. Scharff. 1987. *Object Relations Family Therapy*. Northvale, NJ: Jason Aronson.

Scharff, J. S. 1992. *Projective and Introjective Identification and the Use of the Therapist's Self.* Northvale, NJ: Jason Aronson.

Sori, C. E. F., and D. H. Sprenkle. 2000. Training family therapists to work with children and families: A Delphi study. Ph.D. thesis, Purdue University, West Lafayette, Indiana.

Zilbach, J. J. 1986. *Young Children in Family Therapy*. New York: Brunner/Mazel.

11

Divorce Terminable and Interminable

Roberto Losso and Ana Packciarz Losso

Why do marriages end in divorce? Among multiple factors, we note the disappointing expectations of the other into whom aspects of the ego ideal (or the ideal ego) have been deposited; claiming or submitting to power and possession; and developing in different ways during critical phases in the family life cycle. Added to those, there is a rupture of a shared illusion, which is called *a collusion*, a term that refers to *unconscious links* (Kaës 1993).

We know that each couple is organized (and maintained) around positive elements: mutual investments; a certain degree of mutual admiration and being in love; common identifications, ideals, and beliefs; styles of functioning in which desires can be met in a fairly satisfactory way, where the partners can achieve an acceptable degree of confirmation and reaffirmation of their narcissism and can express a reasonable level of aggression. But it also is organized and maintained by relinquishing or putting aside certain psychic contents—referred to by Kaës (1989) as *le pacte dénégatif* (p. 130) (translated as *pact of denial*). This happens through an unconscious agreement that certain aspects of the couple's link remain repressed, denied, split off, and embedded in the mental space of both subjects. That agreement has two functions: as an organizer of the link and as a defense. The dissolution of the couple's bond permits the emergence of that which was part of the agreement but remained silent. For this reason, after separation, the link frequently acquires characteristics of great violence because the individuals feel their psychic integrity about to explode. Reproaches, disqualifications, verbal or bodily aggression, paranoid fantasies, and in certain cases, homicidal hatred all may appear. Intense suffering and impoverishment may be denied because it is less threatening or disorganizing to maintain such a *dénégatif* link than face the possibility of the emergence of the more primitive and undifferentiated aspects of each subject (or, as Bion would say, the "psychotic parts" of each person) that had lain silent.

Separation is seldom reached by mutual agreement. While one spouse seems to be in good shape (or has the desire) to separate, the other one appears not to be. Each one deposits in the other their respective aspects of desire for or against the separation. Generally, guilt predominates in the partner who "abandons" and the narcissistic wound predominates in the "abandoned" partner. Spouses who had functioned as "the child" within the couple can, when the couple dissolves, fall into a situation of abandonment, as a re-edition of primary abandonment. The real accord will come only when the partners untie the collusive links and develop the process of link transformation.

Each divorce involves the partners in a long process. First of all, it confronts them with situations of loss not only of individual objects, but also of the viability of the family organization and the structure of the family institution—together with all that offers reassurance to the fear of a return to the state of helplessness—the uncertainty and renewed menace of incestuous fantasies. "Each divorce is the death of a small society," Judith Wallerstein (1997) has pointed out. Divorce also implies the loss of objectives—illusional or not—that led to the formation of the couple.

An individual's identity is always constructed from interaction with others. This process that constituted the subject during infancy continues throughout life. Clinical experience demonstrates the vulnerability of the sense of identity and its dependence on the group and on social context. Freud (1921) referred to this when he described how the sense of identity, the person's own ego, is lost in the crowd. Throughout life, identity develops in reference to others and to the group. Identity is constituted above all from the other's recognition, and that is why separation from an intimate partner is so threatening to self-cohesion. In the formation of the couple, confirmation of one's own existence, value, and identity is sought, particularly sexual identity. Falling in love accomplishes that, too: if the other, who is my ideal, loves me, it is because I am worthy of being loved.

Separation always implies a crisis. The destabilizing of a previous equilibrium brings a crisis of identity for both spouses and threatens the psychical equilibrium of the family as a whole and of each of its members. There is a loss of what was known and a new necessity to face an unknown future. This can lead to regressive behavior. A couple may try to maintain stable links to reassure themselves emotionally. The children may show a regressive attachment to one of the parents or to another member of the family, or the parents may look for a regressive attachment, too, to one or several children or to members of the previous generation. In some cases, a new and intense love relation may be sought prematurely, in order to fulfill the void left by the spouse's absence. In other cases, divorcing people seek an enlargement of the network in the extended family or in the social network. Frequently, the place that was occupied by the couple's link is filled by permanent acrimony that has the function of keeping the ex-spouses united through conflict in denial of their respective separation anxieties.

Children of divorce may be left to do the mourning of the parental couple. For children, the separation is an invasive and imposed reality that they cannot control. This imposition reactivates regressive fantasies and behaviors of different levels. Frequently, the children show symptoms, as "spokespersons" (Pichon Rivière 1971) of the group anxiety unleashed by the separation.

THE MOURNING OF DIVORCE

According to Freud (1917), the mourning process is work developed by the psyche to face the loss or death of a significant object, in order to re-introject into the ego the different kinds of links with that lost object, and to be able to resign oneself to accepting that reunion will not happen. The mourning process of divorce is an *intersubjective mourning.* Each partner partially facilitates or fails to facilitate the other's mourning. One of our patients illustrated this situation through the following analogy, saying, "I am like a moth that moves around the light [his ex-wife], a moth that moves, goes up, goes down, but is always flying round the light. It cannot go near, nor can it leave."

Each member should carry the complicated process of withdrawing the cathexis deposited in the partner, in the marriage, and in the family structure, in order to re-introject what has been deposited in the object, in the link, and in the ego, and to re-invest cathexis in new hopes and expectations. It is frequently difficult for a divorcing spouse to figure out which aspects of the self are deposited in the other. The sense of loss is related to the qualities of the link, the sense of group security, family identification, and the prospects for the family. The object of the loss remains alive, stimulating conscious and unconscious fantasies of reunion, revenge, and possession.

Pichon Rivière compared depositing personal aspects in one another to depositing money in the bank. He called it the *DDD theory* (depositor, depository, deposited). When the couple separates, it is time to withdraw the investment. There is a complex interplay between the subject (the *depositor*), the other (the *depository*), and that which has been *deposited.* If aspects of the body scheme are deposited in the other, too, separation can be experienced as an amputation of body parts. There is frequently a predominance of paranoid anxiety: The other becomes an enemy who must be attacked and destroyed with homicidal fantasies, sometimes acted on in extreme cases.

More or less transitory depersonalization sensations can emerge; organic diseases such as cancer and auto-immune disorder can develop. The body takes on the task of expressing what is unthinkable—the denied, repudiated aspects of unconscious alliances. Accidental body damage frequently occurs as a symbolic expression of laceration of the skin surrounding the couple (Anzieu 1993). Other times the eruption of the denied unconscious material is expressed through actions that are harmful for the subject and the family, such as failed business deals, diminution of assets, or loss of work.

As we said above, mourning at times of marital separation has typical family and social characteristics. After the death of a loved one, the family tends to increase multigenerational support, and the extended social network lends emotional support to the mourning family. In the case of divorce that support is frequently absent. People often remain at a distance from the divorced person. Disappointed friends may deliver strong attacks, families may pursue litigation or demand compliance with loyalty pacts. Divorcing spouses often relive experiences of early life abandonment. Then, this process tends to reactivate feelings of physical and emotional deprivation, as well as psychic phenomena derived from uncompleted mourning in the families of origin. They may feel that they have lost external and internal support because they have failed to measure up to their own ideals. They may feel diminished self-esteem, hopelessness, and despair. They find others' criticism and ice-cold silence difficult to accept, because they pour salt in the couple's narcissistic wounds. All this increases persecutory feelings. Objects of support are alive but their support is unobtainable, at least in the manner previously possible. Family members must bear their feelings of loss when the impact of the loved-but-also-hated or previously loved object is still active. The mourning process also suffers interference because the live object can stimulate conscious or unconscious reunion fantasies related to desires for possession. The spouse is thinking, "This person is no longer mine, but I cannot tolerate that he (or she) belongs to another." Retaliation, revenge fantasies, and ideas of destruction of the abandoned or abandoning subject are common. Clinical experience shows that these fantasies are often expressed through the children.

Our social organization does not authorize spouses to untie the marriage links themselves. Moreover, it authorizes a new marriage after divorce somewhat unwillingly. This can activate unconscious feelings of transgression, guilt being stimulated and fed by the divorced spouse. At the same time, behaviors of one of the partners can be misinterpreted so that the one accuses the other of abandoning the children.

Moreover, the ramifications of divorce spread through multiple generational levels to the extended family and social network. When the process of divorce develops in a climate of confrontation, hostility and revenge invade not only ex-spouses and children in the nuclear family but the extended family as well, carrying ramifications of the threat of loss of historical continuity into the separating spouses' connections with their families of origin.

TRANSFORMATION OF LINKS

The aim of intersubjective mourning is the dissolving of the conjugal link. But at the same time, especially when there are children, other forms of the link must be reconstituted. We have called this particular work *link transformation*. After libidinal divestment of the other as an object of desire, there is a reinvestment of the other as a parenting partner.

In some cases, the difficulty of facing this slow painful process induces a search for a sort of "final solution" to the problem—an effort to obliterate the other through a duel to the death, denying its existence and re-creating a new family that ignores the previous one. Generally, attempts to do this fail, sometimes with severely deleterious long-term consequences.

Separation bereavement is not only shared by ex-spouses, but also by the children, and in a great measure by the members of extended families who must elaborate their own current and prior bereavements, including the possible loss of historical continuity with one or both families of origin. Then, the process of link transformation affects not only the link between those who divorce, but all the links between members of the larger family. At the same time, these links are intertwined with the social context, which may induce guilt and incomplete acceptance of the new situation. In the social field, class and cultural differences determine the particular characteristics of this process.

DIVORCE TERMINABLE AND INTERMINABLE

The divorce process is essentially a mourning process for the formerly loved spouse and the formerly valued pairing. Perhaps the process of de-investment of the conjugal object is never totally complete; the man or woman with whom a lasting relationship has been had will probably always have aspects that set them apart from other men and women. Nevertheless, the divorce may be said to be a "terminable" divorce when the couple, after a certain period of time (such as one to two years), is able to mourn the loss of the conjugal link, achieve an emotional separation of the intimate partners while preserving continuity of the parental couple, and tolerate being alone or become open to the possibility of developing new erotic links. They are also helped by the orderly function of the law, and through these processes achieve link transformation.

In cases of "interminable" divorce, this process of link transformation is not possible. A link persists that prevents sharing the mourning process, a particular type of link modality in which transpersonal defenses predominate. The ex-spouses continue to be united by resentment, rancor, and desires for revenge. They remain prisoners of their collusive links. The rupture of the unconscious agreements can frequently unleash intense violence (Kaës 1989).

THE ROLE OF THE LEGAL SYSTEM

The role of the formal system of justice and how it lives in the social imagination is significant in each divorce case. When people have serious difficulties that begin the process of separation and continue in subsequent mourning, they can request help from the legal system. In many of these cases, there is a fantasy that judges can decide for the spouses so as to solve the *impasse* they have created. A lawyer acting as defender of the justice of the ex-spouse's cause often functions as an ally in battles against the other ex-spouse, a role that is assumed in collusion with the lawyer's own family myths. Spouses frequently seek the presence of a third person who can assume the emotional holding and self-organizing functions. Because they invest this third party with a parental authority, they trust them to make decisions—which, on the other hand, they generally systematically violate. This expresses the difficulty finishing the process from an emotional point of view.

Divorced couples are often referred to us from the judicial field. It is often impossible to help them reach agreement or to respect agreements already mandated by the court because of a serious emotional disjunction making it virtually impossible to work toward link transformation. When we contend with situations of "interminable divorce" we must consider processes in which the lawyers of both the ex-partners are frequently engaged, as well as the respective families of origin. In some cases, judges and other representatives of the judiciary system can also be engaged as active participants in a system of multiple collusive links. Couples involved in these "interminable divorces," although consciously seeking the legitimate intervention of the law, unconsciously seek to vindicate narcissistic ideals. So, presentation before each legal audience can become a re-edition of scenes of family life in which collusions, resentments, reproaches, or revenges are displayed. Thus, magistrates are faced with repetitive transgressions of agreements that the divorcing partners supposedly reached, transgressions ranging from violation of common norms of behavior, to repetitive nonobservance or apparent ignorance of compromises that, theoretically, had been agreed upon. All these violations lead to chronic conflict.

PSYCHOANALYTIC THERAPY OF
INTERMINABLE DIVORCE

In recent years, mediation techniques have been developed and disseminated, generally practiced by lawyers who have done specific training in the area, and, in a few cases, by psychologists. Beyond the value of these techniques in certain cases, psychoanalytic therapists do not work in mediation in the usual sense of the word. We practice psychoanalytic work as couple co-therapists in collaboration with legal professionals. Frequently our intervention follows failed attempts at mediation. Other times, we intervene when the agreements obtained during the mediation are not respected, or when conflicts appear that originated in unforeseen situations.

In most cases, ex-spouses do not consciously ask for psychological assistance. They have displaced their conflicts to the judiciary area (sometimes with the lawyer's support), and they deny the emotional difficulties that prevent them from achieving link transformation. In our experience, in these cases it is helpful for the therapist to begin by seeking the support of the judge's authority, from the one who recommends psychological treatment. However, one of the first problems that we have as analytic couple therapists is the necessity of working on the transferential fantasies that are nearly always present. The therapeutic team represents the extension of the judge's authority and role, and therefore, should be understood dynamically in this way. Sometimes it is necessary to return to examining this aspect of the transference during the therapeutic process in order to differentiate the legal from the psychoanalytic field.

In all cases of "interminable divorce" a profusion of narcissistic aspects and a deficiency of ego resources predominate. The role of the judge gives therapists a guarantee of continuity of care because they are temporarily vested with the power that the legal system bestows. We have observed that even if the proposal for treatment comes from the court without a request for therapy from the couple, we often find a positive response that leads to acceptance of a therapeutic process. Surprisingly, a genuine desire for help can emerge even though it had been hidden or repressed until then.

In general, our task is directed at trying to modify impasses that have developed as a consequence of unconscious determinants. Therapeutic work creates conditions in which both members of the couple are able to begin a process of reflection on the collusive bonds that tie them together and undermine the avowed purpose of reaching a separation. Through making possible the naming of the emotional matters at stake, we can facilitate a process of link transformation.

Psychoanalytic family therapy offers a way to reveal the myths and hidden scenes of the family history, which have determined a singular destructive "truth" for each family. Working this way leads the family to free themselves of repetitive behaviors in which each subject of the disturbed link acts on the other according to unelaborated conflicts of the individual and the family of origin via exploring the family myths that have been transferred to the present.

In these cases we have to deal with many technical problems such as limitations on our time and, when there is serious hostility, limitations on our freedom to maintain objectivity by interviewing both ex-spouses (Isaacs, Montalvo, and Abelsohn 1986). We feel that it is necessary that both members participate, whether together or alone. In some cases, we convene meetings with subgroups: the ex-spouses of the couple, each parent with the children, or the children as a group (see next chapter). It is also important that at a certain moment we get both ex-spouses together, both as a couple and with their children. In the first sessions, sometimes the difficulty in talking can be overcome by the therapists, who, by alternating sessions with the divorcing spouses, function as intermediaries.

INTERDISCIPLINARY WORK

Working in an interdisciplinary way, lawyers, judges, and psychoanalytic couple therapists can participate in a process that forces each of these helping parties to accept their own limits for intervention, and, in a certain sense, to tolerate the narcissistic wound on facing the insufficiency of their function when they work alone trying to solve the problems that are presented.

We have worked with magistrates, lawyers, guardians for the children, and other legal professionals in psychoanalytic process groups. These groups allow those professionals to reflect on their respective work experience and explore the way their emotional involvement in these experiences frequently exceeds their rational understanding. This fruitful meeting of legal and psychoanalytic minds is similar in many respects to the experience developed for many years in Balint groups for health professionals (Balint 1964).

A COUPLE AWAITING A DIVORCE DECREE

José (thirty-eight), a systems analyst, and Paula (thirty-six), a professor of humanities, had been separated for two years and were engaged in a contested divorce hearing. They had been sent by the children's lawyer because of custody litigation concerning their daughters. Both spouses were in individual therapy. José maintained that Paula "was a borderline, who is threatening to commit suicide and kill the girls." The elder daughter, Cristina (thirteen), had gone to live with her father and his new partner because, she said, "I can't put up with my mother." The younger daughter, Laura (three), wanted to go live with her sister. After Paula's repeated phone calls, saying that she had a gun and would kill herself and the children, José decided to change the lawsuit from uncontested to contested, and to request custody of his daughters.

José said that at the beginning of the relationship he had felt attracted to Paula physically, to her complexity, and to her intense dependence on him. "She was cast out by her family and I was going to vindicate her." Paula was attracted to José as "a sportsman who was enterprising and protective." "I liked him to show me things. I felt very small, and he was the one who knew everything. I liked adventure with him."

The History of the Marriage

They married in 1985. He had just graduated and she had finished first year at university. Shortly afterward, José got a scholarship to a university in X, another country in Latin America. They decided that he would travel while she stayed in Buenos Aires until she completed her second year, and then transfer to a university in X. But one month later, Paula decided to go and join him, because, she said, "I couldn't bear to be apart from him." She was equally central to José, but in a different way. José said, "I always felt like a moth flying round a light; the moth has mobility, it moves, it goes up and down, but it always moves round the light."

After two years, their first child, Cristina, was born. They started to have difficulties that led to their first separation of eight months in 1989. By now, Paula had graduated in humanities and had started to work in her profession where she made a good salary. During this period of career success for both of them in X, they frequently traveled separately for work. During that time, Paula did not depend totally on José. José said "I didn't see a coming together for us as a couple." They worked a lot and rarely saw each other.

After another separation, they started to think about getting back together in 1993. José was more insistent that she would be better off in Argentina with him. Apparently referring to the economic situation, he claimed, "everything was collapsing in X." Paula did not agree: "I didn't want to get back with him; it was a trap with no way out." She felt fulfilled in her work in X, and feared she would not be able to find a job in Argentina. Finally they decided to return. He travelled to Buenos Aires with Cristina (who was six) and went to live at his mother's house. She traveled to Europe for a post-graduate course of six months, but only twenty days after her arrival, she decided to return to Argentina to be with José and Cristina. José then informed her that he had decided "not to be part of the couple anymore," and she found herself having to go, with Cristina, to her parents' house. Paula now started to show signs of deep psychological disturbances and started going to therapy five times a week. After two years of separation they decided to live together but Paula continued to be unwell. Three years later Laura was born and one year later they separated again. One year after that Paula's father died.

The Therapy

The couple's initial choice of one another as a life partner was based on the fantasy that each one could help the other repair the childhood deficits. José offered himself to Paula as a mother for a little girl; she, collusively, played the part of "abandoned woman-child," offering him her childish dependence and her need for a protective figure. Idealizing him allowed her to deny her own deficits and re-create a primitive bond with a mother.

At the beginning, the task of the therapists consisted above all in the containment of intolerable anxieties, which were being acted out up to this point. The therapists started by assuming a paternal, organizing function, facilitating the opening of a reflective space in which nonverbal language could be understood. That is to say, they lent the family their preconscious. The therapists worked with the couple to construct an extended envelope that permitted the development of a therapeutic process (Houzel 1996).

This more reflective climate allowed the deepening of the analysis of the influence of the pair's respective individual histories, of unconscious motivation for their original choice of each other, and of the collusive links that had kept the two united for so long. José had defined Paula as "borderline." He needed Paula's madness to maintain his sanity. This dynamic hid his propensity to madden her, or to be driven mad by her and be revealed as mad himself. When Paula had been able to find her own space and make changes that allowed her to study, graduate, and work, she achieved an emotional distance from José and began to break her idealized childish dependence on him. Then the marital relationship became more conflicted. José felt her distancing as abandonment and expulsion and was filled with fury. This probably accounted for José's feeling that "everything was collapsing," and it was at that time that they started to think of the possibility of returning to Argentina. Neither of them could maintain the relationship any longer, but their absences from each other also repeatedly led them to reunion. This problem was represented in the transference through continuous phone calls (made with various excuses) to the analysts between sessions.

On the other hand, they continuously ignored agreements achieved exhaustingly during the sessions, as they suffered the constant emergence of urgent persecutory experiences, which they had difficulty reflecting upon. Both needed to maintain and provoke difficult behaviors in the other in order to sustain their own psychic equilibrium through the application of transpersonal defenses (Laing 1961). In consequence, the divorce, at first requested by common accord, proceeded to become contested.

The couple could not separate because of the same unconscious patterns that organized their marriage. José had chosen Paula because she was the excluded one of the family and he wanted to rescue her. In his original family, José seemed to have been placed unconsciously in the role of one who had to rescue his mother whose father had disappeared, whereas her son José went back to his mother's house in Argentina with his daughter. He had to look after his mother as her abandoning father had not.

José carried an emotional burden from the paternal side of his family as well. His paternal grandfather was an alcoholic who had ruined the family, generating a symbolic debt that his son, José's father, had to repay, and he could settle it only partially. The remainder of the task was passed on to José. José became responsible for the remains of the debt handed down by the paternal grandfather and the emotional debt of his maternal grandfather and for rescuing his father's family's good name.

As they battled over the custody of their daughters, José was "the moth that flew around the light," trapped by a destructive "fatal attraction." His weak father, undervalued by his mother, could not exercise his paternal function, from which he felt compelled to escape through having affairs. José tried to escape this fate through marriage and emigration.

Paula's mother had serious psychic problems, due to which her submissive and weak father had to remain permanently by her side. The mother demanded that everyone take care of her. Every attempt at autonomy was interpreted as abandonment, led to the emergence of destructive, vindictive reproaches, and was punished by emotional distancing. This contributed to Paula's psychic disorganization, an expression of the identification with the *maddening object* (García Badaracco 1985). Paula was "trained" to take care of and protect her mother from the emergence of madness. The reproaches directed at José were similar to those she had experienced concerning her mother. José acted as the *maddening object* that generated hatred. But Paula needed to have this kind of object so as not to fall into the breakdown she dreaded, and so that she could sustain her denial of all that had happened in the past (Winnicott 1974).

Paradoxically, at the same time the pattern was supported by José's rescue of Paula's true self from her destructiveness. To find limits and containment, she needed to fuse with him. The couple's initial collusion was broken when Paula partially managed to escape the childish dependence on José, who then could no longer maintain his role as protector of the woman-child, and therefore separated from his wife and returned to his mother. However, with the final rupture of the matrimonial link, she became disorganized.

During therapy, the couple committed emotional blackmail, by making reciprocal threats that reinforced the climate of fear. Paula threatened, "I'll kill myself and the girls." José threatened, "I'll abandon you and take the girls!" The transference threat made by the couple to the therapists was, "A suicide and/or a homicide is going to take place here and the responsibility will be yours." Our anxiety in the countertransference alerted us to these threats. We explored the underlying emotions and provided for reflection and narrativization, through which we could understand the pathogenic and alienating identifications. We came to see that in her acting out, Paula repeated the behavior of a mother who caused scenes, while José repeatedly paid the transgenerational debts due his mother by the maternal grandfather who abandoned his wife and daughter, and by the alcoholic paternal grandfather who had ruined his family.

When the couple repeatedly injected us with their fears of separation and reunion, the resulting countertransferential experiences gradually inoculated us against identifying with the couple's paralysis, and we were able to interpret the couple's repetitive emotional blackmail, and move the therapy forward. The older daughter, Cristina, returned to the mother's house, and the couple agreed again to an uncontested divorce. As hostility diminished, a different climate emerged concerning the care of their children, and Cristina left behind her role of "parentified daughter" responsible for the needs of her mother.

This couple began treatment without any motivation for analysis themselves. Nevertheless, during the course of an analytic therapy, they were able to own the desire to understand the things that united them in discord, initiating in this way a long process that could finally dissolve the collusive links that entrapped them.

SUMMARY

In psychoanalytic therapy of divorce, the therapist looks at positive and negative aspects of couples' bonds and focuses on the guilt and narcissistic wounds of the multiple losses. Interactionally structured aspects of identity are especially difficult to mourn in the interminable divorces where separation is incomplete. The case example demonstrates work with families to transform collusive links, which often includes consultation with the legal system and work with the children.

REFERENCES

Anzieu, D. 1993. Introduzione allo studio delle funzioni dell'Io pelle nella coppia. *Interazioni* 1:75–79.
Balint, M. 1964. *The Doctor, His Patient and the Illness.* Second edition. New York and London: Pitman Medical.
Freud, S. 1917. Mourning and melancholia. *Standard Edition* 14:237–58.

———. 1921. Group psychology and the analysis of the ego. *Standard Edition* 18: 65–144.

García Badaracco, J. 1985. Identificación y sus vicisitudes en las psicosis. Importancia del objeto "enloquecedor." *Revista de Psicoanálisis* 42:3, 495–514.

Houzel, D. 1996. The family envelope and what happens when it is torn. *International Journal of Psycho-Analysis* 77:901–12.

Isaacs, M. B., B. Montalvo, and D. Abelsohn. 1986. *The Difficult Divorce. Therapy for Children and Families.* New York: Basic Books.

Kaës, R. 1989. Le pacte dénégatif dans les ensembles trans-subjectifs. In *Le Négatif, Figures et Modalités*, ed. A. Missenard et al., pp. 30–169. Paris: Dunod.

———. 1993. *Le Groupe et le Sujet du Groupe.* Paris: Dunod.

Laing, R. 1961. *Self and Others.* London: Tavistock.

Losso, R. 2001. *Psicoanálisis de la Familia.* Buenos Aires: Lumen.

Losso, R., and A. Packciarz Losso. 1997. Le "nuove famiglie," studio psicoanalitico. *Psiche, Rivista di Cultura Psicoanalitica* 5(1): 91–99.

Pichon Rivière, E. 1971. *Del Psicoanálisis a la Psicología Social.* Buenos Aires: Galerna.

———. 1978. Neurosis y psicosis. Una teoría de la enfermedad. *Revista de Psicoanálisis* 35:407–19.

Wallerstein, J., and D. Resnicoff. 1997. Parental divorce and developmental progression: An inquiry into their relationship. *International Journal of Psycho-Analysis* 78:135–54.

Winnicott, D. W. 1974. The fear of breakdown. *International Review of Psycho-Analysis* 1:103–112.

12

Therapeutic Supervision with Families of High-Conflict Divorce

Katherine E. Scharff

Divorcing parents who fight over custody and visitation are a challenge to psychotherapists and the family law system. Locked in bitter, entrenched struggles, unable to stay together yet unable to separate emotionally, these parents persistently antagonize, accuse, rage against, and attack each other, and emotionally run rampant over their children. Families of high-conflict divorce usually do not seek help voluntarily but are sent by frustrated judges or attorneys who see therapy as a last resort. If the parents do bring themselves to treatment, it is usually for the father or mother to garner support for his or her side in court. The traditional psychotherapeutic stance fails to penetrate these families' emotional armor, and no one, least of all the families themselves, has much confidence in the therapist's ability to help.

To work with any couples and families in crisis, clinicians must sort through a web of transferences, countertransferences, projections, and projective identifications while attending to the needs of family members as a group and as individuals at varying cognitive and developmental levels. Before family members can make changes in ineffective patterns of relating, they must recognize the painful aspects of themselves projected into others. They must realize that it is futile to expect new outcomes while continuing to treat each other in the same ways. They must accept that they will never metamorphose into versions of each others' ideal fantasies or compensate each other for pain suffered at the hands of primary objects. When they admit the hopelessness of their illusions, families can be helped to recognize and reclaim disavowed parts, and new paradigms of relating can be established.

Change is difficult for all families, but highly conflicted families hold on for dear life to old patterns of relating. When the pain of early loss and deprivation is too great, and when the couples' psychopathology is too severe, divorce can become a war in which caring for the children is the principal battleground. The divorce trauma reawakens earlier traumas and calls forth powerful strategies to ward off internal attacks from persecutory objects. Often, the couple is composed of one spouse who is emotionally or physically abusive (usually with a borderline personality disorder), and another who is a self-styled victim with a passive, masochistic character. Both members of the couple are invested in the battle and continue to perpetuate conflict. What they are fighting for is a fantasy. Each member of the couple unconsciously clutches at a fantasy of extracting from the spouse recompense for the inadequacies of their own internalized primary objects. Propelled by these fantasies, high-conflict divorcing couples and their families share a quality that I call *primitive toxic hopefulness.*

High-conflict families are referred for treatment at all phases of the divorce process, and all levels of involvement with the court system. They may come voluntarily or subsequent to a court order. Frequently they are not sure that they want the services that are recommended, or do not ask for services they need. Often the fitness of one of the parents is under question following allegations of abuse, neglect, substance abuse, custody disputes, or inability to establish a co-parenting relationship. The therapist may be asked to provide forensic evaluation, psychotherapy, supervised visitation, or parenting coordination. The court may or may not grant decision-making power. Although a family may be initially referred for a discrete service, they usually need a combination of services.

Because emotions run high and the cast of characters is large (composed of the family, lawyers, custody evaluators, and other professionals), countertransferences are powerful. The legal system, which encourages each party to exploit the vulnerabilities of the opponent, is frequently antagonistic to psychotherapy and supportive of paranoid-schizoid modes of relating. As a clinician, it is easy to be drawn into the fray by siding with one parent and becoming overwhelmed with emotion, confused, or identified with projected hopelessness. From the beginning, it is crucial to establish the parameters of the therapist's role.

When I work with families with high-conflict divorce I ask, "Will I be expected to testify? Will I be asked to report to attorneys about my ongoing work?" I always make clear that while I will testify if subpoenaed, I will not testify voluntarily. Testimony or reports that I do provide are limited to direct clinical observation. I will not provide recommendations on custody or visitation unless specifically hired to do so. In each case, I make it clear initially that my goals are to improve communication, reduce the level of conflict that the children are exposed to, and promote a healthy adjustment to the reality of the divorce. My goals are not reconciliation, obtaining apologies, or making the couple friends. This helps me to avoid feeling de-skilled or, in a momentary identification with the couple's unrealistic fantasies for the marriage, seduced by fantasies of succeeding where others have failed.

Clinical research on the impact of divorce on children is inconclusive (Wallerstein and Blakeslee 1989, Heatherington and Kelly 2002). Yet, there is agreement that children's adjustment to divorce is largely determined by parents' ability to shield them from parental conflict. Except in cases of severe abuse, the capacity of each parent to foster a loving relationship between the child and the ex-spouse helps the child to adapt to the new reality. By helping the warring spouses to collaborate as parents, the therapist can make a difference to the mental health of the children. Unfortunately, the treatment of these families has traditionally been left to the least experienced clinicians who, without guiding principles, may become overwhelmed.

I have experimented with new therapeutic approaches to facilitate collaboration and healthy adjustment during a difficult period in the life of the family. Out of these experiments a design has emerged that I call *therapeutic supervision*. Therapeutic supervision derives from psychoanalytic theory and technique adapted to the unique needs of this population. Therapeutic supervision is indicated when supervised visitation between a parent and child has been agreed upon or mandated, or when traditional family therapy has failed. It requires a strict frame and clear rules for engagement.

PRINCIPLES OF THERAPEUTIC SUPERVISION

The operating principles that I have developed for therapeutic supervision concern making agreements before the work can begin, setting the frame of the supervision, including any concomitant individual or family therapy, and establishing acceptable behavior in therapeutic supervision sessions. There must be an initial triage phase during which the therapist meets with all parties—parents, caretakers, children, attorneys, and custody evaluators. During this phase, the therapist works to establish a frame for the treatment and rules of conduct to protect the emotional and physical safety of children during sessions. She defines her role within the context of ongoing legal proceedings and she establishes the boundaries of confidentiality. The parents must agree to her being in communication with their attorneys as needed, and they must agree to compensate her for time spent on the telephone with them or with their attorneys. The parents must agree on who will be responsible for paying her fee (I recommend collecting a retainer for one month's work in advance). In short, the therapist and the family reach an agreement on conditions for working together in therapeutic supervision.

Then therapist and parents discuss how they will work together in therapeutic supervision sessions and in concomitant therapy. There will be flexible movement between therapeutic modalities (individual, couple, family) in various combinations of family members. The therapist reserves the right to terminate any session at any time for reasons of safety or propriety of behavior. The length of the therapeutic supervision session will frequently be extended to several hours, and it may take place in clients' homes or an agreed-upon neutral, and sometimes public, setting. The custodial parent must be available by phone during visits with the noncustodial parent. Finally, the parents must agree to observe fundamental rules, such as not disparaging each other or mentioning legal proceedings in the presence of the children.

Setting up the conditions in a directive way establishes a frame within which the therapist can apply psychoanalytic principles of treatment in a nondirective way. The model for working with the highly conflicted divorcing family is based on a dynamic object relations model of personality and interaction and psychoanalytic theories of child development to inform therapeutic interventions, including interpretation, parenting advice and education, and recommendations about visitation and custody. The therapist assesses parent/child attachment (Bowlby 1969). She helps the parents to develop a capacity for mentalizing as together they reflect on and contain internal experience (Fonagy et al. 1991).

The therapist contains powerful affects evoked in her, uses countertransference to inform interpretation and guide movement between modalities, and understands the family as a projective identification system that has run amok and now functions to maintain psychic stasis. She studies the splits between exciting and rejecting object relating in parent-child relationships, notices the ways that they are behaviorally expressed, and embodies her psychological containment of splitting in the physical movement of herself in action with the child and the parents. She studies defensive mechanisms employed by the family as a group and by each member individually, and she notes the way in which the early traumas of parents and children are reawakened by the current crisis. At moments of high affect, she makes here-and-now interpretations, and uses interpretations-in-action when verbal ones are ineffective (Ogden 1994).

The clinical vignette that follows illustrates new applications of traditional psychoanalytic techniques to therapeutic supervision, designed to meet the needs of this population. The family was referred for supervised visitation after the father was charged with both violence against the mother and molestation of the children. Some of the techniques, particularly my willingness to conduct therapeutic interventions in public settings over an extended period of time, will seem unorthodox to the analytically trained therapist, but these modifications were necessary to meet the needs of this family.

CLINICAL EXAMPLE: THE SULLIVANS

I was contacted about the Sullivan boys, aged eight and ten, by their psychiatrist, who asked me to provide supervised visitation with their father. Mr. Sullivan had recently been arrested in front of the boys and removed from the home, following a telephone call by his wife alleging that he had assaulted her. She had since filed for separation on grounds of domestic violence. She further charged that her husband was alcoholic and addicted to Internet child pornography, and that he had molested the children. Mr. Sullivan had been barred from seeing his children for the two weeks since the arrest. The psychiatrist hired by Mrs. Sullivan to evaluate and treat her children recommended court mandated, supervised visitation between Mr. Sullivan and his children pending further investigation, as much to protect Mr. Sullivan from further suspicion as out of concern that he might hurt the children. Since there had been a traumatic rupture in the children's relationship with their father, and great conflict between parents, the psychiatrist thought that supervision should be conducted by a mental health professional.

I began by meeting individually with each parent and with the two children together. This is different from the way that I work in ordinary family therapy—accepting the family in whatever configuration it presents, and following the unfolding narrative and transference. This deviation is itself a behavioral intervention that says to the couple that I am not supporting their fantasy of being locked in as a couple. In these meetings I hear each member's side of the story and try to develop an alliance with each of them. The situation has echoes of the strange situation of infant attachment research (Ainsworth and Wittig 1969, Ainsworth et al. 1978), and it provides an opportunity to assess parent/child attachment styles. I conduct these meetings in my office to frame my professional role, which I know will later come under attack when I move with the family out of the office.

In our first meeting, Mrs. Sullivan discussed concern for her children and fear of her husband. She said that her husband had been a hard taskmaster who expected her to be the perfect wife and mother. She claimed that her ten-year marriage was ruined by his emotional and physical abuse toward her, and that she had felt strong enough to call the police only when abuse had occurred in front of the children. She feared her husband's sexual fetishes had become directed toward her children. She said that her older son had told her, "Daddy touched me down there, and asked me to touch him."

Mrs. Sullivan made several seductive comments flattering my appearance and the decor of my office. She asked about my professional qualifications, particularly in matters of domestic violence and sexual abuse. She attempted to extract from me a statement that I believed that the abuse she alleged had happened. I said, as I always do with such unproven allegations, that while I could not take a position on facts, I could certainly empathize with her concern for her children's safety. I assured her that their safety was my primary concern, too.

In joint sessions with their mother, the children were quiet and made little eye contact. In response to her prompting, they confirmed her allegations, and said they were afraid of their father, "because he is a bad man who yells and hits and drinks too much." They showed an anxious attachment to their mother, keeping close track of her visually as they played. When she spoke of their father, she switched to a stage whisper, or referred obliquely to the abuse and the arrests ("You know, when he did *that thing* to me, and he was taken to, you know, *that place* . . ."). When I suggested that the children seemed to be quite aware of the things that she was speaking about, she said that she was careful never to speak ill of their father. In the presence of the children, I said that the children had certainly been exposed to a lot of scary, confusing things, including seeing their father arrested. Mrs. Sullivan was upset by my direct reference to the arrest. She said she tried not to talk about it for fear of upsetting the children. She was unmoved when I suggested that talking openly about events might help them feel less afraid.

When I saw Mr. Sullivan, he seemed dazed by events and devastated at being separated from his sons. He was reeling from being ousted from his home, his sons having witnessed his arrest, and worrying about what their mother must have been telling them in his absence. He denied ever having assaulted his wife or children. He acknowledged past alcoholism, but denied a current problem. He denied interest in child pornography, but acknowledged that he had recently visited adult Internet pornography sites. Mr. Sullivan said that while there had been problems in his marriage, he felt that things had been generally good in recent years. However, he went on to complain that his wife was domineering and quick to anger. He and the boys had learned to walk on eggshells to avoid provoking her. He felt that she had withdrawn from him sexually in recent years, and he worried she had married him only to serve as a sperm donor.

Without taking a position with regard to the allegations, I empathized with Mr. Sullivan's frustration, shame, fear, and desperation. I suggested that supervised visitation served not only Mrs. Sullivan's interests but his as well, by protecting him from further allegations. We discussed ways for him to address the issue of supervised visitation with the children during the first session without putting them in the middle between their mother and him, or putting ideas in their heads. I said that he and his children had faced a trauma that had to be addressed directly, and that part of my role would be to help them face it.

In sessions without their parents, the children admitted that their mother said "bad things about Daddy that aren't true." They said that their mother had driven them to Mr. Sullivan's house to peek in his windows to see how much money he was spending on new furniture, even though she had taken out an order of protection against his coming to her house. The children's play was riddled with themes of death and destruction. The dolls in my doll house were tossed out windows, beheaded, or stuffed in cabinets and forgotten. When I said that the doll household was scary and confused, and that the children were unsafe and scared, the boys abruptly interrupted the play. As I spoke about their worries, the boys talked loudly to drown me out. I suggested that lots of things were happening between their parents that were not talked about. It must be confusing to know that I would be joining them on visits with their father. I explained that I had to be present as a supervisor because their mother said that Daddy was not safe. The boys continued their play, as if I were not there.

It is worth noting that it is common initially for both parents and children to ignore my presence when I am functioning in the role of supervisor. My presence is a consequence of the divorce and dramatic evidence of the family's inability to function. By locating their grief, disappointment, and shame in me, and by disavowing me (either by treating me as a friend, or by ignoring me), they ward off pain. My insistence on discussing my presence and the feelings about it supports my role as container of split-off projections, and it models a way of thinking about mental life.

APPLYING PSYCHODYNAMIC PRINCIPLES IN THERAPEUTIC SUPERVISION

I structured the supervised visitations so that Mrs. Sullivan would drop her children off at my office fifteen minutes before their father was to arrive, stay for five or ten minutes before leaving, and pick them up fifteen minutes after he left. This typical structure shields the children from the parents' fighting and allows me to observe changes in the children's affects and behaviors during the transitions from one parent to another and in the first moments with each parent.

When Mrs. Sullivan brought the children for supervised visitation with their father, she gave them detailed instructions about what to do if he threatened or hurt them, and if they missed her or felt unsafe. She repeatedly hugged and kissed them, said she would be nearby, and told them that she loved them "to the moon and back." Mrs. Sullivan's exciting object behavior was designed to cast their father as a persecutor by giving the message he was to be feared and hated, and that she alone was to be trusted and loved. I could see how she heightened their anxieties before the visit, and how they gratified her by clinging to her and begging her not to leave. She then looked to me helplessly, and asked what she should do. I said it was hard to say good-bye, but that it was time for her to leave. She asked me to call her on her cell phone if there was any trouble. I said I knew she was concerned about the children, but that it was time for the drop-off, and she would have to go. She left reluctantly.

I was initially surprised to find that, despite their mother's warnings (which were so threatening as to alarm even a trusting person) the children were affectionate and comfortable in the presence of their father. Mr. Sullivan had brought toys for the children. I allow this, unless it becomes excessive. When he became tearful as the children opened his gifts and was unclear about what it would be appropriate to say, I urged him to begin by speaking about the uneasiness of the visit in the presence of a stranger. He looked helplessly toward me, silently imploring me to fill in for him. I said that he might be upset because he had missed the boys, and must have been worried about them and about what they might be thinking about him since their mother thought he was dangerous.

The boys said that they had been terrified when their father was taken away by the police. They imagined terrible things happening to him in jail. With my encouragement, he explained that his arrest was upsetting for him, too. Although he had had to stay in jail overnight, he had been released the next morning without harm. When his children asked him why their mother was saying the bad things about him, Mr. Sullivan looked lost again. I said that their parents were disagreeing a lot and that their mother was angry at their father, but we did not really know why. With support, Mr. Sullivan said that despite what their mother said, he had never physically hurt her and would never hurt them. He loved them and wanted to be with them. I asked him to clarify that he had not seen them for two weeks because of a court order, not out of choice. I said that the children were in a difficult position: their parents disagreed about important things, but the children loved and needed both of them.

In custody cases where there is legal involvement, it is common and even wise for parents to be inhibited in speaking to their children about disputed matters for fear of legal backlash. Sometimes parents like Mr. Sullivan do not stick up for themselves because they are inhibited for emotional reasons. In many high-conflict cases, the parents being accused have internal conflicts that are manifest in a masochistic tendency to leave themselves vulnerable to their spouse's attack. Mr. Sullivan had been unable to see how troubled his marriage was. Now he felt paralyzed in addressing his children about the allegations. He latched onto the golden rule of divorce: never disparage your spouse in front of the children, but to such a degree that he enabled his wife's bullying of him.

During the first supervised visitations, Mr. Sullivan looked for help as he struggled with ways of putting powerful feelings into words and moving away from his masochistic position. In individual sessions, I helped him to verbalize his narcissistic injury over his arrest for what he felt were false accusations, and his fears over the children's alienation. With urging, he began to talk about his devastation over the impending divorce.

Because the children were not afraid of their father, I agreed that we could leave my office during subsequent visitation sessions. The visits began and ended in my office, but in between we went to playgrounds, restaurants, and to Mr. Sullivan's new home. When I announced my agreement with expanded visitation, Mrs. Sullivan realized that I was not going to support her wish for her children to discontinue contact with their father. She now refused to come for individual appointments. Her allegations of abuse intensified and became more detailed. She telephoned me several times per day, intimating that I was inadequately supervising the children, as if I were a disobedient babysitter. She questioned my qualifications and accused me of overcharging, even though Mr. Sullivan, who was paying the bill, made no such accusation.

Mrs. Sullivan brought the children late to my office for visitations. She extended her leave-taking, and her declarations of love became hyperbolic. Inevitably, Mr. Sullivan arrived before she left, despite my careful planning that they not meet. Mr. Sullivan hung back awkwardly, while she clung to the children and shot deadly looks at him, or tried to provoke an argument. When I insisted on keeping her farewells to the allotted time, Mrs. Sullivan requested an emergency hearing and requested I be fired—which the court denied. When the children's psychiatrist, largely in response to evidence contained in reports generated from the supervised visitation, was unable to corroborate Mrs. Sullivan's allegations against her husband, Mrs. Sullivan attempted unsuccessfully to fire him. When she did not garner support from her own attorney to fire the psychiatrist, she fired her attorney and found one specializing in domestic violence and sexual abuse.

Such attacks are difficult for inexperienced therapists to withstand. Newer clinicians performing therapeutic supervision under my direction have required support and encouragement to tolerate their countertransference responses and make them clinically useful. Despite my previous experience with situations like this, several times I found myself so enraged with Mrs. Sullivan that I wanted to drop the case. In calmer moments, I understood that these feelings represented my temporary identification with her disavowed persecutory object. The rage and humiliation that dogged her internally turned on me, and I felt shame, frustration, and helplessness—similar feelings to those experienced by Mr. Sullivan. I wanted to abandon the family, which would have confirmed that she alone could care for the children. I stayed.

I obtained reports from both of the children's schools and spoke to their teachers. Both children had become increasingly inattentive and oppositional. The younger one had regressed to thumb sucking and enuresis. Mrs. Sullivan angrily dismissed my concern when I called to suggest the boys' difficulties might be connected to parental conflict that we should be working on. I said I understood that she did not wish to come to see me, but I would be sharing my thoughts with the children's psychiatrist. Mr. Sullivan *was* concerned about his children's symptoms. He had not been receiving school reports because Mrs. Sullivan had told the school not to communicate with him. With my support, Mr. Sullivan set up a meeting with the school, clarified the family context for the children's behavior, and was reassured that the school did not have a distorted view of him.

I held two four-hour visits per week with Mr. Sullivan and his children. The most striking difficulty was his inability to set limits. The children repeatedly provoked each other and him. Once I accompanied Mr. Sullivan and the children to a toy store, where he bought them yo-yos. On the way home, the boys opened the car windows, and began to dangle the yo-yos out, banging the side of his new car. He became upset, saying to me, "I don't know what to do. They won't stop." I said, "Your kids are banging up your car, but you feel powerless." He began to cry, saying, "I feel powerless. I can't say *no* to my children." I suggested that perhaps he was worried that if he set limits the boys would hate him, confirm their mother's view of him as abusive, and so feel closer to her. Continuing to cry quietly, Mr. Sullivan realized that he felt afraid of being like his own mother. She had an explosive temper and suffered bouts of suicidal depression. He remembered that as a child he had felt desperately afraid of upsetting her. I said that his worry over losing his children's love made him hostage to their demands and abusive behavior. With my encouragement, Mr. Sullivan stopped the car and took the yo-yos away from the boys. Although the ensuing temper tantrums tortured him, he weathered the storm, and the boys calmed down.

The moments of transitions are usually the most anxiety-producing for children in visitation situations. The Sullivan children were particularly vulnerable as the time to leave their father approached. They often became violent and out of control, or asked to take home a toy bought for them to keep at their father's house. Verbal interpretations alone were ineffective, and I had to augment them with behavioral interpretations. After one visit, as his father prepared to leave, the younger boy asked for money. His father reflexively reached for his wallet. I said, "These good-byes are still really hard, but money is not going to solve that." Mr. Sullivan took his hand out of his pocket. The boy then reached into his father's pocket himself and took out a handful of change. When Mr. Sullivan did nothing, I said to the boy, "Lee, give me the money." When he refused, I took his hand and removed the money. Handing the money back to Mr. Sullivan, I said, "The boys are letting you know in lots of ways, that they do not want to leave. So you feel you have to let them take whatever they ask for. You have a hard time holding onto the idea that it is actually you that they want. How about offering a hug, instead of the money, and saying you will call them tomorrow?"

Over the course of many visits, Mr. Sullivan became able to make use of interpretation, coaching, and emotional support. He became able to make sense of his children's behaviors, set appropriate limits, and respond to emotional needs. I joined their play when invited to do so, otherwise I remained an observer, offering occasional commentary. Sometimes I made group interpretations. At other times when the children were playing at a distance, I made individual interpretations to Mr. Sullivan. As he struggled with setting limits, Mr. Sullivan began to see that he felt hostage to his children in the same way he had with his wife. He had dealt with his wife's emotional storms by trying to be above reproach, just as he had tried to be above reproach in his mother's eyes. Now he began to understand why he had been terrified of feeling or expressing anger, and was so invested in his wife's bullying. His unwillingness to see how the problems in his marriage affected his children had represented a toxic hopefulness. He unconsciously hoped that if he behaved well enough, he might preserve the love of his wife and children, and of his disapproving internal mother. Mr. Sullivan accepted my referral for individual psychotherapy to a colleague, which he had resisted until now. This degree of differentiation and acceptance was an achievement of the therapeutic visitation.

On the legal front, data gathered by a therapist from direct observation, particularly around the transfer of the children from the care of one parent to another, are more accurate than the conflicting data from individual interviews. My reports were taken seriously by the custody evaluator and the judge. They contributed to Mr. Sullivan eventually being granted shared custody of his children. My observations also put other ambiguous information in a context that made them comprehensible For instance, Mrs. Sullivan reported that the children were "always quite upset" when they returned home from visits with their father. Custodial parents in high-conflict cases often offer such information as evidence of an impaired relationship with the noncustodial parent. In the Sullivan family, I observed the children with each parent individually and at the points of transfer. My reports documented that the children's discomfort was due to their difficulty with the transfers, particularly because of Mrs. Sullivan's anger at the children's love of their father.

As is often the case in high-conflict families where there are false allegations of abuse, I was ultimately unable to maintain an alliance with the accusing parent. Mrs. Sullivan was invested in vilifying her husband and in promoting the children's alliance with her against him. She had made what we came to understand were false allegations against her husband at a point in their marriage when she felt the tide of her children's allegiances turn toward him. When Mr. Sullivan moved beyond his masochism and saw the toxic results of his passivity, Mrs. Sullivan became enraged at her children for their unwillingness to form an alliance against him—a pull toward her that they were able to resist only with the support of their father and after they had all been in treatment. In this case, as in many others, the only therapy that Mrs. Sullivan would allow was that which occurred during the supervision. While Mr. Sullivan was able to recognize the futility of his repeated attempts to win love and approval (of both internal and external objects) through submission to Mrs. Sullivan, she was unable to face her unconscious hope of warding off frustrating internal objects and achieving love through constraining his relationship with the children and demanding the children's unswerving loyalty.

Faced with having to share the children, Mrs. Sullivan eventually retreated from them instead. She moved to the West Coast, leaving them in the de facto custody of her ex-husband after all, and seeing them infrequently. Future psychotherapy with the children will need to focus on strengthening their skills at coping with their father's insecurities and their mother's assaults on their attachment to him, their grief at losing her, and their experience of her intense splitting, paranoia, and attacks on their minds.

BENEFITS AND DIFFICULTIES OF THERAPEUTIC SUPERVISION

The principal benefits of the therapeutic supervision in this case stemmed from repeated interventions at moments of affectively charged conflict in the course of visits. These broke through the father's masochistic defenses, which in-office individual work had not done. My access to the children allowed me to speak to their anxiety when it was most stimulated and to model ways for their father to help them. In addition, my data enabled the custody evaluator and judge to make well-informed decisions.

The proposed model for therapeutic supervision carries many difficulties. When I present this material, colleagues say, "I don't know how you do that awful work." Indeed, families of high-conflict divorce challenge us by presenting the nightmare of a world where love turns to hate, and parents emotionally abandon their children. Working with these families, we become the targets of brutal rage. We are barraged by urgent telephone calls from myriad sources, accused of incompetence and unethical behavior, and suffer daily pangs of countertransference. We have to hold onto the idea of the children's need for relationship with both parents, sometimes in the face of tremendous pressures to the contrary. We must leave the comfort of our offices to work in unfamiliar settings. We are subpoenaed to give expert testimony, and occasionally we face legal action from disgruntled parents. And, in the face of all this, we must maintain a therapeutically neutral stance. From the client's perspective, the cost of therapeutic supervision is significant. It is, however, not as high as protracted litigation, and it is far more helpful to the family.

Every time I take that first step out of my office with a new family I feel anxious, as though I must push through the membrane protecting my professional comfort zone. As I work with this new paradigm, I feel unsure. But my willingness to take that step allows me to enter the family's life. As one child put it, "You are the only one who goes through what I go through. You see it all. You *get it*."

CONCLUSION

The model for therapeutic supervision with families of high-conflict divorce is derived from psychoanalytic principles applied to the study and treatment of dysfunctional families. Therapeutic supervision offers a naturalistic setting in which to study conflict and vulnerability at times of transition for the children from the care of one separated parent to another, and then to intervene in the form of powerful verbal and behavioral interpretations. At the same time, it allows the collection of rich, accurate data about the family's functioning, data that inform the court's custody decisions. Therapeutic supervision offers the therapist a way of representing that which has been unimaginable for the family going through a high-conflict divorce. In her physical and psychic willingness and capacity to move between split-up and split-off parts of the family, the therapist offers containment to the family's disconnected objects that had been projected into one another, the legal system, or the therapist. In her willingness to bear and then confront the hopelessness expressed in the family's current functioning, the therapist comes to represent hope for new object relations and a new way of life. My hope is that this model of therapeutic supervision might open our minds and extend our practices to this suffering and needy population.

REFERENCES

Ainsworth, M., M. Blehar, E. Waters, and S. Wall. 1978. *Patterns of Attachment.* Hillsdale, NJ: Lawrence Erlbaum Associates.

Ainsworth, M., and B. Wittig. 1969. Attachment and exploratory behavior in one-year-olds in a stranger situation. In *Determinants of Infant Behavior*, ed. B. M. Foss, 4:111–36. New York: Wiley.

Bowlby, J. 1969. *Attachment and Loss. Volume 1: Attachment.* New York: Basic Books.

Fonagy, P., G. S. Moran, H. Steele, and H. C. Higgitt. 1991. The capacity for understanding mental states: The reflective self in parent and child and its significance for security of attachment. *Infant Mental Health Journal* 13:200–216.

Hetherington, E. M., and J. Kelly. 2002. *For Better or Worse: Divorce Reconsidered.* New York: W. W. Norton.

Ogden, T. H. 1994. *Subjects of Analysis.* Northvale, NJ: Jason Aronson.

Wallerstein, J., and S. Blakeslee. 1989. *Second Chances: Men, Women and Children a Decade after Divorce (Who Wins, Who Loses—and Why).* New York: Ticknor and Fields.

13

Expanding the Frame in Therapy with a Stepfamily

Carl Bagnini

My thoughts on families branch out from two object relations concepts: Fairbairn's idea that the object in which the individual is incorporated is then incorporated within the individual; and Sutherland's concept that the mind is an open system in which development establishes order through fluctuation (Fairbairn 1952, Sutherland 1983, Scharff 1994). Their ideas fit with the way infants interact with others within and across generations in their families—a social basis for object seeking. The infant experiences, internalizes, and projects into the family group. This process shapes the internal object relationships in the endopsychic structure of the self. Impingements from the family environment on the infant's autonomous strivings foster non-thinking and lead to aggression, or dissociated forms of it, and they affect the nature of the internalized objects. But this is true not just for infancy. Object construction is a lifelong, cybernetic process of reconfiguring the self.

When I work with families, I use these ideas and extend them to understand individual conflicts and the dynamics of the family group. I illustrate the family therapy application of object relations by describing an unusual, complex, and possibly controversial treatment arrangement for relationship difficulties and problems with self-regulation in the family of a divorced couple and their two adult children—twenty-eight years after the parents' divorce. The design of the treatment called for moving gradually and thoroughly, back and forth, from past to present, interpersonal to intrapsychic, individual to group, and family to stepfamily.

THE OBJECT RELATIONS
FAMILY THERAPY APPROACH

As a family therapist, I can see firsthand how current symptoms are the reliving of the problems of earlier relationships, which prevent authentic individual and family relatedness. I help the family toward a healthy acknowledgment of the limitations of the past, with hope for the future. I join with the family as a special witness to their living history by a process of careful and attentive listening and empathic responsiveness. Identifying the defensive patterns, and noting the countertransferences that they evoke, I experience the family transferences and underlying anxieties about disappointing relationships, and I am then in a position to interpret them from inside my own experience. The therapeutic process of holding and containing allows for the painful aspects of the disturbed unconscious family conflicts to emerge and be detoxified by discussion and reworking. The aim of this therapy is to enable the family members to relocate and heal lost aspects of themselves and others.

The specific approach taken with the divorced family to be presented is highly controversial, for it involved reassembling a family that had dissolved twenty-eight years before. The symptomatic adult children, their long-divorced parents, and their stepfamilies called for an adaptation to the standard frame of therapy. I brought the divorced couple back together for sessions to rework their breakup and repair the trauma they had inflicted on their children. I had sessions with current stepfamily spouses and adult stepsiblings. And I met with the adult children of the divorced couple, whose disturbed relationship I saw as an identification with the predivorce parental couple. This unusual therapy arrangement took place with the generous cooperation and occasional participation of the members of the parents' new families because their current spouses recognized that the unresolved issues of the originally divorced partners had continued to haunt the development of the two adult children and create tension in their marriages.

I developed this flexible treatment approach after experience in early sessions with the divorced family. There the parents' discussions concerning the two adult children were repeatedly pulled into a long-standing undertow of unresolved marital and child rearing issues that remained from earlier years. I realized that intensive sub-unit reconstruction of the original family's relationships would be needed to release the emotional logjam preventing individuation of the adult children in meaningful postdivorce relationships.

THE FAMILY

The parents, here referred to simply as Father and Mother, are both in their fifties, divorced, and now in their third marriages to others. The adult children from Father and Mother's first marriage were the focus of the treatment. These adult children are Megan, twenty-nine, and George, thirty-two. George has temper tantrums and gambling issues; Megan has severe depression, anxiety, employment problems, and interpersonal difficulties; both have serious credit card debt. George and Megan continued to relate to their parents as helpers and draw them into unsuccessful situations. This drained their parents financially and emotionally and angered their respective spouses, especially Mother's husband, whose three children barely endured Megan and George's extended dependencies on Mother.

The stepfather's children, who live independently, have accepted Mother and him as a couple, but Father and Mother's children cannot adapt to stepfamily life. The tension between Father's commitment to his stepfamily and the children's escalating demands grew, fueled by unconscious fantasies of a return to a nurturing nuclear family that in fact they had never known.

The complexity of the family situation called for an expanded, flexible approach, alternating between twelve sibling sessions for Megan and George, eighteen parent sessions for Father and Mother, family sessions for the four of them, and extended stepfamily sessions to include the stepparents, and at times the stepfather's three children. After giving the history of the treatment, I present material from a late session with Father and Mother (now each remarried to others) and their two adult children from their first marriage, Megan and George.

EXPANDING THE APPROACH TO TREATMENT OF A STEPFAMILY

Extending the psychoanalytic object relations approach to family work, the Scharffs recommended a combined and conjoint model in which the children are seen alternately with each parent to help them integrate and differentiate their dual family experience (Scharff and Scharff 1987b). The approach includes repairing the bond with the alienated parent, grieving the loss of the wished-for family, accepting the custodial parent's new marital partnership, and moving on. With adult children of divorce and remarriage I enlarge the frame by alternating sibling sessions, sessions with both biological parents, and the original nuclear family as a whole. I study sibling connections, too, because they reveal particular internalized object representations paralleling and reflecting the nature of the parents' marital relationship (Bank and Kahn 1982). Expanding the frame accommodates and recognizes the subgroups. Attunement to their needs builds safety and trust—a vital requirement.

A FLEXIBLE TREATMENT APPROACH

The need for flexible treatment combinations in this case was determined by the ambiguities and ambivalences within the current group of the multiply remarried adults and the two adult children of the primary parents. Although twenty-eight years had elapsed since the primary family went through divorce, much emotional reactivity remained, with little understanding of how to deal with it. The nuclear fallout was impeding everyone's abilities to move ahead. Father and Mother's third marriages were improvements over their first and second choices. Even so, Megan and George were in turmoil and had trouble bonding with their current stepparents. They felt left out of the loop concerning their parents' choices about whom they married, and the reasons for divorce. Both parents expected the children to adapt to their new spouses and deal with the loss of prior ones. At the same time they both expressed concern and caring for their children but felt frustrated about helping them feel better. The family could not remember a time when caring was adequate for any of them to move through life's challenges with confidence.

George and Megan made attempts at bonding with others outside the family but only alienated everyone, none more desperately than each other. They shared an apartment but could not get along. Megan clung to the living arrangement, and George wanted to move on—a pattern of disruption stemming from early childhood, similar to the entering and leaving of their father and then their stepfather. George maintained a close and consistent relationship with his mother, but at the price of listening to her tearful confessions and complaints about her depressing life, and absolving her of guilt. As adults the children still had insecurities in trusting themselves in a world that forces adjustment after adjustment, with little recognition of what has been lost.

INTERGENERATIONAL TRAUMA AND NEGLECT

The couple's divorce had occurred when Megan was eighteen months and George was three years old. Father and Mother had met at university in the early 1970s, and each was seeking independence and a higher power for understanding themselves in relation to the political and social world. They lived together in a religious commune for some months. As soon as they married, they realized that they differed with respect to security, with Mother being the more serious about preparing for a family and financial stability, and Father so involved with the religious movement that he gave up a fellowship to participate. The couple elected to move ahead in having children, despite considerable tension between them regarding Father's freedom to find his own way, and Mother's nesting requirements. They moved east and Father took up a low-paid, but steady teaching job in token adherence to Mother's family values. The children were born, arguments intensified about money and family versus individual values, and the relationship deteriorated further. Mother got depressed and Father, unable to cope, became violent toward mother. Father's physical abusiveness led to the separation and continued to prevent co-parenting for many years after the tumultuous divorce.

The children hung on to whatever nurturing was available, largely from Mother, even though she was usually depressed and enraged at Father's irresponsibility in failing to maintain child support payments through periods of their greatest dependency. Nevertheless, they had managed, and the children, who were bright, had had a good education. George was in a dental residency, while Megan was a college graduate. They had been able to apply themselves academically, which gave them a sense of accomplishment.

In the assessment sessions, George and Megan listened attentively, but said little, often looking down when Mother revisited Father's hurtfulness and neglect. Each parent acted as though their lost marriage was the only issue even now, and still minimized the impact on the children. Father showed almost no regret for the suffering of Mother and the children. George's gambling and credit card debt, and Megan's depression, underemployment, and intermittent periods of clinging to her brother and mother when unable to live on her own did not claim sufficient attention. The children seemed insecure and helpless because they were not able to defend themselves by thinking. I found myself empathizing with the children more than with the parents, a countertransference wish to supply the missing attention to the least-nurtured members with whom I identified.

I learned that Father had been physically abusive to George during bitter arguments with Mother, beginning at age three and continuing during visitation after the divorce. Even though she was physically spared herself, Megan, a terrified witness to this abuse, erected a mental fortress in which anger in any form was intolerable. George felt that she had been spared because she was their father's favorite. Unmet longings for parental nurturing had been displaced onto each sibling in the form of rivalry and demands that could not be met. The resulting high levels of frustration caused major regressive pulls between depression and aggression. The children didn't understand that their parents' rejecting behavior was related to events, not to them, and so they placed themselves as a couple at the center of what caused their rejection (Fonagy 2001).

Examining the sibling bond unlocked and treated the secret ways that the siblings became a couple caught in the web of their parents' marriage (Bank and Kahn 1982, Kahn and Lewis 1988). Working back and forth with the sibling unit, across the generations, from past to present, sub-unit to sub-unit, and from parts to the whole, I understood the "reactive identities" (Horner 1999) introjected by the brother and sister. Then in whole family sessions, the siblings could share this understanding of what they were carrying for their parents, and so release themselves from the grip of the parental projections.

This was more easily thought than done. Father was unwilling to admit that his aggression and inconsistency had contributed to the children's future difficulties. From the parents' standpoint, they, not their children, were at the center of their hurt feelings. From each child's point of view, the parents were emotionally lacking, overinvolved, or unavailable. Megan was currently hateful of George, but remembered being protective of him when his father was punishing him. She did not fully understand how these events and feelings helped to shape their lives, and often went blank when approaching the subject.

I saw this as Megan's dissociation from her emerging affects and from her mother and brother's repressed rage at their father, and as her identification with the helpless mother, who clung to George, but who did not protect him or Megan in the early years. The parents each took on the victim's role, projected the blame, and evacuated the shame. In this way they had little emotional space to take in the children's needs or experiences, and little recognition of inner and outer aspects of reality or of their own part in the situation.

The children were huddling *inside* their own experience as a sibling couple in which they felt the attributes of each parent projected on each other. Everyone suffered the divorce fallout. The children could not learn to master thoughts and feelings in relation to their parents' unexplained states of depression or disengagement, and so resorted to clinging and identification. There were no conversations to clarify what things meant, and, due to their individual narcissistic hurts and angers, each parent ignored the significant communications of each child.

WORKING WITH THE FAMILY UNIT

My impression was that what they all wanted was not so much to be understood, but to be agreed with. Megan and Mother expressed being hurt by the tantrums that George and Father rationalized as outbursts justified by not being understood. George saw the link between his father's corporal punishment of him and his own quick temper; but this was not so much an insight for his own benefit as it was a way of placating Megan and his mother. Megan felt that she had to make up for her mother's loneliness and lost love and to quell her mother's depression so that it did not engulf Megan and make her feel helpless. Mother and Megan saw that their mutual clinging was connected to making up for deprivations across three generations of women, all of whom thought that the way for a woman to get love from a man was to give in to his demands. This family assumption exacerbated Megan's difficulty in decision making, and in finding a proper partner.

More recently, however, Mother became annoyed that Megan was not making an independent life for herself, while she herself was in the midst of trying to salvage a troubled third marriage. Mother's turning away brought out Megan's strained relationship with her neglectful father and revealed her abandonment anxieties. She felt that she couldn't expect anything at all from a man. The parents began to express disappointment openly with the children about the way they were sucking them dry. Persecutory feelings increased family defensiveness, made discussions tenuous, and emptied the atmosphere of all hope.

TREATING SEPARATE SUB-UNITS

Working separately with Mother and Father in parent sessions, and with Megan and George in sibling sessions, I enabled both pairs to work on the historical derivatives of the current problems.

The Parents

The parents more fully located the unconscious bases for their selection of each other. Father realized that he had been attracted to Mother's selflessness and commitment to his lofty spiritual pursuits. In this way she was like his own mother who had given in to his father's demands, and she was compliant in the face of his temper. Father was hungry for a woman who would not only make his wishes her priority and submit to his temper outbursts, but who would also take his side, something his mother had not done for him when he was hit by his own angry father. Mother's father was aloof, and she sought the opposite, a man who would supply her with closeness, even if she felt controlled by his temper. Recognizing these projections brought Father and Mother in touch with the needs that they each carried into the choice of partner, and that led to unsatisfied longing, rage, and eventually despair.

Father and Mother addressed their fears of opening up further. Father was afraid of losing control, as he was in such a rage at Mother's attachment to the children's needs. The intensity of his reaction stemmed from his hatred of his parents' relationship in which his father demanded and received undivided attention from his mother, and so as a boy he had to go without.

Father's own father abused his wife, while he, as a small boy, could do nothing. Mother could relate to these dynamics as they were repeated in the current situation when George abused her verbally during family get-togethers, and Father did not intervene. Each parent expressed anger at the other in relation to the children's adult problems.

Mother brought her frustration over money into the present, challenging Father to own up to being a wimp about George's debts. Father responded with the accusation that Mother had had no compassion for the financial problems that interfered with his child support, and in retaliation had prevented him from seeing the children. Thus the children had seen their father for only one week in each of two summers, and infrequently during the elementary school years.

Father and Mother realized that their relationships with their own parents in childhood were filled with childhood fears of physical and emotional punishment, which meant that they didn't dare complain. Therapy was different. Having experienced my empathy, they stopped justifying their mistakes, and became able to allow Megan and George to voice their grievances. They were on their way to establishing a more effective, responsive parental attitude.

The Sibling Sub-unit

I then expanded the treatment to allow sessions for the siblings separate from the parents. This opened up a more comfortable space for full sharing of each child's hurts and conflicts. Until then, the parents had blocked each child's interpretations of current and childhood difficulties, any time either parent was criticized for inflicting emotional pain, whether by neglect or intrusiveness.

Megan and George's sessions focused on the ruptured sibling bond, and its origins. George revisited his assumption that Megan was his father's favorite. In tearful sessions Megan recounted how, when terrified of her father's treatment of George, she used to fear for George, and cry in hopes that Father would stop. All the while George had believed that she was spared because she was her father's princess, and he had been made the scapegoat. George's attitude to Megan softened when he realized how his sister had felt for him, but being the younger child, Megan had had no option but to cling to her mother, and submit to her father.

George and Megan each recognized that neither of them was the special one, and both had suffered in their own ways. The sibling work reduced the rivalry and provided them with a means for uniting to confront their parents with what they had learned when nuclear family sessions resumed. Competitive feelings had modified enough to make this possible.

EXPANDING THE FRAME TO
INCLUDE THE STEPFAMILY

In the expanded family sessions, the two current spouses and the stepfather's children encouraged the four original family members to face up to each other and deal with the past.

THE EFFECT ON THE DIVORCED
FAMILY AS A WHOLE

My benign attention softened the pain of prior deprivations. The sibling pair and the parental pair separately developed a trusting relationship with me. Each pair expressed curiosity about what the other pair was doing, and then empathy. The parents' good faith efforts offered renewed hope to George and Megan that at last they could mend their relationship as parents, and bring the children a unity of concern. If the children could get along better, the parental burden of obligation might be lessened. However, the road continued to be bumpy.

The family was frustrated that Father had shown no remorse in therapy over physical violence to Mother and George years ago. Father had made it clear that he would have to have a safe forum for telling his own side of things first. Mother and the children saw this as his rationalizing, but they were all capable of denial like that, and they went along with him for a time. It amazed me that they were so patient. There were moments where I was filled with an angry countertransference as Father's refusal to be accountable continued the destructive denial at the center of their lives. They hoped that a full hearing of his experience might set the stage for forgiveness, but he hadn't found the right time for it, and they didn't force the issue. Violence not acknowledged or repented cast a long shadow on this family's ability to rework the past.

EXAMPLE OF A FAMILY SESSION

Father and Megan had not been getting into anything deep, as Megan put it, and so she was not feeling close to him. Single, feeling unattractive, soon to turn thirty, and underemployed as a youth worker, Megan had no real prospects in her love life or career. She had failure after failure in independent living, and was hard pressed to afford remaining in the apartment on her own when George left.

As the session began, Megan tearfully related examples of being cut off from her father. Father said that because of her long-standing depression and her rejection of him over the years, he felt cautious about finding his way back to her and was not about to expect too much too soon. Mother insisted that Father had always feared Megan's need for a genuine relationship with him, and his elusiveness left Megan disposed to choose only those men she thought she could control. Megan said that she lost her father before the age of three, and then she tried to please him by putting up with his inconsistent visits, his "bad mouthing" her mother, and never having separate time for her. She was in deep pain, crying openly, and communicating freely with me, but unable to look at him, or at her mother or brother.

I asked if in addition to these early losses and longings there were fears as well. George said that he was scared when his father punished him physically, and he felt protected when Megan had cried. At this, Megan could no longer speak! I told her I would pay attention to her pain and continue looking at its causes; to find words that might help label the experience.

My attention turned to Mother. I thought of the terror of a little girl whose safety was falling apart. Mother and Megan shared the assumption that a man would not stay, and if he did he would turn violent. Megan could not express the anger associated with her torment, and so she trivialized men, by selecting those she could control, but never love. I surmised that she desperately needed her father to own up, in order to be angry with him safely. Otherwise there would be no possibility of forgiveness.

I asked if Mother could validate Megan's childhood experience. Mother was able to recount the instances of her own depression, and her anger at Father in the years lasting through the children's adolescence, but she couldn't acknowledge Megan's pain. George had done so in his own way, but not Mother. I felt irritated with her use of time for her own purpose, although I knew that she needed a forum for her hurts as well. I worked with my countertransference, realizing that I identified with the child who needs sympathetic parental understanding of her deep anguish. I would, if needed, go to Father, George, or Mother for a bridge back to Megan if she could not speak for herself as yet.

The direction of the therapy had to be toward mourning the lost needed objects, recognizing the hurts and how they occurred, and creating a space for shared experiences of denied affect. With the family array of narcissistic wounds, much work would be needed if taking responsibility for past injuries were to be accomplished. Experiencing shared sadness might be a modest step in that direction.

Father had been quietly listening to Mother's account of the separation and the divorce's tumultuous effects on her. As Mother spoke, his facial expression was one of disbelief. I noticed that Megan had recovered and was listening attentively to Mother. I asked Megan to tell me about any scary time in the past.

Megan said, "I used to be terrified when Dad gave it to Mom. I had to hide under the bed."

Father remained pensive for a few moments, lowered his head, looked over at Mother, and said, "I'm sorry for what I did to you in my helpless rage."

This was far from a full apology to his family, but it was as close to remorse as he could get, and the others acknowledged his healing step.

PROGRESS

Over the course of the treatment there was a gradual improvement in the family's holding capacity. The members engaged in a complete accounting of their many hurts and losses and a full expression of their sadness. Appropriate boundaries with decreased clinging and ambivalence were established. Mother and Father continued to respect each other's input as they worked together to help the children continue their adult development. Megan's self-esteem improved, her depression lifted somewhat, and she found a better job. George's finances came under control due to a creative debt consolidation and budgeting arrangement that Mother, Father, and he came up with. Mother and Father continued to work on improving their relationship as parents of their adult children, and their current marriages improved. Sibling conflict lessened in intensity.

CONCLUSIONS

Even though twenty-eight years had elapsed since the first divorce, this group experienced tremendous difficulties in adapting to stepfamily life after multiple remarriages. The expansion of the object relations family therapy frame to include various subgroupings at significant points in the process provided a holding environment for addressing individual, couple, family, stepfamily, and intergenerational problems. The parents' inability to address the children's needs during the marriage and since the marital breakup had prevented them from achieving satisfying relationships with each other and compromised their attempts at bonding with others.

The custom-made design demonstrates the flexibility of an object relations approach but remains controversial. I arrived at an unusual frame for the treatment in response to Mother and Father's investment in their children and in each other as their parents, the long-standing nature of the problem, and their current families' support. The wisdom of the approach seems to be validated by the resulting therapeutic process. The family translated the emotions and psychic structures derived from the prior disturbed relationships into a shared language. Competing demands gave way to more satisfying compromises and relative improvements within the parental pair, sibling pair, and stepfamily.

Expanded object relations family therapy with a stepfamily requires us to move gradually and thoroughly, back and forth, from past to present, interpersonal to intrapsychic, individual to group, family to stepfamily. Ample time for therapeutic attention to the pathological underpinnings, reworking, and accepting the new reality propels postdivorce movement into the potentially healing embrace of stepfamily life.

REFERENCES

Ahrons, C. R. 1979. The binuclear family: Two households, one family. *Alternate Lifestyles* 2(4): 499–515.

Ahrons, C. R., and M. S. Perlmutter. 1982. The relationship between former spouses: A fundamental subsystem in the remarriage family. In *Therapy with Remarriage Families*, eds. J. Hansen and L. Messinger, pp. 31–40. Rockville, MD: Aspen Systems Corporation.

Bagnini, C. 2003. Containing anxiety with divorcing couples. In *Self Hatred in Psychoanalysis: Detoxifying the Persecutory Object*, ed. Jill S. Scharff and Stanley Tsigounis, pp. 165–78. London: Routledge.

Bank, S., and M. Kahn. 1982. *The Sibling Bond*. New York: Basic Books.

Bowlby, J. 1973. The place of separation and loss in psychopathology. In *Attachment and Loss, Volume II, Separation: Anxiety and Anger*, pp. 25–32. New York: Basic Books.

Fairbairn, W. R. D. 1952. *Psychoanalytic Studies of the Personality*. London: Tavistock.

Fonagy, P. 2001. *Attachment Theory and Psychoanalysis*. New York: Other Press.

Hodges, W. 1986. *Interventions for Children of Divorce: Custody, Access and Psychotherapy*. Wiley Series on Personality. New York: John Wiley and Sons.

Horner, A. 1999. *Being and Loving*. Northvale, NJ: Jason Aronson.

Kahn, M., and G. Lewis, eds. 1988. *Siblings in Therapy: Life Span and Clinical Issues*. New York: W. W. Norton.

Kantor, D. 1983. The structural-analytic approach to the treatment of family developmental crisis. In *Clinical Implications of the Family Life Cycle*, ed. J. Hansen and H. Liddle, pp. 12–33. Rockville, MD: Aspen Systems Corporation.

McCormack, C. 2001. *Treating Borderline States in Marriage*. Northvale, NJ: Jason Aronson.

Rice, J., and D. Rice. 1986. *Living through Divorce: A Developmental Approach to Divorce Therapy*. New York: Guilford.

Scharff, D. E., and J. S. Scharff. 1987a. *Object Relations Family Therapy*. Northvale, NJ: Jason Aronson.

————— 1987b. Families of divorce and remarriage. In *Object Relations Family Therapy*, ed. Scharff and Scharff, pp. 367–93. Northvale, NJ: Jason Aronson.

Scharff, J. S., ed. 1994. *The Autonomous Self: The Work of John D. Sutherland*. Northvale, NJ: Jason Aronson.

Sutherland, J. D. 1983. The self and object relations: A challenge to psychoanalysis. *Bulletin of the Menninger Clinic* 47(6): 525–41 and in *The Autonomous Self: The Work of John D. Sutherland,* ed. J. S. Scharff, pp. 285–302. Northvale, NJ: Jason Aronson.

Thies, J. M. 1977. Beyond divorce: The impact of remarriage on children. *Journal of Clinical Child Psychology* 6(2): 59–61.

Visher, E., and J. Visher. 1988. *Old Loyalties, New Ties: Therapeutic Strategies with Stepfamilies.* New York: Brunner/Mazel.

Winnicott, D. W. 1952. Anxiety associated with insecurity. In *Collected Papers: Through Paediatrics to Psychoanalysis,* pp. 97–101. New York: Basic Books, 1958.

14

Family Dynamics and AIDS Phobia: A Case Study

Hans-Jürgen Wirth

The spread of AIDS (auto-immune deficiency syndrome) due to HIV (human immuno-deficiency virus) has caused terror in our society and created a new neurosis, AIDS phobia. AIDS phobia has affected a significant number of people and must be considered a serious problem (Ermann 1988). People may fear that they or their relatives might become infected. Some imagine that they might already have been infected. Others become delusional. The phobia of getting infected and the hypochondriac belief of already having the disease tend to merge into each other, and so the term *AIDS phobia* covers *AIDS hypochondria*, too (Jäger 1988). The third type of psychopathological reaction is *AIDS paranoia*.

AIDS PHOBIA

Reactions to AIDS include panic, disgust, and wishes to stay away from infected people. Some of those who fear infection practice strategies of phobic avoidance and precaution (Richter 1987).

AIDS HYPOCHONDRIA

The AIDS hypochondriac is unshakably convinced that he is suffering from a weakness of his immune system that will soon be fatal. He avidly watches all the normal and usually harmless bodily symptoms. Any fatigue, spots on the skin, swelling of the lymphatic glands, diarrhea, night sweats, or slightly increased temperature causes panic and endless visits to doctors' offices and tests. A negative result of an HIV test provides relief for only a few days. AIDS hypochondria is accompanied by insomnia, decreased work drive, severe relationship problems, and impoverished quality of life. AIDS hypochondriacs tend to imagine that they will be rejected and excluded by their family and friends, but they accept it as a justified reaction to their imagined disease and a suitable punishment for their usually single sexual misadventure. Their behavior becomes increasingly incomprehensible for the people around them, and so the fear of being infected with HIV is not only a psychological problem for the individual: It becomes a family issue requiring couple or family therapy.

AIDS PARANOIA

In AIDS paranoia, the fear of getting infected involves feelings of hatred for, and persecution by, those who are infected, and wishes to scapegoat and attack them (Richter 1987). Those who suffer from AIDS paranoia control their own sexual conflicts by means of aggression against HIV-positive people whom they stylize as their enemies. They tend to pursue their aims politically rather than to present for therapy.

AIDS Phobia in the Context of Other Phobias

Many studies have looked at the connection between AIDS phobia and other phobias (Jäger 1988, Hirsch 1989) such as cardiac neurosis or phobia and hypochondria (Rosenfeld 1964). A few case studies consider the family (Neraal 1988, Woidera and Brosig 1990), but most of them offer only glimpses into the problem and omit the relevance of family therapy. The following case study of a combined individual, couple, and family treatment offers insights into the dynamics of the AIDS-phobic individual, his family relations, and treatment difficulties. The psychodynamics of behavioral patterns in the microcosm of a single treatment are illustrative of how society at large deals with AIDS.

A COMBINED INDIVIDUAL
AND FAMILY TREATMENT

This example discusses treatment for an AIDS phobic (hypochondriac type) individual, Heiner, and his family.

The Intake Interview

Heiner is a thirty-two-year-old engineer for the German National Railway Company. He feels wasted as an engineer and would rather be a forest ranger to fight for the preservation of the environment. His boyish face makes him look younger than his age even though he is balding. He has cold sweats, night sweats, fatigue, skin lesions on his thigh, slightly increased temperature at night, and burning sensations on his tongue. Two lymphatic glands have been removed without benefit. Previously an avid soccer player, since falling ill he has abruptly stopped all sports activities and has become flabby.

Spontaneously, he told me that his mother's overprotectiveness, which he attributes to her having lost her own mother, means that she cannot stay alone in the house at night. Her anxiety has had an inhibiting effect on everybody in the family. Like her, Heiner is an anxious type, not as severely anxious as she is, but still cautious and health minded. He does not smoke and tries to lead a healthy life.

His father is the exact opposite of his mother, namely tough and ambitious. He got Heiner and his brother involved in sports, especially in the local soccer team. The whole family is now involved with the soccer team. For six years, Heiner has had a girlfriend, Karin, with whom he has a one-year-old daughter. At first, his girlfriend's pregnancy was an unwelcome surprise because he still wanted to be single, and so he refused to marry her. His parents didn't like her. Even though he and Karin come from the same village, he demanded that they live together in another town. The arrangement didn't go well, and he often went home to his mother. For six years he tried to "please everybody but he got nowhere." When he used to complain about Karin, it was only to escape his parents' criticism. He said that he felt "like a relay station" whose function it is to transmit information from one side to the other.

Heiner told me more about his sporting life as a member of the soccer club, a men's club noted for its chauvinism and enormous group pressure. "There," he said, "being a man is everything. We travel together to away games, and after we've had a few drinks, each man wants to make the best impression on the women. As a result, people do things they really don't want to do. These men are really wild." He went with his soccer teammates to Ibiza, and there he was egged on to have his first one-night stand. Not to appear like a "a nerdy intellectual" he felt obliged to drink, do dumb things, and fornicate like the others so as to "be one of the guys." Throughout the return flight he experienced "hellish anxiety" and lots of guilt about sleeping with a "hippie," and he had to get drunk to calm himself. He still feels guilty and ashamed that he was so weak. He partly blames his parents, arguing that, had he married his girlfriend two years ago, then he could have avoided Ibiza altogether. He thinks that he allows people to influence him too much and that he does not listen to himself. He believes he is HIV infected, even though all the doctors have told him that he is clear, and this fills him with anxiety and depression. He believes that this is his punishment from God.

Recommendation

Heiner refused inpatient treatment because he wanted to keep his illness hidden from his employer. I recommended a combination of individual and conjoint outpatient sessions. There were sixteen sessions in five different therapeutic settings in the following order: two individual, two couple, one with parents, brother, and girlfriend, one with parents and brother, three couple, two mother alone, five couple. Heiner was able to arouse my sympathy, engage my scientific curiosity, and think critically about his social relationships. I thought that he was ready to work in psychotherapy.

During the two sessions with the mother alone it became clear that for years she had been suffering from a massive anxiety neurosis, which she barely managed by means of various family arrangements. By offering her individual therapy sessions, I meant to strengthen her insight into her illness and help her to take personal responsibility for her anxieties and her conflicts and not to burden her family, especially Heiner, with her psychosocial defense strategy. It was my hope that this would be a source of relief for Heiner. To further Heiner's separation process from his parents, the treatment concluded with five sessions for Heiner and Karin.

The Family as Stronghold

The parents see the girlfriend Karin as the main cause of Heiner's problems. The mother suspects that Karin got pregnant against Heiner's wishes so as to catch him. Turning to her son she said, "Be honest, you didn't want that child, did you?" Heiner agreed and added that he was indeed overwhelmed by Karin's pregnancy. The father believes that Heiner's illness broke out after he got back with Karin, who had left him three months earlier. The brother is brutally honest about how unattractive Karin is and how wrong she was to have left Heiner. The mother believes that her negative attitude toward Karin is justified because Karin was mean to have left him and not even once did she prepare breakfast for him, despite the fact that he was traveling all day long. Since Heiner always brought his laundry to his mother and ate meals at her house she thought that Karin did not really take care of his needs and that he really deserved a better woman.

Formulation

AIDS anxiety broke out after Heiner made up with Karin. By embracing his girlfriend and child again, Heiner separated and differentiated from his mother, but the continuing conflict between loyalty to his mother and attachment to his girlfriend brought about deep unconscious guilt feelings for which AIDS would be the perfect punishment. His illness defends him from further reproaches by his mother because he appears punished and he needs mercy. The "sick" body is both the punished self and the mother against whom his deathly aggression is directed. By remaining ill and misunderstood, he is protesting his role as a relay station and thereby wins the strength to stand up for his opinions, even at the cost of self-injury.

I have the impression that the brother stubbornly sticks to his demeaning and wounding statements about Karin and her unappealing looks in order to prove that he, unlike Heiner, is able to keep his distance, to be independent, to have his own opinions. At any rate, he achieves this at the cost of excessive harshness. Whereas Heiner oscillates between various opinions, the brother shows a brutal certainty.

The Mother-Son Relationship

The mother is a traditional domestic homemaker, and subservient to her husband. She feels that her sons view her as the bad mother if she doesn't pamper them. She quells discord. Otherwise she falls apart. She sees Heiner as kindhearted like her and quite different from his brother. She feels sorry for her son because he is so kindhearted, unable to say no, and therefore gets exploited by his girlfriend. Like Heiner, she finds her trust betrayed. When someone disappoints her, she remains offended and hurt.

In response to my question whether she was disappointed as a child, she told me about her mother's sudden death from a dental abscess, when she was ten years old. She said, "I have no anger against my mother, but I was enormously disappointed." From that time on, she experienced anxiety. She is never alone at home without "one of her three male defenders." Her own anxieties are so great, she said, that she really needs to be in therapy herself.

After her mother's death, her father remained single, and so she found it difficult to leave him to marry. When she got married, her mother-in-law told her that she had to polish her husband's shoes. She accepted this because in her own family, she polished everybody's shoes. Her father was jealous of her husband and this caused many fights. Shortly after they had stopped fighting and he was invited to live with them, the father died.

Formulation

The mother's structural conflict is the same as Heiner's. She, too, is ambivalently tied to her mother as the ten-year-old girl who loves her mother and needs her protection, but is deathly disappointed and hurt for having been abandoned by her. Unconscious hatred against her mother reappears in the sharpness and coldness toward Karin. Since the age of ten, Heiner's mother fought against her hatred of her mother by projection of evil into the environment and by reaction formation in the form of special love, care, and sacrifice for the sake of her family.

The Father-Son Relationship

Father and son describe their relationship as harmonious and motivated by shared interests in soccer and books. They do, however, oppose each other heatedly on the topic of politics. Heiner has told his father he should be shot for his opinions, and yet he is concerned that his father will have a heart attack from being overweight. Heiner had passed a difficult examination to be a forest ranger like his uncle, but his father made him choose engineering. The father describes himself as an ambitious man who had to drop out of high school just a year short of obtaining the diploma because of financial difficulties. In his job as an employee of the state he feels restricted and unfulfilled. That's why he is disappointed that Heiner is "working for the state for life."

Heiner is completely devoid of ambition. He no longer "harbors any illusions about a big career." He said, "In the best of cases you become a cabinet minister and do something, but I gave up on that idea." He feels sad but resigned, disillusioned, and withdrawn into a "safe employee mentality."

Heiner's father always tried to bring him up as a tough man, ready to "play hardball." Heiner told me that he used to play soft, and had to teach himself to be aggressive and finish the opponent off before he got wounded himself. Better than playing softly and defensively, playing hard was a principle to apply to the rest of life where the stronger guy is always the winner. One day his father reacted contemptuously when he saw Heiner and Karin cleaning the apartment together, and he described the scene with disgust to his own father, a man who also believes that a man must play hard. Father's education in manliness went so far that he jokingly threatened to shoot Heiner if he ever found him acting in feminine ways. The family thought of Heiner as a weakling and a softy.

Formulation

Heiner is quite impervious to applying my interpretations of his psychosomatic illness to himself, and yet he uses psychosomatic hypotheses as a weapon against his father. He hides his true feelings behind a complex system of strategies of denial, distancing, and turning into the opposite. For instance, he turns his rage toward his father into its opposite, concern for his health. They are close, yet both refer jokingly to shooting each other.

The father has secured his son's loyalty with a mixture of threats and support of masculine pursuits. The son subjugated himself to his father in order to avoid aggressive conflicts with him. In order to please the father, he had to deny the softness, weakness, and anxiety that his neurotic mother had inspired in him. He is trapped between his mother's anxiety-neurotic relationship and his father's ambitions. Identifying with masculine and feminine elements, Heiner embraces his parents' differences, desperately trying to find a compromise between his father's and his mother's expectations.

An increased leaning toward the mother aroused symbiosis anxiety, whereas a more intense relationship with his father would stimulate passive homosexual feelings. Heiner feels contempt for his passive and anxious tendencies, which he sees as unmanly, weak, and ultimately as indicative of homosexuality. His AIDS anxiety is connected to an unconscious homophobia.

Heiner became fat, lost his bulky muscles, felt weak, and became anxious about having AIDS, a physical embodiment of his psychological state of softness, anxiety, and weakness. In this way he turned into the image of a man that his father has made him feel contempt for. By hurting himself, he is taking revenge on his father, who has weighed him down with extreme ideals of manliness, confronting Heiner with his repressed fears of weakness, and Heiner reacts by throwing himself back on his mother's mercy.

According to Richter's (1972) family typology, Heiner's family is phobic, borderline between anxiety-neurotic and paranoid. Clinical studies show that such a phobic family climate fosters heart-neurosis and hypochondriac ideas in children (Richter 1972, Rosenfeld 1964). The mother has organized the family like a sanatorium ruled by harmony and togetherness (Richter 1972) in which conflicts and tensions are to be resolved as quickly as possible, and a healthy lifestyle is supposed to ban all evil, which then is found in others such as Karin. Evil then returns from the outside persecutor and since it cannot exist inside the psyche must be projected into the body (Hirsch 1989).

The Treatment Process

In the course of family sessions, Heiner increasingly gained the ability to distance himself from his parents and have his own opinions. However, he was still influenced by his former close relationship with his parents and still enjoyed his mother's cooking, which gave her ammunition against Karin. The father admitted, "We are an exclusive group. We may argue, but we stand together against outsiders. We have seen Karin as an intruder." Heiner became increasingly able to stand up for his relationship with Karin and set up boundaries between himself and his parents. About a year after the beginning of treatment, Karin became pregnant again and she and Heiner got married. Nevertheless, he remained obsessed with his AIDS hypochondria and worried that he might have infected her and his children.

Heiner liked to show off in the sessions with Karin. Heiner alternated between laughing off his conviction of suffering from AIDS and stating that he will die soon. He said that he came back to Karin because the "hippie" woman had been much too challenging for him, especially sexually. He had no awareness of how humiliating all this was for his wife. Heiner didn't respond to my confronting him with his aggressive and sadistic behavior. He just sat there, straddle-legged, presenting his now big belly, laughing inappropriately and trying to ask me questions and debate medical matters with me. Karin told me that she is suffering so much from the situation that she herself has started to develop symptoms of anxiety and depression and is no longer able to drive a car alone. Heiner said that he thinks Karin is the one who is mentally ill and needs psychosomatic treatment, and therefore she should come to the sessions alone to discuss the tensions with his mother without him.

By this time, I have accumulated a great deal of anger inside me and can hardly stand Heiner anymore. I've tried being friendly and giving benevolent interpretations that appeal to his ability to understand and be insightful, but he cleverly turns to defensive maneuvers. Stubbornly and cunningly, he keeps trying to get onto a buddy-buddy basis with me or into a debate. Discussing matters rationally only strengthens his defenses. Now I blow my top. I confront him with his inappropriate laughter and his dumb talking. Heiner instantly surrenders masochistically. He says that he did not expect anything other than being kicked out of their apartment by his wife and that it would be best to get a divorce. I remind Heiner that his wife has demonstrated sufficiently that she does not want a separation but wants to communicate with him, and yet he hasn't said a single word to her in earnest, only dumb jokes and superficial stuff. I give free expression to the emotions of my countertransference, but I would not call this countertransference acting out. I believe that it is possible to touch the patient inwardly only by such a direct and strongly affective confrontation.

Soon after that, our conversation takes a positive turn. Heiner stops his silly grinning and tells me something personal. He was afraid of being alone in a forest as a child. As a child, he had been seriously ill twice, and his mother had been afraid that he would die. As an adolescent, he became closer to his father, to follow his model of manliness. Now he tells me that he is afraid of flying, taking elevators, and all sorts of mechanical devices. I talk to Heiner about his feeling torn between his mother and his father. To meet his father's and his own adopted standards, he can't allow his soft side to develop and tries to escape into a macho attitude that actually does not suit him. Heiner agrees with that. For the first time it is possible to talk to him about such things.

Half a year after the termination of treatment, Heiner's psychic state has become more stable. He is not as depressed anymore, can go to work, and has started to exercise again. He and his wife have bought a house in a far-away town where he is working, and soon his wife and children will join him. He had distanced himself from his parents for some months and is now talking to them again. Although Heiner is now feeling much better, he has not given up his fixed idea that he is suffering from AIDS. When he had a high fever due to influenza, he went to research institutes specializing in AIDS, was convinced that he was dying from AIDS, and made his parents come and see him. The institutes are still busy testing him for some unique virus that has not yet been identified. Heiner speaks very well of the institutes. He feels accepted and taken seriously. Maybe the positive transference that he has developed for the head of the institute will provide a transference cure for stabilizing his psychic state.

AIDS Hypochondria as Relief and Defense for the Individual

Why were Heiner's hypochondriac ideas so tenacious and why did they bring relief? He could locate his anxiety in an object that he could understand more readily than his parents' contradictory and partially unexpressed expectations. He could feel victimized by fate. He could blame himself for a single instance of moral failing and accept his punishment for that, but since it was a family secret he didn't need to hear remonstrations and reproaches from his friends. All the aggression he didn't dare acknowledge toward his mother and father he could redirect into raging against fate and fighting his lethal disease or attacking his body fatally because he deserved punishment and rejection for his moral failing.

Heiner gained freedom from family expectations and interference. His fixed idea that no one wanted him because he had AIDS made him an independent person for the first time. Whereas he usually shaped his opinions according to his parents' point of view, he could now stick to his own ideas of what was wrong and what to do about it, regardless of the personal cost, becoming the strong man that his father wanted and avoiding causing his mother unbearable anxieties. At the same time, being ill, he was constantly betraying his adopted ideal of manliness. He couldn't direct his anger at his father because he was stronger, and he couldn't direct it to his mother because she was weak and might break down, and then whom would he depend on? Hating and destroying himself let him express his hatred for his parents indirectly and cause them tremendous pain and guilt. His illness says to them, "Look, here is the monster you have made me!"

By remaining immune from all attempts to being talked out of his fixed idea of an AIDS infection, Heiner created a sense of himself as a stable and autonomous person, even if unstable in everyday situations. The mere fact of having an opinion that others doubted and opposed made him feel strong, brave, and independent. The more people objected to his disease, the more self-confident he felt. At the same time that he felt bad and weak from psychosomatic illness, he felt strong being connected to the greatest authorities in the field of AIDS research. Heiner's AIDS hypochondria was armor against his ego weakness and feelings of inferiority. As the cause for his desperation and depression, the fear of AIDS was more acceptable to Heiner than the fear of the breakdown of his ego, and the fear of its dissolution if cut off from his mother. He projected all his fears into his flabby body and his illness to avoid being frightened or sad. In order to recover, he would have to be brave enough to feel the fear, the rage, and the sadness appropriate to his inner life, his history, and current family situation.

AIDS Phobia and the Collective Defense System of the Family

The family therapist usually meets the family at a time when the neurotic family configuration is changing (Richter 1972). Heiner's AIDS phobia shows that the collective neurotic defense system within the family has become unstable. Throughout the years, the family had centered around the anxiety-neurotic mother to cover for her illness. As Heiner tried to separate from the family, the incompatibility between his desire for independence and the family's ideology became obvious. Heiner had to suppress his separation and individuation wishes and to punish himself for that in keeping with the family rule that nobody should do anything that could endanger the mutual dependence of the family members, especially their dependence on the mother as the leading figure. The family lived according to the motto: "We are a closed society and live in beautiful harmony in our nursery-like world. Evil exists only on the outside." He who tries to separate destroys this family consensus and destabilizes the entire family-neurotic defense system. Heiner paid for his striving for autonomy with massive feelings of guilt and fear due to the internalization of previously projected persecutory feelings, which led to the development of individual symptoms.

Previously stuck together pseudoharmoniously, its eyes closed to the evils of violence, cruelty, hatred, and injustice within its family relationships, the family is now being confronted with evil in its midst—in the form of AIDS. Heiner's imagined AIDS infection brings back the suppressed family aggressions that before had been projected onto the outside world. The family dynamic is responding to the threat of the return of the abandoning bad mother embodied in the image of the unpopular wife who left Heiner, by its opposite, that of the anxiously attached, pampering and controlling mother, and ultimately of the grandmother who catastrophically left a dependent family prematurely on account of her untimely death.

SUMMARY

I define AIDS phobia and illustrate the hypochondria type of AIDS phobia. I describe a combined individual, couple, and family treatment process and outcome to connect the individual manifestations of the index patient's illness to the family dynamics. I conclude with an analysis of the multigenerational contributions to the individual's psychopathology.

REFERENCES

Ermann, M. 1988. AIDS-Phobie. In *Münch. med. Wschr.* 130:12–14.

Hirsch, M. 1989. Hypochondrie und Dysmorphophobie. In M. Hirsch, ed., *Der eigene Körper als Objekt. Zur Psychodynamik selbstdestruktiven Körperagierens*, p. 77 ff. Berlin: Springer.

Jäger, H., ed. 1988. *AIDS-Phobie. Krankheitsbild und Behandlungsmöglichkeiten.* Stuttgart: Thieme.

Neraal, T. 1988. Der irrationale Anteil der AIDS-Ansteckungsangst. In H. Jäger, ed., *AIDS-Phobie. Krankheitsbild und Behandlungsmöglichkeiten*, pp. 68–72. Stuttgart: Thieme.

Richter, H. E. 1972. *Patient Familie. Entstehung, Struktur und Therapie von Konflikten in Ehe und Familie.* Reinbek: Rowohlt.

———. 1987. Gesellschaftliche Auswirkungen von AIDS. Statement für die Sitzung der Enquete-Kommission des Deutschen Bundestages "Gefahren von AIDS und wirksame Wege zu ihrer Eindämmung" vom 29.9.1987 in Bonn.

Rosenfeld, H. 1964. Die Psychopathologie der Hypochondrie. In H. Rosenfeld (1981), *Zur Psychoanalyse psychotischer Zustände*, pp. 209–33. Frankfurt: Suhrkamp.

Woidera, R., and B. Brosig. 1990. AIDS-Hypochondrie. Intrapsychische und intrafamiliäre Konstellationen. In M. Wirsching and H. E. Richter, *Neues Denken in der Psychosomatik?* Frankfurt (in Vorbereitung): Fischer.

15

Consulting to a Family Business

Michael Stadter

All mental health professionals know that both the workplace and the family can evoke powerful and primitive responses and interactions among their members. Family businesses combine the dynamics of the family and the workplace to produce uniquely intense phenomena (Levinson 1971, Gage 2002). To understand the complexity of family business we need a theory that bridges individual, couple, group, and organizational dynamics. Object relations theory is a theory grounded in clinical psychoanalysis and intensive psychoanalytic psychotherapy (Greenberg and Mitchell 1983, J. Scharff and D. Scharff 1998) that has been applied to group psychotherapy, couple and family psychotherapy, and brief therapy (Ashbach and Schermer 1987, D. Scharff and J. Scharff 1987, 1991, Stadter 1996) and to the study of group dynamics in institutions (Bion 1959, Obholzer and Roberts 1994, Menzies-Lyth 1988). Concepts of family dynamics, power, authority, responsibility, containment, and processes of projective identification are particularly helpful in understanding the difficulties of family businesses.

Consider Shakespeare's presentation of the dynamics among three brothers in the royal family business—Richard, Clarence, and Edward, the king:

> Plots have I laid, inductions dangerous,
> By drunken prophecies, libels and dreams,
> To set my brother Clarence and the king
> In deadly hate the one against the other . . .
> Clarence still breathes; Edward still lives and reigns:
> When they are gone, then must I count my gains.
>
> *Richard III* (act 1, scene 1)
> (Shakespeare 1989)

173

Few family businesses proceed to actual murder, but many involve strong and regressive forces and some are quite persecutory.

There are multiple definitions of a family business. For the purposes of this discussion, I define a family business as an organization (profit or non-profit) largely owned by two or more members of a family and where two or more family members are in management positions.

FAMILY DYNAMICS AND FAMILY BUSINESSES

In the workplace as in other settings, people interact at various psychological levels. One level involves conscious interaction that is task-oriented, rational, and good enough to be gratifying. Another level involves transference to figures from one's family of origin. For example, a man's supervisor may evoke reactions in him that are intensified by his unconsciously relating to the boss as if he were his father. However, in a family business the man's boss may actually *be* his father. A son or daughter may be treated like, or may act like, a child rather than like an adult employee. Siblings may replay their childhood roles. A parent-manager may avoid making necessary staffing decisions because he is afraid of seeming to show favoritism by appointing one son or daughter to a higher-level position than those of siblings. Unconscious re-enactments occur universally in the workplace through transference relationships, but when the "real" family members are the actual participants there is an additional level of intensity to the interactions, not uncommonly reaching persecutory proportions.

RIVALRY, GUILT, ENVY, AND HOSTILITY: COMMON AFFECTS OF PERSECUTORY STATES OF MIND

Competition over power and resources, envy toward those who appear to be more favored, hostility toward rivals or winners, and guilt over these states of mind are often prominent in the unconscious life of family members in the business. Not only do family dynamics intensify such states of mind, but the states may also be disavowed. For example, one hard-charging CEO had no difficulty acknowledging his own ruthlessness and aggression toward nonfamily employees. He actually seemed proud of it. However, he denied that he treated his employee/son the same way. "I don't do that, I love my son," he thought. The son and other company staff, however, saw this same aggressive pattern directed toward the son.

Family members in business together may try to promote the fantasy that they are or should be "one, big, happy family." This fantasy and the denial of the real interactions often cause damage to both the family and to the business. When family members can face these uncomfortable feelings and states of mind, they can be freed to work and interact with each other more successfully.

FAMILY BUSINESSES MANAGED MORE LIKE FAMILIES THAN LIKE BUSINESSES

Family members may try to deal with their family issues through workplace decisions and strategies. For instance, all the siblings may be given the same degree of status and authority despite their differing levels of competence and motivation. A father regrets that he neglected his daughter when he was young so he gives her a position as senior vice president even though her experience and training make her ill-prepared for this position. A brother resents that his younger brother was always the favored son and he will even the score by keeping the younger brother in a lower-level position. A mother feels guilty because the family did not do enough for her son with severe learning disabilities and so she appoints him to a high-level finance committee despite his ignorance of this area. A father appoints two brothers to be equal CEOs of the company as a way for them to be forced to work together as an ill-advised remedy for the fact that they had never gotten along well with one another.

Trying to resolve family conflicts or problems through business decisions often works to the detriment of both the family and the business.

THE FAMILY BUSINESS THAT CAN IMPAIR FAMILY LIFE

The different roles that family members fill in the workplace—for instance, manager and subordinate, sales representative and manufacturing chief—complicate the already complex interactions among family members. Lack of separation and space between the family members can be problematic when they work together and live together. Workplace conflicts and discussions can spill over into home life and vice versa.

Example: Charles and Cynthia

A husband and wife who came to me for couple therapy struggled with this issue. Charles was a lawyer in solo practice and Cynthia was the office manager in their six-person office. Working together proved to be a chronic and serious strain for their marriage. Cynthia hated Charles's style of management—authoritarian, like her father's style of parenting—which was not the way he was with her at home. Charles often felt that she should agree with him when conflicts arose among employees. Their marriage dramatically improved when Cynthia chose to leave the firm and Charles grudgingly accepted her decision. Then couple therapy helped them to deal with her guilt over leaving and Charles's feelings of abandonment.

FAMILY DYNAMICS IN THE ORGANIZATION RESONATING AMONG NONFAMILY MEMBERS

The powerful, unconscious forces of projective identification can induce nonfamily members to play out roles in the family's drama. This can greatly intensify the conflicts among these employees, and the effects cascade throughout the organization.

Example: David and Diane

Two vice presidents in an office furniture company, David and Diane (nonfamily employees), were referred to me because of their inability to work together. At the conscious level, they did have real clashes of opinion over company policy. Out of their awareness, their conflicts were exacerbated by their unconscious identifications with family members. David was identifying with the founder-CEO of the company who espoused a more conservative, low-tech approach to business and who was having a great deal of difficulty turning over more responsibility to his son, the ambitious company president. Diane was unconsciously aligned with the son in promoting an aggressive business plan that involved more computer and Internet activity and that pushed decision making down to lower-level employees. When the two vice presidents became aware of how they were playing out the father-son conflict, they became able to work more collaboratively. Although they still had frequent conflicts, these struggles no longer had the previous level of primitive regression and aggression. If the father and son had dealt more successfully with their differences, this resolution probably would have had a further beneficial impact on Diane and David's conflicted working relationship.

Like nonfamily employees, organizational consultants may be drawn into taking roles in the family drama unconsciously. The enactment gives the consultant valuable information about the unconscious power of the projective identificatory system of the family business and offers a position of personal engagement from which to arrive at an interpretation geared toward change.

DIFFERENT SETS OF RULES FOR FAMILY MEMBERS THAN FOR NONFAMILY MEMBERS

In a midsized sporting goods company owned by a father and two brothers, one brother embezzled $35,000 to cover gambling debts. Even though this was the second time that he had stolen from the company, he remained in his position. The only consequences that the family imposed on him were closer supervision over his access to corporate funds and the requirement that he begin psychotherapy. A nonfamily member would have been fired and probably arrested.

In another business, a nonfamily member complained to me that he would never be able to reach a certain level of responsibility in the company, no matter how outstanding his performance, because he was not a member of the family. "I'm not royalty," he explained. The different sets of rules for family members (or the perception of different rules) can increase tensions in family businesses and decrease the motivation and commitment of nonfamily members.

DIFFICULTIES IN SUCCESSION PLANNING IN FAMILY BUSINESSES

Most owners of family-owned businesses want the business to remain owned and operated by their future generations. In one survey, 87 percent indicated that they wanted the business to stay in the family. Most new businesses do not endure beyond their first year and only about 30 percent actually make it into the second generation of family ownership and operation (Higgins 1998). As for the other 70 percent, these businesses fail, merge, or are sold.

The founder of a successful business is typically a rather dynamic, highly assertive, maybe even charismatic individual who tends to create a dependency culture in the company with strong forces inhibiting other individuals, including those of the next generation, from taking leadership.

For instance, let's say a father wants to turn the business over to his son. At the surface of his consciousness, he feels that he is doing everything he can to pave the way for him, but the transfer of power doesn't happen. At deeper levels, the father may have unconscious fantasies that impede him from letting his son take control of it. For instance, where the man relates to his company possessively and protectively as a mother would relate to her baby, the fantasy is at the pre-Oedipal level. Where the father is enthralled with his company as a lover or bound to it for better or for worse as a spouse, he may equate giving his son control of the company with loss of manhood or death of the self. Here the fantasy is at the Oedipal level. All of these unconscious fantasies could cause the father to sabotage all attempts to let anyone else take charge of his business. Clearly, the dynamic forces of parental possessiveness and the Oedipus complex can change a business succession into a life-and-death struggle.

As for the son, consciously he may be feeling ready to take control of the company and be eager to do so. Unconsciously, he may be feeling anxious and insecure about his ability to take over the reins. He may also feel guilty over his desire to take charge and move his father out. The son may see the father as holding him back by being hypercritical and infantilizing. He may also feel guilty for being angry at his father's behavior. As for the father, he may be angry with his son for being ungrateful, for not doing it his way, and for not being strong enough. If these unconscious dynamics remain unexamined they can easily prevent an effective succession from occurring.

EXAMPLE: COM.COM, A FAMILY BUSINESS

At the time of the consultation, Com.com was a family-owned business in its first generation of ownership. The company sold specialized computer hardware and software to businesses over the Internet. It had just begun its fifth year, it had twenty employees, and for the first time it registered profits, but barely. There were four owners, Arnold, Ann, Bill, and Betty. They were all in their forties and each had a 25 percent share in the company. Betty is the oldest and Ann is the youngest of three sisters. Ann is married to Arnold and Betty is married to Bill. There are three pairs in charge: Arnold and Ann, Bill and Betty (husbands and wives), and Ann and Betty (sisters). Arnold is the president of Com.com in charge of managing operations. Bill is the executive vice president and manages sales and marketing. Ann is the office manager and reports to Arnold, her husband. Betty is a sales representative and reports to Bill, her husband. Interestingly and problematically, Arnold and Bill really report to no one.

In the first consultation meeting, the owners identified the following issues (see table 15.1):

Table 15.1. Presenting problems in a family business

- Tense atmosphere and lack of communication: Arnold and Bill literally had not talked to each other in two months.
- Lack of decision-making: The conflicts were so severe that the owners were not able to make any major decisions.
- Stagnation: The business was in a state of paralysis.
- Survival: The owners wanted an opinion on whether the partnership could survive and, if so, how.

The Consultation

I consulted with Com.com as part of a consultant team for Business Mediation Associates (Gage, Martin, and Gromala 1999), a consulting group that specializes in working with family-owned and closely held businesses. The consulting model blends mediation, organizational consultation, and family therapy approaches and so calls for a multidisciplinary consultant team: a psychologist paired with a professional from the fields of law, accounting, financial consulting, or organizational development. My consulting partner in this case was Melinda Ostermeyer, an experienced organizational consultant with expertise in decision-making models and alternative dispute systems. This consulting model does provide recommendations and opinions, but it places greater emphasis on facilitating a negotiation process whereby the principals develop their own solutions.

The consultation unfolded in four sessions with the four owners and the two consultants:

Session 1: (At a conference center away from the office) One half-day meeting with the four owners as a group

Session 2: (One week later) A full-day meeting with the group and the partners individually

Session 3: (One week later) One half-day meeting with the owners as a group

Session 4: (Five weeks later) One half-day meeting with the owners as a group

Session 1: The Initial Engagement

We met with the four owners in a preliminary meeting for three hours to see if they wanted to work with us and to assess whether we could work with them. Neither Arnold nor Bill addressed each other in the meeting but talked to each other through us or through their wives. They agreed to work with us but specified that due to financial constraints they could only invest two days. This is much shorter than a typical engagement and while we had misgivings, we agreed to do it.

As the preliminary meeting was ending, we reviewed the written contract for our consulting engagement. Arnold balked. "I'd be willing to do this," he said, "but I'm not sure everybody else wants to do it. Do we have enough information?"

I intervened and said that they didn't need to sign today and that we could schedule another hour next week to decide whether to proceed or not. I then polled the group to see where they were. The other three said they definitely wanted to proceed with the consultation. Arnold said it was now clear to him what the others thought. He acknowledged the partnership was in dire straits and he agreed with the others that what we said sounded good. Still he wasn't sure about going ahead with the plan.

Melinda and I were both frustrated when Arnold put up the roadblock as the meeting was ending. It had seemed to us that the owners had agreed to proceed and that we were set to go. I felt a pull to do as the other owners had often done with Arnold in the past—argue with him that he had already made a decision. Instead, I noted that we didn't have to decide in that meeting and that seemed to settle Arnold down, but removing the pressure didn't enable him to act. I concluded the discussion about whether or not they could work with us by saying that: (1) Arnold was wary of beginning a process solely designed to get him to change; and (2) the other three owners were worried that Arnold wouldn't take it seriously.

Reminding Arnold that the others said that he paralyzes decision making by demanding more and more information obsessively and by saying that he isn't sure everybody is behind a decision, I showed him that this exact dynamic was operative right now. He was actually quiet for a moment, smiled, accepted my observation, and signed the agreement. I said to the group that this type of interaction—using a here-and-now experience to recognize the owners' dynamics—was something that we would be doing with them as we worked together to understand the business.

The interpretation of Arnold's fear that he would be targeted as the sole problem and the others' fears that he wouldn't take the process seriously calmed the situation. Frequently, when one man or woman is helped to see that someone else can speak for his or her issue, the distressing feeling of being alone is lessened for that one person and for the group.

In this vignette, we show how we experienced the pull of projective identification with the owners' problem dynamics. By resisting the pull, containing the group's anxiety and aggression, and interpreting the process, we made a start on detoxifying the situation in which the struggling business had become a persecutory object to the couples and conversely the couples' dynamics were strangling the business.

Session 2: Individual Dynamics and Beginning Group Work

During the morning, we interviewed each partner individually. We were able to understand their conflicts and hopes more clearly. Betty displayed a steady, reasonable, trustworthy presence. Ann came across to us as having the same down-to-earth practicality but she also showed considerable anxiety and an edgy sense of humor. All four owners saw the business as a timely opportunity to make a significant amount of money. Additionally, Betty and Ann had entered the business to work more closely with each other. They felt that they had a good relationship and valued the chance to be even closer.

They had also hoped that being owners would allow them to work part-time so as to spend more time with their children but found instead that Com.-com placed more than full-time demands on them. This overwork repeated a family pattern that they had wanted to avoid. They described their father as a good man and a creative entrepreneur, but he had been away from the family too much trying to turn around a series of businesses that were barely profitable. Their mother worked in the companies too. As Ann said rather bitterly, "We've lived family businesses." In that family, Betty had been the mediator and was closer to their parents. Ann never felt as successful as Betty. We sensed unacknowledged competition between them.

The sisters were overwhelmed by every aspect of their lives. Both were dealing with significant health or behavioral problems with their children and both of their marriages were suffering severe strain during the last few years. The conflict between their husbands was extremely difficult for them. Both women often found themselves acting as messengers between Arnold and Bill—in "no man's land," as Ann called it—and they felt torn by conflicting loyalties. Throughout it all, however, they felt that their relationship as sisters had not significantly suffered. Although she was functioning effectively at work, Betty was clinically depressed. Moreover, the specter of cancer hung over both sisters. A year prior to our consultation, Betty had completed a course of chemotherapy for breast cancer. Several years before that, her middle sister had been diagnosed and treated for breast cancer, too. Ann did not have cancer, but she feared with good reason that it would eventually strike her as well. Even Arnold was worried that some fatty lumps he had found under his skin might be cancerous.

We had found Bill to be quite engaging in our first meeting and so were surprised by how unlikable he seemed when we met with him individually. Of the four partners, he was the most defensive in our individual meeting and we were able to learn the least about him. He deflected questions smoothly and continually returned to complaining about and blaming the problems on Arnold. He had felt humiliated by Arnold regularly and had periodically threatened over the previous six months to quit the partnership. Bill acknowledged that he had failed two years ago to bring in the business that he had promised. By getting additional training and then intensifying his marketing strategies, he had been much more successful in the past year. He was bitter that Arnold and Ann did not appreciate what he had done and did not realize how hard it had been to overcome the difficulties involved.

In contrast, Arnold surprised us by being more appealing than expected. A man with narcissistic vulnerabilities, he nevertheless presented openly in the individual meeting. The appeal to Arnold of starting up the company was to be his own boss and to have the opportunity to make a good deal of money. His parents had divorced when Arnold was five and he never really knew his father. He said he was like his mother. As he put it, "She's controlling but she gets the job done." His job history was one of quick successes followed by intense interpersonal conflicts that meant that he had to move on to the next job. He presented himself as a heroic martyr who had to work seventy-five hours a week despite the physical toll on him. "If I don't do it," he said, "it won't get done." He did acknowledge that he could be too much of a micromanager and that his temper was, at times, abusive and uncontrolled.

That afternoon, we worked with the owners as a group in what proved to be a rather steady, productive session. Bill and Arnold talked directly to each other and the owners agreed upon several ground rules to guide their interactions.

Session 3: The Drama Intensifies during Group Work

The third session was quite different. For an hour and a half, it was a difficult, contentious meeting. Finally the owners worked out an agreement for Bill and Arnold to have a weekly meeting. They eventually agreed upon the time, duration, format, and agenda for these meetings. We then took a break and moved on to address a particular business issue: how to determine if a price for software was a good one and how to determine the speed of follow-through on delivery and service for that product.

As the discussion of the group task progressed, the group dynamics actually regressed and overtook the consultants temporarily. I was taking the lead in facilitating this part of the meeting and Arnold was becoming hostile to me. He was yelling, at times, and was frequently cutting me off. Melinda and I tried to deal with this as a group issue but we got nowhere. As the process moved on Ann, Betty, and Melinda became very quiet. Arnold, Bill, and I became increasingly active and intense. For about thirty minutes, I became downright hyperactive and Melinda became extremely quiet. Like a detached spectator I could see what was happening, but as an involved participant I became so captured by the process that I couldn't get out of it. I couldn't stop overfunctioning. Melinda was equally captured by it and she couldn't emerge from her passivity. In situations like this, when the process becomes too intense and spins out of control, we typically call for a brief break for process and review, but both of us were so disabled that we didn't think of doing that. Finally, Betty found her voice and screamed at Arnold to listen to what I was saying. This was very unusual for her and it broke the regressive cycle and lessened the tension somewhat. Melinda and I recovered sufficiently to call for a break and the two of us met briefly to regroup and reorient ourselves to the consulting task.

For the last thirty minutes we worked on the agenda for the following meeting, our final half-day with this business. Arnold said angrily that he sure didn't want another meeting like this one. Melinda and I agreed. I said that the second half of this meeting had been very difficult and that we would work with them to make the next meeting more productive. I asked if what we had all just been through was very much like life at Com.com. They all agreed it was. Betty said, "I thought we were back at the office."

During the break and after this difficult meeting, Melinda and I processed our experiences. We had both been caught up in an intense and rather primitive projective identification. As Ogden (1982) has noted, one function of projective identification is as an unconscious, nonverbal form of communication. In this meeting the partners didn't *tell* us about their own experience. Through projective identification, they had us *experience* it.

In the meeting, I had come to feel frustrated, isolated, and alone. Since I was operating predominantly from a paranoid-schizoid mode (Ogden 1989), I was not reflecting on these feelings but rather was bombarded by them and so was unable to think. Asking for help didn't even occur to me at the time. I thought angrily, "Where's Melinda? Why isn't she helping out here? Do I have to do this whole damn thing on my own?" I was also experiencing wide swings in my narcissistic equilibrium. At times I was feeling absolutely hopeless and woefully inadequate. Alternately I was experiencing myself as incredibly creative and articulate, uniquely capable of turning this meeting around, and even defiant. Especially at some points when Arnold was cutting me off, I was aware of feeling, "If you're not going to listen to me, fire me. Go ahead, make my day!"

Just like Arnold, I was feeling alone with the burden of responsibility. With too little time for the consultation, I was laboring under a tight deadline. Like him, I felt that I had to be heroic, take charge, and solve the problems myself. No one else could do it, I thought.

Melinda, for her part, was experiencing an equally desperate yet very different state of mind. Like me she felt pressured by our time rapidly diminishing, but unlike me she felt unable to speak. She was thinking, "How do I get in here to help out? I can't find a way in." She felt guilty that she was letting me down. At times she thought angrily, "This is ridiculous. What in the hell is Mike doing?" At other times, she thought admiringly, "Yes, that's just the right comment. That'll work." She also felt that the emotional intensity was just too high and that, since she wasn't a therapist, she should let me deal with it. Just like Betty and Ann at the office, Melinda in the consultation was seeing a turbulent drama but she felt powerless to do anything about it.

The intense psychological states that the consultants were experiencing had caused a temporary paralysis of our consulting function. These were states of mind that dominated the four partners' experience together. Our own reactions gave us a powerful sample of some of their experience and helped us to understand the business.

The Consultants' Insights about the Business

1. The dynamics at Com.com obviously made it difficult for the owners to think and reflect rather than to react. The dynamics had that effect on us, the consultants, as well. Just as the owners were having a difficult time coping with their tumultuous experiences at Com.com, the consultants were temporarily unable to contain the family group anxieties. We all needed to find a way to be able to think again.

2. Intense but unconscious attacks on pairing were part of the psychological environment for the partners at Com.com. It became part of the consultants' psychological environment, too. One of the wonderful aspects of co-consulting is that the two consultants can contain and support each other when the going gets tough. Our consultant pair was so disrupted during this point in session 3 that we were no longer functioning as a couple but rather as individuals under attack. This gave us empathy for the owner pairs. Both marriages were under severe strain. Arnold and Bill, the two top people in the business, were not even talking to each other. The only couple that seemed to be doing well was the sister couple.

3. Although their generally united approach was helpful for the company, their consciously denied sibling rivalry intensified some of the battles between Arnold and Bill. The husbands were acting out their wives' unrecognized conflicts. Moreover, Arnold seemed to be reliving the pain of his parents' divorce. Bill had not given us enough information so we could not be sure of the contribution of his internal couple except to say that he was fully engaged in the enactment. After the consultation was completed, I realized some other family dynamics that were probably persecuting the business. Both married couples were acting out rage against their parents and the sisters were acting together as if to break up their parents who had been wedded to their work.

4. The business was hampered by a dynamic of male hyperactivity and female passivity. One intensified the other, driven by the attacks on pairing and by the sisters' resisting acknowledgment of any significant struggle between them. During a portion of session 3, all three men were overfunctioning and all three women were silent. Betty finding her own voice and breaking out of her projective identification-induced role was an important step in bringing about a new ending for old experience (Stadter 1996).

5. All of the owners were struggling with narcissistic issues involved in regulating self-esteem. Fears of doing something wrong, of failing, and of being shamed kept them from being able to make decisions. Mistrust and rivalry made it difficult for them to take responsibility and to give authority to each other.

6. The owners' group dynamics were pushing Arnold into an aggressive executive role. Admittedly, Arnold had a high valency for it, and that was

why the unconscious group process recruited him for it successfully (Bion 1959). Particularly, Bill's smooth, engaging style and the sisters' avoidance of conflict pressed Arnold into the role of the abrasive boss.

The Consultants' Strategy

Melinda and I grappled with these points. We regained our thinking capacity and planned our work as a consultant pair for the final meeting. Given that we expected only one more meeting, it was unlikely that we could interpret much. Depending on the participants' psychological mindedness, in a longer consultation we would try to bring more of these dynamics to a conscious level. However, we did resolve to keep aware of the forces attacking pairing and promoting male hyperactivity and female passivity. We set as a priority the need to function in a balanced way and, as a team, to contain the process and the affects more adequately. We planned to be a model of cooperation and containment in the final meeting and to talk about the impact of the forces of destruction on us and on the owners. We would watch any distortions in our own self-concepts in the meeting and quickly ask for a break for process and review if either of us felt uncomfortable in our role. Also, if Arnold again took on his obstructive, antagonistic role, we would immediately comment on that, suggest that he was performing a group function, and ask the group to think about what might be going on.

Bion (1967, 1970) has written about attacks on the analyst's thinking capacity in analysis and on the difficulty of containing primitive psychic contents. One of the necessary conditions for effective functioning as a business owner, as a consultant, and as a therapist is to be able to think clearly and creatively. Bollas (1987) has written about occasions in psychoanalytic psychotherapy when the therapist becomes "situationally ill." This occurs because of the therapist's receptivity to countertransference states that involve reliving disturbed portions of the patient's psyche through projective identification. The therapist's situational illness is a version of the patient's own illness. The same process happens to the organizational consultant. With family businesses, the synergistic power of family and workplace dynamics creates a fertile ground for recruitment by such primitive processes. In session 3, Melinda and I had become situationally ill. Now our job was to try to think about it, talk about it together, and treat our own "illness."

Session 4: Group Work and Termination

Through phone calls to the business, together with the owners we set the agenda for the final meeting (see table 15.2).

We started the meeting by acknowledging how difficult the last meeting

Table 15.2. The agenda for the final meeting

- Give a summary and final recommendation
- Work to develop a trial agreement for a decision-making process
- Help to set regular partner meetings

had been and how unbalanced the participation had been, ours and theirs. We said we would do our best to give them contributions from both of us and urged them to do the same. We acknowledged the powerful forces acting on us and on them that can produce such a disruption in the ability to work together. Melinda and I were pleased to learn that Arnold and Bill had kept to their agreement to meet weekly and that the meetings had been productive and were going well. At first we felt surprised, but we soon realized that this positive outcome reflected the potentially detoxifying effect of our engagement in the process. Although we had not put into words an interpretation of our countertransference, our painful identification with the owners' struggles had begun to metabolize some of the toxicity.

The Final Meeting: Impressions and Recommendations

Melinda and I both presented the following summary of our impressions and our recommendations (see table 15.3).

All four owners responded well and were in agreement with our recommendations. The process was calm and collaborative. I had a feeling that their experience of hope for the business as a money-making concern and as a sisterly collaboration had shifted significantly. I thought that they had lost hope of ever being able to make the partnership work in the long run and instead had developed a new and realistic hope that they could find a way in the short run to tolerate working together and to do it effectively.

We then moved to the topic of developing a decision-making process. At the heart of this problem lay their difficulty with taking and giving responsibility and authority. They recognized the urgency of this since they had been unable for months to decide on anything other than the most immediate of operational issues. Yet, the loss of trust among them and the fear of attack for making a wrong decision were paralyzing them. Half of the morning meeting was spent on this. It was a difficult and conflicted meeting with the owners several times almost giving up on the process. In fact, at one point, they became so discouraged yet so clear that they had to break this decision-making paralysis that they seriously entertained the idea of flipping a coin to make a decision. During this work I intermittently felt the pull to become more active as I had in the previous meeting but it was not nearly as compelling. Moreover, Melinda and I were actively keeping an even balance in our

Table 15.3. Summary of recommendations to the family business

- Given the intense conflicts and dynamics, it was a credit to all of them that the company had been able to turn a profit.
- The partnership as presently configured could not last. For their partnership to endure, they would need to do much more work on their partnership structure and process.
- Com.com, a family business, was being conducted like a family and not like a business. The owners needed the following organizational structures: a legal partnership agreement (remarkably, they did not have even a minimal contract), planned performance reviews, clear written definitions of authority for decisions, a decision-making process, and a strategic plan.
- Neither Bill nor Arnold should report to each other. They needed to report to the ownership as a group of four with each having clear, separate responsibilities.
- Ann and Betty needed to become more active in their roles as owners rather than as employees of Com.com.
- The owners had made significant progress by defining a list of guidelines for effective, respectful communication and interactions in the second meeting. They needed to adhere to these guidelines.
- The owners needed to keep the business in perspective and at the office. Com.com was harming their marriages and their health. We urged them to make their health and relationships their top priorities and not to allow discussion of business to take place at home.

participation. Also, we commented repeatedly on the difference in the tone of this meeting and frequently facilitated Ann and Betty to stay active in the process. Eventually, they agreed to a six-month trial period of a decision-making process that authorized particular partners to have final authority on specific issues.

Finally, we spent a short period of time helping them to set up monthly partner meetings. At termination, the partners expressed appreciation for the process even though it had been much more painful and difficult than they had expected. They were surprised and impressed with how we were all able to work in such a different manner in this meeting compared to the previous one. Melinda mentioned hopefully that perhaps they could work differently at the office just as they had done in this meeting.

Follow-up Seven Months Later

Arnold and Bill were still meeting weekly and their meetings were going well. Arnold had not yelled at anyone at the office since he had yelled at me in our third meeting. Owners' meetings were occurring, although infrequently. The four owners had been able to make decisions as a team and the new management process was continuing to work. Profits were up and they had even bought out a competitor. They continued to agree with our observation that the partnership could not hold together in its present form.

However, they had hope for the future since they were now being wooed by a potential buyer. Although the atmosphere at work had improved it was still tense. Ann and Betty were taking a more active role as owners and working less hard as employees. Betty was in individual psychotherapy, was taking antidepressant medication, and was feeling much better. Both marriages were calmer.

Twelve Months Later

The Com.com owners had sold their business for what they felt was a good profit. Bill and Arnold had employment contracts to continue with the new company for three years. Each of them would be reporting to a third individual. Arnold was feeling some anxiety and loss, but the other owners were pleased with the outcome.

CONCLUSION

Even though our consultation with this highly dysfunctional organization was brief, we did manage to help the owners break the organizational paralysis, improve their functioning, and decrease their level of interpersonal stress. The detoxification was incomplete, however, and the owners still had not found a way to be a family business for the long run. They had agreed with our observation that the partnership could not hold together as it was constituted, but they did not act to change that fundamental fact. Instead, they looked for and found a successful exit strategy—selling the company. Our practical consultation and mediation techniques did provide help to the owners, but it was our experiencing their inner world and, once there, struggling to think and act effectively as a couple in working with them that began the detoxifying process. In a longer consultation, we could have brought the issues to consciousness through verbal interpretations and then helped the owners work through toward a more benign organization of their inner and outer worlds. In brief interventions like this, many of the dynamics cannot be expressed verbally in interpretation. Instead, we use "interpretations-in-action" (Ogden 1994). The consultants' nonverbalized activities and their "way of being" function as the interpretations in action that foster a shift in the transferences (Stadter 1996). Within the limitations of the time frame of this consultation, the ways that we worked together to detoxify the bad objects projected into us functioned as the interpretations in action that facilitated change.

REFERENCES

Ashbach, C., and V. L. Schermer. 1987. *Object Relations, the Self, and the Group.* London and New York: Routledge.

Bion, W. 1959. *Experiences in Groups*. New York: Basic Books, 1961.

———. 1967. *Second Thoughts*. London: Heinemann.

———. 1970. *Attention and Interpretation*. London: Tavistock.

Bollas, C. 1987. *The Shadow of the Object*. New York: Columbia University Press.

Erikson, E. H. 1950. *Childhood and Society*. New York: Norton. Revised paperback edition, 1963.

Gage, D. (manuscript in preparation). Shoulder to shoulder: How business partnerships can succeed.

Gage, D., D. Martin, and J. Gromala. 1999. What partners often leave unsaid. *Family Business* 10(2): 21–28.

Greenberg, J. R., and S. A. Mitchell. 1983. *Object Relations in Psychoanalytic Theory*. Cambridge: Harvard University Press.

Higgins, M. 1998. Passing the torch in family owned businesses. *American Business Association Journal*, pp. 48–53.

Levinson, H. 1971. Conflicts that plague family businesses. *Harvard Business Review* 49:90–98.

Menzies-Lyth, I. 1988. *Containing Anxiety in Institutions*. London: Free Association Books.

Obholzer, A., and V. Z. Roberts, eds. 1994. *The Unconscious at Work: Individual and Organizational Stress in the Human Services*. London: Routledge.

Ogden, T. H. 1982. *Projective Identification and Psychotherapeutic Technique*. Northvale, NJ: Jason Aronson.

———. 1989. *The Primitive Edge of Experience*. Northvale, NJ: Jason Aronson.

———. 1994. *Subjects of Analysis*. Northvale, NJ: Jason Aronson.

Scharff, D. E., and J. S. Scharff. 1987. *Object Relations Family Therapy*. Northvale, NJ: Jason Aronson.

———. 1991. *Object Relations Couple Therapy*. Northvale, NJ: Jason Aronson.

Scharff, J. S., and D. E. Scharff. 1998. *Object Relations Individual Therapy*. Northvale, NJ: Jason Aronson.

Shakespeare, W. 1989. *The Unabridged William Shakespeare*. Philadelphia: Running Press.

Stadter, M. 1996. *Object Relations Brief Therapy: The Therapeutic Relationship in Short-Term Work*. Northvale, NJ: Jason Aronson.

16

Holding On and Letting Go: From Family to Couple Therapy

Jenny Berg and Penny Jools

The birth of a child is a developmental challenge, a normative crisis, for any couple. How the parents cope depends on their psychological maturity and the nature of their internal objects, good and bad, built from experience with their families of origin. When the baby arrives, the couple may feel intruded upon rather than joined and enriched. Then the couple functions as a dyad provoked by an intrusive third. Such a couple has a narcissistic marriage, with autistic-contiguous and paranoid-schizoid features underpinning their Oedipal anxieties about the intrusion of the third. Therapy enables the couple to contain these anxieties and progress toward a depressive position adjustment to the developmental challenge of becoming a family unit, including their first-born.

THE DEVELOPMENTAL SEQUENCE

The developmental sequence includes the narcissistic marriage; autistic-contiguous position anxiety; paranoid-schizoid and Oedipal anxieties at the intrusion of the third; and the depressive position and containment. These are discussed below.

1. The Narcissistic Marriage

The spouses project repressed parts of themselves into each other and then relate to each other in a part-object way. They pressure each other to see the

191

self as the self wishes to be seen. They do not see themselves or each other realistically. They collude to idealize and denigrate themselves and each other, by the use of splitting and denial.

2. Autistic-Contiguous Position Anxiety

In such marriages, anxiety is extreme. The spouses defend against it by merging to avoid the annihilatory anxiety that separateness brings. They do this with the use of projective identification and mirroring. They may appear physically close, but the marital container is inflexible. The merger produces psychosomatic symptoms, particularly disturbances at the level of the skin, and genital sexuality is problematic.

3. Paranoid-Schizoid and Oedipal Anxieties: Intrusion of the Third

The arrival of a child upsets the couple's homeostasis, and precipitates the return of split-off and repressed rejecting object relationships that threaten their relationship. Using more splitting and projection, the couple projects their bad feelings into the child. The couple is now in the paranoid-schizoid position. If they take their projections back from their location in the child, they then face their mutually rejecting object relationships. Bitter conflict usually ensues. The arrival of the child activates feelings of rivalry and competition in an already volatile relationship. The couple is now in a stage of Oedipal anxiety, and the resulting murderous rage, directed toward self or other, can lead to a destructive outcome for the couple unless they learn how to contain it.

4. The Depressive Position and Containment

Therapy offers an experience of containment, which facilitates the reintrojection of destructive feelings and improves the capacity to bear Oedipal anxiety, but the ferocity of these conflicts may threaten the viability of the therapy as much as of the couple relationship itself. When therapy can proceed, the couple must mourn what has been lost and acknowledge the presence and value of the therapist and of their child to their relationship. This develops a more objective appreciation of self and other and acceptance of the threesome, the couple, and the individual as equally vital contributions to the family. When the spouses make reparation in this way, they are functioning in the depressive position.

CASE EXAMPLE

We outline the psychological shifts, developmental anxieties, and associated defenses that emerged during the therapy of a couple who got stuck after their first child was born.

Background

Wendy and Hilton sought help because five-year-old Stephen had primary encopresis. After six months of family therapy, the focus shifted to the couple's relationship, and conflict escalated. Wendy and Hilton elected to work with a couple therapist (JB) and Stephen was referred for individual therapy.

In family therapy, we had learned that Wendy and Hilton found their child excessively demanding. Under the strain of dealing with him, their relationship had deteriorated, and they slept in separate rooms. Sexual problems were evident, but not openly discussed. Wendy idealized her hard-working, and therefore somewhat absent, father and criticized her mother for being unsupportive. Wendy was afraid of being too much for her critical, depressed mother, and so she developed a compliant false self: an indispensable, compulsive caregiver. Like Wendy keeping up a compliant façade, Hilton's mother kept up the façade of a happy family, even though Hilton's father was emotionally and physically abusive. Hilton kept up a false self that was charming and urbane, but devoid of true feeling, and in fact he didn't have a voice. Neither Wendy nor Hilton was positively identified with their same-sex parent. Wendy's father was a good father figure for Hilton, too, but he had died when Stephen was a toddler.

The Early Marriage and the Autistic Contiguous Position

Initially Wendy and Hilton had a life of togetherness, full of entertainment and joint activity. She spent a lot of time looking after Hilton devotedly, as she had done proudly for her baby sister. She projected her own neediness into him and looked after it there. With this taken care of, she found time for herself and quietness of mind. She said, "When it was just us, I put a lot of effort into the relationship—I pushed it along. I could think about what we wanted and . . . get it organized." Hilton was happy to receive Wendy's loving attention, which was such a contrast to his early care. However, Hilton was hypersensitive to touch and found embracing aversive, despite being filled with desire. Wendy was patient and persistent, even though their sexual life was compromised by his psychosomatic skin disturbance. She said, "It was hard not to feel rejected, but it worked okay after a while."

On the other hand, Hilton was unable to touch Wendy in a satisfactory sexual way. Wendy had had good sexual experiences previously, but her only other sexual relationship was with an older married man who did not intend to leave his wife. She became extremely frustrated about remaining anorgasmic with Hilton, and he reacted by decreasing the frequency of his attempts at pleasuring her. So, their sex life was dysfunctional, but Hilton received Wendy's patient, nonsexual care gratefully, and she cared for herself in him. This suited them both: for they had a shared defense, and it held them together but it was brittle. It lacked a containing function.

Before the birth of their son, Hilton and Wendy were linked via a mutually exciting object relationship that was narcissistically gratifying. They nurtured their fragile senses of self through idealization of their relationship, through persistent attempts at sexually stimulating experiences even though they were ultimately frustrating, and through having lots of time for themselves. These are defenses at the autistic-contiguous level.

The Birth of the Child Fractures the Narcissistic Couple

> Hilton: In the past we had a fantastic life together with lots to talk about and do—theater, movies, dinner, trips. Now we only talk about Stephen.
> Wendy: I am afraid that we're not doing things together. With Stephen, he doesn't know what to do. And frankly by the time he comes home, I've had it. When he comes in to bed, he interrupts me. Then he goes straight to sleep, and I am left awake thinking over things.

Wendy and Hilton's difficult infant, Stephen, left them each feeling uncared for. At the same time Wendy's father died and left them without a good father figure to support them. Their previously idealized relationship began to crumble. They clung to their preoccupation with Stephen, without which they felt disconnected from each other. Their Oedipal difficulties, due to poor identification with their same-sex parents, made accommodating a "third" in the relationship fraught with anxiety.

Early Couples Therapy: Paranoid-Schizoid Anxieties

In the early sessions, the threat of danger and destructiveness is clear, as anxieties from the paranoid-schizoid level are exacerbated by Oedipal issues.

> Wendy: Hilton turns into a volcano about to blow, and then I'm wiped for days. I don't understand his anger. It must be something from his childhood he is dumping onto me.
> Hilton: I know Wendy is devastated by the anger. I know what she means, and I feel badly about it. The distance to the surface seems a long way off—it seems a long time to go without oxygen.

JB: You both use language that suggests danger. Hilton, Wendy feels you to be like a volcano, and you feel short of oxygen. There is fear in you both of how threatening emotions can be. Wendy, you say Hilton has unresolved feelings of anger to his father, but I think you do, too. For instance, when Hilton withdraws, perhaps it reminds you of when your father was unavailable through work.

Wendy: (*Shaking her head*) My father was a good father.

The words they use vividly evoke images of destruction—reflecting their own projected anxieties and fear of annihilation. Families of origin issues are raised but are unacknowledged or denied. Their shared defense has failed now that they are parents and must meet the needs of their child when they feel lost without their own good father.

Splitting and Acting Out in the Marriage: The Affair

After fifteen months of therapy, Wendy and Hilton are still full of mutual recriminations.

Wendy: I can't even chew my food without being attacked! Nothing I do is okay anymore!

Hilton: Now you know what it feels like! That's what life's been like for me for years.

Wendy: Well you don't have to cope with Stephen every day. I feel so unsupported. Why can you never get home when you say you will? You're always late. I feel like you don't care, like you don't love me anymore.

The next day Hilton rang JB to make a confession. Hilton revealed that he had become accidentally involved in a six-week affair, now ended. With his mistress, with whom he was emotionally fully engaged, he had felt awake to his feelings for the first time. However, he now saw how badly he treated Wendy. He recognized that ignoring Wendy and being fully present with his mistress were indications that he had split himself into two, and he wanted to have his new feelings with Wendy. JB insisted that the information be shared in the next session.

When she heard about the affair, Wendy was enraged. She felt the aggrieved partner. She did not accept that it related to difficulties within the marriage. It was not possible to discuss the meaning of the affair in the couple therapy setting. Hilton started individual therapy and became depressed. He began to mourn his childhood experiences, and made reparation with his parents. He was negotiating the depressive position in a satisfactory way, but Wendy saw his depression as further betrayal. She complained that he attacked her with silence, didn't let her in, and kept the gift of himself for others. Meanwhile, she could not let Hilton in sexually.

Splitting and Acting Out in the Transference: Resistance

Wendy's idealization of Hilton had failed, and her narcissistic investment in herself had taken a body blow. Wendy became clinically depressed and suicidal. She refused referral for psychiatric assessment on the grounds that this would be admitting responsibility for the marital problems. During a particularly bad fight, Hilton left their home. Wendy decompensated, and made threats of suicide and homicide. There were four emergency phone calls one weekend, but Wendy would not agree to safety plans. Feeling attacked by concern for her, Wendy attacked JB.

> Wendy: *(To JB)* I feel like you don't hear how distressed I am. What you say doesn't help. It's like you're not there for me either!
>
> JB: You feel I'm not there for you, but I have been trying to help you. It seems you can't help yourself here because you feel it means accepting all the blame for what is wrong in the marriage.
>
> Wendy: *(Crying)* I am so afraid Hilton won't be there in the future—it's unbearable, the pain is too much.
>
> JB: You fear the pain is too much for Hilton, and so he will leave forever. Perhaps it is safer to be angry with me.
>
> Wendy: Hilton's been good since I've been so terrible, helping in practical ways. *(Smiling seductively, then in a distressed tone)* We were happy before, there was so much good. Where has it gone? I now have a partner who can't bear to touch me.
>
> Hilton: *(Shaking his head)* I wasn't happy. I know that now. And you were always stressed out. I don't remember much happy time. We've rarely slept in the same bed since Stephen was born.
>
> Wendy: *(Flipping into anger)* There's plenty of shit in the past, which I don't wish to rake over anymore. We either go forward positively or not at all.
>
> Hilton: It's not just the past, it's been dreadful lately, and you've been saying alarming things about killing us all.
>
> Wendy: *(Shouting)* That's outrageous, as if I would ever hurt Stephen. He's calling me a murderer.
>
> JB: But you did say those things and Hilton is still reeling from them.
>
> Wendy: Well, I've been able to make a complete flip and leave all that behind me, so I don't want to dwell on it anymore. It needs to be positive from here. I'm sick of sessions where nothing gets resolved.

Wendy, unable to accept her destructiveness, denied that it was in her. When JB confronted this, she seemed like a rejecting mother. Wendy retaliated by acting out. Hilton rang to say Wendy was refusing to attend, and that he didn't want to pressure her. JB interpreted Wendy's acting out their shared destructive feelings and Hilton's collusion: destroying therapy was safer than destroying the marriage. They both returned to the next session.

The splitting within their relationship was now mirrored in the transference. JB had resisted the splitting and attacks of the paranoid-schizoid phase.

By providing a containing space for the murderous rage and the attacks on self and others to be metabolized, JB lessened the intensity of Oedipal anxieties. Depressive integration was beginning to be possible in therapy.

Beginning of the Depressive Position

Hilton, sick of being emasculated in the relationship, had moved out. After two weeks he returned home, because he was concerned by the level of Wendy's despair. Wendy, buoyed, came to the next session with a written list of conditions titled, "How the relationship can best work." Wendy's conditions were a manic attempt at controlling the object of her desire.

Wendy: Can I go on and read my list of conditions?
Hilton: I'd rather read them later, so I can think about my responses to them.
Wendy: *(Frustrated, to JB)* Well, can I put forward my conditions?
JB: With you giving conditions and Hilton making responses, we wouldn't collaborate in thinking together. Perhaps you still feel I am doing a poor job, so you have to take over, like when your sister was born.
Wendy: Oh, this is hopeless. You are biased to Hilton. It's always my stuff, never his. I'm not coming here anymore. I'd be prepared to go and talk to someone else, but this is stupid. Nothing has changed, it's only gotten worse. Hilton has been extremely depressed for months now.
Hilton: I feel like I've been doing a lot of changing. It's hard to be in touch with feelings and not be depressed, but I feel more than I've felt before, and I thought that was what you wanted. And you have been extremely depressed, too.
Wendy: How do I know you won't go off again with somebody else? That could change everything.

During this phase Wendy wanted to be sexual with Hilton, who could not respond. However, when Hilton was sexually motivated, Wendy would get angry, because she felt that he just wanted sex, not closeness. The exciting and rejecting poles of the object relationships oscillated between the couple. Their sexual desire rarely coincided, and when it did it had a manic quality that denied their mutual depression and hostility. Sex was a way of possessing the other by fusion, thus denying the loss of the idealized relationship. For them, sex was not a meeting of two separate individuals.

Working Through to the Depressive Position: Anger Projected at the Therapist, and Mourning the Idealized Marriage, and the Maternal Grandfather

Wendy secretly commenced weekly individual psychotherapy and antidepressants. Hilton began to utilize the couple therapy space effectively, but

Wendy claimed that he talked so openly only in therapy. Her mistrust of him intensified, and she got angry with JB, the good therapist, as if she were a rival wife. Wendy turned away from the marriage, and the therapy, and became obsessed with buying a house, a symbol of the lost marriage.

Hilton: *(to JB)* Wendy saw a financial planner yesterday. *(To Wendy)* Later, when we talked about it, you gave me a barrage about overspending. The fact is I don't spend much. And I still believe the finances are all right.

Wendy: I don't believe you. You've lied to my face about the affair and about money. We're eating into capital. The debt has gone up steadily every year.

Hilton: I've asked you not to accuse me of lying.

Wendy: Well, you've fucked up everything good and proper.

JB: I think the "everything" you refer to is your dream house. Hilton thought he could fund this eight years ago when he was working like a maniac. Part of you, Wendy, was very happy to accept this offer. Now Hilton has cut his workload down to be more available to you. And you have known about the increasing debt, you have mentioned it before. Despite this neither of you has budgeted. I am wondering here about a need on both your parts to deny the losses you have had. Perhaps the house represents that for you, Wendy, and Hilton also finds it difficult to let go of the dream, to admit he can't give you that right now.

Wendy: *(Crying)* I wanted to plan eight years ago. It could have been different. I only want a house to live in.

Hilton: I am prepared to renegotiate all our financial decisions. How would you propose we proceed? You like expensive restaurants . . .

Wendy: *(Interjecting)* I won't have you put that onto me. *(Referring to Hilton taking his mistress out)* I haven't been to the most expensive restaurants in the city for lunch.

JB: Well, I think that you both like nice restaurants. And why wouldn't you? However, this is connected to the previous idea—overspending to mask loss. You have both shared a fantasy of a good providing father, who makes all things possible. And now you share bad feelings because this fantasy is fading.

Wendy: *(Crying)*.

JB: And if I'm not mistaken, Wendy, it's the anniversary of your father's death.

Wendy: *(Crying)* Yes, we went to the cemetery on Sunday.

JB: I recall you didn't have time to grieve properly. And Hilton said Wendy's father was more like a father than his own.

Hilton: Yes, that's true.

JB: So you both have lost a good father, someone you both wanted Hilton to be like, and you lost your good relationship before Stephen was born. There has been a great deal of grief, and since you didn't understand the source of these bad feelings between you, you felt persecuted by them.

Wendy: *(Crying)*.

Hilton: *(Emotionally)* Thank you, that feels important.

The couple's collusive manic defense against loss has become clear. Hilton overspent due to his investment in being the idealized husband. Wendy could have budgeted, but wanted to be indulged. When they stopped blaming each other, they began to understand their own contributions to their shared predicament, and the stuck cycle of mutual recriminations shifted. All that the death of Wendy's father represented—the loss of their shared fantasy of an idealized parent—could be thought about.

CONCLUSION

This clinical example shows a fragile couple relationship operating at narcissistic, autistic-contiguous, and paranoid-schizoid levels as the couple deals with the challenge of adding a baby to their twosome, and then with the destructive impact of the husband's affair. In relation to the therapist as a new edition of the challenging "third," the couple becomes able to operate more consistently at the depressive position. The therapist works with the partners' resistances and transferences to her, and this enables the couple to give up their shared manic defense, acknowledge their shared delusion, and so reach the possibility of a more objective and satisfying shared reality.

II

COUPLE THERAPY

Introduction to Part 2: Couple Therapy

The infant's cry for the mother reverberates in the mind of the adult the infant has become. The adult manages the distress of this internal infant by holding and containment in identification with the mothering person's love. Normal adaptation is skewed when the mother is not attuned and the self in adulthood is not mature. Then when that adult is ready for marriage, he or she looks for a spouse who can provide the attunement and understanding that was not found in the mother, but often ends up with a spouse who is similarly unresponsive to emotional cues. The infant in the adult continues crying unheard and unresponded to. Then annihilatory anxiety calls for defenses that challenge the security and intimacy of the couple's relationship and the adjustment of their children.

The children introject their version of the parents' way of relating, and even as adults, create a fighting sibling pair to keep their attachment to their parents, even after their parents are divorced and relating happily to other spouses. Older siblings of crying infants whose cries are attended to empathically may feel in touch with their own satisfactory early experience, but if they feel painfully excluded from their parents' intimate relationship, they are more likely to feel excluded, envious, or jealous. This feeling of being left out of the sexual couple or the nursing couple creates a major vulnerability if it is imported into the couple relationship.

Couples and families defend themselves against annihilatory and Oedipal anxieties in various ways: merging to avoid mutual rejection, avoiding intimacy, projecting badness into a child, using a spouse as a mother substitute not a wife, feeling depressed, inhibiting sexual pleasure, overspending, abuse, affairs, false allegations of abuse against spouse or child, and, when all else fails, divorce.

Part 2 opens with two chapters by David and Jill Scharff of Washington D.C. and Yolanda de Varela of Panamá, which return to basics as a starting point for the chapters that follow. David Scharff and Yolanda de Varela orient the reader to the model of couple therapy and illustrate it through close inspection of a session. Jill Scharff and Yolanda de Varela show how the object relations approach differs from a more phenomenological one. Together these opening chapters provide a shared clinical experience in which to ground the elaborations in subsequent chapters.

Chris Clulow of England expands the concepts on adult attachment, spawned by John Bowlby's groundbreaking child attachment theory, by applying it to couple therapy. He applies findings concerning the infant's sense of presence and absence of the mother to understand a couple's behavior at times of reunion after separation experienced in therapy.

Attachment theory is also featured in the chapter by Sondra Goldstein and Susan Thau. They use attachment theory to conceptualize their approach to couples. They give vignettes from couple therapy to show the techniques of maintaining a state of attunement, providing a secure base, recognizing nonverbal signals of unconscious associations, and processing emotionally charged interactions. Their approach teaches couples to apply research findings on attachment and entrainment to understand and normalize their couple dynamics and so relieve guilt and shame when they take responsibility for personal contributions to the quality of their relationship.

But many analysts are not comfortable with couple therapy. Richard Zeitner, a training and supervising analyst of the American Psychoanalytic Association, catalogues the many conscious and unconscious factors that operate against analysts' learning how to do analytic couple therapy. He argues for the value of couple therapy as a useful extension of individual analysis and a valid analytic methodology in itself.

The Italian analysts Anna Maria Nicolò, Diana Norsa, and Teresa Carratelli need no persuading of the value of analytic work with couples. In their exposition of dreams reported in couple therapy, they show how dreams not only communicate multiple aspects of couples' selves and the state of their relationship but also introduce a third element into the transference, as the couple works toward the possibility of re-creating a loving bond.

Jim Poulton, Chris Norman, and Merritt Stites also introduce a third element in couple therapy technique. From the field of intersubjectivity they draw the concept of cotransference. This term describes what happens in the dynamic between therapist and individual patient, and it can be equally useful in conceptualizing what happens between a couple and their therapist. Poulton and his colleagues describe the construction of *the analytic third, intersubjective processes,* and *cotransferences* in the complex interactions between the partners of a couple and between the couple and the therapist, and illustrate their ideas in a clinical example of a couple therapy that had a less than optimal outcome.

One of the interferences with re-creation of a loving bond is the influence of narcissism. Healthy narcissism is important for good self-esteem, but excessive narcissism produces omnipotence, a need to be special, and disregard for the feelings of others that lead to tremendous problems in marriage. Jill Scharff and Carl Bagnini describe the impact of narcissistic pathology in severe cases and they propose that narcissistic issues lie at the heart of all marital difficulties. Walt Ehrhardt shows how sexual fantasy and actual affairs are narcissistic individual defenses against the demands of being in a couple. In addition, a narcissistic collusion of the partners bedevils the establishment of intimacy—unless it is interpreted successfully in couple therapy.

The couple link may be maintained but not in a loving way. The tie to the bad object is particularly durable. Using the movie *The Night Porter,* Hugh Joffe from Australia looks at the sadomasochistic bond that persists (after liberation) between a concentration camp inmate and the prison guard who had made her his lover.

Now that society is more accepting of, or at least more open about, homosexual unions, therapists are beginning to write about the problems of gay and lesbian couples. Their issues are different, especially in terms of the political and social challenges they face, but what we know of unconscious factors that create turbulence for heterosexual couples applies to homosexual couples as well. Susanne Iasenza describes "peer marriages"—those gay, lesbian, and heterosexual couples who live and work together amicably as best friends but with little or no sexual life—and illustrates an approach that goes beyond traditional behavioral sex therapy techniques to explore the antisexual impact of early family relations.

Sexual difficulties that accompany marital distress reflect a couple's internal object relations. Norma Caruso demonstrates an object relations model of treatment of sexual and marital dysfunction that goes beyond behavioral sex therapy by centering on understanding couples' internal object relations, focusing on the return of the repressed, and making extensive use of countertransference.

Opposites do attract, and with greater opportunities for international travel and work abroad in the global economy, more marriages are now exogamous. But compatibility at one level may bring together two people who do not fully appreciate one another's culture and its influence on their lives. Joan Soncini elaborates the issues faced by partners who suffer from cultural value conflicts because they are of different nationality, race, and religion, and she emphasizes special considerations regarding their couple therapy.

Couple therapy rarely lasts as long as individual analysis. Some couples work in an open-ended format but others give the therapist and the couple relationship only a limited investment of time. For them, we need an effective short-term format. Mike Stadter and David Scharff adapt the object relations approach used in individual brief therapy to work with couples and families.

Not all couple therapies end with the couple relationship intact. Sometimes a therapist is called upon to help a couple secure a good divorce, or at least understand their contributions to the failure of their marriage so that they can each proceed to healthier relationships instead of repeating the old mistakes. Carl Bagnini gives examples of hatred, splitting, and ambivalence in divorcing couples in which an older woman is left against her will, a younger woman leaves to differentiate, and one woman's obsessive longing for a child and another's insistence on forgiveness destroy two marriages.

Yolanda de Varela from Panamá points out the destructive effect on the intimate life of a couple when they create need-gratifying primitive dyads in which the partners deal with one another as parental substitutes for the lost loves of childhood instead of coupling with the adult partner in the here and now. She shows how analyzing their projection of desire onto their therapist can relieve the impasse and allow the unhealthy dyad to evolve into a mature couple. The book ends with hope for the couple relationship.

17

A Clinical Introduction to Couple Therapy

David E. Scharff and Yolanda de Varela

Object relations couple therapy integrates in-depth individual dynamics with a systemic understanding of couples and the larger family. It stresses the intergenerational origins of development, and the centrality of relationships. The couple has an overarching relational personality that contributes to the evolution of each individual. Their relationship lies within the system of the larger family that includes children or aging parents and extends to the social groups in which the couple and family exist. We believe this way of thinking provides the most in-depth way of understanding—and of intervening with—couples, both within the larger ecological situations in which they live, and in relation to the partners' individual issues.

Object relations therapy is centered on the relationship between the partners, considering both their patterns of interaction and the contributions of each individual. We focus on helping the couple achieve the level of function appropriate to their stage in life (for instance, when they are newly wed, becoming parents, or facing retirement) and the intimacy that they seek—rather than on symptom relief alone.

Object relations theory builds on the work of Ronald Fairbairn (1952), a Scottish psychoanalyst who modified analytic theories of development from the drive-centered, linear thinking of Freud and created a cybernetic view of psychic structure with internal parts in dynamic relation, in keeping with the general systems theory developing in the late 1950s. He proposed that the need for relationships is more important to children and adults, rather than for gratification as Freud had proposed. The child, centered on the mother (or other primary caretaker), inevitably experiences dissatisfaction because no mother can be perfectly attuned. The infant internalizes (or introjects) the image of the mother in order to get control of the pain of rejection, but now experiences similar hurt inside that resembles the external relationship. Then the child performs a second set of defensive mental functions, splitting off the painful part of the mother—not the mother herself, but an internal image that is now the internal object of the infant's longing, love, hate, or interest. Once this painful internal object is split off from the main core object, it is repressed, put out of central awareness because it is too painful to be kept conscious. Splitting and repression continue unconsciously, powered by the main core of the self known as the Central Ego. However, it is not possible to repress just the object. A part of the ego that is in internal relationship to the painful part-object is also split off and repressed, and the relationship between ego part and object part is marked and given meaning by the affects that characterize it, in this case the affects of pain, anger, sorrow, and frustration. This constitutes the rejecting internal object relationship.

At the other end of the continuum is what Fairbairn called "the need exciting object relationship" or "exciting object" for short. The mother who overstimulates, overfeeds, anxiously hovers, or is sexually seductive evokes in the infant unsatisfiable, painful neediness. The infant takes in, splits off, and represses an image of the experience of this tantalizing mother, and splits off the part of the self that longs for her, constructing an internal relationship marked affectively by unrequited longing, unsatisfiable desire, and frustration.

These two classes of unconscious object relationships (exciting and rejecting) feel bad to the child. The more conscious relationship between the Central Ego and its Ideal (or Good-Enough Object) is characterized by fuller, acceptable feelings stemming from experiencing the satisfaction of desire and its regulation by acceptable limits in relationships.

These six internal structures (shown in figure 17.1) are the parts of a dynamic organization. The antilibidinal object constellation attacks and secondarily represses the libidinal (desiring) constellation as it presses to be reconnected with the Central Ego. That means it is easier to hate someone than to long for them in a situation that will never give satisfaction. Some couples fight so fiercely that we wonder why they stay together. They do so because their unsatisfiable libidinal longing for each other is further buried from awareness by an attack by the antilibidinal or rejecting ego. Likewise, a sugar-sweet, cloying couple can leave therapists feeling annoyed when they use libidinal, exciting relationships to further disguise the rejecting antilibidinal system.

Figure 17.1 gives an overview of Fairbairn's model of psychic organization and its internal dynamic quality.

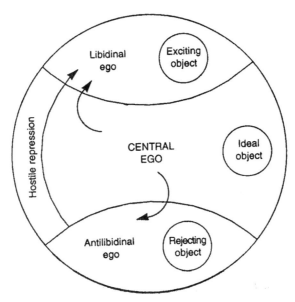

Figure 17.1.   Fairbairn's model of psychic organization

The central ego in relation to the ideal object is in conscious interaction with the caretaker (or spouse). The central ego represses the split-off libidinal aspects of its experience of others along with corresponding parts of the ego and accompanying affects that remain unconscious. The libidinal system is further repressed by the antilibidinal system. © David Scharff, reprinted by permission Jason Aronson/ Rowman & Littlefield.

Example: Dennis and Christie

Dennis, forty-three, called asking for an urgent appointment on the point of divorce after an eight-year marriage. Christie, forty-two, was fed up with his verbal abuse, and now Dennis had pushed her. Dennis was scared that Christie had gone mad and might walk out.

Christie represents alternately both the exciting and fearful internal object for Dennis as he craves and then attacks her. Dennis represents an internal rejecting object for Christie. She longs for him but immediately experiences him as a persecutory object and rejects him. Their relationship reproduces individual internal issues in their interaction, producing a joint personality that is fearfully dominated by their shared rejecting object relations.

A THEORY OF UNCONSCIOUS COMMUNICATION

In order to make an object relations theory of individual development applicable to conjoint therapy, we need a theory of unconscious communication.

Melanie Klein (1946), a Hungarian analyst who developed the Kleinian school in London, coined the term "projective identification" for the way a person evacuates part of the mind into another in order to rid the self of excessive anger or other unacceptable, dangerous elements. We now believe that all persons in intimate relationships use projective identification not only to protect themselves, but also to communicate in depth (J. Scharff 1992). Infants put unthought feelings, needs, and fears into their mother through bodily gestures, vocal intonation, and subtle eye movements. The mother takes in these communications through *introjective identification*— through resonance with her own internal object organization, thereby joining with the infant's experience. Her past experience of distress, fear, or happiness lets her understand the infant's experience. The experience of getting to know each other occurs through endless iterations of these cycles of projective and introjective identification, which also go on in both directions: The mother also puts her anxieties about being a mother into the infant, who identifies and, if things are going well, projects back reassurance. In infancy, the quality of these interactions is the major component in determining the security of the infant's attachment to the parents (Fonagy et al. 2003). In adulthood, these cycles are equally important and more reciprocal. Couples engage continuously in cycles of projective and introjective identification that are by nature largely profoundly unconscious. Therapy makes these matters more conscious so that a couple has new choices about how to relate.

Figure 17.2 shows the cycle of projective and introjective identification between a mother and infant. This cycle could equally well be between spouses. The infant unconsciously seeks an exciting object identification with the mother, for example by crying for more to eat, but meets a rejecting object when she refuses, and identifies with the rejecting object. Rejecting the infant's excess neediness enlarges the infant's rejecting object constellation.

Example: Mutual Projective Identification

Dennis came from a prominent family whose secret is his mother's illegitimacy. Raised by her father, she refused to acknowledge her mother, and rejected her mother-in-law, too. Dennis grew up longing for his mother's exiled mother. In this way Dennis unconsciously experienced his mother's hatred of her mother-in-law as a reaction to her repressed longings for her mother. The unexpressed longing hidden beneath her hatred came through as though it were his longing for the mother she could not be.

Christie was the youngest of four girls. Her parents, married to others, met in a celebrated, scandalous affair. Disinherited and banned socially, they escaped to Europe where their first child was born before they could get divorces. Years later, and three children later, they married while Christie's mother was carrying her.

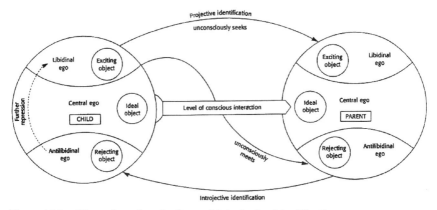

Figure 17.2. The action of projective and introjective identification

The mechanism here is the interaction of the child's projective and introjective identifications with the parent as the child meets frustration, unrequited yearning, or trauma. (The same situation could apply to two adult partners.) The diagram depicts the child longing to have his needs met and identifying with similar trends in the parent via projective identification. The child meeting with rejection identifies with the frustration of the parent's own antilibidinal system via introjective identification. In an internal reaction to this frustration, the libidinal system is further repressed by the renewed force of the child's antilibidinal system. © 1982 David Scharff, reprinted by permission Jason Aronson/Rowman & Littlefield.

In a system of mutual projective identification, the couple replays both kinds of repressed bad objects described by Fairbairn, living out in their relationship both the longing and rejection they absorbed from their parents during painful childhoods in emotionally impoverished families.

HOLDING AND CONTAINMENT

The mother-infant relationship is marked by two processes central to couple therapy. The first, psychological *holding*, is analogous to the way a parent holds a child in an "arms around" attitude in order to provide for safety, growth, and development. We call this the *contextual relationship*. Within this envelope of safety, the parent offers herself in a focused eye-to-eye relationship that is subjectively I-to-I, that is, a direct communication of the intimate couple's inner feelings and inner worlds. The mother is also the object of the child's love, hate, and interest, and the child uses her to fashion an internal world of internal objects in the *direct* or *focused relationship*. As the infant spends less time in the parent's arms, a space opens between infant and parent that we call the "transitional space" because it mediates between the inner and outer world of both parent and child and between the contextual and focused aspects of the relationship (Winnicott 1951; Scharff and Scharff 1991). Figure 17.3 forms a conceptual basis for our use of transference and countertransference in couple therapy.

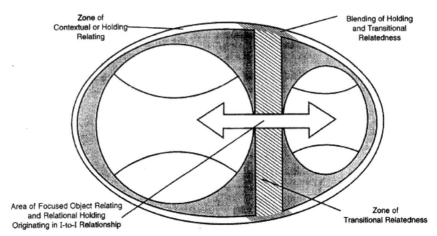

Figure 17.3. Contextual holding, the transitional space, and focused relating

Focused (or centered or I-to-I) relating occurs in and across the transitional space. The transitional space is in contact with both contextual relating and focused relating, and is also the zone which blends the two. © 1991 D. Scharff and J. S. Scharff, reprinted by permission Jason Aronson/ Rowman & Littlefield.

Example: Holding

I found that Dennis and Christie's capacity for holding was severely compromised. In the first three years of weekly treatment, progress was slow, largely because they could not hold themselves psychologically. It was difficult for me to get in a word, as they spilled out details of dreadful interactions without any effort at thinking or at analyzing the consequences for each other. They only slowly allowed me to demonstrate their mutual projective identifications and their individual defenses and anxieties.

I said, "Dennis, I have come to feel that when you shout at Christie, you are secretly feeling she has rejected and wounded you. If you understood and said that, she might be more sympathetic." Christie nodded vigorously.

This interpretation produced relief from their shared persecutory objects, and, as if waking from a trance, they began to see each other differently. The problem was that I became an exciting object who represented the hope that now tantalized them because it seemed unattainable. All possibility seemed to reside in me, not in the couple's own potential for understanding. A shift to twice-weekly therapy improved the holding. They started to bring dreams and beginning attempts at analysis.

A concept closely related to holding is *containment* (Bion 1970) in which the mother accepts the child's projective identifications unconsciously and allows them to resonate with her own internal object relations, understanding them intuitively through her maturity and tolerance of anxiety. Bion called this unconscious process the parent's *reverie*. Then the mother feeds the altered mental contents back to the child, through her own projective identification, and the child experiences mental growth. Similarly, therapists constantly have to tolerate couples' fears. Often, we do this through conscious thinking, but mostly it happens through unconscious resonance and understanding. In the growth of the individual, containment occurs through continuous, mutual cycles of projective and introjective identification, forming the basis of both the child's mental growth and the parent's maturation. The child's mind itself is therefore a product of personal interaction. In neurobiology, Schore (2003 a and b) has described the *entrainment* of unconscious cycles of communication between infants' and mothers' right brains (where emotion is processed) during the first eighteen months of life. The rapid reading of facial gestures, vocalization, and shifts of body position are decoded instantaneously as parent and child read each other's emotional states. These processes happen rapidly and continuously below the level of conscious understanding. They color everything else that happens in infancy, and throughout life. Couples provide unconscious containment for each other while also relating consciously. In therapy we also receive constant signals from the couples we see, most importantly affective signals we process unconsciously, as we make unconscious understanding conscious, first to ourselves, then in work with the couples. We give verbal and emotional meaning to experience. We use our reverie to make things thinkable that were previously unthinkable because they were rooted in early experience, in their bodies, or were too frightening to locate anywhere.

Example: Unconscious Containment

Dennis came to a session upset at Christie's unladylike dancing and her absurd love for ethnic music. What kind of example is she giving to their young daughter—who, by the way, is more feminine than Christie?

I saw the humiliation in Christie's face as she screamed that she was tired of this abuse.

Dennis appealed to me, "Look how she's, like, crazy. Please calm her down." He had no conscious awareness that his own anxiety had fueled hers. It was only when she shouted at him that he became anxious, as if anxiety had arisen only in reaction to her.

I felt invaded by their anger, not understanding (in identification with Christie's confusion) what it was that Dennis wanted from her. It seemed to me that her dancing was a spontaneous expression of vitality that he attacked, scared of the sensuality that others admired. He must have been carrying an identification with his own mother, scared of people finding out about his family's sexual past.

Identifying unconsciously with his mother, Dennis projects this hated identification into Christie, thereby trying to control the sexually exciting object part of his self in her. On her side, Christie feels rejected and humiliated through identification with her mother. Between them, they share a need to protect many painful internalized objects.

Once I processed this formulation silently, I was able to help them see it, too. It immediately brought more insight to the sessions.

ATTACHMENT

Henry Dicks (1967) began the process of putting together a depth psychology of interaction by combining the ideas of Fairbairn on the relational organization of mind with Klein's theory of projective identification. Adding the ideas of Winnicott and Bion has augmented the theoretical support for this approach.

Recent developments in attachment theory (Bowlby 1979, Clulow 2000, Fonagy et al. 2003) augment the ways we describe the bond between infants and parents, and between couples. The classification of infants' attachment to their mothers is based on a research procedure called the "strange situation" in which the infant's response to separation from the mother is coded by looking at the infant's behavior when the mother returns. Infants are classed as (1) secure (goes to mother, may protest, but uses her well), (2) ambivalently insecure (alternates clinging and angry protest), (3) distancing-insecure (walks away from mother, avoids her), or (4) disoriented and disorganized (darts away from the mother, then toward her, looks at her furtively and looks away, a pattern that shows fear in response to her) (Ainsworth et al. 1978; Main and Solomon 1986).

Recent work by Main and her colleagues (Main and Goldwyn 1991) has allowed us to describe adult attachment styles in a similar way using a structured interview about the person's development and family. The interviewers are coded by the style of language in the narrative, not by the content of the story of development. The best predictor of an infant's attachment style is the attachment classification of the parent (true even if that style has been tested *before* the infant's birth), giving our first research evidence of intergenerational transmission of internal object relations. Attachment styles are mediated by each person's internal object set. Fonagy and coworkers (2003) have studied how the mothers teach infants to "mentalize" experience, to grow understanding of other persons' mental states facilitated or hampered by the attachment process. Similarly, adult couples are either secured in a relationship of mutual understanding, or are impeded by their insecure attachment status, a situation studied clinically by researchers of attachment in couple therapy (Clulow 2000).

Example: Styles of Attachment

Christie and Dennis's attachment styles are expressed during the times Christie visits her family in Europe. Prior to her trips, they become abusive to each other and threaten each other with divorce.

Dennis's attachment is ambivalent-insecure. He could never separate from his mother, because of his concern for her depression and emotional deadness. He often tried to anger her to bring her to life. Now he relates similarly to Christie, requiring instant satisfaction of his needs. When she often fails, he angrily distances from her. Then he cannot tolerate being away from her, but he makes sure she understands that he is never satisfied with her. Thus he re-creates the unsatisfying relationship to his depressed inner mother. Failing to understand this impact on Christie, he remains childishly centered on reject-ing her, even though he triggers the very rejection he fears. He has a limited capacity to reflect both on her state of mind and his own.

Christie's style is primarily dismissive-insecure. Her happy early childhood was abruptly destroyed when her father got into serious debt. The continual threat of being thrown out of their house was due not so much to lack of income as to the way her father failed to pay the bills. They were not so much poor as irresponsible. When the parents withdrew from the children in their own preoccupation, Christie learned to do for herself. Although her style of attachment corresponds to the dismissive-insecure classification, she also shows clinging and fearful insecurities that alternate with feeling more secure. When things are difficult, she does not allow herself to feel need, but walks away from situations she interprets as rejecting. When Dennis tries to engage her through angry blaming, she often turns her back, leaving him more frus-trated and seeking to cling to her.

SEXUALITY

Sexuality plays a central role of the *psychosomatic partnership* that ties psy-chological relating to bodily intimacy in adolescent and adult love relations (D. E. Scharff 1982). Marital therapists need a working knowledge of the role of physical sexuality in adolescence, in partner choice, in the maintenance or breakdown of marriage, and in the ways children both draw on the parents' sexual bond and impinge on it. For many couples, a specific focus on sexual difficulty requires that therapists switch to sex therapy or refer to a colleague who is proficient in sex therapy. We recommend all therapists learn about sexual development and the dynamics of sexuality (Kaplan 1974, Scharff 1982, Scharff and Scharff 1991, Levine, Risen and Althof 2003).

Example: Sexuality

When Dennis and Christie are on good terms, they enjoy sex. But when Christie refuses, Dennis often talks about other attractive women. Christie reacts by further distancing.

Christie says she does not like anal intercourse, which Dennis pushes for. He does not understand her refusal, since she sometimes suggests it. She says she does it to please him, but she resents it, as when he surprises her by inserting his finger in her anus during intercourse.

Dennis's desires de-repress her fantasies of anal sex, childhood fantasies that were stimulated by memories of pornographic print materials featuring anal sex, which were left around the house by her father while she was growing up. Combined with the painful memories of her mother's social ostracism, this makes her feel like a prostitute when Dennis requests anal sex.

Discussion of the family history of these matters led to increased understanding and an enhanced capacity to differentiate their situation from the one with Christie's father. She decided that she could tolerate Dennis's finger in her anus during intercourse if he would warn her, but that she could not tolerate anal intercourse. With my help, he was able to understand why and move to a position of feeling they could have a good sexual life without it.

When we see couples from varying ethnic and cultural backgrounds, we look for similarities of pattern extending from the culture, to the social group, the extended family group, the nuclear family, the couple, and the individual. We look to the partners to inform us about their cultural differences, and to work with us toward understanding of those matters as much as toward understanding their individual and couple dynamics. This is true with couples of any ethnicity, even when one of the partners appears to share our own culture. We must let their experience penetrate us, and open ourselves to sharing their in-depth experience in order to let our therapeutic reverie help them with culturally saturated projective identifications and interactions. (See chapter 29.)

CLINICAL TECHNIQUE

We have many functions in mind while working with couples, but relatively few specific techniques. Object relations theory is principally a way of working together with couples toward understanding and growth. The major functions are:

1. Management of the Space within a Frame

We do not tell a couple what to do, but we work to maintain a psychological space in which they can tell their story and work on their conflicts. This therapeutic activity is analogous to the environmental provision the parent offers the infant for safety and space to grow. To this end we offer regularity of boundaries and conditions, fee, times of meeting, length of sessions, and other logistical matters that provide the consistency to frame a reliable psychological space within which we work.

Initially, it was difficult to hold Dennis. Even though a steady frame of work had been established through setting up regular appointments, and beginning and ending on time, his anxious insecurity was expressed by his frequent urgent phone calls to me, trying to stay past the end of the sessions, and, sometimes, even appearing at my office between sessions. Slowly, he internalized the regularity and continuity of the appointments, and adapted to the frame I offered.

2. Management of the Environment

Within the frame, we do not tell patients what to do, where to sit, whether to face each other, or what to say. We ask them to work with us in an environment in which unspeakable things can be voiced and difficult matters can gradually be tolerated and then understood. It is up to us to manage the holding environment—analogous to the parents' ongoing environmental provision for the child through the years—and then to work toward the understanding that is the analogue of the parents' in-depth understanding. We also want to assess the couple's developmental level of function and note if it is appropriate to their current age and stage in the life cycle. We assess whether there are deficits preventing them from adjusting to what is required of them at their stage in life and whether they cling to old dysfunctional patterns out of fear of change and growth. Developmental levels will change over time and often will oscillate within a session.

At first, it seemed that Dennis had more difficulty dealing with emotion than Christie. He was frightened of expressing sadness, and it was easier for both of them to fight than to cry. But as the sessions evolved, it was Dennis who first started to bring scraps of his own history. One session, he broke down crying. He immediately rose from his seat and went to stand by the window, hiding his tears. Christie laughed at him for crying. Containing my own feelings about her reaction, I tried to make sense of it in such a way that both could feel contained. The incident was a defensive replay of early experience. Being the only boy, Dennis was expected to behave like a strong, emotionless man. His family made fun of his tears. Christie's seemingly heartless reaction came from fear. In the session, she had suddenly seen in Dennis her father's vulnerability. To avoid the danger of an unreliable man, she laughed to distance herself from danger.

3. We Demonstrate Our Ways of Working

We encourage communication and tolerant listening toward developing the couple's capacity for reverie and in-depth understanding. We want our own reverie and that of each partner to be a receptive space in which each partner may speak and be heard. We do not ask for genograms or a set history, but look for the object relations histories at moments of affective intensity. Then we ask, "What was it like growing up?" when certain issues are stirred up. For instance, if a couple argues about one keeping the other waiting, we ask what it was like for each of them growing up around this issue. That way we get a living history connected to the session's here-and-now. We value slips of the tongue as clues to unexpressed ambivalence, just as in individual therapy. We ask for dreams from both partners. We do not ask "What does the dream mean?" but we help the couple to unpack the condensed dream images by letting each of them associate freely to the dream images and affects. Dreams in couple therapy belong to the couple and to the therapy process itself, not to the individual.

Christie's defensive facade was unmasked by working on recurrent dreams. In them, she was falling from an airplane or a bridge, looking desperately for something to hang on to. In one dream, her mother was falling with her. We came to see that these represented the anxiety that led to her distancing behavior that gave Dennis, too, the feeling of not having someone to hang on to.

4. Tracking the Affect

Within each session we follow the fluctuations in emotion. These shifts in color and intensity let us know when we are in the territory of an excited or rejecting repressed relationship, and note defensive shifts between differing organizations accompanied by heightened anger, sadness, fear, or arousal.

Christie's intense anger was the frequent clue to her more painful longing for her father. Her chronic difficulty working through losses led her to take on busily taking care of others so as to avoid her own sadness. I pointed out this maneuver frequently before she began to recognize it herself.

5. Noticing Bodily Signals

Some of the most profound or traumatic issues are only sensed by observation of somatic cues, either in the couple or, because of projective identification, at times in the therapist. Noting when one of the partners is ill, has muscle soreness, or is sleepy can lead to deeply buried issues. Similarly, noting physical expressions of the therapist's responses during sessions can indicate that the therapist is resonating with profound, traumatic memories.

Christie uses an IUD and therefore has bloody spotting between periods. She does not want more children, but she does not want a tubal ligation. She wants Dennis to have a vasectomy. Dennis refuses, being clear about the body-damage anxiety that this request stirs up in him. Christie has the same fear. She refuses surgery because, if they got divorced, he could have more children, but she could not.

Meanwhile, her bleeding is an excuse to curtail intercourse. Dennis says she is punishing him. She answers that he knows what he has to do. Here we see how the undercutting of each other expands concretely from affects and verbal communication to the physical arena.

6. Giving Feedback

We give feedback in many ways, an activity we generally group under the category of *making interpretations*. We give support or advice because sometimes couples can use it, particularly parenting advice. But these are not the engines that drive object relations therapy. All our activities are aimed at improving the couple's capacity for thinking cognitively and emotionally. At the simple end, we observe things the couple has not noticed. We link two or more events that belong together, or underscore something the couple has not appreciated. In the more complex levels of understanding and explanation, we construct narrative hypotheses of the partners' individual development, which have contributed to patterns in which they are stuck, and we interpret bodily symptoms and messages in terms of the memories encoded in them, and so develop a picture of the couple's unconscious assumptions that power conscious behaviors. Finally, we work from their transferences to each other and their shared transference to us, in order to understand underlying unconscious issues.

Christie's periodic visits to her sisters in Europe were always a cause for fighting, Dennis thinking that she preferred to be out at some bar or dancing with them and their friends, while he was at home with the children and the bills. He maintained that Christie's sisters always try to convince her she would be better off without him. For many years, to avoid an extended fight, Christie worsened the situation by waiting until a week before her trip to announce it. After a while, they agreed on some conditions for these trips, although Dennis still got upset.

By linking how Dennis felt and how Christie avoided the issue, I showed them the dynamic: These trips remind Dennis of his sisters' ruthless teasing of him as his father's favorite to which he had responded by hiding in his room doing his homework. Now he imagines Christie plotting against him with her sisters, leaving him alone again, doing his (and their) homework.

Nonanalytic therapists criticize object relations therapists for relying on interpretation. They think that object relations therapy is too focused on the emotional, and too weak an instrument to achieve change. For us, interpretation is the analogue to the way a mother speaks to her child about what is happening and conveys to her infant that she is working to understand. While she does not always get things right, the process of working together toward understanding builds a relationship of mutual concern and signifies continuing containment. In therapy, showing the couple that we are working with them cements our alliance, encourages them to work, and facilitates the unconscious right-brain resonance that carries the emotional side of the work.

7. Working with Transference and Countertransference

Transference and countertransference form the central guidance mechanism of our work. When patients see in us aspects of their inner experience concerning both their individual object relations sets and their issues about environmental holding, we call this transference. With couples, we focus mostly on the contextual issues that convey the way the couple cannot provide holding that is adequate to the partners' needs. This is communicated to us through our own introjective identification, which we feel as our countertransference—that is, the whole range of feelings and thoughts evoked in relation to the couple. Some of these will feel benign, but the ones that give us the most important clues will feel painfully excited or rejecting.

Training, supervision, therapy, and clinical experience help therapists develop a baseline for understanding the nuances in their internal responses to couples, but even the most experienced therapist will have to analyze the situation each time. We do this by surrendering to the process of allowing countertransferences to develop in us and create discomfort in us, which is what helps us to understand the couples' experiences from inside a shared situation. Interpretation from the experience of countertransference of the couple's transferences in the here-and-now of the therapeutic session forms our most powerful tool. Constant monitoring of countertransference also acts as a Global Positioning System that informs our understanding.

Dennis had a dream: Coming home after work, he finds Christie with another man whom he beats up. Next, he is outside the house, walking around the neighborhood with me. I say he has to ask Christie for an explanation instead of jumping to conclusions. He regains control and feels better.

I said that the dream portrayed the way in which they both use me to ward

*off bad objects: I helped Dennis avoid the threat of being ignored and aban-
doned (like by his mother), or envied for what he has (like by his father). I
helped Christie with the threat of being the unfaithful woman (like her
mother) or sexually depraved (like her father).*

*Usually during sessions, I feel I have two children who need mothering.
Christie expresses the rejecting object constellation, often threatening to leave
therapy, but I do not feel animosity because I also see her intense longing.
Dennis expresses the other side, wanting to stay in therapy—the longing of
the exciting object constellation. I feel that they want me as the mother they
both longed for, but this interferes with therapy, as they cannot get better if
they want to keep me.*

*I interpreted this in a moving session. They agreed, and began to discuss
this legacy of early unfulfilled needs.*

8. Working Through

Object relations offers an in-depth, long-term approach for couples, who
typically see us for months to years. We strive to help them "work through"
their issues. They circle around to cover overlapping territory again and
again, each time using slightly different ways of addressing problem areas
from different angles, contributing slowly to building new patterns with
more adaptability. The human need for this kind of growth process makes
long-term therapy a more beneficial process than most short-term interventions.

The therapist is trained to think in depth, but sometimes long-term work
is not desired or is not called for (Stadter and Scharff 2000). Some couples
come for a single consultation, or for a few sessions, and some of them derive
considerable benefit. Some come for serial brief therapy, perhaps three to
twelve sessions at a time, returning several times over the years. The only
time short-term therapy is as effective as long-term therapy is when we are
dealing with life crises that derail the couple from a previously healthy
adjustment such as sudden illness, loss of a job, or death of a child, and normal developmental crises such as marriage and birth, which challenge them
in ways for which they are unprepared. Then a brief intervention may get
them back on track so that their normally adaptive skills take hold again.

*Both Dennis and Christie are strongly in the grip of their bad, rejecting,
and exciting internal objects. In those moments when they are able to see each
other differently, they feel lucky to have each other, but usually the potential
space collapses and they go back to criticizing and complaining. They need to
mourn the losses in their lives over and over, before they can accept their own
family as good enough.*

9. Working with Loss and Termination

Object relations therapists see loss as the most frequent issue derailing development: losses in the early life of one or both partners, or in their shared life, as in the case of loss of a child or in previous divorces (Scharff and Scharff 1994). Clinically, an opportunity to mourn comes in the separations and reunions that are intrinsic to the ending of each session. This rhythm prepares couples for the loss of the therapy and therapist at the end of therapy.

Over the years, Dennis and Christie have made many changes in the way they relate. They have considerably lessened their abusive behavior, and threats of divorce rarely come up. Dennis now tolerates Christie's taking yearly trips to her family and she has been good in sticking to their agreements. They increasingly express tenderness, and Dennis is more empathic about Christie's sexual preferences. They are ready to terminate.

Studying the anxiety of ending sessions and mourning these losses—which are often felt in the transference-countertransference exchange—is a major focus of our work, leading to the work of terminating the therapy, which centers on reviewing the course of therapy and dealing with the anxiety of proceeding without the therapist as guide.

During the termination phase, Dennis and Christie worked on re-owning their projective identifications. In the face of anxiety about going on alone, Christie fell back on holding Dennis responsible for derivatives of the corrupt sexual activities of her father and the dismissive attitude of high society. Dennis fell back on holding Christie responsible for his renewed insecurities and anxieties, and again expressed demands that she have everything ready for him to arrive, so that he did not risk finding in her once more the neglectful mother who fails to take care of him when I was not there to look out for him. Reviewing these symptoms, which recalled the beginning of our work, allowed them to mourn the therapy itself and to achieve a sad but satisfying termination.

SUMMARY

The couple's relationship is central to both nuclear and extended family organization. It is the place where individual issues come into focus and it is the foundation stone for the entire human relational system. It draws on the history of each partner to create something new from which they both draw sustenance. Difficulties in their relationship pose formidable obstacles to their continued development and to their offering a secure base for the next generation and the wider family.

As couple therapists, we draw on the various interactions that are the ways the couple relationship is played out in the session. The therapeutic relationship vitally parallels the couple's relationship as the partners re-create their difficulties in the transference-countertransference interaction. We depend most on our growing understanding derived in this way, but we also use other tools—focusing variously on a living history of the couple's internal objects evoked at times of heightened affect in sessions, examining the couple's sexuality, making use of their dreams, establishing links between apparently disparate issues and events. The multiple losses suffered by most couples warrant special attention. All of these factors combine to give object relations couple therapy poignancy and efficacy.

REFERENCES

Ainsworth, M. D. S., M. C. Blehar, E. Waters, and S. Wall. 1978. *Patterns of Attachment: A Psychological Study of the Strange Situation.* Hillsdale, NJ: Lawrence Erlbaum.

Bion, W. R. D. 1970. *Attention and Interpretation.* London: Heinemann.

Bowlby, J. 1979. *The Making and Breaking of Affectional Bonds.* London: Tavistock.

Clulow, C. 2000. *Adult Attachment and Couple Psychotherapy.* London: Brunner-Routledge.

Dicks, H. V. 1967. *Marital Tensions.* London: Routledge and Kegan Paul.

Fairbairn, W. R. D. 1952. *Psychoanalytic Studies of the Personality.* London: Routledge.

Fonagy, P., G. Gergely, E. Jurist, and M. Target. 2003. *Affect Regulation, Mentalization, and the Development of the Self.* New York: Other Press.

Kaplan, H. S. 1974. *The New Sex Therapy.* New York: Quadrangle.

Klein, M. 1946. Notes on some schizoid mechanisms. In *Envy and Gratitude and Other Works: 1946–1963*, pp. 1–24. London: Hogarth, 1975.

Levine, S. J., C. B. Risen, and S. E. Althof. 2003. *Handbook of Clinical Sexuality for Mental Health Professionals.* New York: Brunner/Routledge.

Main, M. 1995. Attachment: Overview, with implications for clinical work. In *Attachment Theory: Social, Developmental and Clinical Perspectives*, ed. S. Goldberg, R. Muir, and J. Kerr, pp. 407–75. Hillsdale, NJ: Analytic Press.

Main, M., and R. Goldwyn. 1991. *Adult Attachment Classification System, Version 5.* Berkeley: University of California Press.

Main, M., and J. Solomon. 1986. Discovery of an insecure/disorganized/disoriented attachment pattern. In *Affective Development in Infancy,* ed. T. B. Brazelton and M. W. Yogman, pp. 95–124. Norwood, NJ: Ablex.

Scharff, D. E. 1982. *The Sexual Relationship.* London: Routledge. Reprinted Northvale, NJ: Jason Aronson, 1998.

Scharff, D. E., and J. S. Scharff. 1991. *Object Relations Couple Therapy.* Northvale, NJ: Jason Aronson.

Scharff, J. S. 1992. *Projective and Introjective Identification and the Use of the Therapist's Self*. Northvale, NJ: Jason Aronson.

Scharff, J. S., and D. E. Scharff. 1994. *Object Relations Therapy of Physical and Sexual Trauma*. Northvale, NJ: Jason Aronson.

Schore, A. N. 2003a. *Affect Regulation and the Repair of the Self*. New York: Norton.

———. 2003b. *Affect Dysregulation and Disorders of the Self*. New York: Norton.

Stadter, M., and D. E. Scharff. 2000. Object relations brief therapy. In *Brief Therapy with Individuals and Couples*, ed. J. Carlson and L. Sperry, pp. 191–219. Phoenix, AZ: Zeig, Tucker and Theisen.

Winnicott, D. W. 1951. Transitional objects and transitional phenomena. In *Through Paediatrics to Psychoanalysis*, pp. 229–42. London: Hogarth, 1975.

18

Object Relations Perspective on a Phenomenological Case History

Jill Savege Scharff and Yolanda de Varela

THE TREATMENT MODEL

Object relations couple therapy is a psychodynamically oriented way of working with couples (Scharff and Scharff 1987, 1991). It derives its methods from the classical psychoanalytic principles of technique handed down from Freud, namely: following unconscious themes by listening to words, silence, and gesture; responding to unconscious material; developing insight; interpreting dreams and fantasies; and working with transference. Object relations couple therapists do not function as a blank screen in the classical analytic way, however. Instead, they are interactive with the couple, and yet, at the unconscious level, they are nondirective. This shift in stance from the classical analytic position is required by the therapeutic focus on the relationship, not on the individual, and is made possible by adopting, integrating, and applying the principles of various object relations theories, not classical Freudian theory.

These object relations theories have in common the view that a person's current relationships take shape from the structure and functioning of the unique pattern of internal relationships that were set down as the person interacted with and adapted to others early in life. Psychic structure is viewed as an internal system of relationships, an internal group that functions as a prototype, a working model of relationships, and a map of what to expect from others. This innerscape determines the choice of the partner and the nature of the couple relationship—for better or worse.

225

The couple is not simply a pair of individuals. The couple relationship is a tightly organized, closed system of interacting individual internal relationships, which are experienced in the interpersonal arena of the couple relationship in ways unique to the couple at conscious and unconscious levels. The outward manifestations of these ways of being recur often enough that the couple therapist can detect the patterns of interaction and show how they embody old ways of feeling and behaving rooted in earlier experiences with the families of origin.

Object relations couple therapists offer a therapeutic relationship that creates a *psychological holding environment* similar enough for old patterns of relating to important figures in the family of origin to be re-created, and yet different enough to allow for their detection. The couple therapist will have plenty of opportunity to *identify patterns of interaction* and, over time, to rework them. The therapist brings the capacity for listening and following, for sharing the couple's experience, for tolerating anxiety and loss, and for being different from the original figures in the life of each member of the couple. The gap between the couple's experience of the therapist as a re-edition of the early objects of their dependency, love, and aggression, and their experience of the therapist as a new object in the here and now, provides space for understanding that allows room for the couple to grow and develop in healthier ways.

To understand object relations couple therapy further we need to note the building blocks of object relations theory upon which this therapeutic method is based (J. Scharff 1989, D. Scharff 1995, J. Scharff 1995, D. Scharff and J. Scharff 1991, J. Scharff and D. Scharff 1992).

THE MAJOR CONCEPTS OF OBJECT RELATIONS THEORY AND THEIR APPLICATION TO COUPLES' RELATIONSHIP FUNCTIONING

Ronald Fairbairn (1952) challenged Freud's theory of human motivation based on instincts. Fairbairn believed that the infant was born with an ego capable of relatedness, and that there was no id full of undifferentiated impulses, as Freud had suggested. Fairbairn argued that the human infant was driven, not by sexual longing and aggressive drives, but by the need for attachment. As the infant develops a relationship, naturally there will be some frustration. A manageable amount of frustration can be coped with and in that case a relatively satisfying view of the experience is taken into the ego. Intolerable features of the relationship need to be repressed because they are too painfully rejecting or too exciting of need to be borne in consciousness. The unbearable experience is controlled by being taken inside the central ego in the form of an internal object that has then to be rejected by consciousness because it is painful. Splitting of the object into rejecting and exciting objects and their repression into unconsciousness occurs together with splitting and repression of parts of the ego that have been in relation to them (called antilibidinal and libidinal egos respectively), along with the appropriate affects of rage and longing. In this way, human experience is transformed into psychic structure through the action of introjection, splitting, and repression. Closest to consciousness lies the central internal object relationship, while the antilibidinal and libidinal internal object relationships are mostly in unconsciousness, the libidinal being the most deeply repressed of all. *The resulting personality is then a system of parts of ego, object, and affect joined in these internal object relationships, all of them in dynamic relation* (see figure 17.1, Fairbairn's view of the endopsychic situation, in chapter 17).

Donald Winnicott (1958, 1965, 1971) used the image of the nursing couple as a guide to understanding child development. The mother has two basic functions: to safeguard or hold the environment for growth (*the environmental mother*) and to be the object of the child's love and hate (*the object mother*). Similarly, in couple therapy, the couple therapist offers a psychological holding environment in which he or she can be experienced as a representative of both the holding mother and the object mother. Winnicott also said that there had been a somatic partnership between the pregnant mother and her fetus, and that at the point of birth this partnership developed into a *psychosomatic partnership* that organized the infant's psyche, and also the psyche of the mother of that infant as she related to and learned about her child. In the transitional space between mother and infant, interpersonal interaction gives rise to experience and expectations that create internal structure. We find this concept helpful, particularly when we are considering the quality of the sexual relationship in the couple. Like the nursing couple, the romantic sexual couple has a partnership with psychological meaning, heightened physical sensation, interdependence, and commitment over time in which growth and development of both parties will occur. Husband and wife relate to each other and contribute to each other's growth through the life cycle.

Melanie Klein (1946, 1975) reconstructed the child's infantile fantasy about the earliest relationship during those anxious months of infantile dependency. She suggested that the infant imagines parts of its own feelings to reside in the caretaking person so as to protect itself, the loved and needed other person, and the relationship between them from the force of the death instinct that might otherwise overpower the life instinct. She went on to say that this mechanism of displacement for which she borrowed Freud's term *projection* would be followed by a more extensive process for which she coined the term *projective identification* in which the infant misidentifies parts of the self in the other person. In projective identification the child finds a part of the self in the parent and thinks that this self-state is emanating from the parent. For instance, when aggression has been projected from the child into the parent, the child experiences the parent as aggressive. This misperceived persecutory object is then introjected and identified with so that the child's aggression is reinforced. If the mother is also available to accept projections of positive, loving feelings, by which she is colored positively, this leads to an introjection of warmth and goodness that counteracts the introjection of a persecuting object (see figure 17.2, The action of projective and introjective identification, in chapter 17).

It was Henry Dicks (1967) who first described the process of projective identification in the selection of a partner and the maintenance of the marital relationship. Dicks applied Fairbairn's concept of psychic structure and Klein's mechanism of projective identification to the marital couple. He found that each partner projects unwanted or endangered parts of the self into the spouse, leading to *a system of mutual projective identification*. The partners choose each other not just for conscious reasons of compatibility but because they offer the possibility of unconscious connection to repressed parts of the self that can be discovered in the partner. Protection of the self and the relationship is intended, and in the healthy marriage it may work that way, at least for some time. But in the unhealthy marriage, deterioration of the couple relationship results when the projective identifications are too concretely cemented or when they are rejected (see figure 18.1).

Figure 18.1 shows the wife looking to her husband to meet her need. If he meets the need, then she learns that it is all right to express the needy part of herself (her libidinal internal object relationship). If she misidentifies him as

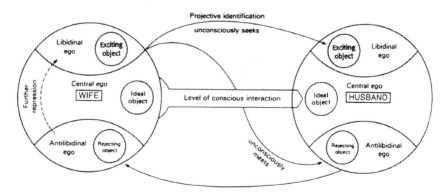

Figure 18.1.   The projective-introjective system of a marriage

Reprinted from *Clinical Handbook of Couple Therapy*, ed. N. S. Jacobson and A. Gurman, courtesy of Guilford Press; and modified from *The Sexual Relationship: An Object Relations View of Sex and the Family*, © 1982 David E. Scharff, reprinted with permission of Routledge and Kegan Paul, and Jason Aronson 2005.

nurturing at that moment, she meets a frosty response (emanating from his internal antilibidinal internal object relationship). She deals with this by introjective identification: She becomes like the rejecting object that she met in her interaction with him. She finds that it is better not to express her need, and this amplifies her internal rejecting object system. She then represses her internal libidinal object relationship as before. The projective-introjective identification system is always mutual. He has simultaneously misidentified his own needy self in his wife's approach and attacked it there to keep it from emerging to his conscious awareness. If he has less need to repress his needy self so thoroughly, he will be able to respond to the need that he finds in her. These dynamics are found in homosexual couple relationships as well, with the additional factor of gender similarity driving the projective-introjective identification system.

The partners (heterosexual or homosexual) must have a balance of unconscious communication that permits a degree of feeling of at-one-ness so that a joint personality can form from the fusion of the two intrapsychic structures, and at the same time enough separation and difference from the original objects that growth can occur in the couple context. Understanding and interpreting the mutual projective and introjective identificatory system of the couple relationship is the basis of the therapeutic action of object relations couple therapy.

Wilfred Bion (1959, 1962, 1967) applied Kleinian theory to his study of groups. He noted that projective identification occurs between the group and the leader in which some individuals are drawn to create an unacknowledged subgroup operating not in pursuit of the group task but in hopes of meeting shared unconscious needs which he named *basic assumptions*. Individuals take the leadership for expressing one or another basic assumption because of their valency to relate to others in this way—either to express a dependent relation to authority, a fight or flight reaction against authority, or a tendency to substitute magical pairing between two individuals as an alternative to the group's task of working out its relationship to the leader. Similarly, we find that in marriage spouses are chosen because of their valencies to accept the projective identifications of their spouses, and in the small group of two they deal with dominance and submission, with leadership through the exercise of authority or the assumption of power, through depending one on the other, fighting, fleeing from the issues, and pairing. Pairing generally supports the task of the marital dyad, but it becomes a destructive defense when the pairing involves a lover, a parent, a child, or an unskilled therapist.

THE THERAPIST'S SKILLS AND ATTRIBUTES

The object relations couple therapist needs to learn the skills listed in table 18.1.

Table 18.1.   Skills of the object relations couple therapist

- Setting the frame
- Maintaining a neutral, but not remote, position of involved impartiality
- Creating a psychological space for sharing thoughts and feelings
- Developing negative capability in the therapist's use of self
- Interpreting defense, anxiety, fantasy, and inner object relations using the "because clause"
- Working with transference and countertransference
- Working through to termination

The primary skill is setting the frame. *Setting the frame* refers to the process of conducting the interview, establishing the fee schedule and the arrangements, managing the anxiety of the initial session, and establishing a working alliance. In an attitude of *involved impartiality*, we maintain friendly but nonintrusive interest and concern in the couple as a partnership without taking sides or holding ambition about how they should change. We simply create a *psychological space* in which they can share thoughts and feelings that they could not do without our help, because we are trained to be able to bear pain and to think about feelings. We are in a state of *negative capability*, which is to say that we are not bound by our memory of what has gone before or blinded by our desire for their relationship—or for us as therapists—to be a certain way. We are not trying to force things or to guess at meanings prematurely. We remain open to whatever may transpire.

We will recognize repeated patterns of interaction. Then we ask ourselves what protective purpose they serve. For this laborious work of excavating from surface to depth, we have found useful the *because clause,* a concept borrowed from the group therapy work of Henry Ezriel (1952), who showed that the first level of defense is to involve the therapist in a particular type of relationship called the *required relationship* that succeeds in covering over a feared and *avoided relationship*. This in turn covers over a *calamitous relationship* that is feared above all. We show the couple how they require each other to behave in a familiar way that hides their avoidance of true intimacy because they are afraid of catastrophe. The avoidance of intimacy shows up in various relationship problems and the catastrophe is imagined in many different forms. Ultimately the couple's deepest fear is that the relationship will die or will kill one or both partners. In short, the calamity is loss of the relationship, loss of the object, or loss of the self. This technique of the because clause enables us to *interpret the couple's defenses and the underlying anxiety* that makes them necessary.

But we do not simply look at the behavior of the couple before us. We attend closely to how the couple perceives us and involves us in their experience (their transferences to us), and we observe our reaction to the being with them (our countertransference). The transference-countertransference dynamic depends on projective and introjective identificatory processes. Projective identification that occurs between the mother and her infant, or between the husband and his wife, also occurs between the couple and the therapist. Temporarily, we become part of the couple's projective and introjective identification system, and then we *interpret the couple's transference from our experience in the countertransference.*

We find that countertransference is of two major types, *contextual* and *focused countertransference.* The contextual countertransference occurs in response to the couple's attitude toward the treatment context and to us as the provider of help, where we are experienced as the environmental mother, while the focused countertransference stems from the resonance between our internal objects and those of the members of the couple, where we are experienced as the object mother. In couple therapy there is an oscillation between these two types. We aim to receive the couple's projective identifications of us so as to understand their dilemmas from inside our experience of focused and contextual countertransference.

Working through involves repeating the work of detection and interpretation until the defenses and anxieties are understood and worked through. At that point the couple has internalized the therapeutic space and can provide psychological holding, intimate relating, and understanding of each other.

The interpretive work of object relations couple therapy is not arrived at by intellectual formulation alone, but relies on the use of the therapist's self. We use our countertransference (our personal reactions) for the detection, understanding of, and conviction about the projective and introjective identificatory system of the couple. Therefore, therapists need to have undergone enough personal therapy, supervision, and peer supervision to be aware of their own internal object relations set so that they can observe its interaction with the couple's system. Even though self-revelation is not called for in this approach, the therapist's self is interacting and remains vulnerable to resonating with the full panoply of emotions. The therapist who wants to use the object relations approach with couples needs personal attributes of honesty, courage, insight, and commitment to ongoing reflection, process and review, and self-analysis.

COUPLE ASSESSMENT, CONCEPTUALIZATION, AND TREATMENT PLAN

We begin with a case conceptualization written by Frank Dattilio and Louis Bevilacqua (2000) and follow with our object relations perspective on their case. (The editors are grateful to Frank Dattilio and Louis Bevilacqua for generous permission to reprint their case conceptualization.)

Introduction and Case Conceptualization of Mike and Jan

The following is a case study of a young married couple, Mike and Jan. A brief narrative containing basic information is provided, including data on psychiatric, medical, and social history; and history of substance abuse, child abuse, and criminal involvement. A description of the presenting problem and a history of the couple's difficulties is explained in detail.

Case Study

Jan and Mike are a middle-class Caucasian couple residing in a suburban neighborhood of the northeast central states. Jan is a forty-nine-year-old sales associate for a pharmaceutical company. She has been a sales representative with the same company for the past fourteen years. Prior to this career, Jan was employed as a receptionist for a dental office and was also working part-time as a salesperson in a major clothing department store. Jan enjoys reading mystery novels and taking care of her animals, which include three horses, two cats, and two birds. Jan has been married to Mike for the past twelve years. They have had no separations to date. They also do not have any children from this union. Jan was married once before for three years. Her marriage ended in divorce due to her husband's continued drug abuse and infidelity. There were no children from Jan's previous marriage.

Mike was also married one time before. His marriage of one year ended in divorce due to his drug abuse. There were no children from this union. Mike is forty-four and currently employed as a welder/fitter. He acquired this trade while in high school and has maintained various employment in this field for the past twenty-five years. He has been employed by four different companies overall, the longest period with his present employer, which has been for the past ten years. Mike enjoys taking care of animals and working on computers.

Mike and Jan met through a mutual friend during a summer outing. They dated only four months before deciding to marry. They decided to skip the formalities and were united by a justice of the peace in a rather impromptu fashion. They described their courtship as a fun time that they will always remember. While dating, Mike and Jan enjoyed seeing new films, dining out, attending parties, skiing, and taking care of Jan's animals. When they initially met, Mike had relatively few friends. When they went out together with other couples, Mike and Jan generally socialized with Jan's friends, who, Mike claims, eventually became his friends as well. Rarely did they socialize with any of Mike's acquaintances.

Psychiatric History

There is no prior history of psychiatric treatment for Mike. He has never been prescribed psychotropic medication, nor has he been hospitalized for any mental health reasons. Mike reports that during his adolescence, his mother received individual treatment for depression after divorcing his father. She was not treated with any medication that he could recall. Mike's brother received individual therapy for "behavioral problems" as a teenager. His father viewed therapy as something that only "crazy" people needed and looked upon therapy with disdain. Mike states that he is interested in initiating therapy in order to reduce the tension that exists between himself and Jan, and he denies maintaining any of the same type of biases that his father held about therapy.

Jan reports that she received individual therapy for depression approximately twenty years ago after undergoing a hysterectomy. She recalled this as being part of the aftercare plan recommended by her gynecologist. Jan attended approximately twelve sessions and viewed her time in therapy as being very helpful. She has never been prescribed psychotropic medication, nor has anyone in her family. Jan reports that no one in her family, including herself, has ever been hospitalized for mental illness, and she is unaware of any psychiatric history with her extended family.

Medical History

Mike has a history of hypertension and elevated cholesterol levels. He inconsistently follows a diet plan to address these two conditions under the care of his family physician. His father had one heart attack, five years ago, and is still living. There is a family history of cancer and glaucoma on his mother's side of the family. His mother is currently in good health.

Jan has no current medical problems. There is a family history of cancer and diabetes on both sides of Jan's parents' family. At the age of twenty-nine, Jan underwent a hysterectomy as a result of ovarian cancer. Her first reaction to the news of having cancer was devastation. She was scared of dying. She said that, fortunately, her friends and family were very supportive and the surgery was successful. She also reported that having a child was never something that she was really interested in doing, yet the idea of having a hysterectomy bothered her. Jan recounted, "I did my share of parenting when I was raising my younger brother, John. I used to have occasional thoughts of what it might have been like to have a child, but not for the past twelve or thirteen years." Jan said what really helped her was when she met Mike and he expressed his lack of interest in children. This was a big relief to Jan and was one of the characteristics that she found attractive about him.

Social History

Mike is the youngest of two boys. His older brother, two years his senior, received part-time special education classes due to weaknesses in reading and math. His brother also had "behavioral problems," which became a central focus in the family during his upbringing. While growing up, Mike and his older brother Mark were not very close. Mike tended to stay more to himself, while Mark had lots of friends but tended to get in trouble for not doing his homework and being disrespectful to teachers. Mike was in regular classes and maintained a C average. He recalls not enjoying school very much. In fact, Mike reports that there was never anything he really liked to do.

One of the things his mom always complained of was that Mike rarely finished anything he started. He remembers taking piano lessons and drum lessons, but quitting each one after a few months. He also tried out for a local baseball league, but quit after the second practice. Throughout elementary school, he was often teased for being the biggest kid in his class and for not being very coordinated. Finally, as Mike entered high school, his father made the suggestion that he become involved with football. This altered his reputation with his peers somewhat and enhanced his social skills. Mike states that he was teased less by the guys but still felt very uncomfortable and somewhat afraid of females. He dated on and off throughout high school but never maintained any serious relationship with a girl. His mother never approved of any of the girls that he expressed an interest in. He recalls one of his mother's typical responses being, "Don't get serious, Michael, it will never last."

Mike describes his parents as being supportive, but to a limited degree. His father attended every one of his football games, and was very lenient in disciplining the children. When Mike had a problem, however, his father's usual curt response was "Get over it." Mike's mother was always there to discuss any problems Mike encountered in life, but tended to be very critical of him in general. He said that no matter what problem he was experiencing, his mother always pointed out that it was somehow related to something that Mike did to cause it. This created a great deal of conflictual feelings toward his mother, whom he views as very controlling and maintaining the power in the family.

In describing discipline, Mike reports that his mother set the rules in the house and that everyone was expected to follow them, even his father. Mike remembers one time that the family was having company. His father spilled a drink on the living room carpet and his mom reacted by yelling at his father and calling him a slob in front of the guests. Mike said his father just left the room and walked out of the house. He did not return home until the next day.

The year Mike graduated from high school, he pursued his trade in welding—something that he trained for in vocational classes and has practiced ever since.

That same year Mike's mother filed for divorce after twenty years of marriage, due to her husband's numerous affairs. Mike described his parents' marriage as involving frequent arguments and several separations. Mike was aware of his father's affairs, and he believed they were due to his mother's constant "nagging" and "put-downs." When Mike's mother decided on the divorce, his father moved out.

Mike was very surprised and angered by this decision but never shared his feelings with anyone. Mike rarely saw his father after he moved out, although they did talk over the phone every couple of weeks. He described his mother as becoming more and more critical and demanding of him. Mike said two years later, his brother Mark moved out of the house to live with his girlfriend. Mike lived with his mother until he got married for the first time at twenty-nine years of age.

Mike has maintained contact with both of his parents throughout the years. His father never remarried. The year before Mike married his first wife, his mother married her second husband, to whom she has been married for the last twenty years. Mike describes his mother's second marriage as good, and he currently maintains a fairly positive relationship with his step-father.

Jan is the oldest of two children. Despite being five years his senior, Jan reports a close relationship with her brother, John, during their upbringing. Her parents both had careers, and had little time for Jan and her brother during their childhood. She describes her parents as very lenient and supportive in a remote sort of way. Her parents rarely denied her anything, and frequently bought her and her brother whatever they wanted. Her parents placed a great deal of responsibility on Jan, since she was five years older than John. As a result, Jan spent a large portion of her childhood as a caregiver to John. She recalls that often, after school, she would make a snack for her and her brother before they began their homework. Sometimes when her mother was running late, Jan would make dinner for the entire family. She reports having enjoyed this type of responsibility until John started high school and became involved with drugs. Jan had been experimenting with marijuana herself, but saw her brother's use as extensive and clearly destructive. This led to frequent heated arguments between herself and her brother. Her parents were quite liberal regarding the drug use, and saw experimentation as "normal." Jan remembers one time that she was expressing her concerns about John's drug use to her parents. Her parents responded by saying, "As long as he only smokes it on the weekends, we don't think he has a problem."

Throughout high school, Jan did well academically and had a number of friends. She reports that her friends were her "real supports." Anytime she had a problem, it was her friends whom she went to. After graduation, Jan attended college and received a bachelor's degree in philosophy, with a minor in marketing. Upon graduating from college, Jan began working full-time in a local clothing department store.

Substance Abuse History

Throughout his senior year in high school, Mike drank alcohol quite heavily on the weekends. At the age of twenty, he was introduced to marijuana by a co-worker. His alcohol and marijuana use continued on and off for approximately ten years. At one point during this time, Mike lost his job as a result of coming to work late and frequently hungover. Unfortunately, his dismissal did not change his frequency or quantity of substance use, which continued. This did not change until Mike became involved in an auto accident due to his drug use. After running over and killing a dog, he crashed into a telephone pole, totally destroying his car. He was charged with driving under the influence and spent one night in jail. This also resulted in Mike's dismissal from his second job. That same year, Mike's first wife divorced him.

At that point, Mike began thinking that his drug use was becoming out of control. He decided to stop using all substances except alcohol. This lasted for three years, until one day a co-worker offered Mike some marijuana after work and he accepted it. He explained this relapse as a result of stress from work. In particular, Mike described experiencing difficulty getting along with a female co-worker with whom he was competing for a position. Mike claims that the last straw to this conflict was when his co-worker was finally chosen for this position over him and received a substantial raise. Mike believed that she was underqualified for this position, and consequently he resigned from his position two weeks later.

Mike continued to use alcohol and marijuana for another ten years. One night, after using alcohol rather heavily, Mike was driving home from a friend's house when he passed out and remained unconscious for several hours. When he awoke, Mike realized that he was in the middle of a cornfield and could not remember how he got there. Following this blackout period, Mike went through a twenty-eight-day inpatient drug and alcohol treatment program. As a result he has been substance-free for the last seven months, and has also been attending Narcotics Anonymous meetings on a weekly basis.

Jan experimented with marijuana and alcohol while in high school and college. After graduating from college, she stopped using controlled substances, except for an occasional glass of wine. During her first marriage, she began using marijuana again. She and her first husband used together frequently. One year prior to separating from her first husband, Jan stopped using and began attending Narcotics Anonymous meetings.

Child Abuse

Mike was sexually molested between the ages of seven and nine by a paternal aunt. This involved her fondling and kissing Mike on a sporadic basis.

He reports that this ended when his aunt moved away. He has not disclosed this information to anyone besides his wife, Jan, and the therapist.

Jan reports no history of any type of child physical or sexual abuse.

Criminal History

Mike was arrested for driving while under the influence and spent one night in jail. His license was suspended for six months.

Jan has no criminal history.

Presenting Problem

Jan made the initial call for an appointment for marital therapy. She stated that she and her husband were experiencing difficulty achieving emotional intimacy due to continual conflicts and lack of effective resolutions. Jan and Mike tend to avoid discussing conflicts with each other. When they do argue, Jan tends to criticize Mike, and he simply dismisses what Jan says as being trivial. At times, Mike will avoid being around the house, particularly when Jan is at home. He does this to avoid tension in the relationship. This conflict-avoidance pattern of interacting has led to a lack of trust and emotional distance between them, which has naturally affected their intimacy. There have been times when attending therapy was discussed, but neither followed through due to periodic improvements.

For the past seven months, Jan and Mike reported, they were getting along fairly well. Mike was calling Jan and letting her know where he was and what time he was coming home. Jan felt that she had begun to trust Mike again. This trust was violated, however, when two weeks prior Mike came home at 2:30 A.M. Mike said he went to Jennifer's house for a party. Jennifer has been a family friend for the past twenty years and the party was for those who helped her to relocate to her new residence. Jan did not want to go to the party and secretly wished that Mike would decline as well. Unfortunately, she never told Mike her true feelings, and Mike ended up going by himself. Mike said he had fallen asleep while at Jennifer's home and did not wake up until 1:00 A.M. Jennifer lives an hour and a half away and Mike said that he drove straight home when he realized what had happened. Jan felt that Mike should have called her immediately and had erred in his judgment. Mike said he just wanted to get home as fast as he could, and knew in advance that Jan would be upset. This incident resulted in a heated argument that included a discussion about divorce. Jan told Mike she was not willing to continue the relationship because she didn't feel as though she could trust him any longer. Mike felt this was totally unfair of Jan. Mike pointed out to Jan that in the last six weeks he has done everything he said he would and that Jan should still be able to trust him. Despite Mike's efforts, Jan said she still wanted to pursue a divorce. Mike angrily responded by saying "Fine, if you want a divorce, go for it. Let's do it tomorrow." The next day Jan reconsidered her position and apologized to Mike but did admit that she was confused about her feelings. Mike acknowledged Jan's confusion and admitted to his own frustrations with the marriage. It was at that point that Jan suggested they begin couples therapy, and Mike agreed.

History of Presenting Problem

Throughout their marriage, Mike and Jan have avoided discussing any conflicts and do not recall ever really resolving any of their disagreements completely. Usually, arguments would end with Mike leaving the house for several hours. When they would reconvene, they would avoid bringing up the issue of contention, and the matter would simply be dropped. The majority of their arguments involved Jan's complaints about Mike's being undependable, and especially concerning his drug abuse. Mike would rationalize that he continued to use substances because of Jan's "nagging." Whenever there would be disagreements, Mike would tell Jan to "just drop it." This tended to infuriate Jan, and she would yell and cry more profusely. Eventually, Mike would leave the room and, sometimes, the house. Unfortunately, the matters would never be resolved and would only be tucked away until they resurfaced in another argument and continued to erode the relationship.

Critical Life Events Time Line

1948 Jan is born
1951 Mike's brother, Mark, is born
     Mike's parents are married
1953 Mike is born
     Jan's brother, John, is born
1966 Jan graduates high school
1970 Jan graduates college—B.A. in Philosophy
     Jan begins working at a clothing department store
1971 Mike graduates high school
     Mike's parents divorce
1973 Mark moves out of his mother's home
     Mike begins using marijuana
1977 Jan is diagnosed with cancer and has a hysterectomy
     Jan attends twelve sessions of therapy for depression
1980 Jan marries her first husband
1981 Mike's mother remarries
1982 Mike gets married for the first time
     Jan stops using marijuana and starts attending N A
1983 Mike is charged with a D.U.I. and loses his second job
     Jan divorces her first husband
     Mike separates from his first wife

1984 Mike and Jan meet through a mutual friend
1985 Mike and Jan get married
1986 Mike begins using marijuana again
      Mike quits his job
1987 Mike starts working at his fourth and current job
1997 Mike attends inpatient drug and alcohol treatment program
      Mike starts attending Narcotics Anonymous meetings
      Mike and Jan begin couples therapy

Source: Dattilio and Bevilacqua (2000), pp. 13–20. Reprinted with permission of Springer.

THE OBJECT RELATIONS PERSPECTIVE ON THE CASE

The background information that Dattilio and Bevilacqua gave us was of the sort that a colleague might prepare for making a referral, introducing a case for discussion at a case conference, or orienting a supervisor. What follows is a description of how we would proceed as couple therapists working with the case ourselves, or as supervisors recommending to others how to proceed with this couple.

Specific Assessment Tools

The report of Mike and Jan is rich in data concerning the history of the individual partners and their couple relationship, but it does not convey the affective tone of their relationship. If one of us were to be the new therapist, we would have to see them in person to assess their resistance, defensive process, and underlying anxiety. We would see how they respond to us and how we feel about them, so that we could use our countertransference to their behavior to form a hypothesis about their transference. If one of us were the supervisor we would have to ask the therapist what it felt like to be with the couple in the session.

What we will do here with Mike and Jan's material is to use it to illustrate how we might gather more information from our experience as therapists with the couple or what we might learn as supervisors from the observations of the student who is presenting their ongoing couple therapy to us, and begin to develop hypotheses about the case from the object relations perspective.

In order to get the information we need, we would arrange a series of clinical interviews to complete an extended assessment for this couple. We would study how they deal with the therapist and the entry into the treatment process, and how the therapist responds to each of them individually and as a couple. We would not tend to do a home evaluation but would arrange to see them in the office setting. The office provides a controlled therapeutic space where the therapists are able to manage the frame of a treatment. Within this frame we create a safe environment in which the couple feels held and where the partners can enter a psychological space in which they can face their anxieties. We would set a fee, a time to meet, and we would start and stop the session on time. Then we would look at Mike and Jan's way of dealing with the frame of treatment. Were they compliant with our expectations, or did they seek to bend the frame, and if so, in what ways? These behaviors would give clues as to how they felt about the prospect of therapy with us.

We would be attentive to our own reactions to detect our contextual countertransference to their contextual transference. We would look out for focused transferences to us which would help us understand from inside our own experience difficulties in how they related to each other. Speaking from inside our own experience gives us a better chance of connecting with the couple and getting through to them in a nonjudgmental way.

During this assessment we would inquire more about the couple's sexual history (D. Scharff 1982, 1989). The information given so far suggests that their sexual relationship was entirely satisfactory; in fact, it was excellent. All the more peculiar then is the fact that it has virtually ceased. We would want to know why. How did each partner feel about its cessation, and how do they understand that a sexual relationship that was pleasurable has now gone into abeyance? If it turns out that the couple had a great deal of difficulty talking about sex, and that was why the information was so cryptic, then we might give them a sex questionnaire to discover their sexual histories and their attitudes toward sexuality in a shared situation, masturbation, sexual fantasies, and reaction to their own and their partner's nudity. It might be found at this point that the description of excellence in the sexual relationship was defensive and that the couple requires adjunctive behavioral sex therapy. If it turns out that a good sexual relationship has been destroyed by marital conflict, then we would feel secure in going ahead to recommend couple therapy without specific behavioral sexual intervention.

Mike and Jan Individually and as a Couple

Mike as an Individual

Mike's brother Mark was placed in special education classes because he had attention deficit disorder and difficulty with reading and math. Mike was in regular classes where he got C's, felt dumb, and tended to quit things. Mike now asks whether he might have attention deficit disorder, too.

On our first reading of the case study, we mistakenly remembered that Mike, like Mark, had been in special education classes. This slip in comprehension may have been an attentional problem on our part due to other factors in our work or personal lives, but it may also be evidence of a specific countertransference response to Mike's depression and low self-esteem in the area of intellectual functioning. We might have identified with Mike's self-diagnosed attentional deficit disorder. We might be picking up a fusion in Mike's unconscious between Mike and his brother, a defense organized to eliminate Mike's guilt over being better endowed. We might have identified with a projection of Mike's ego that feels weak and dumb. We might have identified with a projection of his object that criticizes him and exaggerates his weak points. If we made an error like this in a session, we would look into its relevance for understanding at the unconscious level.

Mike's drug abuse history points to a search for heightened stimulation that can be a marker for attention deficit disorder and for mood disorder. Diagnostic psychological tests of attentiveness are needed but should be combined with testing of intelligence, personality, and cognitive style. It seems that Mike has good coordination of large motor functioning, as shown in his ability to play football and to do welding and blacksmith work. He has the fine motor coordination to manipulate the keyboard, but it is possible that his competence with the computer masks a difficulty with the hand-eye coordination needed for writing. Mike is bright enough to be of interest to an educated woman like Jan, but it seems quite likely that an attention deficit, perhaps complicated by a subtle specific learning disability, has seriously limited Mike's capacity to achieve his potential. The results of intelligence testing, projectives, attention deficit scales, and learning disability assessment tests such as the Woodcock-Johnson could be helpful.

It seems to us that Mike was depressed during school. He tended to quit activities, perhaps because he lost heart due to the effects of undiagnosed weaknesses less obvious than his brother's. He almost quit his marriage when he responded to Jan's suggestion of pursuing a divorce by saying "fine, let's go for it, do it tomorrow," which did not reflect his true feelings at all. Here he shows counterphobic defenses in addition to hopeless responses.

We would ask for more reflection on Mike's early drug use and self-destructive behavior. What triggered the first drink? What events were happening in his family at that time? Was his self-destructive behavior an attempt to punish himself? Was he guilty about something? Even though he is now sober, he still seems to push himself in a self-mortifying way as if only that will keep him free from the self-destructive impulses. After abusing alcohol and marijuana steadily for twenty years, Mike has been substance free for seven months and attends Narcotics Anonymous meetings. We would continue to support his attendance there. He has made a major change in terms of accepting his addiction and working on his recovery. His recent absence from work for a twenty-eight-day hospital inpatient stay seems to have been acceptable to his employer. Apparently substance abuse, or treatment for it, did not compromise his ability to maintain employment, but it probably did compromise his ability to branch out on his own and work for himself, which he would have preferred.

A related problem in the area of oral behavior is Mike's difficulty in managing his food intake. Despite having raised levels of cholesterol and high blood pressure like his father who has already had one heart attack, Mike is not following the diet his doctor recommended. He is waiting to add oral medication to his intake, instead of modifying his present intake. Mike wants his blood chemistry to be controlled by the doctor's prescription of medicine rather than by Mike's taking control of himself. His self-destructiveness is evident in his negligence toward his physical condition.

Mike spends a lot of time working on his home computer, but it is not clear from the record what he does. We would want to know much more about his computing activities and the purposes that they serve. Is he exercising his intelligence in a private way, or is he playing games? Is he transferring his addictive behavior to the Internet? Does he have a secret sex life there? We have been told that in real time, Mike is not a particularly social person and that he has been fairly quiet and keeps himself to himself. So we wonder if he is using his computer to provide a virtual social reality by joining discussions in chat rooms.

Mike seems to have been quite dependent on his parents. He maintained an attachment to his mother, staying at home until he was twenty-nine. As an adolescent, he was quite dependent on his father's approval through attendance at his football games. It is unclear how Mike responded to his parents' relationship, but he was certainly angry when they got divorced. Incidentally, it is notable that Mike did not marry for the first time until a year after his mother remarried, which raises the question of guilty inability to pursue his own needs if his mother's were not met. Could this be an underlying dynamic preventing him from being more successful in relation to Jan? Mike recognizes the value of the good marriage that his mother has had for the last twenty years and has been able to form a relationship with his stepfather. His relationship with his father remains rather tenuous.

Mike's mother was critical of him. She was the disciplinarian, whereas his father was lenient and not particularly involved. He tended to deny problems and to leave when confronted. Mike has picked up his father's habit of avoiding confrontation and he is identifying with this lost father when he emotionally abandons Jan. As far as we know, he has not picked up his father's habit of having affairs. Mike conceptualizes affairs as a response to nagging and belittlement. The story of Mike's coming home late from a party which was the event that precipitated consultation would need to be investigated further, to see whether Mike was acting on an affair fantasy.

We would want to know more about Mike's first marriage, during which his wife became unexpectedly pregnant but miscarried before the couple's ambivalence about bearing a child could be worked through. We are told how the first wife felt about Mike's reluctance to have a child. But we do not learn enough about Mike's reaction to the miscarriage. We wonder whether his increased drug abuse and failing to sleep in the marital bed were responses to unhappiness in the relationship with his wife, or whether they were responses to his resentment regarding his ambivalence concerning the child. It is striking that they separated after nine months, this being the duration of a pregnancy. We find that there is not enough material in the record to help us understand Mike's reluctance to have children in either marriage. Although he enjoys taking care of Jan's animals, Mike has not wanted children. Perhaps he felt that a pregnancy would ruin his marriage, and he might have got this idea from perceiving that his older brother's difficulties ruined his parents' marriage.

The record does not provide enough information about Mike's sexual molestation. Although we know that his aunt fondled and kissed him, we do not know what parts of his body she touched and kissed, or indeed what kind of requests she made of him. Nor do we know why he did not ask his parents for help in understanding or dealing with this situation. In further consultation interviews we would want to open up this topic, because it could shed light on the couple's sexual difficulties and on Mike's fears of intimacy. If it was too difficult for Mike to talk about this topic with his wife present, we might agree to parallel individual interviews, where he could deal with this subject along with the possibility of affair behaviors and the effect of the child abuse on his sexual adjustment. Jan could use her individual session to talk more freely about her reproductive losses and her present feelings about her husband. The history of sexual abuse and the issue of intimacy would be evaluated in depth in ensuing couple sessions.

Jan as an Individual

Jan has a good work record. Her social development is much more satisfactory than Mike's. Her previous marriage lasted three years and ended because of her husband's drug abuse and infidelity. We would want to know much more about her first marriage. It is interesting to consider why her marriage to Mike did not also end over the issue of drug abuse. Perhaps this means that infidelity is the critical issue for her, as it was for Mike's mother. Like Mike, Jan has maintained strong attachments to her family. She uses the opportunity when Mike is busy at work to visit with her parents. Perhaps she is adapting to his unavailability, or perhaps his involvement in work is a response to her primary attachment remaining with her family.

As a young woman, Jan was successfully treated by hysterectomy for ovarian cancer, following which she had depression which responded to short-term psychotherapy. Jan is able to remember her fear of death at the time of her cancer diagnosis, but she is less able to talk about the loss of her fertility. It must have hurt to sustain such enormous damage to her young adult body so that she could not create a child. Jan loves to care for animals and seems to have no idea that they are a replacement for the children that she cannot have. She was glad to find a man like Mike who did not want to have children and so did not face her with conflict over the damage to her reproductive system. She appears to take care of him as her child, just as she took care of her drug-abusing first husband, and before that her drug-addicted brother, who is the same age as Mike. Jan is repeating her history of taking care of a damaged boy. What else is she repeating in her relationship with Mike? We would inquire about feelings of loneliness, abandonment, and fear in her childhood to try to get in touch with her needy self which she splits off into her objects.

Perhaps Mike senses her need to take care of him and keeps his distance so as not to be totally inhabited by her projections. He keeps up a threat of imminent breakdown to keep her interested in curing him. When Mike makes a spontaneous, autonomous gesture, Jan panics. This suggests that she needs him to need her so that she can take care of her own needy self that she projects into him, while denying her own longings to be mothered and to have real babies to mother. She tries to heal him and repair his flaws, as if to prove that she can be creative and the damage to her maternality was not total. Nevertheless, she finds herself sadly unable to repair the damaged couple and create an atmosphere of sexual intimacy.

Jan was raised in a family whose parents were lenient, supportive, liberal, indulgent, and denying of problem areas. At the same time, they expected a great deal of autonomy from their children, and especially from Jan, who was five years older than her brother. Jan seems to have been a parentified child who filled in for her mother as housekeeper, nurturer, and limit setter. This arrangement guaranteed that Jan turn to her peer group for support and for company. Nevertheless, she remains close to her parents, and talks freely about her marital problems with them and with her best friend. Despite being fully informed, her parents deny the gravity of Jan's marital problems, just as they denied their son's drug abuse problem when he was a teenager. Jan feels emotionally abandoned by them, even if they are socially present in her life.

Jan and Mike as a Couple

The manner in which the case is presented puts most of the responsibility for the couple's difficulties on Mike. It does not give a clear take on Jan's contribution to the conflict. The report tells us that the majority of the arguments involve Jan's complaints about Mike not being dependable and especially about his drug abuse. In the past seven months, however, he has become more trustworthy and has stopped using substances. Whereas Mike is impulsive and shows addictive patterns that have led him into trouble, Jan has been able to control her addictive behavior.

Jan is clearly more confident in her intellectual achievements than is Mike, and yet she chose him because she found him fascinating. She feels comfortable being the bigger earner in the couple. We learn that Jan does tend to criticize Mike, a way in which she is like his mother, and Mike avoids dealing with her critical comments, which resembles the way his mother behaved toward his father. Mike's conflict-avoidance manner contains a passive/aggressive stance that supports his fragile sense of autonomy but that leads to a serious breach in their intimate relating. Whereas Jan does raise issues, Mike ignores them and avoids dealing with her. She is unable to push through to resolution because his technique is successful in shutting her up. He also defends himself by leaving the scene until she stops bringing up the topic.

Mike and Jan's social life has deteriorated and has not recovered. Jan has been Mike's avenue to a couples' social group. It seems likely that substance abuse was his other, less desirable avenue to social relatedness. Although the presenting problem is said to be Jan's wish that she and Mike could discuss conflict and reach resolution, rebuild trust, and avoid divorce, it seems to us that the precipitant for Mike and Jan's seeking therapy is shared anxiety over the unfamiliar possibility of having a relationship that is not clouded by the use of substances and the repetitive interactive pattern of nagging and avoidance.

Mike always felt "dumb" compared to girls, who seemed smarter than he was. And yet he chose to marry Jan, who has a college degree. The report does not indicate any feeling of belittlement that Mike might feel in relation to Jan. The only mention of competition concerns his wish to make up the differential in their incomes by working extra on the weekends. We would want to know much more about this area.

Strengths to Build On

Mike and Jan have both had experience with substance abuse and can empathize with each other in dealing with addiction. Both enjoy taking care of animals, which indicates a capacity for nurturing and a weakness in dealing with verbal confrontation. Both of them enjoy solo activity: Jan likes reading; Mike likes computing. In the past they have enjoyed shared activities: going to the movies, going out to dinner, and going to parties, in addition to taking care of the animals. These shared activities could be revisited to rebuild social areas for mutual enjoyment. Their social life could be improved by reconnecting with Jan's couple friends. We need to know more about Mike's social group. Apparently his friends are single, rowdy, and raucous, which suggests that they are a group of drinking buddies. He needs a different, independent social group, which he may find in Narcotics Anonymous.

The couple might rediscover some shared physical activity, such as skiing, or walking, or horseback riding, and lastly they would need to make time to rebuild their sexual relationship. We have the impression that the blocks to sexual intimacy reside in history that predates the lack of trust in the marital relationship. We think that Jan has unresolved issues concerning her sexuality due to the assault on her reproductive tract and that Mike has unresolved issues of intrusion by females due to the sexual abuse he sustained as a child.

Dynamic Formulation of Mike and Jan as a Couple

As a couple, Mike and Jan have developed a marital projective and introjective identificatory system based on Jan's projection into Mike of the needy part of herself that she formerly projected into her younger brother, and Mike's projection into Jan of the critical and controlling part of his mother to whom he remains attached. This sets up a dynamic where Mike is like a troublesome child over whom Jan helplessly frets and fusses, while Jan is like a nagging mother whom Mike avoids, tunes out, and frustrates. Jan feels abandoned by Mike the same way that she feels abandoned by her parents. In this way she expresses her internal couple in her current marriage. The early fascination, enjoyable sex, shared physical activity, and leisure pursuits with friends operated at the level of adult equality during courtship, but this has been invaded by a regressive mother-child dynamic, exacerbated by the self-sustaining substance abuse problem.

Mike and Jan both struggle to repair something, but they do not know what it is. Jan works as a pharmaceutical sales associate who sells medicine to help sick people get well. In this way she can continue her efforts to help weak and damaged objects, like her brother, and her cancer-mutilated self. Mike works as a welder and blacksmith who puts together hard objects so that they will hold against force and not come apart. Symbolically, his work represents his attempt to keep his parents together inside him and not allow his disrupted internal couple to fall apart like his parents did and destroy his relationship with Jan.

The Goals in Treating Mike and Jan

In the short term, Mike and Jan would work toward restabilizing their social network and rebuilding their context of shared activities. Facing and analyzing their conflicts and reversing their sexual withdrawal would be medium-term goals. Rebuilding intimacy would be the ultimate goal. The goals of object relations couple therapy are distinguished from the goals of short-term approaches to couple therapy in not aiming for symptom resolution. Our goals are to help the couple to face their conflicts, re-evaluate their choice of partner, consider whether to recommit to the marriage, or arrive at a decision to separate with concern for each other.

How would we know when Mike and Jan had done enough work in therapy to finish? The criteria that indicate readiness for termination are described in table 18.2. Our goal is to effect a return to the appropriate developmental phase of family life, with improved capacity to master developmental stress, an improved ability for work as a team, and an improved ability to differentiate between, and to meet the needs of, husband and wife.

We tend not to use specific measurements to determine when these goals have been met. We have, however, participated in a research project in which a self-administered questionnaire, known as the Persons Relating to Each Other Questionnaire (Birtchnell 1993), gives couples a score before and at the end of treatment in terms of their ways of relating along the dimensions of upperness, lowerness, closeness, and distance (Scharff and Scharff 1998). When these goals are met, it then remains for the couple to consolidate their gains by engaging actively in the final piece of work, the process of the termination of therapy.

Specific Techniques and Interventions

We do not use specific techniques and strategies, directives, homework, or paradoxical instructions. Our technique consists in maintaining an attitude of listening, following, recognizing patterns, observing our own feelings, and making interpretations. The *use of countertransference to interpret transference* is at the heart of the technique of object relations couple therapy, and yet it may be hard to understand in a single reading. Without burdening the couple with telling them how they make us feel, we use the information from our reactions (our countertransference) to arrive at an understanding of what it is like to be with each of them, and with them as a couple. Our technique is to enter a state of unconscious communication with them, and note and then analyze our feelings and associations. In countertransference, we receive the couple's projective identifications and feel affected by them. There is a resonance between the object relations set of the couple and our inner objects, especially including our internal couple when we are dealing with a couple in therapy.

We are particularly interested in the couple's resonance with our own internal couple. The *internal couple* is a psychic structure that is based on our experience of the relationship between our father and mother as they cooperated together in their marital relationship and as they dealt with us as parents at various developmental stages. This original construction is then modified as we interact with other couples. Mike has a fractured internal couple that is partly intrusive and partly neglectful and so arouses anger in him. Jan has a secure internal couple that is somewhat oblivious and leaves her feeling helpless and overlooked.

The therapist also has an internal couple which interacts with the couples being treated. Our internal couple derives from our earliest, oral level experience of our parents as a couple whom we imagine to be enjoying an orgiastic feeding frenzy. In the toilet training years, we see them as a fighting, sadistic couple, and then in the Oedipal phase we are aware of their romantic excitement at the genital level, and so on until we are mature enough to detach from them as our primary pair of love objects. Becoming familiar with this internal structure is important for the couple therapist. Trouble in this area may lead the couple therapist to feel like quitting so as to avoid feeling excluded, guilty, envious, competitive, and rejected, like a child in relation to the parents who have each other. Or the couple therapist may use the defense of identifying with the omniscient parents so as not to re-experience painful childish feelings.

The couple's shared transference to us stems from the projection onto us of their difficulties in providing holding for each other and is elicited in response to their expectations of the therapist. The *contextual transference* expresses attitudes toward the therapist's responsibility for the therapeutic context. In therapy, Mike and Jan might have a positive contextual transference if they trusted us, as Jan trusted her social worker, or a negative contextual transference if together they felt as uncertain of the value of therapy as Mike and his parents do. Individual *focused object transferences* stemming from the internal objects of husband or wife seek to experience early object relationships with the therapist in the here and now. The therapist becomes both a representative of the environmental mother who will provide safety and continuity and the object mother who is there for direct relating to expressed needs, wishes, and fears. The direct focused transference may attempt to substitute for the contextual transference when the couple cannot sustain confidence in the therapeutic context. In couple therapy we expect oscillation between focused and contextual transference. For instance, Mike might have a focused transference in which he experienced one of us as critical and might wish to quit rather than discuss this, or Jan might feel critical of our approach, might express worry about our reliability, and feel that we are not addressing her concerns.

Pitfalls and Limits

Any unrecognized transference creates a potential pitfall. The best way to address these difficulties is to be on the lookout, ask for reactions, comment on our perceptions of the clients' views of us, and interpret their defenses against therapy. A major route of acting out could be substance abuse that went unrecognized.

We would make our support for sobriety clear. We set limits by meeting only at the agreed-upon times, and we expect prompt payment of the agreed-upon fee. Attempts to change the parameters of the treatment are quickly explored, related to underlying feelings, and made conscious, so that the couple can choose to exercise control over their choices.

Areas to Avoid

We cannot imagine any area as being off limits for our work. Therapy has to deal with all aspects of a couple's life, including secrets. As always, tact and timing determine when and how to bring up a sensitive topic for discussion or to confront difficult defenses and anxieties. We work with the clients' reluctance, embarrassment, ignorance, or shame. We try to understand why these defensive postures are still needed. This helps them to develop comfort when approaching their trigger points.

Inclusion of Others in the Treatment

We do not include other family members, friends, or therapists in the couple therapy, but we would collaborate with other treating professionals. We conceive of couple therapy as a private space for the couple to deal with each other and with the influence of their internal figures on their current relationship. On the other hand, there may be a good reason to deal with one of Jan's or Mike's actual family members whose support or input is regarded as essential. This, however, is not usual in our practice, since our focus is internal not external.

The Role of Homework

We would not use homework or special assignments unless sex therapy exercises were found to be necessary. Our only suggestion is that the couple make time between sessions to talk to each other.

The Time Line of Mike and Jan's Therapy

We would see Mike and Jan as a couple once a week, or twice a week if they wanted to intensify their commitment to therapy. Our sessions would be forty-five minutes long unless Mike and Jan had to travel some distance to see us, in which case a longer session every other week might be more realistic. We would prefer not to see Mike and/or Jan individually unless they showed their need for individual privacy to discuss an issue that could not yet be raised with the other present. It would be our intention to use the individual session to prepare for shared discussion. A pitfall here is that the therapist may receive a piece of confidential information and be stymied in the next couple sessions. Better to make it clear that confidentiality pertains to the couple. A marriage with secrets cannot grow and develop in therapy. If one of them clearly had internalized problems that dominated the couple sessions, then referral to another individual therapist would be arranged.

Termination and Relapse Prevention

Mike and Jan have a good prognosis. They have already stayed together through hard times, and Mike has stopped using drugs. They are in agreement about wanting to avoid divorce. They have had a good sexual relationship to draw on to hold the center of their relationship together if the sexual bond can be reawakened. It is not clear from the limited information presented how committed Mike and Jan are to facing their conflict. An extended four-session assessment in the object relations approach would let us see how they attempt to discuss their problems in the shared interview situation. But only a course of therapy would let us see if they could tolerate the anxiety of disagreement and the necessary expression of feelings of anger, hurt, and frustrated desire until the goals of therapy had been met. We use the criteria listed in table 18.2 to determine when the couple is ready for termination.

We would not build in follow-up interviews because we think that this might suggest that the couple would not manage by themselves. When Mike and Jan terminate, we want them to feel secure in the couple's ability to provide a good holding environment for each of them and yet to feel that they could come back to see us if future experience should lead them to think that they needed more help. The best relapse prevention comes from the couple's continued practicing of the lesson learned in therapy: They need to make time to communicate their feelings to each other, to listen respectfully, and to own their individual contributions to shared difficulties.

Table 18.2.   Criteria for termination

- The partners have internalized the therapeutic space and now have a reasonably secure holding capacity.
- Unconscious projective identifications have been recognized, owned, and taken back by each partner.
- The capacity to love and work together as life partners is restored.
- The sexual relationship is intimate and mutually gratifying.
- The partners can envision their future development and provide a vital holding environment for each other and for their family.
- The couple can differentiate between and meet the needs of each partner.
- Alternatively, the couple recognizes the failure of the marital choice, understands the unconscious object relations incompatibility, and the partners separate with some grief work done and with a capacity to continue mourning the loss of the marriage individually.

REFERENCES

Bion, W. 1959. *Experiences in Groups.* New York: Basic Books.

———. 1962. *Learning from Experience.* New York: Basic Books

———. 1967. *Second Thoughts.* London: Heinemann.

Birtchnell, J. 1993. *How Humans Relate.* Westport, CT, and London: Praeger.

Dattilio, F., and L. Bevilacqua. 2000. Introduction and case conceptualization of Mike and Jan. In *Comparative Treatments for Sexual Dysfunction,* ed. F. Dattilio and L. Bevilacqua, pp. 13–20. New York: Springer.

Dicks, H. V. 1967. *Marital Tensions: Clinical Studies Towards a Psychoanalytic Theory of Interaction.* London: Routledge and Kegan Paul.

Ezriel, H. 1952. Notes on psychoanalytic group therapy ii: interpretation and research. *Psychiatry* 15:119–26.

Fairbairn, W. R. D. 1952. *Psychoanalytic Studies of the Personality.* London: Routledge and Kegan Paul.

Klein, M. 1946. Notes on some schizoid mechanisms. *International Journal of Psycho-Analysis* 27:99–110.

———. 1975. *Envy and Gratitude and Other Works 1946–1963.* London: Hogarth Press and the Institute of Psycho-Analysis.

Scharff, D. E. 1982. *The Sexual Relationship: An Object Relations View of Sex and the Family.* London: Routledge and Kegan Paul. Reprinted 1997, Northvale, NJ: Jason Aronson.

———. 1989. An object relations approach to sexuality in family life. In J. Scharff, ed., *Foundations of Object Relations Family Therapy,* pp. 399–417. Northvale, NJ: Jason Aronson.

———, ed. 1995. *Object Relations Theory and Practice.* Northvale, NJ: Jason Aronson.

Scharff, D. E., and J. S. Scharff. 1987. Couples and couple therapy. In *Object Relations Family Therapy,* pp. 227–54. Northvale, NJ: Jason Aronson.

———. 1991. *Object Relations Couple Therapy.* Northvale, NJ: Jason Aronson.

Scharff, J. S. 1995. Psychoanalytic marital therapy. In *Clinical Handbook of Couple Therapy,* ed. N. S. Jacobson and A. S. Gurman, pp. 164–93. New York: The Guilford Press.

———, ed. 1989. *Foundations of Object Relations Family Therapy.* Northvale, NJ: Jason Aronson.

Scharff, J. S., and D. E. Scharff. 1992. *A Primer of Object Relations Therapy,* 2nd edition (formerly known as *Scharff Notes*). Northvale, NJ: Jason Aronson.

———. 1998. *Object Relations Individual Therapy.* Northvale, NJ: Jason Aronson.

Winnicott, D. 1958. *Collected Papers: Through Paediatrics to Psycho-Analysis.* London: Hogarth Press.

———. 1965. *The Maturational Processes and the Facilitating Environment.* London: Hogarth Press.

———. 1971. *Playing and Reality.* London: Tavistock.

19

Couple Psychotherapy and Attachment Theory

Christopher Clulow

ATTACHMENT THEORY
AND PSYCHOANALYSIS

Psychoanalysis has been slow to acknowledge attachment theory as one of its own. Yet findings from observational and representational research shed light on intrapsychic as well as interpersonal phenomena dealt with in clinical work. For instance, attachment theory is relevant to couple therapy and is especially useful in thinking about behavior and mental representations associated with the experience of reunion in therapy sessions.

Historically, attachment theory and psychoanalysis have been uneasy bedfellows. The reasons for this are many and complex, and it is relatively recently that progress has been made in integrating this "black sheep" of the psychoanalytic community back into the fold (Fonagy 2001). Because scepticism remains about the claim to membership of a theory that has been influenced by nonpsychoanalytic approaches (evolution, ethology, control systems, and cognition), it sometimes needs to be restated that attachment theory *is* a branch of psychoanalysis. In understanding human development and behavior it takes account of unconscious processes, defense mechanisms, the formation of an internal world of object relations, and the relationship of reciprocal influence that exists between this and the social environment of the individual. Today, attachment theory research is providing an empirical basis for many of the clinical assertions made by practitioners of psychoanalysis.

At the heart of attachment theory lie two interrelated propositions that apply to the adult couple as well as to the nursing couple: The felt security of an individual is a product of social relatedness; the development of social relatedness is a product of the felt security of individuals. Herein lies the paradox of partnership: Intimate involvement with others is a precondition for developing a capacity to be alone; the capacity to be alone is a precondition for developing intimate involvement with others. Herein also lie the different starting points of attachment and object relations theories (individuation as a product of intimate relating) and Freudian dimensions of ego psychology (primary narcissism giving way to intimacy) in charting human development.

Intimacy has been defined as "making one's innermost self known, sharing one's core, one's truth, one's heart, with another, and accepting, tolerating the core, the truth, of another" (Cassidy 2001, p. 122). Since the development of intimacy is at the very heart of the psychoanalytic enterprise, and the capacity to be intimate is related to secure attachment, psychoanalysis has reason to be informed about attachment theory. However, a further problem in effecting a rapprochement has been that for psychoanalysis the site of learning about the vicissitudes of intimacy has been clinical practice, whereas for attachment theory it has predominantly been empirical research.

Insofar as attachment theory has become associated with a tradition of observational research, doubt has been raised about its claim to share the same field of concern as psychoanalysis. There is a vigorous debate in psychoanalytic circles about the relevance and utility of observation for therapeutic practice. On one side of the debate there is the argument that unconscious processes and the transference cannot be "seen," in any observable sense, but only experienced within the clinical setting. Meaning results from the processing of experience, and therefore what is of importance follows rather than accompanies events. Everything of clinical interest is then contained in the *après coup*. From this perspective, observational research falls outside the psychoanalytic paradigm and constitutes a potential threat to "the spirit of psychoanalysis, the specific mental state that inhabits the psychoanalyst during his or her work and thinking" (Green 2000, p. 26). An alternative view is that from the earliest stages of infancy there is a capacity for intersubjectivity that can be captured in the present "moment of meeting," and that this present fleeting moment contains aspects of an experienced past and anticipated future that may be communicated through enactments and patterned behavior. The difference then is between a "psychology of presence," infant observation focusing upon an interaction, and a "psychology of absence," exploring what is in the infant's mind when the object is absent (Stern 2000).

Stern's distinction between the "observed infant" and the "clinical infant" is helpful to this debate (Stern 1985). He writes that the "observed infant" is a direct construct of what can be directly observed in the present—movements, facial expressions, language, patterns of behavior, and so on. The "clinical infant" is a construct of the therapist and adult patient as they re-create infancy from memories, enactments in the transference, and theoretically guided interpretations. The "clinical infant":

> is created to make sense of the whole early period of a patient's life story, a story that emerges in the course of its telling to someone else. This is what many therapists mean when they say that psychoanalytic therapeutics is a special form of story-making, a narrative. The story is discovered, as well as altered, by both teller and listener in the course of the telling. Historical truth is established by what gets told, not by what actually happened . . . real-life-as-experienced becomes a product of the narrative, rather than the other way around. The past is, in one sense, a fiction. (p. 15)

Stern argues forcefully that both kinds of infant are needed in pursuing the quest for truth, the "clinical infant" breathing subjective life into the "observed infant," and the "observed infant" pointing toward general theories upon which the inferred subjective life of the "clinical infant" can be built.

OBSERVING MOTHER-INFANT PATTERNS OF BEHAVIOR

The concept of maternal mirroring provides an insight into the process by which secure attachment and the "truth" about the infant's self become known through observation (Winnicott 1974). When an infant looks at her mother, what she sees is herself reflected in her mother's expression. The mother's capacity to focus on her infant, to attend to her and be sensitive to her gestures in the responses she makes, provides the infant with a picture of who she, the infant, is. Winnicott's insight has been developed through observations that show how attuned mothers help their infants identify their feelings by mirroring behavior that has two characteristics: "marking" and "contingency" (Gergely and Watson 1996). "Marking" allows for the infant's experience to be distinguished from that of the mother, and may be communicated by the mother's facial expressions being exaggerated—playfully allowing her to convey that she has recognized and is responding to the *infant's* signal. "Marking" is therefore a bulwark against the excessive use of projective identification. "Contingency" is related to the "truthfulness" of the response, the response being contingent upon the emotional communication of the infant. When the mother reads the situation accurately, "contingency" gives "marking" a coherence. Both form the basis of the beginnings of a sense of an inner world, a "place" in which experience can be projected, represented, thought about, and creatively assimilated. "Untruth" is introduced into the relationship when the mother can afford to respond to only part of the infant's signals and ignores other communications that might disturb her own psychological equilibrium and state of mind. Parents can be unconsciously "untruthful" with their infants when they deny their reality, attack it, or attempt to convert it into something else. The title of the paper, "On knowing what you are not supposed to know and feeling what you are not supposed to feel" (Bowlby 1988), speaks precisely to this condition, one that is manifested most dramatically in relation to events of loss and trauma.

Implicit in this account is the developmental significance of a process in which successions of encounters with the mother provide confirming or disconfirming responses to the infant's experience and nascent sense of self. These encounters might be thought of as reunion episodes, when the infant is not only reunited with the physical presence of the mother but also with an experience of self.

The significance of reunion behavior was emphasized by the results of an attachment-based research process designed to capture and classify the "truthfulness" or "security" of attachment in the infant-parent dyad. Mary Ainsworth, a close colleague of John Bowlby, developed her naturalistic observations of infant-mother relationships in Uganda into similar home observations and a laboratory-based procedure for infants and their mothers in Baltimore known as the Strange Situation Test (Ainsworth, Blehar, Waters, and Wall 1978). This procedure allowed observers to study the responses of infants to being separated from and reunited with their primary caregiver (usually mother). The procedure exposed infants aged between twelve and eighteen months to a stressful sequence of events designed to activate attachment behavior. In a playroom setting the parent twice left and twice returned to her child. A stranger twice entered the room. The infant was once left alone with the stranger and once left entirely alone. The whole procedure, lasting about twenty minutes, was recorded on film.

While Ainsworth and her colleagues had assumed this test would demonstrate the universality of attachment behavior—expecting infants to cry and protest about being separated from their parents, and to run to and be comforted by them upon their return—this was true of only thirteen of the twenty-three infants originally studied. Six showed little or no distress at being left alone or with a stranger, and then ignored or avoided their parents when they returned to the room. The remaining four responded with a mixture of anxiety and anger, clinging ambivalently to the caregiver on her return but unable to engage in exploratory play even when she was present. From these responses a classification of attachment behavior was created. The first, and largest, group of infants were classified as securely attached.

The remaining two groups were deemed to be insecurely attached, the first being classified as avoidant and the second as anxious/ambivalent. Attention later turned to disorganized/disoriented patterns of behavior in which the infant appeared both drawn to and fearful of the mother, but this will not be elaborated upon here.

It is important to remember that while only the infant's behavior was being rated, that behavior was specific to a particular relationship. The infant could behave differently in different contexts. In that sense, what was being observed was a relationship. When insecure behavior was organized (in contrast to the disorganized/disoriented category that was created later) it was understood as a strategy developed by the infant for maintaining proximity with the caregiver in less than optimal conditions. As a result of countless interactions it was assumed that the infant was responding to cues from the caregiver, "reading" how best to avoid outright rejection, or how to be close to her without being intruded upon. This was in contrast to securely attached infants, whose behavior was highly correlated with maternal sensitivity to the infant's signals as evidenced at home over the preceding year.

What is of greatest significance from the Strange Situation Test is that the episodes in which the infant was reunited with the mother provided the strongest evidence for the classification of attachment security. In other words, the infant's inferred state of mind with regard to attachment was most visible at the point of reunion with mother.

REPRESENTING FAMILY EXPERIENCE

The tradition of attachment research has not confined itself to observation. The shift from analyzing the detailed behavior of infants and mothers to examining the pictorial communications of older children and the representation of early family relationships by adults is documented in a seminal paper on attachment research (Main, Kaplan, and Cassidy 1985). From an attachment perspective, narratives constitute important emotional communications and mechanisms for transmitting—and, importantly, from a psychotherapeutic perspective, transmuting—patterns of attachment across the generations (Holmes 2001). Restricted stories are too bounded and rigid to allow the truth out or others in; unbounded stories can have the same effect by confusing the listener and encouraging an enmeshment that allows no coherent theme to emerge.

For adults a sophisticated system has been devised to classify individual attachment security from the way subjects represent their early family experiences in the semistructured task posed by the Adult Attachment Interview (George, Kaplan, and Main 1985). Secure subjects have a narrative style that fulfills four indices of coherence: quality (being "truthful" and having evidence for what you say), quantity (being succinct and yet complete), relation (being relevant and collaborative in presenting what is said), and manner (being clear and orderly). Ratings of security also take account of spontaneity in the telling of stories, and the openness of the teller to reviewing and revising the story as it is being told (the distinction between narrative and story being that between form and content).

Through an analysis of discourse it is possible to discern how language and syntax are used to regulate attachment-related anxieties, much as the observed infant uses behavior to the same end. Insecure patterns take two main organized forms: *dismissing* and *preoccupied* narratives. *Dismissing* narratives attempt to limit the influence of attachment experiences in the way they represent past family relationships. Idealization, lack of recall, abstraction and, sometimes, denigration serve to keep attachment systems deactivated. Contradictions between semantic and episodic accounts fail to provide internal consistency in the narrative which, combined with its brevity, operates to keep the interviewer at bay. *Preoccupied* narratives are confused, passive, vague, sometimes unconvincingly analytical or angrily conflicted. The teller often gets lost in his or her story, fails to find an autonomous perspective in relation to events being recounted, and unconsciously invites the interviewer to become similarly enmeshed in the experience.

The task of the Adult Attachment Interview (AAI) is comparable to that of the Strange Situation Test (SST). It is designed to expose subjects to a stressful situation in order to activate and make evident their orientation toward attachment. There is a reunion dimension in both procedures, the AAI inviting its subjects to re-encounter themselves and their internalized object relationships, rather than actually re-encountering an attachment figure as happens in the SST. However, both procedures are concerned with accessing patterns of attachment in the domain of child-parent relationships. Can the adult couple be construed as an attachment relationship, and if so, what might be taken from the traditions of observation and representation that might be useful for therapeutic practice?

ATTACHMENT AND THE ADULT COUPLE

It was 1987 before adult romantic relationships were formally conceptualized in attachment terms (Hazan and Shaver 1987), although clinicians such as Weiss (1975) and Mattinson and Sinclair (1979) had previously used attachment theory to illuminate patterns of behavior in couple relationships. Subsequently, there has been a growing interest in researching couples from an attachment perspective, especially within the discipline of social psychology (Feeney 1999). Significant differences between attachment in the parent-infant and adult couple dyads have been described in terms of the latter being reciprocal, and being sexually motivated to seek physical proximity—the sexual relationship creating conditions in which attachment can develop (Hazan and Zeifman 1999).

The reciprocal nature of couple attachment has attracted interest from couple psychotherapists and researchers. A distinction has been drawn between simple (uni-directional) and complex (bi-directional) attachment in the couple (Fisher and Crandell 2001). The hallmark of secure attachment for these authors is the capacity of each partner to move between the positions of depending upon and being depended on by each other in a flexible and appropriate manner, what they term complex attachment. In insecure partnerships the direction of attachment may become uni-directional and rigidified, with partners competing with each other for care, denying their need to be cared for, or settling into a quasi-parental pattern where one partner is designated as the carer and the other as being in need of care.

Reciprocity in giving and seeking care is also implicit in the criterion of attachment security for researchers investigating the behavior of adults in couple relationships, although it is not used as a measure of security (Crowell and Treboux 2001). Building on Ainsworth's observational methods for capturing patterns of infant behavior, these researchers have developed a measure of attachment security that examines the quality of secure base use (the "child" role) and secure base support (the "parental" role) displayed by partners in their partnership. In optimal secure base use a partner signals his or her needs clearly and consistently until there is a response. The response received is comforting and enables emotional equilibrium to be established in the partnership. Equally, in providing secure base support the other partner recognizes the distress signals, correctly interprets the need, and provides a response that is timely and appropriate.

Observational and representational measures for capturing attachment security in the domain of the adult couple are still in the early stages of development, but available results indicate that the domains of early family relationships and the adult couple do not map identically onto each other. In other words, there are indications that support the clinical contention that relationships in later life can influence patterns of attachment established during childhood. This is generally encouraging, but more specifically, the methods used to capture patterns of attachment may have real clinical utility.

ATTENDING TO REUNIONS IN PSYCHOTHERAPY WITH COUPLES

Whatever their modality, therapists in the psychoanalytic tradition have long been aware of their significance as attachment figures in their patients' inner and outer worlds. Working with the experience of separation in the therapeutic relationship, whether owing to breaks in the therapy or its ending, is recognized as having tremendous therapeutic potential. This stems from an awareness of how frequently patients manage separations by falling back on characteristic defensive strategies. The loss of, or anxious regard for time boundaries at the end of sessions, the fear or dismissed significance of impending holiday breaks, and the idealization of, or attack on therapy at its close can be understood and worked with as manifestations of, and defenses against, separation anxiety.

The fear of separation, and separateness, lies at the heart of many couple problems. Attempts to control behavior, to plan ways forward, and to structure relationships—whether in the context of the couple or the therapy—can represent attempts to avoid anxiety associated with needing and depending upon others. The failure of one partner to turn up for a session may generate anger in the other that conceals the distress of being left behind. The act of leaving, or not turning up, may be to protect against the fear of being left. The absence of one therapist (in situations where there are two), or sessions missed through therapist absence, can similarly raise anxiety, eliciting angry, dismissing, or fearful responses to the prospect of loss.

The rhythm of weekly sessions, with their regular separations, also brings a cycle of reunions. In this respect therapy sessions can be regarded as having some of the properties of Ainsworth's Strange Situation Test (Clulow 2001). The reunion dimension of the therapeutic process is likely to activate fears about intimacy which, in turn, are linked with internal assumptions and anxiety about the prospect of future loss. The task of therapy means that partners will re-encounter each other—and themselves—in ways that are different from the usual routines of everyday life. Their inner world assumptions about the nature of relationships are tested against those of their partner in an actual relationship. Any dissonance between the two is likely to be stressful, and the couple will work toward arriving at a modus operandi in their partnership that "fits" (as distinct from "meets") the needs of each partner. Together they are likely to fashion and share defensive systems to protect them from threats to their individual and collective representational worlds. It is these dimensions of experience that constitute the focus of attention for couple psychoanalytic psychotherapy (Ruszczynski 1993, Scharff and Savege Scharff 1991).

Because reunion behavior tests conscious expectations and the unconscious premises of the representational worlds of each partner against the reality of an actual social experience (in the contexts of the partnership and in the therapy) there is much potential for learning to occur. The articulation of a shared internal world allows for partners to re-encounter themselves as well as each other, and so provides opportunities for moving from narcissistic object relating toward real intimacy in the partnership and the therapy. In this process the therapist might be regarded as the stranger in the Strange Situation Test. She or he may constitute a threat by appearing to come between the couple, raising the possibility of separation or divorce by engaging the partners in discussions about areas that threaten their sense of security. She/he may also diminish that anxiety by making the process safer—creating for the couple a "secure base" or psychological "container" that facilitates change.

The therapist is also a potential attachment figure, akin to the caregiver in the SST, although in couple psychotherapy he or she is likely to be of less significance than the partner in the room. Nevertheless, in working with the transference it is to be expected that some of the patterns operating between the couple will apply also in relation to the therapist. Here there is scope for a more subtle and intricate series of separations and reunions to be attended to. The therapist's gaze of attention, when turned toward one partner, may break a sense of connection with the other, replicating an Oedipal dilemma that he or she may need to notice and respond to in order for the couple as a whole to stay engaged with the process. The therapist will also need to be alive to how each partner turns away from or intrudes upon the other (and the therapist) at moments of potential emotional engagement, when being reunited with aspects of their experience that cause discomfort or anxiety. Therapists will also need to take into account how countertransferential pressures and their own attachment orientation may result in patterns of relating that avoid real engagement with the dynamic issue that is waiting for recognition and a response.

CASE ILLUSTRATION

In the illustration that follows an attempt is made to show how observing behavior and attending to representations contained in a couple's narrative in the opening stages of a therapeutic consultation has potential for providing access to material that is relevant for making a clinical diagnosis and indicating a possible focus for therapeutic work. The spouses were seen in the context of a pilot research project exploring the feasibility of testing associations between attachment status and conflict management strategies among those approaching the Tavistock Centre for Couple Relationships, London, for help with their partnership.

Alan and Anne are a couple in their midfifties whose children have left home. Prior to the consultation they had completed a fifteen-minute research task in which they were videotaped trying to make headway on their own with the problem that had brought them for therapy. With their consent, the video camera was left running for the consultation. The consultation begins with the therapist saying how long the session will last and asking how he might help.

Alan begins: "The main thing is the last two months." They had left a restaurant where they had been having a meal with their daughter and she had annoyed him. His daughter was driving them home from the restaurant, but as they made to leave a car had pulled out in front of them. He got out of the car to face the driver, fearing he might be in a rage and wanting to protect his wife and daughter. Anne became hysterical. He lost his temper and hit her twice on the arm. The second occasion was when they were on holiday. The holiday was his treat for her. They had run out of money at the hotel, he went to get more, was locked out of their room by her on his return. He had to ask the concierge to let him in. They then had a "totally irrational" fight about where he had been. To prove his position he had even produced the timed receipt from the cash machine. He had withdrawn into another room with a book, she had pursued him, not satisfied with his answer. He had pushed her ("hit me on the head," she says), then she had smashed a lamp and left. He didn't know where she had gone, checked the airport, telephoned his daughter at home, and it was the next day before she returned having slept elsewhere in the hotel. She was "totally irrational—that's my story."

The therapist, anxious about the violence, asks Alan if he is worried about his behavior. He says yes, but excuses himself by saying that he thought he was doing the right thing in each case. He was trying to protect them in the car, he hadn't run away. The therapist asks how he had felt at the time. "Totally angry," Alan replies, "because I was given no explanation by Anne." "Had they tried talking about this?" enquired the therapist. "They had," he said, "but still I got no answer."

Anne comes in at this point saying she had stopped talking because he might become violent, and he had threatened to leave her rather than have that happen again. She refers back to a time some ten to fifteen years previously when she had threatened to take out an injunction against him because of his violence. The children had seen it and been damaged by it. This was news to Alan, and Anne says the children hadn't told him about it because they were scared of him. He says he can't believe this, and comments on all he's done for them, adding that she has been violent, too, even cutting up his clothes. He then protests that the session is getting too adversarial and he feels as if he is in a court of law—like "trying to put my case." His fear is that if he comes out on top from the session then she'll think it is a waste of time, so the only option open to him is being the bad guy.

The therapist picks up the "court of law" experience, commenting on how difficult it must be to talk and listen together in that frame of mind. He asks what they want to come out of the session. Anne responds by saying she thought he had been having an affair when he had been violent before, explaining his behavior by inferring that he had felt guilty then as now. She fears the violence means the same thing is happening again. She feels they have lost their good relationship with the children, and that they need to talk about the past, perhaps with their grown-up children present. The therapist picks up on Anne's fear of Alan having an affair. She agrees, saying they were not as close as they used to be.

Commentary

In this illustration there is evidence of a patterned interaction in the marriage that might be described as a shared defense. The observed dynamic is of a frustratedly angry man being arraigned and controlled by his wife for behaving violently. Alan's gestures, expressed in exaggerated body movements—arms gesticulating wildly and repeatedly slapping the top of his legs as they fall in his lap—convey just how agitated he has become. This is in marked contrast to Anne's stillness as she studies her notes and pursues her arguments. Observing his countertransference, the therapist was aware of feeling anxious about a potentially violent threat, coerced into taking sides, and left in a position where there was little space to think laterally about what the couple might be most anxious about in seeking help.

As we have seen, it is important not only to observe behavior and subjective responses to it but also to understand how couples represent their experience, and to consider what they are trying to communicate through the stories they tell. Here, the truth of a story may not correspond with the truth of the narrative. What is important for the therapist is listening to how the story is told and accessing what it is being used to convey. In this latter respect it has been argued that the stories couples tell in therapy sessions can be regarded as couple "dreams"—sometimes "nightmares": pictorialized communications of emotional experience (Fisher 1999).

Alan and Anne's opening stories suggest roles that each partner takes up in response to an experience of threat. In the first, Alan perceives himself to be both the potential victim and perpetrator of an attack on his family, threatened and frustrated by his exit being blocked by a stranger (the threat of coming to therapy?). In the second, he conveys his response to the experience of being shut out and abandoned. Anne's exclusion of him suggests that this may have been an enacted communication about how she was feeling, having been left on her own at the hotel without explanation. There is a victim-victimizer interaction between them, but the roles are ambiguous and move between them, concealing key emotional communications around the experience of leaving and being left.

Their story and narrative style depict a man who wishes to be in the position of protector and provider for his family and in the marriage, but whose actual experience in relationships falls short of this ideal. He avoids expressing his feelings directly, except through his behavior and in relation to his uncomprehending frustration with his wife. He is prepared to be the "villain of the piece" if that will protect both the marriage and his need for emotional distance. Anne finds it difficult to speak to her own feelings and needs, instead triggering them in Alan. Her ambivalent bids for attention (pursuing, provoking, and protecting herself from him) suggest her underlying anxiety about her entitlement to be loved and wanted for herself, and a belief that she will only be able to keep Alan if she controls him. Their story can be taken as indicative of a shared fantasy that being loved carries conditions, and that intimacy is potentially dangerous in the violent engagement it can provoke. So they keep their distance, but in different ways. This is both a protective strategy and one that can itself trigger a crisis. What they seek is some validation of themselves by each other, but this turns into an appeal for judgment from a third party (therapist, camera, children) that they believe can only be satisfied at the expense of one of them.

CONCLUSION

It is reasonable to assume that couples seeking professional help will find talking about their problems stressful. Attachment theory proposes that such threats will activate both attachment behavior and strategies of relating that individuals assume (often unconsciously) will protect them against the threat of intimacy when that has become associated with the prospect of loss. Strategies relied upon to manage such conflicts are likely to be evident in the "reunion" behavior at the start of therapy, the start of sessions, and the moments of potential encounter within sessions.

By drawing from traditions of attachment research it may be possible for therapists to become more attuned to detecting the nature of the anxiety that underlies a couple's defensive strategies, especially by processing what is said and done in the opening stages of a therapy session. This is likely to involve observing the behavior of couples and the therapist's emotional responses to them, as well as attending to the stories partners recount as representations of the shared unconscious fantasies that bind them together as a couple, and decoding the emotional communications that they contain.

Whether observing or listening, therapists need to take account of the context they create for couples as partners re-encounter themselves and each other in the session. That context, including the therapist's own attachment status, will influence the gestures made and the responses they receive in the fine-grained process of the session. What they create together then becomes open to being experienced and thought about. Given that an optimal level of anxiety is necessary for therapeutic change, creating "secure base" conditions in which exploration is neither understimulated nor inhibited by anxiety becomes an important objective of the work. Attending to behavior and narratives associated with the reunions that are part of the fabric of every therapeutic relationship may then have real practical utility in helping therapists think about and work with insecure patterns of attachment in the couple.

REFERENCES

Ainsworth, M. D. S., M. Blehar, E. Waters, and S. Wall. 1978. *Patterns of Attachment: A Psychological Study of the Strange Situation*. Hillsdale, NJ: Lawrence Erlbaum.

Bowlby, J. 1988. On knowing what you are not supposed to know and feeling what you are not supposed to feel. In *A Secure Base. Clinical Applications of Attachment Theory*, pp. 99–118. London: Routledge.

Cassidy, J. 2001. Truth, lies, and intimacy: An attachment perspective. *Attachment and Human Development* 3(2): 121–55.

Clulow, C. 2001. Attachment theory and the therapeutic frame. In C. Clulow, ed., *Adult Attachment and Couple Psychotherapy. The "Secure Base" in Practice and Research*, pp. 85–104. London: Brunner-Routledge.

Crowell, J., and D. Treboux. 2001. Attachment security in adult partnerships. In C. Clulow, ed., *Adult Attachment and Couple Psychotherapy. The "Secure Base" in Practice and Research*, pp. 28–42. London: Brunner-Routledge.

Feeney, J. 1999. Adult romantic attachment and couple relationships. In J. Cassidy and P. Shaver, eds., *Handbook of Attachment. Theory, Research and Clinical Applications*, pp. 355–77. New York: Guilford.

Fisher, J. 1999. *The Uninvited Guest. Emerging from Narcissism towards Marriage*. London: Karnac.

Fisher, J., and L. Crandell. 2001. Patterns of relating in the couple. In C. Clulow, ed., *Adult Attachment and Couple Psychotherapy. The "Secure Base" in Practice and Research*, pp. 15–27. London: Brunner-Routledge.

Fonagy, P. 2001. *Attachment Theory and Psychoanalysis*. New York: Other Press.

George, C., N. Kaplan, and M. Main. 1985. The adult attachment interview. Unpublished manuscript, University of California, Berkeley.

Gergely, G., and J. Watson. 1996. The social bio-feedback theory of parental affect-mirroring. *International Journal of Psycho-Analysis* 77:181–212.

Green, A. 2000. What kind of research for psychoanalysis? In J. Sandler, A. Sandler, and R. Davies, eds., *Clinical and Observational Research: Roots of a Controversy*, pp. 21–26. London: Karnac.

Hazan, C., and P. Shaver. 1987. Romantic love conceptualized as an attachment process. *Journal of Personality and Social Psychology* 52(3): 511–24.

Hazan, C., and D. Zeifman. 1999. Pair bonds as attachment: Evaluating the evidence. In J. Cassidy and P. Shaver, eds., *Handbook of Attachment. Theory, Research and Clinical Applications*, pp. 336–54. New York and London: Guilford.

Holmes, J. 2001. *The Search for the Secure Base. Attachment Theory and Psychotherapy*. London: Brunner-Routledge.

Main, M., N. Kaplan, and J. Cassidy. 1985. Security in infancy, childhood and adulthood: A move to the level of representation. In I. Bretherton and E. Waters, eds., *Growing Points of Attachment Theory and Research. Monograph of the Society for Research and Child Development. Serial No. 209, Vol. 50, Nos. 1–2.*

Mattinson, J., and I. Sinclair. 1979. *Mate and Stalemate: Working with Marital Problems in a Social Services Department*. Oxford: Blackwell.

Ruszczynski, S., ed. 1993. *Psychotherapy with Couples: Theory and Practice at the Tavistock Institute of Marital Studies*. London: Karnac.

Scharff, D., and J. Savege Scharff. 1991. *Object Relations Couple Therapy*. Northvale, NJ: Jason Aronson.

Stern, D. 1985. *The Interpersonal World of the Infant. A View from Psychoanalysis and Developmental Psychology*. New York: Basic Books.

———. 2000. Empirical infant research. In J. Sandler, A. Sandler, and R. Davies, eds., *Clinical and Observational Psychoanalytic Research: Roots of a Controversy*. London: Karnac.

Weiss, R. 1975. *Marital Separation*. New York: Basic Books.

Winnicott, D. 1974. *Playing and Reality*. Harmondsworth: Penguin.

20

Integrating Attachment Theory and Neuroscience in Couple Therapy

Sondra Goldstein and Susan Thau

ATTACHMENT STYLES IN COUPLES

Bowlby wrote that the human attachment patterns noted in infant-caregiver interaction continue to play a vital role in human development "from the cradle to the grave" (1979, p. 129). Following the seminal work of Bowlby and other infant researchers, there has been growing recognition that the quality of childhood attachments is intimately linked with patterns of interpersonal relatedness throughout life (Clulow 2001). Attachment theory provides a theoretical framework for understanding adult couple relationships, and a valuable perspective for assessing and treating couples. An attachment perspective shifts the focus of concern of couple therapy from the security of the individual to the security of the couple relationship. Central to a couple's sense of security is the ability to regulate affect within the relationship. Schore's (2001) findings from neuroscience provide evidence that attachment patterns influence interactive affect regulation in dyads.

We find parallels between the defining features of infant-caregiver attachment behavior and adult couple attachments. Bowlby (1969, 1973) proposed that attachment bonds are characterized by: (1) proximity-seeking; (2) safe-haven behavior; (3) separation distress; and (4) secure-base behavior. All of these features of infant-caregiver bonds may be observed in couple relationships (Weiss 1991). The partners derive comfort and security from each other. Each partner wants to be with the other, particularly in times of stress. When one partner in a relationship threatens to be physically or emotionally unavailable, the other partner may protest. However, in adult romantic bonds the asymmetry of early bonds is replaced by symmetry, mutuality, and sexual intimacy (Hazan and Zeifman 1994).

Adult styles of relating to primary attachment figures parallel the attachment styles identified in infant-caregiver relationships. Hazan and Shaver (1987) presented groundbreaking research, which showed that the three major childhood attachment styles (secure, insecure-avoidant, and insecure-ambivalent) are also found in adult romantic relationships. Hazan and Shaver taught that attachment styles of couples can be viewed in terms of the answer to the question "Can I count on this person to be there for me if I need them?" If the answer is "Yes" in a positive and secure way, the partners feel confident that they may rely on each other, have open communication, and experience a flexible, cooperative relationship. If the answer is "Maybe," partners tend to have an insecure-ambivalent style, with vigilance about loss, and alternating clinging and angry demands for reassurance. If the answer is "No," the partner's past history of abuse, neglect, or rejection may have left no hope for a secure relationship. In the resulting insecure-avoidant attachment style, the partner avoids closeness or dependency, denies the need for attachment, and views others with mistrust.

Hazan and Shaver's findings are consistent with Bowlby's (1982) hypothesis that children develop internal working models about relationships. These relatively stable working models are implicit, nonconscious guides for later adult attachment relationships. Bowlby (1982) hypothesized that these childhood attachment patterns could change later in life as a result of new emotional experience, and new mental representations of attachment relationships. Thus, internal working models may be altered and updated, allowing the child to earn a secure attachment style as development goes on (Hesse 1999). These ideas provide a rationale for therapeutic efficacy.

NEUROPHYSIOLOGY AND
AFFECT REGULATION

Additional understanding of attachment relationships is found in neuroscience. Attachment drives and depends on the right brain regulation of biological synchronicity between organisms (Schore 2001). Infant right brain to adult right brain psychobiological transactions, mediated by mutual gaze, promote the attachment bond between infant and caregiver. Early emotional regulation, established via infant-caregiver synchrony, leads to the organization and integration of neural networks and eventual self-regulatory capacity in the child. Attachment experiences directly influence the wiring of the orbitofrontal cortex into the limbic system. The orbitofrontal cortex mediates emotional responses and coordinates the activation and balance of the sympathetic and parasympathetic branches of the autonomic nervous system (Price et al. 1996). A balance between sympathetic and parasympathetic arousal is found in secure attachments, while an imbalance is found in insecure attachment patterns (Schore 1994). In insecure-avoidant infants, the autonomic balance is parasympathetically dominated, and geared to respond maximally to low levels of socioemotional stimulation (Izard 1991). In insecure-ambivalent infants, the autonomic balance is biased toward the sympathetic excitatory system over the parasympathetic inhibitory system, creating a vulnerability to underregulation disturbances (Schore 2003b).

The prefrontal system generates internal working models, which guide interpersonal behavior and affect regulation. These attachment schemas become implicit, nonconscious procedural memory networks, which are evoked in interpersonal experiences, particularly attachment relationships. Attachment schemas guide the selection of significant others and influence the emotions experienced within relationships. When a couple's attachment schema is challenged, or the attachment bond is breached, a couple may seek treatment (Cozolino 2002). An understanding of attachment styles and internal working models of relationships provides a perspective in couple therapy for understanding the underlying needs and longings that are readily evoked in intimate relationships. The overarching work of therapy is to "replace silent, unworkable intuitions with functional ones" (Lewis et al. 2002, p. 179).

SECURE BASE AND EMOTIONAL ATUNEMENT

Couple therapy has traditionally been associated with building communication skills as a means of increasing intimacy between partners. But frequently, this approach does not create lasting improvement. Couples may relapse into familiar patterns of conflict that become increasingly destructive. The integration of attachment theory with neuroscience and its application in couple therapy places the emphasis on dyadic affect regulation. By understanding how each partner's nervous system is affected by "emotional reverberations" triggered in dyadic interactions (Lewis et al. 2002, p. 131), couples can work to create greater emotional attunement and the hope for a secure base within the relationship.

The newly emerging field of developmental neuropsychobiology provides a road map of how emotional patterns develop and a window into the interpersonal patterns of intimate relationships (Schore 1994, 2001, 2003a). This perspective emphasizes the complex interactive experience that includes both the individual's internal process as well as the co-constructed reciprocal interactions between the two partners. It also focuses on the therapist's role in this interactive sequence as a consideration. In attachment-based couple therapy, the therapist is committed to creating a secure enough environment in which partners can explore each individual's attachment schemas, enacted in their ongoing intimate relationship (Clulow 2001). Partners' relational needs are best addressed within a psychotherapeutic relationship, which honors the belief that the offer of secure attachment is essential to the curative possibilities of psychotherapy (Amini et al. 1996). Each partner is encouraged to become aware of personal and dyadic nonverbal communication patterns and reach beyond them to discover the unconscious implicit memories that drive them (Schore 2003a). The therapeutic emphasis is on creating a safe base, which permits joint investigation by couple and therapist. Within the secure base of therapy, each partner may feel more balanced, thereby contributing to an enriched and attuned relationship that enhances neural plasticity and learning (Schore 2003a).

Scharff and Scharff (1991) describe the therapeutic base in different terms. They see it as "a transitional space in which the couple can portray and reflect upon its current way of functioning, learn about and modify its projective identificatory system, and invent new ways of being" (p. 108). They emphasize that the therapist creates this environment in order to manage and metabolize the couple's anxiety through holding and containment.

There has been a proliferation of research involving the relational patterns between mothers and infants (Beebe and Lachmann 2002). This has shown that a baby initially needs the interactive presence of an attuned mother in establishing the ability to regulate affect. This finding is validated in couple dynamics, too. In couple treatment, the partners are dependent on the therapist to provide the affect regulation that has been eroded by unrepaired continuing conflict. As the partners are helped to understand their unresolved yearnings, they can begin the process of establishing interdependency in which each takes turns as the benign caretaker, especially in stressful life conditions (Solomon 1994). There is hope that by deepening each partner's understanding of the other, by learning to read each other's verbal and nonverbal cues, and by gaining a deeper appreciation of their own level of arousal, the partners will become more adept at interactive affect regulation, thereby strengthening the security of their attachment bond.

In attachment-based couple therapy, the partners learn about the language of emotion. They are taught to appreciate both verbal and nonverbal communication, including the multitude of signals that are bodily and viscerally based. In any dyad the individual is affected by his own behavior and by his partner's behavior, and each partner is influenced on a moment-to-moment basis by the other (Beebe and Lachmann 2002). By becoming sensitive, partners learn to pay close attention to their own visceral changes and to be curious about what these bodily signals may mean in identifying nonconscious emotions.

NONVERBAL COMMUNICATION

Nonverbal aspects of communication reflect right hemisphere emotional and implicit processes. Quality of eye contact, tone and volume of voice, nature of body movements, facial expressions, and posture are examples of nonverbal aspects of communication that provide avenues of insight into underlying nonconscious emotion. For example, when the couple therapist asks a man to notice his eyes rolling upward as his wife speaks, the man may become aware of the contempt and disdain nonverbally communicated to his wife. When the therapist calls attention to the husband's stroking his face, the man may recover memories of soothing himself after being slapped by his mother, a sensitivity reactivated when he feels criticized by his wife.

The following vignette from sessions in which Anne and Ed meet with one of us as their couple therapist illustrates how the focus on nonverbal aspects of couple communication allows access to nonconscious emotion in dyadic transactions.

Example: Anne and Ed

Anne: *(Beginning the session)* I can't believe how far apart I've felt from Ed this week. It all started when he discovered the $75.00 late fee from Visa. He thought that I paid the bill, and I thought that he had done it. So, we ended up with a late fee. For the rest of the week, he's been so distant and quiet.

Ed: *(His face hardened, jaw and teeth clenched, but speaking in a measured tone)* I hate to waste money and the late fee is $75.00 wasted. She's so careless with money. Just like her family that always lived beyond their means. No one in her family ever paid a bill on time. She's going to get us into the same financial mess.

Anne: *(Slumped into the sofa, crying)*

Ed: *(Continuing to clench his teeth, his face hardened and tense)*

Therapist: *(Thinking that Ed's tone of voice does not match his facial expression of anger, noting that he is speaking so calmly, yet his face looks furious, wondering how to help him have a connection with his emotion, and deciding that his facial expression seems to be the key)* Ed, can you pay attention to your face, and touch your lower face? What do you feel in your face?

Ed: *(Looking surprised, and touching his face hesitantly)* My jaw is clenched, and my teeth are grinding together. The muscles in my face are tense and they almost hurt. I am so embarrassed. I did not know that I was so angry, and I'm embarrassed that you see it in my face.

Anne: And this is what happened at home. Ed had that look on his face all week, but didn't talk to me about how he really felt and how mad he was about the late fee.

Ed: I guess I didn't want to admit to Anne or myself how mad I've been about this. It's really hard for me to be angry out in the open.

Therapist: For you, Ed, anger is not an emotion that you allow yourself, and you feel embarrassed that others may see it on your face. But Anne always senses when you are angry, and pulls away.

This sequence in treatment of Anne and Ed became a reference point in our talking about feelings expressed between them nonverbally, for instance, in gestures, facial expressions, and visual cues. The concept of being attuned to each other's nonverbal communications has been extremely helpful to this couple in creating attunement, recognizing misattunement, and developing the ability to repair breaches in their attachment relationship. Good enough attunement is defined in current research as 30 percent of mutual time spent in a good psychic place (Giannino and Tronick 1988). This concept of "good enough attunement" is helpful to couples. While learning to value balance and harmony, the couple also learns to process the pain of their periods of misattunement, enduring these lapses by remembering that conflict is a normal part of any couple relationship as a reflection of the differences between the two separate partners (Gottman 1991). Couples can feel hope about resolving their conflicts by thinking of them as opportunities for engaging in the process of mutual repair and so achieving greater closeness. Often neither partner has experienced his negative emotions as tolerable or understandable. Thus, when there is an attachment breach, a cycle of shame is triggered with one partner feeling that he or she is being held responsible for being unreasonable and demanding. Couples are taught how the intense state of interactive dysregulation is maintained by both partners, and how this dysregulated state can undermine their attachment bond if it is not interrupted by more reparative approaches. When conflictual feelings are seen as a normal part of a couple's interaction, then each partner can be more interested in what is being activated to create his or her personal contribution to their interactive stalemate. Each partner is encouraged to learn how to self-regulate and so become more sensitive to the partner's affect regulation. This builds mutual awareness and empathy within the dyad and interrupts the ongoing negative cycle.

In this approach to treatment, there is a continuing emphasis on how each partner is processing the emotionally charged interactions that frequently occur in the relationship. By deepening the understanding of one's own internal conscious and nonconscious systems, each partner has a greater capacity to explain his emotional state and needs. The couple learns about the unique subcortical emotional system that they have constructed. They are shown that the automatic rapid and nonconscious appraisal of danger and frightening stimuli can be slowed down when conscious thought and language are used to interrupt this rapid fear cycle (Cozolino 2002). By emphasizing the neuropsychobiological basis of automatic, rapid fear and shame responses, the therapist is able to normalize conflictual states. This type of shaming sequence begins when a young child is socialized, and can become a chronic pattern in adult relationships. Schore (1994, 2001, 2003a) describes shame-based responses moving in a sequence from negative affect to reestablish the state of positive affect, a state of equilibrium and calmness. Healing of the couple's attachment needs is brought to the foreground when these frightening moments are made conscious, then given form, substance, and language allowing joint examination of the interactive process (Johnson 2002). The healing process of repair begins with making a commitment to engage in the examination of fearful moments and goes on to include the co-creation of a shared narrative of the couple's history and manner of emotional processing (Siegel 1999).

MODIFYING ATTACHMENT MODELS AND SECURING THE BASE

We propose that couple therapy based on the integrations of attachment theory and neuroscience provides a secure base for the couple, allows the possibility of updating old internal attachment schemas, and creates new neuronal connections with altered ways of thinking about experience (Siegel 1999). From a neuropsychobiological perspective, the dysfunctional right-brain-to-right-brain transactions between the two partners are replaced with more balanced and considered transactions (Schore 1994, 2001, 2003a). Partners no longer engage in unconsciously traumatizing each other. Being capable of navigating these lapses in connection actually creates resiliency and hope at the foundation of the partnership. All of this is fundamental to the creation of a secure base in which each partner can experience his or her emotional needs, with a sense of well-being, and the state of feeling loved.

Example: Sue and John

Conjoint therapy with Sue and John offers an opportunity to examine these principles from attachment theory and neuroscience in a treatment sequence. Sue and John sought couple therapy because they were having frequent crises regarding their professions as university professors. The following vignette is from a session in which Sue became extremely upset about her overwhelming responsibilities, both at home and at the university.

> Sue: *(Her voice escalating, becoming increasingly shrill)* You just can't imagine how burdened I feel. All I do is work, work, work. John has his tenure track appointment, so he can just work on his research and the book he is writing without having to do anything else. *(Yelling at John who sits passively in his chair staring straight ahead.)* I'm the one who is expected to pick up and take care of whatever is necessary in our family. It just isn't fair. I have no life.

(Looking at him for some sign that he had taken in what she had been yelling about, for some sign of recognition and concern, but finding none, becoming even angrier and more rageful.) You are so mean and uncaring, I can't take it any more.

[Upon hearing these words, John's eyes were filled with disgust and he scowled, and then quickly turned away. He seemed impervious to her cries. Sue saw this and bit her lip, fighting back her rage which soon turned to tears.]

Therapist: *(thinking) I saw this coldness and felt the tension in the room as each partner retreated into a closed down space. I wondered what John was feeling that made him react to Sue in this way. Was it just that he was feeling blamed, and if this was so, why didn't he say something to her? Both seemed so angry. I felt powerless to be able to calm their vibrating nerves down. I wanted out of there, too. Wasn't this what both of them felt?*

[The partners were exhibiting their individual insecure-avoidant attachment styles which were dismissive and rejecting. Their outward behavior suggested that neither believed that the other wanted to be there. In this evocative moment, neither was able to bridge the gulf because both carried the internal view of themselves as someone who is unlovable. This insecurity left each partner vulnerable to being easily disrupted. The continuing occurrence of attachment breaches without the ability to repair created pessimism and despair in the couple.]

Therapist: *(thinking) I had to do something to interrupt this escalating situation and that was a challenge when I too was feeling threatened. I told myself that I could manage my fears as long as I kept away from absorbing theirs. I was there to provide a holding environment for them, and I had to begin relating to them. I began by speaking quietly to each one separately about the rapid shaming that had just occurred. I was extremely careful about the tone and tempo of my voice, knowing that it could negatively impact one or both of them.*

Therapist: This was really an intense time, and we all had our own reaction to how quickly feelings were triggered. *(Looking at John)* You were so overwhelmed by Sue's anger that it looked like you wanted to get away from her. Each of you feels as if you're being made into the bad one while your partner gets to walk away untouched. Each of you feels the hurt and pain of being unwanted so it is hard for you to want to look at your contribution to this moment. You both want me to bear witness to how poorly you have been treated, so that maybe I'll get you, John, to think about how much you have hurt Sue by ignoring and how much you, Sue, have hurt John by complaining.

Sue: I am feeling upset, and then I look at your blank face, John, and it makes me feel absolutely so alone that all I can do is feel rage and fury. I want to get as far away from you as fast as I can. You just don't seem to care at all.

John: *(Attentive, quiet, listening, watching Sue, his face no longer like a mask)* I guess that when you begin to talk like that, it makes me so upset that I don't want to have to hear you.

Therapist: Sounds like Sue's tone and expression make you tense and nervous.

John: I guess I never like to think of myself as a nervous person, but you're right, I feel weird and kind of shaky. Like, I really don't know what to say or do.

Therapist: *(thinking) I could see that this was causing a reaction in John because it was too close to his experience with his parents who had frequent rages over the fact that his father was usually out of work and unable to support the family. I waited for him to begin to make the connection as we dealt with his feelings of helplessness.*

John: I guess that I am more upset with the way you tell me things than what you are actually saying. You do have to do a great deal, and we have to work out a way to manage all these responsibilities better together. But I can't think when you start raging at me.

Sue: I am amazed, John. You are actually talking to me. That's what I have been wanting and thought was so impossible. Maybe this therapy thing really can help us to learn to listen to each other after all. I thought it never would happen.

Therapist: Well, now we have a beginning. *(Trying not to overtalk this point, but wanting to lay the groundwork to explore their co-constructed unconscious patterns of the dismissive attachment I am seeing.)* We have to begin to unravel why you revert to the particular patterns of relating that have become so automatic and habituated in your relationship.

This brief moment is an example of the rapid cycle of fear and anger that becomes a regularly enacted pattern when each partner's insecurity is being repetitively triggered by both verbal and nonverbal cues. Additional couple therapy with Sue and John allowed them to become increasingly aware of emotional triggers in words and gestures that escalated conflict and eroded their sense of a secure attachment bond. As this example illustrates, the therapist has to manage her own feelings, which are being triggered by the continuing enactment of the two partners.

CONCLUSION

The goal of couple therapy based on an integration of attachment theory and neuroscience is to explore and identify the interaction patterns of affect regulation that are the basis of either enhancing or diminishing the emotional connection between the partners. This type of couple therapy is not just about verbal communication patterns and the words used to convey emotion. Nonverbal and nonconscious communication allows us to observe how partners are affecting one another's psychophysiological reactions on a moment-to-moment basis. These patterns of interaction are maintained by the nonconscious attachment schemas that organize each partner's sense of himself in the relationship. There is an ongoing struggle for the couple to answer the question, "Can I count on this person to be there for me?" (Hazan and Shaver 1987). In effect, the answer to this question provides an important perspective for the couple in understanding attachment schemas. This profoundly complex work is about helping both partners understand their part in interrupting the attachment connection, both in overt as well as nonconscious ways. Each member of the dyad must endeavor to make sense of personal attachment needs, understand that perfect attunement is not the goal, and aim for the repair of inevitable moments of disruption. We propose that this resiliency is the essence of a truly loving and enduring relationship.

SUMMARY

Findings from neurophysiology, affect regulation, and attachment research are applicable to treating couples. Adult styles of relating to primary attachment figures parallel the attachment styles identified in infant-caregiver relationships. Informed by these findings, therapists work with couples on maintaining a state of attunement, providing a secure base, recognizing nonverbal signals of unconscious associations, and processing the emotionally charged interactions that frequently occur in the relationship. In couple therapy an understanding of attachment styles and internal working models of relationships provides a perspective for dealing with the underlying needs and longings of intimate relationships.

REFERENCES

Amini, F., T. Lewis, R. Lannon, et al. 1996. Affect, attachment, memory: Contributions towards psychobiologic integration. *Psychiatry* 59:213–39.

Beebe, B., and F. Lachmann. 2002. *Infant Research and Adult Treatment: Co-constructing interactions.* Hillsdale, NJ: Analytic Press.

Bowlby, J. 1969. *Attachment and Loss, Vol. 1: Attachment.* New York: Basic Books.

———. 1973. *Attachment and Loss, Vol. 2: Separation, Anxiety and Anger.* New York: Basic Books.

———. 1979. *The Making and Breaking of Affectional Bonds.* London: Tavistock.

———. 1982. Attachment and loss: Retrospect and prospect. *American Journal of Orthopsychiatry* 52:664–78.

Clulow, C. 2001. *Attachment Theory and the Therapeutic Frame in Adult Attachment and Couple Psychotherapy: The Secure Base in Practice and Research.* Philadelphia: Brunner Routledge.

Cozolino, L. 2002. *The Neuroscience of Psychotherapy: Building and Rebuilding the Human Brain.* New York: W. W. Norton.

Gianino, A., and E. Z. Tronick. 1988. The mutual regulation model: The infant's self and interactive regulation. In T. Field, P. McCabe, and N. Schneiderman, eds., *Stress and Coping,* pp. 47–68. Hillsdale, NJ: Lawrence Erlbaum.

Gottman, J. 1991. Predicting the longitudinal course of marriage. *Journal of Marital and Family Therapy* 17(1): 3–7.

Hazan, C., and P. R. Shaver. 1987. Romantic love conceptualized as an attachment process. *Journal of Personality and Social Psychology* 52:511–24.

Hazan, C., and D. Zeifman. 1994. Sex and the psychological tether. In K. Bartholomew and D. Perlman, eds., *Advances in Personal Relationships: Vol. 5, Attachment Processes in Adulthood*, pp. 151–77. London: Jessica Kingsley.

Hesse, E. 1999. The Adult Attachment Interview. In J. Cassidy and P. Shaver, eds., *Handbook of Attachment*, pp. 395–433. New York: Guilford Press.

Izard, C. E. 1991. The *Psychology of Emotion*. New York: Plenum.

Johnson, S. 2002. *Emotionally Focused Couple Therapy with Trauma Survivors*. New York: Guilford.

Lewis, T., F. Amini, and R. Lannon. 2002. *A General Theory of Love*. New York: Vintage Press.

Price, J. L., S. T. Carmichael, and W. C. Drevets. 1996. Networks related to the orbital and medial prefrontal cortex: A substrate for emotional behavior? *Progress in Brain Research* 107:523–36.

Scharff, D. E., and J. S. Scharff. 1991. *Object Relations Couple Therapy*. Northvale, NJ: Jason Aronson.

Schore, A. N. 1994. *Affect Regulation and the Origin of the Self: The Neurobiology of Emotional Development*. Mahwah, NJ: Lawrence Erlbaum.

———. 2001. The effects of a secure attachment relationship on right brain development, affect regulation and infant mental health. *Infant Mental Health Journal* 22:7–66.

———. 2003a. *Affect Regulation and the Repair of the Self*. New York: W. W. Norton.

———. 2003b. *Affect Dysregulation and Disorders of the Self*. New York: W. W. Norton.

Siegel, D. J. 1999. *The Developing Mind: Towards a Neurobiology of Interpersonal Experience*. New York: Guilford Press.

Solomon, M. F. 1994. *Lean on Me: The Power of Positive Dependency in Intimate Relationships*. New York: Simon & Schuster.

Weiss, R. S. 1991. The attachment bond in childhood and adulthood. In C. M. Parkes, J. Stevenson-Hinde, and P. Marris, eds., *Attachment Across the Life Cycle*, pp. 66–76. London: Tavistock-Routledge.

21

Obstacles for the Psychoanalyst in the Practice of Couple Therapy

Richard M. Zeitner

In this chapter, I discuss the usual psychoanalytic approach to couple consultation and therapy and point to its limitations. For the assessment and treatment of patients who present with a disturbed intimate relationship, I propose an approach that addresses the vicissitudes of the intermingling of unconscious processes in the partners. The detection of unconscious collusion is a fundamental criterion determining the recommendation of couple therapy over psychoanalysis or psychoanalytic psychotherapy. I elaborate my understanding of various obstacles, some of them determined by emotional responses and others by analytic ideals, any of which may limit the analyst's freedom to assess the couple's situation, prescribe the most appropriate modality, and conduct couple therapy within the psychoanalytic model described.

Little has been written about the clinical criteria for recommending psychoanalysis or intensive psychoanalytic psychotherapy versus couple treatment. It has been estimated that fifty to sixty percent of patients presenting for psychological treatment do so for a disturbance in intimate relationships, or other significant relationships (Sager 1976). Even when the presenting complaint is an affective illness or other syndrome, the clinician commonly finds a circumscribed relationship difficulty that is either a major catalyst for, or component of, the symptom complex. Individual symptoms and relationship strain coalesce into a mutually reinforcing pathogenic interaction with the partner—an unconscious collusion—which fuels the symptom expression. With such a large percentage of patients presenting in this manner, it is surprising that so few psychoanalysts are trained in, or at least well versed in, the merits of couple therapy.

Finkelstein (1988) remarks that analysts who have written on marriage and marital therapy have unfortunately published their work predominantly in journals and texts of marital and family therapy rather than psychoanalytic journals. He does not specifically address, however, the variables that contribute to this divergence between the practice of couple and marital therapy and psychoanalysis (Finkelstein 1988). Brody (1988) notes that psychoanalysts who have traditionally focused on expanding the knowledge base of individual treatments have found it harder to achieve the venerated goal of analytic insight in couple treatments, especially when one partner views the other as the source of all problems. This may be why analysts have applied the psychoanalytic method predominantly to the individual rather than to the troubled dyad.

In the foreword to the 1993 reprint of Henry Dicks's (1967) classic, *Marital Tensions,* Sander writes:

> The fields of psychoanalysis and family therapy were and remain curiously disengaged and unintegrated. This is unfortunate, in that, psychoanalytic theory remains the most comprehensive theory of the human mind while remaining limited in its application to a small percentage of patients. One of the causes—and there are many—of the current crisis of psychoanalysis has been an unwillingness to deal with the analysis of transferences and resistances where they are most often encountered: in everyday family life. (Sander 1993 in Dicks 1967, p. xv)

Paradoxically, in spite of this divergence between the fields of couple therapy and psychoanalysis, many analysts will actually utilize some form of couple consultation in their work, although not necessarily as the primary treatment modality. It may be used in the diagnostic phase of consultation, and again during individual psychotherapy and sometimes even psychoanalysis, either sporadically or at planned intervals. Analysts, however, usually view couple therapy as supplemental or even second-rate treatment which is palliative, supportive, informative, or preparatory for the real therapy—psychoanalysis or psychotherapy.

Many analysts recognize the need for couple therapy. Gabbard's (1994) book on the psychodynamic aspects of psychiatric practice devotes a chapter to the psychoanalytic group treatments, including a substantial section on the marital therapies. More recently, Graller and his colleagues addressed the issue of referral for couple therapy and gave a specific model for the collaboration process between the psychoanalyst and couple therapist (Graller et al. 2001). Split transferences are significantly reduced when there is effective communication between the analyst and couple therapist to whom the analysand is referred (Graller 1981). Scharff and Scharff (1991) have shown how a psychoanalytic approach based in object relations theory is particularly applicable to couple therapy. Using this approach, analysts have a way of working with couples that is compatible with their individual analytic theory.

In a unique, inspirational work on developing and maintaining a successful psychoanalytic practice, Arnold Rothstein, a classical analyst, describes the interface of couple therapy and psychoanalysis. He seems to agree with my position that couple dysfunction is in part a manifestation of a couple's externalization of intrapsychic difficulties onto one another but he does not go so far as to describe an unconscious collusion. His work in couple therapy is geared toward the amelioration of externalizing defenses or projective identifications in a manner in which the partners eventually shift to their individual internal conflicts. It is at this juncture that Rothstein will refer one or both individuals for analysis. In this sense he views couple therapy as preparatory for analysis, one way to build an analytic practice (Rothstein 1995).

My position is that in the actual work of couple therapy an approximation to analytic work is actually accomplished, as each individual takes more ownership of his or her psychological conflicts, thereby reducing externalization and projective identifications. Some partners perhaps should go on for analysis, but realistically, many will not. It is the work of the analyst–couple therapist to help the couple make this determination. Once the couple conflict is sufficiently reduced, many couples may have attained their goals of treatment.

In my experience, many and perhaps most analysts actually espouse the need for and value of couple therapy, yet paradoxically relatively few actually practice it as the primary treatment. Indeed, many analysts have little knowledge of or training in couple therapy. When the need for couple consultation or therapy becomes especially apparent, these analysts will frequently refer to a colleague who is skilled in this area of practice. Many couples are referred to me by colleagues who are already treating one member of the couple in psychotherapy or psychoanalysis. In the preponderance of these cases the problematic couple symptom has become more apparent after the individual analysis is underway. In some cases the analyst did assess the couple symptom in the initial consultation, but viewed it as a manifestation of individual character pathology. If analysts did originally consider the possibility that an analysand was skewing the report of couple conflict, or viewed the relationship problem as a function of a collusion or projective identification, they tended to assume that individual analysis would reveal and resolve it. A careful exploration of a patient's significant relationship should occur during the diagnostic consultation. The extent to which the reported disturbed relationship is affected by projective identifications indicates the need for a couple therapy in addition to, or instead of, analysis. Too often, it is later in the analytic treatment that analysts recognize that interactional processes and mutual projections are likely to be better addressed within a couple therapy format because those problematic interlocking dynamics are not accessible in analysis despite their individual analysands' stated desire to work on and improve their couple relationships.

Some analysands will openly express their frustration that expanded insights and analytic gains do not generalize to their couple relationship. Some complain that in spite of their having made changes, their spouses continue to react to them as if they were still controlling, helpless, stubborn people. Analyst and analysand then become aware of the presence of interlocking pathology, which is unlikely to improve without couple therapy. It is at this point that the referral to the couple therapist is frequently made.

OBSTACLES DERIVED FROM CONCEPTUAL RIGIDITIES AND THEIR LIMITATIONS

I describe here couple consultation and therapy as typically practiced by those trained in individual psychoanalysis. I demonstrate how the frame of the individual dynamic lingers, interferes with placing the dysfunctional couple onto center stage, potentially limits the possibilities for individual psychological growth, and may even aggravate the symptoms and disrupt the intimate relationship.

The Partner of the Identified Patient Is Used by the Analyst as an Informer

In the diagnostic phase, the couple session may be used to acquire information about the identified patient's presenting problems or to seek the partner's support of the analyst, the patient, and the individual treatment process. The partner may be included intermittently to provide information about the patient's symptoms and progress, during the course of which there may even be momentary glimpses into the problematic interactions that the presenting patient has described. Often, in an alliance with the patient's partner, the analyst views the patient's intrinsic psychopathology as the real source of difficulty and minimizes the patient's perceptions of the spouse. Schafer (1985) emphasizes the importance of having a balanced view of a patient's objective and psychic realities, an essential prerequisite for making decisions about referral for individual or couple treatment.

The analyst tends to make interpretations about the identified patient's difficulties while the partner is encouraged—and sometimes explicitly advised on how—to manage the patient's problems. Even when the couple interaction is a significant feature in the etiology of a symptom or characterologic difficulty, it may be unconsciously minimized by analyst, patient, and partner. This is especially common when identified patients are of a masochistic or depressive character organization in which their suffering evokes sadism or persecution in their partners and analysts in order to assuage unconscious guilt. The analyst and the partner may then collude unconsciously in playing out the sadistic counterpart of the masochist's sadistic part object, and actually maintain the presenting symptom and keep the identified patient in the sick role.

A suboptimal recommendation for individual therapy

Mrs. A presented for consultation complaining of depression. She immediately discussed her concern about her marriage and especially her husband's unhappiness with management of their family's finances and children's activities. She openly acknowledged her timidity and linked her apprehension in dealing with him to her reaction to the dominance of her physician father. She saw herself much like her mother; self-sacrificing, dutiful, and compromising. Dr. B was struck by the patient's capacity for insight, and commented that her alliance with her mother, coupled with her fears of her father, were revived in her relationship with her husband. Mrs. A readily agreed, and commented that her husband wanted to better understand her depression and would accompany her on the second visit. On that occasion, however, and in the presence of her husband, Mrs. A emphasized how tolerant her husband was of her desire to stay home with the children, and her unwillingness to work outside of the home. She commented that he was an excellent provider, and chided herself for not properly managing the finances. Mr. A appeared affable and concerned, and eloquently described what he felt was his wife's need to do everything perfectly, and that if she would go along with his plan for managing the children's activities, she might feel less burdened. Several subsequent visits included Mr. A in the session. Dr. B continued to be impressed with Mr. A's willingness to support Mrs. A's therapy, and his encouragement of his wife toward more self-tolerance. When Mrs. A finally provided several examples to illustrate her husband's subtle but insistent way of doing things his way, Mr. A remarked that he was merely attempting to support her by providing her with alternative strategies. Following several minutes of Mr. A's justifications, Mrs. A said quietly that she could see his point of view. Dr. B commented that perhaps some additional work on her unreasonable self-expectations would enable her to work through her depression. Mrs. A smiled and said that she knew her husband was right—that she expected too much of herself and would try to ease up on herself. Mr. A thanked Dr. B for his skill and insight, and assured him that Mrs. A would continue her therapy. On the following visit, Mrs. A complained of feeling more depressed as she described her attempts to comply with her husband's "excellent plan."

The clinician indeed focused on the essential dynamics of Mrs. A, while attending to her psychic reality. Mr. A's contribution to Mrs. A's problem areas, however, and Dr. B's collusion with Mr. A, privileged a recommendation for individual treatment over couple therapy and contributed to a worsening of her symptoms.

The Couple Dysfunction as a Psychosocial or Environmental Problem, or a Symptom of Character Disturbance

The analyst may correctly detect the impact of a troubled relationship but then relegate it to the status of a mere stressor. Then the analyst sees the couple dysfunction as something to be addressed, but not in a systematic and well-conceptualized couple treatment format per se, but instead within the context of an individual treatment and/or disease model. In this case the DSM-IV multiaxial system and the insurance company requirements to use it contributed to the clinician's propensity to regard relationship difficulties as secondary to a disease process. Many insurance companies refuse payment for family and couple therapy and so skew diagnosis in the direction of an individual symptom disorder or mental illness calling for an individual treatment that is reimbursable.

During supervision, Dr. B above presented the case of Mrs. A as a possible case for individual psychotherapy, or for analysis. In his initial report, Dr. B's case formulation included a DSM-IV for the clinic record and Mrs. A's insurance company. The diagnosis read as follows (see table 21.1):

Although the fourth axis hints at the couple problem, the focus is on the patient's depression and personality disorder, within a medical/disease model. Even though technically correct, the five axis diagnosis implies that depression with personality disorder is an individual illness aggravated by the psychosocial stress of family upset. Furthermore, the diagnostic label itself determines the recommendation for individual treatment over couple therapy.

Table 21.1.　DSM-IV diagnostic record

Axis I:	Major Depressive Disorder, Single Episode, Moderate, without Psychotic Features
II:	Dependent Personality Disorder
III:	None
IV:	Family Relational Problem
V:	GAF85 (highest level past year)
	60 (current)

Ironically, many psychoanalytic treatments will proceed to explore the patient's experiences with the partner and the partner's contribution to the relationship problems. Analyst and patient may look at unconscious factors in the patient's responses to the partner (and in the transference to the analyst) and may even speculate about the partner's conflicts and developmental difficulties that fuel the interactional problems and aggravate the patient's symptoms. Although these considerations about the partner's contributing unconscious issues may assist the analytic patient in establishing more empathy for the partner, this does little to promote a corresponding and sometimes necessary change in the partner. Partners' conflicts and potentials for problematic projective identifications remain unmodified. It is rare for the analytic patient to be able to make such sweeping changes as to induce such change in the partner that conflict ceases.

Analysis produces favorable results in the area of work difficulty and less clear improvement in the quality of intimate relationships, many of which were subsequently dissolved (Gedo 1984). Many researchers, analysts, and couple therapists would regard dissolution of a bond as an unfavorable outcome. Gurman and Kniskern (1978) found that when spouses were in conjoint treatment the negative effects of therapy (including divorce) were approximately half of those where only one spouse was in treatment. Their conclusions suggest that there is an enhanced outcome of therapy when both members of the dyad have the opportunity to address intrapsychic and interpersonal issues in treatment.

In my view, a change or dissolution of a relationship may indicate a negative therapeutic effect. Few people do not have some capacity to change their intimate relationships, either with or without treatment. Dissolution of a relationship may be a function of intrapsychic improvement and growth, but more likely it is the result of conflict that might not have stayed irreconcilable if both partners had had effective psychoanalytic couple therapy in which to review their personal contributions to the marital problem.

Instead of seeing the couple problem as a psychosocial or environmental problem, the analyst may construe it as a symptom of character pathology. The analyst may be sophisticated and unfettered by diagnostic descriptive criteria of the DSM-IV, and yet conceptualize emotional symptomatology in a predominantly linear cause-and-effect way. For example, when the analyst conceptualizes the problem area from the perspective of ego psychology, aspects of character, overall ego strength, impulse-defense organization, level of introspectiveness, and the patient's capacity to verbalize internal experiences will be the focus. Let's say the analyst views the patient as having an inherently poor capacity to manage aggression, the focus on the patient's unstable affective management overlooks how the partner provokes or aggravates the aggression, retreats in hurt or retaliates, or externalizes aggression onto the partner for containment by a partner who may have a valency for this affect, but who is actually unable to contain it. The couple problem is then obscured by the diagnostic process. What might also be obscured is the patient's inclination to provoke particular responses in the partner in order to perpetuate pathogenic parental relationships. These unconscious processes may come to light in the transference paradigm of individual treatment, but become much more difficult to observe, interpret, and resolve in couple therapy. If the patient presents with essentially good verbal ability, some capacity for introspection, and a desire to understand, the analyst evaluates positively the patient's potential analyzability and the possibilities for psychoanalytic treatment. Again, the dysfunctional couple relationship is overlooked or conceptualized as a manifestation of one individual's intrapsychic pathology. Psychoanalysts having no training in couple therapy, and having a bias toward psychoanalysis or psychoanalytic psychotherapy, are more likely to recommend analysis or psychoanalytic psychotherapy and fail to consider which treatment modality might actually be most helpful.

Psychoanalysts might respond to these concerns with the rationale that whatever characterologic or interpersonal problems exist within the couple relationship will ultimately manifest within the analytic therapy anyway, either by self-report or within the transference. This response, however, fails to consider the intersubjectivity of human relationships as well as the rigidity and elusiveness with which projective identifications function in marriage. The reality of treatment is that many individuals report interpersonal conflicts with scrupulous consistency in their description of the behavior of the partner or spouse. Depending upon the patient's capacity for introspection and the extent of projective identification and externalization, the analyst may get a view of the partner that is greatly different from the partner's actual contributions (Willi 1982). The analyst needs to maintain a balanced view of the patient's psychic and objective realities if the patient's so-called character problems are ever to become part of a transference paradigm. To the extent that the patient's marital concerns are an objective reality, they may be more fully expressed in the marriage than in individual treatment. Depending upon the actual behavior, style, and interventions of the analyst, as well as the way in which the spouse serves as the conduit for the "neurosis," the patient's troublesome issues may not be manifest in the transference. Furthermore, the projective distortions are less accessible for analytic work if the analyst functions in collusion with the patient to reinforce the patient's rigid views of the spouse in accordance with the patient's inner objects. In *Analysis Terminable and Interminable*, Freud recognized the problem of not being able to evoke a latent conflict in the psychoanalytic work. He noted that it could lead to an interminable analysis, unless a fortuitous outside event arose to activate it in the transference. In couple therapy, the focus on the interlocking dysfunction reveals mutually evocative unconscious agencies that the individual transference to the analyst cannot activate in the same way. Without conjoint treatment the couple may not have the opportunity to escape their tightly ascribed roles, nor will individual distortions and other contributing factors be adequately addressed. Conjoint treatment provides the analyst with a unique setting for addressing the contributions of inner objects to distortions in perception that affect a couple relationship and for maintaining a more balanced view of the psychic and objective realities of both partners.

In a well-conducted consultation, the analyst carefully explores the specific manifestations of a patient's conflicts and interpersonal struggles across a wide range, and then patient and analyst arrive at a consensus regarding the best treatment option, individual or couple therapy. There are times, however, when patients will resist a recommendation for couple treatment in spite of apparent couple dysfunction, for instance, to avoid revealing secrets that might damage or destroy the relationship. Analysts need to interpret these resistances to couple therapy with the same tact, empathy, and regard for the individual and the couple as in analysis or psychotherapy.

The Couple Problem Is Treated within a Conjoint Format but without a Focus on the Interlocking Pathology

When the couple problem is focal, analysts with experience in some form of couple therapy will feel reasonably comfortable in making a recommendation for couple treatment rather than individual treatment or analysis. Each of the partner's dynamics will be explored, which expands affect expression, cognitive insight, and understanding of how one is entangled with and annoys the other. What is often overlooked, however, is the way in which each partner projects repressed toxic bad objects onto the other.

Klein first introduced this concept of projection as a defense which initially occurs in the paranoid-schizoid position during the first several months of life in which the infant is dealing with his aggression toward the mother by externalizing his hatred into her (Klein 1946). Thereafter, the infant experiences the hateful part of himself as if the mother were attacking him. This perception of an attacking mother thereby reinforces the infant's aggression. These primitive projective identificatory processes from early life are repeated in the intense couple interaction and collusion, and must become a focus for the therapeutic work with couples.

Here is a typical intervention addressing the closed system of the couple's interactive pattern, but it lacks a dynamic focus:

> Therapist: John, when you feel neglected you resort to sarcastic remarks about Mary's work. Mary, you then distance by becoming remote, quiet, and resentful.

Here is a more complete intervention, which includes the collusion and the manner in which each person attempts to rid himself or herself of unwanted inner objects:

> Therapist: You, John, make subtle, clever, and sarcastic remarks to Mary in order to mask the deeper hurt you experienced when your mother attended first and foremost to all of her social obligations and abandoned you emotionally. But you, Mary, get quiet to avoid expressing the fury you feel at John for his comments about your work, because they remind you of your father's insults when he persistently chided you for never quite doing enough for the family. What you both share here is the hope that the other one will repair your respective injuries by responding more compassionately. . . .

In another version of the closed system paradigm, the analyst addresses the psychodynamic issues of each person within the couple—essentially two individual therapies conducted simultaneously, albeit in a single treatment setting. When one of the partners is unable to attend a session and the analyst sees the other to work on individual issues, the absence of the partner may hardly be noticed and perhaps not addressed as a resistance. The absent partner's issues might be referred to in the hour but are subordinate to the present partner's material.

These forms of treatment may even be somewhat helpful, at least temporarily, as one or both members of the dyad experience the benefits of catharsis and support. Tension and aggression within the couple's relationship are attenuated, but largely as a function of the triangulation with the analyst or therapist, similar to the way in which extramarital affairs or talking with a friend will temporarily stabilize a disturbed marriage. What is lacking in this treatment is the proper analysis of the resistance. The sine qua non of psychoanalytic couple therapy is the simultaneous focus on the collusive interactional problems and on the underlying mutual projection process in which each partner attempts to disavow repressed, conflicted aspects of the self by behaving in ways that unconsciously activate the other's bad objects (Dicks 1993; Willi 1982; Scharff and Scharff 1991). The therapist must specifically address the individual projective identifications of each partner and their unconscious collusion for each of them to finally own and ultimately reinternalize their painful inner object relations. This point is inherent in the theory of object relations couple therapy, but it is frequently minimized in the actual practice of psychoanalysts and therapists as elucidated above.

ANALYTIC IDEALS, EMOTIONAL RESISTANCES, AND DISTORTIONS

Having considered conceptual rigidities and their limitations on the analyst's practice of couple therapy, and factors that contribute to an analyst's preference for recommending analysis or therapy over couple treatment, we must also consider some of the emotional variables within the analyst, as well as ideals that are intrinsic to analytic theory and practice and that contribute to an analyst's reluctance to practice analytic couple therapy.

Transference, Neutrality, and Anonymity

Fundamental to the classical psychoanalytic position, transference is the ultimate modality by which conflicts and developmental difficulties come into focus. Many analysts assume that the transference will be inaccessible in couple therapy because the subject of therapy is the relationship of the couple rather than the transference to the analyst. They fail to appreciate that interactional problems are frequently determined by *mutual transferences.* These become apparent when the analyst focuses on the central unconscious collusion and the projection of bad inner objects onto each other. In this way of working, the transference is then dealt with in the couple therapy as well.

Equally fundamental today are the classical ideals of neutrality and anonymity, even though doubt has been cast recently on the actual attainment of these highly cherished variables (Hoffman 1998). Some analysts question whether, as advocates of the relationship in the practice of couple therapy, they can remain neutral and address the removal of unconscious conflicts and neurotic choices toward the goal of self-development (Willi 1982). Hoffman's work convincingly casts doubt equally on the possibility of attaining a pure analytic frame and the impossibility of the value-free analyst. Even in classical analysis the analyst's bias exerts an influence, albeit unconsciously. Hoffman gives countless examples to show how the analyst's interventions shape the direction of an analysis and even the patient's responses. In analysis we attempt to attain neutrality by telling and demonstrating to patients that we will not advise, guide, or tell them what to do. But the very nature of our interventions unconsciously communicates opinions, values, and even choices. Why then would a treatment format in which the analyst presents as an advocate for the relationship or marriage be any less neutral than a framework in which the analyst is an advocate of self-development and personal growth?

In couple therapy, the goal is to work toward analytic understanding of each person and their interacting dynamics, their projections, and the manner in which their relationship has become stalemated because of their mutual attempts to master and rid themselves of bad or unwanted inner objects. We demonstrate over and over again how each partner thereby shapes the other's behavior, but in ways that have become inflexible and conflicted—thus defining their collusion and interlocking pathology. I tell a couple that this kind of understanding and disentanglement is what couple therapy has to offer. I explain that the goals of the treatment are not specifically to restore the marriage, and yet it is common for couples to think of couple therapists as advocates for marriage, when in fact we are advocates for individual growth within adult relationship. I emphasize that I will not give advice and that separating or remaining together will be the couple's decision, which may indeed become at least partially determined by the couple work: As they come to understand their issues, they will be better able to make a decision.

Even this valiant attempt to remain loyal to the established tenet of analytic neutrality and with no stake in whether the couple remains together or married, falls short of its intended goal, however. It is quite common, for example, for a person in couple therapy to make comments which imply a perception that the analyst is an advocate of marriage and whose "real" goal is that they remain married. If they separate, they feel that their case might be considered by the analyst as a therapeutic failure.

I am an analyst who practices both analysis and couple and family therapy in a suburban office suite. Many people in the community know me as an analyst, married man, and father. My anonymity is already compromised. Patients may comment on the fact that I wear a wedding ring, and my wife has her name on the door of the adjoining office. I am often perceived as an advocate of marriage with a stake in the continuation of the marriage of the couple before me in my office. The known facts about my professional life, marital status, and even life circumstances play an enormous role in the development of a couple's beliefs about my values and what they imagine I want for them. Analysts doing couple therapy must address these fantasies as resistances, as they would in individual treatment.

Analysts who assume that their anonymity and neutrality are more attainable in individual therapy fail to consider that complete neutrality and anonymity are probably as difficult to preserve in analysis as in couple therapy. Consider a patient whose analyst is known to be divorced and currently single. This patient's transference may be infused with the fantasy that the analyst is liberated and highly independent and does not require marriage in order to be fulfilled. Or the patient may have the fantasy that the analyst is a great lover, or perhaps even a loser. The well-attuned analyst would address any fantasy in order to understand the nature of the patient's experiences and their genetic roots, and to analyze a developing transference identification that would affect the patient's life adversely. Couple therapists and analysts alike must remain alert to all transference fantasies which might potentially affect a patient's relationship system and even decisions about marriage versus divorce.

The Analyst's Attitudes toward Marriage

I am not aware of any empirical data on the percentage of analysts who have themselves been divorced correlated with the percentage that practice couple therapy. I would like to see research on analysts' attitudes toward marriage, divorce, couple therapy, experience in conducting couple therapy, and the outcome of couple therapy that they do. My hypothesis is that the degree to which analysts consider themselves to have been successful in marriage and intimate relationships will correlate positively with attitudes to refer for couple therapy, and possibly with their willingness to practice couple therapy themselves.

The Analyst's Countertransference and Tolerance of Intense Affect

Like psychoanalysis, psychoanalytic couple therapy requires evenly suspended attention. Unlike analysis, however, the couple therapist must monitor the partners' communications and transferences to one another, as well as their communication and transferences to the analyst. With communication flowing freely between two people other than the analyst, there is simply more data to monitor than in individual therapies. In general, the analytic couple therapist is required to be considerably more active than in analysis or psychoanalytic psychotherapy. Extensive conflict, both blaming and arguing, must be addressed, and often actively interrupted by the analyst in order to enhance the couple's working alliance and ability to look at themselves and the dynamics between them. Many analysts are uncomfortable with this necessary level of activity. Yet, couples' frequent use of projective identification and externalization requires a level of tolerance that is certainly not unknown in analysis, but which may be less frequent or less striking than in couple therapy.

Arguing and blaming, which are common in couple therapy, are manifestations of projective identification. As I said above, in projective identification the partner appears to be affected by the other partner's projections, so that a repressed part of the self is unconsciously evoked in the other (Williams 1981). The partner then responds to that projection in ways that irritate the other. The very behavior each of them consciously wants from one another is paradoxically denied or aggravated by the other's behavior. Attending to the couple's arguments and mutual blaming, the couple therapist discerns these more primitive mental states and is ultimately able to make interpretations about early object relations and their representation in the troubled marriage.

Example

Mr. and Mrs. C presented for couple treatment ostensibly because of anger with one another and lack of communication. Mr. C considered himself to be a financially capable person whose success in life was due to exceptional hard work and success in the "school of hard knocks." He complained that Mrs. C did not acknowledge his expertise and accomplishments. Mrs. C, whose self-esteem was low, already felt diminished by his constantly berating her for what was lacking. She said that Mr. C's constant complaints about her lack of affirmation of him, coupled with his constant braggadocio, made it impossible to compliment or consult him in any way. Mr. C remarked that he enjoys it when Mrs. C asks him his views on politics, financial matters, or other areas in which he has some interest and expertise. Mrs. C responded that whenever she does, however, she feels diminished since Mr. C always draws attention to her ignorance. She complained that it felt very much like interactions in which her father would criticize her for her inadequate school performance.

As therapy progressed, Mr. C acknowledged that his wishes for Mrs. C's compliments were essential for him to feel good about himself. He regretted not graduating from college, yet felt that his vast reading on many subjects and his hard work had helped him compensate for the embarrassment of leaving school. "Secretly," he said, "I fear that I won't measure up in this very competitive world." The collusion was observed as Mr. C projected onto Mrs. C a narcissistically fragile self. The unconscious belief was, "I can feel capable and brilliant if only you will tell me so." In constant reminders to Mrs. C that she had erred on this or that business matter, which would not have happened had she consulted him, Mr. C criticized Mrs. C for her ineptitude. He projected onto her aspects of his own vulnerable self-worth which represented re-creations of her father's criticism. Mrs. C, feeling diminished when Mr. C either bragged about his "better way" or openly criticized her, felt trapped. Instead, Mrs. C opted for doing things without discussion or consultation with Mr. C. "Furthermore," she said, "why would I give you the satisfaction of asking your opinion, when each time I do, you make me feel worse about myself by acting like my father?"

In the case of Mr. and Mrs. C, I observed a collusion in their presentation of arguments and blame. Each of them shared the wish for the other's affirmation, but instead they offered one another accusations, criticism, withholding, and braggadocio, each partner paradoxically aggravating the pain of one another's wounds through the projection of hurtful objects.

Unlike many psychoanalytic treatments in which patients are operating in the depressive position, patients in couple therapy are frequently immersed in the paranoid-schizoid position. The vignette of Mr. and Mrs. C above portrays open conflict, arguing, attacks on one another for perceived injuries, and rationalizations for retaliatory responses. Although both partners separately may be exceptionally successful in relationships and be capable of introspection and empathy outside the couple, they do not show this toward one another at home or in the consultation room. The psychoanalytic couple therapist must tolerate times of protracted conflict while monitoring and interpreting the projective distortions and hurtful retaliations.

The analyst bases interpretations, therefore, on observation and understanding of the mutual transferences and projective identifications, which are inferred from observing the communication between the couple as well as from gathering the patients' histories, rather than relying on analyst and analysand contributions to the process of analytic understanding. Couple therapy, therefore, requires that the analyst tolerate intense affect in the therapeutic field as these primitive needs, wishes, and various responses are demonstrated.

Treating couples, the analyst often has intense countertransference reactions. These may include a sense of dread as a particular hour of treatment approaches, fatigue following an hour in which projective processes were especially apparent, and even a sense of profound confusion and disorganization, or weary withdrawal in which the analytic couple therapist either defends against certain intense affective experience within a treatment, or experiences a concordant or complementary identification with an internal object of the couple (Racker 1968). It is not uncommon that a couple therapist leaves an hour feeling enervated, even when an hour did not abound with apparent conflict. Engaging in this rapid-fire display of primitive internal objects, while maintaining empathic immersion and analytic vigilance, reawakens within analysts doing couple therapy their own paranoid-schizoid issues. At one moment, for example, the analyst may covertly or even overtly side with one partner against the other. The analyst might make an intervention that is consciously intended to make one partner more aware of a behavior hurtful to the other. The partner who is confronted, however, may experience the analyst as implying blame. Here the analyst may have formed a complementary identification with an internal object of the other partner, and quite likely a persecutory part object. These interactions occur in analysis as well, but with much less frequency than in couple work. Furthermore, the consequences in couple therapy are more dire. To the extent that one partner continues to experience the analyst as more allied with the other partner, without careful interpretation and rectification, the continuity of the treatment is endangered. Analysts with less mastery over their own paranoid-schizoid issues, therefore, are more susceptible to a variety of countertransference enactments in couple therapy than in analysis. They may refer for, or practice, forms of couple therapy that are less intense and less helpful than the model I propose, or they may avoid working with couples altogether.

CONCLUSION

I have outlined the more usual ways in which couple therapy is practiced and conceptualized by psychoanalysts. I address the disadvantages and determinants of limited modalities and interventions. I emphasize the importance of a firm knowledge base and psychoanalytic understanding of couple interaction, the interdependency of partners in a couple, and the mutual shaping process that occurs in couple formation. The psychological fields have thankfully evolved to include postdoctoral and postresidency training and specialization. Understanding the vicissitudes of the underlying projective identification processes is indispensable for all practicing psychoanalysts. To say that all psychoanalysts should also be couple therapists would be like saying all surgeons should also be internists. It is not going to happen, and perhaps it should not. Nonetheless, I argue for the importance of psychoanalysts having a firm grasp of what Henry Dicks calls a "psychology of interaction," which is based substantially, but not exclusively, on object relations theories (Dicks 1993). In addition, a sound understanding of family systems theory, group processes, adult development, and even self-psychology are highly relevant when the clinician addresses a significant couple or marital conflict in an assessment or ongoing treatment.

As a couple therapist who is also a psychoanalytic institute faculty member involved in teaching, I strongly believe in the importance of couple therapy training as a component of institute curricula. This might include at least one didactic course, possibly accompanied by a supervised case. This facet of analytic training should be geared not just to couple treatment per se, but to teaching the psychoanalytic candidate about the very obstacles delineated in this chapter. The recent proliferation of postmodern and object relations theories has already enlightened us about the extent to which human behavior and emotion are in part determined by interpersonal factors. The psyche is not a closed system. Working with couples provides compelling evidence in support of Sanders's concepts of transferences and resistances in family life and Dicks's psychology of interaction in which emotional difficulties are seen as being determined in part by relational factors. Psychoanalytic curricula might include a sequence of courses on object relations theories, self psychology, and postmodern theory, followed by a course on couple theory and therapy. Addressing the couple's interlocking dynamics in a state of unconscious collusion is a way to bridge the gap between traditional psychoanalytic theory and treatment and couple-family theory and treatment. A course sequence such as this would increase the analytic candidate's flexibility in understanding and treating clinical problems in a comprehensive and effective manner. Ultimately, such a curriculum would also assist the clinician to be more effective in making recommendations to patients for couple therapy as a primary treatment, couple therapy as an adjunct to individual therapy, and couple therapy as a preparation for psychoanalysis.

REFERENCES

Brody, P. R. 1988. Couples psychotherapy: A psychodynamic model. *Psychoanalytic Psychology* 5:47–70.

Dicks, H. V. 1993. *Marital Tensions: Clinical Studies towards a Psychological Theory of Interaction.* London: Routledge and Kegan Paul. Reprinted London: Karnac.

Finkelstein, L. 1988. Psychoanalysis, marital therapy, and object-relations theory. *Journal of the American Psychoanalytic Association* 36:905–31.

Freud, S. 1937. Analysis terminable and interminable. In *Standard Edition* 23:211–54. London: Hogarth Press.

Gabbard, G. O. 1994. *Psychodynamic Psychiatry in Clinical Practice: The DSM-IV Edition.* Washington, D.C.: American Psychiatric Press, Inc.

Gedo, J. E. 1984. A psychoanalyst reports: Fifty consecutive cases. In *Psychoanalysis and Its Discontents*, pp. 20–34. New York: Guilford Press.

Graller, J. 1981. Adjunctive marital therapy: A possible solution to the split transference problem. *Annual of Psychoanalysis* 9:175–87.

Graller, J., A. Nielsen, B. Garber, L. G. Davison, L. Gable, and H. Seidenberg. 2001. Concurrent therapies: A model for collaboration between psychoanalysis and other therapists. *Journal of the American Psychoanalytic Association* 49:587–606.

Gurman, A. S., and D. P. Kniskern. 1978. Research on marital and family therapy: Progress, perspective, and prospect. In S. L. Garfield and A. E. Bergin, eds., *Handbook of Psychotherapy and Behavior Change,* 2nd ed., pp. 817–902. New York: Wiley.

Hoffman, I. Z. 1998. *Ritual and Spontaneity in the Psychoanalytic Process.* Hillsdale, NJ: Analytic Press.

Klein, M. 1946. Notes on some schizoid mechanisms: In *Envy and Gratitude and Other Works,* 1946–1963, pp. 1–24. London: Hogarth Press and the Institute of Psycho-Analysis, 1975.

Racker, H. 1968. *Transference and Countertransference.* New York: International Universities Press.

Rothstein, A. 1995. *Psychoanalytic Technique and the Creation of Analytic Patients.* Madison, CT: International Universities Press.

Sager, C. J. 1976. *Marriage Contracts and Couple Therapy.* New York: Brunner/Mazel.

Schafer, R. 1985. The interpretation of psychic reality, developmental influences, and unconscious communication. *Journal of the American Psychoanalytic Association* 33:537–54.

Scharff, D. E., and J. S. Scharff. 1991. *Object Relations Couple Therapy.* Northvale, NJ: Jason Aronson.

Willi, J. 1982. *Couples in Collusion.* New York: Jason Aronson.

Williams, A. H. 1981. The micro environment. In S. Box, ed., *Psychotherapy with Families: An Analytic Approach*, pp. 105–19. London: Routledge and Kegan Paul.

22

Dreams and the Introduction of a Third into the Transference Dynamic

Anna Maria Nicolò, Diana Norsa, and Teresa Carratelli

In the hundred years since the publication of *The Interpretation of Dreams* (Freud 1900) in which Freud introduced the idea of the dream as a wish fulfillment, continued study of the unconscious through dream analysis has centered on the function of the dream, the construction of a psychic space capable of dreaming, the so-called good dream, the incapacity to dream, and the use of dream narration in the analytic relationship (Flanders 1993). Freud's other idea of the dream as a repetition of traumatic experience that is seeking an internal path of communication has become more prominent over time. Detailed work on dreams has shown that the dream is a reactivation of forms of representation of undifferentiated psychosomatic areas that connect to memory traces and day residues of sensations-emotions-images. The dream has a function of caring for the self. Winnicott (1971) (and later Masud Khan 1974) thought of the "good dream" as the type of dream that modulates internal experience and self-integration by connecting intrapsychic trauma representations with other internal self and object representations through an affect link. Bion's (1992) idea was that the "work of the dream" is the expression of a specific mental transformation of unelaborated sensory elements. In this sense Bion therefore speaks of the "work of the dream" as an activity that is no longer confined to sleep but is a continuous re-elaboration of experience during wakefulness as well.

The dreaming function transcends the intrapsychic sphere to occur across relationships, as in the case of maternal reverie. Analysts engage in dreaming their patients' material. In the intrapsychic dimension the work of the dream

297

stabilizes the emotional sense of the experience of living and conveys and modulates profound unconscious experience in intersubjective relationships.

VERSIONS OF THE SELF AND PATHOLOGICAL LINKS

Various levels of organization of our representational world exist and these levels may change. The location of the unconscious is not always traceable to the individual but may be found externalized in the couple's shared reality. As Nicolò wrote some years ago,

> The classic theory of defenses is centered on the study of the individual mind; we may begin to include the theme of interpersonal defenses and the use of the other in order to comprehend the phenomena which interact in the development of the individual mind and of the collective organization like that of the family, where the child is engaged in the construction of the world of his internal relationships through his interaction with external objects. Therefore, we are speaking not only of detachment, splitting or denial, but also of the movement or "transportation" of mental suffering, and not of a simple defense against it. (Nicolò 1993)

And as Meltzer (1979) put it, "we are much more aware of the fact that although it is possible, through the mechanism of detachment, to remain unaware of the pain inside ourselves, there are other methods for internal disposal of various objects in the external world. The transport of mental suffering is not just a simple defense against the self. Its location may be shifted rather than its existence denied" (p. 95, Italian edition).

Individual and relational defenses do not compete for dominance. Both may be dominant at one moment and at another both may be obscured in a continuous oscillation, depending on the observer's point of view and whether they become apparent because of the context (Nicolò 1996).

This formulation shifts the focus from the diagnosis of the individual onto the assessment of the quality of the individual's relationships, whether with internal objects or external objects. It also facilitates comprehension of dissociative phenomena inasmuch as it enlarges the concept of a self to one that is no longer seen as unitary. Mitchell (1992) and others have paved the road to this modification with their idea of the self as a relational, multiple, and discontinuous configuration as well as having a unitary aspect. In different relational contexts such as significant relationships, other versions of the continuous and integral self are activated which, to use Mitchell's expression, are ways of being, functional activities forged around representations.

Links that are particularly significant, like the bond of the couple, activate some versions of each person's self, leaving others silent (Norsa and Zavattini

1997). The analytic process in couple therapy creates a dynamic relationship in which each individual self is delineated, coherent, and constant over time, and at the same time shows itself in multiple and discontinuous relational configurations. Couple therapy is a privileged observatory for the comprehension and management of disturbances in the consistency, continuity, and emotional congruity of the self and its various versions. The real-life context of the couple and the psychotherapeutic context in the here and now contribute to the revisiting of sensation and meaning and so to the construction of new psychic formations.

Being part of a couple may bring out aspects of the self that delude and disappoint, and lead to illness in the individual and the relationship. The couple's bond produces a new intersubjective formation beyond, and separate from, the characteristics of each individual.

Couple therapy is a viable treatment to encourage the transformation of such formations, which are sustained by, and implicitly shared between, the partners. Individual analysis leaves intact the area of the personality involved in the collusive relationship with the partner, and so is less effective than couple therapy.

THE DREAM IN THE COUPLE'S SESSION

The dream is one of the privileged modes for the co-construction of sensation and meaning by the couple. The dreamer is the carrier of this construction on behalf of the couple. The recounting of a dream in a session represents a desire to communicate not only something of one's self, but also to search for an emotional response in the other. The dreamer enters the area for exploration and invites the other to participate and play with the unconscious, an activity that has its own contraindications, traps, and misuses. For Berenstein and Puget (1997), introducing the dream in the session as an individual production of one partner has a double meaning: it permits access to an individual's "visually dramatized scene," and it offers the possibility of entering more deeply into the unconscious dimension of the bond (Berenstein and Puget 1997).

As one of us has previously indicated (Nicolò 1998), there are multiple uses of the dream in couple therapy sessions (see table 22.1).

Two clinical examples, one from a preliminary diagnostic interview, the other from couple therapy, will illustrate how the dream is useful.

Case Example: Patrizia and Lorenzo

Let us now refer to a clinical vignette from a couple session in a preliminary diagnostic consultation with D. Norsa.

Table 22.1. Uses of dreams in couple therapy

- One partner may dream on behalf of the other or illustrate the actions of the other (as demonstrated in the first case).
- Both partners may present dreams that show complementary or collusive aspects.
- One partner may dream the same problem brought, discussed, or dreamed by the other, but shows different defenses.
- A dream may signal the beginning of differentiation in a couple.
- The telling of a dream may express an exhibitionistic-voyeuristic aim toward the partner or the analyst.
- A dream may be an attempt to influence the emotional experience not only of the analyst, but also of the partner.

After the failure of their previous marriages, Patrizia (thirty-eight) and Lorenzo (fifty) became a couple and married. Each had already had a beneficial personal analysis, but both were left with a few central problems unresolved. They were facing a crisis in their marriage because Lorenzo is impotent unless sexual intercourse is preceded by precise sadistic rituals, which irritate Patrizia. In the first diagnostic session the possibility of referral for more analysis and a recommendation for couple therapy were discussed.

In the second session, the couple reports having discussed their therapy options. Patrizia says that that morning they had had intercourse, which had gone well. She explains that it went well because of a fight the previous evening, as if that made sense. She had been compelled to fight because Lorenzo refused to do so and rationalized everything as usual. Lorenzo then speaks of his previous analysis, in which he discovered the extraordinary capacity to fall in love with Patrizia and have an ongoing relationship with her, and in which he hid his persistent sadistic rituals from his analyst. He also discusses the prospect of resuming individual therapy with his analyst who has been in doubt about the value of couple therapy for such long-term, complex pathology.

Patrizia then interrupts anxiously, telling of a dream that she had during

Table 22.2. Three features highlighted in two couples

- In pathological narcissism the pathological tie can:
  - ○ cover a schism,
  - ○ highlight the precariousness of the boundary of the self, and
  - ○ reveal the parasitic use of the partner for maintaining consistency of the self.
- Dreaming by the couple highlights nature of the couple link.
- The transference/countertransference dynamic effects a transformation toward a new psychopathological formation in the couple.

the night: "I was in the kitchen, together with Lorenzo, but he was a small child. I realized, in confusion, that the kitchen appliances looked enormous to me and I wondered why."

She realizes that in the dream she has been seeing the world as if she were Lorenzo as a child. In the session, she cries and comments on this aspect. When Lorenzo, who has not understood, asks for an explanation, she tries to make him understand by saying that she has had a dream in his place.

Comment

The communication of the dream is first a response to the analyst, who is questioning herself about the therapeutic indications for couple or individual therapy. It is as though Patrizia were telling the analyst that the problem directly involves her, aspects of her own childhood being so annihilated that she can only see the world through the eyes of her child-partner, Lorenzo.

The kitchen is the maternal world full of mechanical objects that at the same time recalls both the world of the couple and the therapeutic space, where instruments for cleaning, washing, and cooking (metabolizing) are found, but they are dehumanized and rendered emotionless.

The dream is not confined to the dream space, but it has a function in the psychic space of the therapeutic relationship, in which the spouse is also a privileged participant.

Lorenzo does not understand; the dream and its dynamics seem foreign to him, he says. He describes himself during the session in the same way that he does in the couple, as the one with the sadistic and sadomasochistic bent. He is the split-off pole of perversion. Patrizia can dream for both; she is the pole of the possibility of representation for the couple. She can dream of the child who is the other. At the same time, she sees through her husband's eyes, showing a confused level of functioning in the couple. Through the representation of the child-husband, Patrizia's dream also shows her problem of nonintegration of an undifferentiated psychosomatic aspect for which she has no internal images unless they borrow from the inner child of her husband.

Patrizia suffers the anguish of the parasitic guest in her internal world, the child-husband, instead of him suffering, but this does not produce the curative effect for which Patrizia had been hoping. She had not created a dimension free of suffering in which to refind adult sexual libido. Nor does she manage to impart to Lorenzo a profound knowledge of the denied affects of his inner child. On the contrary, the repeated and parasitic use of her husband's inner world traps Patrizia inside a masochistic kind of suffering, preventing her from connecting to an authentic experience of her own self.

The child-Patrizia "parasitizes" the child-Lorenzo for the purpose of being able to represent her prohibited, libidinal, and aggressive affects toward the grown kitchen-body of the mother. This is also what happens in Lorenzo's perverse sexual fantasies toward his wife's adult female body. The way that Lorenzo behaves in reality, Patrizia behaves in her dreams. But there is no intrapsychic space for the elaboration of a problem in which they mirror each other. What Patrizia is asking the analyst for, through her dream, is help in unraveling the aspect of the couple's bond that has been utilized in an illusory expectation of care, and that continues to function according to the repetition compulsion, instead of in healthy pursuit of adult libidinal and sexual aims. The couple's bond is characterized by a level of intimacy equivalent to an exclusive dialogue between two unconscious states. The couple shares an area of cooperative play, but also one of confusion, nondifferentiation, and pathological collusion (Balint 1963).

In reviewing Patrizia and Lorenzo's diagnostic material, the therapist considered the indications for analysis or couple therapy. Patrizia's dream is the equivalent of an unconscious request for the analyst to intervene where a therapeutic impasse has been produced in individual analysis, and couple therapy is the treatment of choice. In the case of dissociated behavior, perverse, psychotic, or psychosomatic functioning based on the dissociation of aspects of the self and dissociation of those aspects that are realized in the other or activated by the presence of the other, the couple setting offers the chance to collect in vivo the evolution of these transpersonal disturbances.

Case Example: Lilli and Pedro

As may occur in individual analysis, a patient's dream serves as a sort of summary of the work done in analysis. It offers the opportunity to follow the internal world of the dreamer and the setting the couple construct; observe the couple's conscious and unconscious relationships; and detect varying versions of the transference.

Lilli and Pedro, both in their forties, have been in therapy with D. Norsa for two years. They have two children, Camilla, five, and Luca, three. Camilla shows general malaise, problems with sexual identity, and heightened irritability. Before her marriage Lilli was in analysis for a period of depression. Pedro, who has always been sceptical about psychoanalysis, has a narcissistic personality that constantly causes him to flee from an internal feeling of death.

The first phase of the therapy was characterized by interpretations that focused on the couple's vicious cycle in which Lilli, afraid of falling back into depression, reacts by hyperinvesting in the children, so that the children's lives are full of needs which she says are never met by Pedro, while Pedro vacillates between seeking refuge in Lilli's supermother care and claustrophobic reactions that lead to panic attacks. Lilli developed a better awareness of Pedro's latent state of anguish. The development of the psychopathological formation in the couple transference and its analysis allowed the detachment of Camilla from the parents' destructive projections. Once the couple arranged analysis for their daughter Camilla, a more open libidinal area in the couple emerged and activated conflict and resistance.

We now describe the appearance of a dream involving the dynamics in both partners activated by their relationship. The session in which this dream was presented signaled the beginning of an important developmental step for the couple.

A couple's pathological link is sustained by some versions of the self, while other versions remain silent. In the session in question, new versions of each individual self begin to integrate and, as they do, the partners form a tender and caring bond, while in the dream the pathological link finds an effective representative form that is separate and distinct. We may consider this an example of a dream of the fourth type: "dreams that signal the beginning of differentiation in the couple." This dream also shows the transference relationship that the couple, but not the individual dreamer, develops with the analyst for the couple (Norsa and Zavattini 1997).

During the session, Lilli appears calmer than usual and cheerfully says she had a silly dream, which she recounts:

> There is a rich person's house, many invited guests, a large living room like a theatre, but there is no stage. Where the stage should be, there are large windows looking out over the garden. I am also among the people, but I think that somewhere else, upstairs, there is the theatrical production room, where there is a private party going on, and where the hosts have invited their closest friends; so I wonder why they are allowing all these guests to enter. I keep walking about. The children are also there. As I walk on I notice a man with a white scarf who suddenly hurls it at the guests, and as he does so, it turns into a very sharp blade, just as I am passing. I become very frightened. I think how he could cut people's heads off with that blade. I run off and find Pedro in a nearby room. I ask him to do something, to protect me, and cowering, I shelter myself between his feet. He tells me there is nothing to be afraid of, but in the meantime I see the man coming over, looking for me, because he has understood that I was the one who reported him. I realize that Pedro will never confront him, so I will have to do it.

Pedro is very interested while his wife speaks, and he seems particularly touched when she says she has taken refuge between his legs so he can protect her.

Together they joke a bit about a few elements of the dream.

> Lilli: The dream in that house reminded me of that place—do you remember?— where we went before the children were born. The scarf, I don't know, it seemed so light as though it were silk.

Pedro: Like the one I gave you last year.
Lilli: No. Which one? You didn't give me any scarf!
Pedro: But don't you remember? I gave it to you for your party, but you didn't like the colour, and you gave it to your sister.
Lilli: I don't know! I don't remember.

This brief dialogue, which is also characterized by careful, mutual listening, is interrupted. Lilli's mood darkens. She begins to speak of practical matters. Pedro justifies himself. When they speak together about the period before the children, Lilli seems able to make contact with something relaxing and enjoyable, connected to the soft and light sensual quality evoked by the scarf.

However, the theme of the recent gift mentioned by Pedro, once again brings about a hardening on Lilli's part. Her undifferentiated sensuality is principally autoerotic, and she cannot accept such a rapid transformation into a desire to share with the other. While she resumes the usual relationship, comprised of roles, accusations, and rigidity, she toys with a bracelet made of colored strings that she wears tied to her wrist.

The couple's analyst thinks that her bracelet is like the multicolored bracelets that teenage girls often wear: every color recalls a significant affective area. Love, health, happiness, hope, and desires, represented by the knots in the bracelet, will come true when the knots are undone. While the analyst is engaged in these thoughts, the couple again start speaking of the children in the usual contentious way, even though they both end up by agreeing on the necessity of placing some sort of limits on them. While Lilli yet again shows her irritation, Pedro moves his chair toward the heater, in search of contact and support.

Comment

In this couple, the dreams and their associations clarify how the other is attacked as a potential libidinal object that also represents libidinal aspects of the self. The relationship with the object is merged and confused with problems of the self's own intrapsychic conflict. The attack on the object is an attack on the libidinal bond, and at the same time is an attack on one's own capacity to experiment with libido. Therapy is felt as potentially dangerous in that it threatens change.

The dream narrative mobilizes the attention and involvement of the husband, who recognizes himself in a version of his positive self; so the dream has signaled a change in respect to the predominantly evacuative use of sensations and emotions which has characterized the exchanges and communication of the couple up to that moment.

Further confirmation is also offered by the countertransference involvement of the analyst who is especially attracted by the nonverbal behavior in the session, and who now finds herself engaged in the type of mental functioning Bion describes as "dream work," similar to maternal reverie, which is indispensable for picking up the mood of a session. In short, we might say that the analyst is in the presence of a "good dream" because of its capacities for evocation and communication, and for its power of representation.

The Dream, the Couple, and the Transference

We now stop and analyze, in particular, the representative power of this dream in regard to the pathological nucleus of the bond between the couple and its implications for the transference. There are numerous questions we might ask ourselves, such as: What is the affective engine of the dream? Where does the analyst figure into the transference-countertransference dynamic? What has the dream to tell us about the dreamer, the couple, and the analyst's transference dynamics?

The dream stages the drama of the sadistic and narcissistic dissociated self, in the form of the dominant image of the man with the scarf. At the same time, the dream represents desire and curiosity connected to the potential for change. The therapeutic space is also represented as the negation of a primary scene: It is a theater, but there is no stage; children and adults are mixed together; there is no performance, and in its place a man appears with feminine elements (the scarf) with which he charms and betrays the audience. The internal space of the primary scene is located in the production room, which is the most special parental space but which nonetheless proves inaccessible.

The bizarre and dangerous character is a combined masculine and feminine phantom object that at the same time represents Lilli and Pedro's transference projection onto the analyst. The couple's psychopathological formation lies precisely here with the threat of death, castration, and the annihilation of creative and procreative capacities, and the fear that this is unassailable. When this new formation is projected onto the analyst in the transference, it runs the risk of blocking her work by signaling that any intervention aimed at change is impracticable. In this formation, which the couple is only now starting to contain and recognize, we can also find the roots of the disturbance of identity of Camilla, the couple's daughter.

We want to emphasize that the dream represents both the pathological nucleus and the therapeutic space. In light of this new representation of the therapeutic setting, the appearance of the collusive nucleus warns that the therapeutic work risks running into an impasse or interruption. At the same time various hypotheses concerning the meaning of the analyst's intervention are presented in this scenario.

Lilli and Pedro secretly compete with the analyst, now that they have substituted the dream object for their daughter. The new dream object has characteristics that are potentially more suitable than their daughter was for constituting the transformative object they need, but at the moment at which it presents itself, it arouses feelings of envy, impotence, and a wish to attack.

Last of all comes the question as to how the analyst may quietly observe the dream during the session, allowing herself to vacillate from one vantage point to another, rapidly following first one path, then another (see table 22.3).

Through the therapeutic process, the dream documents the way the dreamer's anguish organizes itself into a signal of threat to the couple's bond, but one that also has developmental and transformative potential. Finally, thanks to the viewpoint of the analyst who functions with the perspective of a third party who neutralizes and modulates the libidinal and aggressive investments of the couple, the process of working through the dream in a session opens up the possibility that, with time, Lilli and Pedro can develop a less envious and more admiring attitude toward the couple and allow it to be made up of creative good parents, who, for the time being, are misplaced in the production room upstairs.

All this means that careful work must be done on the various configurations of negative transference in order to allow the couple access to a capacity for recognizing the partner as other than the self, and to use the third person of the analyst as a curative and transformative function of each individual self and of the couple link, thereby allowing other versions of each self to emerge and replace the ones previously suffocated by the pathological collusion.

Table 22.3.   Vantage points from which to observe the dream

- The analyst may feel that Lilli is inviting her into the production room, so as to experience the delicate function of tolerating and absorbing the ambivalence and destructive hate that emanate from the scene's central character.
- The analyst may feel pushed into assuming the centrality of the man with the scarf, helping the patients with the possibility of rendering the antilibidinal organization as an object, so that they may take it back in small, transformed doses within the self.
- The analytic space may become this living-room environment that is not yet a stage, but which favors the definition of boundaries between an interior and an exterior, with a view and a garden.
- The analyst may finally stop on the threshold at the French windows leading into the large living room, and lend the couple her capacity for 180-degree perspective, permitting them to survey the various spaces, characters, and interactions that are explicit and implicit in their relationship. Within the shared illusion, in the here and now of the session she may strengthen her insight into how the couple has been committed to rejecting and facing the pernicious invasion of this psychopathological formation that has now become evident in the shared therapeutic setting.

CONCLUSIONS

Listening to the dream narrated by one partner as though it belonged to both allows us to pick up the shared sense of that pathological area which is actively sustained by versions of the self of each of them, and which, in turn, keeps these versions of the self in the foreground, leaving other, more reparative versions hidden in the background. Concentrating on the concept of the link between the couple brings into focus the psychopathological formations that represent the couple's unconscious bond, dominate the course of treatment, and also emerge in the dream space. The dream space therefore becomes the privileged place in which there is a continuous oscillation between dream thought and transference. Through the dream work, the couple's individual and shared dynamics enter and enliven the transference relationship. In its content and manner of narration, the dream activates the emergence of versions of the self different from the ones usually activated by the couple's bond and this transforms the emotional life of the couple.

In the first case, Patrizia's dream illustrates the use of the partner's internal interpersonal defenses, and it is an exact mirror of the bond between the partners, whereas Lilli and Pedro's dream demonstrates that working on the collusive bond reactivates various versions of each individual self, and this then modifies the rigid pathological order.

Lorenzo's powerful, perverse pathology, which missed the chance of cure in a dyadic analytic context, has been transferred to the couple's shared bond where it is now exposed for work. The unconscious often appears more clearly in an intimate relationship than it does in an individual. It might be said to acquire substance, to materialize. Patrizia reveals a good capacity for insight, but at the same time she is still unable to produce a co-construction of meaning with Lorenzo. However, she can acquire a sense of communication when unconscious issues are first directed toward the analyst. She and Lorenzo can then help build the foundation for therapeutic work by using the analytic third. Working around the construction of the "third," the intrapsychic dimensions of the one and the other are freed to engage in an authentically libidinal exchange that moves the couple toward a cure.

Whereas Patrizia fails with Lorenzo, Lilli is able to recruit Pedro's participation, because a new version of Lilli's self is also present in the dream, laden with the search for a good object relationship. Lilli's capacity for insight succeeds in providing a metaphor for the couple's psychopathological formation. For his part, Pedro can now feel relieved in recognizing a version of self that is more sincerely affective, and that attracts him toward greater participation in a new form of relationship with Lilli. In couple sessions like this one, the analyst's attention is directed to nonverbal communication, and using her maternal reverie and doing the dream work, tunes in to the emotional atmosphere produced in the here and now.

Table 22.4. Three elements and "the third"

- The construction of a "third" therapeutic space characterized by an analyst listening to the dreams of each individual as though they were generated by the bond of the couple.
- The use of the transference to activate and represent a psychopathological formation as a projection from the couple's collusive pathology.
- The aim of the therapeutic work is to produce a "third" element that facilitates the freeing up of different versions of the self in the couple, which gives access to new affective levels and supports the search for a more loving bond.

In this chapter we have attempted to show the correlation between the three concomitant elements (see table 22.4).

SUMMARY

Dreams in couple therapy are expressions of the multiple discontinuous selves of partners and of interpersonal defenses. Two dreams offered during analytic couple therapy illustrate the use of transference and countertransference to observe disturbances in self-cohesion, communication of self-states, and attempts to influence the partner's emotional state. Dreams communicate the state of the couple relationship and the state of the transference, and activate the analytic third, a space in which shared pathology can be expressed and transformed, and which facilitates the growth of new aspects of self seeking a more loving bond.

REFERENCES

Ardizzone, I., A. M. Lanza, and T. Carratelli. 1999. "L'integrazione somato-psico-mentale e la costruzione dell'oggetto interno." (The somato-psycho-mental integration and the construction of the internal object.) Congresso EFPP, Roma, 1–3 ottobre 1999. *Richard e Piggle.* Rome: Il Pensiero Scientifico, 2000.

Balint, E. 1963. Unconscious communications between husband and wife. In S. Ruszczynski, ed., *Psychotherapy with Couples,* pp. 30–43. London: Karnac, 1993.

Berenstein, I., and J. Puget. 1997. *Lo Vincular.* Buenos Aires: Paidos.

Bion, W. R. 1992. *Cogitations.* London: Karnac.

Carratelli, T. I. 1998. "La ricerca di una visione bidirezionale nella comprensione della psicopatologia evolutiva: Il pendolo tra asse intrapsichico e relazionale." *Corpo Mente. Studi clinici sulla patologia psicosomatica in età evolutiva* (a cura di), T. Carratelli, A. M. Lanza, cap. IV, pp. 79–113. Rome: Borla.

———. 1997. "The matrix of psyche-soma." Commentary on papers presented by Raquel Zak De Goldstein. London: Karnac, 2001.

Flanders, S., ed. 1993. *The Dream Discourse Today.* London: Routledge.

Freud, S. 1900. *The Interpretation of Dreams. Standard Edition* 4–5.

Giacolini, T., and T. I. Carratelli. 2000. "La psicopatologia del figlio adolescente tra contesto coniugale e perturbante genitoriale." Congresso Nazionale *Quale psicoanalisi per la coppia e la famiglia?* Napoli, 1–3 dicembre.

Khan, M. R. 1974. *The Privacy of the Self*. London: Hogarth. (Trad. It. *Lo spazio privato del sé*. Turin: Bollati, 1979.)

Losso, R. 2000. *La Psicoanalisi con la Famiglia*. Rome: FrancoAngeli.

Meltzer, D. 1979. *The Kleinian Development. 1: Freud's Clinical Development*. Perthshire: Clunie Press.

———. 1979. Un approccio psicoanalitico alle psicosi. *Quaderni di Psicoterapia Infantile* 2: 31–49. Rome: Borla, 1982.

———. 1979. Lutto e melanconia. In *Lo Sviluppo Kleiniano* 1:92–102. Rome: Borla, 1982.

Mitchell, S. A. 1992. Contemporary perspectives on self: Toward an integration. *Psychoanalytic Dialogues* 1(2): 121–57.

Monniello, G., G. Mattivi, and T. Carratelli. 2000. "Dreams and self-narrative in diagnostic work with adolescents: 'reminiscences in hysteria.'" (Sogni e narrazione di sé nel lavoro diagnostico in adolescenza. "Le reminiscenze nell'isteria.") *The Italian Journal of Psychiatry and Behavioural Sciences, Official Journal of the Italian Psychiatric Association*. New series, 10(2): 131–45.

Nicolò, A. M. 1992. Versioni del sé e interazioni patologiche, *Interazioni*, no. 0 'Legami e affetti,' pp. 37–48. Rome: FrancoAngeli.

———. 1993. Countertransference in the psychoanalysis of the couple. Presented to the 38th IPA Congress, "The psychoanalyst's mind: from listening to interpretation," Amsterdam, July.

———, ed. 1996. *Curare la Relazione: Saggi sulla Psicoanalisi e la Coppia*. Rome: FrancoAngeli.

———. 1998. Dream and family. *Funzione Gamma Journal*, no. 2, ottobre 1999 (www.funzionegamma.edu).

Norsa, D. 1999. The parental couple: Intrapsychic organizer of affects between change and stability. Third European Congress of Psychoanalytic Psychotherapy of Children and Adolescents, Rome.

———. 2000. Memories of primary relations and thinking disorders. 5th European Psychoanalytic Federation Conference on Child and Adolescent Psychoanalysis, May 12–14, Paris.

Norsa, D., and G. C. Zavattini. 1997. *Intimità e collusione*. Milan: Raffaello Cortina Ed.

Winnicott, D. W. 1971. Dreaming, fantasying, and living. In *Playing and Reality*. New York: Basic Books (Trad. It. *Sogno, fantasia e vita reale*. In *Gioco e Realtà*. Rome: Armando, 1974).

23

The Analytic Third and Cotransference in Couple Therapy

James L. Poulton, Christine C. Norman, and Merritt W. Stites

In many forms of contemporary psychoanalysis the concept of the analytic third is widely used (Ogden 1994). In analytic treatment, the analyst works in a dialectically interdependent relationship with the analysand. The analytic third is jointly created by individual subjectivities of analyst and analysand and by their intersubjective interdependence, and the analytic process is the outgrowth of a dialectical interplay between these three "subjectivities": analyst, analysand, and the analytic third.

In couple therapy, too, we note the construction of the analytic third, and of other related intersubjective processes, as they occur in the complex interactions between the partners and in relation to the therapist. We also find essential the concept of *cotransference*, which was introduced through the work of Donna Orange (1994) in the self psychology tradition. We describe some of the intricacies of the analytic third and the process of cotransference in a couple therapy that had a less than optimal outcome.

TRANSFERENCE, COUNTERTRANSFERENCE, AND TRADITIONAL CONCEPTS OF THE SUBJECT

The phenomenon of transference, defined as the "expression of the internal object relations" of the patient in relationship with the analyst (Racker 1957, p. 161) in such a way that the "present goes back into the past, and *is* the

311

past" (Winnicott 1956, p. 298), has long been considered fundamental to effecting change through psychoanalytic therapy. Similarly, the analyst's countertransference, "based on identification with the patient's id and ego and his internal objects," is recognized as an essential tool in understanding the analysand (Racker, p. 161). Transference and countertransference do not occur in separate vacuums, but rather play off each other in complex ways. Countertransference in reaction to the analysand's transference is not the only way it plays. As Racker said: "just as countertransference is the psychological response to the analysand's real and imaginary transferences, so also is transference the response to the analyst's imaginary and real countertransferences" (pp. 161–62).

Recognizing an interplay between transference and countertransference did not go far enough for some theorists. With his concept of the analytic third, Thomas Ogden goes beyond thinking of an interplay between two separate individuals, and blurs boundaries between the two. What were originally two separate subjectivities become merged in the analytic third, in a dialectic that actually creates a new and unified subjectivity. Ogden conceives of the analyst and analysand as both separate *and* interdependent. As separate, they are "subject" and "object" to one another. And yet, as they are each confronted by the "otherness" of the other's subjectivity, a third subjectivity, the analytic third, is formed. This represents an intermediate ground that is created by the joint contributions of the analyst and analysand at the same time their subjectivities are also being created by it.

Ogden relies on this concept of shared subjectivity in his analysis of what he calls the "matrix of the transference-countertransference" (Ogden 1994, p. 137). In this matrix, the analysand does not simply speak *about* her experience and how she creates it in her life. Rather, she

> contributes to an intersubjective construction within the analytic setting that incorporates *in its shape and design* the nature of the psychic space within which the patient lives (or fails to come to life). Invariably, the analyst unconsciously participates in the creation of the intersubjective construction within the analytic setting. It is in part through this avenue (i.e., through countertransference analysis) that the analyst gains access to the nature of the states of being, comprising the matrix of the patient's internal world. (Ogden, p. 164)

This shift away from concepts that presuppose two separate subjectivities (such as transference and countertransference in their original meanings) toward concepts that entail a more radical view of shared subjectivity or intersubjectivity has been paralleled by similar transformations in philosophy, theories of language, and hermeneutics, all part of a growing recognition of the inadequacies of traditional views of the self or, more specifically, of the subject.

The traditional concept of the subject is marked by what Daniel Dennett calls "the intentional stance": the subject is presumed to stand separate from other subjects, from objects, and even from its own thoughts and emotions, in such a way that it can manipulate them according to its own detached deliberations. As Richard Rorty says, it is the view of human beings as "not simply networks of beliefs and desires but rather beings which *have* those beliefs and desires" (Rorty 1989, p. 10).

The concept of the subject in the intentional stance has long been associated with analytic concepts of projection, transference, and countertransference. Consider, for example, the hidden implications in the following passage:

> The patient in analysis projects aspects of his internal world into the analyst so that he may explore the nature of whatever aspect of his internal reality he is projecting into the analyst. The question he poses is "if I do this to him, what will happen?" but more precisely it is "if I make him feel what I feel, what will he do?" Will he explode (i.e., "is what I am projecting explosive?") Will he find it pleasurable, annoying, incomprehensible (i.e., "is what I am projecting pleasurable, annoying, or incomprehensible?") The analyst's response to the patient's projective probe tells the patient about the probe—his own projection, a piece of *his* internal world. (Caper 1996, p. 860)

In this passage, which is not uncharacteristic of the ways that analysts speak, two related properties are imputed to the subject: First, that the subject is *separate* from its own projections, and presumably from the rest of its internal states; and second, that it stands in a deliberate, decisional, and manipulative relationship with those internal states, so that they become vehicles for its strategic testing of its relations with others. While these imputations are particularly visible in this passage, they can be found, to varying degrees, in many analytic writings about the nature of the communicative processes between subjects. This posture harkens us back to the Cartesian and mentalistic image of the self as a homunculus sitting behind phenomenal experience making decisions about what will be perceived and not perceived, thought or not thought, in serene and omnipotent deliberateness. The growing sense of this concept's absurdity, heralded by the ascendance of existential, postmodern, and deconstructionist thought, has led to considerations of other, more radical paradigms of the subject. The analytic third, with its implications of the merging of selves into shared subjectivities, is one such paradigm.

THE DECENTERED SELF

Perhaps the most damning criticism of the traditional view of the subject pertains to the inherent isolation in which it places the self. Malpas, in discussing the traditional view, states that "subjectivity itself is viewed as constituting an internal private realm of meaningfulness that requires no reference to anything outside itself. The subject is a solitary individual locked within the private space of his or her own thoughts. . . . From this position, it becomes questionable how such an isolated subject could ever know anything other than itself" (Malpas 2000, pp. 588–89). In other words, if subjectivity is viewed as consisting of the traditional subject taking an intentional stance toward its own internal states, then the meaningfulness of those states must be determined only by that subject's deliberations. But if this is so, then the only language that subject could understand would be a *private* language, one designed only to describe that subject's experience. In this case the language of others, in their own isolated internality, would be incomprehensible, since there would be no superordinate criteria for the translation of one subject's meanings to another's (Glynn 2003). As Malpas says, if the subject is *metaphysically* isolated from others, objects, and the contents of its own experience, then it is also *epistemically* isolated (2000). Rorty adds: if there is no such thing as a private language, then there is also no such thing as a private self (1989).

The solution to this problem depends on a reworking of the subject so that it is no longer grounded in metaphysical isolation, but in an intersubjective community. One solution was that of Lacan, who defined a subject as that which arises in the act of speaking, but went on to observe that, since language is a system whose rules are established by a community of speakers, the subject reveals itself as intersubjective at the moment it comes into existence. Rudolph Bernet puts this point succinctly:

> The experience of self in speaking is necessarily connected to the experience that the significance of everything that I say about myself has its origin simultaneously and undecidably both inside and outside myself. (Bernet 1996, p. 176)

The subject being described here is a *decentered* subject, in that it is no longer the subject of the intentional stance—a metaphysical presence in and to itself (one could also call this the Wittgensteinian subject, for whom all meaning depends on references to other texts, and hence does not depend on a central metaphysical presence). Rather, it is an "inter-subject," one whose meaning depends on references to other subjects and the speaking community to which they belong. If meaning can only arise from a community of words and the system of rules that differentiate between them, then, as Derrida said, "the central signified," that is, the self, "is never absolutely present outside a system of differences" (Derrida 1978, p. 280).

COTRANSFERENCE

The decentered subject now sets the stage for a modernization of the notions of transference and countertransference, and the matrix from which they arise, since it allows us to speak more explicitly about the dialectic inherent in the analytic third—that is, about the *shared-subject* interplay between analyst and analysand by virtue of their participation in the decentered realm of the intersubjective (Orange 1994). As the analyst and the analysand begin their work together, they each experience their developing relationship from multiple perspectives, as Ogden observed. They each experience themselves from the standpoint of their own presumed individual subjectivities, and at the same time, from the decentered perspective, they co-occupy a unifying process that does *not* rely on separate, deliberate, or decisional individuality. This process, moreover, is unified around *themes*—about how the world, the self, and any particular moment in the analysis is to be seen. The source of these themes lies in the *valencies* (Bion 1961) that both analyst and analysand bring to the analysis. These valencies are constructed by the historical experiences of each that have helped to determine both the superficial and the deep ways that meaning (emotional, verbal, motivational, and so on) is assigned to the specific elements of their experience. When the valencies between analyst and analysand are complementary, *the valencies* form a bond that leads to a structured, although decentered, experience. The joined valencies function together to create a local inscribing function (local to the analyst and analysand) that co-constructs, in a true intersubjectivity, the joint experience between the two.

Note that we are effectively describing the transference-countertransference matrix, with one major difference: we have eliminated, or at least attempted to eliminate, the forms of language that carry hidden commitments to the traditional concept of the subject. The result is a process that bears all the marks of what we have known as the transference-countertransference matrix, but that is yet remarkably different. For this reason a new designation—*cotransference*—is appropriate. Cotransference, then, is to be defined as that process in which analyst and analysand project onto, or rather co-construct into, themselves jointly created experiential elements, arising from conscious and unconscious valencies, that contribute to the determination of *what* they find meaningful, and *how* they find it meaningful, in the analytic situation.

In the following section, a case is presented that illustrates the basic workings of cotransference. The case was selected precisely because it had a less than desirable outcome, which was due to the cotransferences occurring between the four key people involved.

CASE ILLUSTRATION

The couple, Mr. and Ms. Y, had been married approximately seventeen years when they first sought psychoanalytic psychotherapy. Ms. Y, age thirty-eight, contacted Therapist A because she'd had a romantic, although nonsexual, friendship with one of her professors. Ms. Y had told both her religious leaders and her husband about the relationship, and she had submitted to a reprimand by her church. Ms. Y thought she had resolved her feelings of guilt and anger about these events, but now felt she had merely pushed them aside.

Ms. Y described her husband as disciplined, hard on himself, rigid, and judgmental of others. She felt that he was terribly insecure, which he could manage only if she was completely approving of him. He would sacrifice anything to make her happy, and she felt smothered and angry at his constant concessions. His solicitousness triggered shame in her and made her feel that she was the source of all the problems in the marriage. She clung to her anger as a way of creating separation, both from Mr. Y and from her remorse and self-condemnation.

Ms. Y was the third of six children. She described her father as gentle and quiet, and not very involved in child rearing. He played in a jazz band and had given up a dream of owning a restaurant because it seemed too risky to her mother. At a point deep into the therapy, she learned that her father had a nervous breakdown during World War II and was counseled not to marry or have a family. Ms. Y's mother came from an alcoholic home and was a perfectionist in many things. Ms. Y was afraid of her mother's moods and became confused when they shifted without warning. She felt that she couldn't talk to her mother about anything important. She had been uncertain about marrying Mr. Y, but her mother said she was letting a good thing get away and she felt the choice was made for her.

One month after Ms. Y began individual therapy with Therapist A, Mr. Y also agreed to begin individual therapy. Therapist A referred him to her friend and clinic partner, Therapist B. Mr. Y, age forty, described himself as a rigid perfectionist who yelled at his children, pushed too hard, and was often defensive. He said that he liked things to be in order, and he was confused about how he had been so disappointing to his wife. He felt he had tried to be helpful in her recent pursuit of a college degree, but found that he could "never do anything right" and only felt anger from her. He said that he was committed to his religion and its beliefs that marriage, since it is eternal, should not be abandoned.

Mr. Y was the fifth of six children. He had been premature at birth, and had to spend his first week of life in the neonatal intensive care unit. He described his childhood as hard, mostly due to his fear of his alcoholic father's paranoid behavior, explosive outbursts, and unpredictable mood swings, and to his feeling responsible for protecting his mother and his sisters. He allowed very little contact with his father, since he felt he had to set tight boundaries around his father's intermittently needy and manipulative behavior.

Two aspects of the cotransferential relationships between these four individuals are considered: the nature of the relationships within and between all four people pertaining to religion; and their relationships to paired parental images of submission and aggression.

Some background information about Therapist A and Therapist B and their relationship is necessary to understand the cotransference. Therapist A is a devout member of the same religion as Mr. and Ms. Y. She came from a devout family, with a father she saw as passive and disengaged from his children. She had experienced and worked on her anger at her father's passivity. In addition, at the time she was working with Ms. Y, her husband's business had failed and she was angry with him for having jeopardized the family.

In contrast, Therapist B is an atheist who has expressed some disdain for conservative religions and Therapist A's religion in particular, for its rigid rules, its judgmental attitudes, and its sometime brutal treatment of people. Therapist B was brought up as a Unitarian in the suburbs of Boston, in a family with an angry mother who scared her and a father who died of exhaustion in the face of his wife's anger and disappointment in him, or so the adult children conjectured. Despite their differences, Therapists A and B have been best friends for twenty years and have been practicing together in a private psychotherapy clinic for almost as long.

The course of therapy for Mr. and Ms. Y was intermittent, and marked by multiple attempts at, and withdrawals from, conjoint couple therapy with both individual therapists as cotherapists. The multiple cotransferences between the couple and Therapists A and B are most visible in a sequence from a conjoint session that occurred midway through the treatment. Mr. and Ms. Y had taken a break from therapy because they were satisfied that they had achieved a better understanding of their relationship. Three months later Ms. Y began a new flirtation with a man she had met through her church, and therapy was resumed. This flirtation became sexual and resulted in another reprimand from their church. The sessions were often strained, in part because of Mr. and Ms. Y's own emotional patterns, but also in part because of a growing tension and defensiveness between the partners and between Therapists A and B, as can be seen in the following sequence.

Mr. Y had arrived on time for this session, but Ms. Y was running late. Initially, both therapists checked the waiting room and then returned to their offices. Therapist B then checked the waiting room a second time, found Mr. Y there and invited him back to her office where the conjoint sessions were usually held. Waiting for Therapist A and Ms. Y to arrive, Mr. Y went ahead and told Therapist B of a recent dream in which Mr. Y's father sat on him, in an attempt to smother him, and Mr. Y had responded with rage.

Therapist B connected Mr. Y's dream to his feeling of being smothered by his wife's anger. When Therapist A and Ms. Y arrived five minutes later, Therapist B, excited and energized by the dream work, suggested that it might be an important dream relating to the couple's process. Therapist A felt impatient with Therapist B and did not respond to her suggestion. Instead she picked up a thread of a discussion from the previous week concerning Ms. Y's need to maintain her anger in order to protect her separateness from Mr. Y. Ms. Y was afraid of losing track of herself in the face of his neediness and pain, resulting in what she feared would be a loss of her self, or of her individuality. After Therapist A reintroduced this topic in the current session, Ms. Y said: "Mr. Y thinks he is so above me. He acts like nothing has happened, that we can just go on being a happy couple. It is so infuriating—he has all the answers and takes no responsibility for any of this." Mr. Y responded, "I'm angry and I don't like what has happened, but I also don't want to lose my family. I *do* want to leave the neighborhood and I don't want to have the constant reminder of your affair." To this, Ms. Y recoiled with shame. "How could you want to be with me?" she said. "Don't you think I know how bad I am?" Therapist B interjected at this point, saying, "I think Mr. Y is telling you how he feels," at which Ms. Y now became visibly angry with Therapist B and, instead of expressing it directly, collapsed into another moment of shame, saying, "It's all my fault." Shortly after this exchange, Therapist A turned to confront Mr. Y with his simplistic ways of thinking and his failure to appreciate all that Ms. Y was going through and trying to communicate to him. Mr. Y then seemed to experience a collapse of his own, including confusion and a constricted way of speaking. When the session ended, Therapist B was angry with Therapist A for dismissing the dream and taking over the session.

There are three arenas in which cotransference is occurring in this exchange.

COTRANSFERENCE BETWEEN MR. AND MS. Y

Mr. and Ms. Y are co-constructing a complex set of presumptions about the nature of their relationship. Ms. Y, on the one hand, vacillates between hating the submissive in herself, since it implies being dominated by objects that do not necessarily have her interests in mind, acting out her rebellious individuality as a partial act of aggression against those objects, and then experiencing the punishment from those objects in the form of shame. Mr. Y, on the other hand, also vacillates between multiple positions. He is a demanding perfectionist who uses aggression against his children in order to manage the anxieties arising from an overly punitive superego (arising from identification with his father). On the other hand, he is a submissive, passive, and solicitous husband who protects his attachment with his idealized mother/wife through "doing anything" to please her. Together, Mr. and Ms. Y have cotransferentially co-constructed a relationship in which each is as comfortable enacting identifications with aspects of their own internal object world as they are enacting aspects of the other's. For example, Mr. Y's strategy of submission, developed from his family of origin, is also an identification with the submissiveness that Ms. Y hates in herself. Ms. Y, on the other hand, in the expression of her anger at being controlled by Mr. Y's emotions, also identifies with and enacts Mr. Y's father's rage that he himself carries unconsciously.

The real cotransferential aspect of their relationship, however, doesn't pertain as much to their trading of identifications as to the atmosphere they have created in their marriage through them. For Mr. and Ms. Y have constructed together a psychic environment in which the fundamental issue that each faced in childhood continues to be played out, although never resolved. That issue is, of course, the question of how to be: submissive and dependent, or aggressive and autonomous. Through agreement of their fundamental valencies, derived from prior experience, they have reached a kind of social contract, unconsciously elaborated, that submission versus aggression will be the dominant existential question facing their relationship. And they have also agreed that they will find no way to transcend it.

The cotransference between Mr. and Ms. Y has occurred within the analytic third, since it arises from a different kind of subjectivity than Mr. or Ms. Y's individual subjectivities. Here is where the concept of the decentered self becomes important, for this "different kind of subjectivity" is precisely an intersubjectivity in which the intentional stance from each self has been eliminated. Neither Ms. Y nor Mr. Y deliberately constructed this environment, but it was constructed through them, through their cotransference.

COTRANSFERENCE BETWEEN THERAPIST B AND MR. Y, AND THERAPIST A AND MS. Y

If the events that occurred between each therapist and client were to be described using traditional concepts, employing the intentional stance, then we would use such language as "Therapist B introjectively identified with Mr. Y's maternal object which he needed to protect him from the angry outbursts of his father/wife"; or "Therapist A enacted an identification with Ms. Y, originating in Ms. Y's projective identifications, which endorsed Ms. Y's contempt for submissiveness and passivity, both in her husband and in herself." Such descriptions would be valid *to an extent*, in that they would capture the events as they could be viewed from the standpoint of the clients as separate and independent from the therapists. If we think in terms of cotransference, however, then the valencies that each therapist brought to the therapy must also be included in our descriptions. In other words, from a cotransferential perspective, it makes a difference that Therapist B had her own history that had primed her to be protective of the one perceived as submissive and victimized by an angry wife. It also matters that Therapist A's history had formed her so that she would feel some justification for anger at men who were too passive to stand up for themselves, or for what was right. The construction of Therapist B's identification with Mr. Y's internal protector was actually a *co-construction*, performed without intent or deliberation, and arising from a shared space, an analytic third, in which the "subjectivities" of therapist and patient worked in such concert that they must be conceived of as having been unified. A similar point can be made for Therapist A's identification with the angry Ms. Y.

COTRANSFERENCE BETWEEN THERAPIST B AND THERAPIST A

Elements of cotransference between the cotherapists affected the therapeutic transactions. Historically, the religious conflict between the two therapists has at times led to injuries suffered by both, for example when Therapist A had felt discounted by Therapist B's dogmatic criticism of religion, or when Therapist B felt excluded by what she regarded as Therapist A's blind adherence to religious tenets. The conflict emerged primarily in two ways in the sequence with Mr. and Ms. Y. First, Therapist B had, in her own words, an "excruciatingly difficult time managing the church's discipline of Ms. Y and making her shame public in front of their children." This meant that, cotransferentially, some of the frustration Therapist B experienced with Therapist A around the issue of religion was now making its way into the treatment environment, in the form of Therapist B's discounting of Ms. Y's position because of her blind adherence to a church that was mistreating her. This, of course, only served to augment Therapist B's tendency, already developed through her cotransference with Mr. Y, to protect him from Ms. Y's angry attacks. Second, Therapist A reports that, when she came into the session and found that not only had Therapist B already started meeting with Mr. Y, but that Therapist B proposed his dream as the agenda for the meeting, Therapist A became upset and steadfastly refused to participate in Therapist B's plan for the meeting. This refusal in part originated in the long history of their dispute over the basic role of belief in one's life. Specifically, Therapist A had often resisted Therapist B's dogmatic moments through the very strategy she chose here: a steadfast adherence to her own path despite Therapist B's advocacy for thinking about, or taking, other directions. Therapist A's response in the session was also augmented (in a similar way as was Therapist B's response) by her cotransference with Ms. Y, in which they both had become committed to angry resistance as a way of preserving independence and individuality.

A complex set of cotransferences had arisen among and between the four people involved in this session. Their complexity makes them quite difficult to describe, but the basic elements can be seen in multiple unconscious agreements: (a) Therapist A and Ms. Y agreed that anger at passive men is justified and necessary for individuation, (b) Therapist B and Mr. Y agreed that he needed a protective female who would shield him from feared angry attacks, (c) Mr. and Ms. Y agreed that the dominant issue that they would use their relationship to try to work through was that of submission and dependence versus aggression and autonomy, and (d) Therapist A and Therapist B agreed that the conjoint therapy with Mr. and Ms. Y would be an arena in which issues around religious belief would continue to be worked through. Finally there was an unconscious and nondeliberate agreement among all four that all of the above issues would be the primary focus of the conjoint therapy.

CONCLUSION

The cotransferences in this case functioned like social contracts, unconsciously and unintentionally determining which "selected facts" were to be found meaningful and would be utilized in the course of the therapeutic interaction. In essence each individual contributed to the co-construction of these cotransferences according to the valencies established by their personal histories, in such a way that they were operating not from the position of the traditional subject in an intentional stance, but from that of the subject decentered by participation in an *intersubjective* sequence.

Understanding the intersubjective processes in which therapists participate with patients in cotransferential ways provides one more tool for gaining perspective on unconscious dynamics, helps both to contain and transform them, and so benefits the course of treatment. The concepts of cotransference and the decentered self imply that the therapist is not just an accidental part of the patient's characteristic patterns, but is an essential part. This observation argues for constant and vigilant questioning of how the therapist's presence contributes to the constructions of the patient, and of how both are inscribed by the intersubjective. It also suggests that case reports that exclude the personal role of the therapist are not scrupulously "objective" but are a defensive attempt to conceal the therapist's contributions, as if including them would constitute a narcissistic airing of oneself in public. Indeed, an argument can be made that from the perspective of the decentered self, the concept of objectivity is outmoded and needlessly restrictive. For therapists to reveal themselves in reports of interactions with patients takes courage, but not to reveal themselves—if only to themselves—

obscures a significant source of influence over their patients' clinical presentations.

REFERENCES

Bernet, R. 1996. The other in myself. In *Deconstructive Subjectivities*, ed. S. Critchley and P. Dews, pp. 169–84. New York: State University of New York Press.

Bion, W. R. 1961. *Experiences in Groups*. London: Routledge.

Caper, R. 1996. Play, experimentation and creativity. *International Journal of Psycho-Analysis* 77:859–69.

Derrida, J. 1978. Structure, sign and play in the discourse of the human sciences. In *Writing and Difference*, pp. 278–93. Chicago: University of Chicago Press.

Glynn, S. 2003. "Identity, intersubjectivity and communicative action." Article published on the Internet.

Malpas, J. 2000. Between ourselves: Philosophical conceptions of intersubjectivity. *International Journal of Psycho-Analysis* 81:587–92.

Ogden, T. 1994. *Subjects of Analysis*. Northvale, NJ: Jason Aronson.

Orange, D. M. 1994. Countertransference, empathy, and the hermeneutic circle. In *The Intersubjective Perspective*, ed. R. Stolorow, G. Atwood, and B. Brandchaft, pp. 177–86. Northvale, NJ: Jason Aronson.

Racker, H. 1957. The meaning and uses of countertransference. In *Essential Papers on Countertransference*, ed. B. Wolstein, pp. 158–201. New York: New York University Press, 1988.

Rorty, R. 1989. The contingency of language. In *Contingency, Irony, and Solidarity*, pp. 3–22. Cambridge: Cambridge University Press.

Winnicott, D. W. 1956. The clinical varieties of transference. In *Collected Papers: Through Paediatrics to Psycho-Analysis*, pp. 295–99. New York: Basic Books, 1958.

24

Narcissistic Disorders in Marriage

Jill Savege Scharff and Carl Bagnini

THE INDIVIDUAL
NARCISSISTIC PERSONALITY

Narcissistic personality disorder is defined as "a pervasive pattern of grandiosity, need for admiration, and lack of empathy that begins by early adulthood and is present in a variety of contexts" (DSM-IV, p. 658). The pattern is inflexible, persistent, maladaptive, disabling, and distressing. This diagnosis is estimated to affect 1 percent of the general population and is found in up to 16 percent of the clinical population. Half to three-quarters of the group diagnosed with narcissistic personality disorder are male. In our view, this percentage is tilted toward males because the greater emotional expressiveness of narcissistic women tends to generate diagnostic categorization in the borderline and histrionic groups.

Adolescents are narcissistic, being self-centered and impervious to their parents' needs, but normally they grow beyond it. Some narcissistic traits may appear in normal adults. Only when these traits are distressing and impairing is the diagnosis of narcissistic personality disorder made. In later years, narcissistic traits may emerge as full-blown personality disorder when declining mental ability and physical competence puncture grandiosity and the required admiration is harder to attract.

Narcissistic individuals are self-important, boastful people who aggrandize themselves and belittle others. They are entitled, exploitative, and insensitive. They think that they are unique and should be appreciated as being special. They often prefer to associate with people whom they regard as brilliant, beautiful, or famous in order to emphasize their own superiority.

Beneath this veneer of overinflation of self lies a weak self-esteem system. They waste time seeking praise and feel unduly hurt if it is not forthcoming. They are often described as having huge egos but in fact their egos are extremely fragile and need constant boosting. They appear to be self-sufficient but they are really hugely dependent on others for emotional supplies. They may be quite charming and seductive, but below the exterior they are cold and unresponsive. They are arrogant, haughty, selfish, disparaging, and envious.

In the world of work they may perform at a low level in order to avoid competition that could lead to defeat and humiliation. On the other hand they may perform at an outstanding level, pushed on by ambition. At some point they experience a downfall as they react badly to adversity, criticism, and unfavorable decisions. In social life they feel vulnerable to slights and rejections (real or imagined). They either withdraw in a state of hurt and shame or fight back with contempt and rage.

THE ORIGINS OF NARCISSISTIC PERSONALITY FEATURES

Traumatized children who are not given words to encode their memories of the trauma and are not encouraged to express their reactions may develop a narcissistic cocoon to shield them from further trauma (Scharff and Scharff 1994). Children raised as extensions of self-absorbed parents instead of feeling valued for their individuality become narcissistic. Whether the parent has overvalued or denigrated the child depends on how the parent has felt about the part of himself or herself that the child represented at any one moment. The child builds a narcissistic personality in identification with the parent, worshipped on the surface but beneath the bravado, denigrated. When the child's self is treated as a part of the parent, it cannot be autonomous and self-determining. The self creates a defensive, grandiose state of self-sufficiency and seeks admiration from others to confirm its worth. Narcissism is a result of the miscarriage of the normal process of identification (Modell 1993).

NARCISSISTIC PARTNERS IN LOVE AND MARRIAGE

Narcissistic personality disorder may be commoner in men than women, but many women have narcissistic features that cause them as much trouble in their work and social lives even if other features skew the diagnostic picture. Narcissistic traits create a cocoon that protects from further hurt and prevents closeness (Modell 1975). Narcissistic people are afraid that intimacy means fusion with the spouse and loss of the self (Solomon 1989). So, when the narcissistic person marries, the spouse is up against a formidable challenge. He or she is likely to feel frustrated by the elusiveness of the perfect butterfly that is promised but never emerges. Narcissistic people have great difficulty in achieving an intimate marriage, since they do not relate to the spouse as a person having needs and personality attributes. They attempt to regulate distance and avoid humiliation (Lansky 1985). Their sense of entitlement and superiority means that the spouse must either kowtow to the narcissistic mate and accept a denigrated position or must aspire to ideals of perfection that keep threats to self-esteem at bay. Being afraid of not existing as an independent entity, the narcissistic spouse seeks agreement and validation from the spouse. There is no concept of mutual interaction and shared development.

Narcissism may be expressed in hypomanic behavior, overspending, drinking to excess and overeating to feed the hollow ego, verbally abusive scolding, physical abuse, having affairs, and pairing emotionally with a child to exclude and hurt the denigrated spouse. The narcissistic traits may be colored with histrionic features that dramatize the self and secure the attention of onlookers to ward off fears of being empty and uninteresting. Narcissistic traits may be associated with paranoid and antisocial features when withdrawal is the form of defense that is dominant. Narcissistic traits may be expressed as substance abuse in the form of drinking or snorting cocaine to get a physical feeling of needs being met. When narcissism reveals itself in the form of preoccupation with appearance it may lead to excessive exercise, anorexia, and purging as the perfect body is hatefully pursued inside the self rather than being sought and enjoyed in the body of the loved one.

In the average courtship, a state of narcissistic overvaluation happens normally. People fall in love and each thinks the other is wonderful. When one of the lovers is narcissistic, this state of finding the self and the other wonderful may be prolonged into the marriage to a ridiculous extent that does violence to the reality of the spouse, or it may give way to profound disappointment when expectations are not met. During the courtship, the narcissistic fiancé might ooze with charm and romantic appeal. Another woman might hate it, but his inhibited, unselfishly good fiancée finds in him an attribute that she cannot find in herself, and she cherishes it in him. Such hero worship is short lived because the other side of the narcissistic persona is abusive and demanding (Glickhauf-Hughes and Wells 1995). After the marriage, he cannot remain charming and the wife no longer finds him to be everything that she is not. Then the spouses have to accept each other as they really are, and that means accepting aspects of oneself, too, which may prove impossible in a narcissistic state of nonawareness.

If there was an intense sexual courtship an exciting attachment may last for a while, but only if the narcissist is viewed as the great lover. Should the other spouse require attention to detail, or express preferences not within the narcissistic partner's lovemaking repertoire, deep feelings of inadequacy may result and take the form of complaints, withdrawal, or excuses. Disillusionment is painful for the narcissistic personality. Since only one lover is truly wonderful, the other must be bad.

What type of marital partner is suitable for the narcissistic individual, and what kind of marital pattern will result from the bonding of the two personalities? The other spouse's personality may be narcissistic also, or it may be borderline (Lachkar 1992, McCormack 1989, 2000, Slipp 1984), obsessional (Barnett 1975), or masochistic (Glickhauf-Hughes and Wells 1995). The borderline is loved for expressing emotionality that the narcissist is not capable of, but trouble comes when emotionality turns to rage and escalating bids for attention. The obsessional spouse tries too hard to be perfect and feels driven by increasing demands from the narcissist who cannot be satisfied. The masochistic spouse submits to the denigration that keeps the narcissist's self-esteem propped up by comparison. The narcissistic spouse succeeds in aggrandizing the narcissistic partner until their mutual envy tears the marriage apart.

To put it simply, the ideal partner for a narcissist is either a stunning knockout, or a devoted audience! But such a partner does not lead to growth. The narcissist's spouse seeks an ideal love object in order to mend deficiencies in self-esteem and to meet unacknowledged infantile needs, not to grow through an appreciation of difference and a mutual, loving negotiation.

In every marriage there is tension between the needs of the self and its strivings, and the needs of the loved one. Spouses want to be together but they need to feel separate, too. For marriage to work the couple must find a way to transcend the tension of opposing forces between two different psyches (Colman 1993). A person with a secure self brings substance to the couple relationship. He doesn't lose his individuality and yet he adapts to the personality of the woman he loves. A person with a narcissistic self is both insecure and apparently self-sufficient. This interferes with bonding and intimacy in marriage. When the couple then seeks therapy, the narcissistic state complicates the establishment of a therapeutic alliance.

THE NEED FOR AN INTENSIVE PSYCHODYNAMIC APPROACH

Couples with a narcissistic spouse (and there may well be narcissistic issues in both members of the couple) are hard to engage and difficult to treat. The therapist must take a long-term view of the case. A few sessions getting at the symptoms and the couple's complaints about each other may make a dent in the armor, but this will only increase the need for better armor. We advise the therapist to take time to get to know the couple and to let the couple build trust. That means asking more about every sign of distrust and nonengagement in the opening sessions so that emerging anxiety can be put into words and faced in relation to the therapist as assessment and therapy proceed. What helps the narcissistic person to emerge from the cocoon is a favorable environment in which past traumas can be remembered, unhooked from their present incarnation in the marriage, reworked in safety over time, and so detoxified. This calls for an intensive, long-term, psychodynamically oriented approach. Within that spectrum, we recommend object relations couple therapy for narcissistic issues in marriage.

THE OBJECT RELATIONS APPROACH TO COUPLES

Our approach to couple therapy is based on the Scharffs' (1991) integration of the individual object relations theories of Fairbairn (1952) and Klein (1946) and the theories of Bion (1959, 1967, 1970) on mother-infant and group interaction. In object relations theory, we think of the individual personality as a system of parts built up from experience with the mother and others in the family of origin. The infant is born as a whole self that is ready to engage with the mother and the family. In the course of infantile dependency, the child encounters both satisfaction and frustration of the drives to be autonomous and to be in a relationship. Satisfying experience is recorded in a conscious area of the self in the form of an accepted internal object. Infants deal with unsatisfying experience by taking the unmanageable aspects of frustration into the self where they are repressed as bad internal objects. The self divides into parts of the ego that relate to these objects and the frustrated, craving feelings that they elicit. We call these *unconscious internal object relationships* and we find that they are constantly seeking to return to consciousness and be integrated into the self.

The state of being in love offers hope of acceptance of these hidden parts of the self. When two people fall in love, they do so in response to an attraction between these internal object relationships of which they are unaware. The fit between these internal object relationships, and whether they are open to modification by learning from experience with the spouse—new experience that is different from that of infancy—determines the nature of the marriage and its long-term quality. The spouses form a small group of two that is greater than the sum of its parts. Belonging to this group shapes the continuing development of each partner's personality.

Kleinian theory attributes the baby's anxiety to the force of the death instinct overwhelming the life instinct within the baby. Kleinians think that the infant deals with this threat to the self by the defense of projection. The infant gets rid of anxiety and the feelings that go with it (such as rage) by locating them outside the self and inside the mother instead. When the infant successfully fills the mother with feelings, she may seem to be angry. Then the infant misidentifies her demeanor as the cause of anxiety. The infant deals with the persecutory object that she has become by taking it inside the self and splitting the perception of the mother into a good mother (experienced under the force of the life instinct) and a bad mother (under the death instinct). Projective identification is a way of communicating a state of mind, as the mother feels acutely the distress her infant can't describe to her. The empathic mother is able to contain the infant's distress and return it to the infant in a more manageable form. The unresponsive mother is not available to help the infant who may keep up a barrage of crying to engage her or may slump and withdraw into a self-protective narcissistic cocoon.

Projective identification is the basis of empathy and the means for communicating distress in adult relationships, too (J. Scharff 1992). In marriage, union of two personalities threatens the autonomy of the self. In defense, one spouse uses the other spouse as the repository for parts of the self that become riddled with anxiety and evokes a state of mind in the spouse that re-enacts the drama of the internal object relationships.

For example, in a family described more fully by J. Scharff (1992), a wife who is illiterate because of learning difficulties and poor self-esteem resulting from sexual abuse in second grade chooses a highly competent husband who feels good about himself. He gets validation of his competence from helping her and that protects his ego from experiencing his own problems in self-esteem, stemming from a family that valued bravado and mocked competence. By having a helpless wife he can disavow the lack of bravado in himself because he has to be strong for her. She does not develop her own skills, remains dependent, and stays home. So he always has a secure base for taking care of his needs, while thinking he is doing that for her.

In adulthood, spouses use projective identification for communicating deeply with the personality of the spouse and for defense against anxiety by getting rid of it into the other person without acknowledging it. To put it another way, in marriage unwanted parts of the self such as unacceptably needy or aggressive parts are projected outside the self and refound in the spouse where they may be hated or cherished (Dicks 1967). If hated, the spouse hates the other spouse with all the force directed against the bad objects that would otherwise remain internal to the self. On the other hand, these projected parts of the self may be cherished. If cherished, the spouse whose personality resonates with these attributes is met with indulgence—perfect for the narcissist. With commitment, love, and satisfying experience in marriage, the defensive aspects of projective identification become less necessary and the communicative aspects predominate so that the other spouse can experience and so understand what one is feeling and care about it. A capacity for concern is essential for mature relating.

We believe that for a marriage to be mutually satisfying, self-centered aims have to be subordinated in favor of intimacy. Narcissistic spouses can't do that. They remain self-involved. They have a rigid outlook and they do not relate to each other as whole persons (Klein 1946). Instead, they overuse the mechanism of projective identification to get rid of painful aspects of themselves and project them into the spouse. Then the narcissistic husband deals with his wife as if she has traits that need a cocoon around them like he does and he may overwhelm her with his wish to be the same as her or frustrate her by keeping his distance.

A narcissistic man who is always working rarely sees his wife except when they go out to entertain clients. She amuses herself by spending the extra money he earns on expensive clothes and personal grooming. He enjoys the way she looks as a trophy on his arm. He doesn't confront her on her overspending but secretly he holds her in contempt. In this way he fails to acknowledge his own greed and exploitiveness and attacks it in his wife.

These deficits reduce the capacity for intimacy with spouses and for working with therapists. The therapist needs to observe how the narcissistic wife uses her husband and the couple therapist to support her functioning, and how the narcissistic husband craves the unconditional support of his wife. Such couples come for therapy when the spouses who previously fulfilled their projected needs fail to cope with the feelings that they have to bear in doing so. The projective identificatory system of the marriage breaks down. Then the couple therapist is needed to release the gridlock and help the couple to adapt and develop a more flexible system for defending themselves, communicating their anxieties, tempering their needs, and satisfying each other's longings for understanding, connection, and pleasure (Ruszczynski and Fisher 1995).

It is not easy for a marriage—or a therapeutic relationship—to modify malignant narcissism. Instead of putting themselves into the healing mix of the loving marriage, narcissistic people require their spouses to mirror and validate their uniqueness so that their shameful insecurities can remain underground. The spouse is called upon to admire sufficiency and to overlook the narcissistic spouse's inherent selfishness and entitlement based in neediness. Hidden are longings, dependencies, and deficiencies, but beneath the surface lies tremendous shame about selfishness and neediness. These longings and fears are uncovered when the narcissist is faced with possible loss of the other, for instance when infidelity or divorce threatens.

The narcissist is prone to deny any and all disturbing attributes. Fantasy rules. Feelings make perceptions about self and other real; projections are experienced as realities. The constant need for affirmation precludes carefully appraising the reality of the other person. Dealing with the differences that should enrich the marriage is particularly difficult.

THE CHALLENGE TO THE THERAPIST

As we've said, narcissistic people have difficulty engaging in treatment. They want, and they feel they deserve, only the "best" doctor. Anything less is an insult to their self-evaluation. Yet, they are terrified of depending on the doctor, even if they do convince themselves they found the best. They want us to feel impressed by them. They want us to want them as patients and to dedicate ourselves to their every need, to gratify their requests for special treatment, and to provide them with phenomenally intuitive understanding. We may find their expectations daunting. We may feel flattered. We may feel unbelievably appreciated for our work as their therapists, but more often we feel bored and irritated, as they are unable to take in our interpretations. Loaded with honor, we may then be sunk without trace. We feel frustrated when we are unable to reach them or help them see beyond their own narrative. Any intervention can be felt as an assault, destructive to the ego and its peculiar wrappings and sensitivities to slights. We have to tread softly when we tread on this particular psychopathology and we have to be alert to the ever-present likelihood of our sincere efforts at understanding leading instead to a degree of shame that threatens the continuity of the treatment.

THE TASKS OF COUPLE ASSESSMENT FOR THE NARCISSISTIC PERSONALITY

Setting the Frame

We establish the arrangements for meeting, the length of the session, and the fee. Then we note how the couple responds to the frame. How they deal with the boundaries of the professional relationship reflects the way they deal with each other, with significant members of their families of origin, and with authorities in their community. Any couple may ask to be seen in the evening or to have a reduced fee, but the narcissistic couple may expect it and be overly hurt or furious if special consideration is not offered.

Creating Psychological Space

We want to hear about whatever is on their minds. We do not take sides. We do not lead the session with many questions on standard inventories. We ask occasional questions for clarification as need arises, and other questions to link history to current experience in this marriage and this couple therapy.

We do not pounce with astute observations, clever interpretations, or behavioral recommendations. By letting the partners take the lead in determining how to use the session and by listening attentively to the thoughts and responding to the feelings of both partners approximately equally we ensure that the session becomes a space for thinking psychologically about their issues. The narcissistic couple may seem to dismiss the therapist's efforts but that is only because they cannot admit to how much they need a secure, dependable environment in which to unwind their cocoon.

Listening to the Unconscious

We listen in a relaxed yet attentive way to the words, of course, but we also follow the backstory, the unspoken conflict behind the narrative, by attending to silences, pauses, hesitations, and gestures. We listen for the associative flow between the paragraphs of their speech to detect the underlying theme. The narcissistic couple may have trouble communicating because they block feeling.

Following the Affect

We assess the feeling tone of each communication and the atmosphere of the session. Rare moments of affect in the here and now give us access to earlier moments of heightened tension in the families of origin.

For example, Mrs. A is nagging Mr. A to get rid of years of accumulated papers, childhood possessions, and mementoes of his bachelor life to which he is attached and for which he has plenty of storage space. He claims that she is piling on the pressure and it is driving him crazy. Suddenly she gets very agitated. The therapist asks whether her husband reminds her of anyone she had to deal with before. Now she says that her mother is a packrat, a schizophrenic who refuses treatment, and who can't have relationships. Mrs. A gets rid of everything she doesn't need so as not to be like her mother. Mrs. A owns her own anxiety instead of projecting it onto Mr. A's similar but different behavior. Mr. A keeps everything to be like his mother and to hold on to his memories of her.

For our way of working, this is a more effective way of learning about the relevance of family history than taking a genogram or a formal family history inventory.

Transference and Countertransference

We connect with the couple at the deepest parts of our personalities. We notice how we feel in their presence (Scharff and Scharff 1991). Our personal reaction gives us a mirror image of their marital joint personality (Dicks

1967). We can then interpret their repetitive, behavioral patterns and their impact on each other from inside our own experience.

Mrs. A recites long lists of things to be got rid of. The therapist notes that the domestic problems she asks for help with represent a conflict over intimacy and old attachments. But Mrs. A doesn't leave any room for comment. At first, the therapist can't find the space to make this interpretation but if she doesn't succeed they will not get much from their session. She interrupts to say that, like Mr. A, she found the long list overwhelming now as it is in real life and that, like Mrs. A, she had great difficulty in finding space for herself. Then she says that Mrs. A is trying to find a way to express her feelings about her husband's not making room for her and his new marriage and Mr. A is reacting against the fear that she will leave no room for him. This intervention moves the discussion forward, at least temporarily.

To work in this way, we need to prepare ourselves as a finely tuned, therapeutic instrument by having our own analysis or therapy, subjecting our interactions to process and review, and engaging in supervision, peer supervision, and consultation (Scharff and Scharff 2000).

Interpreting Defense

These patterns of behaving, communicating, thinking, and feeling defend the couple from deep anxieties, the most primitive of which are the possible death of the couple and the negation of the hope of creating a family.

Confronting Basic Anxiety

Once we recognize the defenses we can figure out what anxieties they protect the couple from facing. Once the anxieties are named, the couple can connect them to their histories, disconnect them from their interactions with each other, and then develop strategies and solutions together for moving on securely to the next developmental phase of the couple's life.

CLINICAL ILLUSTRATION: CISSY AND PATRICK

I (JSS) set the frame by agreeing to a one-hour consultation. Because this was a consultative service to the low-fee clinic, there would be no fee. I began to create a psychological space by asking the couple to tell me about themselves and the problem they were working on and then I waited to hear from them.

Cissy and Patrick told me that they had been married for only a short time. They came for couple therapy because conflict over Patrick's passion for his hobby and Cissy's longing for intimacy that had troubled them during their courtship had not been resolved by being married. Patrick denigrated marriage but he valued highly the commitment of being together exclusively.

I waited to hear more. I noted that Patrick looked at me apparently defiantly and Cissy looked at Patrick with a resigned look of frustration. Here I was attending to a nonverbal communication that expressed their dynamic before their words put it together for me.

I learned that they had met at a prestigious university where they felt superior to the other students. They thought of themselves as gifted in a highly complex area of study. When I heard that neither of them were working full-time in their field, I began to suspect narcissistic dynamics. They said that they had enjoyed getting together to laugh at everyone else. Now I felt sure of it. Cissy and Patrick began trying to tell me what Patrick's hobby was and how Cissy felt about it, which should have been simple, but they used language that was so general and highly intellectual that I had no idea what they were actually talking about. I felt that Cissy wanted a close relationship with Patrick and that Patrick wanted to be free to follow his own path.

Using my countertransference I noted that I felt excluded. I also felt like an idiot, too inferior to comprehend their discourse. I had experienced the way that Cissy and Patrick were defending themselves by locating feelings of inadequacy not in themselves, or even projecting them into each other, but locating them in other people, finding them to be inferior, and excluding them from their circle. Examining my feelings, I deduced that what they were defending against were probably anxieties about self-worth. What I said was that their highly intelligent way of talking left me feeling confused and left out of their tight circle and then I couldn't understand their pain. They were pleased to have their intellect admired, and I think that is what let them listen to the problem I was addressing of my being excluded from a position in which I could develop empathy.

Cissy and Patrick responded by telling me about a specific marital problem of lack of empathy. Extremely hesitantly, Cissy explained that Patrick is thoughtless, neglectful, and dismissive of her feelings. I thought that she was holding back a tremendous amount of rage at her attachment needs not being met by him, and that probably had not been met in her family of origin. She said he is constantly late, not minutes late, but hours late. Patrick said that he can't understand why Cissy worries if he is late, why she expects him to call her if he is detained, and why she feels neglected and depressed. She thinks he doesn't care about being together or making her happy. He thinks that she doesn't care about letting him do his work and do things his own way and so making him happy. For instance, he complained that she insisted that he buy a good suit to get married in without regard to the fact that buying clothes from arrogant salespeople and dressing up make him extremely uncomfortable. He concluded that she is not thoughtful about his concerns either but that he is the most thoughtless. He seemed proud of his accomplishment in being the worst.

Cissy is masochistic and depressed. Only Patrick qualifies as having narcissistic personality disorder. However, Cissy and Patrick as a couple have a shared narcissistic defense in which they bond against the helpless, inadequate people in their world and hold them in contempt. Patrick attempts to escape the bond by staying out late. When Cissy expresses longing to be with him or the wish to be considered when he can't be with her, Patrick feels that Cissy is trying to control him. Neither one feels cared about. Each of them thinks less about the other's needs, fears, and wishes than they do about their own. The therapist begins to wonder about how neglected or dismissed they felt in their families of origin, but waits to see if the information will emerge spontaneously. If it does not she will ask.

Cissy volunteered that she hated herself for being resigned to Patrick's behavior as her mother had been resigned to the callousness of her father. Her own marriage was conforming to the destructive image of her parents' marriage. This led to a discussion of Cissy's pain as a child who was responsible for keeping her parents together and who was the only reason that one of them was alive, but still she couldn't make them happy. Patrick illustrated the pain of his childhood with an example of being punished viciously when his behavior outside the home had upset the prominent neighbor that his parents admired. He said that his parents always cared more about their standing in society than about his physical and mental health. Now I could understand that Cissy was glad to have a husband who had more to live for than her, and Patrick was glad to have a wife who did not insist that he conform to her standards. Patrick and Cissy's narcissistic defenses were identifications with and against the parents they were dependent on but about whom they were ambivalent.

OBJECT RELATIONS COUPLE THERAPY TECHNIQUE

In therapy the aspects used in assessment to establish a basis for working with the couple continue to apply. Over time, the therapist's capacity for holding and containment become the main ingredients of a successful treatment.

Holding

Holding refers to the therapist's task of providing a safe psychological space over time in which the couple can feel accepted, not judged or blamed, and in which each member will be viewed as equally important and held equally accountable for the state of the marriage. We listen without intervening at first. We follow the affect and use it as a guide to the core issues of the relationship and their connection to early individual experience. We notice defensive patterns that repeat and, when the time is right, we point them out and ask the couple to think about what purpose they serve. This leads us gradually to a discussion of deeper issues, once the couple trusts our capacity to hold their anxieties and help them to put them into words. We call this our holding capacity.

The therapist's self is our most useful tool. We train ourselves in personal analysis or psychotherapy, in supervision, in discussion with peers, and in constant personal process and review of the clinical situation to be receptive to the manner in which the couple uses us as their therapist. As we experience, think about, and react emotionally at a deep level to the personality structures of the couple, we respond by reflecting back what we have noticed, relate it to the historical context, and interpret it in the here and now (Joseph 1985). We attend to their responses to separation at vacation time and between regularly scheduled sessions to learn how the couple deals with loss and separation anxiety. We work with a spouse's dream, listening for associations by the dreamer and by the other partner. We regard the individual's dream as a communication from the couple to us.

The narcissist wants to be loved unconditionally, but the therapist offers only acceptance. We form an alliance on the basis of a nonjudgmental attitude, good reality checking, an appreciation of the separateness of minds and the value of differentiated thinking, thoughtfulness, and concern. One spouse will often want the narcissism of the other spouse confronted. We will do that but we will also look out for narcissistic traits in both of them. We will always find that the spouse who is not diagnosed as narcissistic does have some narcissistic issues too that are buried in the more obvious problems of the narcissistic spouse. Perhaps they are not as crippling, but they are there contributing silently to problems of inaccessibility and entitlement. In fact, we find that more subtle forms of narcissism lie at the root of many marital problems.

How do we deal with a narcissistic wife who appears overly concerned for the health of her spouse and yet she doesn't really sense what he is feeling at all? We think about what she is avoiding in herself. Perhaps she focuses on improving his comfort so as to avoid experiencing his pain, examining her role in causing his pain, and acknowledging her own pain. Perhaps she does not allow suffering since the relationship may be threatened if responsibility is sought for actual hurts or slights. As therapists we cannot afford to collude with this. We have to hold on to our own separate view and to face pain where there is pain. Having attended to our own individuality, we are in a better position to help the couple move out of their state of complementary narcissism and face the reality of their separateness and their need for mutuality (Strean 1985). We help them toward a state of individuation with improving capacities for empathic attention to losses, rage, sadness, and grief, and eventually to mature relating.

Containing

Containing refers to the therapist's task of tolerating the couple's anxieties over time and allowing them to resonate at the deepest levels of the therapist's psyche so as to understand the couple from inside her own experience. She is then able to respond in words that give shape to nameless fears. As she creates with the couple a narrative of their marriage and of their childhood experiences, she shows them how to process their experience and meet the developmental challenges at the present stage of their marriage. As the couple works with her, the partners learn to do this for themselves. They identify with her containing function.

To work in this way with such couples, therapists must study their own reactions, their countertransference to the couple's transference. As therapy proceeds, therapists find that they unwittingly play a role in re-creating the couple's defensive patterns to avoid underlying anxieties. They may experience feelings, thoughts, fantasies, or sensory experiences such as visual or olfactory images that give a clue to the underlying dynamics of the couple. The therapist's analysis of how she feels helps her to understand what is being projected from one spouse to another and from the couple to her. Her observations of contradictions between a spouse's supposedly benign motives and the actual effects of the behavior on the other spouse and on the therapist supply the basis for reality-based mirroring and interpretation. In a real sense the provision of a space for thinking anew is the single most powerful tool in working with primitive abandonment anxieties, the narcissist's deepest dread.

EXAMPLE OF TREATMENT OF THE MARRIAGE WITH A NARCISSISTIC SPOUSE

We here present an example of holding and containment and the interpretation of mutual projective identifications in object relations couple therapy. We emphasize the therapist's internal thought process as he works to understand the couple.

Background

Paul and Anne C. had been married for one year before Paul arranged for couple therapy in which he hoped I (CB) would cure his wife. Paul is forty,

Anne forty-five. This was their first marriage. Paul and Anne had the same goals and wishes: a marriage, children, achievements, physical health, and the acceptance of each spouse's family, but the real draw was tremendous physical appeal and instant sexual chemistry. They looked like Pierce Brosnan and Sharon Stone. Anne became hurt and enraged when Paul noticed how attractive Sharon Stone was (the actress, not the wife who resembled her) even though it was Anne who liked to imagine that Sharon Stone would find Paul attractive. Then Anne became convinced that Paul was no longer faithful to her. Paul referred to Anne as "my wife," which suggested to me that he thought of her as a possession that was no longer under his control.

First Session

Anne was hysterically accusing Paul of having an affair, removing his underwear from the home, and comparing himself to young movie stars. Paul was expressing fury that she was raging irrationally and threatening to divorce him because of things that meant nothing. Paul said that his spiritual advisor/therapist advised him that his wife's behavior was bizarre and needed therapy and medication if he was to get back his marriage. He insisted that she was the sick one and the cause of the problem. Anne said she had wanted marital therapy six months ago and Paul had refused. He had little idea of a collaborative approach to them as a couple.

Each partner's mirroring of the other as an exciting, idealized, romantic object was severely tested by shared attraction to Anne's enviably admired look-alike. This diminished self-esteem and led to fears of competition and loss.

I asked for more details about their first year of marriage. They told me that Paul's father died of cancer, Anne's mother fell ill and her male companion died suddenly, Paul lost his boss, and his new boss tried to force him out. All through this they had been supportive, sympathetic, and available to each other. The marriage hadn't fallen apart then.

Anne and Paul had clung to each other desperately in the face of attack by stressors outside the marriage. Now their bond was threatened by attraction to a competitor. Recovery could not be complete because they didn't know how to mourn.

Anne demanded that Paul own up to his selfish and flagrant betrayal, or get out. Paul demanded that Anne get treatment for her crazy ideas about him.

Neither spouse took responsibility for any of the charges being hurled about. Paul viewed himself as the helpless victim of what he called his wife's "incipient psychiatric breakdown." Anne viewed herself as the victim of a distancing, self-absorbed, betraying spouse. Paul looked to me for constant validation. Anne wanted me to confirm her perception of herself as the victim and justify her experience of rage and terror.

Using a technique of empathic mirroring, I commented that it was no wonder they were struggling after the trauma they had been through in their first year of marriage. They paused briefly and looked at each other, but they could not take in what I said. Neither of them could connect to any process that led to this derailment of the marital relationship. Emotions continued to run high. Complaints and counteraccusations escalated.

They wanted me to be like Solomon, wise in judgment of their case, but I viewed myself like a dormouse, stunned by the craziness of the Mad Hatter's tea party. I felt besieged with their demands that I take sides with no regard to separate thoughts or personality of my own. I found it difficult to provide good psychological holding or to think coherently about them, but I did attempt to tune in to each of them.

My feeling of ineptness and incoherence stemmed from a countertransference response to the narcissism. I reminded myself that the narcissistic person who seems psychically removed from the human environment, encased in a cocoon of grandiosity, omnipotence, and in Paul's case, pathological certainty, is not able to provide flexible and robust psychological holding for his fragile self. The narcissistic man is terribly fearful of compliance with the wishes of the woman he loves because it threatens his independence. However, he is also in desperate need of nourishment and fears losing her as the person he really depends on. Love relations require comfort with depending on each other and so do sexual relations. Because of dependency conflicts in the narcissistic personality, love and sexuality in marriage threaten the integrity of the self.

Paul's demands that I comply with his point of view were charged with aggression. His demands on me were a defense against my detecting in him the narcissistic vulnerabilities that he wished to deny (Modell 1975). Underneath his aggression lay a secret helplessness in response to the threat of complete loss of the woman I was expected to transform for his use.

Like many narcissistic people, Anne and Paul don't listen well and so had to repeat my interpretations and comments. I said again that there had been too much trauma for such a young marriage to handle, and I guessed that the family had been under strain as well and less able to support the young couple. I said that they were upset with each other because their emotional bond had been under attack from too much fallout to bear and that I believed that their rage and terror spoke for a powerful helplessness that could not be verbalized—at which Anne sobbed, and Paul went numb. This offered me a moment of emotional connection before Paul retreated to his imperious style and threatened divorce if Anne did not get the help I must give her. And Anne said he'd have to admit to the affair if she were to forgive him.

I felt some anger at their stubborn refusals to accommodate. I felt most anger at Paul's intrusive, demanding, infantile attempts to manipulate the marital therapy contract and continually try to get me to see Anne as sick. I balanced this reaction by feeling empathy for him being in such a panic, unable to convince his wife that he was faithful.

Narcissistic people like Paul want a spouse (and a therapist) who are in complete agreement with them. An independent position produces abandonment anxiety and rage.

Second Session

I said that Paul couldn't reduce his wife's threats to end the marriage if he didn't own up to having an affair. He said he wasn't having an affair. He confessed to getting rid of his underwear and explained that it was because he had a slight leakage sometimes. Indignant, he complained that he was being blamed for taking six pairs of underwear outside the home as if he was seeing another woman!

Anne had interpreted the leakage as sexual infidelity and Paul had hidden his insecurity by trying to throw it away. Each of them was aggrandized by the projection of ideal parts of the self and then admired for their film-star looks and also envied and distrusted. Each of them was threatened by the other's excessive projection of disavowed bad parts of the self—Anne with being excluded, betrayed, unreasonably jealous, and sick, and Paul with being irresponsible, imperious, self-centered, and abandoning. They held on to this projective identificatory system stubbornly rather than recognize their shared sense of threat, their shared helplessness in the face of trauma, and their fears of abandonment. They didn't want to admit their dependency on each other for security and regulation of self-esteem. I wrestled with questions as I pondered the gridlock. What was the intolerable threat to Anne? Was there something beyond infidelity that terrified Anne so much that she had to threaten divorce from Paul? Was this panic perhaps a manifestation of a narcissistic object choice leading to escalating disappointment as each partner's performance in the marital task failed to serve grandiose motives?

I asked Anne to tell me more about the threat.

She said that she couldn't help feeling Paul was up to no good. He brings home magazines of men and compares himself to them. He was always telling her how handsome he is, like the models in the magazines. She used to think he was self-centered, but not that much. And, they hadn't had sex in four months!

I asked them what they thought that meant.

Paul said that they used to play a game of imagining they could be movie stars since they were so attractive. Paul justified his use of the magazines as just another game like that.

I asked if this game with fantasies had fostered better sexual relations. They looked at each other as though they had been found out doing something illicit. But they cautiously went ahead to explore their memories of imagining love scenes between movie stars and how that increased their mutual sexual desire.

I made little comment so as to allow them the space to begin their work and to enjoy the improved feeling that was now entering our work space. Capitalizing on the improved tone of the relationship, I asked Anne and Paul to hold off on their threats of divorce since they added more trauma to a situation that was already full of trauma, and the constant threat would prevent working with the marriage and sorting things out. Anne explained that she threatens divorce when she feels violent, or fears that Paul will divorce her, as his therapist seems to be encouraging.

Both members of the couple were using the threat of divorce in a desperate attempt to modify the other's use of them.

I asked Anne and Paul to tell me more about their sexual relationship now and in the early days.

They described a tenuous beginning. Intense passions were kept inside, with desires (and even affection) strictly limited in family surroundings. Playful affection and kissing were minimal in their love life. The sexual bond was purely functional, they said. Sex consisted of manual touching of genitals toward orgasm. Intercourse was infrequent and short, just sufficient for Paul to achieve ejaculation. Anne was satisfied with the pleasure that she gave him.

The mood during this discussion was serious and halting. These facts were told with shame, as though I were a religious authority figure who might be looking for ways to censure them. I did not ask much, letting them add or subtract to each other's statements. Nor did I comment. It was becoming painful for me to hear of so much insecurity, anxiety, and adolescent uncertainty. The couple's lack of emotion and of playful intent made me sad. The more I heard, the more I had to tolerate a dysphoric state in myself.

The mourning process for their losses and traumatic experiences had become frozen. Mourning had to begin in me before they could become capable of it themselves. Once they could feel sadness and grief initially through their therapist and then in themselves, they would be able to experience feelings of love.

Paul and Anne continued discussing the lack of sex. As we ended, Paul shook my hand as they left the office. I think he was thanking me for my silent acceptance.

As a young couple Anne and Paul had been confronted with the impermanence of bonds. This had disrupted their confidence in the longevity of marriage. They had not developed a secure sexual relationship to maintain their marital bond and to provide pleasure and relief from stress. The threat to Anne of losing Paul to an affair and the threat to Paul of divorce from Anne provoked major anxieties and a sense of crisis that filled the therapy space week after week. This was an expression of their despair and their resistance to sharing the therapy space for the good of the couple. They had to test me with threats of divorce and termination before they could trust in my ability to work with them at the deepest levels of their anxiety and for as long as they needed me. We will continue to work on resolving her paranoid anxieties about his betrayal and his delusion that she is mentally ill before we are able to work on more fundamental anxieties about loss, damage, and lack of generativity.

Concurrent Therapies

During the course of my assessment of the couple, their therapist did not detect a level of anxiety or depression that would warrant medication. Behavioral sex therapy might become relevant to help them sustain vaginal intercourse more reliably, but not before Paul's fears of needing Anne and feeling persecuted by her accusations and Anne's inhibition of desire and envious projection of desire into other women had been fully addressed in couple therapy. The question of other psychotherapy approaches crossed my mind, especially in the face of the couple's deep resistance to sharing the therapeutic space for exploring how they each contributed together to impede their marital satisfaction. Individual therapy might seem a much easier choice for each of them. However, when an individual therapist supports a one-minded, one-sided point of view that one spouse is the victim of the marriage (as Paul's advisor did), this creates in the patient an infantile attachment to the therapist and a nonselective identification based on adhering to the therapist's biased view. This is a major impediment to establishing couple therapy (Fisher 1995). Individual therapy can be carried on concurrent to couple therapy if the couple therapist and the individual therapists trust and respect each other's work. It is possible to integrate what has been learned in the couple's individual therapies into our joint work to good effect.

THE GOALS OF OBJECT RELATIONS COUPLE THERAPY

We do not aim for symptom removal. We aim for fundamental character change. We are not teaching the narcissistic person to avoid expressing those traits. We are working toward their being unnecessary in the context of a loving marriage. On the other hand we do not privilege marriage over divorce. Our role is to help the couple appraise their marriage, explore what can be done to bring satisfaction to each partner, and arrive at a commitment to marriage or divorce. Divorce is not necessarily a failure of couple therapy. For instance, in the case of Paul and Anne, their therapist had to be prepared for the possibility that couple therapy might lead to divorce, given the degree of the narcissistic pathology, the resistance, the short duration of the marriage before trouble hit, and the tenacity of Paul's defensive strategy of scapegoating Anne. Only if couple therapists can face the possibility of failure of the marriage, can they deal with the anxieties that compromise the couple's relationship.

IMPLICATIONS FOR RELATED THERAPEUTIC APPROACHES

We believe that object relations theory of the narcissistic personalities and their marital interaction can be useful to extend understanding in other psychodynamic couple therapy models where personality change and adaptability is the goal. Even if the treatment goals are for cognitive mastery or behavioral restructuring, our way of thinking and working can enhance the establishment of the alliance. We have emphasized that the defensive, fragile nature of narcissistic personalities and their marriages requires special attention to the holding environment, sensitive pacing of interventions, and the careful creation of the therapeutic alliance. Systems and strategic therapy models that do not take account of this are prone to stalemate. Then the therapist may try interventions when bored, flooded, or unable to remain impartial and detached. Therapeutic interventions under these conditions reflect an anxious response to being ignored or deprecated. The therapist tries too hard to think up things to do so as to feel effective, rather than experience the deadening feelings of being with a narcissistic spouse or spouses. It is more beneficial to the couple for the therapist to tolerate the feelings of boredom and worthlessness and use the experience to understand and talk about the couple's effect. Couples may have highly charged emotional reactions or may leave treatment because of therapist-directed action-oriented interventions that do not take account of narcissistic resistance and vulnerability. Of course, negative therapeutic reactions may occur at any time and within any treatment, but techniques that ignore resistance and vulnerability will surely fail.

We advise trying to maintain a state of mind that follows the aims of the narcissistic spouse and their impact on the other spouse. We recommend looking out for the other spouse's hidden investment in the narcissistic spouse's narcissistic equilibrium. We track the affect, monitor frustrations, and detect the aims of various behaviors. We pay particular attention to the infantile origins of the current mode of relating in the marriage.

With narcissistic personalities the holding and containment deficits in the relationship and the individual spouse's past derivatives present a regressed and pain-driven situation. Our theory and clinical experience guide us to tread softly and gradually with these patients. We attend to the developmental deficits, cotransferences between the spouses, and projections onto the therapist. Most importantly, we work with the couple's conflict over longing for intimacy and fearing intimacy, wanting to give love but needing to protect the self from imagined attack and depletion. This powerful ambivalence presents the greatest challenge to the holding and containing function of all types of therapies. Without a secure alliance, no treatment can occur, whichever school of therapy is at work.

CONCLUSION

The study and treatment of narcissism in marriage requires careful, lengthy assessment of developmental, interpersonal, and intrapsychic dimensions. Because couple therapy is extremely difficult with this narcissism-dominated population, therapists have tended to conclude that individual therapy of the self-psychology school is the treatment of choice. On the contrary, individual therapy may collude with the narcissistic problem. We find that object relations couple therapy provides a perspective on the inner world of narcissistic relating that is useful for an in-depth understanding of marriages that present this pathology. The intrapsychic lens enlarges our view of the interpersonal world of the couple and vice versa. Our knowledge of the marital joint personality translates into technique in which we provide a psychological holding space in which the couple can express their narcissistic defenses, explore, and then modify them. Couples on the brink may be unable to share in couple therapy no matter how receptive the therapist is to their narcissistic issues. Nevertheless, receptivity and knowledge of early object relations maximize the couple therapist's effectiveness in engaging and sustaining therapy with the couple threatened by unhealthy narcissism.

REFERENCES

Barnett, J. 1975. Narcissism and dependency in the obsessional-hysteric marriage. *Family Process* 11:75–83.
Bion, W. 1959. *Experiences in Groups.* New York: Basic Books.
———— 1967. *Second Thoughts.* London: Heinemann.
———— 1970. *Attention and Interpretation.* London: Tavistock.

Colman, W. 1993. Marriage as a psychological container. In S. Ruszczynski, ed., *Psychotherapy with Couples* (pp. 70–96). London: Karnac.

Dicks, H. V. 1967. *Marital Tensions: Clinical Studies towards a Psychoanalytic Theory of Interaction.* London: Routledge and Kegan Paul.

Fairbairn, W. R. D. 1952. *Psychoanalytic Studies of the Personality.* London: Routledge.

Fisher, J. 1995. Identity and intimacy in the couple: Three kinds of identification. In *Intrusiveness and Intimacy in the Couple*, ed. S. Ruszczynski and J. Fisher (pp. 74–104). London: Karnac.

Glickhauf-Hughes, C., and M. Wells. 1995. *Treatment of the Masochistic Personality.* Northvale, NJ: Jason Aronson.

Joseph, B. 1985. Transference: The total situation. In E. Bott Spillius and M. Feldman, eds., *Psychic Equilibrium and Psychic Change: Selected Papers of Betty Joseph* (pp. 156–67). London: Routledge, 1989.

Klein, M. 1946. Notes on some schizoid mechanisms. In *The Writings of Melanie Klein, Vol. 3* (pp. 1–24). London: Hogarth Press, 1975. (Reprinted London: Karnac Books, 1993.)

Lachkar, J. 1992. *The Narcissistic/Borderline Couple: A Psychoanalytic Perspective on Marital Treatment.* New York: Brunner Mazel.

Lansky, M., ed. 1985. *Family Approaches to Major Psychiatric Disorders.* Washington D.C.: American Psychiatric Press.

McCormack, C. 1989. The borderline/schizoid marriage: The holding environment as an essential treatment construct. *Journal of Marital and Family Therapy* 15:299–309.

———. 2000. *Treating Borderline States in Marriage.* Northvale, NJ: Jason Aronson.

Modell, A. 1975. A narcissistic defense against affects and the illusion of self sufficiency. *International Journal of Psycho-Analysis* 56:275–82.

———1993. The narcissistic character and disturbances in the holding environment. In G. H. Pollack and S. Greenspan, eds., *The Course of Life, Vol. 6* (pp. 501–17). Madison, CT: International Universities Press.

Ruszczynski, S., and J. Fisher, eds. 1995. *Intrusiveness and Intimacy in the Couple.* London: Karnac.

Scharff, D., and J. Scharff. 1991. *Object Relations Couple Therapy.* Northvale, NJ: Jason Aronson.

Scharff, J. 1992. *Projective and Introjective Identification and the Use of the Therapist's Self.* Northvale, NJ: Jason Aronson.

Scharff, J., and D. Scharff. 1994. *Object Relations Therapy of Physical and Sexual Trauma.* Northvale, NJ: Jason Aronson.

———. 2000. *Tuning the Therapeutic Instrument.* Northvale, NJ: Jason Aronson.

Slipp, S. 1984. *Object Relations: A Dynamic Bridge Between Individual and Family Treatment.* New York: Jason Aronson.

Solomon, M. 1989. *Narcissism and Intimacy.* New York: W. W. Norton.

Strean, H. 1985. *Resolving Marital Conflicts: A Psychodynamic Perspective.* New York: John Wiley and Sons.

25

Couples in Narcissistic Collusion: Sexual Fantasy and Acting Out

Walton Ehrhardt

THREE CASES OF NARCISSISTIC COLLUSION

I illustrate the concept of narcissistic collusion with brief descriptions of three couples in which both partners present with sexual fantasies and enactments.

Case 1: The Silvers

Roger and Dee presented for therapy both admitting to extramarital relationships. As parents of two young children, aged nine and seven, each was receptive to my advice that they discontinue these relationships and focus on their marriage. This treatment took place many years ago and I was not yet doing object relations couple therapy. I used a Bowenian therapy model stressing overfunction and underfunction. Insurance limitations necessitated a treatment protocol of twenty-four sessions, and in that short time the couple ended the affairs, reconnected, and began a more productive lifestyle together. Following a six-month break, Dee returned to work with me in individual therapy, and over the next six years made significant gains for herself. Recognizing that she tended to devalue herself by taking care of her family and her husband's family, she reduced her role in her husband's extended family of origin and their family real estate business, and left all that to Roger. She completed her college education, obtained a significant professional position with a local business, and terminated therapy. Six

345

months later, she returned to therapy now expressing serious ambivalence about continuing the marriage with Roger. Roger entered individual therapy with a colleague. While Dee was considering divorce, Roger, believing that she was having an affair with a colleague, attacked her with a stun gun. She separated immediately and sought a restraining order against him. Tragically he proceeded to kill her and himself.

Case 2: The Golds

Jim and Jana had been married twenty-three years and were the parents of college-age children. Both of them had active fantasies of specialness and were pulled toward a sexually addictive pattern of affairs. Both partners expressed difficulty in joining the therapy process and in establishing and maintaining the time frame, in trusting one another to relinquish an extramarital sexual partner, and in developing a capacity to listen to the other instead of interrupting and attacking.

Case 3: The Greens

Married seventeen years, David and Ruby were parents of three sons. David had admitted to a brief affair with his spouse's younger sister, Marilyn. Ruby had had no sexual affair, but she was deeply involved in a relationship of intense sibling rivalry with Marilyn and one of parenting her younger married sister. After two and a half years of therapy, Ruby angrily left the conjoint therapy and ultimately stopped therapy altogether, refusing to own any aspect of responsibility for a failing marriage.

TWO GENERALIZATIONS ABOUT NARCISSISTIC COUPLES AND A NARCISSISTIC CONTINUUM

Psychotherapy with a narcissistic couple is extremely challenging and entails learning, including how to accept failure (Kernberg 1975, 1995). The therapist feels overburdened, confused, and sometimes hateful, wanting to slap someone or exit from the couple. It is difficult to hold and contain the primitive object relations of such a couple whose primitive states of mind reflect malignant envy and borderline pathology (Bollas 2000). Narcissistic pathology in couples includes selfishness, self-sufficiency, superiority, grandiosity, hysteria, and borderline features (further described in chapter 24).

Narcissism is ubiquitous in human development. It contributes to normal self-esteem but it also leads to serious pathology (Freud 1914, Spreuill 1975). Otto Kernberg described those with serious pathology as a "special group of patients":

I am referring to those narcissistic personalities who, in spite of a clearly narcissistic personality structure, function on what I have called an overt borderline level, i.e. present the nonspecific manifestations of ego weakness characteristic of borderline personality organization. . . . These narcissistic patients present severe lack of anxiety tolerance, generalized lack of impulse control, striking absence of subliminatory channeling, primary process thinking, and proneness to the development of transference psychosis. (Kernberg 1975, p. 266)

Working in individual therapy with narcissistic characters is hard enough. They need perfect mirroring, stroking, and responses. They want to be in control. They feel omnipotent and always right. They want to be special, and they become injured when their specialness is not recognized and outraged when they do not feel understood. Narcissists range from being "thick-skinned" in some matters to being "thin-skinned" in others (Symington 1993). When injured or insulted, they typically withdraw physically, emotionally, or both, and may quit therapy in a huff.

Narcissistic pathology in couples lies along a continuum (Grotstein 1980, Kernberg 1995), from those whose narcissism makes the couple relationship impossible (Kohut 1971, Lachkar 1992) to those whose pathology appears to be the basis of their long-term involvement (Grotstein 1980, Kernberg 1995, McCormack 2000, Ruszczynski 1993, Scharff and Scharff 1991). These collusively joined couples present with a mixture of narcissistic and borderline features. Addressing the difficulties for couples, Kernberg notes that the marital relationship is filled with narcissism that is far more than the sum of the individual narcissism: "We . . . have to deal with two problems: narcissistic psychopathology in one or both partners and the 'interchange' of personality aspects of both, bringing about the couples' pathological relationship that does not correspond to the individual pathology of the partners" (Kernberg 1995, p. 143).

OBJECT RELATIONS OF COUPLES: THE BRITISH SCHOOL OF THERAPY

Couple therapy is a complex undertaking. It calls for a theory that can address unconscious processes at the heart of the individual personality and extend to understanding the nature of the couple's relationship. I look to British object relations theory for the concepts that support in-depth couple therapy. I lean toward the Independent tradition but I blend in Kleinian ideas and concepts from object relations couple therapy—introjective and projective identification, focused transference and contextual transference, holding, and containment (Scharff and Scharff 1991, Siegel 1992, McCormack 2000).

Dynamics of transference and countertransference exist between the marital pair in their relational zone and between each member of the dyad and the therapist in the contextual zone of relating to therapy and the therapist. As the partners re-present their longing for relationship, the therapist feels connected and accepted. However, as they present their rejection, the therapist feels walled off.

In each of the three couples that I discuss, the type of narcissistic object choice is governed by unconscious states of mind involving primitive object relations of splitting (Fairbairn 1954, Guntrip 1971, 1989), projective identification (Klein 1946, J. Scharff 1992), and collusion with the internal couple of each partner (Kernberg 1995, Scharff and Scharff 1991, Willi 1982). The endopsychic structure of the person affects the development of both ego ideal and superego, both of which are problematic in narcissistic couples.

THE ESSENCE OF NARCISSISM: SPLITTING AND PROJECTIVE IDENTIFICATION

Kleinian theory holds that everyone relates through the use of the basic psychodynamic process called projective identification. Personalities with a greater need for defense use projective identification to an extreme, and this can result in narcissistic control of, or retreat from, objects. The term *narcissism* refers to a particular type of object relationship in which the use of projective identification involves massive splitting and idealization.

Fairbairn's thinking developed in relation to his work with schizoid patients whom he experienced in the transference as unconsciously splitting the frustrating caregiving object into exciting and rejecting aspects. He realized that these corresponded to internal structures formed during the vicissitudes of infantile dependence. The key dynamic is this: good (satisfying) and bad (exciting and rejecting) affect-laden experiences are *introjected* into the internal world as internal good and bad objects to which good and bad aspects of self must relate inside the self. Fairbairn's major contribution here lies in his emphasis on the *dissociation* and *repression* of object experience, thereby rendering parts of experience and parts of self unconscious. Some of Fairbairn's schizoid patients might today be called narcissistic. Guntrip correctly observed that "narcissism is a disguised object relation" (Hazell 1994, p. 57). Narcissism is essentially a *retreat from objects*.

MAJOR THEMES IN THESE NARCISSISTIC COUPLES ARISING FROM PROJECTIVE IDENTIFICATION

Some Functions of Projective Identification

Projective identification fulfills two basic functions: (1) communication and (2) defense (Steiner 1993). The projection communicates what the projector finds to be intolerable, lacking, painful, or frightening. It may derive from a fear of separation or loss, a fury over imagined or real damage, a sense of deficiency, a need to feel understood, or a need to wound the other as the projector feels wounded. Various reasons for their projective identifications are shown in the couple vignettes, elaborated below.

To Relieve Anxiety and Pain

Roger and Dee Silver eloped as high school graduates in order to avoid the misery of their alcoholic families of origin. Each had formed a caretaking transference to needy parents and disowned their own neediness. Roger's father owned about three dozen houses and expected his son to assist in the maintenance of these properties while continuing his firefighter position with the city. Dee kept the books for the real estate business and kept the family needs satisfied. But Dee and Roger could not express and respond to their own needs. They were miserable. As their repressed libidinal selves became frustrated, they each had turned outside the marriage to an "exciting" other to get their needs met and to escape from pain.

To Avoid the Experience of Separateness or Loss

David and Ruby Green were each avoiding terrible feelings of separation and loss. David was avoiding his grief over the death of his college sweetheart, the first and only woman by whom he felt loved. Ruby had lost her father and, encouraged by her needy mother, had taken over his position of authority in the family instead of taking time to mourn him. The Greens' marriage formed around a unique rule: "It is right for us to join together. We are as one. Don't dare to notice difference. Don't disagree with me. If you disagree with me, you will be wrong. If you are wrong, I may leave you!"

To Place the Intolerable Aspects of the Internal Self and Object Representations into Another, Where They May Be Dominated or Controlled

Ruby was not aware of her own neediness disguised in her need to be needed. The couple formed around someone being ill. First, it was David's father, and then, his mother. David experienced Ruby as unavailable, and in frustration turned to her sister. Following the deaths of the parents, it was David who was ill. He was being treated for a rare blood condition and for benign prostate enlargement. Ruby insisted that he was gravely ill and needed her desperately, to the extent that he was frightened for his life. Ruby seemed just like his mother who had insisted that David's alcoholic father was too ill to leave. So, they colluded in this domain of control over one another's freedom, just as his parents had done. David's way of experiencing relief was to turn to his wife's little sister, who understood him and agreed with his way of thinking and feeling and who, for her own reasons, supported his anger at being controlled by Ruby.

To Damage or Destroy the Object

Roger Silver's self-hatred led him to perceive Dee as unloving and unfaithful, even though this was not the case. He enacted his fantasy of punishing her by zapping her with a stun gun. She ordered him out of the house, thereby validating his fear that he had damaged his beloved object-possession. He ultimately destroyed that possession and himself in a vicious act as if to say: "If I cannot possess you, then no one else will, nor will you!"

To Get into an Object in Order to Take Over Its Capacities and Make Them One's Own

The Gold couple, Jim and Jana, idealized lots of other people. Jim idealized his father out of his own need to feel important by association. He enacted this self-importance in the business world. Jana idealized the emotive, seductive therapist who introduced her to the ecstasy of Tantric sexuality, the merger of souls, and communion with a deity. Each of these spouses used the "other" in an attempt to take over admired capacities of the other in order to make them one's own. In the Silvers and the Greens, affairs were attempts to feel raised up by the personality gifts of the other.

As a "Direct Communication," to Imbue the Other with One's Own Unrecognized Feelings

Each of the Greens projected an element of misery into the other which was palpable to the therapist. If David were not feeling well, he would expect Ruby and the therapist to feel ill, too. If they did not, he would respond with disappointment, and wish for the return of a lover who would join in his feeling state of mind. This dynamic is: "I feel bad. You are part of me. Therefore you feel bad."

Collusion and Formation of Joint Ego Boundaries

These couple dynamics operate within a collusion system. Two individuals join as partners when they experience an unconscious valency of attraction (Scharff and Scharff 1991). As they pursue a relationship of intimacy and sexuality, unconscious aspects of their self and object constellations begin to emerge in the body-mind connection of the reawakened psychosomatic partnership (Winnicott 1965, Scharff and Scharff 1991). The couple forms a joint marital personality in which there are expanded joint ego boundaries, a collusive attribution of unconsciously shared feelings, splitting and repression of the reacting self, and split-off object relations remaining charged with psychic energy (adapted from Dicks 1967, pp. 68–70). In other words, the process of splitting and repression leaves the central ego impoverished because it is lacking relational potentials, which remain locked up in the split-off aspects of libidinal and antilibidinal egos and corresponding objects.

Implications for Therapy: Blurred Boundaries and the Sense of Oneness

In couple therapy partners spoke for one another and reacted angrily when contradicted. There was little appreciation of "me" and "not me," each spouse failing to relate either to self or other as a whole person. The primary motivations for the relationship were the pursuit of survival, the need to use the other to complete the deficiencies in the sense of self, and above all the necessity of maintaining a feeling of oneness. Frustration quickly mounted between them as each talked over the other. When one partner spoke from an anxious pole expressing fear of abandonment or chaos, the other spoke from the pole of intrusiveness, and a few minutes later in the same session these positions reversed.

NARCISSISM AND SHARED INTERNAL WORLDS

Relationship difficulty arises as the *repressed* aspects of each partner's self-system *return* from unconscious repression into conscious states of mind owing partly to the emergence of individual pathology and partly to the effect of two personalities joining (Kernberg 1995). Disappointment occurs when the partner and the self fail to match the rigidly held fantasy expectations of how each should play their marital roles. According to Dicks:

> Fantasies . . . are based on direct or contrasting parent images and the unreal expectation in the marriage is that partners must be "all-in-all" to each other, make good all defects and offer perfect gratification of all needs. It is the return of the repressed that causes trouble. It breaches the idealizations. (1967, p. 71)

The return of repressed material undermines the unconscious quid pro quo of the joint collusive relationship determined by their shared dependency issues.

IMPLICATIONS FOR THERAPY

Via primitive introjective and projective identification, the partners re-create and confirm their respective internal self and object relationships in the external reality of their marriage. Each spouse then attempts to control the other, hoping to master in the marriage what was beyond the ability as a child.

The following clinical manifestations commonly occur:

Common Clinical Manifestations

Hurling Identical Paranoid Projections and Accusations at One Another

The initial sessions with the three clinical cases are marked by attack and blame to defend against persecutory anxieties. These antilibidinal ego responses lead to a feeling of wariness and weariness in their feelings for one another.

Alternately Presenting a "Need for the Other" as if the Other Is Part of Oneself

Split off and repressed libidinal aspects of self are disowned and projected into the other. These are terribly lonely people, but they do not allow themselves to *feel* the presence of the otherness of others. They withhold connection, yet they hang on to the other only to complete the self. For example, Roger and Dee Silver had not participated in sexual intercourse with one another for seven years since the conception of their last child. Jim and Jana Gold had not had intercourse with one another for four years, as satisfaction was sought outside the marriage.

Cherishing and Persecuting the Partner When Identified with Aspects of the Self

Ruby Green idealized her husband as a good father and dutiful husband. Her way of loving him was to take charge. His compliance to her controlling ways was his way of loving her. She projected her libidinal, needy self into him and managed it there. His affair with her hated sister took him right out of her control and destroyed her mechanism for repression of her neediness. His response was to indulge her with hugely expensive gifts.

The Silvers presented a somewhat different clinical picture. Roger Silver's envy of his cherished spouse was augmented by the arrival of their two children whom she mothered as lovingly as she had attended to her husband's need for nurturance. Later, terrified of abandonment when she considered divorce, he unleashed his fury in a premeditated act of murder and suicide, the final gesture of a malevolently envious state of mind (Williams 1997, personal communication, and text 1998).

NARCISSISM AND THE THREESOME STATE OF MIND

The Ubiquity of Triangulation

Triangulation occurs in all dyadic relationships, and is related to the relationship between the self and the internal couple (Scharff and Scharff 1991). Ian Suttie's early thinking about the formation of triangles is helpful in conceptualizing the development of an affair. Working from the perspective of the dyadic relationship of the love-seeking infant in relation to mother, Suttie noted that this love bond is primary and has the quality of tenderness (1935, p. 44). This companionship of love, expressed in pleasurable mother-infant play, gradually expands to a companionship of interest/rapport in relation to her and many others. Suttie concludes: "The function of the interest rapport has this in common with love: that it affords a sense of companionship and dispels that of *loneliness*. It is thus *social* not sexual in origin. It may unite with 'sexual appetite'" (1935, p. 46f.).

Suttie's thinking suggests that the earliest formation of object relationships results from the welcome experience of tenderness in response to vulnerability. Fairbairn also referred to vulnerability, but he called it dependence, and focused on the formation of internal object relationships that arise to control nontender experiences by taking them inside the self and repressing them. Using concepts from Bion and Winnicott, I think of it this way: the mother who provides a good environment and is the focus of her child's existence mediates tenderness through her capacity to contain her baby. When this capacity is compromised, the infant registers a betrayal felt as a trauma, and defensively responds with splitting and repression.

An Affair Is about Fantasy, Not Reality

As children mature they use the transitional space for play and imagination to recognize their dependency and their capacity to be alone and experiment with being separate from mother. In my opinion narcissistic people are greatly in need of play space in which to practice relating to themselves and others. Without this, they become vulnerable to sex (with the self or with partners) as an impersonal way of relating, based on the search for the elusive psychosomatic partnership. This is the narcissistic edition of the Oedipus complex, arrived at following an envious relationship with mother, and then with father, which leads to a sense of secrecy and specialness. The internal ideal ego reflects ideal fantasies of becoming special to someone, and the ego is split into a part that does feel special and a part that is not special at all. In relation to a partner, the person with an ego in two parts is in a triangle, and this may lead to a tendency to triangulation, which in many cases takes the form of affairs (Khan 1995).

Affairs Are about Triangulation

Person (1988) suggested two basic forms of triangulation: split-object triangles and rivalrous triangles.

Split-object triangles are those that form around one partner being experienced as the "good" lover, the other partner as the "bad" lover. Such a split-object triangle is based on a fantasy of a conflict-free relationship in which the ideal partner provides perfect emotional support. This dynamic was present and active in the three couples under consideration.

Rivalrous triangles are a reversal of the child's Oedipal relation to the internal couple. The child who felt rejected as the loser in the Oedipal struggle becomes the sought-after object by two potential lovers who are in competition for the affection of the child, now an adult. David Green's affair with his wife's sister presented him with the fantasy of being pursued by *two* lovers, Ruby and Marilyn. That was his way of feeling special. Ruby's ongoing spiteful relationship with her sister was a form of persecutory revenge in which she took pleasure in how much David bought for her, really rubbing it in on her sister.

Affairs Are about Betrayal

In Fairbairn's system, when the self has been betrayed in its deepest need to experience receiving and giving of love, it responds by believing itself to be unlovable and unimportant (1954). The early promise of the pristine self is betrayed. In adulthood that self continues to betray itself. The betrayals will first be manifest in the contextual transference through lateness, issues around payment of fees such as outrage at the cost, forgetting appointments, and broken promises. The three couples all manifested the symptoms of betrayal of themselves, each other, and of the therapy.

An Affair Indicates Activity of a Parasitic Part-Object Relationship

Bion referred to a parasitic quality in some relationships: A parasitic relationship is one in which one "depends on another to produce a third, which is destructive to all three" (Bion 1970, p. 95). A parasitic quality of relating dominates the joint marital personality in all of these couples.

An Affair Involves a "Pairing" within a Family or Community Group

The affair is the creation of a special pair that offers the narcissistic person a magical solution to relational problems, just as two people may pair up excitedly to do something else instead of working equally with all the members of a work group (Bion 1961). The partner in the affair is a messianic deliverer, a wished-for ideal parent. Just as the twosome takes away from the energy of the work group, and the work group also looks to the pair to divert it from its work, the errant spouse dilutes the marriage, but the marriage also has an investment in the affair. The affair is parasitic on the marriage, and the marriage is parasitic on the affair.

How does this parasitic pairing apply in the clinical cases? Each partner has some conflict between superego, ego ideal, and ego. When partners come together there is normally a struggle between the superegos, and when conflict arises there is ambivalence. Grunberger says: "In a well balanced relationship, both partners can keep their own superego and their own narcissistic defense without fear and without arousing anger in the other" (1971, p. 81, f.50). But in the narcissistic collusion, the resolution is compounded by envy of the ideal.

Jim Gold was envious of his wife's independence. She owned a successful business, traveled, and enjoyed a lover with whom he did not believe he could compete. In his eyes, Jana was superior. Surprisingly, Jana Gold was envious of her husband's personal and professional position as a community activist and powerful attorney in a prestigious law firm. He was so self-sufficient, he acted as if he had no need of her. He was not interested in her body, in her sexual pleasure, but only in his own. Each had brought an aspect of part-self in relation to part-object. Each in their own busy self-involved worlds had become libidinally starved. They remained a couple, they said, "for the sake of the children." But the child parts of themselves were in need of equal consideration, and they did not know how to care tenderly for those vulnerable parts. So the child in them was clinging to the idealized "other man" who would serve as the "messianic deliverer."

THERAPY WITH COUPLES IN NARCISSISTIC COLLUSION: SOME PRINCIPLES

Need for Structure: Response to Chaos

The couple presents in a collusive state of mind and they need to find clarity and structure in their couple therapy. Their area of centered holding and relating at the outset of therapy is full of defenses against internal chaos, which shows up in their transference as attack and blame, difficulty with words, and general avoidance of awareness. The primitive nature of their organization as a couple requires that the therapist be in charge from the very first connection with them.

The therapist must establish rules right away, especially regarding how to keep their agreements with one another and with the therapist regarding appointments. For example, with the Gold couple, they were so casual in relation to their commitment to therapy that I found it necessary to construct a written contract that specified their individual responsibility for payment and for rearranging appointments instead of simply canceling. They learned that their passivity had been an act of betrayal to themselves and to me.

The *therapeutic goal* is to wean the partner who clings and the partner who idealizes away from clinging and idealizing. Developing healthy reliance on one another (as opposed to alternate clinginess and dismissiveness) is a slow and tedious process.

Containment: Response to "Oneness"

The development of a therapeutic container is difficult because of narcissistic defenses against intrusiveness, control, and failure of containment. The therapeutic focus must first be on the more narcissistic partner, the supposedly logical one who is less capable of connecting with feeling states. For example, Jim Gold emphatically responded to me that his work was far more important than anything I might consider of importance regarding the couple's psychotherapy. I felt I had to endure this until I was able to build enough understanding based on using my countertransference to provide information about the activity of defenses and the state of mind being projected. I said, "You are wanting me to know how insignificant you felt in relation to your powerful, busy, self-important father. I am having to teach you another way of being important."

A Process: From Oneness to Twoness

In couple therapy the partners are invited to identify their states of mind and look at the functioning of their selves. The movement from collusive oneness toward the separate twoness of differentiated and self-defined beings is a slow unfolding process. The therapist respects the couple's pace and revisits the defenses that reassert themselves to attack this process because it is unfamiliar and difficult to sustain. The partners work toward having a life other than through the partner, and at the same time recognizing the partner's otherness, and valuing the privilege of being together.

A few words of caution to the therapist in this phase of the work. One partner may take flight from therapy altogether and return to the status quo. The therapist feels the sense of trauma and abandonment that the narcissistic person has been dealing with and is not given the chance to help. The parasitic relationship to the partner is very strong. As one therapist counsels: "Unhealthy parasitic relationships lead to hiding, fears, darkness, persecutory anxiety, clinginess, and emptiness" (Lachkar 1992, p. 169). The therapist must respect the fact that the healing process takes hard work, is slow going, and takes steps backward. The therapist is constantly returning to the point that external gratification, boundary intrusion, and blaming do not develop a sense of self.

Arrival at Thirdness

The couple arrives at the third position. The capacity for thirdness correlates with the development of subjectivity and potential space (McCormack 2000). In this position of thirdness, in this potential space, experience of the other as a whole person reflects the movement from paranoid/schizoid to depressive relating in which taking account of the needs and feelings of one another can lead to a more meaningful relationship. The couple experiences the satisfactions of their relationship and the therapeutic process. The partners recognize one another as separate and valuable, they can relate to their marriage as a valued entity, and they can appreciate their therapist as a useful person, they can see the therapy process and what they have learned from it, and then they prepare to leave therapy by agreement.

SUMMARY

I illustrate in this chapter the clinical dynamics of narcissism in couples, in particular their acting out of fantasy through extramarital affairs. I broaden Kernberg's concept of narcissism on a continuum to a continuum of types of narcissistic collusion in couples. From a British object relations theory perspective, I present basic aspects of splitting, projective identification, collusion, Oedipal difficulty with frustrating internal object experiences leading to triangulation, and aspects of working through in conjoint marital therapy. Using my work with three clinical cases I illustrate the difficulties of the therapeutic process, show therapeutic failure and successful outcome, and develop some principles for working with this clinical population.

REFERENCES

Bion, W. 1961. *Experience in Groups.* London: Routledge.
———. 1970. *Attention and Interpretation.* London: Karnac, Maresfield Edition.
Bollas, C. 2000. *Hysteria.* London: Routledge.
Chasseguet–Smirgel, J. 1985. *The Ego Ideal.* New York: W. W. Norton.
———. 1984. *Creativity and Perversion.* London: Free Association Books.
Coleman, W. 1993. The individual and the couple, in S. Ruszczynski, ed., *Psychotherapy with Couples,* pp. 126–41. London: Karnac.

Dicks, H. 1967. *Marital Tensions.* New York: Basic Books.

Fairbairn, W. R. D. 1954. *An Object Relations Theory of the Personality.* New York: Basic Books.

Freud, S. 1914. On narcissism: An introduction. *Standard Edition* 14:73–107.

Grotstein, J. S. 1980. A proposed revision of the psychoanalytic concept of primitive mental states. *Contemporary Psychoanalysis* 16:479–546.

———. 1983. A proposed revision of the psychoanalytic concept of primitive mental states. II. The borderline syndrome. Sec. 1. *Contemporary Psychoanalysis* 16:570–604.

———. 1984. A proposed revision of the psychoanalytic concept of primitive mental states. II. The borderline syndrome. Sec. 2. *Contemporary Psychoanalysis* 20:77–118.

———. 1984. A proposed revision of the psychoanalytic concept of primitive mental states. II. The borderline syndrome. Sec. 3. *Contemporary Psychoanalysis* 20:266–343.

Grunberger, B. 1971. *Narcissism: Psychoanalytic Essays.* New York: International Universities Press.

Guntrip, H. 1971. *Psychoanalytic Theory, Therapy, and the Self.* New York: Basic Books.

———. 1989. *Schizoid Phenomena, Object Relations and the Self.* Madison, CT: International Universities Press.

Hazell, J., ed. 1994. *Personal Relations Therapy: The Collected Papers of H. J. S. Guntrip.* Northvale, NJ: Jason Aronson.

Johnson, S. 1987. *Humanizing the Narcissistic Style.* New York: W. W. Norton.

———. 1994. *Character Styles.* New York: W. W. Norton.

Kernberg, Otto. 1975. *Borderline Conditions and Pathological Narcissism.* Northvale, NJ: Jason Aronson.

———. 1995. *Love Relations.* New Haven, CT: Yale University Press.

Khan, M. 1995. Secret as potential space. In S. Grolnick and L. Barkin, eds., *Between Reality and Fantasy,* pp. 257–70. Northvale, NJ: Jason Aronson.

Klein, M. 1946. Notes on some schizoid mechanisms. *International Journal of Psycho-Analysis* 27:99–110.

Kohut, H. 1971. *The Analysis of the Self: A Systematic Approach to the Psychoanalytic Treatment of Narcissistic Personality Disorders.* New York: International Universities Press.

Lachkar, J. 1992. *The Narcissistic/Borderline Couple.* New York: Brunner/Mazel.

Laplanche, J., and J. B. Pontalis. 1973. *The Language of Psychoanalysis.* New York: W. W. Norton.

McCormack, C. 2000. *Treating Borderline States in Marriage.* Northvale, NJ: Jason Aronson.

McDougall, J. 1995. *The Many Faces of Eros.* Northvale, NJ: Jason Aronson.

Person, E. 1988. *Dreams of Love and Fateful Encounters.* New York: Penguin Books.

Pittman, F. 1989. *Private Lies.* New York: W. W. Norton.

Ruszczynski, S. 1995. Narcissistic object relating. In S. Ruszczynski and J. Fisher, eds., *Intrusiveness and Intimacy in the Couple,* pp. 13–32. London: Karnac.

———. 1993. *Psychotherapy with Couples.* London: Karnac.

Scharff, D. E. 1982. *The Sexual Relationship.* London: Routledge.

———. 1992. *Refinding the Object and Reclaiming the Self.* Northvale, NJ: Jason Aronson.

———. 1996. *Object Relations Theory and Practice: An Introduction.* Northvale, NJ: Jason Aronson.

Scharff, D. E., and J. S. Scharff. 1991. *Object Relations Couple Therapy.* Northvale, NJ: Jason Aronson.

Scharff, J. S. 1992. *Projective and Introjective Identification and the Use of the Therapist's Self.* Northvale, NJ: Jason Aronson.

Siegel, J. 1992. *Repairing Intimacy: An Object Relations Approach to Couples Therapy.* Northvale, NJ: Jason Aronson.

Spreuill, V. 1975. Three strands of narcissism. *Psychoanalytic Quarterly* 44:577–95.

Steiner, J. 1993. *Psychic Retreats.* London: Routledge.

Strean, H. 1980. *The Extramarital Affair.* New York: The Free Press.

Suttie, I. 1935. *The Origins of Love and Hate.* Middlesex: Penguin Books.

Symington, N. 1993. *Narcissism: A New Theory.* London: Karnac.

Willi, J. 1982. *Couples in Collusion.* New York: Jason Aronson.

Williams, A. H. 1998. *Cruelty, Violence, and Murder.* Northvale, NJ: Jason Aronson.

Winnicott, D. W. 1965. *Maturational Processes and the Facilitating Environment.* New York: International Universities Press.

26

Dynamics of Sadomasochism in the Film *The Night Porter*

Hugh Joffe

What is it that makes the mind so curious about, and occasionally even aroused by, thoughts of domination and submission? Equally, why do these concepts appear so regularly in dreams, social relationships, and erotic life? By the same token, why is it so difficult for men and women to interact as equals without being attracted to the age-old archetype of master/slave?

Men who find something sinister in the female body are terrified of losing their sense of power and influence over women. Consequently, many choose to take up a dominant position in heterosexual relationships. Females are comparatively far less preoccupied by ideas of hierarchy, but tend to prefer trying to relate meaningfully. Deep-seated envy of the other gender appears common to both males and females. Gender-based access to power and control varies from society to society, but in any society overwhelming power relations may be entered into, as one gender tries to leave its mark on the other.

In the pursuit of a loving relationship, we are likely to pair with a partner whose capacity to enhance our existence comes with a capacity to torture and destroy us, depending on the circumstances. Obviously, we hope that both partners will come to that much sought-after position of integrated self-fulfillment. However, it does not take a great deal to turn the relationship into one that is vicious, competitive, or aggressive. Failure to regulate or balance love and hate is toxic for the future of the relationship. Unfortunately, the statistics on partnership, and marriage in particular, do not look encouraging, as evidence indicates that interpersonal levels of conflict and violence are on the rise.

Goldberg (1993) reports that half the women in America are physically or emotionally abused by the men in their lives. Likewise, children are being exposed to acts of violence. Additionally, Goldberg suggests that some form of hitting, beating, and abuse are as much a part of the American dating scene as arc loving flirtations and affections. Emotional abuse in couples is often denied or made light of by reducing it to a simple question of dominance, but issues of power, control, rage, and cruelty all form part of the clinical picture. Hirigoyen (1998) contends that emotional abuse is set in motion when a loved one is somehow found lacking or the relationship is too symbiotic. Narcissists, for example, try to control and regulate social distance. Too much psychic space for them proves anxiety provoking, whereas too little is suffocating and can terrify them sufficiently into trying to destabilize or destroy their partner's self-esteem.

Why do women who are the targets of abuse return again and again to abusive situations? Is it their need for security in the face of emptiness? Do they fear scorn or expect shame if they separate? Socially and psychologically speaking, many women feel as if they are nothing without a man.

The experience of regaining the freedom to start over seems too daunting. Many women cannot bear to be separate and prefer to take whatever physical and emotional abuse is meted out to them rather than experience the pains of freedom or those associated with independence. For those who take up a submissive stance, it seems that it is the case of "better the devil you know." Rasmussen's (1988) study on battered women reveals that this gravely endangered sector of society fears abandonment far more readily than it fears pain or even death.

Freedom, which so appeals to the mind and watchful gaze of the philosopher, is seldom explicitly referred to in psychoanalysis. Freud, for instance, was much more preoccupied by the concept of power and hardly ever mentions the word *freedom* in the *Standard Edition*. Speaking of sovereignty and liberty, the philosopher Rousseau suggests mankind is quite prepared to "sacrifice pleasures, repose, wealth, power and life itself for the preservation of this sole good" (May 1981, p. 4). Likewise, Fromm (1942), a psychoanalyst with a particular bent toward political philosophy, mentions how the oppressed classes of both Europe and America were willing to die on the battlefield to secure and sustain their freedom from those who might oppress them. While there is tremendous support and advocacy for freedom, some argue that we cannot bear the existential angst that attends it. The pain that escorts regulated compliance or submission is deemed preferable to the pain of freedom.

Fromm goes on to comment on an interesting paradox. Man's industrial and technological advances, in conjunction with the development of a more complex urban lifestyle, have not resulted in a greater self-assurance and independence. Rather, we now seem plagued by more intense feelings of powerlessness and anonymity, both of which foster a strong need to attach to someone worthwhile even though, at times, this attachment may turn out to be abusive.

Because few of us have the capacity to stand alone, at the first sign of distress we seem only too prepared to cede control to someone who appears stronger or acts more authoritatively than we do. In fact, somebody who is able to offer some form of safety or protection even if it is manipulative, becomes that much more desirable. Perhaps it is a throwback to our earliest states of infancy, where nurture, security, and dependency are all inextricably linked.

By becoming part of a system or couple that appears firm and unshakable, a person feels that the sense of self becomes strengthened, and therefore, more formidable. Usually in these circumstances, one party is solicited or chosen to lead, dominate, or control the other, as if by unconsciously immersing oneself in the psycho-soma of the other, it is possible for the weaker partner to find some comfort and temporary respite from the searing pains of loneliness.

The desires to either sexually subjugate and possess one's love object or alternatively to surrender one's personal separateness and individuality for the sake of some security forms the basis of a sadomasochistic way of relating. While this way of connecting may hold out a seductive promise of belonging, it actually fails to provide the necessary parameters for psychic growth.

In couple relationships where pathological dependency is favored over freedom, the partners seem to fuse to prevent or deny the psychic existence of the other. Analysis usually reveals that one or both parties have experienced some unbearable early childhood trauma. Rather than contemplate our trauma, we tend to search for other distractions. There is a powerful wish to escape the limitations or finiteness of our existence, and replace this stark world with one where all things are possible. In this space, pleasure always seems to supercede pain.

I turn to the medium of film for the opportunity to witness the psyche and its torments and the means to study it from a psychoanalytic point of view. As Gabbard (2001) suggests, "the cinema and psychoanalysis have a natural affinity" (p. 1). It is here that the mind comes alive, to be experienced and to be explored.

The film I have chosen portrays a young woman who, having been sexually and emotionally traumatized by her sadistic Nazi captor, later fails to embrace freedom, but opts to remain perversely attached to him instead. As such, it provides us with an interesting vista into some of the questions raised and, in particular, allows greater insight into the dynamics of power and powerlessness as well as dominance and submissiveness in couple relations.

THE NIGHT PORTER

Liliana Cavani's (1974) *The Night Porter* delves into a relationship between Max, a former SS officer, and Lucia, a Jewish adolescent girl whose life he saved, and consequently whose fate he controlled in the concentration camps. The conditions of the camps and the instinct to survive led many ordinary people to engage in extraordinary activities. In this instance, Lucia enters into a sadomasochistic tryst where she is forced to participate in polymorphous perverse sexual relations with a German captor for the right to some continuance, especially when those around her are being sent to the gas chambers of Auschwitz.

The movie is set in 1957 Vienna, where a secret organization of former Nazis meets regularly at a well-known hotel to expunge its Holocaust past, through a self-styled truth commission. The group aims to "work through" residual shame and guilt, hopefully removing any incriminating evidence from ever falling into the hands of the Nazi war hunters being sent to Europe at the time to round up and prosecute former war criminals.

Max works in this hotel as its night porter. It is here, some eleven years after the war, that he becomes reacquainted with Lucia, his former camp girlfriend. Trying to put the past behind her, she had left Europe to live in America where she had married a refined man. Her husband, a successful conductor, was about to perform a number of summer concerts in Vienna, and despite some obvious posttraumatic concerns at returning to Europe, she had volunteered to accompany him.

As she approaches the hotel reception desk to request the keys to her room and locks eyes with none other than Max, an intense hypnotic state is rekindled, which opens the door to a vast store of repressed memories. Through these, we, the audience, become privy to their previous relationship and quickly realize that the lurid details of this relationship have been buried deep inside her. Unable to turn anywhere for help, she panics as she is affronted by a troubling dilemma. While she is terrified to go anywhere near this man for fear of further abuse, a significant part of her feels an irresistible urge to resume an active sexual relationship with him.

Through her flashbacks, we witness the first time Max made her acquaintance. Posing as a Nazi doctor, he stumbled upon a stunning Jewish teenager, as he was engaged in filming naked prisoners as they stood in line awaiting medical examinations that would determine their outcome.

Stirred by this girl's virginal innocence and naïve facial expressions, Max fixed his camera on Lucia, violating her space, moving from head to foot, as she blinked in confusion and looked away in embarrassment. Rather than being put off by this behavior, her shyness actually inflamed him to want to see more of her intimate parts, and in turn stimulated strong cravings to sexually penetrate and possess her. Plagued by these irresistible urges, Max eventually led his charge to a room where they could be alone, and then forced her to perform oral sex. Thereafter, she was forced into frequent perverse sexual encounters with this man.

The Night Porter explores the compromises and sacrifices that this adolescent is forced to make during her internment as she battles cold, hunger, abuse, and shame in order to survive. It seems that the film director decides not to portray Lucia's responses to this depravity clearly as her facial expressions are indeterminate, leaving us uncertain as to whether she hates and abhors these sexual acts of violence, or gives her consent willingly, underscoring a degree of pleasure in being debased (Scherr 2000). Perhaps the somewhat lifeless expression that emanates from her eyes depicts a defensive dissociation that she has developed in order to cope. We are left puzzled, if not outraged, by her postwar decision to resume a steamy sexual relationship with a man of such dubious character, who had raped her body and mind.

In Max's apartment, to the dismay and outrage of his Nazi friends, the pair re-creates a delusional world of tormenting love. Addictive sadomasochism unites this couple in a common enterprise, as both seek to complete themselves through the realization of a perfect union. However, they soon discover that they have to pay a heavy price for their predilection. That is, freedom and individuality are sacrificed for a symbiotic attachment, which brings about disaster.

To make sure their story is never told, Max is given explicit instructions to assassinate Lucia, but he refuses, forcing the two of them to hide and barricade themselves inside a "love-nest." This is a psychic retreat, a place of refuge from the world of real relationships, where those who enter feel protected, even though they are still in the throes of unconscious psychic pain (Steiner 1993). Driven by the need to find food, the two become exposed, and eventually, are shot dead.

Prior to their demise, it is particularly interesting to note how Lucia manages to turn the tables on her lover, intentionally inflicting pain on him. By making him walk over freshly broken glass, purely for her own sexual excitement, we observe that she, too, is capable of sadistic attributes (Siegel 1995). Traditionally, poststructuralist film theory has defined the male as the active sadist and the female as a passive masochist. Clearly, this movie confronts us with the fact that masochism is not simply the prerogative of the feminine. Nor can a woman be denied the pleasure of making a man the subject of her own cruel gaze.

Cavani deliberately leaves much of the complex interplay between the two characters open to interpretation, refusing to pigeonhole the characters or their relationship. We are asked to rethink some preconceived notions about victims and their victimizers, especially in times of war.

WAS THE DECISION TO REUNITE PERVERSE?

The audience would have been far happier if on meeting Max again, Lucia had preferred to repudiate him publicly and charge him with sex crimes. This would have allowed us to feel that she had transcended her abuse and was now psychologically healthy enough to demand retribution. Instead, we are forced to witness and endure the enslaving passion she feels for this sadist who cannot love but only express hatred or aggression in his sexual life. She is traumatized, tied to her abuser, and now perverts pain into sexual excitement.

Perversion implies an internal process that fails to differentiate between, and actually reverses, good and bad. Perversion turns things completely upside down or inside out, and in so doing, distorts the truth. Perversion deviates from what is perceived to be right because it does not accord with the laws and expectations of human nature, and it impedes a person's capacity to thrive.

In Shakespeare's *Macbeth,* the witches' incantation, "Fair is foul and foul is fair," summarizes the essence of the perverted state. Perversion is a phenomenon that leads people from the true depths of their emotional pain by distracting them with something that is far more pleasurable. Since they are outside the realm of moral acceptance, perverted images always have a primeval power to stir up feelings. Yet it is equally possible to argue that these are nothing more than a series of strong defenses against traumatic losses not adequately mourned.

Despite this, many people believe Cavani's film warps the historical facts of the Holocaust. Rather than re-creating some factual account of the atrocities perpetrated by the Nazis against humanity, *The Night Porter* perversely waters down actual traumatic memory into an erotic spectacle that uses Nazi atrocity merely as its vehicle. In so doing, it actually "decontextualizes the concentration camp from its historical facticity" (Scherr 2000 p. 5).

In all probability, if we add something to the truth, we will no doubt take something away from it. Why then does Lucia try to disguise and distort her feelings of absolute horror at seeing her parents wrenched from her side? Is her heartbreak so profound that she cannot contemplate this phenomenon, but rather feels the need to dissociate herself from the bald truth and institute a lie instead? Perhaps her sadomasochistic attachment to Max is one of the mind's attempts to preserve its own sanity and re-establish control in a world denuded of morality. It certainly seems to have provided her with some means of dealing with traumatic feelings of helplessness and hopelessness. If this were not so, she may well have become acutely psychotic or died of a broken heart.

What does Max signify for Lucia? Perhaps he is nothing more than a symbol of absence, representing everything in Lucia's past life that she has previously lost. Some might say he is symbolically like the angel of death, who entices and seduces her so he can do as he pleases. Sex and death are now equated in her mind. While this unconscious link is too painful to accept, it has to be kept secret from consciousness. Yet it is from this dark space that Lucia's sadomasochism emanates. A perverse defense was the best way for her to maintain this secret, while desperately trying to keep her trauma at bay.

In the face of trauma, when psychic life becomes bereft of meaning, and where the victims' only available link to life is through an aggressor, it is highly likely that they will turn to their abusing object for continued support. As Van der Kolk (1987) states, "the most powerful asset in overcoming psychological trauma seems to be the availability of a helpful and trustworthy caregiver" (p. 34). In order to survive her concentration camp experience, Lucia decides to turn to Max.

Graham (1994) suggests that if a captor shows some benevolence toward the captive, this perceived kindness allows the victim some hope as well as some space to defend against abject terror. Victims do not stay with their abusers because they have bonded with them. Rather, they bond with their abusers because they see no way to escape.

Equally, one may raise the question as to whether Lucia's spellbound need to submit to Max's depraved sadomasochistic antics was because they dulled or masked some other intense psychic pain. Stolorow, Atwood, and Brandchaft (1994) reported a clinical case in which a psychotic, deprived nineteen-year-old incessantly implored her analyst to beat her. For a while, this was the only communicative exchange that she could articulate. The analyst eventually managed to help her to realize that this wish was addictive, underscoring the fact that in her situation, "physical pain [was] better than spiritual death" even though it was violent and abusive. It is not uncommon to learn from masochistic patients that the only time their parents became emotionally invested in them was when they were being punished.

Borrowing heavily from Bion's (1970) work, Abel-Hirsh (2002) similarly contends that there is a distinct difference between pain suffered and pain felt. According to her, "pain felt but not suffered may be believed to carry information about the torturer and hold no meaning for the self." In light of this, it would seem that those who are not able to endure or experience the psychic pain that accompanies everyday life and loss cannot grow and develop. Instead, they become forced to, or choose to, engage in activities that pervert the truth and in some cases compel them to adopt extreme measures as a means of survival.

In order to stave off a deep personal sadness resulting from all her losses, Lucia chooses rather to submit herself to a perverse ritual, incorporating subjugation and humiliation at the hands of a tormentor. The ensuing sexual abuse allows her to disavow and/or numb the emotional pain of her parents' death in favor of being able to focus on a physical stimulus instead, which has become erotically exciting. In an imaginary merger with some abusive figure, where the laws of space and time are suspended, separation, death, and mourning simply do not exist. Rather, sadist and masochist are able to form a bond that is united in its common enterprise.

The obsessive search for a caretaker or lover, even an abusive one, is experienced as essential for emotional survival. The expressed purpose in this instance is to win love, at any cost, and against all odds. It can often remain in the mind long after the loss has occurred and customarily becomes a way of dealing with, or filling up, an empty space. In fact, one may argue that it is a self-soothing remedy to treat the posttraumatic state.

The fact that unholy alliances between captors and their victims occur so regularly has forced those of us working in mental health to acknowledge it as a particular disorder, called "the Stockholm Syndrome." This occurs when a victim is in the presence of—and cannot escape from—a threatening person who is at least temporarily stronger or more powerful. The development of this syndrome actually increases a victim's chance of survival. To all intents and purposes, it is a reinstatement of the extreme dependency so characteristic of one's early childhood, at a time when secure attachment is needed and when trauma is devastating. The fears and pleasures of infancy are reawakened in the adult victim who is terrorized by captors, and yet thankful to and dependent on them (Franzini and Grossberg 1995).

GUILT

In my opinion, surviving the initial trauma of rape in conjunction with being forced to engage in ongoing abusive sexual relations in an atmosphere of death and destruction may well have caused permanent damage to Lucia's mind. Besides altering her fundamental assumptions about life and reducing her capacity to trust, it is highly probable that she may have felt extremely ashamed if not terribly guilty for her actions. Not being able to stand up to one's captors creates a deep sense of inadequacy. By tacitly agreeing to become a camp prostitute and then developing positive feelings for her sadistic captor, it is highly likely that she would have not only shamed herself but felt as if she had betrayed the honor, ethics, and moral codes of her deceased parents. Therefore she felt any abuse received was thoroughly deserved because of her wickedness.

In making love to Max, it is quite likely that Lucia felt that she had not only crossed over religious and ethnic lines but was in breach of incest laws, too. In the family romance of the Oedipal period, the daughter is a proactive agent in explicitly looking for her father to become the object of her love. The mother is seen to be cold and rejecting of the child's needs and desires, which in turn stimulates the child to seek out the father as a source of security and affection through some sexualized play. The child is seen as active seductress, whereas the father is perceived to be a passive, if not innocent, bystander in the daughter's quest to establish union. So Lucia could experience her effect on Max as a repetition of an early childhood wish to be with a forbidden man.

The fact that Lucia chose to repeat and restage the trauma in Vienna a few years later with the man who had abused her is likely to have stripped her of any sense of morality. Failing to live up to her own ideals no doubt promoted a strong wish to be punished, so as to avoid the loss of her parents' love. Punishment might have seemed the only path toward some genuine reparation.

In many religious traditions, the desire to be beaten and whipped underscores a strong wish to do penance for such wrongdoing. Assuaging one's guilt through participation in sadomasochistic rituals, acts of asceticism, and self-abuse, people believe that they can effect a cure for their evil deeds or intentions. Some religious men and women still believe that this is the only way to purge a guilty soul of its transgressions.

The sadomasochistic interactions between Lucia and Max strip the ego of its defenses, ambitions, self-consciousness, and success. In the ensuing trance, the ego dissolves in order to become subservient to the master. Whether in submission to the will of God or to the sexually dominant, the masochistic position emphasizes the wish to serve, or to abandon oneself sexually, physically, and emotionally to the power, authority, and control of another. Masochism may be seen as a strategy for escaping guilt and holding on desperately to the love and attention of a significant other, when all seems lost. Furthermore, it may be perceived as a universal technique employed through the ages by human beings for dealing with the problems of guilt, helplessness, and hopelessness.

For me, the saddest thing about the entire *Night Porter* saga is that Lucia could not really face thinking about or confronting the inherent truth of her situation. As a consequence of some terrible inner emptiness, she fails to feel any pain or develop the appropriate links between the trauma of the Holocaust and her strong need for attachment. Unfortunately, her character has not matured adequately over time, but remains primitive and disconnected instead, resulting in an absolute terror of helplessness and insecurity. By failing to atone properly for her own unconscious violence and hostility, she cannot effectively mourn for her external losses but is forced to adopt a series of destructive, sadomasochistic rituals instead. This in turn produces ineffectual guilt, which at the end of the day cannot be used productively by the personality to facilitate its own growth or development. As Carveth (2001) so aptly states, "the guilty subject who cannot bear feeling guilty will evade guilt feeling one way or another" (p. 21), unless the language for facing guilt is learned. Unfortunately, Lucia never learns to do this and has to pay the ultimate price for choosing to remain a child.

DOES A *NIGHT PORTER* SYNDROME EXIST WITHIN THE MIND?

This movie has made me wonder whether there is something in the mind that hypnotizes us to submit to, if not worship, another part of it that is entirely destructive and totally controlling. Perhaps Max, "the Night Porter," is nothing more than a metaphor for our experience of a diabolical inner figure, which inhabits or invades the mind following a traumatic episode. (Some may prefer to associate it with the term *superego* or *inner critic* but what we call it is less important than understanding why it happens.)

It would appear that man's mind can only withstand a measured dose of trauma before rupturing into hundreds of smaller pieces. As such, the inner Nazi, or "the Night Porter," is called upon to prevent a psychosis from happening and indeed preserve the personality from total annihilation. Operating like some commissioned gatekeeper, it protects the soul and the essence of the mind from being overrun by torrents of anxiety, which are part and parcel of any violent change. A symbolic figure of the nature of "the Night Porter" comes along to allow life to continue on the outside with a superficial sense of normalcy. Other dissociative defenses, namely, splitting, projective identification, idealization, depersonalization, and psychic numbing are regulated by the same figure, to ensure the preservation of the species.

Discussing the undisclosed world of trauma, Kalsched (1996) contends that by submitting to its power, the weaker or inferior part of the self is assured some continuance, postponing any need to contemplate its weakness, emptiness, or even badness. This was very much the case for Lucia. However, as we all know, these services never exist without cost. Betty Joseph (1982), for instance, suggests that masochism is based on an infant's belief that the price to be paid for the love of one's parents is the surrender of personal separateness and individuality.

In the face of trauma, the weaker part of the personality is virtually a total slave to the perceived omnipotence of its stronger twin. Terrified of being abandoned to that space where bad feelings prevail, the self engages the services of an inner tyrant and then provides it with the necessary support and the political clout to govern the remainder of the personality, without creating the presence of an effective opposition to regulate the process.

More often than not in the case of societal trauma, concepts of tyranny and totalitarianism substitute for the principles of freedom and democracy. Fascism maintains that it is the duty of the powerful and intelligent to gain control over the state so that members of the proletariat may be organized and governed. Failure to accept or conform to these tenets results in harsh or cruel punishments being administered swiftly. Sadly, in the name of safety and security, dictatorial omnipotence destroys the imagination of the mind, plunging it into conformity, boredom, and a state of subjugation.

Trauma seems to divide the mind into a binary state of opposites, in which the strong and weak parts of the self try to remain connected through a sadomasochistic form of coupling. It is as if the weak cries out to the strong, "You can do anything you like to me, hit me, abuse me, just don't leave me alone to face the darkness or blackness of my existence." The mere presence of a so-called stronger other is enough to ameliorate the panic and distress that an anticipated separation sometimes stimulates. The sadist on the other hand virtually says to the captive, "I can do anything I want without being terrified that you will leave me." This in turn hides some dependence on that inferior or submissive part of the self (Bach 1991).

Interestingly enough, when a strong sadomasochistic narcissistic organization exists, as it does with Lucia, we are not able to hold the notion of a parental couple firmly in our minds (Fisher 1999). As a consequence there is no internal feeding mother to identify with, nor is there the father's penis to support the mother in her rightful place. Then persecutory anxiety runs rife in a self that exists without a container. To all intents and purposes, the person is forced to compromise by managing anxiety through the creation of a deviant act. In the case of Lucia it seems that the only pathway to avoid depression or a full-blown paranoid state was for her to act out sexually. In this way she could exist without a soul.

TAKING MAX AND LUCIA TO THE CONSULTING ROOM

Max and Lucia felt stimulated by the bizarre sexual rituals and behavior of the other, allowing each to withdraw momentarily from the harsh brutality and intrusiveness of war into a mental space that was both exciting and comforting. What had started out as sexual abuse soon developed into a containing, emotional folie à deux, where rather than face the sheer awfulness and insanity of the Holocaust, Max and Lucia managed to create a series of perverse defenses that assisted them to shut out the rest of the world and gain a sense of oneness in their own madness. By engaging in sadomasochistic behavior, they chose to seek out an altered state of consciousness, like taking a drug to obliterate the traumatic circumstances. As long as the drug soothed them, neither of them wished to change. What appears as sick, perverse, or shocking also has multifaceted, adaptive, psychic connections. It is hard to imagine that Max and Lucia would ever have stopped to think about, or question their existence, and so create the need to go for help, even though we may firmly believe it is indicated.

Some scenes in the movie indicate that Max is totally enraptured by this woman's beauty, which not only stimulates his intense desire, but simultaneously introduces him to his need to take possession of her exquisiteness and control it for fear of it abandoning him at a later stage. The fact that she was a Jewess in captivity made the task that much easier. While Lucia's life at that time had depended on complying with his sexual demands, she now manages to take something from the encounter. She enjoys fleeting moments of seeing and experiencing the adulation in his gaze and despite the bleakness in her life, some part of her realizes that she is special to him. This empowers her to demand something from him during their exchanges.

The way she keeps him coming back is to not fully give of herself to him sexually. This sexual aloofness, an autistic defense perhaps, seems to make him far more uncertain of his prowess. Desperately wanting the recognition of being good enough as a lover and therefore as a man, he tries in vain to get her to climax, only to be frustrated time and time again, which allows her to become powerful and demand more from him. In this way, she turns the tables from simply being another little Jewish masochist to becoming a Nazi dominatrix, who demands that he worship her for the chance to gain some genuine sexual release. She has identified with the aggressor, so that she could be the one who *does* rather than the one who is *done unto*.

It would appear that masochists do not simply allow themselves to be tormented. On the contrary, they are able to reverse roles so that it is the tormentor who ultimately becomes the tormented. Not having an opinion of her own, and giving in to his every whim, bar making the affirming psychological and sexual commitment to him that he so needs, allows Lucia to express some of her anger and regain control of the situation. Her passivity makes Max feel like she is a rag doll that can be manipulated, but certainly not psychically or sexually controlled. While this is a source of extreme frustration for him, it excites her. In couple therapy, we find that while anger may be a destructive emotion in a couple's existence, it can work wonders for their erotic life.

At the end of the day, if you were to take Lucia aside and ask her whether she loves Max, I very much doubt if she could answer in the affirmative. In my opinion, because Lucia never completed her mourning process satisfactorily, she did not resolve the ambivalent features of her love and hate. In offering true love, a person does it, not out of fear of being abandoned, but out of goodwill to the other. While Lucia may have been capable of perverse relations with Max, I believe there is insufficient psychic energy available to her for a genuine love affair. At best, we might hear her say, "I make love to him simply because I cannot live without him."

The Night Porter is a film that challenges us to think through many internal contradictions. It certainly makes us consider why some abused women derive pleasure through their sadomasochistic rituals. The irregularities portrayed by Lucia are, in my opinion, simply a defense against a sadness she finds insufferable. Trauma is always a crucial variable to look for when discussing perversion. It invariably obliterates psychic structures, causing mutations to our inner world so as to make sure that the ego does not feel its own pain.

Perhaps what transpires in this case has some bearing for women who find themselves caught up in similar situations. For these women, it feels better to be abused than to be neglected. The fear of falling into a depressive abyss is for them worse than a life filled with cruelty or domination.

POSTSCRIPT

The Night Porter is a complicated, disjointed story about two central characters who should by all accounts despise each other and stay away from each other, but who get together nonetheless. Max and Lucia did manage to form a couple space, but for all the wrong reasons. Their couple space was filled with perverse mating rituals, the imagery of which lingers uncomfortably. After watching *The Night Porter*, I came away with my head reeling. The director did not provide many clues to understanding the couple relationship, but she certainly did bring the topic of sadomasochism to the fore in a vivid way that is hard to ignore.

REFERENCES

Abel-Hirsh, N. 2002. The perversion of pain, pleasure and thought: On the difference between "suffering" an experience and the "construction of a thing to be used." *The Melanie Klein Trust*, pp.1–6.

Bach, S. 1991. On sadomasochistic object relations. In *Perversions and Near Perversions in Clinical Practice*, ed. G. Fogel and W. Myers, pp. 75–92. New Haven and London: Yale University Press.

Bion, W. R. 1970. *Attention and Interpretation*. London: Karnac.

Cavani, L. 1974. *The Night Porter*. New World Pictures.

Carveth, D. L. 2001. The unconscious need for punishment: Expression or evasion of the sense of guilt. *Psychoanalytic Studies* 3(1): 9–21.

Fisher, J. V. 1999. *The Uninvited Guest*. London: Karnac.

Franzini, L. R., and J. M. Grossberg. 1995. *Eccentric and Bizarre Behaviours*. New York: Wiley.

Fromm, E. 1942. *The Fear of Freedom*. London: Routledge and Kegan Paul.

Gabbard, G. O. 2001. Introduction. In *Psychoanalysis and Film*. London: Karnac.

Goldberg, J. 1993. *The Dark Side of Love*. London: Aquarian Press.

Graham, D. 1994. *Loving to Survive: Sexual Terror, Men's Violence, and Women's Lives.* New York: New York University Press.

Hirigoyen, M. F. 1998. *Stalking the Soul.* Canada: Helen Marx Books.

Joseph, B. 1982. Addiction to near death. *International Journal of Psycho-Analysis* 63:449–46.

Kalsched, D. 1996. *The Inner World of Trauma.* London: Routledge.

May, R. 1981. *Freedom and Destiny.* New York: W. W. Norton.

Rasmussen, A. 1988. Chronically and severely battered women: A psychodiagnostic investigation. Unpublished doctoral dissertation. Graduate School of Applied and Professional Psychology, Rutgers University. *Dissertation Abstracts International* 50, 2634B.

Scherr, R. 2000. The use of memory and the abuses of fiction: Sexuality in holocaust memory and fiction. *Other Voices* 2(1): 1–18.

Siegel, C. 1995. *Male Masochism.* Bloomington: Indiana University Press.

Steiner, J. 1993. *Psychic Retreats.* London: Routledge.

Stolorow, R. D., G. E. Atwood, and B. Brandchaft. 1994. Masochism and its treatment. In *The Intersubjective Perspective,* pp. 121–26. Northvale, NJ: Jason Aronson.

Van der Kolk, B. 1987. *Psychological Trauma.* Washington, D.C.: American Psychiatric Press.

27

Low Sexual Desire in Gay, Lesbian, and Heterosexual Peer Marriages

Suzanne Iasenza

Many couples enter sex therapy in states of conflict expressed outside the bedroom as well as in their intimate life. They each fault themselves or blame their partner for their sexual difficulties. The couple therapist begins by emphasizing good communication skills, conflict resolution, and how to negotiate and compromise. These qualities tend to improve the erotic environment of a couple, and the sexual problem may then take care of itself.

THE COMPANIONABLE BUT SEXLESS MARRIAGE

Other couples with sexual problems present as if they have no interpersonal conflicts, and they require a different approach. Each partner describes the couple relationship as satisfying, and they consider themselves to be one another's best friend. Schwartz calls these "peer marriages." Many heterosexual, as well as gay and lesbian couples, in their thirties and forties, fit the description of peer marriages. They have "a marriage of equal companions, a collaboration of love and labor in order to produce profound intimacy and mutual respect" (Schwartz 1994, p. 2).

Schwartz first discovered these "peer marriages" in 1983 when she, with co-researcher Philip Blumstein, conducted one of the most comprehensive studies of couples in the United States, a ten-year project in which she drew on data from twelve thousand questionnaires and six hundred interviews from married and co-habitating heterosexual, gay, and lesbian couples. She hypothesized that gay and lesbian relationships were more egalitarian because unlike heterosexuals the partners did not have to overcome traditional gender roles to develop relationships that felt fair and mutually supportive.

When partners in such a peer marriage enter sex therapy they often do so to gain an understanding about the only area of dissatisfaction—their sexual life. They wonder why, when they are experiencing such high satisfaction in so many other areas—parenting, financial and domestic responsibilities, friendship, intimacy, and communication—their sexual relations are so infrequent. Often one or both partners report low sexual desire. It should be mentioned that some couples with low sexual desire feel fine about it and do not seek sex therapy, because other satisfying qualities of the relationship take priority over sex. Others don't fight about it but enter sex therapy simply to find out why they experience such low sexual desire.

Adult romantic relationships have their roots in infancy and childhood. DiCeglie (1995) holds that our childhood experience of the parental couple influences how we conduct adult relationships. In the best of all worlds we can desire, identify with, and enjoy both members of the parental couple. This enables us to experience the greatest degree of flexibility and richness in adult love relationships. When one or both parents relate dysfunctionally with the child and/or each other, the child's ability to move through all possible internal parental object relations is hindered. These hindrances emerge later in adult love relations as sexual shutdowns, anxieties, or defenses.

Why does this happen? Does all passionate adult sexuality involve the eroticization of power inequities like those first experienced in childhood? Are peer partners ill equipped to deal with the inevitable differences and tensions involved in sex? How might the partners be splitting off bodily shame, hate, or hostility into sexuality and avoiding these disavowed feelings by experiencing low desire?

Thinking of the parent-child relationship, Winnicott discussed the importance of the development of "potential space in which, because of trust, the child may creatively play" (1971, p. 109). Equally in adult relationships that potential space is needed for creative interaction. Helping couples create safe potential space for their erotic life is essential in supporting their ability to reveal unconscious conflicts underlying sexual difficulties and work through them together.

UNDERSTANDING AND TREATING
THE SEXUAL DIFFICULTY

The goal of treatment is to help the couple create an erotic environment in which they may explore, expand, and enjoy their sexual potential. Through a combination of behavioral and educational interventions and psychodynamic interpretations, the couple may discover the unconscious childhood events, couple dynamics, and societal influences that contribute to sexual difficulties (Iasenza 2000; Masters and Johnson 1966, 1970; Kaplan 1974; Scharff and Scharff 1991; Scharff 1998).

Having good sex often mobilizes guilt and anxiety about boundary maintenance, comfort with intimacy, body image, religious and family attitudes about sex, and self-worth. Family life, intimate relationships, and sexual histories of lesbian women and gay men often contain sexual guilt, anxiety, and shame due to societal and internalized homophobia (Buloff and Osterman 1995; Gair 1995; Isay 1989; Loulan 1984). When they meet a therapist who has internalized homophobic attitudes, their shame is compounded.

In the past, some psychoanalysts added to the shame and guilt experienced by lesbians and gay men by characterizing homosexuality as sexual perversion or psychological abnormality. Even in the twenty-first century, therapists may carry residuals of these beliefs unconsciously (Kernberg 1975; McDougall 1980; Siegel 1988; Socarides 1968, 1988). Despite the momentous 1973 decision by the American Psychiatric Association to remove homosexuality as a mental disorder from its diagnostic manual, it has only been within the past decade that a groundswell of gay and lesbian affirmative psychoanalytic literature has emerged (Burch 1997; Drescher 1998; Domenici and Lesser 1995; Glassgold and Iasenza 1995; Gould and Kiersky 2001; Isay 1996; Kirkpatrick 1996; Magee and Miller 1997; O'Connor and Ryan 1993; Schwartz 1998).

This development, fostered by feminist, gay and lesbian, and some senior analytic thinkers, most notably Kernberg and McDougall, is rapidly expanding not only our understanding of normal homosexualities but of gender and sexuality in general. Contemporary thinking is deconstructing gender and sexual dichotomies, expanding the roles of childhood sexual desires and identifications, and examining forms of defensive and symptomatic heterosexualities (Benjamin 1995; Chodorow 1994; Kernberg 2002; McDougall 1995; Person 1999).

Kernberg concludes:

1) In contrast to the perversions, with their rigid and restricted sexual behavior that becomes an obligatory precondition for sexual excitement and orgasm, homosexuality implies a sexual disposition and set of sexual activities that can be as broad, flexible, and rich as can heterosexual commitment.

2) We no longer believe that there exists one homosexuality, but a spectrum of homosexual orientations that reflect different psychodynamics, possible different etiological factors, and that range clinically from severe psychopathology to health. The same spectrum, however, may be described for heterosexuality, although idealized, normative formulations regarding heterosexuality are more readily available. (2002, p. 11)

I approach my discussion of clinical case material involving gay male, lesbian, and heterosexual couples with Kernberg's directions in mind, neither idealizing the heterosexual nor pathologizing the homosexual, and offering each of these cases not as general examples of gay, lesbian, or heterosexual development but as individual expressions of sexual orientations, each containing their own unique sets of psychodynamics. I hope to illustrate the psychodynamic challenges in working with the unconscious roots of low sexual desire in the lives of three otherwise fulfilled, companionable couples. I focus particularly on the effects of the internal parental couple on each relationship.

A Gay Couple: Bob and Carl

Bob and Carl, both in their forties, have a gay peer marriage. Their sexual histories contain ample evidence of enjoyable sexual experiences, both partnered and solo. Bob and Carl think of themselves as intellectually, emotionally, and socially well matched. They bought and furnished beautiful homes in Manhattan and in the country. Carl's parents who live in New York know and welcome Bob as their son-in-law. They enjoy a rich social network of colleagues, friends, and family, to all of whom they are out as a gay couple. Nevertheless, during four of their five years together, one or both of them has refused sex.

Their family histories tell the back story. Bob grew up in a Southern Baptist family where both of his parents abused alcohol and his father was physically and verbally abusive. He became aware of his feelings for boys early on but he knew that given his parents' religious beliefs and his father's obsession with hypermasculinity both in himself and his two sons, his physical and mental survival depended on secrecy and silence. He didn't have much of a social life and throughout his teen years depended on masturbation (fantasizing about boys and girls). As he and his brother entered adolescence, his father's abuse and neglect of his mother intensified, and she regularly turned to her two teenage sons for company and comfort. Bob remembers with disgust and outrage her controlling rituals of demanding that he and his brother kiss her on the lips before leaving the house or hug closely before they retired at night. Bob saved himself by excelling in academics and getting into a college away from home. He decided to come out to his parents at the end of his senior year of high school only to have his father disown him, refuse to pay for college, and proclaim that he never wanted to meet any of Bob's boyfriends. Bob's mother lived in fear of defying his father and silently went along with it.

Carl and his sister were raised in a comfortable New York family where his parents were supportive, attentive, and encouraging of the children's talents and travel. They seemed like the perfect family. His father and mother were civil with each other, highly successful, and well known in their fields. They valued achievement and social prominence. Carl was a straight-A student and was president of the debate club. His family enjoyed many social gatherings with their friends, many of whom were openly gay and lesbian. Carl knew that his parents would probably deal well enough with his homosexuality given their circle of friends but he carried a deep concern about not measuring up and suspected that their politeness might mask feelings of disappointment in him.

From early on as a slightly built boy with no athletic ability, Carl was taunted and bullied so badly that he avoided the showers and left as fast as he could when the "hey faggot" epithets began. He never reported these shaming experiences to anyone, including his parents. He openly dated girls and secretly dated boys throughout his teen years until he fell in love at age fifteen with a boy with whom he thought he'd spend the rest of his life. By senior year the pressure of the secrecy was too much for his boyfriend who abruptly announced one day that he was "going straight." Carl was devastated, more so because he never let on to his parents how wounded he was. One day after college when his mother asked why he was so distant and didn't share his friends with the family, he came out. Both parents were supportive, and Carl felt grief about the time he had spent in loneliness and secrecy.

As Bob and Carl shared their histories in therapy they began to realize that each of them felt pulled into a parental triangle to contain their parents' conflicts, and that they replicated these dynamics with each other. Their "No's" to sex were protective: Bob wanted to feel some control over inappropriate responses from both parents; and Carl had to protect himself from the kind of abandonment that he experienced with his first boyfriend and that he had been afraid might occur with his parents.

Sex therapy helped them begin to break the silences and secrets that characterized their sexual life with each other. As they shared fantasies and wishes first in sessions and then at home, they created a safe potential space in which to overcome sexual shame and express their own particular sexual needs. Bob had to work through his fear and anger about the abuse in his family and Carl needed to grieve the loss of his teenage boyfriend to permit himself to trust "putting all his eggs in one basket" again. As the work proceeded, each needed to escape less and could begin to relate in a mutually engaging sexual way.

A Heterosexual Couple: Mary and David

Mary and David began sex therapy after their second child entered first grade, at which time they found the energy, time, and desire to understand the one area of their relationship that eluded them: their sexual life.

Consciously proud of their peer marriage, these forty-year-olds were well aware of the uniqueness and preciousness of their relationship. They shared child rearing, finances, supported each other's careers, and felt they were best friends. Having been in individual therapy for years, both of them were perplexed about the near absence of sexual activity in their fifteen-year marriage, even before the children were born. "Perhaps," Mary wondered aloud, "we have to put our conflicts somewhere."

And she was right. As we proceeded with therapy their highly problematic dynamics were revealed in their individual family and sexual histories. Mary grew up in a family where her father was a rageaholic and her mother was excessively controlling. She and her two sisters grew up "walking on eggshells" wondering when the next blow-up would occur, her father threatening to leave and her mother collapsing in hysteria. Even though Mary was the youngest, she was the parentified child, the one who would try to calm down her father or soothe her mother, although never succeeding. She learned that couple relationships were precarious. She held herself responsible when things went wrong and felt like a failure when she couldn't fix things. This proved to be a deadly dynamic to bring into her sexual life since sex rarely is simply soothing, easily controllable, or able to be "fixed" by one partner.

David grew up in a family where his mother gave up an acting career to have him and his brother. His father was a successful lawyer, providing well for the family but preoccupied with his work and other women. He reported rocky relationships with each of his parents for different reasons. His mother shared too much about her disappointments with his father, including her distress at his sexual rejections. David felt overwhelmed and scared by these stories, and reacted to them by developing an early precocious sexuality. He began having sexual intercourse in junior high, mostly with older women, and saw himself as a great seducer for whom sex was merely a conquest. His sexuality defended him from his identification with his mother—from their shared feelings of rejection by a man who had no more time for his child than for his wife.

When David and Mary met, they consciously lived a different couple life than did either set of their parents. But unconsciously, David still needed an instant commitment and quick, hot sex to fend off the vulnerability of needing and wanting, and Mary felt overwhelmed by sexual intensity that she couldn't control. After one month he pushed for them to move in together, and Mary started to say no to sex. David at first felt angry and rejected but eventually felt relieved because he no longer had to be exposed to intense desires that reminded him of his mother's.

In therapy they became aware of how they were replicating their parental couple experiences. Mary expected that the intense catastrophes of childhood would play out in their sexual life, making it feel too dangerous and burdensome to enjoy. David anticipated feelings of unrequited yearning and outright rejection. He ensured that there would be no sex by first relentlessly pursuing Mary in ways that put her off, and then by not trying. As they worked through their anger, fear, and sadness, their childhood defenses shifted and they were able to utilize slow sensate focus experiences, building toward a rich and varied sexual life.

A Lesbian Couple: Sara and Joan

Sara and Joan, a couple in their forties, entered sex therapy at a point when they were sadly considering ending their relationship. Having had an extraordinarily compatible, fun, ten-year relationship as soul mates, intellectually and politically in sync, they were at their wits' end to find a way to work out their problem of sexual infrequency. This may have begun with an acute depression that Sara had experienced when she lost an important job, but even when the depression lifted, no improvement came.

As we reviewed their sexual history, it turned out that even though they had sex regularly during the first five years, the quality of their sexual interaction was more defensive than deeply intimate. Their family histories gave some understanding of this. Sara grew up in an alcoholic family where her father's drinking led to losing his job and her mother was clinically depressed and frequently suicidal. Sara took care of her four younger siblings and worried most about losing her mother. For Sara, experiencing a "heart-opening sexuality" with Joan felt too risky. Sara's mother was attracted to death, her father was attracted to other women, and Joan let Sara know that she too was attracted to other women. Sara felt that if she lost Joan, she'd lose herself—just as she felt about her suicidal mom.

Joan grew up seeing her mother and father fighting about her father's infidelities, and she was left feeling mad at her father and sad for her mother. She remembered deciding early in her life that in her own relationships she would never put herself in her mother's situation as the betrayed and abandoned partner. Joan coped with the strife at home by getting involved at school and dating girls early on. She was attractive and experienced herself as powerful in getting girls interested in her. When she met Sara she enjoyed seducing and getting her commitment, but she did not make an equal commitment.

Therapy helped them realize how they protected themselves from experiencing the vulnerabilities associated with their mothers. As they worked through those feelings they were able to revive their sexual life. Sara was able to open herself more emotionally to Joan when they had sex, and Joan was able to give up her imagined affairs with other women—to let Sara be the only one. Their sexual crisis helped them create a potential space where they could be more passionately connected than ever before.

CONCLUSION

These three cases illustrate how unconscious dynamics originating in childhood contributed to low sexual desire in gay male, lesbian, and heterosexual couples. Sex therapy needs to include an understanding of early parental and childhood unconscious sources of sexual problems, especially in "peer marriages" where communication and general relating is often quite sufficient. The literature needs more examples of gay and lesbian couples. The cases presented here show that many of the unconscious contributions to adult sexual problems are similar across heterosexual, gay, and lesbian peer marriages. Couples require an approach that goes beyond traditional behavioral sex therapy techniques, one that helps couples understand the impact of early family relations.

REFERENCES

Benjamin, J. 1995. *Like Subjects, Love Objects*. New Haven, CT: Yale University Press.

Buloff, B., and M. Osterman. 1995. Queer reflections: Mirroring and the lesbian experience of self. In J. M. Glassgold and S. Iasenza, eds., *Lesbians and Psychoanalysis: Revolutions in Theory and Practice*, pp. 93–106. New York: The Free Press.

Burch, B. 1997. *Other Women: Lesbian/Bisexual Experience and Psychoanalytic Views of Women*. New York: Columbia University Press.

Chodorow, N. J. 1994. *Femininities, Masculinities, Sexualities: Freud and Beyond*. Lexington: University of Kentucky Press.

DiCeglie, G. R. 1995. From the internal parental couple to the marital relationship. In S. Ruszczynski and J. Fisher, eds., *Intrusiveness and Intimacy in the Couple*, pp. 49–58. London: Karnac.

Domenici, T., and R. Lesser, eds. 1995. *Disorienting Sexuality: Psychoanalytic Reappraisals of Sexual Identities*. New York: Routledge.

Drescher, J. 1998. *Psychoanalytic Therapy and the Gay Man*. Hillsdale, NJ: Analytic Press.

Gair, S. R. 1995. The false self, shame, and the challenge of self-cohesion. In J. M. Glassgold and S. Iasenza, eds., *Lesbians and Psychoanalysis: Revolutions in Theory and Practice*, pp. 107–123. New York: The Free Press.

Glassgold, J. M., and S. Iasenza, eds. 1995. *Lesbians and Psychoanalysis: Revolutions in Theory and Practice*. New York: The Free Press.

Gould, E., and S. Kiersky, eds. 2001. *Sexualities Lost and Found: Lesbians, Psychoanalysis, and Culture*. Madison, CT: International Universities Press.

Iasenza, S. 2000. Lesbian sexuality post-Stonewall to postmodernism: Putting the "lesbian bed death" concept to bed. *Journal of Sex Education and Therapy* 25(1): 59–69.

———. 2004. Passion, play, and erotic potential space in lesbian relationships. In A. D'Ercole and J. Drescher, eds., *Uncoupling Convention: Psychoanalytic*

Approaches to Same Sex Couples and Families, pp. 141–56. Hillsdale, NJ: Analytic Press.

Isay, R. 1989. *Being Homosexual: Gay Men and Their Development.* New York: Farrar, Straus and Giroux.

———. 1996. *Becoming Gay: The Journey to Self-acceptance.* New York: Pantheon.

Kaplan, H. S. 1974. *The New Sex Therapy.* New York: Brunner/Mazel.

Kernberg, O. F. 1975. *Borderline Conditions and Pathological Narcissism.* New York: Jason Aronson.

———. 2002. Unresolved issues in the psychoanalytic theory of homosexuality and bisexuality. *Journal of Gay and Lesbian Psychotherapy* 61:9–27.

Kirkpatrick, M. 1996. Lesbians as parents. In R. P. Cabaj and T. S. Stein, eds., *Textbook of Homosexuality and Mental Health,* pp. 353–70. Washington, D.C.: American Psychiatric Press.

Loulan, J. 1984. *Lesbian Sex.* Duluth, MN: Spinsters Ink.

Magee, M., and D. C. Miller. 1997. *Lesbian Lives: Psychoanalytic Narratives Old and New.* Hillsdale, NJ: Analytic Press.

Masters, W. H., and V. E. Johnson. 1966. *Human Sexual Response.* Boston: Little, Brown.

———. 1970. *Human Sexual Inadequacy.* Boston: Little, Brown.

McDougall, J. 1980. *A Plea for a Measure of Abnormality.* New York: International Universities Press.

———. 1995. *The Many Faces of Eros.* New York: W. W. Norton.

O'Connor, N., and J. Ryan. 1993. *Wild Desires and Mistaken Identities: Lesbianism and Psychoanalysis.* New York: Columbia University Press.

Person, E. S. 1999. *The Sexual Century.* New Haven, CT: Yale University Press.

Scharff, D. E. 1998. *The Sexual Relationship.* Northvale, NJ: Jason Aronson.

Scharff, D. E., and J. S. Scharff, eds. 1991. *Object Relations Couple Therapy.* Northvale, NJ: Jason Aronson.

Schwartz, A. 1998. *Sexual Subjects: Lesbians, Gender and Psychoanalysis.* New York: Routledge.

———. 1994. *Love between Equals: How Peer Marriage Really Works.* New York: The Free Press.

Siegel, E. E. 1988. *Female Homosexuality: Choice without Volition.* Hillsdale, NJ: Analytic Press.

Socarides, C. W. 1968. *The Overt Homosexual.* New York: Grune and Stratton.

———. 1988. *The Preoedipal Origin and Psychoanalytic Theory of Sexual Perversions.* New York: International Universities Press.

Winnicott, D. W. 1971. *Playing and Reality.* London: Tavistock.

28

A Troubled Marriage in Sex Therapy

Norma Caruso

Couples seeking marital therapy are filled with hurt and anger, as if an early agreement about how the couple would relate has been violated. Each spouse asks the therapist to change their partner back to the person they once knew. These problems and the difficulties in sexual functioning that often accompany them reflect the couples' internal object relations. This chapter examines a model of treatment of sexual and marital dysfunction that centers on understanding couples' internal object relations, with a focus on Fairbairn's (1943) concept of the "return of the repressed" (Dicks 1967, Scharff and Scharff 1987). The treatment of these matters combines psychoanalytic work on the marital and sexual relationship with behavioral sex therapy (Kaplan 1974, Scharff 1982, Scharff and Scharff 1991) and extensive use of countertransference that enables therapists to speak to couples' difficulties from inside shared experience.

RETURN OF THE REPRESSED

For many couples, it is a challenge to maintain a loving bond when anger and rejection replace the longing so characteristic of courtship. From the vantage point of internal object relations, courtship represents a "manic triumph" that allows each partner to project idealized aspects into the lover, and in turn, to have these aspects recognized and admired. Repression serves to keep rejected and persecuting aspects of each partner under cover long enough for the couple to form a loving bond (Scharff and Scharff 1987). However, human beings strive for wholeness in intimate relationships

385

(Sutherland 1963). When individuals risk becoming known, they express denied and repressed aspects of themselves.

Dicks (1967) combined Fairbairn's description of the return of repressed bad object relations (1943) and his model of endopsychic structure (1944) with Klein's (1946) concept of projective identification to arrive at a sophisticated model of marital dynamics. Individuals reclaim lost parts of themselves in marital relationships by locating split-off and repressed libidinal and antilibidinal objects within their partners, and then get them back through introjective identification. When this process miscarries, marital partners are haunted by the unconscious identification with hated parts of the self seen in the spouse (Scharff and Scharff 1991).

THE COUPLE

Lourdes was born in Colombia and raised Catholic. Attending graduate school in the United States, she became friendly with Singh, a man of Indian descent. Lourdes was taken aback when Singh approached her with a kiss and attempted to unbutton her blouse. She felt that Singh had misread her friendly interest as a sexual invitation. Nevertheless, it was not long before their friendship and common interests led them to an exclusive relationship supported by Lourdes's appreciation of Singh's sense of fun, and Singh's love of Lourdes's caring, gentle nature. Several months into their courtship, they began sexual intercourse. As they began making plans to marry, Lourdes began to feel guilty and to experience sex as "boring." Singh reluctantly agreed to suspend intercourse until the wedding. Also at this time Singh's brother was seriously injured in an automobile accident. After dating for about one and a half years, Singh began to have temper outbursts, which he attributed to caring for his ill brother. Frightened, Lourdes briefly questioned marrying him.

At the moment of commitment to marriage, the couple's rejecting object relations surfaced and transformed their relationship. Lourdes's reprieve from sexual relations represented a reawakening of antisexual trends rooted in her repressive cultural and Catholic traditions conveyed by a variety of parental prohibitions, including refusal to sanction dating. Lourdes dutifully complied, while unconsciously harboring resentment especially toward her father, and by extension, toward all men. Lourdes projected her denied anger and sexuality into Singh, then attacked these qualities in him to bolster her view of herself as chaste and gentle. Singh's culture favored dominant men and subservient women. He was responsible for a dependent mother whose needs became more pronounced with his father's death. The unconscious resentment for his idealized mother was displaced onto Lourdes.

MARRIAGE AND SEXUALITY

In marriage, emotional relatedness is interwoven with sexual life. Sexual functioning provides valuable information about the object constellation of each spouse, and serves as a barometer of the couple's capacity for secure intimacy (Scharff 1982). Within marriage sexuality also forms a *psychosomatic partnership* (Winnicott 1960, 1971) that echoes the physical and psychological functioning of mother and infant. A fulfilling sexual life reverberates with early nurturing, while frustrated sexual relations amplify the repressed longing for the exciting object and unappeased anger at the rejecting object. Sex has the potential to invigorate the relationship as the couple encounters the daily stresses of life. But unfulfilling sexual relations can tear apart the threads of love, nurturance, trust, and safety that are so essential to marriage. In the aftermath, each spouse feels hurt, rejected, and angry (Scharff and Scharff 1991).

Although they had had premarital intercourse, Lourdes and Singh had avoided sex since marrying one year ago. Lourdes's phobic avoidance of intercourse was in striking contrast to her description of premarital sex as pleasurable. She presented their sexual difficulties as being a consequence of the couple's emotional relationship. She said Singh's preoccupation with sex and his tendency to be rough and greedy reflected his lack of sensitivity to her needs. She also said Singh was more dedicated to his mother than to her. She acknowledged her sexual withdrawal. Singh maintained that Lourdes's difficulties relating sexually invaded their emotional relationship. He denied insensitivity or preoccupation with his mother, and felt rejected, sad, and angry. He blamed Lourdes, although he acknowledged that he had distanced from her.

The couple agreed that the emotional climate contributed to their sexual impasse and that their sexual dysfunction eroded their capacity to feel connected. Their sexual problem seemed also to stem from Lourdes's developmental conflict about sexuality, and from Singh's conflicts about women and his difficulty tolerating tenderness.

MUTUAL PROJECTIVE IDENTIFICATION IN THE MARRIAGE

In marriage, each spouse contributes hidden aspects to a *joint marital personality* that allows one partner to perceive the other as if they were part of oneself. How this aspect of oneself is perceived influences the way the one treats the other, as spoiled and cherished, or denigrated and persecuted (Dicks 1967). The joint personality also offers an opportunity for "each half to rediscover lost aspects of their primary object relations, which they had split off or repressed, and which they were, in their involvement with the spouse, re-experiencing by projective identification" (Dicks 1967, p. 69). Each member of the marital dyad comes to re-experience in the partner aspects of their primary object relations through projective identification. In marriage, commitment powers projective identification as an integral part of the interaction (Scharff and Scharff 1991).

Lourdes had been drawn to Singh's sense of humor and fun, whereas Singh was attracted to Lourdes's seriousness, caring nature, and gentleness. Unconscious factors, rooted in primary object relations, were also at play in forming their partnership. Lourdes pursued a relationship with someone she initially perceived as too forward sexually, because she was unconsciously drawn to Singh's open expression of sexuality, a lost part of herself. Contrary to the sexual image Singh portrayed to Lourdes, he described himself as a shy bookworm without previous sexual encounters before meeting her. Lourdes represented a woman who could accept his projection of inhibition while he experimented.

Together Lourdes and Singh projected a split between desire and dread into their genital interaction. Singh's genitals represented the exciting and dangerous aspect of desire; Lourdes's embodied dread. She deposited her denied sexual longings in Singh, and he displaced his inhibitions onto Lourdes.

Lourdes's desire to re-own her sexuality, revealed in her fantasies of becoming a wild woman sexually, conflicted with her cultural norms. She projected this feared aspect into Singh, where she attacked and denigrated it in him. Her refusal to yield to Singh's sexual demands supported her identification with her mother and her repressive religious and cultural dictates, while maintaining the illusion of shedding the subservient role of women of her culture.

Singh's impassioned pleas for sex allowed him to feel he had broken with the Old World culture of his childhood. Accepting Lourdes's projections further bolstered this image. Unable to acknowledge controlling, anxious parts of himself, Singh projected them into Lourdes and criticized her for them. He was unaware of his investment in their collusive sexual avoidance for which he blamed Lourdes, but through which Singh continued to be the dutiful son who owed his primary allegiance to his mother.

Lourdes's and Singh's sexual dysfunction formed a *mutually gratifying collusive system* (Zinner 1976) in which unconscious intrapsychic conflicts of each partner are expressed in the relationship. Intrapsychic conflicts stemming from early unsatisfactory personal relationships interfered with the genitals as a vehicle for libidinal energy. The pressure on the couple to form a gratifying sexual union revived repressed object relations. Through psychological conversion the couple's genitals become the medium for their expression. We can spell this out by saying that through projective identification Singh's penis became the physical locus of the exciting and intruding object, while Lourdes's vagina embodied the rejecting object.

Then, further interpersonal conversion resulted in sexual dysfunction when Singh's urgency for sex triggered Lourdes's withdrawal (Fairbairn 1954; Scharff 1982). The couple's inability to form a psychosomatic partnership threw them back unconsciously onto their parental objects.

Despite its unconscious advantages, this pattern produced an undercurrent of mutual remonstrance that permeated their marital joint personality. Each blamed the other, and felt victimized in turn. In sessions, each focused on the other's behavior. Where Lourdes withheld her body and Singh withheld his thoughts, in treatment they censored information so that sessions frequently lacked vitality and I felt disconnected in a way that mirrored their emotional and physical disconnection. Because both of them had thoroughly projected the problem into the other, they believed that it was the other partner who needed to change and there was nothing they could do personally to help the situation. Defeated, each fantasized ending the relationship. In sessions, hopelessness dragged me down. I was judge and jury in a stalemated court case.

TRANSFERENCE AND COUNTERTRANSFERENCE

Freud (1895, 1905) applied the term *transference* originally to the therapeutic relationship. Fairbairn (1952) wrote that repressed aspects of the self are revealed in transference because of the basic need for connection of all parts of the self. For Guntrip (1969) transference served as an instrument through which unconscious elements of resistance unfold interpersonally. From this perspective, transference is a concept that has relevance to all relationships, rather than being limited to the therapeutic relationship (Scharff and Scharff 1991).

Countertransference has as much relevance to work with couples as to individual therapy and analysis. It allows therapists to understand and find meaning in transference communications that take place through the process in which the couple uses projective identification to impart their experience to the therapist (Scharff and Scharff 1987, 1991). Two examples demonstrate the use of countertransference in couple therapy. In the first, material from the early phase of treatment focuses on helping the couple to understand central problems of the relationship and to recognize sexual difficulties embodying their conflicts. The second example also demonstrates the use of countertransference when the treatment incorporates techniques of behavioral sex therapy.

Transference and Countertransference in Early Treatment

Lourdes entered the office and sat in a chair usually occupied by Singh. When he silently stood over her, Lourdes apologized and moved to her customary seat. Noting my annoyance at Lourdes, I waited for the session to unfold without commenting. The couple said they had an uneventful week and, therefore, had nothing to discuss. After some floundering Lourdes suggested they pick up on last week's theme about what each could change about themselves, rather than harping on the flaws of one another. Lourdes proposed that she "be more patient and tolerant, and also make time for physical intimacy." Singh suggested that he "spend more time devoted to Lourdes." Then, he added, "over the weekend I tried to be closer to you, but you really weren't interested."

The couple's initial interaction around where they would sit set the tone of the session and captured features of their transference to each other, and jointly to me. They demonstrated their struggle over dominance and submission. When Singh stood wordless over her as she sat in "his" chair one day, Lourdes apologized and returned to her usual chair. Her behavior expressed her belief that she needed to be patient and tolerant of Singh while covering unacknowledged resentment and anger that I had absorbed through projective identification. In the same way that Lourdes complied with Singh's unspoken demand, I sensed that within the session her initiation of a discussion around change was an attempt to please him and me. Her hollow words gave me the feeling that I was working alone. I imagined that the disconnection I felt was similar to Singh's feeling when Lourdes rebuffed his attempts to be close.

Singh's proposal for change also had an empty ring. Singh worked to connect with me around fixing Lourdes, conveying the feeling that his own relief resided in the efforts of the male therapist he had been seeing for a year, and not with me. Just as he asked Lourdes to relinquish her chair, he seemed to be asking me to give up my position to a man. Feeling dismissed by Singh helped me to connect with Lourdes and to understand the resentment that distanced her from him.

I asked them what got in the way of being more connected. Lourdes attributed their difficulty to busy schedules. I noted their frequent difficulty feeling more connected even when they found time together. Then Singh reported an argument. "Take last night. Lourdes didn't get home until late, but there was still an opportunity to get together. But, it never happened."

Lourdes responded by saying that last evening she didn't want to be around Singh because of the way he was acting. "I just thought, 'Let him have his tantrum. Let him get it out of his system. I don't want to be around him.' So I left. It used to be that I might have said something. Now, I just don't say anything. Why bother?"

Singh replied, "See, I can't get upset or angry about anything. If I do, Lourdes doesn't want anything to do with me."

Lourdes said, "People have asked me about abuse when they've seen you angry. So there must be something about the way you get angry."

Singh turned to me and said, "I don't understand how she can see me that way."

Lourdes replied, "See, he has no feelings about what I'm saying."

I said, "I'm not so sure."

Singh said, "It's gotten to the point that I just say 'whatever' and move on. It used to bother me. Now, it registers, but I just move on."

I observed, "There's a cold war in progress. Each of you has feelings about what the other is doing and has made an effort to let your feelings be known, with the hope that the other would change. But that hasn't happened. So both of you pull back in hopelessness and resignation. Then, passion and vitality are drained from your marriage. You've brought this lifeless state into the session. Despite having had an argument last evening you began the session in a subdued way with nothing to discuss."

Lourdes dismissed my comment by identifying some positive encounters. But Singh agreed, "I think what you're saying is true. I know I feel hopelessness. I've made an effort to change and I have nothing to show for it."

In this segment Lourdes and Singh described the pattern of withholding and illustrated their style of relating in the transference. Initially, they reported that they had nothing to discuss due to an uneventful week. In fact, they had had an argument the previous night that left them feeling disconnected, drained, and hopeless. Rather than discuss these feelings, they talked about what they thought I wanted to hear in much the same way that Lourdes offered Singh the apology she thought he wanted. By avoiding anger, they drained the session of vitality. Having absorbed their projections, I felt dragged down with them. Noting and processing my reactions enabled me to identify with their experience and comment on the process both between them at home and in the session with me.

As the session progressed, Singh elaborated on his hopelessness about whether the couple would ever resolve their difficulties. "I'm wondering if we're ever going to have kids. I think the issue of kids is much more important to me than it is to Lourdes."

Lourdes said, "You know I want kids, but right now we need to sort out our relationship."

Singh persisted, "Well, when will we have children then? Give me a date. I just don't think that it's ever going to happen."

I said, "I hear you asking if you'll ever be a family. It's hard to imagine because right now your relationship feels attacking and unsafe."

Singh said, "I definitely feel that. I frequently feel that Lourdes criticizes my every move. She doesn't even have to say anything." He asked Lourdes if she felt the same way.

Lourdes said, "I have to agree the lack of safety in our marriage makes it difficult to think about being more intimate with you."

I said, "You're also worried the lack of safety in here means that I will criticize your every move. Then you're less willing to discuss troubles."

In response, Lourdes and Singh acknowledged their shared anxiety and seemed calmer. I also was aware that I no longer felt disconnected from them.

I was able to point out to the couple that the underlying fear permeating their emotional and sexual life also got played out in the transference to me as a contextual parent providing safety (Scharff and Scharff 1991). In an effort to manage their fear of assault from me, Singh and Lourdes withheld parts of themselves. In the countertransference, I felt the disconnection that was conveyed through their shared projective identification. By addressing their anxiety about assault, I provided holding and containment. Feelings became more tolerable. Working on the contextual transference, a function included in Winnicott's (1956) concept of "holding capacity," creates space for growth (Scharff and Scharff 1987).

Transference and Countertransference in Sex Therapy

During the first ten months of marital therapy, the couple made strides in understanding how their problem with intimacy manifested in their sexual difficulties. I then introduced behavioral sex therapy techniques into the psychoanalytic work (Kaplan 1974, Scharff 1982, Scharff and Scharff 1991). The behavioral component involves assigning the couple a series of graded home exercises that begin with nonthreatening, nongenital pleasuring of each other. Additional tasks are added as the couple masters each level; and exercises are repeated when they encounter difficulties.

In the first exercise, the couple in the privacy of their own home engaged in nonsexual pleasuring (no inclusion of breasts or genitals) by alternatively massaging each other with oil while nude and reported their experience in the next session. Lourdes reported, "Doing the exercise was great. I could relax, knowing it was not going anywhere." She compared this scenario to what usually transpires, when she tenses as she anticipates intercourse. However, contrary to the instructions, Singh had attempted to fondle her breasts.

Laughing, Singh said, "I knew it wasn't right, but I thought I'd give it a shot." Singh did not like the oil or being massaged and felt frustrated by the limitations of the exercise.

Because this exercise serves as a foundation for the success of the subsequent exercises, I reassigned it for the following week. Again, the couple reported that Lourdes tensed up when Singh tried to touch her breasts, and that he dismissed her anxiety. But this time Lourdes set limits, although in a playful rather than forceful way.

I confronted Singh about the impact of his behavior. I said he had misbehaved for them both. I assigned the same exercise, emphasizing our need to know that they could lower Lourdes's anxiety and establish safety by adhering to the limits before they could move to the next stage. Singh was annoyed. Laughing, Lourdes said she had told Singh his misbehavior would have this outcome.

In the first two sessions the couple demonstrated considerable resistance. Singh dismissed my instructions. His aggressive, demeaning behavior ignored Lourdes's need for safety and compromised her experience. Although I suspected that behind Singh's behavior was his fear of sensuality, nevertheless I felt countertransference anger. His difficulty tolerating his tenderness and his projection of aggression had the effect of creating a controlling stance in both Lourdes and myself. Additionally, Singh's annoyance at being reassigned the exercise engendered in me the feeling that, like Lourdes, I was depriving him of sex. My feelings of being angry and withholding helped me connect with Lourdes's experience of Singh.

Although I was more sympathetic to Lourdes, I believed that Singh's spoiling of the exercise reflected the couple's shared fears. Lourdes's resistance was subtly manifested in her failure to deal forcefully with Singh. Her belief that she needed to be patient and tolerant of Singh covered her underlying anger. I contained her anger and assumed her role of confronting Singh. She seemed delighted at the opportunity to relinquish this responsibility.

In the transference Singh revealed his use of aggression as a defense against tenderness, and Lourdes demonstrated her use of patience and tolerance to avoid her fury. In turn, I understood how they related by denying dreaded aspects in themselves and depositing them in the other.

Over the next weeks the couple's resistance increased. Lourdes complained of fatigue and difficulty maintaining the stamina needed to massage Singh. Physical intimacy seemed to deplete, rather than revitalize, her. While Lourdes's enthusiasm waned, Singh's pleasure increased. Despite these shifts, the overall resistance remained. Often they came late, and in session they seemed depleted. They reported difficulty finding the time to do the exercises. As a solution, Lourdes suggested that they shorten the exercises and that Singh could watch television while doing the massage. In short, there seemed a striking absence of vitality and passion.

Lourdes and Singh displayed the same difficulties within the sessions. They failed to adhere to the scheduled time, and once in the session, they seemed worn out. As I got an inside look, I felt like the teacher making her students do homework. Their resistance was interfering with learning from what I offered them. This difficulty in the contextual transference mirrored their difficulty receiving pleasure from each other.

Faced with their lack of vitality, I felt it was up to me to supply energy and hope. However, because of their frequent lateness, I felt pressured for time. Lourdes's recommendation to watch television while doing massage at once paralleled my experience of trying to get too much squeezed into the time.

During the next few weeks I continued to reassign the same exercise and to explore the couple's difficulty carrying it out. They admitted feeling that they were in the remedial class as they struggled to comply with my instructions and to experience pleasure. My efforts to confront their resistance were dismissed by explanations concerning their busy schedules. The underlying dynamic behind their difficulty had yet to be revealed. Nevertheless, they began to adhere to boundaries and enjoy the massage, so I assigned the second exercise. I told them to continue to massage each other's whole body, but now to include genitals and breasts in passing, but not beyond the point of mild arousal.

In the second exercise, Lourdes crossed her arms over her breasts, closed her legs, and wore underwear. I suggested that we try to understand her need to protect herself.

Lourdes said, "I don't understand. I've never been traumatized and it's not that I don't trust Singh. I'm not thinking that he'll rape me when he is passing over my vagina. Maybe, it just has to do with progressing on to the next exercise."

Noting Lourdes's transferential reference to therapy, I said, "I do have the impression that you feel violated by Singh and so you feel unsafe."

She conceded, "You're right. It's the way he grabs my breasts."

Singh added, "Not just when it comes to sex, but in our relationship in general. Lourdes says I create unsafe situations around driving or spending. Guys don't think about being safe or violated in the same way as women."

I said, "You often feel assaulted by Lourdes's criticisms. The way she finds fault violates your sense of yourself as a responsible man."

Singh said, "It does feel like Lourdes has a rifle and is shooting at me."

I said, "You feel that I'm shooting at you, too, when I challenge your way of relating. Lourdes, you also feel that I push you into unsafe territory so you need to take cover from me, too."

For several weeks in the treatment the couple resisted my efforts to address their difficulties. The pace at which they were able to take in what I had to offer, and in turn, to articulate their struggle mirrored the slow rhythm of their learning to give and to receive from each other. Thus, Singh and Lourdes were giving me an inside appreciation of the unconscious meaning of their timing. In their relationship, each withheld parts of themselves for fear of being violated, and so felt disconnected. Lourdes's vulnerability to feeling violated resided in antisexual trends rooted in her repressive culture and Catholic traditions and expressed in terms of parental prohibitions that interfered with her claiming her body and her sexuality as her own. She worried that Singh would violate her in a similar way. In Singh's family his mother, who had always depended on him and his brother, became even needier after the death of his brother, and as the remaining son, Singh's sense of responsibility for his mother increased and stymied his adult development and capacity to care for his wife. Lourdes represented the threat that once again he would be held captive by a dominant woman. When Lourdes connected her need to take cover from the threat of progress in treatment, I was able to say that they felt threatened by me. They accepted my interpretation and I felt more connected to them.

DISCUSSION

This clinical material illustrates how the couple attempted to reclaim lost parts of themselves. They located libidinal and antilibidinal parts of themselves in each other through projective identification, but suffered interpersonal difficulty through the return of the repressed bad objects. In their quest for wholeness and their longing to have good and bad aspects of themselves accepted, they revealed rejected parts of themselves. Lourdes's inhibitions around sexuality and Singh's repressed anger emerged with the challenge contained in their commitment to marry. Then their difficulty tolerating these dreaded aspects within themselves and within their spouse tested the resiliency of their relationship and brought them to treatment.

This couple's sexual problems were rooted in object relations conflicts that magnified relational marital tensions. An unconscious current of mutual destructiveness undermined the holding capacity within their marital and sexual life. Each partner feared assault and blame. This dynamic, continually played out in their relationship, was then expressed in their shared contextual transference to me as a parent responsible for safety and facilitation of growth. Analyzing countertransference reactions helped me find meanings in the couple's unconscious communications that took place through projective identification. Interpretations based on this understanding advanced the treatment. The combination of behavioral and psychoanalytic techniques worked at multiple levels of the couple's difficulty and was required to take account of the multiple dimensions of their difficulties.

SUMMARY

I demonstrate in this chapter integrating psychoanalysis and behavioral techniques in sexual and marital therapy. I apply Fairbairn's (1943) concept of the "return of the repressed" to helping a couple reclaim lost unconscious parts of themselves. The clinical example is presented to show extensive use of countertransference during sex and marital therapy.

REFERENCES

Dicks, H. V. 1967. *Marital Tensions*. London: Karnac.

Fairbairn, W. R. D. 1943. The repression and the return of bad objects. In *Psychoanalytic Studies of the Personality*, pp. 59–81. London: Routledge.

———. 1944. Endopsychic structure considered in terms of object-relationships. In *Psychoanalytic Studies of the Personality*, pp. 82–135. London: Routledge and Kegan Paul, 1952.

———. 1952. *Psychoanalytic Studies of the Personality*. London: Routledge and Kegan Paul.

———. 1954. Observations on the nature of hysterical states. *British Journal of Medical Psychology* 27:105–25.

Freud, S. 1895. The psychotherapy of hysteria. *Standard Edition* 2:255–305.

———. 1905. Fragment of an analysis of a case of hysteria. *Standard Edition* 7:7–122.

Guntrip, H. 1969. *Schizoid Phenomena, Object Relations and the Self*. New York: International Universities Press.

Kaplan, H. S. 1974. *The New Sex Therapy*. New York: Brunner/Mazel.

Klein, M. 1946. Notes on some schizoid mechanisms. *International Journal of Psycho-Analysis* 27:99–100.

Scharff, D. E. 1982. *The Sexual Relationship: An Object Relations View of Sex and the Family*. London: Routledge. Northvale, NJ: Jason Aronson.

Scharff, D. E., and J. S. Scharff. 1987. *Object Relations Family Therapy*. Northvale, NJ: Jason Aronson.

———.1991. *Object Relations Couple Therapy*. Northvale, NJ: Jason Aronson.

Sutherland, 1963. Object relations theory and the conceptual model of psychoanalysis. *British Journal of Medical Psychology* 36:109–24.

Winnicott, D. W. 1956. Primary maternal preoccupation. In *The Maturational Processes and the Facilitating Environment*. London: Hogarth Press, 1965.

———. 1960. The theory of the parent-infant relationship. In *The Maturational Processes and the Facilitating Environment*, pp. 37–55. London: Hogarth Press, 1965.

———. 1971. *Playing and Reality*. London: Tavistock.

Zinner, J. 1976. The implications of projective identification for marital interaction. In *Foundations of Object Relations Family Therapy*, ed. J. S. Scharff, pp. 155–73. Northvale, NJ: Jason Aronson, 1989.

29

Intercultural Couple Therapy

Joan Massel Soncini

My focus is on intercultural couples, defined simply as those in which the partners are from different cultural traditions. Whether heterosexual or homosexual, the partners come from different countries of origin, different races, and/or religions, and this often leads to cultural value conflicts. I want to clarify the issues faced by intercultural couples, describe their needs in therapy, and emphasize special considerations regarding their treatment. To work with them, therapists need to expand their clinical knowledge by adding crosscultural theories and techniques to the basic object relations approach. Theoretical diversity is essential to arrive at sensitive treatment of these couples.

THE SHIFT TOWARD INTERCULTURAL MARRIAGE

In the United States, spouses were inclined to choose one another on the basis of "like marrying like." They wanted their life partner to be of similar race, religion, and cultural background. With increased opportunities for Americans to study, work, and travel abroad, and for many nationalities to visit or immigrate to the United States, there has been a shift toward interracial, interreligious, and intercultural marriage. These marriages are also referred to as exogamous marriage or out-marriage—two rather unfriendly terms reflecting discomfort with a choice that lies away from what is usual, out of the norm, and not legitimate in years past.

It was not until 1967 in the United States when the Civil Rights movement

397

had gained momentum that legislation made marriage between different races and cultures legal. In August 1996, the U.S. Census Bureau reported that the foreign-born population reached its highest level since World War II. The topic of a growing debate, U.S. immigration laws permitted increased numbers of foreigners to enter the United States permanently (Holmes 1995). Americans clearly have more opportunities to meet and fall in love with people living in, or immigrating from, other countries, and now have a legal basis for marrying them.

PROBLEMS FACING INTERCULTURAL COUPLES

The problems that intercultural couples face may be divided into internal and external sources of conflict.

External Sources of Conflict

Environmental hostility leaves the couple with a sense of social isolation, marginality, and alienation (Bizman 1987, Cottrell 1990, Cretser and Leon 1984, Hutter 1990, Markoff 1977). The environmental response affects how the foreign-born partner negotiates the process of acculturation, which affects the marital relationship.

Internal Sources of Conflict

The environment may support the couple and confirm the validity of the marriage, but the couple experiences tension for reasons internal to the marriage, most commonly because the partners have incompatible worldviews. Ibrahim and Schroeder define worldviews as

> the beliefs, values, and assumptions, which mediate communication, relationships, modes of problem-solving, decision-making, and the life style of the client. Worldviews are culturally based variables, that tend to be implicit, and to some extent we believe *unconscious*. . . . [They are] influenced by ethnicity, culture, religious or spiritual beliefs, language and semantics, educational level, social class, age, life stage, lifestyle preferences, and gender. (Ibrahim and Schroeder 1990, p. 194)

All marriages pass through several stages of adjustment toward a comfortable level of intimacy. The ultimate achievement is a good tolerance for frustration and conflict, a satisfactory development of the self as an individual and as a life partner, and a sense of the couple as the priority. In the intercultural marriage, the partners have an additional task, that of realizing the disconnection between their worldviews and accepting their cultural differences, gaining understanding of them, working through the associated conflicts, and making necessary adjustments. When backgrounds are different—whether on racial, religious, or cultural counts—adjustment and compromise are particularly problematic, according to many respected authors (Barron 1972, Cretser and Leon 1984, Gordon 1964, Ho 1984, McGoldrick and Preto 1984, Romano 1988, Tseng 1977). Disharmony results when the couple cannot resolve issues arising from different cultural values regarding child-rearing techniques, religious practice, appropriate gender role behavior, and boundary issues with in-laws and extended family (see table 29.1). The parties question their love and ask if they are a good enough couple: Should they stay together, marry, separate, or divorce?

Intercultural couples in the United States present for couple therapy with areas of confusion and painful conflict based on some combination of cultural, intrapsychic, and interpersonal issues. Cottrell (1990) advises the couple therapist to explore thoroughly the couple's primary motivations for marriage. This is an essential preliminary to understanding the foundations of the marriage and assessing the couple's strengths, for adjusting to cultural differences, working through conflicts, and participating in the process of therapy. The couple therapist sorts out *what causes conflicts* for the couple. This task is especially challenging with intercultural couples, as they have two risky tendencies: to overemphasize and to overlook their cultural differences. Couples do this to defend themselves from reality.

Falicov (1986) found that those intercultural couples who experience distress in their marriage *minimize* or *maximize* cultural differences, often as an unconscious defense. They may *deny* any cultural differences, due to their determination to show the world that their issues are not cultural, particu-

Table 29.1. External and internal sources of cultural conflict

1) Experiencing family or societal hostility
2) Retaining incompatible worldviews and cultural values concerning:
   - the importance of family
   - gender role expectations
   - relationships with friends
   - emotional expressiveness
   - how to raise children
   - how to spend money
   - food preferences and eating habits
   - politics
   - where to live
   - where to go to seek help: family, church, or a psychotherapist

larly when family and friends have objected to the marriage on those grounds (Falicov 1986, Romano 1988). The couple may blame the easily visible cultural differences for everything that goes wrong, a defense against looking at more serious underlying issues. Each member of the intermarried couple may adhere to the ethnocentric belief that: "My way is the only way to be." Different worldviews lead to the misunderstanding of intentions and the meaning of behavior: The Latino husband misperceives his Asian American wife's respectful restraint as a rejection, and she misperceives her Latino spouse's passionate excitement as a threat of violence.

HIGHLY VISIBLE DIVERSITY

Sometimes the couple's diversity is *center stage*, and highly visible when they are of different races, and this difference causes problems for the family and for each other. When Jack, an Israeli doctor, married Mary, an African American, his mother refused any contact with Mary and did not attend their wedding. Angie, a biracial woman from Kenya, continuously felt belittled by Thomas, her elegant English husband. Belle, a stunning Chinese-born journalist, felt overwhelmed and overpowered by the physical presence of Paul, her tall, athletic Norwegian boyfriend. Katarina, a Greek physics professor and Raj, her Indian doctor husband, argued all the time and could not resolve anything. They complained, "No one likes us; no one sees us as a good couple!" and posed a question to be answered by the expert: "Should we stay married or divorce?" It turned out that Katarina's parents, out of shame, refused to tell friends and relatives in Greece of this marriage. And Raj's father told his son: "Sure, marry the person you love, just don't tell your mother!" Then he went on to tell Raj's mother after the fact, and it took years for her to accept the couple, but first Raj and Katarina had to accept themselves as a good match.

DISREGARDED DIVERSITY

On the other hand, some couples may *think of themselves as monocultural.* Despite appearances, Tomoko, from Japan, and Jack, an American Jew, began couple therapy with a total disinterest in cultural differences, saying, "We've been together for over thirty years. What cultural differences?" Being an expert on Japanese affairs made it more difficult for Jack to assign importance to cultural realities, which he consistently overlooked. Other couples who look similar based on skin color may ignore other cultural differences. Annette and Peter thought of themselves as two black lawyers and showed total disregard for their culturally diverse backgrounds. Learning about their

African American and West Indian heritages turned out to be the key to understanding and resolving their central conflict.

INTEGRATING SENSITIVITY, OBJECT RELATIONS, AND CROSS-CULTURAL THEORIES AND TECHNIQUES

Problems may derive from cultural/value differences, and/or interpersonal conflicts, and/or intrapsychic issues. Cultural discord may be so dramatic that the therapist may miss some or much of the underlying intrapsychic issues. In general, these areas of difference lie along a continuum and melt into one another. It is a challenge to sort out the levels at which conflict is determined, but it is essential.

WHY OBJECT RELATIONS THEORY IS SUITED FOR THIS POPULATION

Object Relations is particularly apt because it focuses on the interplay between external and internal realities, not only between individuals and their families of origin, and other major relationships in their lives, but between aspects of the cultural and societal environment. In my application of object relations couple therapy, I focus on understanding these intertwined and interdependent dynamics, observe their influences on the couple, and anticipate reenactments within the couple dyad in sessions. This is not a problem solving, quick-fix approach. On the contrary, object relations couple therapists work from a psychoanalytic perspective. We listen carefully to conscious and unconscious material, often expressed within the transference/countertransference configuration, and we make trial hypotheses and gradually develop understanding of the conflicts and insight into the dynamics.

Many foreign-born patients are highly uncomfortable with the unfamiliar

Table 29.2. The "Source of Problems" continuum

Culturally Determined
- worldview on intermarriage and marriage/gender role differences

Interpersonally Determined
- projective identification of guilt, badness, shame

Intrapsychically Determined
- narcissistic vulnerability, depression, personality disorders, use of primitive defenses

experience of a therapeutic environment. Seeking psychotherapy for a New Yorker is quite different than it is for a person from the Ivory Coast or Guatemala, two cultures among many in which psychotherapy barely exists, and if it does it is only for those considered crazy. In addition, typically one member of the couple (who does not accept the idea of psychotherapy because of considering couple and family problems to be an intensely private matter) is culturally far less comfortable participating in couple therapy than is the other.

Picture the therapy session when the husband is from Japan or Kenya, his white wife or lover is from mainstream America, and I am their therapist, a white woman born in the United States. Each partner will be attempting to figure out my stance, test me for any Western bias, and check out my ability to identify and understand their values. I will be working to understand their cultural perspectives. I will be careful to provide good contextual holding: establishing trust, containing anxiety, showing how therapy works, earning confidence in the ability to understand and help. I will also be sorting out their projective identifications: namely, how each partner projects out unwanted internal feelings and relationships onto the other partner.

TWO EXAMPLES ALONG THE SOURCE OF PROBLEMS CONTINUUM

Melanie and Harmeet

Barely two months after their wedding, Melanie, thirty-two, a stunning blond and blue-eyed doctoral student from Virginia, and Harmeet, thirty-five, a strikingly handsome and turbaned Indian Sikh, already a bank vice-president, were referred to me for couple therapy. Their problem with family acceptance emerged during a family visit when Melanie had said to Mimi, her young sister-in-law, "Listen, Mimi, I don't see why Harmeet can't cook me a meal! Why should I do all the cooking?" Harmeet's father became outraged, and he began to hurl insults at Melanie: "You slut! How dare you speak this way with my son. What a lack of respect!" When he was driving the couple home to their apartment, Mr. P was still upset. When they arrived at the couple's apartment, Mr. P followed his new daughter-in-law up the stairs and into the apartment to continue the diatribe. She was incensed, and she was scared. "You can't come in here," she exclaimed. At this, Mr. P raged on: "What? This is my apartment, for it is my son's home! You have no right to tell me that I cannot come in here." Harmeet didn't know what to do. Melanie ran into her bedroom, closed the door, called her father, and begged for guidance and help. He told her to call the police, who arrived promptly and told Mr. and Mrs. P that they had to leave, embarrassing them horribly. Mr. P then insisted that his son drive them home, for he was too upset to drive. Melanie pulled Harmeet in the other direction: "You can't possibly leave me alone." In an act of unusual bravery, the torn Harmeet remained with his wife, rejecting his father's command.

Issues Considered along the Source of Problems Continuum

Cultural Mr. P was distraught about his son's marrying Melanie, and he fought against it from the beginning of their courtship. Melanie, from a southern, American family, had grown up with the family value that she should choose whomever she wanted to marry for love. She could not understand why Mr. P was hostile. What was wrong with her? Harmeet had never explained his cultural reality to her. South Asians, that is Indians and Pakistanis, consider it shameful for a son or daughter to marry someone who is not of the same background, religion, and class. The story of this couple's family situation was so dramatic that therapy had to deal first with the cultural misunderstandings between the spouses and between the couple and Harmeet's parents. Only then did we get to the intrapsychic issues.

Intrapsychic Then we could see Melanie's preexisting lack of self-esteem, poor ego control, and mood swings, leaving her vulnerable to distress. Harmeet, in turn, harbored unconscious anger at his father, who was often unreasonable, even outrageous and uncontrollable within his family. The family myth was that Mr. P was *normal*, and his wife and children walked around on tiptoe trying to keep him calm. Having never challenged his father openly, Harmeet's choice of an all-American wife was an unconscious act of rebellion, a way to move away from his father's despotic demands.

The foundation of the choice of an intercultural partner may be healthy for conscious reasons with which unconscious reasons are in sync, or less healthy for unconscious reasons that dominate rational choice. Motivations range from the positive search for personal growth and expansion to the defensive search for enhancement or outlet for rebellion. A man with a solid foundation may seek an exotic wife to widen his horizons and foster his growth, and another man may choose such an exciting wife to repair a flaw in his self-esteem by making him feel special and unique. A man like Harmeet may fall in love with Melanie for her beauty, her warmth, and her keen intelligence, and remain unconscious of his driving wish for emancipation from and rebellion against his background and his overcontrolling, prejudicial, and intrusive family.

Interpersonal Mr. P's hostility toward the couple created intense anger and conflict within the couple dyad. Years of living with his father had left Harmeet with blunted affect and a tendency to squash awareness of conflict. Melanie's valency for crying and hysterical outbursts reminded Harmeet of his irascible father, and he would try to calm her down. Harmeet's parents, protecting their beloved first son's place in their hearts, turned their wrath on Melanie. They saw Harmeet as the perfect, self-contained son and blamed Melanie for causing pain and being bad for him. Melanie distrusted Harmeet, because he wouldn't protect her by standing up to his father, which he had no conscious wish to do. She felt that Harmeet didn't love her as much as he did his family. She could not understand why her in-laws felt that she and Harmeet were "a bad couple." Why did they see her as a bad person? Why couldn't they see how much she loved their son and cared for him? Melanie did not empathize at all with Harmeet's predicament.

Progression of the Therapy

Melanie and Harmeet came to me in crisis, Melanie flooded by feelings of confusion, righteousness, and anger, and Harmeet in a state of emotional paralysis and not knowing what to do. Harmeet had never been in therapy, but he was aware that mainstream New Yorkers seek help in psychotherapy without shame. Melanie had previously had a good experience in therapy. So I felt hopeful that with their attitude and my experience with intercultural marriage, we would be able to work together.

Melanie and Harmeet were attractive and educated. They seemed very much in love and highly motivated to find answers. After an *initial exploration* of the presenting incident, we discussed the way the couple met, what originally attracted them to one another, and how they had experienced their pre-wedding period together. I was particularly struck by Melanie's lack of knowledge regarding South Asian prejudice against outmarriage. Thus, I asked Harmeet to tell me about his parents' reaction to his choice of mate. Harmeet was the first grandchild of four fairly recent immigrants. His father was bombarded by his siblings who feared that Harmeet's cousins might follow his shameful example.

As is typical of my way of working, I requested individual sessions with each spouse, trying to learn more about their object relations' histories. Briefly, Melanie's father, a wealthy Southern farmer, controlled his family with an iron fist, whereas her mother, although more educated and considered to be from a "better" family, catered to his every whim. Melanie, the youngest with three older brothers, always felt singled out as the silly sister, "the hysterical complainer." No one listened to her, she said.

Harmeet plainly needed to understand his wish to marry out as a wish for separation/individuation from his family. We explored how he felt about his father's behavior, before and after the incident. He expressed his anger and resentment of his father's inability to see the point of view of anyone else. He came to empathize and even to identify with Melanie's sense of worthlessness, something he himself might have felt at home vis-à-vis his father but which he successfully kept at bay under cover of academic and professional excellence.

Both of them also gained some empathy for Harmeet's parents, who had to face their Sikh friends' and relatives' fury and fear. Harmeet took on more responsibility for protecting his wife and confronting his father in a firm but noncombative way. Melanie felt listened to, protected, and valued. The couple understood the basis for their intercultural marriage and learned how to deal with its impact on them and their families. They discovered that the contrast between South Asian collectivist and American individualist worldviews on marital choice was key: The Asian culture places the couple as secondary to the collective family; the Western culture supports individual choice and marrying for love. By including a focus on differing cultural backgrounds, intrapsychic and interpersonal realities, Melanie and Harmeet progressed consistently and optimistically in therapy. But the couple's cultural clash was also a smokescreen for Melanie's depression. Melanie came back for some individual work, as she became depressed and stuck in finishing her Ph.D. dissertation, allowing for further exploration into the intrapsychic issues to which I have alluded.

Miguel and Helen

Miguel, a Mexican, and his American fiancée, Helen, sought premarital couple therapy. Helen and Miguel had met in Monterrey, Mexico, while Helen was studying Spanish before returning to her last year of college, and Miguel was working as a doctor. The initial excitement of falling in love in Mexico having waned, the couple had become aware of their numerous differences, already pointed to by both sets of parents who expressed deep concerns and, at times, even prohibitions about marriage. Now living in the United States, Miguel drives a cab while he struggles painfully to improve his English, in order to pass the qualifying examination to practice medicine in this country. Miguel and Helen are in crisis due to rising disagreement, conflicting views of reality, and fears that their decision to marry may be a mistake. They are also in disagreement over the value of couple therapy.

As often occurs with intercultural couples, Miguel agrees to couple therapy only under duress, and can barely hide his disdain for the process. He explains that in his native Mexico, psychotherapy is only for crazy people, "locos." He does not see the sense in talking with a total stranger. In the first session I see that the inability to empathize or compromise is not restricted to him:

> Miguel (to Helen): "What? You think that's right? Es absurdo. No tienes razon! Listen to me. Put on my glasses, and you'll *see* that I'm right and you're absolutely wrong!"

Helen (to Miguel): *You* just don't see. Why don't *you* put on my glasses, and you'll see that I'm right, and you're simply wrong!"

However, hoping to work things out with Helen, Miguel agrees to comply with her ultimatum: therapy or no marriage. Living in the United States culture has precipitated their distress, has forced them to face their differences, and gives them access to therapy. I learned that Helen had changed since coming home. She became more critical. Supported by the surrounding culture, she became more sure of her rights and her perceptions of gender roles. Recently, when Miguel became incensed about their diet, complaining that he missed Mexican food, Helen exploded, complaining to him about what she termed his "male, macho chauvinism," and she threatened to break their engagement. Miguel and Helen are not sure whether to marry or not. Unlike couples from the same cultural background, they see life through very different lenses.

CONFLICT: NORMAL AND PREDICTABLE

Having diverse interpretations of reality is normal for intercultural couples, for their perceptions were developed in different cultural settings. They should not be surprised when conflict arises; it is totally predictable. They should anticipate conflict and be prepared to talk over their differences, especially in the early years of adjustment to their relationship. Falicov (1986) refers to this period as the "cultural transition phase." She states that the couple's developmental task is to "arrive at an adaptive and flexible view of their cultural similarities and differences" including: a balance of individuated values, a capacity to negotiate conflicts, and the creation of a "new cultural code," which integrates parts of both cultural heritages (p. 448).

In general, it is widely accepted that difficulties are more likely to occur in intermarriages, and that it takes more effort to make intermarriages work than marriages of those of similar cultural heritage. In spite of such information, however, little guidance has been given to partners entering into intercultural marriages. Very little advice is available for the mental health professionals who are apt to be summoned to help when difficulties arise (p. 121). Hsu (1977) points to the need to enhance knowledge, skills, and techniques for therapists working with intercultural couples.

With the increased numbers of intermarriage, there have been many changes in the way people perceive and deal with intermarried couples, and in the research and literature on the subject. Americans have swayed back and forth between respecting differences and obliterating them in the melting pot. Some see intermarriage as a deviant choice, a threat, a danger to cultural identity; others see it as an exciting, enviable choice, one that shows lack of prejudice, brings diversity, and so enriches society. Therapists are not immune to the influence of the culture in which they grew up, but they have tools for examining their culture-bound attitudes and correcting for them.

AN EXERCISE IN EXPLORING THE THERAPIST'S CULTURAL IDENTITY

In intercultural couple therapy, there are three (perhaps four, if there is a co-therapist) people in the room, and this means the presence of at least two, if not three or four, different cultural backgrounds. Before attempting to treat these couples, it is important for the therapists to explore their own cultural identity and views on intermarriage. This is basic to understanding the use of the therapist's self and working with countertransference. Therapists need to examine their own situations, and ask themselves some key questions. "Am I in an intermarriage, with differences of race, culture, class, and/or religion? How about my parents, friends, siblings, and co-workers? What are the first words that come to mind when I see a biracial, interreligious, or intercultural couple? Have I ever treated an intercultural couple in couple therapy? Have I noticed any differences between therapy with intercultural versus monocultural couples?"

Imagine you are a female American therapist, treating a Chinese man, who is married to an American woman. In the first session, the American wife, in a fit of rage, denounces her husband for paying far too much attention—and money—to his family of origin. Would you be moved to side with the wife? You might be trained to look for the unconscious motivation for the wife's attitude, perhaps in her feeling uncared for or unloved by her husband, in playing second fiddle to her other siblings, or in hating to acknowledge her debt to her own parents. But would you explore with the couple the cultural significance of the family and the role of the son in the Chinese culture?

How would you react to the above-mentioned Miguel, who ridicules his American fiancée for failing to prepare his favorite meals for him? It is generally easier for an American therapist to listen to a man like Miguel, to feel empathy for him, to understand him, if he does not raise his voice, but speaking at high volume is how he expresses himself. Can you accept that? Working with intercultural couples demands a neutral attitude toward the complaints of each partner and a capacity to contain anxiety rather than act it out. This therapeutic stance is far easier to attain if we anticipate the challenge and always ask ourselves: "Is this a problem created by cultural differences, by interpersonal or intrapsychic problems, or by a combination of both?" "What am *I* feeling?" and, finally, "What is each person and/or the couple dyad putting into me or getting me to do?"

BENEFITS AND RISKS OF
INTERCULTURAL MARRIAGE

Some intermarrying couples prepare more thoroughly for their marriage than other couples, perhaps in response to unsolicited advice and opposition from friends and family. They adopt a "We'll show them!" attitude. Following this preparation, the couple may become more self-reliant, determined, and committed to making it work, or they may become a brittle couple who need adversity for their definition. Before marrying, couples tend to romanticize their differences and similarities, often denying any unpleasant differences. They think of themselves as a wonderful international cocktail of the best ingredients of traditions, customs, art, holidays, cooking, language, music, and friends (Romano 1988, p. 16). How long this rosy glow lasts depends upon the magnitude of the couple's differences, which having been initially attractive may become a source of tension and conflict later.

The couple experiences "the return of the repressed" when individual aspects of the self and the other which the partners have ignored or denied come to the fore. The partners now come face to face with these aspects of themselves as they deal with what they now find in the spouse (Frank 1989). The couple fends off the return of the repressed by fighting, postponing, denying problems, and distancing. On a more positive note, the couple may allow the repressed to become conscious by confronting differences, understanding their meaning, and then seeking solutions or compromises that work for both partners.

On a negative note, there is a higher rate of divorce among intermarriages. Paris and Guzder (1989) attribute the higher risk of divorce in exogamous marriages to the power of unconscious reasons for marrying and resulting unconscious dynamics within the couple. On a positive note, a successful intercultural marriage offers a greater degree of self-other differentiation than may be found in a monocultural marriage: difference may aid in clarifying boundaries, which is helpful for any couple. During one of the interviews for my doctoral dissertation on intercultural marriages, a husband eloquently expressed a positive view of his intercultural marriage. He said, "Being married to someone of another culture has given me an opportunity to grow, to see my own capacity and flexibility in trying to understand another person's cultural values, beliefs, and customs. I daily have to deal with and to respect my wife's differentness. From this, I have a broader opportunity for learning and growth. And, of course, it's never boring!" (S. Ahmad, personal communication, February 12, 1995, in Soncini 1997).

TYPICAL AREAS OF CONFLICT

In intermarriage, the potential for misunderstanding and disagreement is increased. The intermarrying couple will be best off if they anticipate this and understand that it is *normal*. The couple's therapist will do best to regard these misunderstandings and disagreements as basically normal, but simply in need of mediation, whether they are major or minor. In addition to the differences in preferences regarding the daily trivia of deciding who is responsible for the garbage, how to celebrate a birthday, or how to entertain properly, the couple faces major differences concerning gender roles and status, religion, ownership of property, and child-rearing practices (Tseng et al. 1977). When compromise cannot be reached over major or minor differences, then the therapist should work on unconscious contributions to the stalemate. Alternatively, a period of individual therapy may be needed in preparation for couple therapy (Ho 1990). I followed Ho's advice and treated an African-born wife individually, when her husband's negative cultural view of psychotherapy precluded his continuing therapy. It was a difficult choice for me, as the couple's issues were the obvious focus, couple therapy was the treatment of choice, and I am committed to the value of the couple therapy approach. Happily, the wife made progress in achieving an enhanced sense of her own capacity and power, which she then applied to improving the couple's understanding and harmony.

SIX AREAS OF CULTURAL CONFLICT

Each member of an intercultural couple enters the marriage with a mixture of attitudes concerning what is best, what is all right, and what is least valued. These attitudes have particular power to create cultural conflict in six areas defined by Crohn (1995). (See table 29.3.)

Gender role differences cause strain between an American woman and a Japanese man, between an American man and an Indian woman. Even in small culturally diverse populations, an intercultural couple can meet with problems, like Koko, a Polynesian, and John, a Caucasian, who live in Hawaii. For Koko, the family comes first, whereas for John, the individual's needs are the priority. John chose Koko because he fell in love with her, and she with him. But her family was shocked and displeased with her choice, which was perceived as a rebellion. As a traditional family, they expected Koko to agree to a pre-arranged marriage, respecting the supremacy of the extended family within which the new couple would have a specific and well-structured place (Markoff 1977). John considers Koko to be in an enmeshed relationship with her family, whereas Koko feels that John cares little for his family, as he rarely visits them. John tells his wife she should be more independent and have her own ideas and values about various aspects of life. Koko is surprised by how much John has differentiated from his own parents' lifestyle. If they have children before resolving these differences, this

Table 29.3. Crohn's six areas of cultural conflict

1) Time
   present-, past-, or future-orientation
   rushing to make every minute count
   versus
   a relaxed attitude about time
2) The nature of the universe
   trust in the inherent goodness of man and destiny
   versus
   a distrust of others and pessimism
3) Cohesiveness of the family
   belief in cooperation and interdependence
   versus
   independence
4) Emotional expressiveness
   expressing one's emotions, particularly anger
   versus
   holding in anger
5) Interpersonal relations
   respecting age, authority, and tradition, such as in a hierarchical society like Japan
   focusing on the needs of the group before the individual, such as in a cooperative or
   collective society like Mexico and Italy
   versus
   placing the individual, his needs, his independence as primary, such as in an
   individualistic society like the United States
6) Gender roles
   assertiveness and subordination
   versus
   evolved gender relations like in the United States—which is out of step with other
   countries (Crohn 1995, p. 93).

dynamic may create strife between them over how much to promote dependence or independence in their children.

In the United States there has been growing attention to the way men and women differ in their styles of communication in books such as *Men Are from Mars, Women Are from Venus* (Gray 1992) and *You Just Don't Understand* (Tannen 1990). For monocultural couples these communication problems are hard enough, and for intercultural couples they are amplified under the impact of different cultural backgrounds, native languages, personalities, levels of education, and life experiences. Language itself is often highly ambiguous. Gestures, postures, style, physical proximity, and touch have distinctly different meanings from one culture to another. Emotional expressiveness differs, too. There can be quite a contrast between, for example, the fury of a formal and apparently controlled Englishman and that of a loud, obviously angry Puerto Rican. McGoldrick, Pearce, and Giordano (1982) explain that "couples often react to each other as though the other's behavior were a personal attack rather than just a difference rooted in ethnicity. Typically, we tolerate differences when we are not under stress. In fact, we find them appealing. However, when stress is added to a system, our tolerance for difference diminishes. We become frustrated if we are not understood in ways that fit our wishes and expectations" (pp. 21–22). Perel (1995) notes that certain life-cycle events, especially additions (the birth of a child, weddings) and subtractions (divorce, retirement, death), are often stressful, cause conflict, and necessitate renegotiation of previous agreements at a time of emotional upheaval.

Stereotyping is a particularly onerous problem, even within the intercultural couple. "You're Oriental, so of course you think that way; just like your parents!" "You're French, and that's why you never do/always do . . ." Stereotyping disregards individuality, and it tends to be prejudicial. Hand in hand with stereotyping is its pernicious relative, ethnocentrism. When this negative stance exists within the intercultural couple, the scene is set for disaster. Conversely, openness to exploring and understanding the spouse's worldview allows for enhanced understanding and harmony.

Tesler-Gadow (1992) observed conflicts around food and eating habits, friendship patterns, the use and treatment of money, cleanliness, decorating, recreation, holidays, pace, and work. Romano (1988) added to this list: place of residence, politics, in-laws, social class, modes of dealing with stress, illness, and suffering. Ask an intercultural couple what and how they eat, and you will learn a lot about how well they function together. Eating habits vary from culture to culture: frozen dinners versus handmade pasta; Japanese ritual tea ceremonies versus a hot dog on the run in Central Park; supper at six o'clock versus dinner at ten or eleven; and so on. I asked my happily married hairdresser, a New York Jew, what his Filipino wife and he generally ate. He smiled and responded: "We mostly eat Filipino, or Asian, food, as my wife really prefers it and, as for me, I like it tremendously and really don't care that much to eat American food. She's also the one to have left her country, so I figure it's important for her to feel a tie to her culture" (R. Stuart, personal communication, January 20, 1996).

The issue of acculturation to a new country's ways generally has an impact on the couple at one time or another. Several factors affect acculturation: language proficiency, whether the move was voluntary or involuntary, whether the individuals continue at the same socioeconomic level as in their country of origin, and whether the immigrant spouse can continue in the same trade or profession. One aspect of acculturation is the attitude toward receiving help from a doctor or psychotherapist. In some cultures, seeking professional help is normal and valued; others view it as shameful, because they value depending on, first and foremost, oneself, one's family, a

-spiritualist, a faith healer, or God. In many cultures, such as Miguel's, only "crazy people" go for psychotherapy or counseling.

HOW DO INTERCULTURAL COUPLES ADJUST TO DIFFERENCES AND RESOLVE CONFLICT?

Attitude determines where on the continuum from success to failure an intermarried couple will fall. The successful ones show empathy, flexibility, and tolerance. The less successful show rigid ethnocentricity, believing that there is only one right way. The continuum runs from disaster to good adjustment. Several books offer an optimistic view on the potential for good adjustment—*Adjustment in Intercultural Marriage* (Tseng, McDermott, and Maretzki 1977), *Building a Successful Intermarriage between Religions, Social Classes, Ethnic Groups or Races* (Ho 1984), and *Intercultural Marriage: Promises and Pitfalls* (Romano 1988).

One-way adjustment is a solution in which, basically, one partner gives up his/her culture in favor of the other's so as to avoid conflict, but the denial of one's own cultural identity or of any cultural differences at all is not a stable solution and deprives the couple and their children of a heritage. Two-way adjustment involves reaching agreement; accepting culturally bound beliefs, values, and customs; and leaving room for negotiation. The resulting enhanced understanding is founded upon respect for difference, which is not seen as disloyalty, and awareness of individual needs and values. Romano (1988) calls this the "ideal intercultural marriage model" (p. 175). Ho (1984), Tseng et al. (1977), and Romano (1988) list several ingredients for successful adjustment and conflict resolution: an ability to tolerate confusion and anger, to hear the other's views, and to be flexible and open to change; a general liking and respect for the other's culture; a sense of humor; and, last but certainly not least, the support of families and friends.

INTERCULTURAL COUPLES IN THERAPY

Child-rearing Concerns

The arrival of the first child often brings a resurgence of conflicts over culture, due to pressures from the grandparents and from the spouses themselves. New parents revisit their own early childhood experienced in different societies. For instance, a collectivist society may encourage dependency on the family and community, whereas an individualist society supports autonomy and sharpened ego boundaries (Mann and Waldron 1977). As these experiences are quite different for each partner in the intercultural couple, they may create an unexpectedly emotional environment as the partners plan for raising their children or dealing with their questions: Who am I? Am I American, or French, or South African? Am I white, black, Jewish, Muslim, or Catholic? (Perel 1995). The parents who may have dodged the issue before are now forced to decide about religion and the observance of family holidays. Perel (1995) wisely points out that parental harmony in general and agreement on these specific questions are the key to the children's well-being. McGoldrick and Preto (1984) emphasize the importance of integrating the two cultures, which is supported by the couple's maintaining open access to their two families of origin. Thus, the couple can model for their children a pride and respect for their cultural roots.

Special Techniques and Considerations in Intercultural Couple Therapy

Premarital Therapy

Hsu (1977) identifies areas of particular sensitivity that need to be addressed when couples come in for premarital therapy, in particular the opposing or conflicted worldviews of the couple. He encourages the therapist to take an active role in alerting premarital couples about the inevitability of cultural conflict. It is normal and to be expected. McGoldrick and Preto (1984) use premarital therapy to offer techniques to help maintain contact with respective families, especially when one or both are oppositional: They advise the couple therapist to explore gender and marital roles, the meaning of family, and expectations about how a husband and wife fit into the extended family; and to expand knowledge, fascination, and respect for the cultural backgrounds and rituals of each partner and enhance acceptance of difference.

Establishing the Therapy Culture

Working with intercultural couples in therapy calls for some caution in the opening sessions. Ho (1990), an experienced intermarriage therapist, wisely warns: "If [the therapists] are not adequately aware or sensitive to the complex dynamics of the multiracial or multiethnic system, therapists may unknowingly drive away their clients after the initial session" (p. 47). The therapist works on creating a therapeutic relationship, individually and with the couple, and building understanding, confidence, and trust in the therapeutic process.

In working with intercultural couples there often is a clear disparity between the partners regarding the acceptance of therapy. When one spouse is far more comfortable with therapy than the other, there will be different levels of anxiety in the initial sessions. One member (usually the foreign-born partner) may be skeptical, nervous, shameful, negative, or even antagonistic to the culturally unacceptable idea of therapy. The client from a collectivist culture with a strong "present orientation" may not want to recall the painful past nor look forward to the future. Therapists must show an ability to leave their own cultural framework and to be open to exploring and learning the cultural backgrounds of each member of the couple, seeking understanding of them as individuals, rather than as stereotypes of a cultural group. Therapists want to avoid countertransference enactments of colluding with one spouse (especially with the spouse who shares the therapist's gender or culture). They want to guard against presenting a common front against a marginally cooperative, or even oppositional spouse, who may be feeling extremely uncomfortable with the process of therapy.

It's worth it to take the time to talk about attitudes and expectations of therapy and explain how therapy works. When an intercultural couple enters therapy, the therapist's and the couple's ethnicity, race, class, culture, and gender will be highly visible and identifiable as similar or different. This means that therapists must be willing to address this issue and demonstrate an objective stance in the initial sessions, to avoid being accused of being prejudiced or allied with one partner. This is basic to establishing a safe therapeutic environment and building confidence in the therapist.

Then the therapist shows an understanding of the presence of conflicting worldviews, those of the two partners and that of the therapist. It is important not only to understand our own value systems, but also those of each client, paying close attention to exploring their worldview as individuals, rather than incorrectly categorizing or stereotyping them according to ethnicity, race, religion, or class. Therapists' worldviews leave them vulnerable to disagreeing with one of the clients on many issues, privileging the reality of one of the spouses over the other. Within the sessions, enhancing understanding and respect for each other is a prelude to exploring various alternatives or compromises, and expanding horizons from any one cultural stance.

The nature of the relationship between client and therapist varies across cultures. Unlike egalitarian cultures, traditional societies tend to respect authority to the extent that the therapist will be expected to be wise, to know the answers, and to give advice to be followed obediently by the client. Different cultures are accustomed to different strategies for resolving conflict. A British American's belief in self-sufficiency is in conflict with his Asian wife's expectation that the therapist, being regarded as a person of authority, is expected to give advice and guidelines to be followed. Men from some cultures may feel uncomfortable expressing personal problems with a woman therapist, expecting wisdom and authority only from a male counselor. Other men may not wish to discuss private marital matters in public or with any outsider, feeling shame that he is unable to handle his wife and their problems.

When therapists encounter a client whose worldview conflicts with their own, the scene is set for strong emotions, countertransference reactions, and acting out. Peer supervision is extremely helpful in monitoring and learning from countertransference to which the group can give voice when the therapist cannot. When making a case presentation to a group of professional psychotherapists, I described an interaction between an intercultural couple. One of my colleagues responded both angrily and adamantly: "But, you have to tell the husband he can't do that! Tell him he's in America now, and his behavior is outrageous here!" I was quite surprised and taken aback by her vehemence and responded innocently, holding in my anger: "But, if I told him that, he would leave therapy and never come back. Besides, I feel that it's important to explore how his culture supports his behavior and, then, to work through understanding toward a new way of responding to his wife." My colleague was filled with countertransference. Her reaction partially represented my negative feelings that I had split off while trying to maintain neutrality in my dealing with this difficult foreign-born spouse.

Identifying and Defining the Problems

The intercultural couple therapist learns to listen with a special ear tuned into distinguishing between cultural versus interpersonal or intrapsychic issues while assessing problems or issues. We explore together, tease out, and define those *culturally derived, interpersonal, and intrapsychic issues* that undermine happiness and understanding.

At the culture end of the continuum, the therapist might be working with the situational stress of acculturation. Ho (1990) reminds us to consistently keep in mind that the couple should be understood within the context in which they live. For example, being an interracial or intercultural couple is far easier in Hawaii than in a small Southern town not used to, fearful of, or openly hostile to such diversity, but the problems are still there for couples like John and Koko to face and work through.

Then, the therapist may move along the continuum to question how differences in the couple's cultural background and worldviews create conflict regarding issues of gender roles, power, child rearing, communication, and intimacy. Moving over toward the right side of the continuum, the therapist explores the defensive reenactment of previous object relations' conflicts within the present family. Observing what works and does not work in each of the two spouse's cultures and modeling respect for learning about and understanding them, the therapist can offer new ideas and ways of observing reality, while still supporting each individual's style or approach to tackling problems. At the far end of the continuum, the therapist shows which intrapsychic personality traits are active in influencing the extent to which an individual can successfully be part of a couple dyad.

Goals for intercultural couple therapy are divided into three levels described by Ho (see table 29.4).

Table 29.4. Goals of intercultural therapy

intermediate goals
contribute to a climate for continued therapy
help to furnish the basic needs in situational stress

instrumental goals
aid in achieving the ultimate outcome

ultimate goals
directly deal with the problem such as the relationship itself, child-rearing practices, in-law relationships, and so on

Intervention

The couple therapist helps the couple to clarify and respect their similarities and differences of values, expectations, and standards within the marriage, by enhancing each partner's curiosity, interest in, and respect for the other partner's way of understanding or viewing reality; reducing rigid ethnocentrism; teaching improved crosscultural communication strategies; viewing cultural conflict as a *normal* phenomenon, rather than proof of pathology or lack of caring; and working with the couple to create a safer space in which they can explore ways to resolve disagreement by mutual compromise. The newfound understanding and adaptations must be *culturally owned* by the couple. They must become part of their relationship.

Ending

Ho (1990) shows how differently people of various cultures tend to approach the ending of a relationship. The Irish tend to end abruptly, avoiding praise. British Americans may end abruptly when the "business" is done. A Jewish spouse may end unwillingly, complaining, yet maintaining newfound understanding and growth. An Asian from a collectivist culture *may* terminate prematurely so as not to burden the therapist any longer. In intercultural couple therapy, progress in improving relations, learning new ways of dealing with and resolving conflict, gaining and expressing empathy, and even saying good-bye must be done in a way that is culturally acceptable for each individual.

CONCLUDING REMARKS

There are many roads to Rome. In intercultural couple therapy, the therapist's flexibility and openness to learning and respecting how each member of the couple understands reality models the technique for respecting difference and valuing understanding. The model having been taken in and owned, the couple has the technique for maintaining a successful intercultural marriage.

REFERENCES

Barron, M., ed. 1972. *The Blending American Patterns of Intermarriage.* Chicago: Quadrangle Books.

Bizman, A. 1987. Perceived causes and compatibility of interethnic marriage: An attributional analysis. *International Journal of Intercultural Relations* 11(4): 387–99.

Brislin, R., ed. 1990. *Applied Cross-Cultural Psychology,* vol. 14. Newbury Park: Sage.

Cottrell, A. 1990. Cross-national marriages: A review of the literature. *Journal of Comparative Family* 21(1): 151–68.

Cretser, G., and J. Leon, eds. 1984. *Intermarriage in the United States.* New York: Haworth Press.

Crohn, J. 1995. *Mixed Matches: How to Create Successful Interracial, Interethnic, and Interfaith Relationships.* New York: Fawcett Columbine.

Falicov, C. J. 1986. Cross-cultural marriages. In *Clinical Handbook of Marital Therapy,* ed. N. S. Jacobson and A. S. Gurman. New York: Guilford Press.

Frank, J. 1989. Who are you and what have you done with my wife? In *Foundations of Object Relations Family Therapy,* ed. J. S. Scharff, pp. 175–84. Northvale, NJ: Jason Aronson.

Gordon, A. 1964. *Intermarriage: Interfaith, Interracial, Interethnic.* Boston: Beacon.

Gray, J. 1992. *Men Are from Mars, Women Are from Venus.* New York: HarperCollins.

Ho, M. K. 1984. *Building a Successful Intermarriage between Religious, Social Classes, Ethnic Groups or Races.* St. Meinrad, IA: St. Meinrad Archabbey.

———. 1987. *Family Therapy with Ethnic Minorities.* Newbury Park, CA: Sage Publishers.

———. 1990. *Intermarried Couples in Therapy.* Springfield, IL: Charles C. Thomas.

Holmes, S. A. 1995. Surprising rise in immigration stirs up debate. *The New York Times,* pp. A1, A15, August 30.

Hsu, J. 1977. Counseling for intercultural marriage. In *Adjustment in Intercultural Marriage,* ed. W. S. Tseng, J. McDermott, and T. Maretzki, pp. 121–31. Honolulu: University of Hawaii Department of Psychiatry.

Hutter, M. 1990. Introduction to cross-national marriages. *Journal of Comparative Family Studies* 21(2): 143–50.

Ibrahim, F., and D. Schroeder. 1990. Cross-cultural couples counseling: A developmental, psychoeducational intervention. *Journal of Comparative Family Studies* 21(2): 193–205.

Mann, E., and J. Waldron. 1977. Intercultural marriage and child rearing. In *Adjustment in intercultural marriage,* ed. W. S. Tseng, J. McDermott, and T. Maretzki, pp. 62–81. Honolulu: University of Hawaii Department of Psychiatry.

Markoff, R. 1977. Intercultural marriage: Problem areas. In *Adjustment in Intercultural Marriage*, ed. W. S. Tseng, J. McDermott, and T. Maretzki, pp. 51–62. Honolulu: University of Hawaii Department of Psychiatry.

McGoldrick, M., J. Pearce, and J. Giordano. 1982. *Ethnicity and Family Therapy.* New York: Guilford Press.

McGoldrick, M., and N. G. Preto. 1984. Ethnic intermarriage: Implications for Therapy. *Family Process* 23(3): 347–64.

Paris, J., and J. Guzder. 1989. The poisoned nest: Dynamic aspects of exogamous marriage. *Journal of the American Academy of Psychoanalysis* 17(3): 493–500.

Perel, E. 1995. Intermarried couples. Paper presented at the meeting of the Family Therapy Network Symposium, Washington, D.C, March.

Romano, D. 1988. *Intercultural Marriage: Promises and Pitfalls.* Yarmouth, ME: Intercultural Press.

Soncini, J. 1997. Intercultural couples: Cultural differences, styles of adjustment, and conflict resolution techniques, which contribute to marital harmony. Unpublished doctoral dissertation, University of Minnesota, Minneapolis.

Tannen, D. 1990. *You Just Don't Understand: Women and Men in Conversation.* New York: Ballantine Books.

Tesler-Gadow, B. 1992. Intercultural communication competence in intercultural marriages. Unpublished doctoral dissertation, University of Minnesota, Minneapolis.

Tseng, W., J. McDermott, and T. Maretzki, eds. 1977. *Adjustment in Intercultural Marriage.* Honolulu: University of Hawaii Department of Psychiatry.

30

Brief Therapy with Couples and Individuals

Michael Stadter and David E. Scharff

Object relations theory provides a particular perspective on personality, development, and the conduct of psychotherapy. It is one of the four major branches of psychoanalytic thought (Pine 1990). It puts the individual's need to relate to others at the center of human development, the first and most important tendency in the baby. When this experience with the caretaking person is internalized it results in a part of the psyche being structured on the model of that person. It is then called the internal object and becomes a basic building block for continued psychic structuring as aspects of self-organization relate to it internally. No other perspective on the human condition puts as much emphasis on the fundamental need to depend upon and relate to one another.

Many writers have contributed to the development of core object relations concepts. Ronald Fairbairn's theory of object relations (Fairbairn 1952, Scharff and Birtles 1994) began with the axiom that everyone needs relationships from the beginning of life, and that individual development is the story of the vicissitudes of dependency on others, as well as the struggle to be separate within relationships. Fairbairn's theory describes how the mind is structured psychologically by incorporating experience with others (represented by "internal objects"), by splitting off unsatisfactory parts of relationships from satisfactory ones, and repressing those unsatisfactory encounters that were too painful to be borne in consciousness. Melanie Klein (1975a and b) studied the infant's projective processes. She developed the theory that children were born with an excess of aggression which they handled by projecting

419

it out (in fantasy) into their parents, and then unconsciously identifying with that part of the parent they felt was now characterized by this projected excess of aggression. This process, which she called "projective identification," was the hallmark of early mental life in what she called the "paranoid-schizoid" position—or that state of mental organization in which splitting and projection dominate. Later she postulated another, more mature psychic organization, the "depressive position," a state of mind in which a person can tolerate love and hate, envy and gratitude for a person at the same time, and can also be concerned for that person's well-being. Donald Winnicott (1965, 1971, 1977) intensively studied the mother-infant relationship. He described the way that mothers provide a safe, reliable, psychological "holding" of their infants, offering an environment that facilitates growth, and within which they offer to be the object of their baby's love, hate, interest, and use for its own purposes. John Bowlby developed attachment theory (1969, 1973, 1980) describing the use the child makes of the mother as a secure base from which the infant gradually moves to explore the environment, deal with separation, and cope with loss. Most modern infant research takes Bowlby's work as a starting point.

Wilfred Bion (1967) transformed Klein's theory of projective identification into an interactive vision in which the growth of mind is a product of the interaction between child and parent. The parent's mind is the *container* for the child's primitive, unnamed anxieties (the *contained*). When the child projects these unmanageable early anxieties into the parent, she tolerates and transforms them, and returns them to the child in a more structured way through her attitude and actions. Guntrip (1969) wrote of the strivings of a self to find another self to relate to, and Sutherland (Scharff 1994) explored the evolution of the person's self for autonomous functioning, in relation to but not subservient to others. For further reading on object relations concepts see Greenberg and Mitchell (1983) and Scharff and Scharff (1992, 1998).

Object relations theory came out of the depth psychology developed in psychoanalysis and intensive psychotherapy. Since then there has been a long-standing tradition of applying these concepts to a variety of issues and treatment modalities. Two developments within this tradition are especially relevant to this chapter on brief couple therapy. First, Henry Dicks's landmark book *Marital Tensions* (1967) synthesized the work of Fairbairn and Klein to arrive at the idea that marriage sets up a situation of mutual projective identification in which the internal object relations of each spouse join together to form a *joint marital personality*. In therapy, analysis of the patterns of the shared projective identifications help the couple understand what unconscious internal problems they are attempting to solve by creating their partnership. Second, Michael Balint and his colleagues (Balint, Ornstein, and Balint 1972) at the Tavistock clinic in London developed one of the first psychodynamic models of brief therapy, which they called Focal Psychotherapy. This approach was further developed by Balint's Tavistock colleague, David Malan (1976), who carefully researched what works and what does not in brief therapy. Donald Winnicott (1971, 1977) pioneered applying object relations concepts to brief therapy with children in consultation with parents.

These contributors have greatly aided us in the development of our approach to brief object relations therapy with individuals and couples. In-depth presentation of our brief therapy paradigm can be found in Stadter (1996), D. Scharff and J. Scharff (1991), and J. Scharff and D. Scharff (1998).

KEY ELEMENTS OF OBJECT RELATIONS THERAPY

Our object relations approach to brief therapy emphasizes four points:

1) Uniqueness of each individual client, couple, and therapeutic relationship

Careful diagnosis is important, but purely descriptive classifications systems such as the DSM-IV are not as valuable as an assessment that emphasizes the underlying psychodynamics of the client's suffering and symptoms. Any categorization must acknowledge the uniqueness of each client or couple that is not fully accounted for by diagnostic types. The object relations therapist repeatedly asks, "Who is this person or couple in front of me?" No matter how experienced the therapist is, each individual and couple must be approached with an attitude of not knowing and of hopeful discovery. Therefore, training and experience are crucially important, but no "cookbook" approach can really help. Depending on the clients and the situation, five sessions may be too many or two years of three times per week therapy may be too little. Therapy has to be tailored to each situation.

2) Repetition of past patterns of relating

Clients are helped to identify and change unconscious patterns of interacting with others and themselves that have been in place for years or even decades. For these people the past keeps happening over and over again. Object relations brief therapy aims at helping clients to have a present and future that becomes different from that repetitive past.

3) The healing power of the therapeutic relationship

The object relations approach holds that little of benefit can occur in therapy unless the therapist and client develop a positive relationship. The effectiveness of technical interventions depends upon the relationship. Guntrip (1969) writes that the unique therapeutic relationship creates the situation necessary for our technique to address patients' problems successfully. The relationship factor in therapy is just as important whether it lasts for one session or for one year.

4) Studying the therapeutic relationship to reveal ways of relating

Transference and countertransference are the technical terms for the patterns of emotion and ways of relating studied in therapy in order to gain understanding of clients' inner worlds. Even in brief therapy, the therapist is aware of the unconscious forces and patterns in the way clients relate to the therapist (the transference) *and* in the way the therapist is feeling and relating in response to clients (the countertransference). When possible the therapist looks for ways to interpret and to comment upon this. Moreover, the therapist tries to connect these reenactments in the transference-countertransference matrix (Ogden 1994) with clients' past patterns of behavior, feeling, and thinking. This type of interpretive work requires considerable skill and creativity. Even when patterns cannot be fully interpreted in the brief therapy context, the therapist's awareness and internal processing, even when unspoken, should effectively further the therapeutic process.

This is part of the containment function (Bion 1967) that is crucial in the role of interpersonal relationships to facilitate intrapsychic growth. Containment is a special unconscious process in which the person (in this case the therapist) is able to take in and tolerate painful mental states of another person (such as anxiety, frustration, anger) that otherwise cannot be tolerated and understood. The therapist's ability to stay with the difficult affect, take it in, work toward understanding, and empathically communicate with the client helps to detoxify painful, even overwhelming, emotions. Containment is a process that is essentially unconscious but that leads toward conscious understanding. The object relations approach with its emphases on the uniqueness of each client and therapist, the therapeutic relationship, and the value of unconscious reenactments for clarifying internal object relations can deepen the work of therapists from other theoretical orientations.

STRATEGIES

While it is important for clinicians to think in terms of technique and strategy, many therapists overemphasize technique and strategic interventions without adequate attention to the nature and quality of the relationship that has developed between client(s) and therapist. An object relations approach always keeps in mind the context of the relationship. So-called excellent or correct strategies fail when they are implemented within a poor therapeutic relationship. For heuristic purposes we discuss strategies individually. In practice, each strategy has to be considered within the unique holding environment that has developed between the therapist and client or couple. (See table 30.1.) Not all strategies are utilized in every case—but nothing can be accomplished without the first one.

Strategy 1: Develop a therapeutic alliance

Therapy cannot proceed without client and therapist making an alliance (conscious and unconscious) in the service of therapeutic progress. The object relations therapist operates from a stance of empathic attunement, sensitively and nonjudgmentally trying to understand the client's concerns, and interacting with the client in a manner that conveys respect, competence, and compassion. This stance, which is common to that taken by therapists from most orientations, facilitates the development of the therapeutic alliance. First, since brief therapy raises the challenge to develop a working alliance quickly, the clinician must be aware of the common tendency to feel hurried or impatient. Rapid development is different from hasty development. We cannot push the process faster than clients can tolerate. When we try to speed this up without adequate sensitivity to clients' readiness, they will often experience a repetition of earlier unempathic relationships, or may defensively idealize the therapist. Second, when therapists direct attention to describing and understanding the clients' pain, they feel understood and more willing to work. Third, taking a history, a shared process of discovery, increases the alliance. Fourth, collaboratively setting a focus with clients assists in alliance building. Finally, using knowledge of clients by attending to transference and countertransference reactions permits therapists to use clients' internal language better and helps to solidify the therapeutic relationship.

Table 30.1. Object relations strategies in brief therapy

- Develop a therapeutic alliance and engage the client's curiosity in the inner world
- Set a dual focus: symptomatic and dynamic
- Use selected historical material to help with focus setting and to understand repetitive patterns
- Invite the client to examine the way client and therapist are relating
- Interpret dynamics and patterns when possible
- Use nonpsychodynamic techniques as appropriate
- Consider serial brief therapy
- Try to provide a new ending for an old experience

Strategy 2: Set a dual focus: symptomatic and dynamic

Setting a therapeutic focus is the distinguishing difference between brief and long-term dynamic psychotherapy (Stadter 1996). In object relations brief therapy, we set a focus collaboratively with the client on two levels: symptomatic and dynamic. The symptomatic level typically addresses the psychological pain or the functional impairment that brought the client in— for instance, a sexual problem, family tension, poor grades. Sometimes this is all that can be done. However, whenever possible, a dynamic focus is also agreed upon, which centers on the client's underlying psychodynamic structure. The two foci are usually connected, even though that may not be obvious. Work on the dynamic focus assists in the work on the symptomatic focus. We work to understand links between the symptomatic focus and the clients' dynamics. If an appropriate dynamic focus cannot be found, the therapy is usually more limited, supportive rather than interpretive.

Strategy 3: Get selected historical material to help with focus setting and to understand and illustrate repetitive patterns

Even in brief object relations therapy it is essential to develop an understanding of clients' object relations patterns through taking a history. Taking a history is frequently therapeutic in itself (Malan 1976). The client is able to see—sometimes for the first time—that there are understandable patterns where before life seemed chaotic. Table 30.2 highlights some of the most important issues we address in gathering historical data (Stadter 1996).

In long-term therapy, clients usually revise their history over time. In brief therapy, the original history often has to remain unchallenged. However, with couples, partners often have different views of individual and shared history, a discrepancy that may become the focus.

Table 30.2. Taking an object relations history

- Each client's impression of parents, other members of the family of origin, and other important figures that contributed to their personality structure
- Recurring patterns of interpersonal interactions (e.g., repeatedly being in an abused position in relationships), including a history of the couple's relationship when there is a long-term partnership or marriage
- Best and worst levels of past functioning
- Family history of psychological disturbance, substance abuse, and loss
- Past suicidal, self-defeating, psychotic, or other regressive behavior
- Significant issues relating to health
- Previous individual and couple therapy

Adapted from *Object Relations Brief Therapy*, M. Stadter, 1996, courtesy of Jason Aronson.

Strategy 4: Invite clients to examine the way they and the therapist are relating

It is expected that individuals or couples will reenact some past relational patterns. This offers an affectively powerful, here-and-now opportunity for learning. It can be quite anxiety-provoking for clients to do this kind of in-session experiential work; not all clients can do it. However, when tolerable and possible, the therapist directs clients' attention to this arena by saying, for instance, "I noticed something that occurred just now and wondered if you felt that I didn't want to listen to you" or "How did you feel when I made that last comment?"

Strategy 5: Interpret dynamics and patterns when possible

Interpretation is a cornerstone of psychodynamic therapy. Interpretation is a verbal intervention through which therapists make previously unconscious material conscious, or link events in a causal connection in a way that is new to the clients (Lang 1973, Scharff and Scharff 1998). Given the time constraints of brief therapy and particular client dynamics, depth interpretation may not be possible. If we push too tenaciously, we can damage the therapeutic alliance and cause the therapy to fail (Piper et al. 1993). The object relations brief therapist works to understand and interpret the external conflict or situation—the there-and-now—with the internal situation—the here-and-then—and its effect on the therapeutic relationship—the here-and-now (Scharff and Scharff 1998). In all object relations work, the therapist uses transference and countertransference to make sense of the client's situation. The here-and-now of transference-countertransference is used first for facilitating the therapist's understanding, and then for formulating interpretations.

Malan (1963, 1976) in Great Britain and later Davanloo (1980) in the United States devised a way of thinking about the short-term client's issues, termed the triangle of conflict and the triangle of the person, two images that they keep in mind to organize their thinking about clients' issues and guide their interpretive focus. In the triangle of conflict, a concept drawn from drive theory, they trace the connection between impulse, anxiety, and defense. In the triangle of the person, they trace clients' feelings and actions toward the therapist, the feelings toward important figures from the past such as parents, and those toward others in the present or recent past. Then the therapist uses these triangles in formulating interpretations, Davanloo from a more forceful and confrontational interpretive stance than Malan. In line with current thinking in object relations and self psychology, Stadter (1996) added an aspect to the brief therapy process, an evaluation of the client's attitudes toward self and others, now and in the past. That innovation adds "self" as a fourth nodal point to the interpretive thrust of the triangle of the person, and brings a new dimension of immediacy to the process (see figure 30.1).

Here is an example of an interpretation linking past and current external relationships to the client's self. The therapist might say, "You keep away from your wife sexually now (there-and-now relationship) because you are afraid she will take you over (a self experience) like your mother used to do (there-and-then relationship)." However, to link such an interpretation to the transference, the therapist might draw on a sense of the client's reluctance to speak about the transference by adding, "You are also afraid of being here with me (here-and-now transference) in case what I say will somehow put you in danger of being taken over by me (self's fear in here) as you feel dominated by your husband (there-and-now relationship)." In this way, the two interpretations would link all three angles of the triangle with the position of the self in its center.

In couple therapy, interpretation generally moves toward helping understand the partners' shared construction of dynamics, the underlying reasons for their shared reenactments, and their shared transference to the therapist. For instance, a therapist might go on to include the wife of the man in the example above, by saying to her, "In a complementary way, you tolerate his sexual withdrawal (there-and-now) because you are afraid of being an overwhelming person (self experience) as you felt your mother was to you

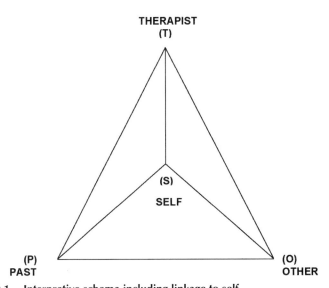

Figure 30.1. Interpretive schema including linkage to self

From *Object Relations Brief Therapy,* M. Stadter, 1996. Reprinted courtesy of Jason Aronson.

and your father (there-and-then)." Then the therapist could link both of these individual patterns to the couple's shared transference by saying "I sense you both are afraid my comments will push you into a destructive pattern and that I will be like the intrusive, know-it-all mothers you both feel you had" (Scharff and Scharff 1991).

Strategy 6: Use nonpsychodynamic techniques as appropriate

To conduct brief therapy from an object relations perspective, the therapist who is trained to do so may complement the psychodynamic listening, interpretation, history, confrontation, and dream work with techniques from cognitive-behavioral, Gestalt, hypnosis, or sex therapy. Other brief dynamic therapy models are similarly integrative (Budman and Gurman 1988, Strupp and Binder 1984, Horowitz, Marmar, Krupnik et al. 1984, Scharff and Scharff 1991).

We do need to be aware of the effect of the role shift when giving directive instructions to clients. For instance, how would teaching clients to reduce anxiety through deep muscle relaxation affect transference? How do clients feel when therapists recommend cognitive therapy techniques to deal with guilt while at another time remaining more silent in order to permit the client to stay with the guilt? Integrating dynamic and nondynamic approaches usually enhances the work: Nondynamic interventions often serve to expedite therapy on particular issues; the dynamic perspective attends to the meaning of the client's suffering and symptoms while providing knowledge about the clients' resistance.

This last point concerning resistance can be crucial with any form of therapy. For instance, consider the problem of lack of client compliance with cognitive/behavioral and sex therapy assignments. Understanding the unconscious dynamics involved in noncompliance is often necessary for effective progress. With many clients, attention to transference, countertransference, and unconscious processes facilitates change. Even when using a behavioral intervention, therapists should remember Heimann's questions that orient the therapist toward the inner world: "Who is speaking?" (that is to say, what part of the client's inner world is being given expression at that particular moment) and "To whom is the person speaking?" (what part of the client's inner world is being represented by the therapist at the moment) (Bollas 1987).

Strategy 7: Consider serial brief therapy

Therapists should consider not only the present work with a client but also how the current experience may affect continued growth and development. Attention to the dynamic focus is helpful in this regard in that it works on a theme or issue that operates beyond the current brief encounter. Seen from this perspective, a single piece of brief therapy is a part of a larger process of change that may include periodic brief episodes of therapy throughout clients' lives. Episodic return for additional therapy can be termed "serial brief therapy" (Stadter 1996). When clients have experienced a process of change in the context of a unique, consistent relationship at one time of distress through a relationship with a reliable therapist, then at another time of future distress or developmental need, they return for further work. In this way, individual episodes of therapy build upon earlier episodes. The whole is greater than the sum of its parts. Serial brief therapy can be viewed as a developmental approach to psychotherapy over a person's life cycle (Bennett 1989, Budman 1990, Budman and Gurman 1988, Cummings 1990, Stadter 1996).

Strategy 8: Try to provide a new ending for an old experience

Many clients, especially character-disordered ones, hardly live in the present. Their lives are strangled by their inability to encounter others directly. Instead, they experience people through the distorted prism of their past experience. Without knowing, they select friends and partners on the basis of similarity to important past people. These unconscious reenactments of past relationships with others limit and trouble their lives. Gaining awareness of this pattern allows them to experiment with new ways of relating. This may be the most important lesson of therapy.

Repetitive experiences are replayed in the therapy relationship, so the brief therapist attempts to respond in a manner that is different from the response of important past objects. In this way therapists offer new outcomes to the old experiences. Therapists must be more than just a projection of good elements in clients' minds; they must, in their own reality as persons, bring something new, something clients have not experienced before (Guntrip 1969). Such interactions can be profoundly therapeutic when therapists disconfirm clients' beliefs (unconscious or conscious) that they will be responded to in a particular way.

CLINICAL INDICATIONS FOR EACH STRATEGY

This form of brief therapy (like many brief therapy models) is the treatment of choice for highly motivated clients in situations deriving from developmental and externally imposed crises where there is relatively little severe underlying disturbance, or in which the resonance with deeper issues does not principally involve entrenched characterologic patterns (Scharff and Scharff 1998). However, external factors such as limited motivation, constrained financial resources, and relocation may also preclude long-term therapy. In these instances, brief therapy can often provide timely if limited help. In keeping with the emphasis on the unique dynamics, strengths, and weaknesses of the particular client, the model does not a priori exclude a client from this form of brief therapy (Stadter 1996). The careful choice of the focus for a particular client is crucial if the therapist and client(s) are to work effectively within the constraints of dynamics, pathology, and external limitation. Table 30.3 lists six selection questions used in object relations brief therapy.

Can a Clear Focus Be Defined?

The single most important difference between brief and long-term dynamic psychotherapy is the setting of a therapeutic focus. If time is limited, then the therapy must be centered in some way. Otherwise, much may be touched on, but nothing resolved. With a focus, quite disturbed clients can be helped even in a few sessions.

For example, object relations brief therapy was able to help Rhonda, a paranoid woman who was at times delusional, in only two sessions. She came in crisis, thinking she should quit her job as a secretary because she was convinced she would be fired. The therapist helped her focus on how to deal practically with the job crisis and how to manage her intense anxiety due to lifelong feelings of incompetence and being undervalued. She was able to work out a plan that enabled her to check out how her performance was viewed externally by her supervisor who actually saw her as an excellent secretary. When seen several years later, she was still able to handle the job, and she was still quite paranoid.

In another example, Mr. and Mrs. D were seen as a couple because Mrs. D had suffered increased anxiety after Mr. D's recent heart attack. She had begun to badger him about his eating and exercise. One result was that he

---

Table 30.3.   Establishing a basis for recommending brief therapy

- Can a clear focus be defined?
- Can clients quickly develop a positive, collaborative relationship with the therapist?
- Can clients tolerate the frustration of a brief approach?
- Are there clients for whom brief therapy is better than long-term therapy?
- Have clients responded positively to trial interpretations or interventions during evaluation?
- Can clients benefit from brief discontinuous courses of therapy, as opposed to needing a continuous long-term relationship with a therapist?
- How do clients' clinical presentations compare with presentations that research has shown to be responsive to brief therapy?

began to avoid her sexually. In brief therapy, the focus on her anxiety and his sexual avoidance (the symptomatic focus) led rapidly to an understanding that Mrs. D had a lifelong fear of loss and abandonment beginning with threats from her parents to send her away, while Mr. D feared intrusiveness from his obsessively controlling parents (the shared dynamic focus). The health crisis had heightened these vulnerabilities, which resolved in three sessions so that the husband and wife were able to find each other sexually again.

Sometimes, as with Rhonda, only a symptomatic focus is possible, one that works exclusively with psychological pain and functional impairment. However, whenever possible, we set a dynamic focus that centers on the client's or couple's underlying psychodynamic structure, as with the D couple. Malan's (1976) research shows that clients who are curious about their inner world do better in brief therapy than clients who are uninterested in their own dynamics. So, an important question for the brief therapist is: How can I creatively engage the clients' curiosity about themselves? Much of the art of psychotherapy lies in the answer to that question. A general rule about focus-setting is the following: The more disturbed the client and/or the briefer the therapy, the tighter and more specific the focus should be.

Can the client quickly develop a positive, collaborative relationship with the therapist?

If the therapist and client do not establish a cooperative alliance quickly, they will need to work together for an extended period of "pre-therapy" until trust and collaboration develop. For instance, Sally, a woman in her forties, moved into dynamic therapy only after many years of supportive treatment. She had been severely sexually abused as a child and had many dissociative symptoms. It took the first three years of treatment before she was able to trust the therapist enough to risk talking about matters that were centrally important and meaningful to her. Abused and hostile clients often require this kind of extended treatment approach. Even then, however, sometimes an agreed-upon focus can lead to more rapid progress.

Can the client tolerate the frustration of a brief approach?

For some clients the yearnings and rage at disappointment that will be stimulated by brief work require the therapist to recommend longer-term treatment. This is especially the case for many clients with borderline and dependent personality disorders. Attention to the focus and the limits of therapy, however, can often make the rigors of brief treatment manageable for some of these clients.

Are there clients for whom brief therapy is better than long-term therapy?

We have noted that clients with an external or developmental crisis may only want—and need—brief therapy. Brief work can also be especially helpful for some clients when it confronts the key issues of loss and dependency by focusing on the limited contact with the therapist. Similarly, the time constraints can help confront obsessive or narcissistic clients with the impossibility of "having it all."

Has the client responded positively to trial interpretations or interventions in the evaluation session(s)?

One of the most accurate methods to determine if the client can benefit from brief therapy is to try out some of the interpretations or interventions that would be used in a brief, focused approach. If the client does not respond positively, then a long-term or modified approach should be considered.

Can the client benefit from brief discontinuous courses of therapy (as opposed to needing a continuous long-term relationship) in order to change in ways that are significant?

Many clients find serial brief therapy effective and convenient for them. The following vignettes illustrate when it was useful (Alan, and Sol and Nancy M), and when it would not have been effective (Sally).

Alan was seen from the ages of eighteen to twenty-five for five episodes of brief therapy ranging from three to twenty sessions in duration for a total of fifty sessions when he was depressed after a breakup with a girlfriend. When he began treatment he was a profoundly schizoid, suicidal, asexual young man. When he was last seen in treatment, eight years later, he had an enthusiasm for life, was professionally successful, had a network of personal relationships, and was dealing with his sexual self. Alan had internalized the therapy process and was continuing to do work on his own. He found it helpful to return repeatedly for "consultations" as he called them, to further his personal journey (Stadter 1996).

Sol and Nancy M first came asking for sex therapy when, in their mid-twenties, they had been married four years. A course of psychodynamic sex therapy twice a week for about four months gave them competent sexual functioning they had not previously had (Scharff 1982, pp. 131–32). They returned to the therapist many times in subsequent years for marital strain when they could not process developmental issues: career change for both Sol and Nancy, issues of child development in their daughter, and ways of relating to their own siblings and parents. They came as a couple, individually, and in one series, Sol came with his brother and father for ten sessions to work on family business matters. Over fifteen years, they were seen for a total of seventy sessions.

By contrast, however, Sally (described above) could not have benefited significantly from serial brief therapy since she needed the extended presence of a therapist in a consistent, nonabusing relationship to be able to modify her old destructive patterns.

How do clients' clinical presentations compare with presentations that have been shown by research to be responsive to brief therapy?

Barber and Crits-Christoph (1991) note three client qualities that brief dynamic therapists typically emphasize when they consider candidates for brief approaches: a history of at least one good relationship, psychological mindedness, and motivation for more than simple symptom relief. Drawing from Steenbarger (1994) and Hoglend (1993a), table 30.4 lists some factors relevant to the success of brief interventions with couples, and individuals, too.

CLINICAL APPLICATIONS WITH AN INDIVIDUAL: CASE EXAMPLE

This case is presented from the therapist's perspective to convey the subjective experience of the relationship, especially the transference-countertransference dynamics. Note not only the use of the strategies, but the way the therapist uses his own countertransference reactions to understand the client and further the therapy. This is a core aspect of any object relations therapy.

Ronald, a twenty-four-year-old single man, had just begun his second semester in law school and was acutely anxious because of his so-so performance during first semester. He was having difficulty sleeping, couldn't concentrate on his studies, felt out of control, and was viciously self-critical. He

Table 30.4.   Research on client variables and brief therapy

- Clients who enter therapy with strong interpersonal skills achieve results faster
- Clients who engage actively change faster than those who take a passive stance
- Clients who are highly motivated change faster
- Change occurs more quickly with a clear focus than when the focus is vague or complex
- Personality disorder characteristics usually take a longer time to change

felt humiliated for being so out of control. His insurance would cover only fifteen sessions of psychotherapy, and he wanted therapy to be conducted within that amount of time. Ronald said that he expected it would take less time than that, "if it helps at all."

In the first session, I (MS) was impressed by Ronald's narcissistic issues, and was also aware of a number of my own feelings and reactions. First, I felt saddened by how hard he was on himself. He talked movingly about almost always being disappointed in himself. I found my own thoughts going toward some of my own lack of self-acceptance. I felt, "I'm going to be disappointing to him because I won't meet his standards." But I also was feeling some irritation with an arrogant, entitled quality to him. For example, when I explained to him that I expected clients to file their own insurance forms, he replied, "I realize that that's the way you do it for other people, but couldn't you make an exception for me?" These reactions of mine were important in giving me some understanding of his inner world. I felt he must also feel unsure of himself and in need of special treatment in order to benefit from help.

At the end of the first session we agreed to work on the symptomatic focus of trying to get his anxiety to a more manageable level and to help him be able to concentrate well enough to study. In law school, a student can easily fall hopelessly behind in just a few weeks. I also made a tentative suggestion to Ronald that I was impressed by the extremely high standards that he set for himself and thought that they may be connected with the intensity of his anxiety reaction. He seemed to accept that idea, so the issue of his high or "all or nothing" standards became the beginning of a dynamic focus on his narcissistic character. In this first session, moreover, the discussion of his high standards evoked his curiosity about his inner world and supported the alliance building (Strategy 1). And we had been able to set the beginnings of a dual focus (Strategy 2).

Also, in this session Ronald mentioned that he had been athletic in college but had not engaged in any exercise since coming to law school because he felt he didn't have the time. I suggested that vigorous exercise is sometimes quite helpful in managing anxiety and recommended that he try some jogging, which he had previously done in college (Strategy 6: nonpsychodynamic intervention). He agreed to try it.

I was aware in this session of a countertransference feeling of pressure to help him reduce his anxiety quickly and to "prove" instantly that therapy could be helpful to him. Earlier in the session he expressed skepticism as to whether therapy would help at all. I thought my plan to direct our attention toward symptomatic relief was sound, but I wondered if I was also responding to his rather critical "show me but I don't think this will help" attitude.

Session 2

I came to understand Ronald's critical attitude better during this session (Strategy 3: history-taking). He was the oldest of four children and was the only son. His parents divorced when he was ten and he described great admiration for his mother who alone raised him and his three sisters. He described her as being "principled and a hard worker" but also as being "depressive and a martyr." He worried about her since she so often seemed to be unhappy.

Ronald hated his father and was estranged from him since the divorce. He was contemptuous of his father for never finishing high school. Also, his volatile father had physically and emotionally abused his mother and him, although not his sisters. His father seemed to want to spend time with Ronald, but things usually degenerated when his father yelled at him or sometimes hit him. His father always seemed disappointed with him.

He had had one serious romantic relationship throughout college but he and his girlfriend "just grew apart." It sounded to me as though he lost interest in her as being not enough for him. A current distress had come with breaking up with a woman he had been dating for three months, an important interpersonal detail that he was only now mentioning.

In the first session, Ronald said he was always disappointed with his performance, but in the next session, he corrected that, saying that during his senior year in college he was "perfect"—popular, good grades, high office in student government. He noted that it was always difficult for him to trust people, and he was ashamed about going through this present crisis. His professional goal was to run for political office in the U.S. Senate, or even higher.

I felt more empathic, as I often do when I learn more about a client's background. I considered that the pressure I was feeling to prove myself was part of a concordant identification (Racker 1968) with Ronald. This was the way his father frequently caused him to feel, and the way he was relating to me was an unconscious identification with his father while I identified with his victimized self. I further reflected that academic success was additionally important to his self-image because it differentiated him from his much less educated father. I wondered about unconscious identifications with his mother's depressive, martyred stance and also about whether he might expect some similar self-sacrificing devotion toward him from any woman that he would be involved with. I did not share any of these speculations with Ronald at this point. However, these insights did help me to maintain my empathy for him in the face of his self-critical attitude. This understanding of Ronald also helped me later in the therapy to resist the projective identification pull to be like his father: I felt it but I did not act it out.

The preliminary foci that we had set in the previous session still seemed apt. He indicated that his anxiety had diminished somewhat and that the jogging had been helpful, but that his sleep disturbance and inability to study were continuing. I proposed that during the next several sessions we work on his anxiety by doing some behavioral relaxation training and he readily agreed (Strategy 6: nondynamic interventions). As I state above, a practical focus on symptom alleviation seemed wise for several reasons: he was directly asking for that, the symptoms were quite disruptive of his functioning, a law student can easily fall hopelessly behind in a semester in a matter of only a few weeks, and he seemed to need "proof" that therapy could help him. On the other hand, I wondered if I was acting out a transference-countertransference dynamic with Ronald being his critical father and me being the Ronald who would inevitably fail in the father's eyes and disappoint him. If that dynamic were prominent, then therapy would inevitably fail. I felt unsure of my decision but was heartened by the benefits he had reported from jogging and by his eager response to the relaxation suggestion.

Sessions 3–7

In these sessions we worked on relaxation exercises and readings on self-help cognitive therapy of depression. As he found these helpful, I relaxed, felt his idealization of me grow, and no longer feared premature termination.

Sessions 8–12

I did mostly interpretive work (Strategy 5) during this phase. By session 8, his functioning had returned to levels prior to receiving his first semester's grades. I felt, however, that unless he became more aware of his narcissistic issues and better able to cope with them that he would likely have recurring crises of this sort. I noted that we were about halfway through our contract but he denied any reaction to that.

We continued to look at how narcissistically vulnerable he was, as we focused on a few interpretive themes. We discussed how his grandiose standards for success intensified his disappointment and suffering when he didn't meet them and how his self-esteem was reactive to such events. We connected his strife-ridden childhood, especially his father's influence, with his labile self-esteem. He had unconsciously internalized his father's abusive, critical characteristics and frequently treated himself as his father had (Self-Past link). He also often treated other people as his father had treated him and his mother (Past-Self-Other interpretation). I invoked the transference/countertransference when we talked about his critical dismissive attitude toward me during the first session (Therapist-Self-Past interpretation). The depression and self-pity he experienced when he defined a situation as a failure was conceptualized as an unconscious identification with his depressive mother (Past-Self connection). During this period he expressed the feeling that I was disappointed in him. I suggested that he felt I was responding to him as his father had (Therapist-Self-Past interpretation). The interpretations concerning me and our discussions about the way we were relating are examples of directing attention to the way the client and therapist are relating (Strategy 4).

Ronald was an active collaborator during these sessions and was at times enthusiastic about being able to understand elements in his personality that had previously been mysterious to him. He had difficulty acknowledging his own critical stance with other people and initially felt criticized when I pointed it out. It was painful for him to consider that not only was he the victim of his father's attacks, but also that he himself had unconsciously attacked others at times as well (Past-Self-Other interpretation). He had organized part of his life to demonstrate emphatically that he was not like his father by becoming highly educated. There were instances when Ronald would feel put down by me when I pointed something out that he hadn't yet seen. We looked at this as a result of the extraordinarily high expectations he had for himself and of his difficulty with envy.

Sessions 13–14

Ronald requested that we schedule our last three sessions every other week to permit an opportunity to deal with his difficulty in getting a summer job. I agreed to meet every other week, with mixed feeling. On the one hand, it would be useful to spread out the last sessions to help him deal with the blows to his self-esteem that were part of searching for a summer job. The approach of less frequent sessions toward the end of the contract can be useful in relapse prevention and in reducing the difficulty of termination for the client. On the other hand, diluting the experience of termination gave me some concern.

Ronald had a history of denying the importance of relationships in his life and failing to mourn their endings. He said, "When it's over, time to move on." This contrasted with his often obsessive preoccupation with other losses—losses of self-esteem and confidence in his academic prowess. Our relationship had been important to him. Losing a supportive connection with a trusted older man had to be meaningful, despite his reluctance to be aware of my importance to him. When we discussed ending therapy (Strategy 4), he discounted the significance of it (see session 15, below). I did not pursue his reaction to termination persistently. After therapy had ended, I felt that I had not done enough on that important issue. I had felt that greater exploration of termination would have evoked strong resistance. Nevertheless, in my countertransference I became aware of my own resistance to dealing with the pain and loss of endings. Through projective identification, perhaps I had come to feel less significant to him than I was, and then acted that projection out. Later, I realized that my feelings of inadequacy about handling his termination were, in part, a projective identification of his own inadequacy.

Session 15

Ronald landed a good summer job. He came to the last session with an air of triumph, but an air of sadness, too. He denied it had to do with this being our last session. He had been thinking perhaps he had not really changed at all, and had not gotten much out of therapy. I felt sad as he said that. I suggested that we look at his impression that he hadn't changed. How did he see himself now compared to when we began five months ago?

Like a lawyer, he cited the evidence: much less anxiety, eating and sleeping well, studying effectively, greater appreciation of his brittle self-esteem, recognition of the tyranny of his all-or-nothing expectations, and awareness of his need to be "special." I thought to myself that this would be pretty impressive in any therapy, but especially so from someone who was disappointed with therapy. Ronald movingly said that he was amazed to note this array of improvements. He hadn't been in touch with them minutes before. We looked at this as a dramatic example of how predisposed he was to be critical of himself. I acknowledged that his life wasn't perfect and that he was still struggling, but noted, too, that it was hard for him to hold on to good experience.

Our discussion of these issues as he terminated provided him with "a new ending for old experience" (Strategy 8). He was able to end with some understanding of the important dynamics of his vulnerability to disappointment and his difficulty in holding on to good-but-imperfect experience. As I was connecting the pattern back to the relationship with his father, I felt particularly saddened that it was so difficult for him to hold on to good experience unless feeling grandiose. This dynamic was a manifestation of a periodic inner sense of emptiness, a state experienced by many clients with prominent narcissistic issues, which can only be thoroughly addressed in long-term treatment.

Ronald's disappointment in therapy and in me was also a way to diminish pain over the loss of the relationship through seeing it as less valuable. I acknowledged the gains that Ronald had listed, and suggested that further work in open-ended therapy on his self-esteem issues might eventually be useful since he intended to be in positions of influence. He agreed, and said that probably the government would be better run if more of our leaders had been in therapy.

CLINICAL APPLICATIONS WITH
A COUPLE: CASE EXAMPLE

In this couple, many years of shared low desire had been complicated by an increasing problem with the husband's impotence. I (DES) was initially concerned that individual therapy or psychoanalysis might be needed because the husband's inhibited desire seemed to be part of a pervasive problem with identity and with fear of a dominating exciting object. Nevertheless, brief sex therapy alone proved sufficient.

Dr. and Mrs. T were both thirty-five when they were referred by an adoption agency just a month after they adopted an infant girl, Tammy. Never sexually assertive at best, Dr. T had experienced erectile failure occasionally during the infertility evaluation and procedures and their attempts to conceive. After that time two years ago, he had shown little interest in sex. Mrs. T had hardly noticed at first, being busy with her own career as a sports executive. Gradually she realized she felt neglected. Eventually the couple admitted to the adoption social worker that their sexual difficulty detracted from their otherwise loving relationship.

During the evaluation with me, Dr. T admitted freely that he had become distracted from sex by his interest in professional and community matters. He was also consciously aware that he withdrew from sexual encounters because of his fear of erectile failure, but he underscored his feeling that he had not been motivated about sex since marriage. This was not true during vacations, when the couple relaxed and enjoyed sex easily. The problem was one partly of erectile instability and performance anxiety, and partly of inhibited sexual desire. In the evaluation, understanding the presenting problem and establishing a symptomatic focus, I moved toward understanding a dynamic focus (Strategy 2) by getting a brief history from each partner (Strategy 3). This process also helped establish a therapeutic alliance (Strategy 1).

Getting the Husband's History

Dr. T's interest in sex had always been rather low. During his years in boarding school, he had several short homosexual encounters, which spoke to his difficulty in establishing an adolescent sexual identity. He had no sexual interest in men, nor any encounters after high school. He said that his relationship to his parents had been good, as was the parents' relationship itself until his mother began to look her age while his father's energy continued unabated. Then, when Dr. T was in college, his father ran off with another woman. Dr. T had felt his mother's hurt although he still got on well with his father.

Getting the Wife's History

Mrs. T told me that she was the baby sister, with an athletic older brother in a loving family. Pushed to be as athletic and competitive as her brother, she never had much confidence as a woman. The difficulty with her sense of femininity left her on shaky ground in now asking Dr. T to be more interested in her sexually.

In the evaluation I saw the couple separately and together. When I saw them for an interpretive session, they brought their one-month-old adopted infant, and I was therefore able to see their physical awkwardness. Mrs. T held Tammy straight out from her body, balanced on the edge of her lap with Tammy's feet crowded in her genitals. She supported Tammy's head with one hand and offered the bottle like a syringe with the other. The stilted scene did not seem cozy or cuddling. While Mrs. T was tender, she handled the child at an unusual distance from her body. I felt I could imagine a similar awkwardness with her body and with her husband's body. When Dr. T took the baby, he seemed lost and overwhelmed, yet he was clearly overjoyed to hold her. The whole uncomfortable situation was not, however, the slightest bit unloving.

Setting Symptomatic and Dynamic Foci

I told the couple that they shared in the avoidance of sexuality because of a shared shakiness about themselves as sexual people. I had already encouraged Dr. T to tell his wife of his anxiety and shame about erectile failure (Strategy 6—nondynamic technique of advice-giving, in this instance, suggesting disclosure). He had done so, to their shared relief. I said now that underneath the performance anxiety that led to the erectile difficulty, there seemed to be a shared difficulty with desire, which Dr. T expressed for both of them. I suggested we begin sex therapy, with the option of turning to marital or individual work, working to further our alliance as I explained what I understood of the link between symptomatic and dynamic foci. I wondered silently if Dr. T would eventually need intensive psychotherapy or psychoanalysis. But as the couple was open, friendly, articulate, and trusting, I felt that my optimistic countertransference should predict a good treatment outcome. That feeling was quickly dashed.

The couple agreed readily to my suggestions for treatment. Before we could even begin treatment, Dr. T said he was scheduled to spend several weeks in an important postgraduate training program during the summer. This required getting them to examine our therapy relationship (Strategy 4). My own schedule dictated that I begin treatment then or else refer them to a colleague. When I told them this, Dr. T became obviously anxious. I spoke about the way this choice required him to face the defensive way he put his marriage second to professional interests. Mrs. T colluded with his avoidance. I could feel my own anxiety and disappointment when she encouraged him to go to the course. Using my own countertransference feeling as a clue to their fear of closeness I said I understood their shared fear of risking closeness. With this help, Mrs. T was able to say that she could hardly bear to ask him to stay in town and put their relationship first. She related this to her guilt about asking for anything for herself, just as she thought her mother would never offend her father by asking for consideration.

This encounter brought the first opportunity to use the nature of our relationship to their therapeutic advantage and to examine the countertransference to good effect.

Their difficulty in making the commitment to get on with treatment was a blow to my excessive optimism about them. At least I was now warned about the extent of their resistance and their false optimism that being nice, warm, reasonable, and nondemanding would be enough for their marriage. Now thinking that it might be difficult to hold them in treatment, I felt on my guard. After considerable distress, Dr. T finally decided to stay for therapy. Within hours of doing so he felt he had passed a crisis of commitment. He said, "I feel like a new man, almost as if I had just made a decision not to leave my wife. It's the decision that makes me different from my father."

The early sex therapy exercises of nonsexual touching gradually increasing to include sexual experience went well (Strategy 6, nondynamic elements). The couple relaxed with the protection from anxiety, and felt the loving feelings they had been missing. But when I assigned genital stimulation, Dr. T reported in several sessions that he could feel no arousal. I asked if he had any dreams, and he obliged promptly.

"Two nights ago I dreamt that a teacher I hardly knew at medical school came over and sat down to talk to me. He never would have then, all the more so because he was arrogant about students. That was the dream. I had read the day before that he had killed himself because he was depressed. That reminded me of my wife's brother, who had been depressed but did not kill himself. He got through it. We used to worry that her brother had an organic condition, just as I worry that my impotence is organic."

I said that since we knew from physical evaluation he had no organic basis for his sexual difficulty, we could look to the dream for help with causes. Mrs. T joined in, "I worry that he is uninterested because I'm just not sexually attractive." And she continued to elaborate on the feeling that she had a boyish figure. She had not had a menstrual period until the age of twenty-one, presumably because of physiological inhibition from the strenuous exercise of college athletics. "I never feel I can be sexy like a real woman. I never got there: I got stuck at fourteen."

I said to them, "You both feel your bodies are deficient. This contributes to your sexual fear and disinterest, Dr. T, and to your feeling, Mrs. T, that you cannot expect any better" (Past-Self dynamic interpretation). They then reassured each other about their mutual attraction to each other's bodies and other attributes.

I thought that they both seemed to be stuck developmentally in midadolescence, a period whose focus is the shaky sense of self as attractive and sexual. I said that we should not underestimate Dr. T's fear about the depth of the problem as evidenced by the life-and-death quality expressed in the dream. In addition, I continued working on strategies 4 and 5 by asking them about the difficulty in their current relationships, in their relationship to me as a therapist and to their shaky self-structures. I pointed out to them the anxiety about me as "the medical school teacher" of the dream. They shared a fear that I might be disdainful of them, and also that their condition would kill me off—making me unavailable to them just when they needed me to work on these issues.

The next two sessions used nonpsychodynamic techniques of prescribing pleasuring exercises and discussing how they went. The couple reported mutual enjoyment. Mrs. T had become easily aroused while Dr. T enjoyed the massage without arousal or erection. Even during the individual sessions of self-pleasuring that I assigned each of them, he had not felt arousal.

I continued to try to solve the puzzle of their stuckness by working in the countertransference. I had begun to worry. I was feeling the anxiety that they shared. The thought seized me that perhaps they would not get far, and that they were less easily treatable than I had thought. This is to say that in the countertransference, I began to absorb their doubts about whether I would help them. I thought that they could kill my efforts to help them. So now, in the countertransference, I was experiencing them as disappointing exciting objects—a complementary identification with the people by whom each of them had felt disappointed earlier in life (Racker 1968). I had the fantasy that they might leave treatment without improvement, and that, if they did, I would be relieved. To use the language of their symptoms, I felt "sick of treating them" and, in a way, lost my "desire" to do so. They had now recruited me, through their projective identification, to join in their shared unconscious view that sexual desire would bring them to a hopeless and potentially lethal impasse. So in this transference-countertransference replay of their internal problem, I now felt seduced by them as exciting objects into an empty hopefulness, and I felt let down by the failure that they also feared.

After the signs of impasse persisted through another few sessions, Dr. T then brought in a second dream. He began by assuring me that it was completely unrelated to the therapy, a warning that alerted me to the probability that it *was* related.

I was standing with ten or fifteen people in a large room with our backs to the wall. It occurred to me that we were going to be executed one by one. My first reaction was to be defeatist. I took off my jacket and rolled up my sleeves, just as I did a few minutes ago in here, and I thought, "If they are going to do it, I hope they'll hurry. Waiting is agony." They were demonstrating how people died by carbon monoxide poisoning, the same way as that teacher of mine in medical school died recently. They showed that you went to a bed covered with garbage bags and you had a gas mask with oxygen until it is changed to carbon monoxide. I realized they hadn't started, and it was a long time. I thought, "I don't want to die, so why not fight?" I asked to use the telephone. I called my mother, but there was no answer. My fight juices were finally going by now, so I just walked out the front door of the office. I took off my shirt because somehow it was a telltale sign, and I started to run. It felt terribly slow. After two or three minutes, I realized a motorcycle policeman was following me. I kept running for my life. I was running past strip places on a highway and gas stations which were closed because it was 2 A.M. The policeman caught up with me. I thought he was going to catch me, but just at that moment, a bad guy came out of a trailer and took a shot at the cop, who took off after him. So I got away.

This dream allowed for a full dynamic set of interpretations and was a vehicle for linking the sexual symptomatic focus and the dynamic one (Strategy 5). Dr. T's association left all three of us in no doubt that the execution he feared was the sexual exposure of the exercises (Strategy 4). Mrs. T was the one to notice that the odd method of execution—on a bed that felt threateningly smothering—recalled the assigned sexual exercises on the bed which she covered to protect it from being stained with oil. In the dream, he had called his mother as he had done in his youth when he felt helpless. He said, "Hers is the one number which hasn't changed all these years. I was counting on her. She should have been home in the middle of the night, but she wasn't there. So I ran for my life." I said that I was the cop he feared. He replied, "No doubt about that!" But Mrs. T joined in to add that she had also identified with the cop, since he often behaved toward her as if she was after him to do things. He talked about fearing being controlled by the demand for sex implied by me in giving exercises, by his wife in being attractive to him, and even by himself since he cared for her.

I asked him about the building in which the dream occurred. It reminded him of his junior high school, the one he had left to attend boarding school to escape his mother. But when he left home, he missed her terribly. When I said he might have felt he had to leave home as a young teenager because of discomfort with his recognition of his parents' sexual life, he replied, "Well, they did have a last child just after I left. In fact, we named Tammy after that sister."

The fear of the persecuting object was now out in the open in a way that fully connected the sexual symptom, the dynamic focus, and the transference, all seen in the dream, in Dr. T's acknowledged fear of sex, in his acknowledged fear of me, and in the person of their infant named for a child born of the parents' intercourse. The couple could also see the way their transference fear echoed the feelings they were trying to keep at bay between themselves (Self-Past-Other-Therapist connection).

I summed up my speculations about this dream in dialogue with the couple. Here I condense our conversation. Dr. T had felt threatened with annihilation by me as the representative of parental sexuality. He also felt afraid of being annihilated by sex itself and by the smothering engulfment of his wife, who now stood for the seductive and threatening part of his mother, but who stood at other times for the cop/bad parent. But he was also expressing (through projective identification) a fear of sex for both of them, for she was identified with the threat of sex that he felt in a more obvious way. He had been on the run, but early in their marriage and early in therapy, they both had. I ended by saying, "You can't get aroused when you're on the run, Dr. T, just as you, Mrs. T, couldn't get pregnant when you ran so much that you had no menses!" Although I was the cop and executioner in the treatment, it was Mrs. T who had been in that role up to now. She had accepted it because she felt no one would willingly have her.

In the exercise following this session, Dr. T was easily aroused, and the treatment followed a rapid course to successful completion. Dr. T found that he was able to relax through any periods of anxiety he felt, and progressively his anxiety and fear receded. Mrs. T also found it progressively easier to avoid backing off lest she be seen as the cop. The couple continued on to a new level of integration of their sexual and emotional intimacy.

This couple got what they came for in therapy. Nevertheless, during termination there were moments of anxiety about whether they could maintain their progress because of the pain of the loss of giving up their former adjustment. This distancing from each other sexually, which they had maintained over the first year of their marriage, had allowed them to enjoy each other's company like a fond and sexually unthreatened brother and sister. Now they worried about whether they could manage a new intimacy. Nevertheless, they said they were willing to take their chances, knowing they could come back to therapy. They brought their daughter, Tammy, with them to the last meeting. She made the perch at the end of her mother's knee a throne from which to command parental attention and joy—a giggling three-month-old with loving and physically more confident parents. There were traces of the awkwardness from two months before, but the exchange between Tammy and her parents had a new, lively rhythm (Strategy 8—a new end for old experience).

The couple's loving relationship and their motivation allowed them to work through their shared problem and their individual contributions to it quickly but thoroughly, taking back individual projective identifications through the improvement of their physical and emotional partnership. We worked on the symptomatic focus of their shared loss of sexual desire through interpretation of dynamic elements of overlapping areas of their internalized worlds, especially that of shaky sexual identification and low self-esteem in regard to sexual functioning.

Follow-Up

I heard from the Ts on two occasions. First, I got an announcement of a birth from them eighteen months after termination. There, pictured with his doting parents and twenty-three-month-old sister, was a baby boy. The note from Mrs. T said, "We never expected this would happen. Thanks for your help!"

Then, three years later Mrs. T came up to me at a theater. She asked to speak to me for a moment, and said that she just wanted me to know that she thought of me often. They had been able to conceive yet another child, and their marriage had remained solid and loving. Treatment had turned their life around.

CONCLUDING SUMMARY

These two cases illustrate the use of the dual focus on symptoms and on psychodynamics in the conduct of object relations brief therapy and the use of the transference-countertransference matrix to link dynamic elements— the past, the self, internal objects—to the here-and-now of the relationship with the therapist. This linking activity clearly distinguishes this mode of brief therapy even when therapy also has a supportive quality by focusing on symptom relief, and even when the therapy draws a significant amount of technique from the nondynamic therapies, as we illustrated by sex therapy in the case of Dr. and Mrs. T and by the cognitive-behavioral techniques with Ronald. Derived from theories mainly tested in long-term therapy, object relations brief therapy is a sophisticated way of relating to and treating clients, a powerful tool for change and growth.

REFERENCES

Balint, M., P. H. Ornstein, and E. Balint. 1972. *Focal Psychotherapy*. London: Tavistock.

Barber, J. P., and P. Crits-Christoph. 1991. Comparison of the brief dynamic therapies. In *Handbook of Short-Term Dynamic Psychotherapy*, pp. 323–55. New York: Basic Books.

Bennett, M. J. 1989. The catalytic function in psychotherapy. *Psychiatry* 52:351–64.

Bion, W. R. 1967. *Second Thoughts*. London: Heinemann.

Bollas, C. 1987. *The Shadow of the Object.* New York: Columbia University Press.

Bowlby, J. 1969. *Attachment and Loss. Volume 1: Attachment.* New York: Basic Books.

———. 1973. *Attachment and Loss. Volume 2. Separation: Anxiety and Anger.* New York: Basic Books.

———. 1980. *Attachment and Loss. Volume 3. Loss: Sadness and Depression.* New York: Basic Books.

Budman, S. H. 1990. The myth of termination in brief therapy: Or it ain't over till it's over. In *Brief Therapy: Myths, Methods, and Metaphors*, ed. J. K. Zeig and S. G. Gilligan, pp. 206–18. New York: Brunner/Mazel.

Budman, S. H., and A. S. Gurman. 1988. *Theory and Practice of Brief Therapy.* New York: Guilford.

Cummings, N. A. 1990. Brief intermittent psychotherapy throughout the life cycle. In *Brief Therapy: Myths, Methods, and Metaphors*, ed. J. K. Zeig and S. G. Gilligan, pp. 169–84. New York: Brunner/Mazel.

Davanloo, H., ed. 1980. *Short-term Dynamic Psychotherapy.* New York: Jason Aronson.

Dicks, H. V. 1967. *Marital Tensions.* London: Karnac.

Fairbairn, W. R. D. 1952. *Psychoanalytic Studies of the Personality.* London: Routledge and Kegan Paul.

Greenberg, J. R., and S. A. Mitchell. 1983. *Object Relations in Psychoanalytic Theory.* Cambridge: Harvard University Press.

Guntrip, H. 1969. *Schizoid Phenomena, Object Relations and the Self.* New York: International Universities Press.

Hoglend, P. 1993a. Personality disorders and long-term outcome after brief dynamic psychotherapy. *Journal of Personality Disorders* 7(2): 168–81.

———. 1993b. Transference interpretations and long-term change after dynamic psychotherapy of brief to moderate length. *American Journal of Psychotherapy* 47(4): 494–507.

Horowitz, M. J., C. Marmar, J. Krupnik, et al. 1984. *Personality Styles and Brief Psychotherapy.* New York: Basic Books.

Klein, M. 1975a. *Love, Guilt and Reparation and Other Works 1921–1945.* London: Hogarth.

———. 1975b. *Envy and Gratitude and Other Works (1946–1963).* New York: Delacorte.

Langs, R. 1973. *The Technique of Psychoanalytic Psychotherapy*, vol. 1. New York: Jason Aronson.

Malan, D. H. 1963. *A Study of Brief Psychotherapy.* London: Tavistock.

———. 1976. *The Frontier of Brief Psychotherapy.* New York: Plenum.

Ogden, T. H. 1994. *Subjects of Analysis.* Northvale, NJ: Jason Aronson.

Pine, F. 1990. *Drive, Ego, Object, and Self: A Synthesis for Clinical Work.* New York: Basic Books.

Piper, W. E., A. S. Joyce, M. McCallum, and H. F. A. Azim. 1993. Concentration and correspondence of transference interpretations in short-term psychotherapy. *Journal of Consulting and Clinical Psychology* 61(4): 586–95.

Racker, H. 1968. *Transference and Countertransference.* New York: International Universities Press.

Scharff, D. E. 1982. *The Sexual Relationship*. London: Routledge and Kegan Paul, reprinted Northvale, NJ: Jason Aronson, 1998.

Scharff, D. E., and E. F. Birtles. 1994. From *Instinct to Self: Selected Papers of W. R. D. Fairbairn, Vols. 1 and 2*. Northvale, NJ: Jason Aronson.

Scharff, D. E., and J. S. Scharff. 1991. *Object Relations Couple Therapy*. Northvale, NJ: Jason Aronson.

Scharff, J. S. ed. 1994. *The Autonomous Self: The Work of J. D. Sutherland*. Northvale, NJ: Jason Aronson.

Scharff, J. S., and D. E. Scharff. 1992. *Scharff Notes: A Primer of Object Relations Therapy*. Northvale, NJ: Jason Aronson.

———. 1998. *Object Relations Individual Therapy*. Northvale, NJ: Jason Aronson.

Stadter, M. 1996. *Object Relations Brief Therapy*. Northvale, NJ: Jason Aronson.

Steenbarger, B. N. 1994. Duration and outcome in psychotherapy: An integrative review. *Professional Psychology: Research and Practice* 25:111–19.

Strupp, H. H., and J. L. Binder. 1984. *Psychotherapy in a New Key: A Guide to Time-Limited Dynamic Psychotherapy*. New York: Basic Books.

Winnicott, D. W. 1965. *The Maturational Processes and the Facilitating Environment*. New York: International Universities Press.

———. 1971. *Therapeutic Consultations in Child Psychiatry*. New York: Basic Books.

———. 1977. *The Piggle: An Account of the Psychoanalytic Treatment of a Little Girl*. Madison, CT: International Universities Press.

31

Containing Anxiety with Divorcing Couples

Carl Bagnini

Instead of being treated as a developmental challenge from which recovery is possible, divorce may be experienced as an unmanageable persecutory object, both for the partners of a broken marriage and for their couple therapist. Divorcing spouses or partners may torment and persecute each other with their hurt, ambivalence, and lost hope. Then the couple relationship appears devoid of any good, and yet the partners with their deep unconscious attachment pursue the "forever" dream. Fused by hate, loss, disappointment, and betrayal, the partners are unable to detach or differentiate. They insist on defending themselves righteously against the accusations of the dying marriage and the disappointed spouse. In a symbiotic partnership or a long marriage with children, the unconscious terror of ending and aloneness prevents exploration and resolution.

Couple therapists may agonize over raging couples who struggle over whether to stay together. Emotion-laden sessions are the norm in working with couples on the brink. Their disturbances press hard on us, as we experience the insanity of love gone wrong. Divorce is a painful outcome for us, too, even though we are more individuated than the partners in the couple relationship. We can use our training to help us deal with loss and dread, and we can think ahead. We can contain our experience, and yet we may long for the moment after they exit the office, so that we can begin our recovery. It is so difficult to help them let go.

Termination anxiety accompanies work with a terminal marriage, and it affects the therapist and the couple. Fear of the end of a marriage brings

447

harshness to the therapy process. Angry protest precedes acceptance, which cannot be arrived at without going through a mourning process. Mourning the lost marriage is difficult to do with the spouse who is about to be lost, and with the couple therapist who is also about to become a lost object. The pain is often too great for the couple to stay with the therapist they originally chose as the one they hoped could help them save their marriage. Couples in a divorce mode seldom stay long enough in couple therapy to grieve their loss so as to move on to individual lives with confidence and understanding of their vulnerabilities.

In cases of divorce, loss of love brings with it a cruel and persecuting superego. Unprepared for dealing with the demise of their wished-for marriage, a couple feels pain and persecutory anxiety. Suddenly the parting spouses have to learn skills that they did not expect to need. They need therapy to adapt to dashed expectations and prepare for the future. Some couples feel so damaged by the time they get to the therapist that they cannot undertake the therapy task. Others can work to detoxify the malignant projective matrix as they mourn the loss of the good and bad parts of the marriage and re-own the parts of the self that had been projected into the spouse.

Some couples arrive for treatment obviously at the brink of marital dissolution. Their verbal attacks are dramatic, unrelenting, violent, and sometimes irrational. Yet, surprisingly, hard work sometimes salvages the relationship. Other couples are rational and cooperative. They seem to respond well in therapy, only to reveal that they are one step from indifference, a death knell for marriage. Detachment of affect implies an emotional separation of long duration without a formal notice. Love is indeed gone.

Some couples present for therapy when one spouse emphasizes the other's vulnerable personality. The individual identified as sick is placed in the therapist's care for the day when the complaining spouse vacates the home. Other couples initially appear to be very much intact, with just a few problems to be worked with, but when one spouse begins to change for the better, a deeper malignancy emerges. The unfamiliar new behavior disturbs the projective identificatory system of the marriage and the marriage deteriorates, despite the therapist's Herculean efforts.

When there is individual growth in one spouse's ability to relate and be intimate, the other spouse experiences an unwelcome jolt in the system. The integrity of the unconscious object relations set of the marriage has now been disrupted. An unexpected new good experience in treatment creates a deep disturbance, as there is now the possibility of reliable dependency. Massive schizoid defenses are mobilized against it. When one spouse becomes self-directed and self-defining, the borderline spouse is torn apart with envy and attacks the possibility of integration. Further individual breakdown then sabotages movement into the depressive position. In other couples, the spouse who longed for improvement in the partner, and finally gets it, cannot accept it because of resentment at how long it took. Sometimes change is too little or too late. Sometimes hope is too painful to bear, for fear of renewed disappointment.

CLINICAL ILLUSTRATIONS OF DIVORCING COUPLES

Some of the examples discussed here include the older woman being left; the baby as savior; being at the ex-spouse's service; and the young woman's folly of forgiveness.

The Older Woman Being Left

Anne called in deep distress. She told me that she had been married to Bob for thirty-five years, and that they are the parents of three successful out-of-the-home children. Three weeks ago, she said, Bob announced that he wanted out of the marriage. He seemed so much in a hurry to get out that she wondered if he had someone else.

Now, on the phone, Anne is close to being out of control. She tells me she is frightened, desperate, clutching herself to hold herself together, her entire existence at stake. All her life she had been taken care of by Bob. They have done everything together—child rearing, business failures and great successes, and now this, an earthquake. She needs help. She says she is willing to do anything to save the marriage and will come in immediately. She is sure Bob will be motivated to come in to "help her get therapy for the marriage." Anne shows no awareness of the implications of stating Bob's motive in this way. I schedule an emergency appointment for Bob and Anne to see me that evening.

As they talk in my office, I see that Bob is self-assured, in control, calm, and articulate. Anne is wide-eyed, high strung, painfully tearful from the start, obviously in shock. Bob restates what Anne related on the phone: he is there for her, he wants to help her through this, but he has reached a decision and wants to move things along as soon as possible.

"Why so fast?" I ask.

"Because I am fifty-six years old and I don't want to waste time. I do still love Anne, and I know she is a good person, but I don't want to be married to her anymore."

This sounds as if Bob is simply dealing with a solution to his personal anxiety over aging, as if it has nothing to do with Anne or the quality of their marriage.

So, I inquire about prior marital problems in this long marriage. Anne reveals she had an affair twelve years ago. When Bob found out about this he had felt persecuted by the images of her involvement with another man and had become violently disturbed. They went together for counseling. After only two sessions they left with the advice to try and get past it. They tell me they never spoke of it again. I note that they are talking about it now with me, in the first session of this, the next treatment opportunity. I ask how they could avoid talking about such an important sign of trouble since then until now. Calmer now, Anne volunteers that there was no sex in the affair: she got to the motel but she couldn't go through with it. Sex wasn't the primary motive for her. I nod for her to continue. Bob is staring at her. She looks away, then at Bob, and tells me sadly that he never believed that she didn't have sex. Bob says he thought that she must have had sex with her lover because she didn't initiate sex in the marriage. Anne firmly blocks the discussion of problematic sex, defensively pressing the point that Bob was so tired with work problems that she thought he needed to sleep. Avoiding this for now, I ask if they differed on other issues, or needs in the marriage, and any other disturbances they never got past.

They continue telling me about their roles in the marriage—he the financial provider and protector, she the home-based provider and child-rearing parent. Anne tearfully relates that she has no other skills, that she is nothing without Bob! He answers with a limp reassurance that she will be okay, because they can sell the house, and the settlement should be quick and easy. I am thinking to myself that he hasn't heard her at all. I ask Anne if she is ready for difficult discussions or decisions. She responds that the room is spinning, this is so fast. I intervene, saying to Bob that if he insists on going this fast harm may be done and a backlash may follow. He nods, saying that he can see how upset Anne is. I ask if there is anyone else in his life that he might be in a hurry to join.

I look at Bob, waiting for him to answer my loaded question. He doesn't look at me. He doesn't answer. Anne says she received an anonymous phone call telling her Bob has a woman in Dallas, but Bob says that the call must have been from a business enemy trying to make trouble. In the face of uncertainty about any hope of reconciliation, I ask if they could they agree to a slowing down of the separation process to give time for thinking about what led to their current crisis, whether Bob wants a new relationship, and how they can adjust to the changes.

Bob says he will come if it will help Anne, but he insists that he wants out of the marriage. He remains calm, self-contained, and adamant. I tell them that "coming to therapy for Anne" will lead to ending the marriage. Anne says she wants to come back anyway to understand what is happening. I close the session by mentioning that thirty-five years together means that much has transpired and needs to be reviewed, and that each of their futures depends on learning as much as possible about themselves in the intimate and sexual relationship of this marriage. We could determine whether they could accomplish this together, or not, in which case individual therapy would be a good option.

I wanted to assess if this was going to be marriage therapy or divorce therapy, a consult to determine individual therapy needs, or no basis for therapy at all. Based on Bob's attitude, I felt little optimism that they could use couple therapy to recover their marriage, or that Bob would accept individual therapy, but I hoped to slow him down a bit. Bob experienced this offer of sessions as an opportunity for relieving himself of a guilty burden and then getting on with his life. Anne saw it as an opportunity to prevent the fragmentation of her self, and perhaps to change Bob's mind. My approach offered time, space, and a holding environment in which Anne might be able to confront the enormity of her plight, or at least reduce the immediacy of her impending loss, and Bob could review his decision without panic. There was still a chance that I might be allowed to help them detoxify the persecutory effects of Bob's lack of sexual desire, Anne's old affair, and the threat of divorce itself.

Guilt and fear complicate the decision to divorce. A spouse may worry that the spouse being left will break down, or become so livid that violence could ensue in the form of suicide, or destructive legal attacks. Here the persecutory superego exerts its wrath over the lost love object (Schecter 1979). The ego is under attack. Previous holding that was good enough in the long marriage is insufficient to sustain a more benign adjustment to its termination. The dependent wife cannot rely on her husband anymore except to the extent that he provides for her financially. If the husband was the ego ideal, the wife being left can no longer count on association to him to maintain her self-esteem.

When the fears of loss of income, loss of companionship, loss of social standing, and loss of self-esteem are intense, narcissistic clinging of one spouse to the other may last for months or years. Even after a legal separation and divorce the persistence of this phenomenon cannot be underestimated.

The Baby as Savior

Dick and Sue had been unhappy in a childless marriage of twenty-four years. They had been in marital therapy for two years without improvement in how they felt because they had little in common to work with toward reconciliation. Termination of the marriage and of treatment seemed inevitable. Sue no longer loved Dick. Nevertheless, she insisted that he give her a baby, even though significant marital problems had not been worked through, including her infidelities, his difficulty in providing financially, and their problems with intimacy and sexuality. Dick refused to provide her with the necessary sperm.

Within three months of moving out, Sue showed up unannounced at the couple's former residence to tell him that she would return to the marriage, if he would relent and give her the baby she required. Dick's life was beginning to take shape, while Sue's was bogged down in continuing anxieties and insecurities, and a desperate longing to have life from the man she could not love.

Partners who cannot love each other may put all their hope into a baby. Unmetabolized aspects of the couple's projective identificatory system get projected into the fetus. In the case of Dick and Sue, the fetus remained a battleground of longing and withholding like the marriage itself. Sometimes a couple may proceed to have a live child who becomes the receptacle for unmanageable parts of the couple relationship. The child is then treated as the elusive but cherished part or as the hated, rejecting aspect of the frustrating spouse. This is obviously a burden on the child of unhappy marriage or of divorce and induces problematic behavioral changes that become autonomous. It is also a burden on the couple whose efforts to deal directly with their marital or postdivorce relationship are diverted to responding to the needs of their child.

At the Ex-spouse's Service

Tony had moved out of the home he had shared with his wife, Alice. After the separation, Tony continued to be available to help Alice prepare and physically set up her art shows, work for which she had had no motivation during the marriage. Alice looked well, she was working out for the first time in her life, she was productive, and her outlook was improved. In contrast to being dependent when she was married, Alice was now on her way to an independent new life without Tony.

Tony's disillusionment with his marriage had led to a long-term affair with a younger, livelier, and more self-directed woman. This had increased his withdrawal and further fueled Alice's depression. Their relationship had clearly been unfulfilling over many years and Tony's decision to end the marriage was final.

Although there was little evidence of love and devotion between them from the earliest days of the marriage, Tony continued, for some time after the separation, to cling to Alice in the role of her assistant. Guilty about leaving her and curious about how she was doing without him, he wanted to help and feel needed.

Couples like Tony and Alice are fearful of individuation. The spouses look after each other, but without passion or growth potential. When one of them leaves, it may be difficult to give up the parental caregiver aspect of the former marital role. Even after divorce, the couple may continue to share the unconscious long-term assumption that the only form of couple is one consisting of an anaclitic, infantile dependency, the parent and child roles oscillating between them. If the abandoned wife copes, the husband who separated from her can't believe that she doesn't need him as before. Her individuation is felt as a psychic injury to him. This may lead to an unhealthy return to the marriage in a caregiver role so as to be reassured of the value of the self.

The Young Woman's Folly of Forgiveness

Rachel, a thirty-six-year-old woman in a three-year marriage to Saul, eventually separated from him after two years of marital therapy. She realized that she had married him mainly to keep her parents happy. Her mother was physically and emotionally abusive (and so was Rachel's sister) and her father was deeply depressed. Her parents' relationship was readily destabilized by any stress and so Rachel acceded to her father's request that she ignore and forgive the ongoing emotional and physical abuse heaped on her as a child by her mother and older sister so that her protests did not cause trouble between her parents. As an adult, Rachel continued to protect her parents at the sacrifice of her own needs by marrying Saul because he was a nice, cute, Jewish accountant who was adored by her family and whose presence kept her parents calm.

Soon Saul neglected Rachel's needs and withdrew from her demands as her father had done. The neglect and withholding of the past were repeated. Her fantasy marriage quickly evaporated. As she got closer to divorce, physical symptoms emerged as if the clamor of protest in her body could no longer be quieted by her association with Saul. Although not an abusive person, Saul nevertheless represented the abuse that Rachel had not been allowed to protest.

After the separation there was tremendous pressure on Rachel to forgive Saul, to see only his good points, and to reunite with him. On the one hand Saul asked Rachel for forgiveness (both a stunning reversal of the childhood pattern in that he asked for this for himself and not for her parents' sake, and yet a repetition in that yet again Rachel is required to forgive to keep the peace), but on the other hand he continued to manipulate her emotionally and to side with her parents who obviously preferred him to her. The therapist was also pressured by phone calls from the mother requesting him to bring the therapy to a happy ending, by getting the daughter to give up her crazy ideas and forgive her husband, and by extension give her parents absolution. Keeping her marriage would require Rachel's constant forgiveness, and she was no longer willing to subordinate her needs in favor of others.

This case illustrates the way that the family's projective matrix may exert a malignant effect on a couple. Marrying to earn a parent's love and staying married to keep both parents together are heavy burdens on a marriage. Marital therapy allows reworking of family dynamics so that the spouses can move out of the projective matrices of their families of origin, deal with the persecutory objects internal to the psyche, and develop autonomy. Only when a spouse is separate from the projections of the past and recognizes the separate other in the spouse can love flourish.

THE PERSECUTORY CHALLENGE TO THE THERAPIST

Few situations are as challenging or persecuting for couples and for therapists as the issue of divorce. It draws into the consulting room our personal value system concerning monogamy and our theories about what makes or breaks a marriage. When faced with the possibility of the end of a marriage, our countertransference may be concordant with the feelings of the children. We may be angry or afraid as if our parents are failing us, or we may grieve for our failure to keep them together. The painful prospect of being involved in a great loss stirs us to the core. Our psychoanalytic paradigm is no insurance against this. Simply tracing each spouse's unconscious precursors of marital conflict and making the individual's unconscious conscious are not sufficient as therapeutic approaches. We have to analyze the interpersonal situation of the couple relationship. Working with here-and-now realities in marriage is as important as dealing with past traumas, neglect, and failed attachments that have influenced premarital life and mate choices. Such issues as hope, subculture, religion, devotion, will, loyalty, and spirituality need to be included when we are exploring couple resilience and potential for reworking the relationship.

We ask couples: To what extent is there a narcissistic preoccupation with the self and its right to be served by the spouse? Is personal sacrifice seen as a restriction of individual needs and strivings? To what extent are communal issues, or the needs of the group, including the family, a major concern for one or the other spouse? The balance between the needs of the individual, the marriage, the nuclear family, and the families of origin is central to the future of the marital institution itself. In one case keeping the family together was the driving force for the husband to remain married, due to his ethnic and cultural values. The wife was not of his background and could have taken the action leading to divorce, but she had accommodated to his views about family values. Shame was a powerful motive for maintaining this loveless marriage.

The literature abounds with discussion of the effects of divorce on children of different ages, the legal ramifications, the economic impact, the problems of remarriage and blending families, and the reactions of extended family members and friends. Not so available to us especially in the psycho-analytic literature are the interpersonal and intrapsychic aspects of marital dissolution, the shared object relations that must be deconstructed in a divorcing process, and discussion of the therapist's role in the process of growth and recovery.

The psychoanalytic literature lacks details of these phenomena because of the clinician's pain in studying and staying with the lingering process of marital dissolution. Therapists need concepts to contain the potentially devastating effects of the fallout of a failed relationship, but there is scant information in the literature. The lack of theory follows from an avoidance of admitting to and thinking about the therapist's pain. With little preparation from psychoanalytically informed training, we are challenged to think our own way through and keep our egos intact when feeling persecuted during such difficult work. Suffering is to be expected in terminations of all types. In dealing with the regression inherent in the divorcing couple, we find ourselves quite alone when we need the most support.

Being so close to couples puts us uncomfortably close to their loss and sense of failure. We may feel like ejecting them from treatment under pressure from our internal objects if our losses resonate with the couple's loss. Each of us has personal and professional feelings that color the extent to which we can approach the object relations of divorce. We may not have mastered all these feelings, but we can work with them if we feel supported. Too few analytic therapists come together to discuss and explore these issues, and so there is not a good containing environment in which therapists can find help with processing their experience.

LOSS AND MOURNING IN DIVORCE

Since divorce is a form of termination, an understanding of loss and mourning may be of help in contemplating the end of a marriage and the end of a couple's treatment. In his paper "Mourning and melancholia," Freud described the process of acceptance of loss at times of grief: "Each single one of the memories and situations of *expectancy* which demonstrates the libido's attachment to the lost object is met by the verdict of *reality* that the object no longer exists; and the ego, confronted as it were with the question whether it shall share this fate, is persuaded by the sum of the narcissistic satisfactions it derives from being alive to sever its attachment to the object that has been abolished" (Freud 1917, p. 255, author's italics).

In her paper "A contribution to the psychogenesis of manic-depressive states," Melanie Klein (1935) wrote that the loss of good objects is a major threat to our security, and fear of this loss is the source of great pain and conflict. Alteration in the external circle of family objects produces insecurity in the internal objects. Threats to good internal objects leave the child feeling filled up with bad, persecutory objects and fears of annihilation of the self. Depending on the nature of the internal objects children and adults can experience manic and depressive responses to anxiety, related to fantasies and affects associated with the internalized mother, and colored by whether she was experienced as helpful or revengeful, loving or angry.

During our development as therapists we have internalized objects based on our experiences with our own internal mothers, our teachers, our therapists, and former clients. These internal objects have attributes that may be dangerous and unpleasant or consistent and helpful. Dealing with divorce in couple therapy, we are faced mainly with the more dangerous and unpleasant ones. We experience sorrow, distress, and feelings associated with failure such as low self-esteem arising from perceptions of ourselves as unhelpful objects.

Any leave-taking regenerates loss and mourning issues for us. Even the cases that we wish would leave treatment cause us pain, since we feel persecuted by our own hate of a particular couple or divorcing partner. We feel guilty to be relieved of the burden of some couples. We are alive, witnessing a death, even though a necessary one if the individual spouses are to develop by beginning anew. If so much of marriage is dependent on a search for lost objects, then when that marriage breaks up, it becomes another lost object compounding a previous, and perhaps deeper, loss. What was never achieved in the marriage cannot be recovered in the marriage, or in the divorce.

During the divorcing process, infantile loss and the painful layering of reactions to frustrated hopes are experienced again. Conscious and unconscious attachments are severed for a second time. No wonder couples often fly into manic attempts to salvage what they can. The denial of psychic reality allows the attachment to persist in the face of tremendous difficulty. In despair, a spouse may become depressed with suicidal feelings, while the other may act out through extramarital flight. Murder or suicide end growth for spouses dramatically, but more commonly unresolved grief cripples future growth in an ordinary way. Defenses, including omnipotence, avoidance, and even idealization may continue to prevent total collapse and assuage one spouse's terror of the depressive position.

HATRED, SPLITTING, AND AMBIVALENCE IN DIVORCE

If hatred of the object and splitting instead of ambivalence dominate the separation process, hate will not then be available to the self for use in differentiation, separation, new realistic boundary setting, and mourning loss. Instead, the hated spouse or therapist takes on an entirely bad persona, in order to preserve the self as good. This is a precarious bargain since the distribution of all-good and all-bad can shift, and then suddenly it is the self that feels bad. Splitting in which only good or bad can be tolerated at one time leads to destructive actions alternately toward the self and the formerly loved partner. While these dynamics frequently accompany divorce to some degree they usually resolve over time to a more mature state of ambivalence. In object relationships dominated by persecutory superego functioning that has not been resolved in therapy, the therapist notes with regret that the primitive and punitive affects will continue to affect individual and family development long after the divorce is final. This knowledge propels us to keep divorcing couples in therapy long enough for them to learn as much as possible about themselves and the nature of the relationship they created so that mistakes in fit are not repeated. Sensitivity to the clients' capacity to endure this type of soul-searching is essential so that we judge correctly the moment when enough is enough. Otherwise the result will be abandonment of treatment, rather than a mature integration of the feelings of love and hate, with resolved grief over past losses and hope for an easier future.

WORKING WITH THE THERAPIST'S SELF

If we have too much anxiety about endings and too much grief about losing divorcing couples from treatment, we may rush them into premature endings. On the other hand, we may deter them from making the decision to end the marriage by rehashing marriage dynamics so as to avoid blaming ourselves for abandoning the couple. We may have difficulty letting the spouses leave each other and us if our self-esteem is insecure. Our professional competence is shaken by termination due to unanticipated divorce if we are not always prepared for that eventuality, even though we should be because we know that it is not our responsibility to save marriages or to break them up. We simply help couples learn, and they are ultimately responsible for the fate of their relationship. Yet, in the throes of flawed couple relating, we may be drawn into an attempt to improve holding so that we do not face the narcissistic injury of not being able to help the couple hold on to their commitment. We may seek object constancy in the face of object sorting and splitting in the couple. In this phase of therapy, the splitting may be a necessary part of dissolution of the marriage partnership and we must learn to accept it.

It is painful for us to recognize that as we succeed in our approach, the couple fails in the marriage. The loss of a meaningful relationship with one couple can cause a crisis of confidence in our professional life. We may obsess over the case. Have we done all we could? Do we ever know for sure? We may turn against ourselves through self-deprecation, self-abasement, or depression. We wonder, question, analyze our reactions, and if necessary seek consultation to ensure that we maintain an impartial sensitivity to the needs of both the divorcing partners.

Divorcing couples force us to work on ourselves, grow in maturity and acceptance, face loss, and confront reality. We do not always welcome the variety of experiences that we have to contend with in the pursuit of a therapeutic ending. We are forced to revisit the unworked through parts of our internal world as the loss of love reaches its emotional peak. The struggle between the benign and persecutory elements in the object relations of divorcing clients evokes our own struggles. The couple's shame, guilt, and low self-esteem resonate with our own. The divorcing partners may regress and attempt to kill off what was once loved, and that may include annihilating us. We learn to accept and forgive ourselves when some marriages, and some treatments, fail.

Comfort with the therapeutic process of the divorcing couple is at best a momentary accomplishment. Detoxifying the persecutory object of divorce is not an easy matter, but it can be achieved by containing the persecutory super ego affects, understanding termination anxiety, and metabolizing the attacks on love as the couple leaves the partnership with each other and with us.

REFERENCES

Freud, S. 1917. Mourning and melancholia. *Standard Edition* 14:243–58.

Klein, M. 1935. A contribution to the genesis of manic depressive states. *Love, Guilt and Reparation and Other Works, 1921–1945*, pp. 344–69. London: Hogarth Press and the Institute of Psycho-Analysis, 1975.

Martin, E., and R. Schurtman. 1985. Termination anxiety as it affects the therapist. *Psychotherapy* 22(1): 92–96.

Schecter, D. E. 1979. *The Loving and Persecuting Superego*. Presidential Address. William Alanson White Psychoanalytic Society, New York, May 23, 1979.

32

The Splitting Function of the Dyad and Containment of the Couple

Yolanda de Varela

From time to time an individual therapist working with an adult patient hears the child's desperate cry for the mother. Similarly, the couple therapist hears that cry when one member of the couple tries to re-create a lost love and fails. The disappointed one then turns to the therapist in a last-ditch effort to refind the mother/infant experience. From this moment, a struggle starts between a desirable, healthy, mature inclusive couple relationship with an equal partner, and a regressive, symbiotic exclusive dyadic relationship with a mother substitute. Will the couple survive, or will the long-lost dyad take over? Will splitting overwhelm the containing possibilities of the couple relationship?

Like individual psychoanalytic psychotherapy, object relations couple therapy is an in-depth approach. The couple is conceived of as a holding environment for the family and as a mental space in which the partners can contain (reflect upon and process) their various past and present feelings, experiences, and expectations, and so reach for growth, connection, and autonomy (Scharff and Scharff 1991). The best results in individual treatment came when "the self was felt to have brought both parents back internally into a good relationship" (Sutherland 1989, p. 174). In couple therapy, the best result is achieved when the couple resolves preoedipal attachments and the partners bring their respective internal couples into good alignment. When the relationship is dominated by needs for gratification, the couple creates multiple dyadic interactions of an exciting and ultimately frustrating nature. These repetitive dyads are limited in scope and cannot evolve to become a satisfying, complex, growth-promoting couple relationship. I have concluded that for adult partners in a relationship, the limited re-creation of the mother-infant dyad serves to gratify early longings, but only the fully realized couple relationship contains and holds together the process of growth, separation, and individuation.

When couple therapy fails, one of the partners may request psychotherapy. This eventuality raises many questions. What's the unconscious goal? Who is the desired object? Where is the transference located? Is it projected into the therapist's internal couple? What is the nature of the countertransference? Does the therapist identify with the lonely child excluded from the couple, and then join in the fantasy of a dyadic relationship with one of the spouses?

I present a case here in which I treated the couple and the wife. I call the couple Bob and Elaine. Bob had his own therapist, a medicating psychiatrist. I give details below from one individual session with Elaine and one couple therapy session to show the action of splitting and the formation of multiple dyads. Bob and Elaine used their individual internal couples destructively to split both their joint internal couple and the therapist's internal couple. I tried to facilitate neutral, nontraumatic psychological penetration of their psyches to lay the foundation for improving the couple's sexual intimacy. But on the way there, I became viewed in fantasy as the desired primal object, which then undermined the couple's integrity. I also show here how interpreting this and so repairing the internal couple led to individual integration and an improved couple relationship for Bob and Elaine.

THE THERAPIST'S NARCISSISM, PREOEDIPAL, OEDIPAL, AND SIBLING RIVALRY ISSUES

Behind the request for combined, concurrent treatment lie both a conscious need that is realistic and justified, and an unconscious plea for gratification. I had been seeing Bob and Elaine in couple therapy. When they wanted individual therapy for Elaine in addition to couple therapy, they asked me to treat her, too, because they lived in a small community with a limited availability of trusted therapists, and they already trusted my work. Acceding to their request, however, raised the danger that I might succumb to the fantasy that I was the only one who could help them. The therapist who is vaunted as special has farther to fall from grace. Having been warmly invited in, she may then be cruelly excluded from the couple. This evokes in the therapist a feeling of childlike longing to be part of the parental couple that echoes the couple's desire to be intimate. When the therapist is under the sway of a narcissistic, omnipotent feeling of having been chosen above all other therapists, she may find that her sense of being special resonates with the couple's narcissism. Her interpretations are then heard as signs of favoritism toward one of the partners, not as interpretations of couple conflict. The therapist becomes for herself, as well as for the couple, the *object of desire*. The stage is set for competition—between the partners, between therapist and colleagues, and between the couple's internal parental couples. From then on, the questions regarding who is better than whom, who has more than the other, and who is going to be left out, hang in the air as obstacles to the integration of the couple.

In a combined, concurrent treatment format, unconscious longing for the primary dyad, sibling rivalry issues, and competition to possess and impress the therapist permeate the sessions. This, however, is not a reason to refuse the request. In fact, the treatment format brings out the hidden force of dyadic splitting and makes it available for work. As both members of the couple fantasize about having primal homosexual or heterosexual relationships with the individual therapist of one of them, these fantasies compete with the couple's heterosexual relationship. Examining this in sessions with Bob and Elaine revealed the repetition of early conflicts and its impact on their coupling: Bob's rejection of his father due to a symbiotic relationship with his mother; and Elaine's fusion with her idealized father to repair damage done by her mother's rejection. These defensive dyads left over from childhood prevented separation, individuation, and dealing with reality, a huge impediment to growth and productivity. Bob and Elaine became an "as if" couple.

TRANSFERENCE, COUNTERTRANSFERENCE, AND THE OBJECT OF DESIRE

The therapist's countertransference responses are the main guide to understanding the couple's dynamics. Each member of the couple stirs up internalized object relations of different significant dyads and couples. Therapists' personal work on understanding themselves, modifying their internal object relations, and mourning losses is crucial. Otherwise the intimacy provided in individual and couple therapy can stir up in the therapists feelings of jealousy, longing, sadness, and anger related to their own former therapists, or envy for pleasant aspects of their patients' relationships with partners, parents, children, and grandparents. The therapist feels like an outsider to the couple and yet is filled with the feelings associated with projected exciting and rejecting objects that need containment.

When individual sessions complicate couple therapy, the partners have to abandon attachments to the primal dyad and mourn the loss of total possession of the therapist's focus in order to establish an internal working couple in good relationship with each other and with the therapist. There is a general fear among couple therapists that individual analysis endangers the couple therapy and that couple therapy compromises individual therapy. The couple therapist may indulge the wish for the dyad temporarily, but only in the service of the couple, not as a default option. The therapist encourages the dyad to give way to the emergence of a well-functioning and integrated couple by maintaining the primary stance toward the couple, and not the dyad.

There is a constant search, both by the therapist and the members of the couple, for the desired object. Then this desired past object must be let go and mourned to welcome a new way of relating, that of the couple. The dyadic relation to the desired object is a manifestation of the paranoid-schizoid position. As couple therapy progresses, therapist and couple negotiate the depressive position, and dyadic relating gives way to true couple functioning. This therapeutic work is impossible unless the therapist has had a good personal analysis, and carries inside a good internal couple (preferably realized as a good intimate personal relationship in the present as well), and especially, if this is a first case, has the help of a supervisor. Therapists need to be armed with a good range of internalized objects and a well-integrated internal couple to ward off the bad internal object relationships that will be located inside them by projective identification. Otherwise, the pain and longing is too much to bear. The capacity to internalize a couple with members in good relationship with each other gives the therapist a sense of internal peace that fosters therapeutic action (Sutherland 1989).

PENETRATION OR DESTRUCTION?

When couple therapy is proceeding in the paranoid-schizoid position, the therapist doubts the wisdom of the patients' decisions, and the patients respond to the same interpretation quite differently from one moment to another. In the case of combined, concurrent treatments, members of the couple often perceive the individual sessions as an attack on the couple or the partner who is left outside the dyad. The themes the couple brings to the session stir up repressed exciting and rejecting object relationships in the therapist, where they reverberate with her vulnerability to dyad formations. These repressed, split-off, and projected dyads are delivered into the treatment space where they can be examined and there shed light on the couple's current dynamics.

THE COUPLE

Bob and Elaine had been living together for the previous five years, and were now married. They were having great difficulty in developing feelings of well-being, intimacy, and sexual satisfaction. Bob was thirty years old and Elaine was twenty-seven. Through the years of working with them, I was torn between two extreme reactions: I felt filled with their sadness and feelings of abandonment, and I felt rejected and angry at them for not letting me in. The atmosphere was warm and cool, even in the same session. Sometimes I was eager to see them, and sometimes I felt loaded with feelings of futility and fatigue. Elaine's individual issues surfaced early in the treatment. She had recurrent symptoms of diarrhea and anxiety for which individual treatment was needed. She had had an unsuccessful experience in therapy years earlier, and now she adamantly refused to see anyone but me. Bob had been seeing a psychiatrist sporadically for medication and supportive sessions for some years. When Bob and Elaine bombarded me with their request that I see her individually, I explained the benefits and difficulties of a combined, concurrent treatment. Unfortunately, differences in professional technique made it impossible for me to have any communication with Bob's therapist—and this was to create another level of difficulty.

In individual sessions with Elaine I was faced with an impenetrable wall, while at the same time receiving a clear and desperate invitation to breach the wall and not leave her alone. A pattern developed: The day after a satisfactory containing and understanding session, an excluding, devaluing patient returned. The strong need to merge brought out her dread, and so she merged with some other object and excluded me from her internal world.

First Contact

Bob felt that he had done his part in individual therapy already. Now Elaine needed to do hers. He knew she would never seek help on her own, and that is why they had been in couple therapy. Elaine was shy and awkward around emotional issues. She could not express her feelings and she doubted her own intellectual capacity. She regarded Bob as the intellectual. Bob carried the narcissistic investment on behalf of the couple, and Elaine carried the devaluation.

Bob was the youngest in his family. He always felt that his mother invested more in his two older sisters than in him. He could not protest because he did not want to be called a "crybaby." He felt that he was a disappointment to his father, who would have liked him to be a surgeon like him. Bob had chosen to be a salesman, and now had his own small department store. He craved his father's approval but got criticism instead, and he reacted by doing the opposite of what his father wanted. Bob liked to think of himself as a solo person with little or no love and affection toward his parents or sisters.

Born overseas, Elaine moved here with her family when she was six years old. She described a happy childhood with all her needs met by her loving extended family. She felt sorry when her husband talked about his childhood, and she could not understand why his parents did not provide for his needs. She was aware that her family suppressed negative emotions, and she resented not being able to express her emotions with Bob. If she tried to, he took over her feeling; for example, if she were slightly tearful about something that happened to upset her, he would soon be sobbing about a tragic situation in his life. She would then swallow her tears and comfort him. She tended to transform her emotions into physical symptoms such as frequent diarrhea and migraine headaches, lack of sexual interest, and inability to have an orgasm.

Each partner suspected that the other one was interested in another love object. For example, Elaine had the fantasy that Bob was having an affair; Bob thought that Elaine would have preferred a man more like her father, with whom Bob could not compete. When Bob was single he had enjoyed good sex, especially when with a woman who wanted to be with him more than he wanted to be with her. Now that he was married to the woman he wanted, he did not have a passionate sexual life, and he missed that.

The Work

The couple greeted me warmly as if they had a good alliance with me, but actually they resisted my interpretations. Bob was openly skeptical. He reported on the couple sessions to his individual therapist, not as a way of integrating insight, but to get a second opinion on the couple and supervise my work. Bob looked to me not for understanding but for friendship and pity—which may have been what he found with his own therapist. He looked for me to mother him, and when that hope was dashed, he tried to make me fail, and so triumph over me. When he saw that his wife made faster progress in her therapy with me than he did with his therapist, he felt rejected and envious, as he had when his mother gave more to his sisters than to him. Bob had the fantasy that Elaine and I had formed a mother-daughter dyad that excluded him, and so he felt that he had lost a wife, a therapist, a mother, and a sister.

Elaine expressed her transference as a resistance—to talking, to having memories, and to free-associating. She disposed of my interpretations aggressively in the form of diarrhea, as if they were toxic. Having little to go on, I found myself guessing with her. While trying to make sense of her silence, I felt like an intruder inside her psyche. Many times, after what I considered empathic interpretations, she went blank, giving me the feeling that a heavy door had been closed in my face. She dealt with her anxieties by keeping busy all the time. Although she was always complaining of not having enough time for herself, she held two jobs, which filled the space and let her avoid thinking and feeling. Her relationship to an internal void was so strong that it prevented the formation of any couple vital enough to destroy this enervating connection.

Elaine's Dyadic Relationships

Elaine was the middle child of three, with an older sister and a younger brother. Born after her parents already had a daughter and would have preferred a son, she felt that she was a disappointment. Her mother doted on her eldest daughter, who married a well-known surgeon and attained the professional and social success that her mother had longed for herself. Being a foreigner, she was obsessed with feeling part of the culture and society of her new country. Elaine's youngest brother was valued as the only son and the carrier of the family name. Elaine felt invisible and unworthy of attention, especially in relation to her mother. Feeling ignored by her mother, Elaine turned to her father with whom she felt comfortable. She admired his erudition and his ability to support his family. She idealized him and the part of herself that belonged to him. She could not find any other man capable of reaching the pedestal on which she placed him.

Elaine knew that her siblings cared for her but she thought that they did not admire her. She thought that they regarded her as efficient and reliable, not intellectually capable. She could get angry more easily with them than with her parents, but she idealized them, too, at the cost of her own sense of worth.

Once she entered individual therapy, Elaine reinvented me as an idealized powerful parent on whom she could depend. She operated according to the fantasy that by merging with me, some of my knowledge or power would adhere to her. Thus, in her view, I was better and more understanding than her husband and his therapist: She could rely on me in a way she never could with her parents. But she did not show any real emotion toward me. It did not occur to her that I might value her in any way. She was just another case, another hour of work.

Bob's Dyadic Relationships

With no siblings and two daughters, Bob's father had hoped for a son, who would become a successful surgeon, be a leader in the professional field like him, take over his practice, and carry on the family name. When he did not fulfill his father's dream for him, Bob felt criticized by his father, a man who liked to have the last word. Bob in turn was highly critical of his father as an unfeeling and castrating man who did not inspire respect or love. Bob felt that his father devalued and ignored Bob's mother and his two daughters as well. Although Bob saw his father as incapable of expressing warm feelings to anyone, he had a dynamic and active relationship with him. He saw his mother as capable of expressing affection, but not to him. He rarely talked about her, and when he did, it was to devalue her. He said she was a nonentity. She regularly bought her daughters clothes and made sure they had everything they wanted, but the occasional gifts she bought for him were chosen on the spur of the moment, without knowledge of his needs or desires. Bob mentioned in passing that when his mother was pregnant with him, she was devastated by the death of her father, whom she had idealized, and named Bob after him. Bob was a pale shadow of the ghost of her father, and unlike his own father, too. Bob hated his oldest sister for being like his father, for being close to his mother, and for having everything she needed. She had the love of her mother, she was successful socially, she was a respected nutritionist, and he resented her every step of the way.

Bob split off his father, his mother, his wife, and myself as bad part-objects and projected all the goodness into his therapist, believing that he was the one who supported him and saved him from depression with magic pills. Bob's idealization of his therapist was seductive. I had the impression that his psychiatrist had identified with it. Bob let him know that it was from him that he received the good milk, the emotional and intellectual nourishment not offered by his parents and not accepted from me. If any of his relationships went bad, Bob called him for an appointment and got validation about himself, his attitude in the conflict, and the benefit of his good individual therapy—and no confrontation. Bob could not imagine me working with the psychiatrist like a parental couple concerned about his welfare and progress (and indeed it was not possible) because he could not bear to feel excluded from such a great couple. Bob could only pair us destructively by presenting my work in couple therapy as defective and collecting his therapist's supervisory responses, spoiling both the integrity of his individual therapy with him and his couple therapy with me. Thus the psychiatrist and I became a new internal dyad for Bob to attack and in which to get stuck.

Elaine's Individual Session: An Attack on Couples

The following vignette from an individual session with Elaine shows the splitting function of the primitive dyad with the effect that she placed me at the center of all her desires. She excluded any other good experience in her life outside therapy. She was preoccupied with fantasies about my private life. She resented any person connected to me, and she wanted to merge with me and eliminate any aspect of my life that did not involve her. She admired my clothes and hairdo, and wanted to become like me.

In the session that I describe, Elaine began by recounting the many times she had lost something valuable to someone else. She had lost her mother's admiration and love to her older sister. She lost her father's admiration to her more precious brother. Due to her sexual inhibitions, she lost her first boyfriend to a sexually attractive girl. She continued to suffer from exclusion in her current relationships, at school, in social events, and in her professional work, and, as if that were not enough to bear, she imagined the loss of her husband's fidelity.

Elaine could only get to the desired man through a woman—her mother, her boss's secretary, and her woman therapist, me. In couple therapy sessions Elaine expected me to talk to her husband for her. She used her mother to speak for her to her father and to her sister. At work, she communicated with her male boss through his secretary. She always found someone to talk for her, and so she made herself invisible. And finally, she met her husband while he was in a relationship with one of her women friends. She had no awareness of her aggression in taking something important away from the other woman and her hidden aggression in not speaking up for herself, but because of this disavowal and suppression of aggression, she felt guilty, ungrateful, and a fake. She felt depressed and deprived because she had been unable to receive love from anyone. And she was unable to give because it felt like giving to a mother who already had everything, including Elaine's idealized father. As soon as Elaine became aware of needy feelings toward me and began to accept what I had to offer, she became afraid of losing me. It seemed impossible that emotional closeness could be obtained without doing damage to the desired object.

Then Elaine told a dream: "Last night, I dreamt that I was diving deep in the ocean, and floating on top of me was a woman who invited me to have sex with her. I didn't want to do it, it seemed wrong, but she convinced me to do it. I didn't see her naked, nor did I feel her touching me. I only had a pleasurable feeling."

Her need to be attached to me was stirring up primal homosexual longings that frightened her but also brought her pleasure. I felt that her fear of losing me was driving a homosexual penetration of my internal world to possess my internal objects. For example, she had been very curious about my husband after meeting him at a business convention. She felt that my internal space was already occupied by him. She wished she could get rid of him.

After this session I had a dream in which I discovered that my husband had had a baby with another woman and was asking me to raise the child as my own. I think my dream represented my countertransference reaction to Elaine's attack on the couple to maintain a regressive, dyadic relationship with me. She was like a ruthless child who has no qualms about biting or kicking anyone who gets between her and her mother. My dream also showed me that her wish to possess my husband lay behind her more conscious longing to create an exclusive dyad with me.

To get clear of her neurotic dilemma, Elaine needed me to receive her sexuality, tenderness, love, aggression, and rejection as projective identifications, to contain them, and to integrate them inside myself. I felt so threatened by her intrusion into my world, that I wanted to separate myself and dodge her merger fantasies. This impulse was expressed in changing my hairdo radically. I was hiding behind a new look; She was looking inside me, and threatening my own internal couple.

The Couple and the Therapist

During sessions with Bob and Elaine, I was often struck by the contrast between them. Bob is light and short, whereas Elaine is heavy and big, giving the impression that she could crush and swallow him with her physique. She is cold and unemotional; he is all feelings and tears. He could overwhelm her with affect but she could overwhelm him by freezing. I often felt like a buffer in the middle of their process and sometimes felt abused and penetrated by their persecutory and exciting objects. At other times I felt pulled in by Bob and Elaine's charm, only to find myself dropped by their shared narcissism as they refused my interpretations. At those times I felt betrayed and devalued. I sometimes ended up attacking my therapeutic skills and resenting my work. Couple therapy with them had the quality of a roller-coaster: I could bask in their esteem, and then find myself catapulted into worthlessness.

From Primitive Dyadic Pairing to Complex Couple Functioning

In an earlier session, Bob had said that he would have loved to have a psychologist like me when he was a boy, because I would have saved him a lot of problems later. Longing was placed in another time and in another dyad, this time into him and me, and not into the married couple. In another session prior to my vacation, Bob expressed his wish to kiss me good-bye. Elaine said she would never dare even to think about kissing me. Bob expressed for both of them their longing for me, while attacking his couple relationship with Elaine. Elaine rejected her love for me and their longing for each other.

A Couple Session

Elaine arrived at this couple session saying she felt less and less like attending. She had more important things to do than to be there. Maybe, I said, she was angry because she was afraid I would make her talk about things she didn't want to talk about. She was silent. Bob responded that he didn't know what she did in her individual sessions, but here he wanted to make her talk about her sexual inhibitions. He felt I took her side, allowing her to talk about unimportant issues instead of their sexual life. She was afraid I would make her talk, when in reality it was Bob who was pressuring her. He expressed for both of them the longing for a good sexual relationship. She expressed their shared conflict in communicating needs and difficulties.

As they continued to use me in different ways to express both neediness and feelings of rejection, both of them projected the responsibility for their shared difficulties into me.

Continuing, Elaine said that she was angry without knowing why. She just knew she didn't want to be here and was finding it harder and harder to come to her sessions. Couple therapy had become another task. She would rather be doing something else. She realized that she was angry with me because she was afraid I would make her talk about things she had told me but was not ready or willing to talk about with Bob. She was upset because he and I would pressure her into talking.

Her use of the term "another task" reminded me of the way she felt about having sex with her husband. I sensed that she was feeling an internal pressure to talk with Bob about her sexual difficulties. I thought that the rejecting objects that dominated her sexual life had now taken over the transference and might be about to emerge.

A silence followed. Then Bob said it was unfortunate that Elaine felt that way when he wanted her to do the talking, but he would go ahead and talk because time was running out and nothing was happening between them—as his psychiatrist had pointed out.

I felt the familiar twinge of devaluation when Bob mentioned his psychiatrist's opinion. I felt annoyed about Elaine's withholding.

Bob went on to say that life was not nice to him. Somehow everything had gone wrong. He didn't want to feel sexually needy all of his life, waiting for her to desire him and feeling rejected. Elaine looked at me as if waiting for me to say something, even though she had warned me not to pressure her into talking.

I was then in a bind, pulled between Bob's desire to confront desire and Elaine's reluctance to join him in this effort. I did not want to be controlled by her. So I decided to ask her if she could answer Bob.

Elaine responded. She told Bob that we had been working on her sexuality during the individual sessions and explained how difficult this had been for her. She had come to accept that her lack of interest in sex was because she didn't want to confront the issue of her inability to reach an orgasm. She didn't know if Bob realized how depressed she had been about this. He looked surprised.

Elaine continued to explain how her anxiety paralyzes her not only by inhibiting her in the sexual arena, but also by preventing her from remembering and making sense of her ideas, even forgetting important things that she wanted to share with me. She was afraid she would never be able to progress.

I asked her what would be the danger behind progressing.

The danger, she said, would be to try and then fail. While she was talking, Bob made a timid attempt to comfort her by caressing her hand, but soon drew back. He said he didn't understand. She had had orgasms many times, hadn't she? What was she talking about? How come she and I knew that she hadn't had an orgasm when he had been there and had seen them?

Elaine said I had suggested she should bring the subject to couple therapy but she hadn't been able to until now. Hesitantly she confessed to faking orgasms so that she would not feel deficient and ashamed. She wanted to please Bob and not risk being rejected by him. Bob was not satisfied with her answer. He continued to insist that there had been times when she had enjoyed intercourse. She agreed that she could enjoy intercourse but was unable to reach orgasm, a depressing reality that made her feel worthless. How come something so basic even to animals was so difficult for her?

Bob spoke sadly about the many years they had wasted. He didn't want to go through life without having a relationship that includes good sex. Elaine said she felt as if she had gotten rid of a heavy burden. Bob added, "As if you had got rid of pounds of feces." Elaine acknowledged that maybe this outpouring connected to her constant diarrheas. Bob said that he wondered how things would be now that Elaine was telling him what he needed to know. They left talking about their need to communicate during sex.

The Dynamics of the Session

This session shows movement between the paranoid-schizoid and depressive positions, and between relating at the dyadic and couple levels. In the paranoid-schizoid position, Bob, Elaine, and I faced our internal rejecting objects. The dangers of good and bad internalized objects and schizoid-paranoid and depressive anxieties were contained and worked through.

For Bob, realizing he was not doing his job by not noticing Elaine's difficulties in reaching orgasm was a devastating narcissistic wound. Bob made me feel that I was not doing my job properly in not forcing Elaine to give up her secret sooner and in bringing it out now. I felt guilty about opening this wound by leading Elaine to her revelation, but I did it because he was right: the job needed doing and it was my job to do it.

Elaine aggressively withheld crucial information from Bob that she gave to me. This kept him isolated from her. By telling it to me alone, she paired with me to create the symbiosis she never had with her own mother. On the issue of sex, she was more available to me than to him, and this left him feeling isolated and castrated. The revelation could have been destructive, but I think that it set the stage for reparation and healing.

The members of the couple had difficulty in becoming a real couple because they lacked the childhood experience of having a containing relationship, so they longed for a symbiotic relationship of pleasure instead, one that necessarily excluded the pain of acknowledging the reality of others. The internalized model of the couple was of a parental couple fused in a pre-Oedipal, dyadic relationship that excluded Bob and Elaine as children. Now Bob and Elaine's relationship was built on the isolation and rejection of a third. Each of them wanted to be the one and only, and yet have no differences between them, no space for separation. Envy, rejection, and anxiety followed in the wake of their re-creation of a primitive dyad in their paranoid-schizoid way of dealing with the experience of being together. Having not had a mature couple to identify with, Bob and Elaine had trouble creating a containing couple where they could share their ideas and feelings and grow together.

CONCLUSION

In individual therapy Elaine discovered that behind her wish to merge with me was her difficulty in mourning a close relationship with her mother that she longed for but had not experienced. This internal pre-Oedipal couple, frozen in time in her internal world, supported her fantasy of a fused couple as the epitome of a perfect relationship in marriage and in therapy. Her dream of an orgasm with me, and my understanding of her need to have an exclusive relationship with me without gratifying it at the expense of the couple, marked a moment of transition in her therapy. An increase in the space for thinking made it possible for her to reveal to Bob both her difficulty and her longing for a mature sexual relationship with him. In individual sessions, Elaine moved from dealing with me in a dyad to allowing for the formation of a couple with Bob without the danger of rejection or expulsion.

This prepared the way for the couple session in which Elaine was able to tell Bob about her inability to reach orgasm. Instead of hearing her confession as proof of his inadequacy as he often did, Bob felt included by her and by me. He felt needed by her to help with sexual issues, and wanted to learn how he could facilitate orgasm. Elaine's individual sessions ceased to be a place from which Bob felt excluded, as Elaine and I became a couple with concern for him. Then in couple therapy, Bob and Elaine identified with my way of containing conflict and including the third position in my thinking about experience.

The function of their dyad had been to create confusion and destruction. It prevented the development of a couple for holding, containment, interpretation, and integration. Once reliance on the dyad gave way to the formation of a trusted couple relationship, Bob and Elaine could discuss and contain their difficulties. Then their more creative and productive aspects emerged.

They became successful in their professional work, she became orgasmic with him, and they began to start a family.

SUMMARY

I describe the destructive effect of two individuals' dyadic internal object relationships on their marriage. In discussion of a combined, concurrent couple and individual therapy, I show the prevalence of need-gratifying primitive dyads and the destructive effect that they have on the couple's hopes for intimate relating. When I had become the object of desire to which the preference for dyadic relating attaches, I made the interpretation that this reliance on dyadic functioning with each other as parent substitutes stems from lost loves of childhood, and so I worked through these losses with the partners until they were functioning as a mature couple of equals capable of holding, containment, interpretation of conflict, and personal integration.

REFERENCES

Scharff, D. E., and J. S. Scharff. 1991. *Object Relations Couple Therapy*. Northvale, NJ: Jason Aronson.

Sutherland, J. D. 1989. *Fairbairn's Journey to the Interior*. London: Free Association Books.

Epilogue

David E. Scharff and Jill Savege Scharff

New Paradigms for Treating Relationships is an array of international applications of psychoanalytic theory to couple problems. We explore the impact of narcissism, sexual dysfunction, and sadomasochism on the couple bond. We illustrate homosexual unions, intercultural couples, divorce, and remarriage. We deal with defenses against functioning as a couple. We cover brief therapy, sex therapy, and intensive analytic couple therapy with dream interpretation. Starting from a base in object relations theory, we then apply adult attachment research, findings from neuroscience, chaos theory, intersubjectivity, and theory of the analytic third to therapeutic strategies with couples.

We show how spouses react to aspects of each parent and sibling that they find in one another, and then treat one another accordingly. We show how a therapist is co-opted to form a dyad with one spouse and works through that transference phenomenon by proving that she can include both spouses in her mind, and so she facilitates couple functioning. We demonstrate in many clinical examples the oscillation of identification with exciting and rejecting objects, and the analysis of symptoms as defenses against the loss of the good object. We show therapists linking clinical work and theory as they think about and learn from experience. We show them talking with adults and playing with children, dealing with resistance to interpretation, being devalued in the transference, interpreting projective identifications, mourning, and working through, as they apply object relations theory and technique in couple and family therapy.

We want to demonstrate the value placed internationally on applying psychoanalytic insight to understanding family dynamics and devising treatment for families and couples. We want to give access to the illuminating ways of thinking about analytic couple and family therapy described in the Spanish, French, and German literature. We widen our focus as much as possible while staying true to the in-depth way of working with the unconscious that is characteristic of psychoanalysis.

A book like this is intended as a report on the field in its current state, and in this we hope to succeed in some measure. Even though we provide a core of practice from which to draw, we will not stop there. We can never exhaust the areas of study that are potentially helpful either to the practitioner or to the researcher. Psychoanalytic couple and family therapy should not be a static subject. To retain its vitality, it must continue to evolve and grow. In that spirit, we hope these chapters will encourage others to apply psychoanalysis to families and couples, and then write about their evolving experience with analytic couple and family therapy.

Credits

The editors would like express gratitude to the following publishers for their permission to reprint or adapt text from papers and chapters listed below:

Whurr

Introduction to Part 1

Scharff, J., and D. Scharff. 2004. Introduction: Psychoanalytic couple and family therapy, Part 2. *International Journal of Applied Psychoanalytic Studies* 1(3): 211–13.

Chapter 10 Play and Family Therapy by J. S. Scharff

Scharff, J. S. 2004. Play and very young children in family therapy. *International Journal of Applied Psychoanalytic Studies* 1(3): 259–68.

Chapter 12 Therapeutic Supervision with Families of High-Conflict Divorce by K. Scharff

Scharff, K. E. 2004. Therapeutic supervision with families of high-conflict divorce. *International Journal of Applied Psychoanalytic Studies* 1(3): 269–81.

Chapter 13 Expanding the Frame in Therapy with a Stepfamily by C. Bagnini

Bagnini, C. 2004. Extending Fairbairn's and Sutherland's socio-intrapsychic model to assessment and treatment of a stepfamily. *International Journal of Applied Psychoanalytic Studies* 1(3): 247–58.

Chapter 16 Holding On and Letting Go: From Family to Couple Therapy by J. Berg and P. Jools

Berg, J., and P. Jools. 2004. Holding on and letting go: Developmental anxieties in couples after the birth of a child. *International Journal of Applied Psychoanalytic Studies* 1(3): 224–33.

Chapter 20 Integrating Attachment Theory and Neuroscience in Couple Therapy by S. Goldstein and S. Thau

Goldstein, S., and S. Thau. 2004. Integrating attachment theory and neuroscience in couple therapy. *International Journal of Applied Psychoanalytic Studies* 1(3): 214–23.

Chapter 32 The Splitting Function of the Dyad and Containment of the Couple by Y. de Varela

Varela, Y. de. 2004. The splitting function of the dyad versus the containing function of the couple: A case of combined couple and individual therapy. *International Journal of Applied Psychoanalytic Studies* 1(3): 234–46.

Routledge

Chapter 15 Consulting to a Family Business by Michael Stadter

Stadter, M. 2003. Persecutory aspects of family business. In *Self Hatred in Psychoanalysis,* pp. 205–224. London: Routledge.

Chapter 31 Containing Anxiety with Divorcing Couples by C. Bagnini

Bagnini, C. 2003. Containing anxiety with divorcing couples. In *Self Hatred in Psychoanalysis,* pp. 165–78. London: Routledge.

Zeig, Tucker, and Theissen

Chapter 30 Brief Therapy with Couples and Individuals by M. Stadter and D. Scharff

Stadter, M., and D. E. Scharff. 2000. Object relations brief therapy. In *Brief Therapy with Individuals and Couples,* ed. J. Carlson and L. Sperry, pp. 191–219. Phoenix, AZ: Zeig, Tucker, and Theissen.

Springer

Chapter 18 Object Relations Perspective on a Phenomenological Case History by J. Scharff and Y. de Varela

Dattilio, F., and L. Bevilacqua. 2000. Introduction and case conceptualization of Mike and Jan. In *Comparative Treaments for Relationship Dysfunction*, ed. F. Dattilio and L. Bevilacqua, pp. 13–20. New York: Springer.

and

Scharff, J. S., and Y. de Varela. 2000. Object relations therapy. In *Comparative Treaments for Relationship Dysfunction*, ed. F. Dattilio and L. Bevilacqua, pp. 81–101. New York: Springer.

Springer (Kluwer Academic Press)

Introduction to Part 1

Scharff, D., and J. Scharff. 2004. Introduction: Psychoanalytic couple and family therapy, Part 1. *Journal of Applied Psychoanalytic Studies* 5(3): 253–55.

Chapter 1 Models of the Mind for Couple and Family Therapy by D. Scharff

Scharff, D. E. 2003. Psychoanalytic models of the mind for couple and family therapy. *Journal of Applied Psychoanalytic Studies* 5(3): 257–67.

Chapter 11 Divorce Terminable and Interminable by R. Losso and A. Packciarz Losso

Losso, R. 2003. Divorce terminable and interminable: A psychoanalytic and interdisciplinary approach. *Journal of Applied Psychoanalytic Studies* 5(3): 321–34.

Chapter 14 Family Dynamics and AIDS Phobia: A Case Study by H.-J. Wirth

Wirth, H.-J. 2003. Family dynamics and AIDS phobia. Trans. Z. Lothane. *Journal of Applied Psychoanalytic Studies* 5(3): 309–19.

Chapter 19 Couple Psychotherapy and Attachment Theory by C. Clulow

Clulow, C. 2003. An attachment perspective on reunions in couple psychoanalytic psychotherapy. *Journal of Applied Psychoanalytic Studies* 5(3): 269–81.

Chapter 22 Dreams and the Introduction of a Third into the Transference Dynamic by A. Nicolò, D. Norsa, and T. Carratelli

Nicolò, A. M., D. Norsa, and T. Carratelli. 2003. Playing with dreams: The introduction of a third party into the transference dynamic of the couple. *Journal of Applied Psychoanalytic Studies* 5(3): 283–96.

Chapter 28 A Troubled Marriage in Sex Therapy by N. Caruso

Caruso, N. 2003. Object relations theory and technique applied to sex and marital therapy. *Journal of Applied Psychoanalytic Studies* 5(3): 297–308.

Wiley

Chapter 17 A Clinical Introduction to Couple Therapy by D. Scharff and Y. de Varela

Scharff, D., and Y. de Varela. 2005. Object relations couple therapy. In *Handbook of Couples Therapy*, ed. M. Harway, pp. 141–56. Hoboken, NJ: Wiley.

Guilford

Chapter 24 Narcissistic Disorders in Marriage by J. Scharff and C. Bagnini

Scharff, J., and C. Bagnini. 2003. Narcissistic disorder. In *Treating Difficult Couples*, ed. D. K. Snyder and M. A. Whisman, pp. 285–307. New York: Guilford.

Index

479

About the Editors and Contributors

EDITORS

David E. Scharff, MD, of Chevy Chase, Maryland, is co-director of the International Psychotherapy Institute (IPI); chair of the Object Relations Theory and Practice program at IPI; teaching analyst, Washington Psychoanalytic Institute; and clinical professor of psychiatry, Georgetown University, Washington, D.C., and at the Uniformed Services University of the Health Sciences in Bethesda, Maryland. He is a past president of the American Association of Sex Educators, Counselors, and Therapists and was director of the Washington School of Psychiatry from 1987 to 1994. His private practice of adult and child psychoanalysis and psychotherapy and couple, sex, and family therapy is in Chevy Chase, Maryland. He is the author, co-author, and editor of many books, including *Refinding the Object and Reclaiming the Self*, *The Sexual Relationship*, *Object Relations Family Therapy*, *Object Relations Couple Therapy*, *Object Relations Theory and Practice*, *The Psychoanalytic Century*, and *From Instinct to Self: Selected Papers of W. R. D. Fairbairn*.

Jill Savege Scharff, MD, of Chevy Chase, Maryland, is co-director of the International Psychotherapy Institute (IPI); chair of the International Institute for Psychoanalytic Training and former chair of the Child, Couple, and Family Therapy Program at IPI; teaching analyst, Washington Psychoanalytic Institute; and clinical professor of psychiatry, Georgetown University, Washington, D.C. Her private practice of adult and child psychoanalysis and psychotherapy and couple, sex, and family therapy is in Chevy Chase, Maryland. She is the author, co-author, and editor of many books, including *Projective Identification and the Use of the Therapist's Self*, *Object Relations Individual Therapy*, *Object Relations Therapy of Physical and Sexual*

Trauma, The Autonomous Self, Self Hatred in Psychoanalysis, The Legacy of Fairbairn and Sutherland, The Primer of Object Relations Theory, 2nd edition, and *The Facelift Diaries.*

CONTRIBUTORS

Sylvie Angel, of Paris, France, is the co-founder and medical director of the Monceau Center for Family Therapy in Paris. She also cofounded the Pluralis and Pluridis Centers. A prolific author of books for professionals and parents in France, she is also senior editor of the *Réponses* collection at Robert Laffont Publishers. She is a chevalier of the Order of the Légion d'Honneur.

Carl Bagnini, MSW, BCD, of Long Island, New York, is a clinical social worker on the faculties of St. John's University Postdoctoral Program in Couple and Family Therapy and the Suffolk Institute of Psychoanalysis and Psychotherapy and is in private practice in Port Washington, New York. He contributed to *Tuning the Therapeutic Instrument: Affective Learning of Psychotherapy* (2000) and *The Clinical Handbook of Couple Therapy*, 2nd edition. He is chair of the Couple, Child, and Family Therapy Program at the International Psychotherapy Institute (IPI) Washington and chair of IPI-Long Island.

Jenny Berg, M.B.B.S., F.R.A.N.Z.C.P., Cert. Child Psych., of Sydney, Australia, is a child, adolescent, and family psychiatrist and an executive member of the New South Wales Institute of Family Psychotherapy. She lectures and supervises in object relations family therapy for the Australian Faculty of Child Psychiatry.

Theresa Carratelli lives in Rome, Italy, and is a psychoanalyst and professor of infant development. A full member of the Associazione Italiana di Psicoanalisi and the International Psychoanalytical Association, she holds the title of Professore di Neuropsichiatria Infantile—Facoltà di Medicina, Università degli Studi di Roma "La Sapienza."

Norma Caruso, PsyD, of Richmond, Virginia, has a private practice in Richmond. She is assistant clinical professor in the Department of Psychiatry at the Medical College of Virginia and serves on the faculty at the International Psychotherapy Institute (IPI) and IPI-Metro Washington.

Christopher Clulow, PhD, of London, England, is director of the Tavistock Centre for Couple Relationships, where he practices as a couple psychotherapist, teacher, and researcher. His books on couples undergoing change, marriage, and family life include *Adult Attachment and Couple Psychotherapy: The Secure Base in Practice and Research*. He is editor of *Sexual and Relationship Therapy*, past chair of the Commission on Marriage and Interpersonal Relations of the International Union of Family Organizations, full member of the Society of Psychoanalytical Marital Psychotherapists, and qualified rater of the Adult Attachment Interview and Therapies.

Robert Cvetek, of Ljubljana, Slovenia, is a specialist in marital and family therapy and serves on the faculty of University of Ljubljana Graduate Program in Marital and Family Therapy. He is the author of several articles on trauma, relational family therapy, and research in martial and family therapy.

Walton H. Ehrhardt, EdD, is from New Orleans, Louisiana. He is a licensed marriage and family therapist and licensed mental health counselor, with professional memberships in AAMFT, AAPC, and AGPA. Currently serving as dean of students in the International Psychotherapy Institute (IPI), he also chairs IPI-New Orleans. He maintains a private practice of psychotherapy in New Orleans.

Katarina Kompan Erzar, PhD, of Ljubljana, Slovenia, is on the faculty of University of Ljubljana Graduate Program in Marital and Family Therapy and is co-director of the Franciscan Family Institute in Ljubljana. She is the author of the articles, "The discovery of the relationship" and "Hidden power of the family."

Tomaz Erzar, PhD, lives in Ljubljana, Slovenia. He is assistant professor at University of Ljubljana Graduate Program in Marital and Family Therapy and is co-director of the Franciscan Family Institute in Ljubljana. He is the author of *Farewell to Freud* and several articles on Lacanian psychoanalysis, epistemology, and structuralist philosophy.

Lilia Gagnarli, of Florence, Italy, is a psychologist, psychotherapist, and senior trainer at the Instituto di Terapia Familiare in Florence, associate member of the Società Italiana di Psicoterapia Psicoanalitica, member of the editorial board of the journal *Interazioni*, and maintains a private practice in individual, couple, and family therapy in Florence. She is a member of the European Family Therapy Association and of the Italian Psychoanalytical Psychotherapy Association.

Sondra Goldstein, PhD, of Los Angeles, California, is clinical associate professor, Department of Psychology, University of California–Los Angeles, and is a clinical psychologist in private practice in Encino, California.

Christian Gostecnik, PhD, of Ljubljana, Slovenia, is associate professor at University of Ljubljana Graduate Program in Marital and Family Therapy and is co-director of the Franciscan Family Institute in Ljubljana. His books include *Modern Psychoanalysis, Psychoanalysis and Religion, Relational Family Therapy, I Met My Family, Let Us Try Again*, and *Parenting Adolescents.*

Suzanne Iasenza, PhD, of New York, is on the faculties of John Jay College– City University of New York and the Institute for Contemporary Psychotherapy and Psychoanalysis and maintains a private practice in psychotherapy and sex therapy in New York City. She is co-editor of *Lesbians and Psychoanalysis: Revolutions in Theory and Practice* (1995) and *Lesbians, Feminism and Psychoanalysis: The Second Wave* (2004).

Hugh Joffe is a psychiatrist in Sydney, Australia.

Penny Jools, PhD, of Sydney, Australia, is a clinical psychologist and psychotherapist. She is secretary of the New South Wales Institute of Family Psychotherapy, Australia. She works as a therapist with individuals and families in Sydney.

Ana Packciarz Losso, of Buenos Aires, Argentina, is a full member of the Argentine and the International Psychoanalytic Associations. She is professor of Clinics of Families and Couples, John F. Kennedy University, Buenos Aires, and serves as a member of the Committee for the Psychoanalytic Investigation of Families and Couples, Argentine Psychoanalytic Association.

Roberto Losso, of Buenos Aires, Argentina, is consulting professor of psychiatry, faculty of medicine, University of Buenos Aires. He is a full member of the Argentine and the International Psychoanalytic Associations, director of the Program in Psychoanalytic Therapy of Families and Couples, CAECE University and Argentine Psychoanalytic Association, and the author of *Psicoanálisis de la familia. Recorridos teòrico-clínicos.*

Molly Ludlam lives in Edinburgh, Scotland. She is a member of the Scottish Institute of Human Relations and associate member of the Society of Couple Psychoanalytic Psychotherapists. Her psychoanalytic psychotherapy practice with adults, couples, and parents draws on experience as a schoolteacher and a social worker in a Child and Family Mental Health Team.

Anna M. Nicolò, of Rome, Italy, is a child and adolescent psychiatrist and psychoanalyst, a full member of the Società Psicoanalitica Italiana and the International Psychoanalytical Association, and the editor in chief of

Interazioni. She is a charter member of Società Italiana di Psicoterapia psicoanalitica dell'infanzia, dell'adolescenza, e della coppia. From 1989, she has been president of Centro di Psicoanalisi Familiare e di Coppia.

Christine C. Norman, of Salt Lake City, Utah, is a licensed clinical social worker and has a private practice in psychotherapy in Salt Lake City. She is a fellow with the International Psychotherapy Institute, Chevy Chase, Maryland, and a faculty member with IPI-Salt Lake.

Diana Norsa, of Rome, Italy, is a psychoanalyst and full member of the Associazione Italiana di Psicoanalisi and the International Psychoanalytical Association.

James L. Poulton, PhD, of Salt Lake City, Utah, is a practicing psychologist in Salt Lake City. He is a member of the faculty of the International Psychotherapy Institute (IPI) where he serves on the executive committee, and he co-chairs IPI-Salt Lake. He is an adjunct assistant professor in psychology and clinical instructor in psychiatry at the University of Utah, and is the co-author of *Internalization: The Origin and Construction of Internal Reality.*

Katherine E. Scharff, MSW, of Bethesda, Maryland, is director of Washington Services for Relationships in Transition, co-director of the International Psychotherapy Institute (IPI)-Metro Washington, and the author of *Therapy Demystified.* She is a clinical social worker and psychotherapist in private practice in Bethesda, Maryland. She specializes in children, families, and high-conflict divorce.

Joan Massel Soncini, PhD, of both New York and Italy, is adjunct professor at the School of Social Work, New York University, and a psychotherapist fluent in four languages and specializing in intercultural couples and cross-cultural psychotherapy. She is a graduate of the Washington School of Psychiatry Object Relations Couples and Family Therapy Program.

Michael Stadter, PhD, from Washington, D.C., is a clinical psychologist and a member of the faculty and board of directors of International Psychotherapy Institute (IPI). He is clinical psychologist-in-residence in the department of psychology at American University in Washington, D.C., and serves on the faculty of the Washington School of Psychiatry. His private practice in Bethesda, Maryland, includes long-term and brief psychotherapy as well as clinical supervision and organizational consultation. He is the author of *Object Relations Brief Therapy* and the editor of *Dimensions of Psychotherapy.*

Merritt W. Stites, MSW, of Salt Lake City, Utah, is a licensed clinical social worker in private practice in Salt Lake City. She graduated in 1992 from the Object Relations Theory and Practice program at the International Psychotherapy Institute, Chevy Chase, Maryland.

Susan Thau, PhD, of Santa Monica, California, is a clinical psychologist in private practice in Santa Monica, and a training and supervising analyst at the Institute of Contemporary Psychoanalysis, Los Angeles, California.

Yolanda de Varela, MA, PhD, of Panamá City, Republic of Panamá, is a clinical psychologist whose PhD thesis is on research into learning object relations concepts. She is in private practice of individual, child, and couple psychotherapy in Panamá City. She is a past president of the Panamanian Psychological Association. Publications include chapters in *Tuning the Therapeutic Instrument: Affective Learning of Psychotherapy* (2000) and *Comparative Treatments for Relationship Dysfunction* (2000). She is a faculty member of the International Psychotherapy Institute (IPI) and founded IPI-Panamá and the Foundation for Healthy Relationships in Panamá.

Hans-Jürgen Wirth, Prof. PhD, from Geissen, Germany, is a psychoanalyst in private practice, a member of the German (DPV) and International Psychoanalytic Associations, lecturer at the University of Bremen, and owner/publisher of Psychosozial-Verlag. His most recently published book in English is *9/11 as a Collective Trauma and Other Essays on Psychoanalysis and Society.*

Richard M. Zeitner, PhD, ABPP, lives in Blue Springs, Missouri, and is training and supervising analyst at the Greater Kansas City Psychoanalytic Institute and chair of its curriculum and faculty committee. His private practice of psychoanalysis, couple therapy, and family therapy is in Blue Springs.